Index of American Periodical Verse: 1980

by

Sander W. Zulauf

with

Jandra Milkowski

The Scarecrow Press, Inc.
Metuchen, N.J., & London
1982

Library of Congress Catalog Card No. 73-3060

ISBN 0-8108-1480-3

To the memory of

Marion Zulauf (1923-1980), John Milkowski (1914-1974), and

James Wright (1927-1980).

CONTENTS

PREFACE

The tenth annual edition of the Index of American Periodical
Verse records by poet the titles of the poems that appeared in the
pages of selected magazines in 1980. Some great remembered lines
from the greatest poets come rippling through my brain and shatter
the morning silence as effectively as an ear-splitting roar from a
747 sixty feet above the runway on takeoff. "The United States
themselves are essentially the greatest poem" (Whitman); "Wisdom
wants nothing more" (Stevens); "had undone so many" (Eliot); "No
ideas but in things" (Williams); "wanting to have the last word"
(Burke); "terrible beauty" (Yeats); "may great kindness come of it
in the end" (Nemerov); "faithful as enemy, or friend" (Bishop); "I
would break/Into blossom" (Wright); "Of which vertu engendred is
the flour" (Chaucer); "Till love and fame to nothingness do sink"
(Keats); "Are you my angel?" (Ginsberg); "like a perhaps hand"
(cummings); "Look carefully into the palm of your hand, it's empty"
(Salinas, translated by Wright); "Let me not to the marriage of true
minds/Admit impediments. Love is not Love that alters when it
alteration finds" (Shakespeare); "Earth's the right place for love"
(Frost); "Familiar as an old mistake/ And futile as regret" (Robin-
son); and "nothing more to say."

Some of these titles that we have happily tracked down and
recorded will be among the great poems of the future and will be
remembered by those to whom such things are important, for whom
the words become that wondrous "momentary stay against confusion."
This enormous job has been accomplished because of the hard work
and dedication of many people whose names have appeared in the
nine previous prefaces; all of those beautiful souls have made sacri-
fices for this service to poetry. There is much that I am thankful
for at this moment in my life, especially that I have been blessed
with such friends and relatives. I thank God for them all. Why
did I do it? What have I learned? I did it with the bravado of
young Ezra Pound: I wanted to know everything I could about con-
temporary poets. I suppose now I could have accomplished that by
reading carefully every issue of a few dozen of these magazines,
reading until I understood what was written there. I have learned
that I "would not trade the song of one brown bird at sunset" for
all the knowledge I have accumulated about poets and poetry in our
time. I have learned that the act of making poems is the act of
committing the soul to paper; through sleight-of-hand, the very
great poets manage to reveal and conceal their very souls at the
same time.

I also know that I will be dragging ten red books with me for the rest of my life, giving them a prominent place on my bookshelf and referring to their pages from time to time. It is my sincere hope that someone is able to continue this work. I am convinced of its intrinsic value and do not want to see it come to a halt. I will do everything I can to see that it continues. But I also must get on with other things, my other lives that wait for me in all of my tomorrows. It is not easy to give up what I have given myself to for ten years. What of it? An old obsession is giving way to a new one. "Oh, do not ask 'What is it?'/Let us go and make our visit." Don't know yet what it is, but I have an idea. And faith. And hope. And love most of all. May God be with you now and ever.

S. W. Z.

Succasunna, N. J.
August 1981

ABBREVIATIONS

ad.	adaptation
arr.	arrangement
Back:	back issue copy price
Ed. (s.)	Editor(s)
Exec.	Executive
(ind.)	price for individuals
(inst.)	price for institutions
(lib.)	price for libraries
p.	page
pp.	pages
Po. Ed.	Poetry Editor
Pub.	Publisher
Sing:	single copy price
SI	Special Issue
(stud.)	price for students
Supp	Supplement
tr.	translation
U	University
w.	with
$10/yr	ten dollars per year
$10/4	ten dollars for four issues
(1:9)	volume one, number nine
(80)	number eighty

Months

Ja	January	Jl	July
F	February	Ag	August
Mr	March	S	September
Ap	April	O	October
My	May	N	November
Je	June	D	December

Seasons

Aut	Autumn, Fall	Spr	Spring
Wint	Winter	Sum	Summer

PERIODICALS ADDED

Annex 21
The Barat Review
Cape Rock
Cream City Review
Crop Dust
The Little Balkans Review
Ontario Review

Outerbridge
Poetry East
Primavera
The Threepenny Review
Visions
Water Table

PERIODICALS DELETED

Chomo-Uri
Cornell Review
Harvard Advocate
Mademoiselle
Modularist Review
Poultry

St. Andrews Review
Texas Quarterly
Thought
Vagabond
West Branch
Yellow Brick Road

PERIODICALS INDEXED

AAR
ANN ARBOR REVIEW
Fred Wolven, Ed.
Washtenaw Community College
Ann Arbor, MI 48106
(-)
 Subs: $6 /3
 Sing: $2

Academe
ACADEME: BULLETIN OF
 THE AAUP
R. K. Webb
Ellen Morgenstern, Eds.
Suite 500
One Dupont Circle
Washington, DC 20036
 (66:1-8)
 Subs: $24 /yr

Agni
AGNI REVIEW
Sharon Dunn, Ed.
Box 349
Cambridge, MA 02138
 (12-13)
 Subs: $9 /2 yrs
    $5 /yr
 Sing: $3

AmerPoR
AMERICAN POETRY REVIEW
Stephen Berg, et al., Eds.
Temple U Center City
1616 Walnut St.
Room 405
Philadelphia, PA 19103
 (9:1-6)

 Subs: $19 /3 yrs
    $13 /2 yrs
    $ 7.50 /yr
 Sing: $ 1.50
 Missing (8:6)

AmerS
THE AMERICAN SCHOLAR
Joseph Epstein, Ed.
1811 Q St., N.W.
Washington, DC 20009
 (49:1-4)
 Subs: $24 /3 yrs
    $18 /2 yrs
    $10 /yr
 Sing: $3

AndR
THE ANDOVER REVIEW
William H. Brown, Ed.
Erica Funkhouser, Po. Ed.
Phillips Academy
Andover, MA 01810
 (7:1)
 Final issue.

Annex
*ANNEX 21
Richard & Lorraine Duggin, Eds.
U of Nebraska at Omaha
Omaha, NE 68182
 (2)
 Sing: $3.95

Antaeus
ANTAEUS
Daniel Halpern, Ed.
The Ecco Press

---

*New titles added to the Index in 1980.

1 W. 30th St.
New York, NY 10001
  (36-39)
  Subs: $14/yr
  Sing: $4

AntR
ANTIOCH REVIEW
Robert S. Fogarty, Ed.
Sandra McPherson, Po. Ed.
Antioch College
Yellow Springs, OH 45387
  (38:1-4)
  Subs: $15/yr (inst.)
            $12/yr (ind.)
  Sing: $ 3.50

ArizQ
ARIZONA QUARTERLY
Albert Frank Gegenheimer, Ed.
U of Arizona
Tucson, AZ 85721
  (36:1-4)
  Subs: $5/3 yrs
            $2/yr
  Sing: $ .50

Ark
THE ARK
Geoffrey Gardner, Ed.
Box 322
Times Square Station
New York, NY 10036
  (14)
  Sing: $10
(Note: The Ark was mistakenly
deleted from the 1979 Index.)

ArkRiv
THE ARK RIVER REVIEW
Jonathan Katz
Anthony Sobin, Eds.
Box 14
Wichita State U
Wichita, KS 67208
  (-)
  Subs: $5/4

Ascent
ASCENT
The Editors
English Dept.

U of Illinois
Urbana, IL 61801
  (5:2-3) (6:1)
  Subs: $3/yr
  Sing: $1

Aspect
ASPECT
Ed Hogan, Ed.
13 Robinson St.
Somerville, MA 02145
  (76)
  Sing: $2
  Final issue.

Aspen
ASPEN ANTHOLOGY
J. D. Muller, Ed.
Box 3185
Aspen, CO 81612
  (9-10)
  Subs: $6.50/yr
  Sing: $3

Atl
THE ATLANTIC
Robert Manning, Ed.
Peter Davison, Po. Ed.
8 Arlington St.
Boston, MA 02116
  (245:1-6) (246:1-6)
  Subs: $45/3 yrs
            $33/2 yrs
            $18/yr
  Sing: $ 1.75

Bachy
BACHY
F. X. Feeney, Prose Ed.
Leland Hickman, Po. Ed.
Papa Bach Paperbacks
11317 Santa Monica Blvd.
West Los Angeles, CA 90025
  (16-17)
  Subs: $10/yr
  Sing: $ 3.50

BallSUF
BALL STATE UNIVERSITY FORUM
Merrill & Frances M. Rippy, Eds.
Ball State U
Muncie, IN 47306

(21:1-3)
Subs: $5 /yr
Sing: $1. 50

BaratR
*THE BARAT REVIEW
Lauri S. Lee, Ed.
Barat College
Lake Forest, IL 60045
(8:1)
Subs: $15 /2 yrs
$ 8 /yr
Sing: $ 4. 50

BelPoJ
THE BELOIT POETRY JOURNAL
Robert H. Glauber, et al.,
Eds.
Box 2
Beloit, WI 53511
(30:3-4) (31:1-2)
Subs: $17 /3 yrs
$ 6 /yr
Sing: $ 1. 50

BerksR
BERKSHIRE REVIEW
Gary Jacobsohn, et al., Eds.
Williams College
Box 633
Williamstown, MA 02167
(15)

Bits
BITS
Robert Wallace, et al., Eds.
Dept. of English
Case Western Reserve U
Cleveland, OH 44106
(11) (Chapbooks)
Final issue; will continue
publishing chapbooks.

BlackALF
BLACK AMERICAN LITERA-
TURE FORUM
Chester J. Fontenot
Acting Ed.
100 English Bldg.
U of Illinois
Urbana, IL 61801
Subs: Statesman Towers West

1005
Indiana State U
Terre Haute, IN 47809
(14:1-4)
Subs: $4 /yr

BlackF
BLACK FORUM
Julia Coaxum, Ed.
Box 1090
Bronx, NY 10451
(-)
Subs: $3 /yr
Sing: $2

BosUJ
BOSTON UNIVERSITY JOURNAL
Paul Kurt Ackerman, Ed.
718 Commonwealth Ave.
Boston, MA 02215
(26:3)
Sing: $4
Final issue.

Bound
BOUNDARY 2
William V. Spanos, Ed.
Robert Kroetsch, Po. Ed.
Dept. of English
SUNY-Binghamton
Binghamton, NY 13901
(8:2-3)
Subs: $15 (inst.)
$10 (ind.)
$ 7 (stud.)
Sing: $ 7 (double)
$ 4

CalQ
CALIFORNIA QUARTERLY
Elliot L. Gilbert, Ed.
Sandra M. Gilbert
Kevin Clark, Po. Eds.
100 Sproul Hall
U of California
Davis, CA 95616
(16 /17)
Subs: $5 /yr
Sing: $1. 50

CapeR
*CAPE ROCK

R. A. Burns, et al. , Eds.
Southeast Missouri State U
Cape Girardeau, MO 63701
   (15:2) (16:1)
   Subs: $1.50/yr
   Sing: $1

CarlMis
CARLETON MISCELLANY
Keith Harrison, Ed.
Carleton College
Northfield, MN 55057
   (18:2-3)
   Sing: $6
   Final issue.

CarolQ
CAROLINA QUARTERLY
Dorothy Coombs Hill, Ed.
Miriam Marty, Po. Ed.
Greenlaw Hall 066-A
U of North Carolina
Chapel Hill, NC 27514
   (32:1-3)
   Subs: $10/yr (inst.)
             $ 7.50/yr (ind.)
   Sing: $ 3
   Back: $ 3

CEACritic
CEA CRITIC
Elizabeth Wooten Cowan, Ed.
Dept. of English
Texas A&M U
College Station, TX 77843
   (42:2-4) (43:1)
   Subs: $18/yr (lib.)
             $12/yr (ind.)

CentR
CENTENNIAL REVIEW
David Mead, Ed.
Linda Wagner, Po. Ed.
110 Morrill Hall
Michigan State U
East Lansing, MI 48824
   (24:1-4)
   Subs: $5/2 yrs
             $3/yr
   Sing: $1

CharR
CHARITON REVIEW
Jim Barnes, Ed.
Division of Language and Litera-
   ture
Northeast Missouri State U
Kirksville, MO 63501
   (6:1-2)
   Subs: $7/4
   Sing: $2

Chelsea
CHELSEA
Sonia Raiziss, Ed.
Box 5880
Grand Central Station
New York, NY 10017
   (-)
   Subs: $6/2
   Sing: $3.50

ChiR
CHICAGO REVIEW
Bill Monroe, Ed.
Marjorie Pannell
Michael Sells, Po. Eds.
U of Chicago
5700 S. Ingleside
Box C
Chicago, IL 60637
   (31:3-4) (32:1)
   Subs: $27/3 yrs
             $18.50/2 yrs
             $10/yr

Chowder
CHOWDER REVIEW
Ron Slate, Ed.
Floyd Skloot, Associate Ed.
Box 33
Wollaston, MA 02170
   (-)
   Subs: $8/3 yrs (inst.)
             $7/3 yrs (ind.)
   Sing: $2.50

ChrC
THE CHRISTIAN CENTURY
James M. Wall, Ed.
407 S. Dearborn St.
Chicago, IL 60605

(97:1-43)
Subs: $45/3 yrs
         $30/2 yrs
         $18/yr
Sing: $ .60

CimR
CIMARRON REVIEW
Neil J. Hackett, Ed.
William Mills, Po. Ed.
208 Life Sciences East
Oklahoma State U
Stillwater, OK 74078
  (50-53)
  Subs: $10/yr
  Sing: $ 2.50

ColEng
COLLEGE ENGLISH
Donald Gray, Ed.
Brian O'Neill, Po. Cons.
Dept. of English
Indiana U
Bloomington, IN 47401
Subs: NCTE
       1111 Kenyon Rd.
       Urbana, IL 61801
  (41:5-8) (42:1-4)
  Subs: $30/yr (inst.)
           $25/yr (ind.)
  Sing: $ 3

Columbia
COLUMBIA
Eva Burch
Harvey Lillywhite, Eds.
Kate Daniels, Po. Ed.
404 Dodge Hall
Columbia U
New York, NY 10027
  (4-5)
  Sing: $3

Comm
COMMONWEAL
James O'Gara, Ed.
Rosemary Deen
Marie Ponsot, Po. Eds.
232 Madison Ave.
New York, NY 10016
  (107:1-23)
  Subs: $35/2 yrs

$22/yr
Sing: $ 1

ConcPo
CONCERNING POETRY
Ellwood Johnson, Ed.
Robert Huff, Po. Ed.
Dept. of English
Western Washington U
Bellingham, WA 98225
  (12:2) (13:1-2)
  Subs: $4/yr
  Sing: $2

Cond
CONDITIONS
Elly Bulkin, et al., Eds.
Box 56
Van Brunt Sta.
Brooklyn, NY 11215
  (6)
  Subs: $15/yr (inst.)
           $ 8/yr (ind.)
           Free to women in
           prisons and mental
           institutions.
  Sing: $ 3

Confr
CONFRONTATION
Martin Tucker, Ed.
English Dept.
Brooklyn Center of Long Island
  U
Brooklyn, NY 11201
Subs: Business Manager
       Eleanor Feleppa
       Office of the Director
       of Public Relations
       Southampton College
       Southampton, NY 11968
  (20)
  Subs: $15/3 yrs
           $10/2 yrs
           $ 5/yr
  Sing: $ 3
  Back: $ 2

CreamCR
*CREAM CITY REVIEW
Henri R. Cole, Ed.
Lynda Olson, Po. Ed.

Box 413
English Dept.
U of Wisconsin--Milwaukee
Milwaukee, WI 53201
 (5:1-2)
  Subs: $6/yr
  Sing: $3

CropD
*CROP DUST
Edward C. Lynskey, Ed.
Route 2   Box 392
Bealeton, VA 22712
 (1-2/3)
  Subs: $8/yr
  Sing: $3

CutB
CUTBANK
Sandra Alcosser
Ralph Beer, Eds.
Dept. of English
U of Montana
Missoula, MT 59812
 (14-15)
  Subs: $7.50/2 yrs
              $4/yr
  Sing: $2.50

DacTerr
DACOTAH TERRITORY
Mark Vinz
Grayce Ray, Eds.
Moorhead State U
Box 775
Moorhead, MN 56560
 (17)
  Sing: $2

DenQ
DENVER QUARTERLY
Leland H. Chambers, Ed.
U of Denver
Denver, CO 80208
 (14:4) (15:1-3)
  Subs: $14/2 yrs
              $ 8/yr
  Sing: $ 2

Durak
DURAK
Robert Lloyd

D. S. Hoffman, Eds.
166 S. Sycamore St.
Los Angeles, CA 90036
or
RD 1   Box 352
Joe Green Rd.
Erin, NY 14838
 (4-5)
  Subs: $7/2 yrs
              $3.50/yr
  Sing: $1.95
  Back: $2.50
  Set: $10

EngJ
ENGLISH JOURNAL
Ken Donelson
Alleen Pace Nilsen, Eds.
College of Education
Arizona State U
Tempe, AZ 85281
Subs: NCTE
        1111 Kenyon Rd.
        Urbana, IL 61801
 (69:5-9)
  Subs: $30/yr (inst.)
              $25/yr (ind.)
  Sing: $ 3

EnPas
EN PASSANT
James A. Costello, Ed.
1906 Brant Rd.
Wilmington, DE 19810
 (10-11)
  Subs: $11/8
              $ 6/4
  Sing: $ 1.75
  Back: $ 1.50

Epoch
EPOCH
James McConkey
Walter Slatoff, Eds.
245 Goldwin Smith Hall
Cornell U
Ithaca, NY 14853
 (29:2-3)
  Subs: $5/yr
  Sing: $2

Falcon
THE FALCON
W. A. Blais, Ed.
Mansfield State College
Mansfield, PA 16933
(19)
    Sing: $2
    Final issue.

Field
FIELD
Stuart Friebert
David Young, Eds.
Rice Hall
Oberlin College
Oberlin, OH 44074
(22-23)
    Subs: $8/2 yrs
            $5/yr
    Sing: $2.50
    Back: $10

Focus
FOCUS/MIDWEST
Charles L. Klotzer, Ed./Pub.
Dan Jaffe, Po. Ed.
928a N. McKnight
St. Louis, MO 63132
(14:85-88)
    Subs: $100/life
            $29/30
            $19.50/18
            $14/12
            $8/6
    Sing: $1.25

FourQt
FOUR QUARTERS
La Salle College
20th & Olney Aves.
Philadelphia, PA 19141
(29:2-4) (30:1)
    Subs: $7/2 yrs
            $4/yr
    Sing: $1

GeoR
GEORGIA REVIEW
Stanley W. Lindberg, Ed.
U of Georgia
Athens, GA 30602
(34:1-4)

Subs: $10/2 yrs
        $ 6/yr
Sing: $ 3

Glass
GLASSWORKS
Betty Bressi, Ed.
Box 163
Rosebank Sta.
Staten Island, NY 10305
(-)
    Note: Suspended w.
    (3:1/2/3) in 1978.

GreenfieldR
THE GREENFIELD REVIEW
Joseph Bruchac III, Ed.
Carol Worthen Bruchac,
Managing Ed.
Greenfield Center
New York 12833
(-)
    Subs: $5/2
    Sing: $3

GRR
GREEN RIVER REVIEW
Raymond Tyner, Ed.
Saginaw Valley State College
Box 56
University Center, MI 48710
(11:1-2/3)
    Subs: $6/yr
    Sing: $2

HangL
HANGING LOOSE
Robert Hershon, et al., Eds.
231 Wyckoff St.
Brooklyn, NY 11217
(37-38)
    Subs: $15/12
            $10/8
            $ 5.50/4
    Sing: $ 1.50

Harp
HARPER'S MAGAZINE
Lewis H. Lapham, Ed.
Hayden Carruth, Po. Ed.
Two Park Ave.
New York, NY 10016

(260:1556-61) (261:1562-67)
Subs: $14/yr
Sing: $ 1.50

Hills
HILLS
Bob Perelman, Ed.
36 Clyde St.
San Francisco, CA 94107
  (6/7)
  Sing: $2

HiramPoR
HIRAM POETRY REVIEW
David Fratus
Carol Donley, Eds.
Box 162
Hiram, OH 44234
  (27-28)
  Subs: $2/yr
  Sing: $1

Hudson
THE HUDSON REVIEW
Paula Dietz
Frederick Morgan, Eds.
65 E. 55th St.
New York, NY 10022
  (33:1-4)
  Subs: $12/yr
  Sing: $ 3.50

Humanist
HUMANIST
Lloyd L. Morain, Ed.
7 Harwood Dr.
Amherst, NY 14226
  (40:1-6)
  Subs: $12/yr
  Sing: $ 2
  Back: $ 2.50

Im
IMAGES
Gary Pacernik, Ed.
Dept. of English
Wright State U
Dayton, OH 45435
  (6:2) (7:1)
  Subs: $3/yr
  Sing: $1

Iowa
IOWA REVIEW
David Hamilton
Fredrick Woodard, Eds.
308 EPB
The U of Iowa
Iowa City, IA 52242
  (10:4) (11:1)
  Subs: $8/yr (inst.)
             $7/yr (ind.)
  Sing: $2

JnlONJP
JOURNAL OF NEW JERSEY
  POETS
V. B. Halpert, Managing Ed.
M. Keyishian, et al., Eds.
English Dept.
Fairleigh Dickinson U
285 Madison Ave.
Madison, NJ 07940
  (-)
  Subs: $3/2
  Sing: $1.50

JnlOPC
JOURNAL OF POPULAR CUL-
  TURE
Ray B. Browne, Ed.
Popular Culture Center
Bowling Green U
Bowling Green, OH 43403
  (-)
  Subs: $25/2 yrs
             $15/yr
  Sing: $5

KanQ
KANSAS QUARTERLY
Harold Schneider, et al., Eds.
Dept. of English
Kansas State U
Manhattan, KS 66506
  (12:1-4)
  Subs: $18/2 yrs
             $10/yr
  Sing: $ 2.50
  Back: $ 2.50

Kayak
KAYAK

George Hitchcock, Ed.
Marjorie Simon, Assoc.
325 Ocean View Ave.
Santa Cruz, CA 95062
  (53-55)
  Subs: $5/4
  Sing: $1

LitR
THE LITERARY REVIEW
Martin Green
Harry Keyishian, Eds.
Fairleigh Dickinson U
285 Madison Ave.
Madison, NJ 07940
  (23:3-4) (24:1-2)
  Subs: $9/yr
  Sing: $3.50

LittleBR
*THE LITTLE BALKANS RE-
  VIEW
Gene DeGruson, Po. Ed.
The Little Balkans Press, Inc.
601 Grandview Heights Terr.
Pittsburg, KS 66762
  (1:1)
  Sing: $3.50

LittleM
THE LITTLE MAGAZINE
Felicity Thoet, Ed.
John Silbersack, Managing Ed.
Box 207
Cathedral Station
New York, NY 10025
  (12:3/4)
  Subs: $7/4
  Sing: $1.50

LittleR
THE LITTLE REVIEW
John McKernan, Ed.
Little Review Press
Box 205
Marshall U
Huntington, WV 25701
  (13/14)
  Subs: $2.50
  Sing: $1.25

MalR
THE MALAHAT REVIEW
Robin Skelton, Ed.
Box 1700
Victoria, BC
Canada V8W 2Y2
  (53-56)
  Subs: $25/3 yrs
            $10/yr

MassR
THE MASSACHUSETTS REVIEW
John Hicks
Robert Tucker, Eds.
Memorial Hall
U of Massachusetts
Amherst, MA 01003
  (21:1-4)
  Subs: $10/yr
  Sing: $ 3

MichQR
MICHIGAN QUARTERLY REVIEW
Laurence Goldstein, Ed.
3032 Rackham Bldg.
The U of Michigan
Ann Arbor, MI 48109
  (19:1-19:4/20:1)
  Subs: $22/3 yrs
            $16/2 yrs
            $10/yr (inst.)
            $ 9/yr (ind.)
  Sing: $ 2.50
  Back: $ 2.00
  Note: (19:4/20:1) is a
  special issue entitled The
  Automobile and American Cul-
  ture and is available for $7.

MidwQ
THE MIDWEST QUARTERLY
V. J. Emmett, Jr., Ed.
Michael Heffernan, Po. Ed.
Pittsburg State U
Pittsburg, KS 66762
  (21:2-4) (22:1)
  Subs: $4/yr
  Sing: $1.50

MinnR
THE MINNESOTA REVIEW

Roger Mitchell, Ed.
Box 211
Bloomington, IN 47402
  (NS14-NS15)
    Subs: $15 /2 yrs (inst.)
                   $11 /2 yrs (ind.)
                   $ 9 /yr (inst.)
                   $ 6 /yr (ind.)
    Sing: $ 3

MissouriR
MISSOURI REVIEW
Speer Morgan, Ed.
Dept. of English
231 Arts & Science
U of Missouri
Columbia, MO 65211
  (3:2-3) (4:1)
    Subs: $12 /2 yrs
                   $ 7 /yr
    Sing: $ 2. 50

MissR
MISSISSIPPI REVIEW
The Center for Writers
Box 5144
Hattiesburg, MS 39401
  (-)

Modern PS
MODERN POETRY STUDIES
Jerry McGuire
Robert Miklitsch, Eds.
207 Delaware Ave.
Buffalo, NY 14202
  (10:1)
    Subs: $9 /3 (inst.)
                   $7. 50 /3 (ind.)

Montra
MONTEMORA
Eliot Weinberger, Ed.
The Montemora Foundation,
  Inc.
Box 336 Cooper Sta.
New York, NY 10276
  (Supp) (7)
    Subs: $12 /3 (inst.)
                   $10 /3 (ind.)
    Sing: $4

Mouth
MOUTH OF THE DRAGON
Andrew Bifrost, Ed.
BIFROST
Box 957
New York, NY 10019
  (2:4-5)
    Subs: $36 /10 (lib.)
                   $15 /5 (ind.)
    Sing: $ 3. 50
    Final issue.

Mund
MUNDUS ARTIUM
Rainer Schulte, Ed.
U of Texas at Dallas
Box 688
Richardson, TX 75080
  (-)
    Subs: $10 /2 (inst.)
                   $ 8 /2 (ind.)
    Sing: $ 4

Nat
THE NATION
Victor Navasky, Ed.
Grace Schulman, Po. Ed.
72 Fifth Ave.
New York, NY 10011
  (230:1-25) (231:1-22)
    Subs: $50 /2 yrs
                   $30 /yr
                   $15 /1-2 yr
    Sing: $ 1. 25

NegroHB
NEGRO HISTORY BULLETIN
J. Rupert Picott, Ed.
1401 14th St. , N. W.
Washington, DC 20005
  (43:1-4)
    Subs: $16 /yr
    Sing: $ 4. 50

NewEngR
NEW ENGLAND REVIEW
Sydney Lea, Ed.
Box 170
Hanover, NH 03768
  (3:2)
    Subs: $12 /yr

Sing: $ 4
Incomplete--issues missing.

NewL
NEW LETTERS
David Ray, Ed.
U of Missouri--Kansas City
5346 Charlotte
Kansas City, MO 64110
  (46:3-4) (47:1)
    Subs: $50 /5 yrs (lib.)
                 $40 /5 yrs (ind.)
                 $21 /2 yrs (lib.)
                 $18 /2 yrs (ind.)
                 $12 /yr (lib.)
                 $10 /yr (ind.)
    Sing: $ 3
    Back: Prices on re-
                 quest.

NewOR
NEW ORLEANS REVIEW
John Biguenet, Ed.
Box 195
Loyola U
New Orleans, LA 70118
  (7:1-3)
    Subs: $19 /3 yrs
                 $13 /2 yrs
                 $ 7 /yr
    Sing: $ 2.50

NewRena
THE NEW RENAISSANCE
Louise T. Reynolds, Ed.
Stanwood Bolton, Po. Ed.
9 Heath Road
Arlington, MA 02174
  (12-13)
    Subs: $7 /3
    Sing: $3. 50

NewRep
THE NEW REPUBLIC
Martin Peretz, Ed. /Pub.
Robert Pinsky, Po. Ed.
1220 19th St., N.W.
Washington, DC 20036
  (182:1 /2-26) (183:1 /2-26)
    Subs: $28 /yr
                 $17 /yr (stud.)
    Sing: $ 1

NewWR
NEW WORLD REVIEW
Marilyn Bechtel, Ed.
Suite 308
156 Fifth Avenue
New York, NY 10010
  (48:1-6)
    Subs: $5 /yr
    Sing: $1

NewYorker
THE NEW YORKER
Howard Moss, Po. Ed.
25 W. 43rd St.
New York, NY 10036
  (55:47-53) (56:1-45)
    Subs: $46 /2 yrs
                 $28 /yr
    Sing: $ 1. 25

NewYRB
THE NEW YORK REVIEW OF
  BOOKS
Robert B. Silvers
Barbara Epstein, Eds.
250 W. 57th St.
New York, NY 10107
    Subs: Subs Service Dept.
           Box 940
           Farmingdale, NY 11737
  (27:1-21 /22)
    Subs: $20 /yr
    Sing: $ 1. 25

Nimrod
NIMROD
Francine Ringold, Ed.
Arts and Humanities Council of
  Tulsa
2210 South Main
Tulsa, OK 74114
  (24:1)
    Subs: $16. 50 /6
                 $11 /4
                 $ 5. 50 /2
    Sing: $ 3

NoAmR
NORTH AMERICAN REVIEW
Robley Wilson, Jr., Ed.
Peter Cooley, Po. Ed.
U of Northern Iowa

1222 W. 27th St.
Cedar Falls, IA 50614
   (265:1-4)
   Subs: $8/yr
   Sing: $2

Northeast
NORTHEAST
John Judson, Ed.
Juniper Press
1310 Shorewood Drive
LaCrosse, WI 54601
   (3:8-9)
   Subs: $15/yr
   Sing: $ 2.50

NorthSR
NORTH STONE REVIEW
James Naiden, Ed.
U Station
Box 14098
Minneapolis, MN 55414
   (-)
   Subs: $7.50/3 (inst.)
            $6.50/3 (ind.)
   Sing: $3

NowestR
NORTHWEST REVIEW
John Witte, Ed.
John Addiego, Po. Ed.
U of Oregon
Eugene, OR 97403
   (18:3)
   Subs: $16/3 yrs
            $11/2 yrs
  $10/2 yrs (stud.)
  $ 6/yr
  $ 5/yr (stud.)
   Sing: $ 2.50

Obs
OBSIDIAN
Alvin Aubert, Ed./Pub.
Wayne State U
Detroit, MI 48202
   (5:1/2-3)
   Subs: $5.50/yr
   Sing: $2

Ohio R
OHIO REVIEW

Wayne Dodd, Ed.
Ellis Hall
Ohio U
Athens, OH 45701
   (24-25)
   Subs: $25/9
            $10/3
   Sing: $ 3.50

OntR
*ONTARIO REVIEW
Raymond J. Smith, Ed.
9 Honey Brook Dr.
Princeton, NJ 08540
   (12-13)
   Subs: $18/3 yrs
            $13/2 yrs
            $ 7/yr
   Sing: $ 3.95

OP
OPEN PLACES
Eleanor M. Bender, Ed.
Box 2085
Stephens College
Columbia, MO 65215
   (29-30)
   Subs: $7/2 yrs
            $4/yr
   Sing: $2

Os
OSIRIS
Andrea Moorhead, Ed.
Box 297
Deerfield, MA 01342
   (10-11)
   Subs: $4/2
   Sing: $2

Outbr
*OUTERBRIDGE
Charlotte Alexander, Ed.
Margery Cornwell-Robinson,
   Asst.
English Dept.
College of Staten Island
715 Ocean Terr.
Staten Island, NY 10301
   (4/5)
   Subs: $4/yr
   Sing: $2

Paint
PAINTBRUSH
Dr. Ben Bennani
Dept. of English
U of Riyadh
Box 2456
Riyadh, Saudi Arabia
Subs: Jelm Mountain Pubs.
         209 Grand Ave.
         Suite 205
         Laramie, WY 82070
   (-)
Subs: $12 /2 yrs
            $ 7 /yr
Sing: $ 4

Pan
PANACHE
David Lenson, Pub.
Candice Ward, Ed.
Box 77
Sunderland, MA 01375
   (21)
Sing: $3
Note: (23) will be a ten
year retrospective issue.

ParisR
THE PARIS REVIEW
George A. Plimpton, et al., Eds.
Jonathan Galassi, Po. Ed.
45-39 171 Place
Flushing, NY 11358
Poetry Mss.:
   541 E. 72nd St.
   New York, NY 10021
   (77-78)
Subs: $20 /8
            $11 /4
Sing: $ 3. 50

PartR
PARTISAN REVIEW
William Phillips, Ed.
Boston U
128 Bay State Rd.
Boston, MA 02215
   (47:1-4)
Subs: $27 /3 yrs
            $19 /2 yrs
            $10 /yr
Sing: $ 2. 75

Paunch
PAUNCH
Arthur Efron, Ed.
123 Woodward Ave.
Buffalo, NY 14214
   (-)

Peb
PEBBLE
Greg Kuzma, Ed.
The Best Cellar Press
118 S. Boswell Ave.
Crete, NE 68333
   (-)

Pequod
PEQUOD
David Paradis, Ed.
536 Hill St.
San Francisco, CA 94114
Poetry Mss.:
   Mark Rudman, Po. Ed.
   817 West End Ave.
   New York, NY 10025
   (11)
Subs: $12 /3 yrs
            $ 9 /2 yrs
            $ 5 /yr
Sing: $ 3

Pig
PIGIRON
Jim Villani, Managing Ed.
Rose Sayre, Associate Ed.
Box 237
Youngstown, OH 44501
   (7)
Subs: $7 /yr
Sing: $4

PikeF
THE PIKESTAFF FORUM
James R. Scrimgeour
Robert D. Sutherland, Eds. /
   Pubs.
Box 127
Normal, IL 61761
   (3)
Subs: $10 /6
Sing: $ 2

PikeR
THE PIKESTAFF REVIEW
   See PikeF above.

Playb
PLAYBOY
Hugh M. Hefner, Ed./Pub.
919 N. Michigan Ave.
Chicago, IL 60611
   (27:1-12)
   Subs: $18/yr
   Sing: Varies.

Ploughs
PLOUGHSHARES
DeWitt Henry
Peter O'Malley, Dirs.
Box 529
Cambridge, MA 02139
   (6:1-3)
   Subs: $10/yr
   Sing: $ 3.50

Poem
POEM
Robert L. Welker, Ed.
Box 1247
West Station
Huntsville, AL 35807
Subs: Box 91
        Huntsville, AL 35804
   (38-40)
   Subs: $5/yr

PoetC
POET AND CRITIC
David Cummings, Ed.
203 Ross Hall
Iowa State U
Ames, IA 50011
   (12:1-3)
   Subs: $7/2 yrs
                $4/yr
   Sing: $2

Poetry
POETRY
John Frederick Nims, Ed.
601 S. Morgan St.
Box 4348
Chicago, IL 60680
   (135:4-6) (136:1-6) (137:1-3)

Subs: $20/yr
Sing: $2 + 25¢ postage
Back: $2.25 + 25¢ postage

PoetryE
*POETRY EAST
Kate Daniels
Richard Jones, Eds.
1909 Jefferson Park Ave. #3
Charlottesville, VA 22903
   (1-3)

PoetryNW
POETRY NORTHWEST
David Wagoner, Ed.
4045 Brooklyn Ave. N.E.
U of Washington
Seattle, WA 98105
   (21:1-4)
   Subs: $5/yr
   Sing: $1.50

PoNow
POETRY NOW
E. V. Griffith, Ed./Pub.
3118 K Street
Eureka, CA 95501
   (26-29)
   Subs: $19/18
                $13/12
                $ 7.50/6
   Sing: $ 1.50

PortR
THE INTERNATIONAL PORT-
   LAND REVIEW
Cindy Ragland, Ed.
Box 751
Portland, OR 97207
   (26)
   Subs: (-)
   Sing: $8.95 for issue
                (26),
   a 504-page international issue.

PottPort
THE POTTERSFIELD PORT-
   FOLIO
Lesley Choyce, Ed./Pub.
Pottersfield Press
RR #2 Porters Lake
Nova Scotia B0J 2S0

15   Periodicals Indexed

Canada
(1-2)
Subs: $3. 75/yr
Sing: $3. 75
Back: $5

PraS
PRAIRIE SCHOONER
Hugh Luke, Ed.
201 Andrews Hall
U of Nebraska
Lincoln, NE 68588
(54:1-4)
Subs: $24/3 yrs
         $16.50/2 yrs
         $12/yr (lib.)
         $ 9/yr
Sing: $ 2.50

Prima
*PRIMAVERA
Janet Heller, et al. , Eds.
1212 E. 59th St.
U of Chicago
Chicago, IL 60637
(5)
Sing: $3.50

QRL
QUARTERLY REVIEW OF
   LITERATURE
T. & R. Weiss
26 Haslet Avenue
Princeton, NJ 08540
(-)
Subs: $20/2 (cloth)
         $10/2 (paper)
Sing: $13 (cloth)
         $ 5.95

QW
QUARTERLY WEST
Michael Dobberstein, Ed.
Joe Alfandre, Managing Ed.
312 Olpin Union
U of Utah
Salt Lake City, UT 84112
(10-11)
Subs: $8/4
Sing: $4.50/2

RusLT
RUSSIAN LITERATURE TRI-
   QUARTERLY
Carl R. Proffer
Ellendea Proffer, Eds.
Ardis Publishers
2901 Heatherway
Ann Arbor, MI 48104
(-)
Subs: $25/3 (inst.)
         $16.95/3 (ind.)
         $13.95/3 (stud.)
Back: Prices on request.
Cloth: Add $10 to each
         rate.

Salm
SALMAGUNDI
Robert Boyers, Ed.
Peggy Boyers, Exec. Ed.
Skidmore College
Saratoga Springs, NY 12866
(47/48-50/51)
Subs: $20/2 yrs (inst.)
         $10/2 yrs (ind.)
         $12/yr (inst.)
         $ 6/yr (ind.)

Sam
SAMISDAT
Merritt Clifton
Robin Michelle Clifton, Eds.
Box 129
Richford, VT 05476
or
Box 10
Brigham, Quebec
JOE 1J0
Canada
(81-103)
Subs: $100/all future
         issues
         $20/1000 pp.
         $12/500 pp.
Sing: Varies.

SeC
SECOND COMING
A. D. Winans, Ed.
Box 31249
San Francisco, CA 94131

(-)
Subs: $6.50/yr (lib.)
           $4/yr (ind.)

SenR
SENECA REVIEW
James Crenner
Bob Herz, Eds.
Hobart & William Smith Col-
leges
Geneva, NY 14456
(-)
Subs: $5/yr
Sing: $3

SewanR
SEWANEE REVIEW
George Core, Ed.
U of the South
Sewanee, TN 37375
(88:1-4)
Subs: $37/3 yrs (inst.)
           $28/3 yrs (ind.)
           $26/2 yrs (inst.)
           $20/2 yrs (ind.)
           $15/yr (inst.)
           $12/yr (ind.)
Sing: $ 2.75
Back: $ 4.50

Shen
SHENANDOAH
James Boatwright, Ed.
Richard Howard, Po. Ed.
Washington and Lee U
Box 722
Lexington, VA 24450
(31:1-2)
Subs: $8/2 yrs
           $5/yr
Sing: $1.50
Back: $2.50

Sky
SKYWRITING
Martin Grossman, Ed.
511 Campbell Ave.
Kalamazoo, MI 49007
(-)
Subs: $5/2
Sing: $2.50

SlowLR
SLOW LORIS READER
Patricia Petrosky, Ed.
923 Highview St.
Pittsburgh, PA 15206
(4)
Subs: $10/4
           $ 5.50/2
Sing: $ 3

SmF
SMALL FARM
Jeff Daniel Marion, Ed.
Route 5 Cline Rd.
Box 345
Dandridge, TN 37725
(11/12)
Sing: $5
Final issue.

SmPd
SMALL POND
Napoleon St. Cyr, Ed./Pub.
Box 664
Stratford, CT 06497
(48-50)
Subs: $13.50/3 yrs
           $ 9/2 yrs
           $ 4.75/yr
Sing: $ 2

SoCaR
SOUTH CAROLINA REVIEW
Richard J. Calhoun
Robert W. Hill, Eds.
Dept. of English
Clemson U
Clemson, SC 29631
(12:2) (13:1)
Subs: $5/2 yrs
           $3/yr
Sing: $2

SoDakR
SOUTH DAKOTA REVIEW
John R. Milton, Ed.
Box 111
U Exchange
Vermillion, SD 57069
(18:1-4)
Subs: $10/2 yrs

$ 6 /yr
Sing: $ 2

Some
SOME
Alan Ziegler, et al. , Eds.
309 W. 104th St.
Apt. 9D
New York, NY 10025
(-)
Subs: $9 /yr (inst.)
          $5 /yr (ind.)
Sing: $2. 50

SouthernHR
SOUTHERN HUMANITIES RE-
  VIEW
Barbara A. Mowat
David K. Jeffrey, Eds.
9088 Haley Center
Auburn U
Auburn, AL 36849
(14:1-4)
Subs: $8 /yr
Sing: $2. 50

SouthernPR
SOUTHERN POETRY REVIEW
Robert Grey, Ed.
English Dept.
U of North Carolina
Charlotte, NC 28223
(20:1-4)
Subs: $4/yr
Sing: $2

SouthernR
SOUTHERN REVIEW
Donald E. Stanford
Lewis P. Simpson, Eds.
Drawer D
U Station
Baton Rouge, LA 70893
(16:1-4)
Subs: $13 /3 yrs
          $ 9 /2 yrs
          $ 5 /yr
Sing: $ 1. 50

SouthwR
SOUTHWEST REVIEW
Margaret L. Hartley, Ed.

Southern Methodist U
Dallas, TX 75275
(65:1-4)
Subs: $13 /3 yrs
          $10 /2 yrs
          $ 6 /yr
Sing: $- 1. 50

Sparrow
SPARROW
Felix & Selma Stefanile, Eds.
Sparrow Press
103 Waldron St.
West Lafayette, IN 47906
(40)
Subs: $6 /3
Sing: $2

Spirit
THE SPIRIT THAT MOVES US
Morty Sklar, Ed.
The Spirit That Moves Us Press
Box 1585
Iowa City, IA 52244
(5:1 /2)
Subs: $12 /2 yrs (lib.)
          $ 9/2 yrs (ind.)
          $ 6. 50 /yr (lib.)
          $ 5 /yr (ind.)
Sing: $ 2

Stand
STAND
Jon Silkin, Ed.
Jim Kates, American Ed.
16 Forest St.
Norwell, MA 02061
Subs: 19 Haldane Terrace
       Newcastle-upon-Tyne
       NE2 3AN
       England
(21:1-4)
Subs: $10 /yr (inst.)
          $ 8. 50 /yr (ind.)
Sing: $ 2. 50

StoneC
STONE COUNTRY
Judith Neeld, Ed.
20 Lorraine Rd.
Madison, NJ 07940
    (7:1-3)

Subs: $5/3 (lib.)
           $4. 50/3 (ind.)
Sing: $1. 75 & $3. 50
Back: $1. 75

SunM
SUN & MOON
Douglas Messerli
Literary Ed.
4330 Hartwick Rd.   #418
College Park, MD 20740
  (9 /10)
  Subs: $15 /3 (inst.)
             $10 /3 (ind.)
  Sing: $ 4. 50

Tele
TELEPHONE
Maureen Owen, Ed.
Box 672
Old Chelsea Station
New York, NY 10011
  (16)
  Subs: $6 /2

Tendril
TENDRIL
George E. Murphy, Jr. , Ed.
Box 512
Green Harbor, MA 02041
  (7 /8-9)
  Subs: $6 /3
  Sing: $3

13thM
13th MOON
Ellen Marie Bissert, Ed.
Drawer F
Inwood Station
New York, NY 10034
  (-)
  Subs: $12 /3 (inst.)
             $ 6 /3 (ind.)
  Sing: $ 2. 25

ThRiPo
THREE RIVERS POETRY
   JOURNAL
Gerald Costanzo, Ed.
Three Rivers Press
Box 21
Carnegie-Mellon U
Pittsburgh, PA 15213

(15 /16)
Subs: $5 /4
Sing: $1. 50

Thrpny
*THE THREEPENNY REVIEW
Wendy Lesser, Ed. /Pub.
Box 335
Berkeley, CA 94701
  (1-3)
  Subs: $7 /2 yrs
             $4 /yr
  Sing: $1

TriQ
TRIQUARTERLY
Elliott Anderson
Jonathan Brent, Eds.
1735 Benson Ave.
Northwestern U
Evanston, IL 60201
  (47-49)
  Subs: $35 /3 yrs
             $25 /2 yrs
             $14 /yr
  Sing: $ 5. 95
  Back: Prices on request.

UnmOx
UNMUZZLED OX
Michael Andre, Ed.
105 Hudson St.
New York, NY 10013
  (21)
  Subs: $8 /4
  Sing: $3. 95

Ur
URTHKIN
Larry Ziman, Ed. /Pub.
Box 67485
Los Angeles, CA 90067
  (-)
  Sing: $3. 95

US1
U. S. 1 WORKSHEETS
Rod Tuloss, Ed.
US 1 Poets' Cooperative
21 Lake Dr.
Roosevelt, NJ 08555
  (12 /13)
  Subs: $4 /8
  Sing: $1. 50

UTR
UT REVIEW
Duane Locke, Ed.
U of Tampa
Tampa, FL 33606
  (6:1-3/4)
  Subs: $9/4
  Sing: $2.50 & $5

VirQR
VIRGINIA QUARTERLY RE-
  VIEW
Staige D. Blackford, Ed.
Gregory Orr, Poetry Cons.
One West Range
Charlottesville, VA 22903
  (56:1-4)
  Subs: $24/3 yrs
             $18/2 yrs
             $10/yr
  Sing: $ 3

Vis
*VISIONS
Bradley R. Strahan, Ed./Pub.
Black Buzzard Press
2217 Shorefield Rd.
Apt. 532
Wheaton, MD 20902
  (1-4)
  Subs: $7/3
  Sing: $2.50

WatT
*WATER TABLE
Sharon Bryan
Linda Gregerson, Eds.
845 Bellevue Place East   #206
Seattle, WA 98102
  (1)
  Sing: $3
  Ceased publication.

WebR
WEBSTER REVIEW
Nancy Schapiro, Ed.
Webster College
Webster Groves, MO 63119
  (5:1-2)
  Subs: $4/yr
  Sing: $2

WestHR
WESTERN HUMANITIES RE-
  VIEW
Jack Garlington, Ed.
U of Utah
Salt Lake City, UT 84112
  (34:1-4)
  Subs: $15/yr (inst.)
             $10/yr (ind.)
  Sing: $ 2.50

Wind
WIND
Quentin R. Howard, Ed.
RFD Route 1
Box 809K
Pikeville, KY 41501
  (36-38)
  Subs: $6/4 (inst.)
             $5/4 (ind.)
  Sing: $1.25

WindO
THE WINDLESS ORCHARD
Robert Novak, Ed.
English Dept.
Indiana-Purdue U
Fort Wayne, IN 46805
  (36-37)
  Subs: $20/3 yrs
             $ 7/yr
             $ 4/yr (stud.)
  Sing: $ 2

WorldO
WORLD ORDER
Firuz Kazemzadeh, Ed.
415 Linden Ave.
Wilmette, IL 60091
  (14:1-3/4)
  Subs: $11/2 yrs
             $ 6/yr
  Sing: $ 1.60

WormR
WORMWOOD REVIEW
Marvin Malone, Ed.
Ernest Stranger, Art Ed.
Box 8840
Stockton, CA 95204
  (77-80)

        Subs: $12/4 (patrons)
                        $ 6/4 (inst.)
                        $ 4/4 (ind.)
        Sing: $ 2

YaleR
THE YALE REVIEW
Kai T. Erikson, Ed.
J. D. McClatchy, Po. Ed.
    (v. 70)
1902A Yale Sta.
New Haven, CT 06520
    (69:3-4) (70:1-2)
    Subs: $12/yr (inst.)
                    $10/yr (ind.)
    Sing: $ 3
    Back: Prices on request.

Zahir
ZAHIR
Diane Kruchkow, Ed.
Box 715
Newburyport, MA 01950
    (-)
    Subs: $6/2 (inst.)
                    $4/2 (ind.)
    Sing: $2.50

THE INDEX

AAL, Katharyn Machan
  "Beverly. " Pig (7) My 80, p. 90.
  "1979. " Outbr (4/5) Aut 79-Spr 80, p. 57.
  "The Train Aisle. " Tele (16) 80, p. 123.
  "Watching the 11:00 News (Ithaca, NY: 2/7/78). " Tele (16) 80,
       p. 123.

AARON, Howard
  "Phosphors. " SlowLR (4) 80, p. 71.
  "Urban Exit, Rural Ingress. " SlowLR (4) 80, p. 73.

AARON, Jonathan
  "Farther Away. " NewYorker (56:13) 19 My 80, p. 100.

ABBOTT, Anthony S.
  "Fool's Paradise. " SouthernPR (20:2) Aut 80, p. 33.

ABERG, W. M.
  "Dividing the Field. " CutB (15) Aut/Wint 80, p. 54.
  "The Lark and the Emperor. " Bits (11) 80.

ABERG, William
  "The Remembering" (for L & L). EnPas (11) 80, p. 11.

ABRAMS, Doug
  "Choice. " CapeR (16:1) Wint 80, p. 34.

ABRAMS, Eric
  "Light Be Nimble. " Focus (14:86) Ap 80, p. 35.

ABRAMS, Judith Ann
  "A Hospital Room. " CimR (50) Ja 80, p. 33.

ABRAMS, Sam
  "Diomedes for President. " Tele (16) 80, p. 85.
  "The Most. " Tele (16) 80, p. 86.
  "Notes from the Plague Planet. " MichQR (19:4/20:1) Aut-Wint
       80-81, p. 758.
  "Proof. " Tele (16) 80, p. 85.
  "Second Homeric Hymn to Paulette Goddard. " Tele (16) 80, p.
       86.

21

ABRAMSON, Neal
   "Dry Heart. " Confr (20) Spr-Sum 80, p. 88.

ABSE, Dannie
   "Lunch and Afterwards. " Iowa (11:1) Wint 80, p. 100.
   "Of Itzig and His Dog. " Iowa (11:1) Wint 80, p. 102.

ABSHER, Tom
   "Pure and Simple. " PoNow (29) 80, p. 1.
   "July. " PoNow (29) 80, p. 1.

ACKERMAN, Diane
   "Sister Juana Ines de la Cruz, Hearing That Her Lover, Giorgio,
      Has Drowned. " AmerPoR (9:4) Jl-Ag 80, p. 35.

ACKERSON, Duane
   "Eating Bread. " PoNow (26) 80, p. 15.

ADAM, Helen
   "At the Window. " SunM (9/10) Sum 80, p. 158.
   "The Hermit. " Ark (14) 80, p. 151.
   "Seven Stars. " SunM (9/10) Sum 80, p. 160.
   "A Tale Best Forgotten. " SunM (9/10) Sum 80, p. 157.
   "Troynovant Is Now No More a City. " SunM (9/10) Sum 80, p.
      156.

ADAM, Ruth
   "In the Night Club. " GRR (11:2/3) 80, p. 7.
   "Mary-mary Poems. " GRR (11:2/3) 80, p. 80.

ADAMO, Ralph
   "Dead Letter and Lotus Centerfold. " Bound (8:2) Wint 80, p.
      316.
   "In My Latest Letter to the Free World I Said. " Bound (8:2)
      Wint 80, p. 315.
   "That Hand" (for RMG). Bound (8:2) Wint 80, p. 314.

ADAMS, Ann
   "To a Teenage Daughter. " PottPort (1) 79-80, p. 29.

ADAMS, David
   from Another Place: "Ohio Clouds" (for Angela). StoneC (7:2)
      My 80, p. 22.
   "Going Home. " Wind (36) 80, p. 2.
   "A Hunter With No Luck at All. " Wind (36) 80, p. 1.

ADAMSON, Robert
   "My House. " NewL (46:3) Spr 80, p. 31.

ADCOCK, Betty
   "Topsail Island. " SouthernPR (20:2) Aut 80, p. 12.

ADCOCK, Fleur
"Influenza. "   PortR (26) 80, p. 101.
"Widowed. "   PortR (26) 80, p. 102.

ADDIEGO, John
"California Radio Frequency. "   CalQ (16/17) 80, p. 45.
"It's Been Good to Know You" (for Woody Guthrie).   CalQ (16/
17) 80, p. 44.
"A Resort on the Warm Springs Reservation. "   PoNow (29) 80,
p. 1.

ADKINS, Carl A.
"The Silence of Recognition. "   KanQ (12:3) Sum 80, p. 91.

ADLER, Jeremy
"Affluence" (tr. of Franz Wurm).   PortR (26) 80, p. 381.

AGBOBLI, Fred
"Fertility Dance. "   PortR (26) 80, p. 149.

AHERN, Maureen
"Boarding School" (tr. of Cecilia Bustamente).   NewOR (7:3) 80,
p. 285.
"A Dead Man" (to Rafael Morales) (tr. of Vicente Aleixandre w.
Virginia Randall).   DenQ (15:3) Aut 80, p. 18.
"For Robert Lowell" (tr. of Antonio Cisneros w. David Tipton).
NewOR (7:3) 80, p. 240.
"If You Stay in My Country" (tr. of Enrique Verástegui).
NewOR (7:3) 80, p. 297.
"Metamorphosis of the Sorceress" (to Remedios Vara) (tr. of
Rosario Castellanos).   DenQ (15:1) Spr 80, p. 91.
"My (Love Poem)" (tr. of Mario Montalbetti).   NewOR (7:3) 80,
p. 255.
"My Night" (tr. of Vicente Aleixandre w. Virginia Randall).
DenQ (15:3) Aut 80, p. 20.
"No Star" (tr. of Vicente Aleixandre w. Virginia Randall).
DenQ (15:3) Aut 80, p. 19.
"Passport" (tr. of Rosario Castellanos).   NewOR (7:3) 80, p.
256.
"Speaking of Gabriel" (tr. of Rosario Castellanos).   DenQ (15:1)
Spr 80, p. 90.
"Story" (tr. of Blanca Varela).   NewOR (7:3) 80, p. 291.

AHSAN, Syed Ali
"Ashohaya. "   PortR (26) 80, p. 40.
"Helpless" (tr. of "Ashohaya" by author).   PortR (26) 80, p. 41.

AI
"Conversation" (for Robert Lowell).   ParisR (77) Wint-Spr 80,
p. 116.
"Four Haiku by Issa. "   Ark (14) 80, p. 155.

"Kristallnacht. " Poetry (135:6) Mr 80, p. 340.
"Pentecost" (for myself). Tendril (9) 80, p. 17.
"The Psychiatrist. " Poetry (135:6) Mr 80, p. 338.
"They Shall Not Pass. " Iowa (11:1) Wint 80, p. 103.
"Winter in Another Country. " Poetry (135:6) Mr 80, p. 336.
"Yellow Crane Pavillion. " ParisR (77) Wint-Spr 80, p. 117.

AIKEN, William
"Adventures in Inventory. " WormR (77) 80, p. 32.
"After Winter Storms. " NewRena (12) Spr 80, p. 81.
"House Image. " WormR (77) 80, p. 31.

AKERS, Deborah
"Watching the Boys Come Home. " BelPoJ (30:4) Sum 80, p. 30.

AKESSON, Sonja
"Autobiography" (tr. by Ingrid Clareus). PoetryE (1) 80, pp.
    25-33.

AKHMADULINA, Bella
"Farewell. " PortR (26) 80, p. 340.
"In a Vacated Sanitorium. " PortR (26) 80, p. 335.
"Innovation. " PortR (26) 80, p. 338.

AKINS, Barbara
"Remember This. " HiramPoR (27) Aut-Wint 80, p. 5.
"Renaissance at the Beach. " HiramPoR (27) Aut-Wint 80, p. 6.

ALBERSHARDT, Marty
"At the Bank. " Vis (2) 80.
"Margaret (19) 1977. " Vis (4) 80.

ALBERT, Alan
"I Am Waiting. " PoNow (28) 80, p. 33.
"Until Now. " SouthwR (65:2) Spr 80, p. 177.

ALBERTI, Rafael
from Between the Carnation and the Sword: (7, 11) (tr. by
    Martin Paul and José Elgorriaga). AmerPoR (9:5) S-O 80,
    p. 34.

ALBRECHT, W. P.
"The Beach. " KanQ (12:1) Wint 80, p. 166.

ALBRIGHT, Jeff
"I Stood There Watching the Sky...." Spirit (5:1/2) Aut-Wint
    79-80, p. 24.

ALDRICH, Elizabeth
"I Am Helios. " PartR (47:4) 80, p. 617.

ALDRICH, Marcia
"Apology to the Thin Man. " PoetryNW (21:2) Sum 80, p. 37.

"Suspense. " PoetryNW (21:2) Sum 80, p. 38.

ALDRIDGE, Richard
"How Goes Is. " PoNow (28) 80, p. 32.

ALEGRIA, Claribel
"Eramos Tres. " Cond (6) 80, p. 160.

ALEIXANDRE, Vicente
"Adolescence" (tr. by David Garrison). DenQ (15:3) Aut 80, p. 16.
"Always" (tr. by Willis Barnstone). DenQ (15:3) Aut 80, p. 15.
"At Last" (tr. by Willis Barnstone and David Garrison). DenQ (15:3) Aut 80, p. 14.
"A Dead Man" (to Rafael Morales) (tr. by Virginia Randall and Maureen Ahern). DenQ (15:3) Aut 80, p. 18.
"Face Behind the Glass (The Old Man's Gaze)" (tr. by David Garrison). DenQ (15:3) Aut 80, p. 17.
"My Night" (tr. by Virginia Randall and Maureen Ahern). DenQ (15:3) Aut 80, p. 20.
"My Voice" (tr. by Willis Barnstone). CutB (14) Spr /Sum 80, p. 105.
"No Star" (tr. by Virginia Randall and Maureen Ahern). DenQ (15:3) Aut 80, p. 19.

ALESI, Eros
"Letter to My Father" (tr. by Jan Pallister and Marisa Gatti-Taylor). EnPas (11) 80, pp. 4-10.

ALEXANDER, Bonnie L.
"La Boheme. " Pan (21) 80, p. 38.
"A Duck by the Road. " Pan (21) 80, p. 38.

ALEXANDER, Paul
"The Marble Elephant. " Im (7:1) 80, p. 3.

ALEXANDER, Robert
"At Night the Street. " CreamCR (5:2) Spr 80, p. 87.

ALI, Agha Shahid
"A Butcher. " CharR (6:2) Aut 80, p. 47.
"To the Painter. " CarlMis (18:2) Sum 80, p. 94.

ALIGHIERI, Dante
from the Inferno: "Canto I" (tr. by Willis Barnstone). ChiR (31:4) Spr 80, p. 171.

ALLARDT, Linda
"Calling Home. " PoNow (29) 80, p. 19.
"Latecomers. " PoNow (29) 80, p. 19.
"Watching Him Disconnect. " PoNow (29) 80, p. 19.
"The Whole, Remembering. " PoNow (29) 80, p. 19.

ALLDRED, Pauline
"Between Parallel Lines. " KanQ (12:3) Sum 80, p. 19.
"Captive. " SoCaR (13:1) Aut 80, p. 49.

ALLEN, Gilbert
"To My Brother at Thirty-One. " Epoch (29:3) Spr-Sum 80, p.
    264.

ALLEN, John
"Moskva" (for Russ). StoneC (7:1) F 80, p. 11.

ALLEN, Judith
"Apart: Both of Us Reading Madame Bovary. " Tendril (7/8)
    Spr-Sum 80, p. 7.

ALLEN, June
"The Almost Ring. " Poem (40) N 80, p. 25.
"Arc. " Poem (40) N 80, p. 26.
"Death of a Bird. " Poem (40) N 80, p. 24.

ALLEN, Michael
"China. " ColEng (42:2) O 80, p. 153.

ALLEN, Paul Edward
"Waiting for My Son's Return. " SouthwR (65:3) Sum 80, p. 265.

ALLMAN, John
"Antonin Artaud in the Land of the Tarahumaras. " PoetryNW
    (21:4) Wint 80-81, p. 9.
"The Fixer. " PoNow (28) 80, p. 21.
"Marcel Proust Leaving Princesse Soutzo's Room at the Ritz. "
    PoetryNW (21:4) Wint 80-81, p. 7.
"Personal. " PoNow (28) 80, p. 21.
"Wives of Geniuses. " PoNow (28) 80, p. 21.

ALLRED, Joanne
"Last Gardenia. " QW (11) Aut-Wint 80-81, p. 17.

ALMON, Bert
"Constitutional. " ConcPo (13:2) Aut 80, p. 62.
"Feedback. " PoNow (27) 80, p. 29.
"The Kruegers Talk About the Dusty 30's. " ConcPo (12:2) Aut
    79, p. 57.
"San Francisco Midnight. " KanQ (12:1) Wint 80, p. 165.

ALOFF, Mindy
"For Anita, Who Dreamt of a White Bird Dying. " AmerPoR (9:3)
    My-Je 80, p. 46.

ALTHAUS, Keith
"On This Side. " VirQR (56:2) Spr 80, p. 264.

ALVARADO, Angela
   "Maitines. " Os (10) Spr 80, p. 19.
   "La pérdida. " Os (10) Spr 80, p. 18.

AMATO, Michael
   from These Blank Spaces: (1, 2).   Wind (36) 80, p. 41.

AMES, Evelyn
   "Fishing Through the Ice. " BelPoJ (31:1) Aut 80, p. 4.

AMMONS, A. R.
   "Design. " Hudson (33:1) Spr 80, p. 36.
   "Distraction. " Hudson (33:1) Spr 80, p. 35.
   "Feel Like Traveling On. " Hudson (33:1) Spr 80, p. 37.
   "Negative Pluses. " AmerS (49:1) Wint 79-80, p. 80.
   "Night Finding. " Hudson (33:1) Spr 80, p. 38.
   "Rapids. " Hudson (33:1) Spr 80, p. 36.
   "Room Conditioner. " Tendril (9) 80, p. 18.
   "Spruce Woods. " Hudson (33:1) Spr 80, p. 37.

AMOI, Fatho
   "Partance. " PortR (26) 80, p. 216.

AMSDEN, Bob
   "Busing. " WormR (77) 80, p. 13.
   "Papa. " WormR (77) 80, p. 13.
   "Reunion. " WormR (77) 80, p. 13.

ANAGNOSTOPOULOS, Athan
   from Maria Nephele: Twelve Poems (tr. of Odysseus Elytis).
       ParisR (78) Sum 80, pp. 62-78.

ANCROM, Nancy
   "Love and Friendship. " Tele (16) 80, p. 103.
   "Rothko Retrospective. " Tele (16) 80, p. 102.
   "Spring. " Tele (16) 80, p. 102.

ANDAY, Melih Cevdat
   "All Things Side by Side" (tr. by Talat Halman and Brian
       Swann). PoNow (26) 80, p. 46.
   'In Those Small Lakes" (tr. by Talat Halman and Brian Swann).
       PoNow (26) 80, p. 46.
   "Lycian Women" (tr. by Talat Halman and Brian Swann).   PoNow
       (26) 80, p. 46.
   "Open Window" (tr. by Talat Sait Halman and Brian Swann).
       CharR (6:2) Aut 80, p. 55.

ANDERSON, Bruce B.
   "Primer for a Princess. " Shen (31:1) 79, p. 94.

ANDERSON, Duane
   "Day Off. " Tele (16) 80, p. 113.

ANDERSON, Gerald
"Haiku. " WindO (36) Spr-Sum 80, p. 5.

ANDERSON, Jack
"The Abyss. " HangL (38) Aut 80, p. 8.
"Departure Gate. " PoNow (27) 80, p. 41.
"Explorers. " HangL (38) Aut 80, p. 7.
"Fire Trucks Returning. " HangL (38) Aut 80, p. 3.
"The Folly of Eating Stones. " PoNow (27) 80, p. 9.
"How to Read Poetry. " MissouriR (3:3) Sum 80, p. 38.
"The Movement of a Statue. " MissouriR (3:3) Sum 80, p. 40.
"My Parents in the Locked Room. " PoNow (26) 80, p. 21.
"The Peace of the Evening. " Field (22) Spr 80, p. 55.
"The Peeker. " HangL (38) Aut 80, p. 4.
"The Play of Affection: A Game in Five Moves. " LittleM (12:
    3/4) 80, p. 73.
"The Sick House. " MissouriR (3:3) Sum 80, p. 37.
"Sock Lust. " HangL (38) Aut 80, p. 6.
"Young Man with a Rifle Leaning from a Window. " PoNow (26)
    80, p. 21.

ANDERSON, James
"Your Song. " NewL (46:4) Sum 80, p. 69.

ANDERSON, Kathy Elaine
"Ahmos. " Obs (5:1/2) Spr-Sum 79, p. 106.
"Derrick. " Obs (5:1/2) Spr-Sum 80, p. 106.
"The Grandpa. " Obs (5:1/2) Spr-Sum 79, p. 107.

ANDERSON, Ken
"The Metamorphosis. " Mouth (2:5) O 80, p. 40.

ANDERSON, Michael
"Doors: A Short History of America. " KanQ (12:3) Sum 80, p.
    62.
"Sociobiology Theory. " KanQ (12:3) Sum 80, p. 52.

ANDERSON, Peggy
"Asunder. " ChrC (97:41) 17 D 80, p. 1246.
"Confessional Poet. " ChrC (97:17) 7 My 80, p. 519.

ANDERSON, Susan
"October Birth" (for Shelly). BelPoJ (30:3) Spr 80, p. 12.
"Suicide. " MassR (21:4) Wint 80, p. 766.
"When We Were Rich. " MassR (21:2) Sum 80, p. 343.

ANDERSSON, Claes
"In Helsinki" (tr. by Lennart Bruce). PoetryE (1) 80, p. 40.
"In This Country" (tr. by Lennart Bruce). PoetryE (1) 80, p.
    41.

ANDRE, Michael
"Crumbs for Lytton Strachey. " PoNow (27) 80, p. 21.

"Dying. " PoNow (27) 80, p. 21.
"Gloria Swanson. " PoNow (27) 80, p. 21.
"Revise, Dear John, Downward Those Hopes. " PoNow (28) 80,
    p. 13.
"What Is Poetry This Is. " PoNow (27) 80, p. 21.
"Why Do the Poor Bleed and Tremble?" PoNow (28) 80, p. 13.

ANDREAE, Christina
"Mahabalipuram. " Ark (14) 80, p. 154.
"Nothing Up My Sleeve. " Ark (14) 80, p. 153.

ANGEL, Ralph
"Anxious Latitutdes. " PartR (47:4) 80, p. 614.

ANGELAKI-ROOKE, Katerína
"The Triumph of Constant Loss" (to Andonis Fostieris). PortR
    (26) 80, p. 164.

ANGELL, Roger
"Greetings, Friends. " NewYorker (56:45) 29 D 80, p. 35.

ANGLESEY, Zoe Rita
"The Latest Thing. " CropD (2 /3) Aut-Wint 80, p. 16.

ANGST, Bim
"Confession. " BelPoJ (30:4) Sum 80, p. 7.
"Driving to Work. " BelPoJ (30:4) Sum 80, p. 9.
"Litany. " CapeR (16:1) Wint 80, p. 28.

ANIAKOR, Chike C.
Eleven Poems. Obs (5:1/2) Spr-Sum 79, pp. 94-105.

ANONYMOUS
"Bible Stories. " Playb (27:12) D 80, p. 249.
"Castaway. " Playb (27:3) Mr 80, p. 165.
"Chloe's Candle. " Playb (27:5) My 80, p. 179.
"The Coachman and His Whip. " Playb (27:3) Mr 80, p. 165.
"Flower Basket" (tr. by Graeme Wilson). DenQ (15:3) Aut 80,
    p. 84.
"it ain't the things. " Sam (86) 79, p. 20.
"Ivies" (tr. by Graeme Wilson). DenQ (15:3) Aut 80, p. 81.
"John the Baptist. " Playb (27:12) D 80, p. 249.
"En Keltisk sång om mötet efter döden. " NewRena (12) Spr 80,
    p. 42.
"The Land of Cocaine" (tr. by R. S. Gwynn). Playb (27:6) Je
    80, p. 181.
"Making Love in Darkness" (tr. by Graeme Wilson). DenQ (15:3)
    Aut 80, p. 82.
from Nineteen Ancient Songs: "Thoughts of Returning Home" (tr.
    by Jon Hansen). ChiR (31:4) Spr 80, p. 159.
"Notes from a Psychiatric Worker. " Playb (27:4) Ap 80, p. 74.
"Ten Commandments Plus. " Playb (27:12) D 80, p. 249.

ANSON, Joan
"Hitchhiker. " SmPd (49) Spr 80, p. 14.
"The Vampire. " HiramPoR (27) Aut-Wint 80, p. 7.

ANSON, John I.
"Autumnal. " ArizQ (36:3) Aut 80, p. 196.

ANSON, John S.
"The Sad Adagio. " PoNow (29) 80, p. 1.

ANTHONY, George
"Passeggiata. " OP (30) Aut 80, p. 62.
"Poem: You yourself the creature you create. " OP (30) Aut 80,
    p. 61.
"SFN. " OP (30) Aut 80, p. 60.
"Weather Report from Monhegan. " OP (30) Aut 80, p. 59.

ANZALDUA, Gloria
"Holy Relics" (to Judy Grahn and V. Sackville-West). Cond (6)
    80, pp. 144-150.

APOLLINAIRE, Guillaume
"The Eel" (tr. by Irving Feldman). ModernPS (10:1) 80, p. 1.

APPEL, Dori
"Mending Basket. " SouthernHR (14:2) Spr 80, p. 141.

APPLE, Tyrone
"Couple Dollars Worth of Reg-lar. " EngJ (69:5) My 80, p.
    59.

APPLEMAN, Marjorie
"Heidi" (for Joan L. and Marilyn M.). Wind (37) 80, p. 3.
"Home Sick. " Wind (37) 80, p. 4.

APPLEMAN, Philip
"Memo to the 21st Century. " Tendril (9) 80, p. 19.

APPLEWHITE, James
"The Scene. " VirQR (56:2) Spr 80, p. 274.
"Trees at Night. " SouthernPR (20:2) Aut 80, p. 13.

ARA, Agneta
"De enda Krig. " PortR (26) 80, p. 126.
"Jag betraktar männis korna. " PortR (26) 80, p. 125.
"November. " PortR (26) 80, p. 125.

ARCHER, Nuala
"Flies Love Me. " Poem (38) Mr 80, p. 56.
"Reacquaintance with Lumbricus Terrestris. " Poem (38) Mr 80,
    p. 55.
"Walking. " CreamCR (5:1) Wint 79, p. 47.

"Your Philodendron, a Frightening Heart, Discusses Our Relation-
    ship. " Epoch (29:2) Wint 80, p. 135.

ARDINGER, Richard
    "Two Poems After Ezra Pound. " PikeF (3) Wint 80, p. 11.

ARENAL, Electa
    "The Mother" (tr. of Gioconda Belli w. Marsha Gabriela
        Dreyer). Cond (6) 80, p. 165.
    "We Shall Beget Children" (tr. of Gioconda Belli w. Marsha
        Gabriela Dreyer). Cond (6) 80, p. 169.
    "We Were Three" (tr. of Claribel Alegria w. Marsha Gabriela
        Dreyer). Cond (6) 80, p. 161.

ARENDT, Erich
    "Prager Judenfriedhof" (für Paul Celan). PortR (26) 80, p. 144.

ARGUËLLES, Ivan
    "crazy horse. " Kayak (53) My 80, p. 39.
    "creusa. " Ark (14) 80, p. 157.
    "silences and distances. " Kayak (53) My 80, p. 40.
    "vocabulary of hands. " Kayak (53) My 80, p. 38.

ARIDJIS, Homero
    "The Dead of the Revolution" (tr. by Eliot Weinberger). Montra
        (7) 80, p. 85.
    "Landscape" (tr. by Eliot Weinberger). Montra (7) 80, p. 89.
    "Mexico City" (tr. by Eliot Weinberger). Montra (7) 80, p. 88.
    "San Miguel in the Backyard" (tr. by Eliot Weinberger).
        Montra (7) 80, p. 87.
    "Tezcatlipoca" (tr. by Eliot Weinberger). Montra (7) 80, p. 84.
    "Zapata" (tr. by Eliot Weinberger). Montra (7) 80, p. 86.

ARMAND, Octavio
    "Possible Love Poem to the Usurer" (tr. by Carol Maier).
        NewOR (7:2) 80, p. 101.
    "The Word Is Still Lip" (tr. by Naomi Lindstrom). NewOR (7:3)
        80, p. 293.
    "You Call" (tr. by Naomi Lindstrom). NewOR (7:3) 80, p. 292.

ARMSTRONG, Lewis
    "Diary. " Wind (37) 80, p. 5.
    "Wind Chimes. " Wind (37) 80, p. 5.

ARNDT, Walter
    "Mr. and Mrs. Knopp" (tr. of Wilhelm Busch). NewEngR (3:2)
        Wint 80, pp. 190-206.

ARNOLD, Bob
    "Approach. " NewL (47:1) Aut 80, p. 11.
    "Bobolink. " NewL (47:1) Aut 80, p. 12.
    "Treeing the Raccoon. " NewL (47:1) Aut 80, p. 11.
    "Turning the Page. " NewL (47:1) Aut 80, p. 10.

ARREOLA, Juan Jose
"Astronomy" (tr. by James Normington). PoNow (28) 80, p. 44.

ARROWSMITH, William
"Death Agony" (tr. of Cesare Pavese). BosUJ (26:3) 80, p. 35.
"Deola Thinking" (tr. of Cesare Pavese). BosUJ (26:3) 80, p. 34.
"The Fringe of Hair" (tr. of Eugenio Montale). WatT (1) Aut 80, p. 87.
"Indian Serenade" (tr. of Eugenio Montale). WatT (1) Aut 80, p. 89.
"Morning" (tr. of Cesare Parese). BosUJ (26:3) 80, p. 33.
"The Old Drunk" (tr. of Cesare Pavese). BosUJ (26:3) 80, p. 38.
"Sultry Lands" (tr. of Cesare Pavese). BosUJ (26:3) 80, p. 36.
"Women in Love" (tr. of Cesare Pavese). BosUJ (26:3) 80, p. 37.
"Your Flight" (tr. of Eugenio Montale). WatT (1) Aut 80, p. 85.

ARTMANN, H. C.
"Craft and Industry" (tr. by Harriet Watts). BosUJ (26:3) 80, p. 98.

ASCHMANN, Charles
"At Evening. " ConcPo (13:2) Aut 80, p. 51.
"A Print from the National Gallery: Two Views. " ConcPo (13:2) Aut 80, p. 51.

ASEKOFF, L. S.
"Dark Targets. " PartR (47:2) 80, p. 229.

ASHANTI, Asa Paschal
"Reading Southern Poetry Review. " BlackALF (14:4) Wint 80, p. 171.
"Trinity. " BlackALF (14:4) Wint 80, p. 171.

ASHBERY, John
"And I'd Love You to Be in It. " PoNow (27) 80, p. 21.
"My Erotic Double. " PoNow (27) 80, p. 21.
"Tide Music. " YaleR (70:2) Wint 81, p. 258.
"Unusual Precautions. " YaleR (70:2) Wint 81, p. 258.

ASHMORE, Charles I.
"The Nuclear Power Plants were removed from the earth centuries ago. " CropD (2 /3) Aut-Wint 80, p. 12.

ASHWORTH, Warren Russell
"The Old Neighborhood. " CropD (2 /3) Aut-Wint 80, p. 13.

ASTOR, Susan
"Circa July. " KanQ (12:2) Spr 80, p. 12.
"Confession. " KanQ (12:2) Spr 80, p. 11.
"Migrations. " Outbr (4 /5) Aut 79-Spr 80, p. 69.

"On the Mortality of Bugs. " Outbr (4/5) Aut 79-Spr 80, p. 67.
"Passing Through. " WebR (5:1) Wint 80, p. 61.
"Pinocchio. " WebR (5:1) Wint 80, p. 60.
"The Road the Crows Own. " Outbr (4/5) Aut 79-Spr 80, p. 68.

ASVAT, Farouk
  "Possibilities for a Man Hunted by SBs. " PortR (26) 80, p. 331.

ATKINSON, Alan
  "Garden. " ChrC (97:25) 30 Jl-6 Ag 80, p. 757.

ATTIAS, Abby
  "(thoughts about) war. " EngJ (69:5) My 80, p. 57.

ATWOOD, Margaret
  "Landcrab. " Field (22) Spr 80, p. 66.
  "Landcrab 2. " Field (22) Spr 80, p. 67.
  "Out. " Field (22) Spr 80, p. 69.
  "Variation on the Word Sleep. " Atl (246:3) S 80, p. 91.
  "Vultures. " Field (22) Spr 80, p. 65.

AUDEN, W. H.
  "The Ball of Fluff" (tr. of Harry Martinson w. Leif Sjoberg).
      PoetryE (1) 80, p. 37.
  "The Butterfly" (tr. of Harry Martinson w. Leif Sjoberg).
      PoetryE (1) 80, p. 36.
  "The Swan" (tr. of Harry Martinson w. Leif Sjoberg). PoetryE
      (1) 80, p. 35.

AUGUSTINE, Jane
  "Rosita Cemetery. " CalQ (16/17) 80, p. 128.

AUSTER, Paul
  "Credo. " Pequod (11) 80, p. 67.
  "Search for a Definition. " Pequod (11) 80, p. 68.
  "A Tomb for Anatole" (tr. of Stephene Mallarmé). ParisR (78)
      Sum 80, pp. 136-148.

AUSTIN, F. A.
  "The Previous Tenant Left Three Bagsful of Pornography. "
      Aspect (76) S-D 79-80, p. 40.

AVES, Jonathan
  "Explaining Leather to My Best Friend from High School. "
      Mouth (2:4) My 80, p. 5.
  "Love Song of Carmen Miranda. " Mouth (2:5) O 80, p. 15.
  "Telescopes. " Mouth (2:4) My 80, p. 15.
  "Waving Hankies Can also Mean Goodbye. " Mouth (2:5) O 80,
      p. 14.
  "Writer's Block. " Mouth (2:5) O 80, p. 16.
  "Writer's Cramp" (for Nate, Nick, Ziggie, Leo, Mephisto,
      Larry). Mouth (2:4) My 80, p. 11.

AVIDAN, David
"Megaovertones, Another Wave" (tr. by author).   PortR (26) 80,
   p. 202.

AWAD, Joseph
from an Epigenethlion: "You will reach for the rosebud, suck
   the pain. " Wind (36) 80, p. 4.
"Love Poem. " ChrC (97:5) 6-13 F 80, p. 137.
"Romantic. " Poem (39) Jl 80, p. 28.

AXELROD, David
"The Odds Makers. " CropD (2/3) Aut-Wint 80, p. 28.
"Virginia Soil. " CropD (2/3) Aut-Wint 80, p. 22.

AXINN, Donald Everett
"The Climbers. " PoNow (28) 80, p. 20.
"Monsters. " PoNow (28) 80, p. 20.
"Saturday Night on the Desert, March, 1938. " NewEngR (3:2)
   Wint 80, p. 262.

AYLESWORTH, John
"The Boy Who Ate Cigarette Butts. " PoNow (27) 80, p. 47.

AYRES, Elizabeth
Seventeen Poems from the Noh. MalR (55) Jl 80, pp. 114-123.

B. , G. N.
"Denial" (tr. by E.W. F.). BosUJ (26:3) 80, p. 159.

BACELO, Nancy
"De vos de mí teñidos habitantes. " PortR (26) 80, p. 446.

BACON, Martha
"The Phantom Helen. " YaleR (69:4) Sum 80, p. 558.

BADER, Anne Louise
"Disenchantment at the Dance. " EngJ (69:5) My 80, p. 56.

BAEHR, Anne-Ruth Ediger
"The Price. " Sam (98) 80, p. 2.

BAER, William
"Books. " Poetry (136:2) My 80, p. 67.
"Von Sternberg. " KanQ (12:4) Aut 80, p. 140.
"When She Is Silent. " Poetry (136:2) My 80, p. 69.

BAGG, Robert
"Hands. " Atl (245:3) Mr 80, p. 69.

BAGLOW, John
Ten Translations. MalR (55) Jl 80, p. 24.

BAILIN, George
"Winter Seminar: The Professor at Seventy. " WestHR (34:1)

Wint 80, p. 38.

BAIR, Tom
"Journal. " SouthwR (65:3) Sum 80, p. 234.

BAIRD, Andrew
"And Something More Than a Sense of Ending. " NewYorker (56: 26) 18 Ag 80, p. 86.

BAKAITIS, Vyt
"Slow down and stop. The sentence falls apart" (tr. of Tomas Venclova). PortR (26) 80, p. 266.

BAKER, Claire J.
"She Said She Didn't Write Poems Because She Was Afraid to Bare Her Soul. " PikeF (3) Wint 80, p. 10.

BAKER, David
"Go On. " Poem (39) Jl 80, p. 51.
"In October. " WebR (5:2) Aut 80, p. 52.
"Late: Long Climb. " WestHR (34:2) Spr 80, p. 158.
"Legacy. " CharR (6:1) Spr 80, p. 11.
"Neighborhood. " Poem (39) Jl 80, p. 52.
"Part of a Story. " Poem (39) Jl 80, p. 53.
"Pilgrim. " CharR (6:1) Spr 80, p. 11.
"Rain. " WindO (36) Spr-Sum 80, p. 38.
"Road to My Old Lover's House. " Sam (92) 80, p. 56.
"Six Days Alone, Trying to Write" (for Robert Bly). Wind (38) 80, p. 19.
"Thoughts Toward Evening. " WindO (36) Spr-Sum 80, p. 38.
"Up Early, ". CharR (6:1) Spr 80, p. 10.

BAKER, Houston A. Jr.
"Color: A Possible Ending. " Obs (5:1/2) Spr-Sum 79, p. 111.

BAKER, James T.
"Seoul City. " ChrC (97:9) 12 Mr 80, p. 288.

BAKER, Mary
"Winter Fire. " CapeR (16:1) Wint 80, p. 23.

BALABAN, John
"Deer Kill. " PoNow (28) 80, p. 11.
"For a Friend Now Far Away. " PoNow (27) 80, p. 29.
"Journey in the Desert. " PoNow (28) 80, p. 10.

BALAKIAN, Peter
"First Nervous Breakdown, Newark 1941. " LitR (23:3) Spr 80, p. 353.
"For My Grandmother, Coming Back. " PoetryNW (21:1) Spr 80, p. 21.
"The History of Armenia. " PoetryNW (21:1) Spr 80, p. 18.
"What My Grandmother Said When It Rained. " LitR (23:3) Spr 80, p. 354.

BALAZS, Mary
"The Camel. " PoetC (12:2) 80, p. 18.
"The Campground at Night: Trailer Row. " KanQ (12:3) Sum 80,
p. 142.
"Compliance. " DacTerr (17) 80, p. 4.
"In the Heart of the Forest. " Wind (37) 80, p. 2.
"Poetry-in-the Schools: for a Fifth Grader, Parents Divorced. "
Wind (38) 80, p. 1.

BALDERSTON, Jean
"Loaves. " SoDakR (18:3) Aut 80, p. 25.
"Summer Corn. " SoDakR (18:3) Aut 80, p. 24.

BALDWIN, Deirdra
"Another Spring. " Outbr (4/5) Aut 79-Spr 80, p. 59.
"The Collective Forces. " LittleM (12:3/4) 80, p. 38.
"Out and Back. " Outbr (4/5) Aut 79-Spr 80, p. 58.
"Their Strange Evaluation. " LittleM (12:3/4) 80, p. 36.
"Why Certain Calls Are Never Answered. " Outbr (4/5) Aut 79-
Spr 80, p. 60.

BALDWIN, Nell
"The Riddle. " Outbr (4/5) Aut 79-Spr 80, p. 66.
"The Visit" (for Thomas Krampf). Outbr (4/5) Aut 79-Spr 80,
p. 64.

BALDWIN, Sy Margaret
"Deer Around the World. " Bachy (17) Spr 80, p. 87.
"Listening for the Cuckoo. " Bachy (17) Spr 80, p. 87.
"The Scars on My Mother's Eyes. " Bachy (17) Spr 80, p. 86.
"Swimming the Catalina Channel. " Bachy (17) Spr 80, p. 85.
"This Photo of My Mother. " Bachy (17) Spr 80, p. 85.
"Woman With Child and Dog. " Bachy (17) Spr 80, p. 86.

BALL, Angela
"Children Swinging. " PoNow (29) 80, p. 1.
"Weekend. " NewOR (7:2) 80, p. 133.

BALLARD, Richard
"Summer in Kansas. " LittleM (12:3/4) 80, p. 61.

BALOG, B. E.
"Indian Pipes" (for Ellen). CapeR (16:1) Wint 80, p. 50.
"My Parent's Argue. " BallSUF (21:1) Wint 80, p. 80.

BANANI, Amin
"Question" (tr. of Forugh Farrokhzad w. Jascha Kessler).
CutB (14) Spr/Sum 80, p. 104.

BANDEIRA, Manuel
"The Art of Loving" (tr. by John Nist). AmerPoR (9:6) N-D 80,
p. 35.
"The Virgin Mary" (tr. by John Nist). AmerPoR (9:6) N-D 80,
p. 35.

BANKS, Stan
   "On 10th Alley Way. " Focus (14:86) Ap 80, p. 34.
   "Shook. " Focus (14:86) Ap 80, p. 34.

BANSET, Elizabeth A.
   "Great Aunt Althea. " Poem (39) Jl 80, p. 46.
   'To My Husband in the Event of My Death. " Poem (39) Jl 80,
      p. 48.

BARAKA, Amiri
   "Reprise of One of A. G. 's Best Poems!" Tendril (9) 80, p. 20.

BARFOOT, James
   "Listening to Berkeley. " ChrC (97:20) 28 My 80, p. 610.

BARGEN, Walter
   "Creation Drunk on Cheap Wine. " Focus (14:86) Ap 80, p. 30.
   "Flat Lander's Dream. " WebR (5:1) Wint 80, p. 63.
   "Listening to the Echo. " WebR (5:1) Wint 80, p. 62.
   'Well Wishing. " PoetryNW (21:1) Spr 80, p. 49.
   'Whipping Post. " Focus (14:86) Ap 80, p. 30.
   'White's Creek Irish Wilderness. " Focus (14:86) Ap 80, p. 30.

BARKER, David
   "Beauty Packs Her Bags. " WormR (78) 80, p. 55.
   'Crime in the Kitchen. " WormR (78) 80, p. 54.
   "Ode, By Way of a General Complaint. " WormR (78) 80, p. 54.

BARKER, Wendy
   "July. " FourQt (29:4) Sum 80, p. 10.

BARNARD, Mary
   "Here Is a Camelia" (tr. of Marco Antonio Montes de Oca).
      DenQ (15:1) Spr 80, p. 93.

BARNES, Dick
   "A Cooking Fire. " Bachy (17) Spr 80, p. 90.
   "Decrepitude Is Wisdom and. " Bachy (17) Spr 80, p. 88.
   "A Lake on the Earth: The Swarm. " Bachy (17) Spr 80, p. 91.
   "Learning Death" (for Bert Meyers). Bachy (17) Spr 80, p. 89.
   'On a Photograph Given Me by My Grandmother. " ParisR (78)
      Sum 80, p. 121.
   "Song. " Bachy (17) Spr 80, p. 91.
   'Trolling: The Truth by Touch. " Bachy (17) Spr 80, p. 88.

BARNES, Jeannette
   "Great-Uncle Jack. " KanQ (12:3) Sum 80, p. 71.
   "Orison. " KanQ (12:3) Sum 80, p. 70.
   "The Ponies. " KanQ (12:3) Sum 80, p. 72.
   'The Terminal. " KanQ (12:3) Sum 80, p. 71.

BARNES, Jim
   "Above the Harbor of Lindos" (tr. of Dagmar Nick). DenQ (14:4)
      Wint 80, p. 127.

"Against Metempsychosis and C. " PoetryNW (21:4) Wint 80-81,
    p. 33.
"Autobiography, Chapter XII: Hearing Montana" (for Bob Con-
    ley). DenQ (14:4) Wint 80, p. 32.
"Autobiography, Chapter XIX: For Andrew Grossbardt, in
    Memoriam. " QW (11) Aut-Wint 80-81, p. 5.
"Choctaw Scarecrow, with Feathers. " DenQ (14:4) Wint 80, p.
    33.
"Driving Through Missouri. " QW (11) Aut-Wint 80-81, p. 98.
"Great Plains Tornado. " DenQ (14:4) Wint 80, p. 31.
"Memoirs of a Catskinner. " MissouriR (3:3) Sum 80, p. 32.
"My Father's House. " DacTerr (17) 80, p. 5.
"Still-Hildreth Sanitarium: Ice Fishing. " Focus (14:86) Ap 80,
    p. 33.
Summons and Sign (tr. of Dagmar Nick). CharR (Supp) 80.
    Entire issue.
"Sundown at Swan Lake, Missouri. " Focus (14:86) Ap 80, p. 33.
"Swan Lake, Again. " Focus (14:86) Ap 80, p. 33.

BARNES, Terri
    "Crossroads. " CarlMis (18:3) Wint 80, p. 33.
    "Melting the Wax from the Honey. " CarlMis (18:3) Wint 80, p.
    32.
    "To Emily Dickinson. " CarlMis (18:3) Wint 80, p. 33.

BARNIE, John
    "The Dog in Us. " LitR (23:3) Spr 80, p. 394.

BARNSTONE, Aliki
    "Mating the Goats. " ChiR (31:3) Wint 80, p. 38.

BARNSTONE, Willis
    "Always" (tr. of Vicente Aleixandre). DenQ (15:3) Aut 80, p.
    15.
    "Archaic Faces on the Wall. " NewL (46:4) Sum 80, p. 20.
    "At Last" (tr. of Vicente Aleixandre w. David Garrison).
    DenQ (15:3) Aut 80, p. 15.
    "Christmas Day. " NewL (46:4) Sum 80, p. 20.
    "A Dancer Meets Her Muse in a Bar. " ColEng (42:2) O 80, p.
    152.
    "Daydreaming of Anne Bradstreet and Her Eight Birds Hatcht in
    One Nest. " CalQ (16/17) 80, p. 147.
    "Emily Dickinson in Her Light. " PoNow (28) 80, p. 5.
    "Father. " Kayak (53) My 80, p. 55.
    "Fever. " NewL (46:4) Sum 80, p. 21.
    "Gandhi. " PoNow (28) 80, p. 5.
    "How and Why I Became a Mime. " Kayak (53) My 80, p. 54.
    from the Inferno: "Canto I" (tr. of Dante Alighieri). ChiR (31:4)
    Spr 80, p. 171.
    "Kids. " Kayak (53) My 80, p. 55.
    "Like the Bull" (tr. of Miguel Hernández). ChiR (31:4) Spr 80,
    p. 148.
    "My Voice" (tr. of Vicente Aleixandre). CutB (14) Spr /Sum 80,

p. 105.
"Song of the Birds." Kayak (53) My 80, p. 56.
"Stained Glass." NoAmR (265:3) S 80, p. 18.
Ten poems (tr. of Jorge Luis Borges). Columbia (5) Aut-Wint
    80, pp. 9-21.
"The Tower." NewL (46:4) Sum 80, p. 21.
"Two Versions of the Aftermath." Kayak (53) My 80, p. 56.

BARRAX, Gerald W.
"The Competitors." GeoR (34:3) Aut 80, p. 495.
Eleven Poems. Obs (5:3) Wint 79, pp. 93-100.

BARRELL, John
"On a Portrait of Wordsworth Engraved in Mezzotint." Stand
    (21:3) 80, p. 42.
"A Preface to the Lyrical Ballads." Stand (21:3) 80, p. 43.

BARRETT, Carol
"Escape from Kansas." KanQ (12:2) Spr 80, p. 24.
"Touchstone" (for Elwin). KanQ (12:2) Spr 80, p. 23.

BARRIE, Jill
"Mother." Sam (101) 80, p. 57.

BARRINGER, Margaret
"Margins." AmerPoR (9:4) Jl-Ag 80, p. 44.

BARROWS, Anita
from The Bridge of the Familiar: "The garden, the unwalled."
    Montra (7) 80, p. 28.
from The Bridge of the Familiar: "the way leaves are more
    transparent at their edges." Montra (7) 80, p. 28.
from The Limits: (7, 8, 9, 10, 11). Montra (7) 80, pp. 23-27.

BARRY, Jim
"Aline." SmPd (49) Spr 80, p. 21.

BARRY, Paul
"Paolo and Francesca." OhioR (24) 80, p. 23.

BARTLETT, Elizabeth
"Attention, Viticians." PoNow (28) 80, p. 30.
"Bachelor Poet, After 20 Years" (to Larry Rubin). Wind (38)
    80, p. 3.
"Forewarned." PoNow (28) 80, p. 30.
"In Days of New." MalR (53) Ja 80, p. 108.
"Mexican Folklorico." PoNow (28) 80, p. 30.
"When Light Rays Bend." MalR (53) Ja 80, p. 109.

BARTLETT, Helen
"Check-Out Counter." MassR (21:2) Sum 80, p. 364.

BARTON, Bruce B.
"A Gift." DacTerr (17) 80, p. 6.

BARTON, David
  "Frogs. " ColEng (41:6) F 80, p. 655.
  "The Humboldt Trail, 1887. " ColEng (41:6) F 80, p. 653.
  "Midsummer. " CarolQ (32:3) Aut 80, p. 50.
  "Missing Persons. " CarolQ (32:3) Aut 80, p. 48.
  "The Procuress. " SouthernPR (20:2) Aut 80, p. 66.
  "Solutions. " CarolQ (32:1) Wint 80, p. 79.
  "Yorkshire. " ColEng (41:6) F 80, p. 654.

BARTSCH, Kurt
  "Poetry. " Stand (21:1) 79-80, p. 48.

BARWELL, Jay
  "Blue Domestic Morning. " CarolQ (32:2) Spr-Sum 80, p. 68.
  "In a Bucket. " PikeF (3) Wint 80, p. 36.

BASCOM, George
  "August Dawn for M. R. " KanQ (12:1) Wint 80, p. 45.

BASHO
  "The Summer Moon" (tr. by Etsuko Terasaki). CutB (14) Spr /
    Sum 80, p. 91.

BASS, Madeline Tiger
  from The Book of Reeds: "Another City. " Outbr (4/5) Aut 79-
    Spr 80, p. 92.

BATES, Cynthia
  "Father the Fire-Maker. " CalQ (16/17) 80, p. 42.
  "The Fish. " CalQ (16/17) 80, p. 43.
  "Sleeping with Great-Grandmother. " SoDakR (18:2) Sum 80, p.
    16.

BATES, Kyle
  "From the Desk of a Bad Bagger. " Aspen (10) Wint 80, p. 79.
  "You Saw Two Foreign Porno Flicks. " Aspen (10) Wint 80, p.
    80.

BATES, Randolph
  "At the Lusher Fair. " PoNow (29) 80, p. 2.
  "Last Word for Master Sergeant Fortinberry. " PoNow (29) 80,
    p. 2.
  "Unc. " PoNow (29) 80, p. 3.

BATKI, John
  "A Vision" (tr. of Attila Jozsef). PoNow (26) 80, p. 45.

BAT-MIRIAM, Yocheved
  "The monasteries lift gold domes. " PortR (26) 80, p. 200.

BAUDELAIRE, Charles
  "I have no convictions as men of my century understand the word. "
    Bachy (16) Wint 80, p. 50.

BAUER, Steven
"Aspen Grove. " PraS (54:2) Sum 80, p. 79.
"Dead Shark at Long Nook. " PraS (54:2) Sum 80, p. 78.
"In a Field. " PraS (54:2) Sum 80, p. 80.
"Tornado Watch. " CharR (6:2) Aut 80, p. 25.

BAUMAN, Cory W.
"Mountain Pond. " ConcPo (13:2) Aut 80, p. 63.

BAUMANN, Susan
"The Garden Green, the Garden Gone. " Shen (31:2) 80, p. 103.
"The Rest. " Shen (31:2) 80, p. 104.

BAUMEL, Judith
"Fibonacci. " ParisR (78) Sum 80, p. 115.
"Message from the Interior: Walker Evans, No. 1, Walpole,
   Maine. " Ploughs (6:2) 80, p. 85.
"Message from the Interior: Walker Evans, No. 2, Scarborough,
   New York. " Ploughs (6:2) 80, p. 88.

BAXTER, Charles
"anecdote: the hitchhiker. " Kayak (55) Ja 81, p. 66.
"Fighting Depression, I Take My Family on a Picnic. " PoetryNW
   (21:4) Wint 80-81, p. 34.
"The Imaginary Mother. " PoetryNW (21:4) Wint 80-81, p. 35.
"meditation on porn. " Kayak (55) Ja 81, p. 67.

BAYS, Bertie Cole
"Honey in December. " LittleBR (1:1) Aut 80, p. 24.

BEALL, Sandra
"In Praise of Hysteria. " PoetryNW (21:3) Aut 80, p. 38.

BEAR, Jan V.
"Midnight. " SmPd (50) Aut 80, p. 32.

BEARD, Cathy
"Any April. " BelPoJ (31:1) Aut 80, p. 5.

BEAUDOIN, Kenneth Lawrence
"Destiny of a Poet" (tr. of Claude Vigée w. J. R. Le Master).
   WebR (5:2) Aut 80, p. 77.
"Michael's Tomb" (tr. of Claude Vigée w. J. R. Le Master).
   WebR (5:2) Aut 80, p. 76.

BECK, Gary
"Snowscape. " CutB (15) Aut /Wint 80, p. 60.

BEENEN, Jennivien-Diana
"Cathedral. " MalR (54) Ap 80, p. 91.
"Morning Poem. " MalR (54) Ap 80, p. 90.

BEHM, Richard
"A Magic Poem" (for Susan). Im (6:2) 80, p. 6.

"On Making a Will in Indian Summer. " Im (6:2) 80, p. 6.
"Midwest Bustrip with a Woman Mad as Any of Us. " PoNow
(29) 80, p. 3.
"Nightswim. " CreamCR (5:1) Wint 79, p. 112.
"Old Man Ferdich. " CreamCR (5:1) Wint 79, p. 111.
"On Recently Having Taken Up Carpentry. " Vis (2) 80.
"Vietnam Fragment. " SouthernHR (14:3) Sum 80, p. 221.

BEICHMAN, Janine
"Haiku" (tr. of Nakamura Kusatoo). DenQ (15:1) Spr 80, p. 47.
"Haiku" (tr. of Masaoka Shiki). DenQ (15:1) Spr 80, p. 47.

BEINING, Guy R.
"Artism. " Tele (16) 80, p. 52.
"Hourglass Fragments. " Tele (16) 80, p. 53.
"ushers at the funeral of a raw-robed member. " PikeF (3) Wint
80, p. 8.

BELASIK, Paul
"Mountain. " Sam (102) 80, p. 36.

BELITT, Ben
"March Willows. " Salm (50/51) Aut 80-Wint 81, p. 9.
"Sumac. " Salm (50/51) Aut 80-Wint 81, p. 3.
"Thoreau on Paran Creek. " Salm (50/51) Aut 80-Wint 81, p. 7.
"Voyage of the Beagle" (for Fred Burkhardt). Salm (50/51) Aut
80-Wint 81, p. 8.

BELL, Charles G.
Eleven poems. NewL (47:1) Aut 80, p. 97.

BELL, John
"Butterflies. " PottPort (1) 79-80, p. 27.
"Epigram for a Novel That I Will Never Write. " PottPort (1)
79-80, p. 26.
"The Infirmary Jesus. " PottPort (1) 79-80, p. 28.
"Untitled: U are. " PottPort (1) 79-80, p. 27.

BELL, Marvin
Eight poems. Field (22) Spr 80, pp. 28-47.
"He Said To. " Tendril (9) 80, p. 24.
"He Said To. " Watt (1) Aut 80, p. 2.
"The Last Thing I Say. " Atl (246:5) N 80, p. 85.
"The Mummies of Guanajuato. " Antaeus (37) Spr 80, p. 46.
"The New Formalists. " Antaeus (37) Spr 80, p. 49.
"That Time in Tangier. " Antaeus (37) Spr 80, p. 47.
"These Green-Going-to-Yellow. " NewYorker (56:37) 3 N 80, p.
56.
"Things I Took. " AntR (38:4) Aut 80, p. 472.

BELLAMY, Joe David
"Electrical Storm. " PoNow (28) 80, p. 21.
"The Sniper. " PoNow (28) 80, p. 21.

"You Would Have Made a Great Champion. " PoNow (28) 80, p.
21.

BELLG, Albert
"Lloyd Reynolds, Calligrapher. " NewL (46:3) Spr 80, p. 83.

BELLI, Gioconda
"Engendraremos ninos. " Cond (6) 80, p. 168.
"La Madre. " Cond (6) 80, p. 164.
"Ya van meses, hijita. " Cond (6) 80, p. 166.

BELLI, Giuseppe Gioachino
"A Bad Moment" (tr. by Miller Williams). Poetry (136:1) Ap
80, p. 8.
"Le bbestie der paradiso terrestre. " Poetry (136:1) Ap 80, p.
4.
"Cain" (tr. by Miller Williams). Poetry (136:1) Ap 80, p. 6.
"Death with a Coda" (tr. by Miller Williams). CutB (14) Spr /
Sum 80, p. 49.
"Good Weather" (tr. by Miller Williams). CutB (14) Spr /Sum
80, p. 47.
"The Grownup Sons" (tr. by Miller Williams). CutB (14) Spr /
Sum 80, p. 48.
"Memory" (tr. by Miller Williams). Poetry (136:1) Ap 80, p. 7.
"Religion Explained and Defended" (tr. by Miller Williams).
CutB (14) Spr /Sum 80, p. 46.
"The Resurrection of the Flesh" (tr. by Miller Williams). Po-
etry (136:1) Ap 80, p. 9.
Thirteen poems (tr. by Miller Williams). QW (10) Wint-Spr
80, pp. 56- 62.

BENBOW, Margaret
"Bride and Bear. " Poetry (136:2) My 80, p. 100.
"High Wind. " Poetry (136:2) My 80, p. 98.
"The Old Biograph Girl. " Poetry (136:2) My 80, p. 99.

BENCK, Ernie
"Blown Away. " BelPoJ (31:2) Wint 80-81, p. 14.

BENDA, Jan
"Elegy on the Eternal Burn in the Heart of Bohemia" (tr. of
Milan Exner w. Clayton Eshleman). Montra (7) 80, pp. 115-
121.

BENEDETTI, David
"Blank Pages in Middle of Book. " Tele (16) 80, p. 39.
"Reverberation. " Tele (16) 80, p. 40.

BENEDIKT, Michael
"The Burning Down of 'Jenny's Restaurant' Jan. 30, 1979 Fol-
lowing a Visit the Prior Sunday Night (Jan. 28) Across
Town in Boston's North End and Also Another Lesson
Learned. " Agni (12) 80, pp. 95-104.

"For Susan Golden, So She Might Walk the Streets in Safety Yet
    Radiant. " Agni (13) 80, pp. 79-84.
"Friendship vs. Conflict-of-Interest: Meditations from a Desk. "
    Confr (20) Spr-Sum 80, p. 93.
"How in Boston One Sunny Afternoon in June Psychology and
    Politics Foul the Literal but Poetry Helps" (for Z.).
    Aspect (76) S-D 79-80, p. 44.
"The Ring I Just Bought, and Wear: My Energy Ring to Salomé
    X, at Her Parents' House, Corpus Christi, Texas from
    Michael X. , at His Mother's Name in No. Hollywood,
    Florida. " MinnR (NS 15) Aut 80, p. 19.
"Some Simbu!" (for Z.). Durak (5) 80, p. 20.

BENGSTON, David
    "Two Men's Rooms--Nine Years Apart. " PoNow (29) 80, p. 47.

BENJAMIN, Jerry
    "No Unhappy Reason. " PartR (47:4) 80, p. 613.

BENJAMIN, László
    "Miért siratni. " PortR (26) 80, p. 174.

BENJAMIN, Saul Hillel
    "At Summer's End. " AmerS (49:3) Sum 80, p. 384.

BENNANI, Ben
    "And He Returned in a Shroud" (tr. of Mahmud Darwish). Bound
        (8:3) Spr 80, p. 200.
    "A Letter from Exile" (tr. of Mahmud Darwish). Bound (8:3)
        Spr 80, p. 203.

BENNETT, Beth
    "An Apology for Melanie. " EngJ (69:8) N 80, p. 72.

BENNETT, Bruce
    "Art and Life. " Wind (38) 80, p. 4.
    "Lying in the Dark. " Wind (38) 80, p. 5.
    "Scene. " PoetryNW (21:3) Aut 80, p. 38.
    "Short Poem. " Wind (38) 80, p. 5.
    "Sour Grapes Revisited. " Bits (11) 80.
    "Vanished. " Wind (38) 80, p. 4.

BENNETT, John
    "The Hare Krishna Boys. " PoNow (27) 80, p. 22.
    "Hornets. " PoNow (27) 80, p. 22.
    "How Talent Gets Discovered. " PoNow (27) 80, p. 22.

BENNETT, Louise
    "Carifesta Rydim. " PortR (26) 80, p. 225.
    "Independance. " PortR (26) 80, p. 224.

BENNETT, Will
    "Coke. " Tele (16) 80, p. 45.

"Present Company. " Tele (16) 80, p. 44.
"Telephone bells ring out in the great community of. " Tele (16)
    80, p. 44.

BENSHEIMER, Virginia
"Little Girl Lost. " Vis (3) 80.

BENSKO, John
"To My Wife. " NewOR (7:2) 80, p. 177.

BENSON, Steve
"A Mystery. " PoetC (12:1) 80, p. 5.

BENTLEY, Roy
"Shirts. " FourQt (29:2) Wint 80, p. 33.

BEN-TOV, Sharona
"Rock Juice. " SouthernPR (20:2) Aut 80, p. 68.

BENVENUTO, Joyce
"Making It New. " GRR (11:1) 80, p. 36.

BERG, Stephen
"Clouded Sky" (tr. of Miklos Radnoti w. Steven Polgar and S. J.
    Marks). PoetryE (1) 80, p. 79.
"Free Variations. " Ark (14) 80, p. 158.
"A Letter to My Wife" (tr. of Miklos Radnoti w. Steven Polgar
    and S. J. Marks). PoetryE (1) 80, p. 78.

BERGER, Suzanne E.
"The Grievers. " Aspen (9) Spr 80, p. 62.
"Lady. " Aspen (9) Spr 80, p. 61.
"Light. " PraS (54:4) Wint 80-81, p. 24.
"Mornings. " Tendril (9) 80, p. 25.
"Still Life, with Apple. " Aspen (9) Spr 80, p. 63.

BERGMAN, David
"Bedside Manner. " Mouth (2:5) O 80, p. 13.
"The Sons of Paracelsus. " Mouth (2:5) O 80, pp. 28-33.

BERKE, Judith
"Office Procedure. " PoNow (29) 80, p. 5.
"A Queen. " WormR (77) 80, p. 6.
"Two Witches. " WormR (77) 80, p. 6.

BERKSON, Lee L.
"dictionary gestures. " SmPd (48) Wint 80, p. 10.
"family portrait. " SmPd (48) Wint 80, p. 9.

BERMAN, Ruth
"Apparent Angular Diameter. " SoCaR (13:1) Aut 80, p. 74.
"The Blessing. " Poem (38) Mr 80, p. 54.
"The Poet Reads to the Women's Poetry Society. " Poem (38)
    Mr 80, p. 53.

BERNARD, Jeanne Alaska
"Evening. " ThRiPo (15 /16) 80, p. 26.

BERNAUER, Carol
"1 /2 /80. " CapeR (16:1) Wint 80, p. 33.

BERNHEIMER, Alan
"Extension Heavens. " Tele (16) 80, p. 7.

BERNSTEIN, Michael André
"Survivors. " NewOR (7:1) 80, p. 42.

BERRY, D. C.
"Anna Italia. " SouthernR (16:4) Aut 80, p. 935.
"If Love's a Yoke. " QW (10) Wint-Spr 80, p. 86.
"Song. " SouthernR (16:4) Aut 80, p. 934.

BERRY, Wendell
"An Autumn Burning. " Ark (14) 80, p. 162.

BERRYMAN, John
from Job: "Job. " Poetry (136:1) Ap 80, p. 35.

BERTAGNOLLI, Olivia
"Critic. " FourQt (29:3) Spr 80, p. 36.

BERTOLINO, James
"Bean Karma. " PoNow (26) 80, p. 17.
"The Beauties of Travel. " Tele (16) 80, p. 11.
"A Walk with Cordrescu. " Tele (16) 80, p. 11.

BERTOLUCCI, Attilio
"Giovanni Diodati" (tr. by Charles Tomlinson). Stand (21:3) 80,
    p. 75.

BETZ, Daniel
"Harris, Iowa. " Sam (86) 79, p. 65.
"One Down; Eight Lives Left. " Sam (92) 80, p. 68.

BEUM, Robert
"An Aging Lady. " Comm (107:5) 14 Mr 80, p. 142.
"Stack Tones. " SouthernR (16:2) Spr 80, p. 424.

BEVERAGE, Mary
"Love. " Sam (102) 80, p. 38.

BEYER, Barbara Langham
"Aunt Mattie Dying. " Pig (7) My 80, p. 73.

BEYER, William
"Emily Dickinson; an Epitaph. " Wind (37) 80, p. 6.
"Mood for Winter. " Wind (37) 80, p. 6.

BIADENE, Carlo
"Ascent" (tr. by Peter Russell). MalR (55) Jl 80, p. 61.
"Hope Gone Dead" (tr. by Peter Russell). MalR (55) Jl 80, p.
     63.
"An Unknown God" (tr. by Peter Russell). MalR (55) Jl 80, p.
     62.

BIDART, Frank
"Catullus: Odi et amo. " Ploughs (6:2) 80, p. 9.
"For Mary Ann Youngren. " NewRep (182:18) 3 My 80, p. 28.

BIEGLER, Beth
"Recall-Epigraphs" (w. Richard Kostelanetz). Im (7:1) 80, p. 6.

BIERDS, Linda
"Cutting the Maple. " ConcPo (13:1) Spr 80, p. 20.
"Dining in the Country. " Wind (38) 80, p. 6.
"Elegy for 41 Whales, Beached in Florence, Oregon, June 1979. "
     NewL (46:4) Sum 80, p. 22.
"The Gypsy Who Sewed for Recitals. " PoNow (29) 80, p. 4.
"Kea. " PoNow (29) 80, p. 4.
"One Hot Day in October. " PoNow (29) 80, p. 46.
"Poem of the Moonpeople. " PoNow (29) 80, p. 4.
"What My Brother Saw. " PoNow (29) 80, p. 4.

BIEREZIN, Jacek
"Chess" (tr. by Grazyna Drabik and Austin Flint). PoNow (28)
     80, p. 45.

BIGGERS, Randall V.
"We Still Wait. " EngJ (69:5) My 80, p. 45.

BIGGS, Margaret Key
"After the Sun on Friday. " UTR (6:3 /4) 80, p. 4.
"May 4, 1970. " Sam (98) 80, p. 43.
"Night Screams. " Sam (102) 80, p. 38.
Swampfire. Sam (95) 80. Entire issue.
"Unstung. " Sam (92) 80, p. 36.

BIHLMAIER, Barbara
"spaces. " Prima (5) 79, p. 12.

BILICKE, Tom
"Recognizing Trees. " Wind (36) 80, p. 5.
"September words. " Wind (36) 80, p. 5.

BILLINGS, Philip
"Birth Announcement (Why Another?). " StoneC (7:1) F 80, p. 34.

BILY-HURD, Michael
"Chinese Screen Painting. " KanQ (12:4) Aut 80, p. 98.
"Linguistic Backwash. " KanQ (12:1) Wint 80, p. 77.

BIRCH, Michele
"In Your Room. " <u>AntR</u> (38:2) Spr 80, p. 182.

BIRDSALL, Jane
"How to Make Baba Ghanoush. " <u>BelPoJ</u> (31:2) Wint 80-81, p. 16.

BISHOP, Elizabeth
"The Bight. " <u>AmerPoR</u> (9:1) Ja-F 80, p. 48.

BISHOP, W.
"Amphisbena. " <u>PoetC</u> (12:3) 80, p. 18.
"Caladrius. " <u>PoetC</u> (12:2) 80, p. 32.
"Diary, Photographer, 1850: The Yucatan. " <u>NowestR</u> (18:3) 80, p. 101.
"Family History. " <u>WestHR</u> (34:3) Sum 80, p. 222.
"The First Man. " <u>PoNow</u> (28) 80, p. 47.
"The Mule, Dead. " <u>NowestR</u> (18:3) 80, p. 100.

BISHOP, Wendy
"The Distance to Rhodes. " <u>Wind</u> (36) 80, p. 24.
"Sirenae. " <u>CalQ</u> (16/17) 80, p. 60.

BISINGER, Gerald
"Stellt euch vor. " <u>PortR</u> (26) 80, p. 32.

BISSETT, Bill
"exposing th core. " <u>PottPort</u> (2) 80-81, p. 20.
"if i told yu. " <u>PottPort</u> (2) 80-81, p. 32.

BIZZARO, Patrick
"Essential Messages" (for Jason). <u>CropD</u> (1) Spr 80, p. 7.
"Good Aim. " <u>PoNow</u> (29) 80, p. 5.
"Making a Kite of Songs" (for Kristin). <u>CropD</u> (2/3) Aut-Wint 80, p. 47.
"Patching the Roof" (for Michael Waters). <u>CropD</u> (2/3) Aut-Wint 80, p. 44.
"Tumbling Dry. " <u>CropD</u> (1) Spr 80, p. 7.

BJERREGAARD, Kevin
"The Sealed Box. " <u>KanQ</u> (12:1) Wint 80, p. 134.

BLACK, Candace
"Textile Worker. " <u>CutB</u> (15) Aut/Wint 80, p. 78.

BLACK, Charles
"Circumstances Surrounding the Disappearance of a Freightcar. " <u>SouthwR</u> (65:3) Sum 80, p. 247.
"Gems and Spells. " <u>ArizQ</u> (36:2) Spr 80, p. 164.

BLACK, Harold
"The Children. " <u>Vis</u> (3) 80.
"Give Us Our Daily Walk. " <u>Vis</u> (2) 80.
"The Last Watchman. " <u>Vis</u> (2) 80.

"Lower East Side Muse. " Vis (4) 80.
"Mexico City Fever. " Vis (1) 79.
"Next Week. " Vis (1) 79.

BLACK, John
"Sensory Cue. " SouthwR (65:1) Wint 80, p. 39.

BLACKBURN, Paul
"My New England Grandmother. " BelPoJ (31:1) Aut 80, p. 30.
"Sirventes" (tr. of Arnaut Daniel). Bound (8:3) Spr 80, p. 149.

BLAKE, William
"Of the Sleep of Ulro!" Bachy (16) Wint 80, p. 26.

BLANKENBURG, Gary
"Fish and Flowers. " EngJ (69:5) My 80, p. 50.

BLASING, Randy
Ten poems (tr. of Nazim Hikmet w. Mutlu Konuk).   PoetryE (3)
    80, pp. 6-18.
"Turkish Spring. " LitR (23:3) Spr 80, p. 387.

BLAZEK, Douglas
"The Forest. " PoNow (26) 80, p. 35.
"The Orange. " Durak (4) 80, p. 47.

BLEI, Norbert
"February. " WormR (78) 80, p. 75.
"The Zen Affair. " WormR (78) 80, p. 75.

BLESSING, Richard A.
"After the Last Poem. " PoetryNW (21:2) Sum 80, p. 25.
"Counting Backward. " PoetryNW (21:2) Sum 80, p. 24.
"A Street in Pennsylvania. " HiramPoR (27) Aut-Wint 80, p. 9.
"Waking. " HiramPoR (27) Aut-Wint 80, p. 8.

BLOCH, Alice
"Naturally Occurring Phenomena. " Bachy (16) Wint 80, pp. 20-
    26.

BLOCH, Chana
"The Converts. " CalQ (16/17) 80, p. 95.
"Eating Babies. " Field (22) Spr 80, p. 63.
"The Gifts of the World. " PoetryNW (21:1) Spr 80, p. 15.
"The Lesson" (for Diana O'Hehir). CalQ (16/17) 80, p. 94.
"Letters Home. " CalQ (16/17) 80, p. 93.
"A Life. " PoetryNW (21:1) Spr 80, p. 14.
"Three Studies for a Head of John the Baptist. " Field (22) Spr
    80, p. 61.
"Vision" (for Stephen Mitchell). CalQ (16/17) 80, p. 96.

BLODGETT, E. D.
"Rumi. " ConcPo (12:2) Aut 79, p. 56.
"Weasel. " ConcPo (12:2) Aut 79, p. 55.

BLOK, Aleksandr
"The Kite" (tr. by David McDuff and Jon Silkin).   Stand (21:2)
    80, p. 8.

BLOOMFIELD, Maureen
"Upham Park. " PartR (47:2) 80, p. 224.

BLOUNT, Roy Jr.
"Cf. Grace. " BosUJ (26:3) 80, p. 119.
"Gryll's State. " BosUJ (26:3) 80, p. 120.

BLUE, Jane
"Queen Anne's Lace. " CalQ (16/17) 80, p. 38.

BLUE-ZWARTS, Janice
"The Fields: For Katherine Heather. " MalR (54) Ap 80, p. 146.
"Return to Prinsengracht. " MalR (54) Ap 80, p. 144.   found
    poem.

BLUMENTHAL, Michael C.
"Astronomical: A Marriage. " Nat (230:15) 19 Ap 80, p. 474.
"Christmas Eve: The Jew and the Ceramic Fish. " LittleM (12:
    3/4) 80, p. 56.
"The Flirtation. " Poetry (136:2) My 80, p. 74.
"The Harbor" (for Charlene Cerny). PraS (54:1) Spr 80, p. 14.
"Life Goes On. " Poetry (136:2) My 80, p. 75.
"Manoxylous. " Nat (230:15) 19 Ap 80, p. 477.
"Melancholy. " PoNow (29) 80, p. 5.
"Praise. " Nat (230:15) 19 Ap 80, p. 473.
"Rain. " Nat (230:24) 21 Je 80, p. 764.

BLY, Robert
"Below Freezing" (tr. of Tomas Transtromer). PoetryE (1) 80,
    p. 7.
"Clarity" (tr. of Goran Sonnevi). PoetryE (1) 80, p. 19.
"Dawn in Threshing Time. " PoNow (26) 80, p. 21.
"Elegy for David Wand. " PoNow (27) 80, p. 38.
"The End of Fall" (tr. of Francis Ponge). OhioR (24) 80, p.
    58.
"The Fallen Tree. " Tendril (9) 80, p. 26.
"Grief and Its Roots. " OhioR (25) 80, p. 85.
"The Grief of Men. " NewRep (183:22) 29 N 80, p. 32.
"Listening to a Fog Horn at Port Townsend. " OhioR (25) 80, p.
    84.
"Love Poem in Prose. " OhioR (25) 80, p. 85.
"Night of First Snow. " PoNow (26) 80, p. 21.
"The Rough-barked Cottonwood. " GeoR (34:4) Wint 80, p. 751.
"Street Crossing" (tr. of Tomas Transtromer). PoetryE (1) 80,
    p. 8.
from Talking All Morning: "Mourning Pablo Neruda. " Harp
    (260:1560) My 80, p. 73.
Twenty poems. Kayak (55) Ja 81, pp. 35-51.

BOBROWSKI, Johannes
"Plain" (tr. by Francis Golffing). PoNow (27) 80, p. 45.

BOCHO, Yamamura
"Curves" (tr. by Graeme Wilson). WestHR (34:4) Aut 80, p.
335.

BOCK, Frederick
"Remembering the Anderson Recitals. " Ascent (6:1) 80, p. 51.

BODINI, Vittorio
"Dead Woman in Apulia" (tr. by Ruth Feldman and Brian Swann).
AmerPoR (9:6) N-D 80, p. 7.
"Stazzema Series" (tr. by Ruth Feldman and Brian Swann).
AmerPoR (9:6) N-D 80, p. 6.
"Study for the Sanfelice Woman in Jail" (tr. by Ruth Feldman
and Brian Swann). AmerPoR (9:6) N-D 80, p. 7.
"Via de angelis" (tr. by Ruth Feldman and Brian Swann).
AmerPoR (9:6) N-D 80, p. 8.

BOE, Deborah
"An Apology to My Lover. " US1 (12/13) Aut-Wint 80, p. 3.
"Because It Pleases You. " HangL (38) Aut 80, p. 10.
"Enchiladas. " US1 (12/13) Aut-Wint 80, p. 3.
"Fire. " HangL (38) Aut 80, p. 11.
"Painting the Body. " HangL (38) Aut 80, p. 9.

BOECK, Johann A.
"Da läuft die Brücke westnordwest. " PortR (26) 80, p. 30.

BOGAN, Jim
"Mrs. Franz: Mother Earth's Daughter. " Focus (14:86) Ap 80,
p. 20.
"Nijinsky's Night. " Focus (14:86) Ap 80, p. 22.

BOGEN, Don
"Pioneer Square. " Nat (230:19) 17 My 80, p. 601.

BOGGS, Mildred W.
"Insight. " Wind (38) 80, p. 7.
"Light from Arles. " Wind (38) 80, p. 7.
"Reflecting. " Wind (38) 80, p. 7.

BOGGS, William O.
"French Creek. " ThRiPo (15/16) 80, p. 27.

BOGIN, Meg
"Book of the Dead" (tr. of Salvador Espriu). AmerPoR (9:3)
My-Je 80, p. 39.
"Don't You Hear the Sound the Hoe Makes?" (tr. of Salvador
Espriu). AmerPoR (9:3) My-Je 80, p. 39.
"Here the Voyage Ends" (tr. of Salvador Espriu). AmerPoR
(9:3) My-Je 80, p. 39.

"Old Brueghel Told It Thus" (tr. of Salvador Espriu). AmerPoR
     (9:3) My-Je 80, p. 39.
"Remember Us" (tr. of Salvador Espriu). AmerPoR (9:3) My-Je
     80, p. 41.
"Song of Afternoon Arriving" (tr. of Salvador Espriu). AmerPoR
     (9:3) My-Je 80, p. 40.
"Song of Triumphant Night" (tr. of Salvador Espriu). AmerPoR
     (9:3) My-Je 80, p. 39.

BOGIN, Nina
"In Bavaria. " CalQ (16/17) 80, p. 156.
"St. Valentin. " CalQ (16/17) 80, p. 157.

BOGUS, S. Diane
"Mayree. " BlackALF (14:4) Wint 80, p. 175.

BOIARSKI, Phil
"Akuszerka. " Aspen (9) Spr 80, p. 37.
"Still Wrestling. " Aspen (9) Spr 80, p. 38.

BOISSEAU, Michelle
"From this Distance. " MissouriR (3:3) Sum 80, p. 12.
"Under My Breath. " MissouriR (3:3) Sum 80, p. 10.

BOJANOWSKI, Ted
"The Car. " SouthernHR (14:3) Sum 80, p. 260.
"Kneeling Figure in a Church of Trees. " CapeR (15:2) Sum 80,
     p. 22.

BOLAND, Eavan
"Anorexic. " OntR (12) Spr-Sum 80, p. 19.

BOLLS, Imogene L.
"Mt. Whitestone. " Bits (11) 80.

BOLTON, Charles
"Bolton's Abbey, Bolton's Landing, Bolton's Grove. " Shen (31:1)
     79, p. 86.
"Smudges. " Shen (31:1) 79, p. 88.

BOMBA, Bernard D.
"Daydream. " Sam (101) 80, p. 60.

BONAZZI, Robert
"Motivation. " NewL (46:4) Sum 80, p. 102.
"On the Road. " NewL (46:4) Sum 80, p. 102.

BOND, Alec
"Fathers and Daughters in the Park. " DacTerr (17) 80, p. 7.

BOND, Harold
"Swallowing. " PoNow (27) 80, p. 40.

BONENFANT, Joseph
   "roulis. " Os (10) Spr 80, p. 2.

BONNEFOY, Yves
   from Un feu va devant nous: "La Chambre. " Bound (8:2) Wint
      80, p. 274.
   from Un feu va devant nous: "La lumière, changée. " Bound
      (8:2) Wint 80, p. 277.
   from Un feu va devant nous: "La parole du soir. " Bound (8:2)
      Wint 80, p. 278.
   from Un feu va devant nous: "Le myrte. " Bound (8:2) Wint 80,
      p. 275.
   from Un feu va devant nous: "Une voix. " Bound (8:2) Wint 80,
      p. 276.
   "Two Colors" (tr. by Susanna Lang). Nimrod (24:1) Aut-Wint
      80, pp. 31-33.

BONNELL, Paula
   "Ancestral Memories. " AndR (7:1) Spr 80, p. 32.

BONNER, Carrington
   "Miss Vivian. " Obs (5:1/2) Spr-Sum 79, p. 91.

BOOK, M. K.
   "Frost ********** Fades. " WormR (78) 80, p. 77.

BOOKER, Betty
   "In Winter. " Wind (38) 80, p. 43.
   "Peace Vigil, 12/79. " SmPd (49) Spr 80, p. 7.

BOOTH, Martin
   "Above Colden Water. " MalR (56) O 80, p. 106.

BOOTH, Philip
   "Continuum. " MissouriR (3:2) Wint 80, p. 33.
   "Dayrise. " AmerPoR (9:2) Mr-Ap 80, p. 35.
   "Eaton's Boatyard. " AmerPoR (9:4) Jl-Ag 80, p. 12.
   "Eaton's Boatyard. " Tendril (9) 80, p. 27.
   "Fog. " Atl (246:1) Jl 80, p. 77.
   "Mary's After Dinner. " AmerPoR (9:2) Mr-Ap 80, p. 35.
   "A Slow Breaker. " Hudson (33:1) Spr 80, p. 77.
   "Thinking About Hannah Arendt. " Nat (231:10) 4 O 80, p. 324.
   "This Day After Yesterday. " GeoR (34:1) Spr 80, p. 51.
   "The Valley Road. " Hudson (33:1) Spr 80, p. 77.
   "Wonder. " AmerPoR (9:2) Mr-Ap 80, p. 35.

BORAWSKI, Walta
   "Direct or Indirect Rebound Tenderness" (for JG). Mouth (2:5)
      O 80, p. 38.
   "For Michael (On the Brink of Depression and War). " Mouth
      (2:5) O 80, p. 16.
   "The Marks of Fairy Tales. " Mouth (2:4) My 80, p. 47.
   "The Poet Falls, Flags and Willowtrees. " Mouth (2:5) O 80, p.

17.
"Silk Scarves and Hard Leather. " Mouth (2:5) O 80, p. 39.
Ten poems. Bachy (16) Wint 80, p. 77.
"Tired Song-and-Dance Act. " Mouth (2:4) My 80, p. 47.

BORDEN, William
"On the Discovery of the $4\frac{1}{2}$-Million-Year-Old Footprints. "
DacTerr (17) 80, p. 8.

BORENSTEIN, Emily
"In Anticipation of the Time. " EnPas (10) 80, p. 8.

BORGES, Jorge Luis
"The Angel" (tr. by Norman Thomas di Giovanni). Atl (246:1)
Jl 80, p. 64.
"A History of Night" (tr. by Norman Thomas di Giovanni). Atl
(246:1) Jl 80, p. 64.
"The Moon" (Maria Kodzma) (tr. by Norman Thomas di Gio-
vanni). Atl (246:1) Jl 80, p. 64.
Ten poems (tr. by Willis Barnstone). Columbia (5) Aut-Wint 80,
pp. 9-21.

BORSON, Roo
"Now and Again. " MalR (54) Ap 80, p. 61.

BORUCH, Marianne
"Diamond Breakfast. " Iowa (10:4) Aut 79, p. 36.
"Memory Biscuit. " Ploughs (6:2) 80, p. 37.
"On Translation. " Iowa (10:4) Aut 79, p. 35.
"Passage. " Iowa (10:4) Aut 79, p. 37.
"Sympathy. " BelPoJ (30:3) Spr 80, p. 18.

BOSLEY, James
"Court. " NewL (46:4) Sum 80, p. 99.

BOSLEY, Keith
"The Assumption of Miriam from the Street in the Winter of
1942" (tr. of Jerzey Ficowski w. Krystyna Wandycz).
PortR (26) 80, p. 302.
"Snow, the weird, " (tr. of Pentti Saaritsa). PortR (26) 80, p.
136.
"The Way to Yerushalayim" (tr. of Jerzy Ficowski w. Krystyna
Wandycz). PortR (26) 80, p. 301.
"Wine does not get drunk, by drinking, autumn does not" (tr.
of Paava Haavikko). PortR (26) 80, p. 133.

BOSQUET, Alain
"Méfait du verbe. " PortR (26) 80, p. 140.

BOSTON, Bruce
"Refugee. " US1 (12/13) Aut-Wint 80, p. 12.

BOSWELL, Charles
"Francis Bacon Confronts the Peter Principle. " PottPort (2)

80-81, p. 39.
"Philosophunculizing. " PottPort (2) 80-81, p. 37.

BOSWORTH, Martha
"The Year of Too Much Spring. " ChrC (97:11) 26 Mr 80, p. 346.

BOTTOMS, David
"Coasting Toward Midnight at the Southeastern Fair" (for Jim Seay). SouthernR (16:3) Sum 80, p. 615.
"The Copperhead. " Atl (245:2) F 80, p. 88.
"Fearing Nightmares." MissouriR (3:3) Sum 80, p. 35.
"The Footwashing. " Iowa (11:1) Wint 80, p. 107.
"Recording the Spirit Voices. " MissouriR (3:3) Sum 80, p. 34.
"Sermon of the Fallen. " Iowa (11:1) Wint 80, p. 106.
"The Tent Astronomer. " ParisR (77) Wint-Spr 80, p. 110.

BOUCHARD, Nanette
"The Seventh Night. " HiramPoR (28) Spr-Sum 80, p. 5.

BOUCHER, Alan
"Atlantis" (tr. of Steinn Steinarr). Vis (2) 80.
"Autumn" (tr. of Jon Oskar). Vis (4) 80.
"Falling of leaves" (tr. of Gunnar Dal). Vis (4) 80.
"From the Circus" (tr. of Johan Hjalmarrsson). Vis (2) 80.
"Search" (tr. of Jon Oskar). Vis (2) 80.
"Winter Day" (tr. of Stefan Hordur Grimsson). Vis (2) 80.

BOUGHN, Scott McKinley
"Ghet to Boy. " Mouth (2:4) My 80, p. 13.
"Kid Clean and Broadway Baby/Times Square Lullaby (Subways Ain't for Sleeping: A Case of Do and Die). " Mouth (2:5) O 80, p. 26.
"West End Blues. " Mouth (2:4) My 80, p. 25.

BOUVARD, Marguerite Guzman
"Luftmensch. " GRR (11:1) 80, p. 63.
"White. " SouthwR (65:2) Spr 80, p. 140.
"A Winter's Room. " Prima (5) 79, p. 41.

BOWDAN, Scott
"Teacher. " Bachy (17) Spr 80, p. 99.

BOWDEN, James H.
"At the Spa. " KanQ (12:1) Wint 80, p. 122.

BOWDEN, Michael
"Yellow Sky Watercolor" (for Marcia). CharR (6:1) Spr 80, p. 29.

BOWEN, James K.
"March Snow. " PoNow (26) 80, p. 30.

BOWEN, Robert
"And So It Seems. " Obs (5:3) Wint 79, pp. 106-110.

BOWERS, Neal
"Notes on Ecology. " BallSUF (21:1) Wint 80, p. 79.

BOWIE, Robert B.
"High Country. " SoDakR (18:3) Aut 80, p. 6.
"Higher. " SoDakR (18:3) Aut 80, p. 8.
"Indentations. " SoDakR (18:3) Aut 80, p. 10.

BOWIE, William C.
"Before the Statue of a Laughing Man. " CimR (51) Ap 80, p. 29.
"The Confession. " CimR (51) Ap 80, p. 48.
"Insomnia: The Face of the Clock. " CimR (51) Ap 80, p. 46.
"Letter to the Office of the Alumni. " CimR (51) Ap 80, p. 64.

BOWMAN, P. C.
"The Difference. " SouthernHR (14:4) Aut 80, p. 330.
"Helen Approaching. " SouthernPR (20:1) Spr 80, p. 33.
"The Partner. " SouthernPR (20:1) Spr 80, p. 34.
"The Recidivist. " PoetryNW (21:4) Wint 80-81, p. 40.

BOYCHUK, Bohdan
"The Stars in Summer" (tr. of Boris Pasternak w. Mark Rudman). PoNow (27) 80, p. 45.

BOYD, Melba Joyce
"Beer Drops. " Obs (5:1/2) Spr-Sum 79, p. 84.
"Gramma Wynn. " Obs (5:1/2) Spr-Sum 79, p. 83.
"Sunflowers and Saturdays. " Obs (5:1/2) Spr-Sum 79, p. 85.
"Why?" Obs (5:1/2) Spr-Sum 79, p. 86.

BOYER, Patsy
"Wet Grapes..." (tr of Circe Maia w. Mary Crow). CutB (14) Spr /Sum 80, p. 101.
"A Wind Will Come from the South" (tr. of Circe Maia w. Mary Crow). CutB (14) Spr /Sum 80, p. 103.

BOZANIC, Nick
"The Crane's Ascent. " CarolQ (32:2) Spr-Sum 80, p. 91.
"Suite" (for Ann Gillis). Wind (38) 80, p. 9.
"Suite (2). " Wind (38) 80, p. 10.
"These Poems Begin. " Wind (38) 80, p. 10.

BRACKENBURY, Rosalind
"On a train, reading Marina Tsvetayeva's letters to Boris Pasternak. " Stand (21:1) 79-80, p. 9.

BRACKER, Jon
"Big Little Things. " Mouth (2:5) O 80, p. 19.
"The Opposites of Straight. " PoetryNW (21:3) Aut 80, p. 7.

BRADFORD, Gigi
"Weather Report. " CarolQ (32:1) Wint 80, p. 62.

BRADLEY, George
"August in the Apple Orchard. " ParisR (78) Sum 80, p. 202.

BRADLEY, Marion Minthorn
"Old Jed. " EngJ (69:5) My 80, p. 48.

BRADLEY, Sam
"After the Stroke. " ChrC (97:34) 29 O 80, p. 1028.
"Great Despot, Predatory Yet. " SouthernHR (14:4) Aut 80, p.
  315.
"Man Made Again. " KanQ (12:1) Wint 80, p. 108.
"A Return. " SouthwR (65:1) Wint 80, p. 36.

BRADT, David
"Song and Dance. " KanQ (12:3) Sum 80, p. 133.
"This Wind. " KanQ (12:3) Sum 80, p. 134.

BRADWELL, Leah
"What Hell Is Like. " Sam (92) 80, p. 44.

BRADY, Dan
"Kerouac Wine. " Wind (37) 80, p. 7.
"Mariner. " Wind (37) 80, p. 7.

BRAND, Millen
"Father. " PoNow (26) 80, p. 20.
"From Josephus Gerhard's Farm. " PoNow (27) 80, p. 6.
"The Sleepwalker. " HangL (38) Aut 80, p. 12.

BRANDI, John
"Mientras la Noche se Oscura. " Ark (14) 80, p. 163.

BRANDT, Jorgen Gustava
"Blå nat på hojene. " PortR (26) 80, p. 98.

BRANIN, Jeff
"Appalachian Travel Log. " Wind (36) 80, p. 17.
"Fort Lauderdale Freight Station. " Wind (36) 80, p. 6.
"Seckel Pears. " WindO (36) Spr-Sum 80, p. 40.
"Ten Landings at Philadelphia International Airport. " CropD
  (2/3) Aut-Wint 80, p. 36.
"Wood Roads. " Wind (36) 80, p. 6.

BRASCH, Thomas
"Cassandra" (tr. by Karin von Gierke). Field (22) Spr 80, pp.
  17-21.

BRASFIELD, James
"Daybreak. " SouthernPR (20:1) Spr 80, p. 17.
"Letter from Germany" (for my father). Iowa (10:4) Aut 80, p.
  25.

BRATHWAITE, Edward Kamau
"At the death of a young poet's wife. " NewEngR (3:2) Wint 80,
p. 257.
"Circles" (for Melba Liston). NewEngR (3:2) Wint 80, p. 259.

BRAUDE, Liza Jane
"For Passacaglia 1968. " Bachy (17) Spr 80, p. 130.
"I Never Will Marry. " Bachy (17) Spr 80, p. 133.
"Trust Your Genitals. " Bachy (17) Spr 80, p. 129.

BRAULT, Jacques
"Encres de chine. " Os (10) Spr 80, pp. 4-10.

BRAUN, Volker
"State of the Nation. " Stand (21:1) 79-80, p. 49.

BRAUTIGAN, Richard
"In Pursuit of the Impossible Dream. " NewOR (7:1) 80, p. 24.

BRAVERMAN, Kate
"In Six Months. " Bachy (16) Wint 80, p. 121.
"Jacaranda. " Bachy (16) Wint 80, p. 120.
"Moths" (for Wanda Coleman). Bachy (16) Wint 80, p. 119.
"West Indies Prayer. " Bachy (16) Wint 80, p. 118.

BRECHT, Bertolt
"A Film of the Comedian Chaplin" (tr. by Michael Hamburger).
BosUJ (26:3) 80, p. 170.
"The Greenhouse" (tr. by Michael Hamburger). BosUJ (26:3) 80,
p. 169.
"In the Second Year of My Flight" (tr. by Michael Hamburger).
BosUJ (26:3) 80, p. 170.
"The Mask of Evil" (tr. by Michael Hamburger). BosUJ (26:3)
80, p. 169.
"Nature Poems" (tr. by Michael Hamburger). BosUJ (26:3) 80,
p. 168.
"The Shopper" (tr. by Michael Hamburger). BosUJ (26:3) 80, p.
171.
"The World's One Hope" (tr. by Michael Hamburger). BosUJ
(26:3) 80, p. 172.

BREINIG, Helmbrecht
from Rückenwind and Zaubersprüche: Ten poems (tr. of Sarah
Kirsch w. Kevin Power). Bound (8:3) Spr 80, pp. 191-197.

BRENNAN, Joseph Payne
"Dust. " Comm (107:19) 24 O 80, p. 585.

BRENNAN, Matthew
"Seeing in the Dark. " KanQ (12:3) Sum 80, p. 141.

BRETT, Brian
"The Point. " Ark (14) 80, p. 164.

BRETT, Peter
"Dream of Mutations After Fall-Out." CropD (2/3) Aut-Wint 80,
    p. 18.
"Manzanilla Heart." CimR (51) Ap 80, p. 16.

BREWSTER, David
"Chant Royale: The Gardener, His Rest." PoetryNW (21:1) Spr
    80, p. 25.

BREYFOGLE, Valorie A.
"Between Rains." Wind (38) 80, p. 49.

BRIGHAM, Besmilr
"The Lake, el lago." SouthernR (16:4) Aut 80, pp. 938-943.
"Mother of the Sacred Dancers." SouthernR (16:4) Aut 80, p.
    946.
"The White Doves." SouthernR (16:4) Aut 80, p. 944.

BRINGHURST, William
"The Greenland Stone." AmerPoR (9:6) N-D 80, p. 34.
"Strophe from Sophocles." AmerPoR (9:6) N-D 80, p. 34.

BRINKMANN, Rolf Dieter
"About Separate Departures" (tr. by Hartmut Schnell). NewL
    (46:4) Sum 80, p. 36.
"Mourning on the Clothesline in January" (tr. by Hartmut
    Schnell). NewL (46:4) Sum 80, p. 36.
"Oh, Peaceful Noon" (tr. by Hartmut Schnell). NewL (46:4)
    Sum 80, p. 35.
"Poem: Destroyed countryside with" (tr. by Hartmut Schnell).
    NewL (46:4) Sum 80, p. 37.

BRITT, Alan
"Places." UTR (6:3/4) 80, p. 9.
"Travel Poem (heading west through Florida)." UTR (6:3/4) 80,
    p. 5.
"West Palm Beach." UTR (6:3/4) 80, p. 11.

BROCK, Edwin
"On Call." Antaeus (36) Wint 80, p. 86.

BROCKLEY, Michael
"Reflections Upon Being Greeted on the Sidewalk." BallSUF (21:1)
    Wint 80, p. 62.
"A Valentine for Cheryl." BallSUF (21:2) Spr 80, p. 80.

BRODA, Ina Jun
"Melody" (tr. of Edvard Kocbek w. Herbert Kuhner). MalR (53)
    Ja 80, p. 29.

BRODER, Dean
"distant wings." UTR (6:3/4) 80, p. 15.
"outside our windows." UTR (6:3/4) 80, p. 18.

"people you belong to. " UTR (6:3/4) 80, p. 19.
"september's child. " UTR (6:3/4) 80, p. 14.
"telephoned silences. " UTR (6:3/4) 80, p. 17.
"Violent Picnics. " UTR (6:3/4) 80, p. 12.
"The Winter Tree. " UTR (6:3/4) 80, p. 16.

BRODEY, Jim
"Alice Ordered Me to Throw up" (w. Kathy Foley). Tele (16) 80,
    p. 69.
"For Chester Burnette" (w. Kathy Foley). Tele (16) 80, p. 70.
"Numb Skull" (w. Kathy Foley). Tele (16) 80, p. 69.

BRODSKY, Joseph
"Cape Cod Lullaby" (tr. by Anthony Hecht). Columbia (4) Spr-
    Sum 80, pp. 36-49.
"December in Florence. " NewYRB (27:7) 1 My 80, p. 10.
"Lagoon. " ParisR (77) Wint-Spr 80, p. 71.
"Letters from the Ming Dynasty" (tr. by Derek Walcott).
    NewYorker (55:50) 28 Ja 80, p. 32.
"Strophes" (tr. by David McDuff). Stand (21:1) 79-80, p. 5.

BRODSKY, Louis Daniel
"Ancestry. " FourQt (29:4) Sum 80, p. 20.
"Death Comes to the Salesman. " Harp (260:1558) Mr 80, p. 22.
"Easter Flood. " KanQ (12:1) Wint 80, p. 53.
"Rear View Mirror. " Harp (260:1558) Mr 80, p. 22.
"Redbuds. " CapeR (15:2) Sum 80, p. 3.
"Running in Packs. " BallSUF (21:1) Wint 80, p. 50.
"Sitting in Bib Overalls, Workshirt, Boots on the Monument to
    Liberty in the Center of the Square, Jacksonville, Illinois. "
    HiramPoR (28) Spr-Sum 80, p. 6.

BROMLEY, Anne
"The Empty Room Is Unimaginable. " Pan (21) 80, p. 15.
"Misreadings at a Desk Near a Window. " PraS (54:4) Wint 80-81,
    p. 9.

BROMWICH, David
"The End of Action. " NewRep (182:17) 26 Ap 80, p. 36.
"Oedipus, Pentheus. " Poetry (136:4) Jl 80, p. 202.

BRONK, William
"From Governor's Island. " Pequod (11) 80, p. 1.
"The Rumination of Rivers. " Pequod (11) 80, p. 93.

BROOK, Donna
"Prophecy. " HangL (37) Spr 80, p. 6.
"The Rose That Desired to Shut Up. " HangL (37) Spr 80, p. 4.

BROOKS, David
"Campo di Fiori" (tr. of Czeslaw Milosz w. Louis Iribarne).
    NewYRB (27:16) 23 O 80, p. 80.

BROSMAN, Catharine Savage
"Clearwater. " SouthernR (16:1) Wint 80, p. 135.
"Route 29. " SouthernR (16:1) Wint 80, p. 137.

BROSOFSKE, Greg
"Untitled: I change your bandage. " PikeF (3) Wint 80, p. 36.

BROSTOWIN, P. R.
"Emily D. " Wind (38) 80, p. 42.

BROUGHTON, James
"Hermes, His Music" (for Kenneth Rexroth). Ark (14) 80, p.
    167.

BROUMAS, Olga
"Absence of Noise Presence of Sound" (for Kim Stafford).
    Tendril (9) 80, p. 28.
"Body. " NowestR (18:3) 80, p. 48.
"Buenos Dias" (for Rob Moore). NowestR (18:3) 80, p. 49.
"Composition. " Agni (13) 80, p. 87.
"Easter. " NowestR (18:3) 80, p. 47.
"Exile. " NowestR (18:3) 80, p. 45.
"Out of Mind. " NowestR (18:3) 80, p. 46.

BROWN, Arthur
"I Want a Memory. " Focus (14:86) Ap 80, p. 28.
"There Is a Man Moving into My Skin. " Focus (14:86) Ap 80, p.
    28.

BROWN, Crystal
"Liberation. " Sam (102) 80, p. 33.
"Living on an Icon Translating Vietnamese Folk Poetry. " Sam
    (102) 80, p. 32.

BROWN, Elizabeth
"False Spring. " StoneC (7:3) D 80, p. 6.
"Pasiphae. " StoneC (7:3) D 80, p. 6.
"Skating Alone on a Flooded Cornfield. " Prima (5) 79, p. 42.

BROWN, Fred
"Leonard. " Spirit (5:1/2) Aut-Wint 79-80, p. 23.
"Nam. " Spirit (5:1/2) Aut-Wint 79-80, p. 26.

BROWN, Harry
"The Sudden Life of a Lion. " BallSUF (21:1) Wint 80, p. 4.

BROWN, Joyce S.
"Homo sapiens. " Comm (107:7) 11 Ap 80, p. 212.

BROWN, Martin
"Nietzsche Remembered. " PartR (47:2) 80, p. 216.

BROWN, Paula
"House Guest. " Prima (5) 79, p. 72.

BROWN, Rebecca
  "In the Stacks. " Tele (16) 80, p. 81.
  "Kibler Valley Bits. " Tele (16) 80, p. 80.
  "Lost in Transmission. " Tele (16) 80, p. 81.
  "West. " Tele (16) 80, p. 82.

BROWN, Steven Ford
  "A Fist of Light. " CropD (2/3) Aut-Wint 80, p. 29.
  "Girl. " CropD (2/3) Aut-Wint 80, p. 26.
  "I Row. " Vis (3) 80.

BROWN, Terry W.
  "Ashes. " KanQ (12:2) Spr 80, p. 43.

BROWN, Thelma
  "Arranging Flowers for My Death. " CutB (15) Aut/Wint 80, p.
    85.
  "Beautiful in Birches. " ConcPo (13:2) Aut 80, p. 50.
  "Ruthie Says 'No.'" NowestR (18:3) 80, p. 23.
  "Stampede. " CutB (15) Aut/Wint 80, p. 15.
  "You Are a Grandpa Named Seth. " NowestR (18:3) 80, p. 21.

BROWNE, Michael Dennis
  "Flood. " Aspen (10) Wint 80, p. 43.
  "Hide and Go Seek" (for Lisa). Aspen (10) Wint 80, p. 44.
  "Lars Jenkins, Aged Two" (for Louis and Ann). Epoch (29:3)
    Spr-Sum 80, p. 263.
  "Neighbor in May. " Bits (11) 80.

BRUCE, Lennart
  from Diary: (1, 2, 4, 5, 6) (tr. of Lars Noren). PoetryE (3)
    80, p. 63.
  "I build small nests" (tr. of Gurli Lindén). PortR (26) 80, p.
    129.
  "I draw a diagram of feelings, fill in the chart, but my lines
    miss the point. " PoNow (26) 80, p. 14.
  "I Watch the People" (tr. of Agneta Ara). PortR (26) 80, p.
    125.
  from The Impossible: (85, 87, 93, 182) (tr. of Goran Sonnevi).
    PoetryE (1) 80, p. 20.
  "In Helsinki" (tr. of Claes Andersson). PoetryE (1) 80, p. 40.
  "In This Country" (tr. of Claes Andersson). PoetryE (1) 80, p.
    41.
  "It Takes a Long Time" (tr. of Gurli Lindén). PortR (26) 80,
    p. 131.
  "November" (tr. of Agneta Ara). PortR (26) 80, p. 125.
  "The Only Wars" (tr. of Agneta Ara). PortR (26) 80, p. 127.
  from Order: (May 9) (tr. of Lars Noren). PoetryE (3) 80, p.
    62.

BRUCE, Rickie
  "Japanese-Plum Picking. " KanQ (12:3) Sum 80, p. 103.

BRUCHAC, Joseph
"Beans. " NowestR (18:3) 80, p. 20.
"Blood Skies. " QW (10) Wint-Spr 80, p. 39.
"Charley. " QW (10) Wint-Spr 80, p. 37.
"Fisher. " NowestR (18:3) 80, p. 19.
"Historical Markers Along Route 90. " Ark (14) 80, p. 168.
"Kaydeross Creek. " CharR (6:2) Aut 80, p. 45.
"One Day in the Frog Moon. " CharR (6:2) Aut 80, p. 44.
"The Plum Tree. " Outbr (4/5) Aut 79-Spr 80, p. 70.
"The Pocket Gopher. " StoneC (7:3) D 80, p. 66.
"Santos. " NewL (47:1) Aut 80, p. 104.
"Snow Falling. " NewL (47:1) Aut 80, p. 104.
"A Solitary Bird. " Im (6:2) 80, p. 11.
"Splitting Wood in Late Winter. " Ark (14) 80, p. 170.
"The Star-Nosed Mole. " DacTerr (17) 80, p. 10.
"swallow follows. " NewL (46:4) Sum 80, p. 44.
"Walking Out of Tsa La Gi" (for Louis "Little Coon" Oliver).
   StoneC (7:3) D 80, p. 65.
"Winter's End in Greenfield Center. " Ark (14) 80, p. 171.
"The Wolf. " Im (6:2) 80, p. 11.

BRUMMELS, J. V.
"River Ice. " CharR (6:2) Aut 80, p. 45.
"Small Change. " PraS (54:4) Wint 80-81, p. 69.

BRUNET, David P.
"A Scared Kid with a Knife Threatens an Old Man. " BelPoJ
   (30:4) Sum 80, p. 42.

BRUNETI, Almir
"One Desire" (tr. by Patricia Donahue). NewOR (7:3) 80, p.
   276.

BRUSH, Thomas
"Another Soft Shoe for Spring. " QW (11) Aut-Wint 80-81, p.
   119.

BRYAN, Sharon
"Use Capricious in a Sentence" (for Charles Hockett). AmerPoR
   (9:6) N-D 80, p. 15.
"With Family Below Albion Basin. " OhioR (24) 80, p. 88.

BUCHANAN, Carl
"Nine-Year-Old in Wichita with Corn. " KanQ (12:2) Spr 80, p.
   12.

BUCKLEY, Christopher
"Candles. " CalQ (16/17) 80, p. 134.
"Clouds in March. " Columbia (5) Aut-Wint 80, p. 56.
"Diffidence" (for S. A. S.). Antaeus (37) Spr 80, p. 55.
"First Afternoon of Fall. " CharR (6:2) Aut 80, p. 18.
"In the Remembering. " CharR (6:2) Aut 80, p. 16.
"Light Rain" (for Steve and Barbara Schiefen). CharR (6:1)

Spr 80, p. 28.
"Pastoral" (for John Van der Zee and Vince Croal). SouthernPR
(20:2) Aut 80, p. 42.
"Prayer Flags. " NowestR (18:3) 80, p. 99.
"Quechua. " NoAmR (265:1) Mr 80, p. 48.
"Smoke" (for the poets of Spain). Antaeus (37) Spr 80, p. 31.

BUCKLEY, Vincent
"Depression" (for Seamus Deane). NewL (46:4) Spr 80, p. 11.

BUDBILL, David
"Ben. " NewL (47:1) Aut 80, p. 20.
"Ghosts. " NewL (47:1) Aut 80, p. 21.
"On Being Native. " NewL (47:1) Aut 80, p. 22.

BUESCHER, Jean
"Lord. " BallSUF (21:3) Sum 80, p. 26.

BUETTNER, Shirley
"Home Brew. " KanQ (12:2) Spr 80, p. 34.
"Kansas Saturday, July 1944. " CropD (2/3) Aut-Wint 80, p. 14.
"Night Festival. " KanQ (12:2) Spr 80, p. 35.

BUISSON, Justine
"Ilium. " HiramPoR (28) Spr-Sum 80, p. 7.
"Other Women" (for Dottie). CimR (50) Ja 80, p. 41.

BUKOWSKI, Charles
"and titles too. " WormR (80) 80, p. 135.
"The Beach Boys. " WormR (77) 80, p. 41.
"Black Sun Black. " PoNow (26) 80, p. 13.
"Burning Bright. " PoNow (28) 80, p. 8.
"Dead Again. " WormR (77) 80, p. 38.
"A Fact. " WormR (77) 80, p. 40.
"The Fucking Horses. " PoNow (28) 80, p. 8.
"Hotel Felix. " WormR (78) 80, p. 83.
"love. " WormR (80) 80, p. 131.
"A Love Poem for All the Women I Have Known. " Tendril (9)
80, p. 29.
"My Style. " PoNow (26) 80, p. 13.
"1984. " WormR (77) 80, p. 39.
"a note upon starvation. " WormR (80) 80, p. 136.
"A Note Upon Waste. " WormR (77) 80, p. 39.
"Overt Population. " WormR (77) 80, p. 40.
"Rock. " PoNow (28) 80, p. 40.
"shopping list. " WormR (80) 80, p. 131.
"time is made to be wasted. " WormR (80) 80, p. 133.
"we're all so wanted. " WormR (80) 80, p. 132.
"Yes. " WormR (78) 80, p. 84.

BULLARD, G. L.
"How I 'Lef' a Lover After One Year. " WindO (36) Spr-Sum
80, p. 33.

BULLER, Galen
"The Ogre's Call. " KanQ (12:2) Spr 80, p. 98.

BULLER, S. R.
"Dead Cat. " Poem (40) N 80, p. 52.

BURDEN, Jean
"The Cemetery. " BelPoJ (31:1) Aut 80, p. 32.
"Sabbath. " Im (6:2) 80, p. 7.

BURGIS, Allan
"Mistaken Identity. " WormR (77) 80, p. 14.
"The Usual Symptoms." WormR (77) 80, p. 14.

BURKE, Stephen
"Wax. " EnPas (11) 80, p. 16.

BURLINGAME, Robert
"The Father. " DacTerr (17) 80, p. 11.
"For Thoreau on an October Evening. " QW (11) Aut-Wint 80-81,
    p. 59.
"South from Nogales. " QW (11) Aut-Wint 80-81, p. 58.

BURNHAM, Deborah
"Two Aubades: November. " CutB (15) Aut/Wint 80, p. 79.

BURNHAM, Philip
"Address of the Soul to the Body. " Iowa (11:1) Wint 80, p. 110.

BURNS, Michael
"At the Landfill. " CimR (51) Ap 80, p. 63.
"Bob White. " CimR (51) Ap 80, p. 30.
"Clear Creek New Year's Day. " CimR (51) Ap 80, p. 15.
"For My Father. " QW (11) Aut-Wint 80-81, p. 118.

BURNS, R. W.
"Hagiwara. " HolCrit (17:5) D 80, p. 17.

BURNS, Ralph
"When Huntington, Indiana Tried to Keep Hogs from the Street. "
    CarolQ (32:1) Wint 80, p. 76.
"Worksong. " MinnR (N S 15) Aut 80, p. 20.

BURNS, William
"Mother?" SewanR (88:4) Aut 80, p. 550.

BURR, Gray
"Preparing to Come About. " PoNow (26) 80, p. 11.
"Two at Brentano's. " PoNow (27) 80, p. 5.

BURRELL, Sophia
"Epigram on Two Ladies. " Playb (27:3) Mr 80, p. 165.

BURROWS, E. G.
"Climbing Grey Crag." Ascent (5:2) 80, p. 1.
"Inverness Walkway." Im (6:2) 80, p. 8.
"Looking for the Greenhouse." CharR (6:1) Spr 80, p. 6.
"The Old Woman's House Not for Sale." Im (6:2) 80, p. 8.
"Snow Shower." Im (6:2) 80, p. 8.
"The Trestle." CharR (6:1) Spr 80, p. 5.

BURSK, Christopher
"Branch Sounds." BelPoJ (30:4) Sum 80, p. 25.
"Finding the Words." WindO (36) Spr-Sum 80, p. 48.
"Get Lost." HiramPoR (27) Aut-Wint 80, p. 10.
"Hilaritas." PoNow (27) 80, p. 12.
"Jerusalem Road." Poetry (137:3) D 80, p. 138.
"The Only Thing Worse Than the Terror Itself Would Be the
    Silence Afterward." Poetry (137:3) D 80, p. 142.
"Plywood." Poetry (137:3) D 80, p. 140.
"Preen Glands." MassR (21:1) Spr 80, p. 174.
"Salt." GeoR (34:4) Wint 80, p. 854.
"The Second Story Window." BelPoJ (30:4) Sum 80, p. 24.
"Storm Warning." PoNow (27) 80, p. 12.
"Town Names for Parts of My Body." MassR (21:1) Spr 80, p.
    174.

BURT, Barbara Swett
"Plum Island." BelPoJ (31:1) Aut 80, p. 18.

BUSCH, Trent
"The Country." NewEngR (3:2) Wint 80, p. 269.

BUSCH, Wilhelm
"Mr. and Mrs. Knopp" (tr. by Walter Arndt). NewEngR (3:2)
    Wint 80, pp. 190-206.

BUSH, Barney
"Design." DenQ (14:4) Wint 80, p. 100.
"Late." DenQ (14:4) Wint 80, p. 102.
"Long Road Back" (for Joy). DenQ (14:4) Wint 80, p. 98.
"Northwest Noon." ConcPo (13:2) Aut 80, p. 36.
"Requiem at the Bar." DenQ (14:4) Wint 80, p. 101.

BUSTA, Christine
"Phases" (tr. by Robert Haiptman). CutB (14) Spr/Sum 80, p.
    62.

BUSTAMENTE, Cecilia
"Boarding School" (tr. by Maureen Ahern and author). NewOR
    (7:3) 80, p. 285.

BUTCHER, Grace
"Survival." PoNow (27) 80, p. 11.

BUTKIE, Joseph D.
"Hunger." Mouth (2:4) My 80, p. 23.

"In Japan. " Mouth (2:4) My 80, p. 40.
"Inside the Trojan Horse. " Mouth (2:4) My 80, p. 16.
"Just Another Healthy Homosexual" (to Dick). Mouth (2:4) My
    80, p. 39.
"#1. " Mouth (2:4) My 80, p. 36.
"Query: Do We Share a Common Joy?" Mouth (2:4) My 80, p.
    7.
"Speeding from Tokyo, Spotting Another Foreign Devil. " Mouth
    (2:4) My 80, p. 41.
"To a Married Man. " Mouth (2:4) My 80, p. 45.

BUTLER, Jack
    "The Mantis. " Poetry (137:1) O 80, p. 18.
    "Timber Rattler. " Poetry (137:1) O 80, p. 17.

BUTLIN, Ron
    "Interior 1978. " GRR (11:2/3) 80, p. 47.
    "Two Composers. " GRR (11:2/3) 80, p. 48.

BUTRICK, L. H.
    "Dangerous to Your Health. " KanQ (12:3) Sum 80, p. 123.

BUTTERS, Christopher
    "Why I Stay in New York. " Tele (16) 80, p. 8.

BYRD, Don
    "Sestina and Commentary. " SunM (9/10) Sum 80, p. 130.

BYRD, Sandra
    "Of the Ocean. " GeoR (34:3) Aut 80, p. 635.

CABRAL, Olga
    "Memory. " PoNow (28) 80, p. 13.

CADDY, John
    "The Quest in This Season. " DacTerr (17) 80, p. 12.
    "Sharing the Cry" (for Owen). DacTerr (17) 80, p. 13.

CADER, Teresa D.
    "On the Edge of a Safe Sleep. " Tendril (7/8) Spr-Sum 80, p. 8.

CADNUM, Michael
    "The Tarantula. " HiramPoR (28) Spr-Sum 80, p. 8.

CADY, Joseph
    "In and Out. " Shen (31:1) 79, p. 42.

CAFFYN, Lois P.
    "Unseen. " KanQ (12:3) Sum 80, p. 62.

CAHN, Cynthia
    "Rage Can Be Fun. " BallSUF (21:1) Wint 80, p. 72.

CAKS, Aleksandre
"At the Daugara. " StoneC (7:3) D 80, p. 30.
"Ballad About My Happiness. " StoneC (7:3) D 80, p. 32.

CALDWELL, Justin
"Detroit. " PoNow (29) 80, p. 19.
"The Sleeping Porch. " PoNow (29) 80, p. 19.

CALEB, Marine J.
"Haiku. " WindO (36) Spr-Sum 80, p. 3.

CALENDA, Eleanor Davidson
"In Memory of Bertrand Russell. " StoneC (7:3) D 80, p. 17.
"A Lonely Crowd. " StoneC (7:3) D 80, p. 17.

CALLAWAY, Kathy
"Letter from Paris. " US1 (12 /13) Aut-Wint 80, p. 13.
"Little Berlin. " US1 (12 /13) Aut-Wint 80, p. 13.
"Love in the Western World. " Nat (231:19) 6 D 80, p. 618.
"Working the Night Board. " US1 (12 /13) Aut-Wint 80, p. 13.

CAMILLO, Victor
"Remembering a Friend. " PoetC (12:2) 80, p. 23.

CAMP, James
"The Alleged Perpetrators. " OP (30) Aut 80, p. 18.
"Echoes of the Masters. " OP (30) Aut 80, p. 19.

CAMPANA, Dino
"Marradi" (tr. by Deborah Woodard). Durak (5) 80, p. 50.
"Night Character" (tr. by Frank Stewart). CutB (14) Spr /Sum
    80, p. 17.
"O Poetry You Won't Return Again" (tr. by Deborah Woodard).
    Durak (5) 80, p. 51.

CAMPBELL, David
"Songs of Chance. " NewL (46:3) Spr 80, p. 17.

CAMPBELL, Deborah
"Mapping Four Points. " NewRena (13) Aut 80, p. 71.
"Nature and the Old Marriage. " NewRena (13) Aut 80, p. 70.

CAMPION, Dan
"Shopwindow. " Tele (16) 80, p. 45.

CANNADY, Criss E.
"Phyllis. " SouthernPR (20:2) Aut 80, p. 20.

CANNON, Melissa
"The Abandoned Shoe's Lament. " Tele (16) 80, p. 6.
"For Pain. " BelPoJ (31:1) Aut 80, p. 29.
"Grandfather. " BelPoJ (31:1) Aut 80, p. 28.

CANTRELL, Charles
   "Children in the Snow. " PoetC (12:1) 80, p. 27.
   "In the Shadows of Stone. " PoetC (12:1) 80, p. 28.

CARACCIOLO, Beatrice
   "Journey Book: Mexico" (tr. by Gustaf Sobin and Eliot Wein-
      berger). Montra (7) 80, pp. 78-83.

CARÊME, Maurice
   "Riddles" (tr. by Dennis Tool). CarlMis (18:2) Sum 80, p. 106.

CAREY, Michael
   "Summer Paean. " Tele (16) 80, p. 53.

CARLILE, Henry
   "The Barber's Fountain. " PoNow (28) 80, p. 9.
   "The Book of the Deer, the Bear and the Elk. " PoetryNW (21:
      4) Wint 80-81, p. 16.
   "The Four Seasons. " Iowa (11:1) Wint 80, p. 108.
   "The New City. " MissouriR (3:2) Wint 80, p. 20.
   "One Book. " AntR (38:2) Spr 80, p. 183.
   "Running Lights. " AntR (38:3) Sum 80, p. 346.
   "Small Hunting Accident. " PraS (54:3) Aut 80, p. 64.
   "Spider Reeves. " ConcPo (13:2) Aut 80, p. 38.

CARLISLE, Jonathan T.
   "Welfare. " ChrC (97:2) 16 Ja 80, p. 46.

CARLISLE, S. E.
   "Mysteries of Glass. " Aspect (76) S-D 79-80, p. 26.

CARLISLE, Thomas John
   "After the Operation. " ChrC (97:16) 30 Ap 80, p. 496.
   "Drop out. " ChrC (97:42) 24 D 80, p. 1270.
   "Fruit Out of Season. " ChrC (97:11) 26 Mr 80, p. 341.
   "Mark on His Forehead. " PoNow (29) 80, p. 5.
   "One Long Quarrel. " ChrC (97:36) 12 N 80, p. 1087.
   "Restoration. " ChrC (97:40) 10 D 80, p. 1220.
   "A Severe Struggle. " ChrC (97:22) 18-25 Je 80, p. 671.

CARLSEN, Ioanna
   "Blood Plant. " Poem (38) Mr 80, p. 50.
   "Salt. " Poem (38) Mr 80, p. 49.

CARMEN, Marilyn
   "Harrisburg Hospital. " BlackALF (14:4) Wint 80, p. 175.
   "invisible black face. " Obs (5:1/2) Spr-Sum 79, p. 78.
   "A Vision from Beneath the Skin. " Obs (5:1/2) Spr-Sum 79, p.
      77.

CARMI, T.
   "Inventory" (tr. by Grace Schulman). Nat (231:22) 27 D 80, p.
      712.

"Story" (tr. by Grace Schulman). Nat (230:14) 12 Ap 80, p.
   438.
"To the ridge like the first rain. " PortR (26) 80, p. 206.

CARMINES, Al
"Aneurisms. " ChrC (97:43) 31 D 80, p. 1286.

CARPENTER, Carol
"The Mass Media. " Poem (39) Jl 80, p. 50.

CARPENTER, David
"Salamander" (tr. of Paul Savoie). ConcPo (12:2) Aut 79, p. 29.

CARPENTER, Lucas
"After a Fiddler Convention at Galax, Virginia" (for T. J.
   Worthington). ColEng (42:2) O 80, p. 151.

CARPENTER, Mack
"Ascensions 1:1. " Sam (86) 79, p. 37.
"Ascensions 1:2. " Sam (86) 79, p. 37.
"Ascensions 1:3. " Sam (86) 79, p. 37.

CARPINISAN, Mariana
"Winter Ritual" (tr. of Nichita Stanescu w. Mark Irwin). Iowa
   (10:4) Aut 79, p. 38.

CARREGA, Gordon
"The Best Friend. " PoNow (29) 80, p. 6.
"Caged. " PoNow (29) 80, p. 6.

CARREL, Ann
"Catching. " ThRiPo (15 /16) 80, p. 28.
"The Treacherous Death of Jessie James. " ThRiPo (15 /16) 80,
   p. 29.

CARRERA, Anton
"Estirp. " PortR (26) 80, p. 345.

CARRUTH, Hayden
"Among That Company. " NewYorker (55:48) 14 Ja 80, p. 83.
"Contra Mortem. " Tendril (9) 80, pp. 31-42.
"Fragment of a Conversation in Bed. " NewYorker (56:37) 3 N
   80, p. 166.

CARTER, Ellin E.
"Omen. " HiramPoR (27) Aut-Wint 80, p. 11.

CARTER, Guy
"Walking You Home. " GRR (11:2 /3) 80, p. 116.

CARTER, Jared
"Landing the Bees. " KanQ (12:1) Wint 80, p. 92.
"Mississinewa Country Road. " PoNow (28) 80, p. 40.

"The Moon That Waxes, the Sun That Wanes. " Im (6:2) 80, p.
    6.
"The Undertaker. " PikeF (3) Wint 80, p. 21.

CARTER, John
  "In the Sculpture Garden. " Vis (1) 79.

CARTER, Robert E.
  "Word Alchemist. " MalR (55) Jl 80, p. 144.

CARTER, Steve
  "A Day Out. " NewRena (12) Spr 80, p. 50.
  "Meditation in Black. " NewRena (12) Spr 80, p. 49.

CARTER, Verne Alan
  "Pound of Pasta. " Atl (246:1) Jl 80, p. 80.

CARVER, Raymond
  "Luck. " Tendril (9) 80, p. 43.
  "The Other Life. " MissouriR (3:2) Wint 80, p. 16.

CASEY, Deb
  "Divergent Horses. " LittleM (12:3/4) 80, p. 63.
  "Enough. " LittleM (12:3/4) 80, p. 62.
  "Of the Tongue and Stf: Wrds. " LittleM (12:3/4) 80, p. 64.

CASHORALI, Peter
  "Audobon and the Birds of North America. " Bachy (16) Wint 80,
    p. 83.

CASNER, Lisa
  "Watching Grandma Cook Dinner. " QW (10) Wint-Spr 80, p. 91.

CASSIDY, Ruth M.
  "Faraway. " CropD (1) Spr 80, p. 10.

CASSITY, Turner
  "Anastasia: Anna Anderson Manahan. " SouthernR (16:2) Spr 80,
    p. 411.
  "Appalachia in Cincinnati. " SouthernR (16:2) Spr 80, p. 409.
  "Berolina Demodée. " YaleR (70:2) Wint 81, p. 259.
  "Death and the Bush Pilot. " SouthernR (16:2) Spr 80, p. 409.
  "The Goblin Market, or, The Sorrows of Satan. " Iowa (10:4)
    Aut 79, p. 40.
  "Wine from the Cape. " SouthernR (16:2) Spr 80, p. 411.

CASTELLANOS, Rosario
  "Metamorphosis of the Sorceress" (to Remedios Varo) (tr. by
    Maureen Ahern). DenQ (15:1) Spr 80, p. 91.
  "Passport" (tr. by Maureen Ahern). NewOR (7:3) 80, p. 256.
  "Speaking of Gabriel" (tr. by Maureen Ahern). DenQ (15:1) Spr
    80, p. 90.

CASTILLO, Fernando Paz
"La Mujer que no Vimos. " PortR (26) 80, p. 453.

CASTRO, Jan
"Dance" (for A. Savage). Focus (14:86) Ap 80, p. 24.
"Solar Eclipse. " Focus (14:86) Ap 80, p. 24.

CASTRO, Michael
"Axeman in the Woods in Winter. " Focus (14:86) Ap 80, p. 23.
"Brown Rice. " Focus (14:86) Ap 80, p. 23.
"Coming Out of Bondage. " Focus (14:86) Ap 80, p. 23.
"Wedding Song. " Focus (14:86) Ap 80, p. 23.

CAVALIERO, Glen
"The Grange. " Stand (21:3) 80, p. 61.

CAVALLARO, Carol
"comma AND" (to my Freshman class). PraS (54:4) Wint 80-81,
p. 96.

CAVANAUGH, William C.
"Hapsburg Goat. " SouthernPR (20:2) Aut 80, p. 56.

CECIL, Richard
"Confession. " PoNow (26) 80, p. 33.
"The Ice Couple. " PoNow (26) 80, p. 33.
"Self Portrait. " PoNow (28) 80, p. 30.
"A Tour of Anatolia. " AmerPoR (9:4) Jl-Ag 80, p. 3.

CEDRINS, Inara
"At the Daugava" (tr. of Aleksandre Caks). StoneC (7:3) D 80,
p. 31.
"Ballad About My Happiness" (tr. of Aleksandre Caks). StoneC
(7:3) D 80, p. 33.
"The Bride" (tr. of Aina Kraujiete). PoNow (27) 80, p. 45.
"Chicago" (to Ellen) (tr. of Astrid Ivask). PortR (26) 80, p.
251.
"In the Field" (tr. of Aina Kraujiete). PoNow (27) 80, p. 45.
"Poem: 'As a hunter you must shoot down the moment'" (tr. of
Astrid Ivask). PortR (26) 80, p. 252.
"Strong Light. " Aspen (10) Wint 80, p. 56.

CEELY, John
"Lone Mind" (tr. of Nezahval coyotl [Hungry Coyote]). Tele
(16) 80, p. 15.
"Never" (tr. of Nezahual coyotl [Hungry Coyote]). Tele (16) 80,
p. 16.
"Stand Up" (tr. of Nezahual coyotl [Hungry Coyote]). Tele (16)
80, p. 17.

CENDRARS, Blaise
"Hotel Notre-Dame" (tr. by Perry Oldham and Arlen Gill).
WebR (5:1) Wint 80, p. 32.

"Strangers Inn" (tr. by Perry Oldham and Arlen Gill). WebR
    (5:1) Wint 80, p. 36.

CERNUDA, Luis
    "Nevada" (tr. by James Schevill). PoNow (26) 80, p. 46.
    "Waiting Alone" (tr. by David Unger). PoNow (28) 80, p. 44.

CERRUTO, Oscar
    from Cantico Traspasado: "Persona subrepticia. " GRR (11:1)
        80, p. 30.
    from Cantico Traspasado: "Poco antes nada, y poco despues
        humo. " GRR (11:1) 80, p. 26.
    from Cantico Traspasado: "Que van a dar a la noche. " GRR
        (11:1) 80, p. 28.

CERVANTES, Lorna Dee
    "Beneath the Shadow of the Freeway. " Sam (101) 80, p. 42.
    "Meeting Mescalito at Oak Hill Cemetery. " Sam (102) 80, p.
        48.
    "Uncle's First Rabbit. " Sam (98) 80, p. 40.

CERVO, Nathan
    "Charity. " EnPas (11) 80, p. 23.
    "The Facts. " PoNow (29) 80, p. 6.
    "The Gypsy. " EnPas (11) 80, p. 22.
    "Rain. " EnPas (11) 80, p. 23.

CESAIRE, Aimé
    "Les Pur-sang. " Montra (7) 80, pp. 98-112.

CHACE, Joel
    "Drought. " SouthernPR (20:2) Aut 80, p. 43.
    "Secrets of Men. " Wind (36) 80, p. 8.

CHALFI, Raquel
    "Tel-Aviv Beach, Winter '74" (tr. by Alexandra Meiri).
        AmerPoR (9:5) S-O 80, p. 33.

CHALLIS, Chris
    "Autumn in Hammersmith. " MinnR (NS 15) Aut 80, p. 33.

CHALONER, David
    "Sun House Propaganda. " PartR (47:2) 80, p. 217.

CHAMBERLAIN, William
    "False Daylight. " PoetryNW (21:1) Spr 80, p. 48.

CHAPPEL, Allen H.
    "Margarete with the Trunk" (tr. of Helga M. Novak). NewOR
        (7:1) 80, p. 59.

CHAPPELL, Fred
    "Cabin in Hill Shadow. " SmF (11/12) Spr-Aut 80, p. 3.

"Earthsleep. " GeoR (34:1) Spr 80, p. 128.
"The Fated Lovers: A Story. " SmF (11/12) Spr-Aut 80, pp.
   6-11.
"Forever Mountain. " SouthernPR (20:2) Aut 80, p. 25.

CHAVEZ, Mario
   "Penance in the Other World. " SlowLR (4) 80, p. 37.
   "The Raza Bar. " SlowLR (4) 80, p. 38.
   "Transient. " SlowLR (4) 80, p. 36.

CHERRY, Kelly
   "At Night Your Mouth. " OP (30) Aut 80, p. 14.
   "Late Afternoon at the Arboretum. " OP (30) Aut 80, p. 16.
      16.
   "Reading, Dreaming, Hiding. " OP (30) Aut 80, p. 17.

CHIASSON, Elias
   "A Close-Knit Family. " Focus (14:86) Ap 80, p. 37.
   "I Shopped. " Focus (14:86) Ap 80, p. 37.
   "A Remembering Man. " Focus (14:86) Ap 80, p. 37.

CHILDS, John Steven
   "Charon in the Desert. " CapeR (16:1) Wint 80, p. 2.
   "Michaelmas. " CapeR (16:1) Wint 80, p. 3.

CHIN, David
   "Scallops" (for Lorna). PoetryE (1) 80, p. 70.

CHIN, Marilyn
   "Adrenalin" (tr. of Gozo Yoshimasu w. author). PortR (26) 80,
      pp. 238-243.
   "No dreams befall my pillow. " NewL (46:4) Sum 80, p. 45.
   "Two Women. " Pan (21) 80, p. 12.

CHING, Laureen
   "Eight Blocks" (for M. H. K.). Wind (37) 80, p. 8.
   "My Father. " DacTerr (17) 80, p. 14.

CHIPASULA, Frank Mkalawile
   "Mzee Maurice" (for Ralph and Fanny Ellison). CarlMis (18:3)
      Wint 80, p. 214.

CHISHOLM, Jan
   "Lifelines. " CalQ (16/17) 80, p. 149.

CHMIELARZ, Sharon
   "The Writing Lesson. " EngJ (69:5) My 80, p. 50.

CHO Wun-che
   "Silence of My Lover" (tr. of Han Yong-un w. David James).
      WindO (36) Spr-Sum 80, p. 32.

CHOWDHURY, Kabir
"An Artist" (tr. of Sanaul Huq). PortR (26) 80, p. 39.

CHOYCE, Lesley
"Fast Living. " PottPort (2) 80-81, p. 52.

CHRISTENSEN, Inger
"Handlingen Kontinuiteter. " PortR (26) 80, p. 82.
"Handlingen symmetrier. " PortR (26) 80, p. 85.
"Scenen transitiviteter. " PortR (26) 80, p. 80.
"Teksten extensioner. " PortR (26) 80, p. 79.
"Teksten integriteter. " PortR (26) 80, p. 83.
"Teksten universaliteter. " PortR (26) 80, p. 84.

CHRISTENSEN, Nadia
"Ghosts" (tr. of Kate Naess). PoNow (26) 80, p. 45.
"Snow" (tr. of Stein Mehren). PortR (26) 80, p. 281.

CHRISTENSEN, Paul
"Come Down Here. " Bound (8:2) Wint 80, p. 138.
"Difficult Mornings. " Bound (8:2) Wint 80, p. 140.
"A Memory. " Bound (8:2) Wint 80, p. 139.

CHRISTIAN, Paula
"In Clifton. " WindO (37) Aut-Wint 80, p. 18.
"song of the ugly duckling. " WindO (37) Aut-Wint 80, p. 19.
"Traveling to Miami. " WindO (37) Aut-Wint 80, p. 19.

CHRISTINA, Martha
"82 in June. " Tendril (7/8) Spr-Sum 80, p. 11.
"Functional. " Tendril (7/8) Spr-Sum 80, p. 10.

CHRISTOPHER, Nicholas
"July 4, NYC. " Ascent (5:3) 80, p. 15.
"On the Meridian. " NewYorker (55:52) 11 F 80, p. 58.
"Walt Whitman at the Reburial of Poe. " NewYorker (56:27) 25
    Ag 80, p. 93.

CHUNG Tin-wen
"Nameless. " PortR (26) 80, p. 387.

CHURA, David
"Fossil. " Mouth (2:4) My 80, p. 13.
"The Names of Birds. " Mouth (2:4) My 80. Front cover.

CHUTE, Robert M.
"The Boat Waits. " HangL (38) Aut 80, p. 14.
"A Dream of Two Zeros. " BelPoJ (30:4) Sum 80, p. 40.
"Lioness. " Confr (20) Spr-Sum 80, p. 27.

CIARDI, John
"Donne Ch'avete Inteletto d'Amore. " AmerS (49:1) Wint 79-80,
    p. 78.

"One for Rexroth. " Ark (14) 80, p. 172.
"Thursday Also Happens. " Poetry (137:2) N 80, p. 71.
"Ward Three: Faith. " Poetry (137:2) N 80, p. 73.

CISNEROS, Antonio
  "For Robert Lowell" (tr. by Maureen Ahern and David Tipton).
    NewOR (7:3) 80, p. 240.
  "The House at Punta Nera (that Empire)" (tr. by David Tipton).
    NewOR (7:3) 80, p. 241.
  "King Lear" (tr. by David Tipton). NewOR (7:3) 80, p. 239.
  "Return Visit to London (Ars Poetica 2)" (tr. by David Tipton).
    NewOR (7:3) 80, p. 237.

CITINO, David
  "After the First Frost. " HiramPoR (27) Aut-Wint 80, p. 12.
  "Apollonia, Virgin and Martyr. " SouthernHR (14:1) Wint 80, p.
    20.
  "Coming Home Again. " Im (6:2) 80, p. 8.
  "Curse. " Aspen (10) Wint 80, p. 42.
  "Doors, Window, Flesh and Bone. " PikeF (3) Wint 80, p. 3.
  "Isaac. " PikeF (3) Wint 80, p. 3.
  "Poem for a Thirty-Third Birthday. " HiramPoR (28) Spr-Sum
    80, p. 9.
  "Punishments. " LitR (23:3) Spr 80, p. 382.
  "The Revenant. " EnPas (11) 80, p. 24.
  "Three Plots for Television. " Im (6:2) 80, p. 8.
  "Visiting. " PoetC (12:1) 80, p. 18.

CLAMPITT, Amy
  "Balms. " Poetry (137:2) N 80, p. 82.
  "Beach Glass. " NewRep (182:16) 19 Ap 80, p. 34.
  "Meridian. " PraS (54:1) Spr 80, p. 56.
  "A Resumption, or Possibly a Remission. " PraS (54:1) Spr 80,
    p. 55.
  "Tepoztlan. " NewYorker (56:4) 17 Mr 80, p. 46.

CLAMURRO, William
  "The Edge of Town. " CharR (6:1) Spr 80, p. 19.
  "Letter to Shawville. " CharR (6:1) Spr 80, p. 20.
  "The Trench. " CharR (6:1) Spr 80, p. 21.

CLAREUS, Ingrid
  "Autobiography" (tr. of Sonja Akesson). PoetryE (1) 80, pp. 25-
    33.
  "Destruction" (tr. of Margareta Renberg). PoetryE (3) 80, p. 67.
  "The Disappointed" (tr. of Margareta Renberg). PoetryE (3) 80,
    p. 71.
  "The Foreign Café" (tr. of Margareta Renberg). PoetryE (3)
    80, p. 70.
  "Hope" (tr. of Margareta Renberg). PoetryE (3) 80, p. 66.
  "An iceclear light" (tr. of Margareta Renberg). PoetryE (3) 80,
    p. 69.
  "Mine" (tr. of Margareta Renberg). PoetryE (3) 80, p. 68.

"Saturated commotion" (tr. of Margareta Renberg).   PoetryE (3)
    80, p. 72.

CLARK, Carolyn
    "Farewell" (tr. of Bella Akhmadulina).   PortR (26) 80, p. 341.
    "In a Vacated Sanitorium" (tr. of Bella Akhmadulina).   PortR
        (26) 80, p. 336.
    "Innovation" (tr. of Bella Akhmadulina).   PortR (26) 80, p. 339.

CLARK, Constance
    "Hospital Visit."   Wind (38) 80, p. 12.

CLARK, Duane
    "Bonner's Ferry Beggar."   KanQ (12:2) Spr 80, p. 64.

CLARK, James
    "Domino King."   QW (10) Wint-Spr 80, p. 29.
    "For Those to Come."   QW (10) Wint-Spr 80, p. 28.

CLARK, Kevin
    "Allan Clark."   EnPas (10) 80, p. 12.
    "Death Comes for the Old Cowboy."   CalQ (16/17) 80, p. 37.
    "Death Comes for the Old Runner."   CalQ (16/17) 80, p. 36.
    "Widow Under a New Moon."   GeoR (34:1) Spr 80, p. 162.

CLARK, Melissa
    "The Bee Wedding: Sylvia Plath."   WindO (37) Aut-Wint 80, p.
        12.
    "The Life of the Virgin."   Comm (107:23) 19 D 80, p. 716.
    "My Husband Smokes Cigars with His Father by Candlelight."
        SmPd (49) Spr 80, p. 20.
    "Preppy."   SmPd (49) Spr 80, p. 18.

CLARK, Richard
    "Invocation."   BelPoJ (31:1) Aut 80, p. 2.

CLARK, Stephen
    "Summer Visitors."   Poetry (136:2) My 80, p. 84.

CLAUDEL, Alice Moser
    "For Philip Larkin, Mourning."   KanQ (12:4) Aut 80, p. 46.
    "Thoughts on Coming In."   Wind (38) 80, p. 14.
    "Unlaid Ghosts."   ConcPo (13:1) Spr 80, p. 32.

CLAUDEL, Calvin Andre
    "Aurore Pradere."   WebR (5:2) Aut 80, p. 58.
    "Louisa Died Last Night."   WebR (5:2) Aut 80, p. 59.
    "Mr. Cayetana from Havana."   WebR (5:2) Aut 80, p. 59.
    "One, Two, Three, Caroline."   WebR (5:2) Aut 80, p. 58.

CLAUDIO, Mário
    "Requiem for Pier Paolo Pasolini" (tr. of Eugénio de Andrade
        w. Michael Gordon Lloyd).   PortR (26) 80, p. 311.

CLAUS, Hugo
"Ulysses. " PortR (26) 80, p. 272.

CLAUS, Jeff
"Self-Portrait of Twenty. " LittleM (12:3/4) 80, p. 8.
"Wife Sleep. " LittleM (12:3/4) 80, p. 5.

CLAUSEN, Jan
"Poem in a Year That Punctuates a Decade. " Cond (6) 80, pp.
    109-119.

CLEAR, Therese A.
"Beyond the Yearlings. " PoetryNW (21:2) Sum 80, p. 6.
"High Kiting at Road's End, Oregon" (for Patty Clear).
    PoetryNW (21:2) Sum 80, p. 7.
"Thunder in the Homestretch. " PoetryNW (21:2) Sum 80, p. 8.

CLEWELL, David
"After the Seance. " MidwQ (21:2) Wint 80, p. 245.
"Bullhead County. " MidwQ (21:2) Wint 80, p. 248.
"What the Doctor Found. " MidwQ (21:2) Wint 80, p. 244.
"The Woman at the Jukebox Isn't Sad. " MidwQ (21:2) Wint 80,
    p. 246.

CLIFF, William
"Being in Love" (tr. by Maxine Kumin and Judith Kumin).
    PoNow (26) 80, p. 44.
"This morning lying in bed some English memories" (tr. by
    Maxine Kumin and Judith Kumin). PoNow (26) 80, p. 44.

CLIFTON, Harry
"Cables. " GRR (11:2/3) 80, p. 93.
"The Student. " GRR (11:2/3) 80, p. 94.

CLIFTON, Merritt
"Blanket-Man. " Sam (98) 80, p. 39.
"Cambodia, 1/1/80. " Sam (103) 80, p. 47.
"Debate, Barnyard, After First Snow. " Sam (103) 80, p. 50.
"Entomology II. " Sam (101) 80, p. 41.
"4/25/80--Dawn Raid. " Sam (98) 80, p. 51.
"I Said, Love Thy Neighbor!" Sam (103) 80, p. 33.
"On Pass from Oak Knoll. " Sam (98) 80, p. 39.
"Pre-Trial Examination. " Sam (103) 80, p. 68.
"Pudgy the Tomcat. " Sam (103) 80, p. 15.
"Tale from De Dark Side. " Sam (101) 80, p. 32.
"They Say. " Sam (103) 80, p. 80.
Three of a Kind. Sam (81) 79. Entire issue.
"Yamaska River Death Poem. " Sam (103) 80, p. 26.

CLIFTON, Nicole
"Adolescence. " Sam (101) 80, p. 47.
"Beach Weekend. " Sam (92) 80, p. 58.

CLINTON, D.
"Quick Songs You Can Learn Easy. " MinnR (NS 15) Aut 80, p.
31.

CLINTON, Robert
"Hymn. " Antaeus (37) Spr 80, p. 58.

CLOMPUS, Bradley
"Before Leaving. " CreamCR (5:1) Wint 79, p. 18.

COBIN, Susan
"in your dream you marry. " Kayak (53) My 80, p. 45.

COE, Dina
"Paradise Hill. " US1 (12/13) Aut-Wint 80, p. 3.

COFFIN, Lyn
"The Affair Is Over. " BallSUF (21:1) Wint 80, p. 55.
"The Blackbird Looks Back. " Wind (38) 80, p. 15.
"A Brilliant Alliance. " LitR (23:3) Spr 80, p. 412.
"Cow, Drowning in Mud. " Bits (11) 80.
"The Death Frog. " LitR (23:3) Spr 80, p. 411.
"The Dream. " PoNow (29) 80, p. 7.
"Elegy Number Seven" (tr. of Jiri Orten). DenQ (15:1) Spr 80, p. 76.
"Force of One" (for Jeff). HolCrit (17:4) O 80, p. 9.
"Inheritance. " DacTerr (17) 80, p. 15.
"Initiation. " SouthernHR (14:3) Sum 80, p. 248.
"Motel A'ubade. " ConcPo (13:1) Spr 80, p. 40.
"Oedipus and the Sphinx. " MichQR (19:3) Sum 80, p. 381.
"A Statue of the Sacred Heart. " Wind (38) 80, p. 15.
"The Thasos Kouros. " SouthernHR (14:4) Aut 80, p. 300.
"You Are Odysseus (But I'm the Hottentots). " BallSUF (21:1)
Wint 80, p. 74.

COGSWELL, Fred
"L'amour la poesie" (tr. of Paul Eluard). PottPort (2) 80-81,
p. 41.
"Against the Love Virus. " PottPort (2) 80-81, p. 47.
"I've Little Patience With...." PottPort (2) 80-81, p. 42.
"Over This Collected Self. " PottPort (1) 79-80, p. 12.
"There Are Two Worlds. " PottPort (1) 79-80, p. 37.

COHEN, Jay
"Afterward. " Poem (39) Jl 80, p. 42.
"Memory. " Poem (39) Jl 80, p. 43.
"Sotto Voce. " Poem (39) Jl 80, p. 41.

COHEN, Marc
"Sheep to Shears. " PartR (47:1) 80, p. 120.

COHEN, Rhea L.
"Spring Night. " Vis (1) 79.

COKER, David
"Column of Figures. " ChiR (32:1) Sum 80, p. 11.

COLBY, Joan
"December 15th. " PikeF (3) Wint 80, p. 27.
"Festering. " PikeF (3) Wint 80, p. 27.
"Fever in August. " PraS (54:1) Spr 80, p. 75.
"A Heartbreak Is a Simple Fracture. " NewRena (13) Aut 80, p.
    27.
"How the Sky Begins to Fall. " EnPas (11) 80, p. 15.
"In the Country of Absence. " NewRena (13) Aut 80, p. 29.
"Infirmities. " Im (6:2) 80, p. 10.
"The Marriage Dream. " Sam (102) 80, p. 39.
"Mother Ann Lee. " Tendril (7/8) Spr-Sum 80, p. 12.
"Nature Story. " Wind (38) 80, p. 16.
"The North Wife's Pillow. " StoneC (7:2) My 80, p. 5; also (7:3)
    D 80, p. 77.
"Rockhounds. " CreamCR (5:1) Wint 79, p. 16.
"The Sea-Changes. " PortR (26) 80, p. 440.
"Submission to Pain. " PraS (54:1) Spr 80, p. 76.
"Those Explicit Poems. " Sam (101) 80, p. 33.
"Working on Our Masters in Communication. " ColEng (41:7)
    Mr 80, p. 803.

COLBY, Wendelin
"Untitled: My childhood portrait. " PikeF (3) Wint 80, p. 16.
"Untitled: Two years ago. " PikeF (3) Wint 80, p. 16.

COLE, Henri R.
"Gardening in Pollard Park" (for Gladys, Beryl and Dottie).
    WindO (36) Spr-Sum 80, p. 46.

COLE, James
"Leaving a Cocktail Party. " YaleR (69:3) Spr 80, p. 445.

COLE, Michael
"Late: Arcs and Semicircles" (for Maureen). StoneC (7:1) F
    80, p. 36.

COLEBATCH, Hal
"On the Death of Ludwig Erhard. " NewL (46:3) Spr 80, p. 19.
"On the Death of Ludwig Erhard. " NewL (47:1) Aut 80, p. 109.

COLEMAN, Elliott
"After so much comes this, the crown of pauses. " Poetry (136:
    3) Je 80. Inside front cover.

COLEMAN, Wanda
Nine poems. Bachy (16) Wint 80, pp. 62-68.

COLES, Katharine
"She Visits Paradise. " QW (11) Aut-Wint 80-81, p. 90.

COLINAS, Antonio
"Giacomo Casanova acepta cargo de Bibliotecario que le ofrece,
en Bohemia, el Conde de Waldstein. " PortR (26) 80, p. 343.

COLLIER, Michael
"The Angel of Memory. " Agni (13) 80, p. 89.
"A Little Night Story. " NewRep (182:26) 28 Je 80, p. 28.
"The Point of No Return." Ploughs (6:2) 80, p. 98.

COLLINS, Billy
"Indian Head. " KanQ (12:3) Sum 80, p. 63.
"Victorian Gardening and Other Subjects. " KanQ (12:3) Sum 80,
p. 64.

COLLINS, Denise
"Faces in the Glass. " US1 (12/13) Aut-Wint 80, p. 19.
"A Stranger Meets the Body. " US1 (12/13) Aut-Wint 80, p. 19.

COLLINS, Martha
"The Car Is Red. " Field (23) Aut 80, p. 74.
"Fidelity. " Tendril (7/8) Spr-Sum 80, p. 13.
Nine poems. Agni (12) 80, pp. 50-61.
"The Orange Room" (for Mary Anne Heyward Ferguson and Al-
fred Riggs Ferguson). Agni (13) 80, p. 5.
"Several Things. " Poetry (137:3) D 80, p. 135.
"The Story We Know. " Poetry (137:3) D 80, p. 137.
"Thinking of Need. " Field (23) Aut 80, p. 73.
"While You Sleep, Perhaps. " Tendril (7/8) Spr-Sum 80, p. 14.

COLLINSON, Charles
"courting in january. " PikeF (3) Wint 80, p. 27.

COLT, George Howe
"Wanted Posters. " SouthernPR (20:1) Spr 80, p. 74.

COLWELL, Robert
"Time to Go. " BallSUF (21:1) Wint 80, p. 78.

COMBS, Bruce
"Drunk Indian. " Sam (102) 80, p. 35.
"Three A. M. " CropD (2/3) Aut-Wint 80, p. 22.

COMEAU, Phil
"Future of a County" (tr. by H. Paratte). PottPort (2) 80-81,
p. 36.

CONARD, Audrey
"To the Interior. " SoCaR (13:1) Aut 80, p. 17.

CONDEE, Nancy
"The Trout and the Intellectuals. " Agni (12) 80, p. 110.

CONDINI, Nereo E.
"Haggadahs" (for Saul Bellow). Mouth (2:4) My 80, p. 2.

"Narragansetts. " Mouth (2:4) My 80, p. 1.

CONDRY, Dorothea
'In the Heart of Winter. " Sam (92) 80, p. 66.
The Latter Days. Sam (91) 80. Entire issue.
"Masada. " Sam (98) 80, p. 50.

CONGDON, Kirby
"Mr. Woodbridge. " PoNow (26) 80, p. 14.

CONNELLAN, Leo
"Starlite Farm. " NewEngR (3:2) Wint 80, p. 210.
"Visiting Emily Dickinson's Grave. " Harp (261:1566) N 80, p.
70.

CONNELLY, Michele
"Apart. " Prima (5) 79, p. 67.

CONNOLLY, Geraldine
"A Farm Letter from Mother in Winter in Pennsylvania. " PoNow
(26) 80, p. 47.
"Polish Dolls. " GeoR (34:4) Wint 80, p. 868.

CONNOR, Tony
"Aubade. " PoetryNW (21:1) Spr 80, p. 47.
"Bringing in the House-plants. " Poetry (137:2) N 80, p. 84.
"Emptying the Fishtank. " Poetry (137:2) N 80, p. 86.
Twenty-one poems. MalR (56) O 80, pp. 18-47.

CONOVER, Reg
'The Egg Lady. " Wind (37) 80, p. 9.

CONRAD, Bryce
"Bricklayer" (tr. of Jovan Koteski). CharR (6:1) Spr 80, p. 30.
"Clumsy Amusements" (tr. of Vlada Urosevic). StoneC (7:3) D
80, p. 29.
"Fatigue" (tr. of Jovan Koteski). CharR (6:1) Spr 80, p. 30.
"Feast Day. " StoneC (7:3) D 80, p. 25.
"Inner Abyss" (tr. of Vlada Urosevic). StoneC (7:3) D 80, p.
27.
"Lust" (tr. of Jovan Koteski). CharR (6:1) Spr 80, p. 30.
"Melancholy" (tr. of Jovan Koteski). CharR (6:1) Spr 80, p. 31.
"Prisovjani" (tr. of Jovan Koteski). CharR (6:1) Spr 80, p. 32.
"Rising. " StoneC (7:3) D 80, p. 25.
"Sisters" (tr. of Jovan Koteski). CharR (6:1) Spr 80, p. 31.
'Two Roosters: Red and Black" (tr. of Radovan Pavlovski).
CharR (6:2) Aut 80, p. 56.
"Village Poverty" (tr. of Jovan Koteski). CharR (6:1) Spr 80,
p. 31.
'Walk" (tr. of Jovan Koteski). CutB (14) Spr /Sum 80, p. 56.
'The Youth Who Sleeps at Noon" (tr. of Radovan Pavlovski).
CharR (6:2) Aut 80, p. 57.

CONTOSKI, Victor
"The Enemy. " PoNow (27) 80, p. 22.
"Entering Kansas. " PoNow (26) 80, p. 19.
"Grief. " PoNow (27) 80, p. 22.
"Return. " PoNow (27) 80, p. 22.
"Teddy Bear. " PoNow (27) 80, p. 22.

CONTRAIRE, A. U.
Eleven Haiku. WindO (37) Aut-Wint 80. On calendar.

COOK, Donald
"When the Blessed Are Wed to Silence. " EnPas (11) 80, p. 18.

COOK, Gregory
"An Altar to Loneliness. " PottPort (1) 79-80, p. 14.
"Gellius' Mother and Son. " Ark (14) 80, p. 173.
"Love Moving Through Backfields. " PottPort (1) 79-80, p. 33.
"Shell-Shocked from the Oldest, Most Forgotten War. " PottPort
    (1) 79-80, p. 19.

COOK, Paul H.
"The Dancers. " PoNow (29) 80, p. 7.
"Divertemento on a Western Theme. " CharR (6:2) Aut 80, p.
    21.

COOK, R. L.
"Tonight the City. " ArizQ (36:1) Spr 80, p. 48.

COOKE, Judy
"He to Her. " PortR (26) 80, p. 108.

COOKE, Robert P.
"The Metal Eater. " SoCaR (13:1) Aut 80, p. 76.

COOLEY, Peter
"Autumn Equinox. " PraS (54:4) Wint 80-81, p. 10.
"Flight Patterns. " SouthernPR (20:1) Spr 80, p. 45.
"Fog. " Northeast (3:8) Wint 80, p. 46.
"Getting Soused With God. " Northeast (3:8) Wint 80, p. 45.
"In Witness. " KanQ (12:4) Aut 80, p. 34.
"The Response. " QW (10) Wint-Spr 80, p. 89.
"Song. " PoNow (26) 80, p. 35.

COOPER, Allan
"The Beginning of Fall. " MalR (54) Ap 80, p. 94.
"The Stillness of a Room. " MalR (54) Ap 80, p. 96.
"The Wing" (for Harley Lawrence). MalR (54) Ap 80, p. 92.

COOPER, Dennis
"Dead Dog. " PoNow (28) 80, p. 22.
"My Type" (for Mike Robarts). PoNow (28) 80, p. 22.
"The School Wimp. " PoNow (26) 80, p. 42.
"The School Wimp. " PoNow (28) 80, p. 22.

COOPER, Jane
"House Poem. " ParisR (77) Wint-Spr 80, p. 46.

COOPER, Jane Todd
"Such Earth. " Wind (38) 80, p. 18.

CORBETT, William
"Marie's irises. " Aspect (76) S-D 79-80, p. 9.
"May Songs. " Aspect (76) S-D 79-80, p. 10.
"Poem: Blood on the cover. " Aspect (76) S-D 79-80, p. 14.

CORDING, Robert
"Fabre Adds a Few Pages on Spiders to the Wonders of Instinct. "
     CarolQ (32:1) Wint 80, p. 77.
"Fabre's Last Vision. " CarolQ (32:3) Aut 80, p. 22.
"The View from the Laundromat. " SouthernPR (20:2) Aut 80, p.
     69.

CORDRESCU, Doug
"Slot-O-Topia. " Tele (16) 80, p. 27.

COREY, Stephen
"The Lovers Visit the Museum. " SouthernPR (20:1) Spr 80, p. 7.
"Tracking Deer With My Daughters. " SouthernPR (20:1) Spr 80,
     p. 8.

CORKERY, Christopher Jane
"La Señora Fernández née Slater, the Editor's Wife, Is Gone. "
     NewEngR (3:2) Wint 80, p. 207.

CORMAN, Cid
"Sooner or Later. " Ark (14) 80, p. 174.

CORN, Alfred
"The Beholder. " NewRep (182:25) 21 Je 80, p. 26.
"A Bid. " Salm (47/48) Wint-Spr 80, p. 48.
"Debates. " Salm (47/48) Wint-Spr 80, p. 49.
"Interior. " ParisR (77) Wint-Spr 80, p. 47.
"Maine Real Estate. " NewYRB (27:5) 3 Ap 80, p. 30.
"One to One. " ParisR (77) Wint-Spr 80, p. 48.
"The Outdoor Amphitheater. " Hudson (33:2) Sum 80, pp. 201-209.
"The Progress of Peace. " YaleR (69:4) Sum 80, p. 557.
"Prophet Bird. " Agni (13) 80, p. 110.
"September Inscription. " Salm (47/48) Wint-Spr 80, p. 50.

CORN, Ellen
"Homeland. " WindO (36) Spr-Sum 80, p. 27.

CORR, Michael
"On Enjoying a Dacha off Empire Way. " Focus (14:86) Ap 80,
     p. 25.
"Redbud Bower. " Focus (14:86) Ap 80, p. 25.

CORRINGTON, John William
"The Anchorite. " CimR (50) Ja 80, p. 64.
"The Baptist. " CimR (50) Ja 80, p. 52.
"Francisco Goya Will Now Point Out the Moral of Painting
    Nudes. " CimR (51) Ap 80, p. 56.
"K. 627. " SouthernR (16:1) Wint 80, p. 153.
"The Rainmaker. " CimR (51) Ap 80, p. 24.

COSCA, Laurie
"Darker. " CutB (15) Aut /Wint 80, p. 55.

COSGROVE, Shelagh
"Hamlet. " KanQ (12:4) Aut 80, p. 98.
"Selection. " KanQ (12:4) Aut 80, p. 97.

COSTANZO, Gerald
"Braille. " MissouriR (3:3) Sum 80, p. 28.
"Halloween in Rhode Island. " PoNow (27) 80, p. 13.
"Stargazers" (In memory of Frank Stanford). MissouriR (3:3)
    Sum 80, p. 29.

COSTELLO, James
"Waiting for Deer. " EnPas (11) 80, p. 30.

COSTLEY, Bill
"Celebrating the Vernal Equinox with Carolin Combs in Berlin
    MA 01705 03/21/79 midday. " SmPd (49) Spr 80, p. 3.

COTTERILL, Sarah
"On the Accidental Death of a Man, Cutting Redbud. " WebR
    (5:1) Wint 80, p. 14.

COUCH, Larry
"The Cathedral. " Vis (4) 80.
"The Decision. " Vis (4) 80.
"The Lecture. " Vis (4) 80.

COUCHOT, Lise
"Zaca Lake. " Ark (14) 80, p. 175.

COUNCILMAN, Emily Sargent
"The Growing Edge. " ArizQ (36:2) Sum 80, p. 100.
"Of One. " ArizQ (36:3) Aut 80, p. 216.
"Road Revisited. " ChrC (97:16) 30 Ap 80, p. 495.
"Waking into Dream. " ChrC (97:33) 22 O 80, p. 1008.
"When I Cry. " ChrC (97:9) 12 Mr 80, p. 287.

COUR, Paul la
"The Water Under the Grass" (tr. by Paul Thorfinn Hopper).
    Vis (3) 80.

COURSEN, H. R.
"October Saturday: 1949. " PoNow (28) 80, p. 32.

COURT, Wesli
"The Rider. " HiramPoR (28) Spr-Sum 80, p. 10.

COUTO, Nancy Lee
"Elegy. " AmerPoR (9:1) Ja-F 80, p. 19.
"I Forgot to Eat My Bread. " PoetryNW (21:3) Aut 80, p. 31.
"Walking on the Water. " Hudson (33:2) Sum 80, p. 231.
"Wetbacks. " PraS (54:1) Spr 80, p. 43.

COVIAN, Marcelo
"Al pie de la ventana. " PortR (26) 80, p. 13.

COVINGTON, Kelly
"Future, Dressed for Evening. " MissouriR (3:3) Sum 80, p. 36.

COWAN, Thomas Dale
"Current River. " Focus (14:86) Ap 80, p. 34.

COX, C. B.
"The Conrads in Brittany. " SewanR (88:2) Spr 80, p. 176.

COX, Carol
"Arrangements. " HangL (38) Aut 80, p. 16.
"Driving Back from New Orleans. " HangL (38) Aut 80, p. 17.
"Set on Course. " HangL (38) Aut 80, p. 15.

COX, Elizabeth
"When the Noise of the Mill Is Low" (for Sasquatch). SouthernPR
   (20:2) Aut 80, p. 51.

COX, Joel
"Falling in Spring. " KanQ (12:1) Wint 80, p. 120.
"Green Hay. " CharR (6:2) Aut 80, p. 19.

CRAMER, Scott
"Relics. " Sam (102) 80, p. 51.

CRAMER, Steven
"Aix-En-Provence: April, 1975. " Ploughs (6:2) 80, p. 64.
"Letter from Boston to Ira Sadoff. " Ploughs (6:2) 80, p. 62.
Ten poems. Agni (13) 80, pp. 60-71.
"Water Rats. " MissouriR (3:3) Sum 80, p. 17.

CRANE, Hart
"Distinctly praise the years, whose volatile. " HolCrit (17:1) F
   80. Front cover.

CRASE, Douglas
"To the Light Fantastic. " YaleR (70:2) Wint 81, p. 261.

CRAWFORD, Tom
"Gray Lodge. " Columbia (5) Aut-Wint 80, p. 58.

CREWS, Judson
  "Blinded. " Wind (36) 80, p. 9.
  "Conrad, I shouted. " PoNow (26) 80, p. 22.
  Eight poems. WormR (80) 80, p. 126.
  "I am. " PoNow (26) 80, p. 22.
  "I Defy You. " PoNow (27) 80, p. 30.
  "If I Was Rigged. " Wind (36) 80, p. 9.
  "Light Years. " CropD (2/3) Aut-Wint 80, p. 35.
  "Objects. " PoNow (26) 80, p. 22.
  "Red-mouthed. " PoNow (26) 80, p. 22.
  "The tip. " PoNow (26) 80, p. 22.

CRICHTON, Jennifer
  "The Genius Defines Himself Through Action. " Tele (16) 80, p.
    55.
  "In the Country. " Tele (16) 80, p. 55.

CRNJANSKI, Milos
  "Life. " PortR (26) 80, p. 480.

CROFT, Greg
  "China Eyes. " PottPort (2) 80, p. 18.

CROSSMAN, Malinda
  "It was an ironingboard summer. " Prima (5) 79, p. 7.
  "Prey. " Prima (5) 79, p. 58.

CROSSON, Robert
  "Answers: The Antiphonal. " Bachy (17) Spr 80, p. 83.

CROSTON, Julie
  "Two Red Looms" (to D. & S.). HangL (38) Aut 80, p. 64.

CROW, Mary
  "The Body That Emits Light and Heat Loses Weight" (tr. of
    Enrique Gomez-Correa). WebR (5:1) Wint 80, p. 37.
  "A Change of Place. " KanQ (12:1) Wint 80, p. 152.
  "Wet Grapes... " (tr. of Circe Maia w. Patsy Boyer). CutB
    (14) Spr /Sum 80, p. 101.
  "A Wind Will Come from the South" (tr. of Circe Maia w. Patsy
    Boyer). CutB (14) Spr /Sum 80, p. 103.

CROWELL, Doug
  "Moonshine and Madness. " GRR (11:1) 80, p. 38.

CSOORI, Sandor
  "Waiting" (tr. by Steven Polgar). AmerPoR (9:4) Jl-Aug 80, p.
    42.

CULLEN, John C.
  "The Attic. " Wind (38) 80, p. 47.
  "The Farmers. " Bits (11) 80.

CULLEN, Paula B.
"Cousins. " KanQ (12:1) Wint 80, p. 78.

CULLUM, J. W.
"Roses, Revisited, in a Paradoxical Autumn. " Poetry (136:2)
My 80, p. 93.

CUMMINGS, Melissa
"birches. " Os (10) Spr 80, p. 22.
"tree. " Os (10) Spr 80, p. 22.

CUMMINS, James
"The Case of the Cincinnati Syndrome. " PartR (47:4) 80, p.
604.
from The Perry Mason Sestinas: "Hamilton Burger cleared his
throat. 'You see, style. '" Shen (31:2) 80, p. 102.

CUNNINGHAM, Carl
"Ode to My Father's Hat" (for Shirley Kaufman). DacTerr (17)
80, p. 16.

CUNNINGHAM, J. V.
"Some Good, Some Middling, and Some Bad. " NewRep (182:6)
9 F 80, p. 36.

CUNNINGHAM, Patricia
"Servant of Spring. " PikeF (3) Wint 80, p. 10.

CURLEY, Daniel
"Your Special Chair. " NewL (47:1) Aut 80, p. 105.

CURRY, Peggy Simson
"Growing Old. " SoDakR (18:1) Spr 80, p. 28.
"The Hunt. " SoDakR (18:1) Spr 80, p. 26.

CURTIS, Mary
from Thistledown: "The Windfall Peach. " UTR (6:3/4) 80, p.
20.

CURTIS, Tony
"Strongman. " SoDakR (18:3) Aut 80, p. 28.

CUTLER, Abbot
"The Angel in the Snowdrift. " Pan (21) 80, p. 40.

CUTLER, Bruce
The doctrine of selective depravity. Northeast (3:9[SI]) 80.
Entire issue.

CZARDA, Elaine
"Coloring. " CropD (1) Spr 80, p. 12.
"The Shack. " CropD (1) Spr 80, p. 12.

DABNEY, Janice
  "Passage" (for L.).   Wind (36) 80, p. 11.
  "Tow Path. " CentR (24:2) Spr 80, p. 189.

DACEY, Florence
  "Flirtation With Ice. " DacTerr (17) 80, p. 19.
  "For Emmett, Who Imagines We Are Robbers Disguised as His
    Parents. " PoNow (29) 80, p. 20.
  "The Good News. " PoNow (29) 80, p. 20.
  "Salamander. " PoNow (29) 80, p. 20.

DACEY, Philip
  "Ass-Thetics. " CreamCR (5:1) Wint 79, p. 104.
  "The Condom. " PoNow (26) 80, p. 22.
  "The Condom Salesman Tries Them on Like Shoes. " BelPoJ
    (31:2) Wint 80-81, p. 21.
  "The Condom's Nightmare. " PoNow (26) 80, p. 22.
  "Emmett. " DacTerr (17) 80, p. 17.
  "First Snow. " QW (11) Aut-Wint 80-81, p. 18.
  "For One Who Received a Chainsaw as a Wedding Gift. " BelPoJ
    (31:2) Wint 80-81, p. 20.
  "For the Poet's Father, on His Taking Up Gardening Late in
    Life. " DacTerr (17) 80, p. 18.
  "Form Rejection Letter. " Tendril (9) 80, p. 45.
  "In Her Ear. " SouthernPR (20:2) Aut 80, p. 15.
  "Jill, Afterwards. " PoetryNW (21:3) Aut 80, p. 4.
  "Remembering Adam and Eve" (for Phil and Stephanie).
    PoetryNW (21:3) Aut 80, p. 6.
  "The Runner. " Hudson (33:2) Sum 80, p. 230.
  "The Scar. " Tele (16) 80, p. 95.
  "The Typewriter. " PoNow (26) 80, p. 14.
  "Zooprophylactico. " PoNow (26) 80, p. 22.

DADIE, Bernard B.
  "Aux Poètes. " PortR (26) 80, p. 221.

DAHL, David
  "on the death of max ernst. " Kayak (55) Ja 81, p. 61.
  "serial portrait" (for Nanas Valaoritis). Kayak (55) Ja 81, p.
    62.

DAIGON, Ruth
  "Like an Ideal Tenant. " SouthernPR (20:2) Aut 80, p. 22.

DAIVE, Jean
  "Fut Bati. " Bound (8:3) Spr 80, pp. 152-160.

DAL, Gunnar
  "Falling of leaves" (tr. by Alan Boucher). Vis (4) 80.

DALLMAN, Elaine
  "Mr. Koalch. " Pig (7) My 80, p. 64.
  "No Wings T Get T a Somewheres Tree. " Pig (7) My 80, p. 65.

DALTON, Phillip
"Easter Lilies. " Poem (40) N 80, p. 10.
"Inside Windowpanes. " Poem (40) N 80, p. 11.
"Rose in March. " Poem (40) N 80, p. 12.

DALY, Christopher
"The Beautiful and the Damned. " WormR (78) 80, p. 51.
"Keep the Fred Astair Far Hence. " WormR (78) 80, p. 51.
"King Gustav and the Dynamite Boys. " Sam (98) 80, p. 60.

DALY, Daniel
"Fishing Report. " PoetC (12:3) 80, p. 22.

DALY, Mary Ann
"In an Artist's Backyard. " CarolQ (32:2) Spr-Sum 80, p. 90.

D'AMBROSIO, Vinnie-Marie
"I Will Sleep" (tr. of Alfonsina Storni). CutB (14) Spr /Sum 80,
p. 99.

DAME, Enid
"Community in P-town. " Tele (16) 80, p. 89.

DANA, Robert
"All This Way" (for Edward Levine). NewL (47:1) Aut 80, p.
66.
"Bread" (for E. L. Mayo). NewL (47:1) Aut 80, p. 62.
"The California Variations" (for Kenneth Rexroth). Ark (14) 80,
p. 178.
"Changes. " PoNow (27) 80, p. 8.
"Dream of Henri. " NewL (47:1) Aut 80, p. 64.
"Low Ceiling. " NewL (47:1) Aut 80, p. 68.
"Transferences. " NewL (47:1) Aut 80, p. 65.
"Winter Frieze: D.C. " CharR (6:2) Aut 80, p. 15.

DANE, Joseph A.
"Railroad Ties. " SoDakR (18:3) Aut 80, p. 23.

DANIEL, Arnaut
"Sirventes. " Bound (8:3) Spr 80, p. 147.

DANIELS, Jim
"Digger Arrives Home from Work. " HiramPoR (28) Spr-Sum
80, p. 13.
"Digger Drives to Work. " HiramPoR (28) Spr-Sum 80, p. 11.
"Going Up and Down. " ParisR (77) Wint-Spr 80, p. 111.
"Killing Boxes. " MinnR (NS 15) Aut 80, p. 7.
"Punk. " Wind (36) 80, p. 27.

DANIELS, M. Cortney
"From a Picture of Theodore Roethke. " CarolQ (32:1) Wint 80,
p. 88.
"What We Do from This Porch. " CarolQ (32:1) Wint 80, p. 86.

DANKLEEF, Richard
 "The Dealer. " PraS (54:4) Wint 80-81, p. 66.
 "Flute Song. " AmerS (49:4) Aut 80, p. 528.
 "The Trail. " AmerS (49:1) Wint 79-80, p. 102.

DANON, Samuel
 from Inclus: Twenty-three poems (tr. of Eugene Guillevic).
   MalR (54) Ap 80, pp. 50-60.

DARLING, Jean S.
 from Words to Johanna in the morning: "When you wake up
   you don't know with certainty" (tr. of Margareta Ekström).
   PortR (26) 80, p. 371.

DARLINGTON, Andrew
 "All Night I Dream of Scorpions. " Vis (4) 80.
 "Eight Thirty P. M. " Vis (4) 80.
 "Last Stanza's from Leeds. " Vis (2) 80.
 "Wintercourse. " Vis (2) 80.

DARWISH, Mahmud
 "And He Returned in a Shroud" (tr. by Ben Bennani). Bound
   (8:3) Spr 80, p. 200.
 "A Letter from Exile" (tr. by Ben Bennani). Bound (8:3) Spr
   80, p. 203.

DAS, Jibanananda
 "Banalata Sen (banalatā sena)" (tr. by Clinton Seely. LitR (23:3)
   Spr 80, p. 369.
 "Beggar (bhikhirī)" (tr. by Clinton Seely). LitR (23:3) Spr 80,
   p. 374.
 "Blue Skies (nīlimā)" (tr. by Clinton Seely). LitR (23:3) Spr 80,
   p. 375.
 "In Camp (kyāmpe)" (tr. by Clinton Seely). LitR (23:3) Spr 80,
   p. 370.
 "In Fields Fertile and Fallow (khete prāntare)" (tr. by Clinton
   Seely). LitR (23:3) Spr 80, p. 376.
 "Naked Lonely Hand (nagna nirjana hāta)" (tr. by Clinton Seely).
   LitR (23:3) Spr 80, p. 373.

DAUNT, Jon
 "Ambush. " Sam (102) 80, p. 23.
 "Coyote Meets Bulldozer. " Shen (31:2) 80, p. 105.
 "Going Blind. " NewRena (12) Spr 80, p. 22.
 "Job's Children. " SoDakR (18:3) Aut 80, p. 18.
 "Los Alamos. " NewRena (12) Spr 80, p. 21.
 "Prometheus in Manhattan. " CapeR (15:2) Sum 80, p. 14.
 "Tornado Country. " CapeR (15:2) Sum 80, p. 11.
 "Visiting a Friend. " SoDakR (18:3) Aut 80, p. 19.
 "Volunteer Army. " Sam (98) 80, p. 27.
 "The Western Dust Bowl, Where Highways Go Mad Before They
   Reach the Panhandle. " CapeR (15:2) Sum 80, p. 12.

DAVID, Almitra
"George: Some Observations. " HangL (37) Spr 80, p. 8.

DAVIDSON, David M.
"Letter to My Father. " DacTerr (17) 80, p. 20.

DAVIDSON, Tommie
"Hope. " Wind (37) 80, p. 10.

DAVIE, Donald
"The Bent. " AmerS (49:4) Aut 80, p. 466.
"Devil on Ice. " SewanR (88:2) Spr 80, p. 177.
"Well-Found Poem. " AmerS (49:2) Spr 80, p. 180.

DAVIS, Dick
"The City of Orange Trees. " SouthernR (16:2) Spr 80, p. 446.
"Desert Stop at Noon. " SouthernR (16:2) Spr 80, p. 448.
"Marriage, as a Problem of Universals. " SouthernR (16:2) Spr
    80, p. 445.
"Memories of Cochin: An Epithalamium. " SouthernR (16:2) Spr
    80, p. 444.
"Night on the Long-Distance Coach. " SouthernR (16:2) Spr 80,
    p. 449.
"Syncretic and Sectarian. " SouthernR (16:2) Spr 80, p. 447.

DAVIS, Helene
"Farmers. " Ploughs (6:2) 80, p. 122.
"The Slide. " Ploughs (6:2) 80, p. 121.

DAVIS, Lloyd
"Armstrong Spring Creek. " KanQ (12:2) Spr 80, p. 40.
"Driving West: Diamond Ring, Montana. " KanQ (12:2) Spr 80,
    p. 40.
"Mingo Cemetery. " PoNow (28) 80, p. 43.
"Sewell in June. " PoNow (28) 80, p. 43.
"W. Va. Roadside Park: Mingo. " PoNow (27) 80, p. 19.

DAVIS, Pam
"Encounter. " Poem (39) Jl 80, p. 12.

DAVIS, Paul
"Afternoon at Cannes. " KanQ (12:1) Wint 80, p. 122.

DAVIS, William Virgil
"Absolution. " Im (6:2) 80, p. 10.
"The Blood. " CropD (2/3) Aut-Wint 80, p. 41.
"The Confidence. " PoNow (27) 80, p. 39.
"The Country of Such Caves. " DenQ (15:3) Aut 80, p. 107.
"Cultivation of Pain. " PoNow (28) 80, p. 22.
"The Ends of the Garden. " CalQ (16/17) 80, p. 155.
"An Evening at Home. " Outbr (4/5) Aut 79-Spr 80, p. 96.
"The Gift" (for my son). Wind (37) 80, p. 11.
"Going Places. " Outbr (4/5) Aut 79-Spr 80, p. 97.

"The Gymnasts. " Poem (38) Mr 80, p. 37.
"A Late Elegy for John Berryman. " SewanR (88:1) Wint 80, p.
    19.
"The Obstruction. " Poem (38) Mr 80, p. 35.
"One October Morning. " Poem (38) Mr 80, p. 38.
"One October Morning. " Poem (39) Jl 80, p. 61.
"Small Town on a Winter Night. " Poem (38) Mr 80, p. 40.
"Snow Dream. " DenQ (15:3) Aut 80, p. 106.
"The Time of Year, the Hour. " PoNow (28) 80, p. 22.
"The Weight Lifter. " PoNow (28) 80, p. 22.
"A Winter Without It. " Wind (37) 80, p. 11.

DAVISON, Peter
    "The Sound of Wings. " Atl (245:5) My 80, p. 50.
    "Wordless Winter. " Hudson (33:4) Wint 80, p. 551.

DAWE, Bruce
    "To Be a Poet in Australia. " NewL (46:3) Spr 80, p. 7.

DAWE, Gerald
    "Distances" (for Kevin and Iarla). GRR (11:2/3) 80, p. 96.
    "Ghosts. " GRR (11:2/3) 80, p. 97.

DAWE, Tom
    "A Consecration. " PottPort (2) 80-81, p. 39.

DAY, Jean Trelease
    "Acquisition of the Facts. " SunM (9/10) Sum 80, p. 32.
    "Casual. " Tele (16) 80, p. 71.
    "The Consequences. " Tele (16) 80, p. 71.

DAY, Lucille
    "Fifteen. " Hudson (33:2) Sum 80, p. 246.
    "Reject Jello. " Hudson (33:2) Sum 80, p. 245.

DAYTON, David
    "At the Laundromat. " PoNow (29) 80, p. 20.
    "Postcard from the Heartland. " PoNow (29) 80, p. 20.
    "The Woman Driving the Country Squire. " SouthernPR (20:1)
        Spr 80, p. 37.

DEAGON, Ann
    "Coming Round. " SouthernPR (20:2) Aut 80, p. 49.
    "Enclosures. " SoCaR (12:2) Spr 80, p. 44.
    "Ladies of the Rapid Eye. " OhioR (24) 80, p. 24.
    "Sing, Coroner. " OhioR (24) 80, p. 25.

DEAL, Susan Strayer
    "Doped With the Dust. " HiramPoR (27) Aut-Wint 80, p. 13.
    "The Shape of Herself. " PraS (54:2) Sum 80, p. 75.
    "Solving the Branches. " EnPas (11) 80, p. 29.
    "Sometimes So Easy. " PraS (54:2) Sum 80, p. 76.

DEAN, John
"The Last Days of Edmund Spenser. " PikeF (3) Wint 80, p. 11.
"The Subterraneans. " PikeF (3) Wint 80, p. 27.

De ANDRADE, Carlos Drummond
"An Ox Looks at Man" (tr. by Mark Strand).   NewYorker (56:30)
    15 S 80, p. 50.

De ANDRADE, Eugenio
"Portrait of a Woman" (tr. by Alexis Levitin).   PoNow (28) 80,
    p. 44.
"Requiem para Pier Paolo Pasolini. " PortR (26) 80, p. 310.

DEANE, John F.
"Island Woman. " PortR (26) 80, p. 191.

DEANE, Seamus
"Adagio. " Ploughs (6:1) 80, p. 32.
"Directions. " Ploughs (6:1) 80, p. 34.
"Exile's Return. " Ploughs (6:1) 80, p. 36.
"Osip Mandlestam. " Ploughs (6:1) 80, p. 30.

De ANGELIS, Milo
"Noon Glare" (tr. by Lawrence Venuti).   ChiR (32:1) Sum 80, p.
    106.

De BALKER, Habakuk II
"Hoe een wijnkelder te beginnen. " PortR (26) 80, p. 268.

De BEVOISE, Arlene
"Good Friday. " ChrC (97:12) 2 Ap 80, p. 370.

De BHAL, Liam
"Beyond Youghal. " Stand (21:3) 80, p. 27.

DeBOLT, William Walter
"Compensation. " ChrC (97:4) 30 Ja 80, p. 99.
"Friends. " BallSUF (21:1) Wint 80, p. 69.
"Funeral. " ChrC (97:33) 22 O 80, p. 1007.
"How Sects Began. " ChrC (97:35) 5 N 80, p. 1052.
"Lions and Politicians. " ChrC (97:31) 8 O 80, p. 938.
"Revised Version. " ChrC (97:3) 23 Ja 80, p. 71.

De BRITO, Casimiro
"A paz. " PortR (26) 80, p. 308.

De CORMIER-SHEKERJIAN, Regina
"Hunter. " Wind (38) 80, p. 20.
"Navigation. " WebR (5:2) Aut 80, p. 50.
"A Woman I Know. " Pig (7) My 80, p. 85.

DeFINA, Allan
"David's Poem. " Mouth (2:4) My 80, p. 24.

"Kiss. " Mouth (2:5) O 80, p. 21.
"Lost Face. " Mouth (2:4) My 80, p. 14.
"Love Poem. " Mouth (2:4) My 80, p. 8.

DEFOE, Mark
    "Early Love and Jury Duty. " QW (11) Aut-Wint 80-81, p. 96.
    "Enid, Oklahoma. " QW (11) Aut-Wint 80-81, p. 97.
    "The Estranged Husband Visits His Son at Recess. " LitR (23:3)
        Spr 80, p. 399.
    "Near Milepost 293. " LitR (23:3) Spr 80, p. 400.
    "New Room. " LitR (23:3) Spr 80, p. 399.

DeFREES, Madeline
    "First-Class Relics: Letter to Dennis Finnell. " Tendril (9) 80,
        p. 47.
    "Imaginary Ancestors: Ernst Barlach. " ConcPo (13:2) Aut 80,
        p. 6.
    "The Register. " Iowa (10:4) Aut 79, p. 34.
    "Settling into the A-Frame. " Iowa (10:4) Aut 79, p. 33.
    "Sifting the Ashes. " PortR (26) 80, p. 434.
    "Where the horse takes wing. " NewL (46:4) Sum 80, p. 46.

DEGENFISZ, Halina
    "Here I Am!" Wind (38) 80, p. 22.

De GRAVELLES, Charles
    "Leaving. " ConcPo (13:1) Spr 80, p. 60.

DeGRAZIA, Emilio
    "A Prayer for My Father's Flight. " DacTerr (17) 80, p. 21.

DELANEY, John
    "E. " OntR (12) Spr-Sum 80, p. 78.
    "Spider Plant. " OntR (12) Spr-Sum 80, p. 80.
    "The Syllogistic Trick. " LitR (23:3) Spr 80, p. 379.

DEL GRECO, Robert
    "Uncle Harold Likes to Draw Hands. " KanQ (12:4) Aut 80, p.
        110.

Del VECCHIO, Gloria
    "The Devil. " CapeR (15:2) Sum 80, p. 37.
    "Old Forms. " StoneC (7:1) F 80, p. 25.

De MARIS, Ron
    "House on a Hill. " SouthernPR (20:1) Spr 80, p. 51.
    "Spring Rain. " EnPas (10) 80, p. 16.
    "The Way the Sun Works Loose. " KanQ (12:1) Wint 80, p. 28.

DEMETRE, Sheila
    "Brushing the Mare. " PoetryNW (21:4) Wint 80-81, p. 36.

DEMON, Andrew
    "Son of the Gods, B-52. " BallSUF (21:3) Sum 80, p. 2.

DEMPSTER, Barry
"Angel Song. " BallSUF (21:1) Wint 80, p. 63.

Den BOER, David C.
"After the Rain in October. " KanQ (12:1) Wint 80, p. 28.
"Breaking into Song. " KanQ (12:1) Wint 80, p. 29.
"John Berryman. " KanQ (12:1) Wint 80, p. 30.

DENEEN, Cathy
"Healing. " PoNow (29) 80, p. 7.

DENISON, John
"Friday Night. " KanQ (12:4) Aut 80, p. 132.

DENNIS, Carl
"The Black Night. " Salm (50/51) Aut 80-Wint 81, p. 39.
"The Chosen. " AmerPoR (9:5) S-O 80, p. 11.
"Columbus Day. " NewEngR (3:2) Wint 80, p. 171.
"The Dump. " Salm (50/51) Aut 80-Wint 81, p. 40.
"Flowers on Your Birthday. " NewRep (182:13) 29 Mr 80, p. 39.
"The Gospels. " Salm (50/51) Aut 80-Wint 81, p. 41.
"Sunday Matinee. " NewRep (182:23) 7 Je 80, p. 26.

DENT, Peter
"Afternoon. " Pan (21) 80, p. 14.
"Huddle. " Pan (21) 80, p. 13.

DENT, Tom
"Ten Years After Umbra. " BlackALF (14:3) Aut 80, p. 114.

De OCA, Marco Antonio Montes
"Here Is a Camelia" (tr. by Mary Barnard). DenQ (15:1) Spr
80, p. 93.

DEREMIAH, Paté
"Scale of My Life. " PikeF (3) Wint 80, p. 16.

Der HOVANESSIAN, Diana
"Abortion. " PoNow (29) 80, p. 21.
"His First Wife. " PoNow (29) 80, p. 21.
"Snow in Yerevan. " LitR (23:3) Spr 80, p. 407.
"Teaching You Armenian. " PoNow (29) 80, p. 21.

DERR, Mark B.
"The Hour Before Midnight. " PartR (47:4) 80, p. 612.
"Scrimshaw. " KanQ (12:3) Sum 80, p. 18.

DE RUGERIS, C. K.
"Monday Morning:" SmPd (48) Wint 80, p. 17.

DESSI, Gigi
"Pages" (tr. by Dominick Lepore). DenQ (15:1) Spr 80, p. 88.
"Reward" (tr. by Dominick Lepore). DenQ (15:1) Spr 80, p. 89.

De STEFANO, John
  "Routes: Notes on the Brownian Movement. " ChiR (32:1) Sum
    80, p. 98.

DEUTSCH, Babette
  "The Gift. " Nat (231:1) 5 Jl 80, p. 27.

DE VAUL, Diane
  "For Brooke. " Vis (4) 80.
  "I Dreamed. " Vis (4) 80.
  "Snowdrop Wind Flower or It All Started in an Adult Education
    Course in Life Drawing. " Vis (3) 80.

De VRIES, Rachel
  "I Call Them Sparrows. " Cond (6) 80, p. 170.

DEWEY, Arthur J.
  "Child Star. " ChrC (97:42) 24 D 80, p. 1265.

DeWITT, Bob
  "Souls. " UTR (6:3/4) 80, p. 21.

De YOUNG, Robert
  "Distances. " ColEng (42:1) S 80, p. 62.

DICKERSON, Mary Jane
  "My Inheritance. " Harp (260:1560) My 80, p. 73.

DICKEY, James
  "Christmas Shopping, 1947. " PikeF (3) Wint 80, p. 13.
  "King Crab and the Rattler. " PikeF (3) Wint 80, p. 13.
  "Sea Island. " PikeF (3) Wint 80, p. 13.
  "The Surround. " Atl (246:1) Jl 80, p. 58.
  "Whittern and the Kite. " PikeF (3) Wint 80, p. 13.

DICKEY, Paul
  "Potted Plant. " KanQ (12:1) Wint 80, p. 93.

DICKEY, William
  "Bare Feet in the Wrong Household. " PoNow (28) 80, p. 41.
  "Being Asked to Define Bourgeois Individuality. " PortR (26) 80,
    p. 431.
  "Cherubim. " CarolQ (32:2) Spr-Sum 80, p. 18.
  "Confidence. " PoNow (26) 80, p. 11.
  "For My Fiftieth Birthday. " PortR (26) 80, p. 430.
  "Horn, Mouth, Pit, Fire. " MassR (21:3) Aut 80, p. 460.
  "Opera. " CarolQ (32:2) Spr-Sum 80, p. 19.
  "The Problem of Pain. " MassR (21:3) Aut 80, p. 461.
  "The Pruned Roses. " NewYorker (55:53) 18 F 80, p. 36.

DICKINSON, Emily
  "He was weak, and I was strong--then--. " Playb (27:3) Mr 80,
    p. 165.

DICKSON, John
"Art Gallery. " AmerS (49:3) Sum 80, p. 308.
"The Contract. " SouthernPR (20:1) Spr 80, p. 62.
"The Family. " Im (7:1) 80, p. 10.
"Silent Night. " StoneC (7:1) F 80, p. 10.

DIERCKS, Lisa C.
"The Telegram. " PoNow (28) 80, p. 11.

Di GIOVANNI, Norman Thomas
"The Angel" (tr. of Jorge Luis Borges). Atl (246:1) Jl 80, p.
    64.
"A History of Night" (tr. of Jorge Luis Borges). Atl (246:1) Jl
    80, p. 64.
"The Moon" (to Maria Kodzma) (tr. of Jorge Luis Borges). Atl
    (246:1) Jl 80, p. 64.

DILSAVER, Paul
"Veteran Cultivates Irony. " Ascent (5:3) 80, p. 22.

DILWORTH, Zelda
"To My Unknown Assailant, Who Waits. " Poem (40) N 80, p.
    58.
"12th Anniversary. " Poem (40) N 80, p. 59.

DIMAN, Roderic
"Bogotá" (tr. of Jorge Bravo Muñoz). PortR (26) 80, p. 57.

Di MICHELE, Mary
"As in the Beginning. " MalR (54) Ap 80, p. 97.
"Happiness Takes a Walk on Bloor Street West. " ConcPo (12:2)
    Aut 79, p. 14.

DiPALMA, Ray
"Ode. " SunM (9/10) Sum 80, p. 39.

DiPASQUALE, E.
"Advice. " Poem (38) Mr 80, p. 3.
"Five Mile Run Through Roosevelt Park in a December Wind-
    storm. " Poem (38) Mr 80, p. 4.
"Gifts. " Poem (38) Mr 80, p. 6.
"June Rainstorms. " PoNow (26) 80, p. 30.
"A Longing. " Poem (38) Mr 80, p. 5.

DiPIERO, W. S.
"The Complete King. " NewOR (7:1) 80, p. 19.
"The day I gave over to the earth" (tr. of Sandro Penna).
    PoNow (26) 80, p. 44.
"False Spring" (tr. of Sandro Penna). PoNow (27) 80, p. 46.
"The Father's Tomb" (tr. of Sandro Penna). PoNow (27) 80,
    p. 46.
"Four Brothers. " NewYorker (56:8) 14 Ap 80, p. 46.
"I Know Now Not to Complain" (tr. of Leonardo Sinisgalli).

NewOR (7:2) 80, p. 121.
"In the city he looked almost" (tr. of Sandro Penna). PoNow
(26) 80, p. 44.
"On Christmas eve the river children torch. " CarolQ (32:2)
Spr-Sum 80, p. 22.
"Partisans. " CarolQ (32:1) Wint 80, p. 30.
"School" (tr. of Sandro Penna). PoNow (27) 80, p. 46.
"September moon on the dark valley" (tr. of Sandro Penna).
PoNow (26) 80, p. 44.
"Tell me, you great dreaming trees" (tr. of Sandro Penna).
PoNow (26) 80, p. 44.
"Woman in a Streetcar" (tr. of Sandro Penna). PoNow (27) 80,
p. 46.

Di SANTO, Grace
"In Defense of Plath, Berryman, Sexton. " SouthernPR (20:2)
Aut 80, p. 37.

DISCH, Donna
"Animal Epitaphs. " Aspen (9) Spr 80, p. 81.
"A Hand Out. " Aspen (9) Spr 80, p. 80.
"Purple Riddle. " Aspen (9) Spr 80, p. 80.

DISCH, Tom
"Aubade. " LittleM (12:3/4) 80, p. 28.
"The Fugitive" (for Judith Clute). ParisR (78) Sum 80, p. 126.
"Riddle. " LittleM (12:3/4) 80, p. 26.
"What to Accept. " PraS (54:4) Wint 80-81, p. 12.

DISCHELL, Stuart
"Celestial Ode. " Agni (12) 80, p. 109.
"Walking. " Ploughs (6:2) 80, p. 75.

DITSKY, John
"Act Natural. " SoCaR (13:1) Aut 80, p. 86.
"Chamber Music. " MalR (54) Ap 80, p. 102.
"The Decline of Courtly Love. " LitR (23:4) Sum 80, p. 576.
"In Defense of Profligacy. " ConcPo (13:1) Spr 80, p. 45.
"Incident. " OntR (12) Spr-Sum 80, p. 58.
"1948. " OntR (12) Spr-Sum 80, p. 56.
"Promise. " OntR (12) Spr-Sum 80, p. 57.
"Repairing. " CropD (2/3) Aut-Wint 80, p. 18.

DITTA, Joseph M.
"The Divided Dark. " Wind (36) 80, p. 12.

DIXON, Melvin
"Harlem Footage. " BlackALF (14:4) Wint 80, p. 176.

DJANIKIAN, Gregory
"The Clearing. " CimR (52) Jl 80, p. 45.
"The Evolution of Possibility" (for Tom). CarolQ (32:2) Spr-
Sum 80, p. 80.

"Michelangelo: "'The Creation of Adam. '" HolCrit (17:2) Ap 80, p. 18.
"Winter: Two Lovers in a Bed" (for Lysa). HiramPoR (28) Spr-Sum 80, p. 15.

DOBBERSTEIN, Michael
"The Engine: A Manual. " CimR (51) Ap 80, p. 54.
"Soldiers. " NewL (46:4) Sum 80, p. 68.

DOBBS, Jeannine
"I Dream of My Mother. " Pig (7) My 80, p. 59.

DOBRIN, Arthur
"Old Hempstead Plains. " Vis (3) 80.

DOBSON, Rosemary
"Waiting for the Postman. " NewL (46:3) Spr 80, p. 10.

DOBYNS, Stephen
"Arrested Saturday Night. " Poetry (135:4) Ja 80, p. 215.
"The Delicate, Plummeting Bodies. " NewYorker (55:49) 21 Ja 80, p. 44.
"The Delicate Plummeting Bodies. " Tendril (9) 80, p. 49.
"Discoveries. " Pequod (11) 80, p. 47.
"Footstep. " Pequod (11) 80, p. 46.
"Geese. " MissouriR (3:2) Wint 80, p. 11.
"How Sweet and Proper It Is. " Poetry (135:4) Ja 80, p. 210.
"In Place of a Letter. " Tendril (7/8) Spr-Sum 80, p. 16.
"It's Like This. " Poetry (135:4) Ja 80, p. 216.
"Letter Beginning With the First Line of Your Letter. " Pequod (11) 80, p. 42.
"Moon Song" (for Frances Gillespie). Pequod (11) 80, p. 49.
"Oatmeal Deluxe. " Poetry (135:4) Ja 80, p. 212.
"The Photographs" (for Roswell Angier). Pequod (11) 80, p. 45.
"A Place in Maine. " Poetry (135:4) Ja 80, p. 213.
"Snow. " MissouriR (3:2) Wint 80, p. 13.
"Song for Falling Asleep. " Pequod (11) 80, p. 48.
"Street at Sannois. " Tendril (7/8) Spr-Sum 80, p. 15.
"What You Have Come to Expect. " NewYorker (56:21) 14 Jl 80, p. 36.
"Winter Branches. " Pequod (11) 80, p. 43.

DODMAN, Martin
"Encounter. " Montra (7) 80, pp. 35-41.
"Fut Bati" (tr. of Jean Daive). Bound (8:3) Spr 80, pp. 153-161.
"Margins" (for Robert Creeley). Bound (8:2) Wint 80, p. 127.
"Venice Triptych. " Montra (7) 80, p. 42.

DODO, Jean
"Au marché de mon quartier. " PortR (26) 80, p. 218.

DODSON, Owen
"Prisoners" (for F. B.). BlackALF (14:2) Sum 80, p. 51.

DOI, Toshijuki
  "Stained Glass" (tr. by C. J. McNaspy). NewOR (7:1) 80, p.
  56.

DOLE, Janet
  "Equinox. " CalQ (16/17) 80, p. 61.

DOLEGA, Christine
  "The Psalter's Song. " BallSUF (21:1) Wint 80, p. 48.

DOMIN, Hilde
  "Letter to the Other Continent" (tr. by Inge Eckert-Judd). DenQ
  (15:1) Spr 80, p. 85.
  "On Reading Pablo Neruda" (tr. by Inge Eckert-Judd). DenQ (15:
  1) Spr 80, p. 83.
  "Question" (tr. by Inge Eckert-Judd). DenQ (15:1) Spr 80, p. 84.
  "Salva Nos" (tr. by Inge Eckert-Judd). DenQ (15:1) Spr 80, p.
  82.

DONAHUE, Patricia
  "One Desire" (tr. of Almir Bruneti). NewOR (7:3) 80, p. 276.

DONEGAN, Nancy
  "The Boy. " Tendril (7/8) Spr-Sum 80, p. 20.
  "A Day with No Name. " Tendril (7/8) Spr-Sum 80, p. 18.
  "Letter for a Stillborn. " Tendril (7/8) Spr-Sum 80, p. 19.

DONNELLY, Dorothy
  "Winged Things. " ChrC (97:29) 24 S 80, p. 878.

DONOVAN, Brad
  "For Your Next Party. " Aspen (9) Spr 80, p. 36.

DONOVAN, Gregory
  "The Calling" (for R. W.). QW (10) Wint-Spr 80, p. 120.
  "The Working Man. " QW (10) Wint-Spr 80, p. 116.
  "The Writer Takes a Photograph. " QW (10) Wint-Spr 80, p.
  117.

DOOLEY, Tim
  "The Hypnopompic State. " GRR (11:2/3) 80, p. 68.
  "Impossible Object. " GRR (11:2/3) 80, p. 69.
  "Self-portrait in an attitude of terror. " GRR (11:2/3) 80, p. 67.

DOR, Moshe
  "The Inner Land. " PortR (26) 80, p. 198.
  "The Panhandle of Galilee" (tr. by Anat Feinberg). Stand (21:4)
  80, p. 9.

DORESKI, William
  "Laser. " Aspect (76) S-D 79-80, p. 29.
  "Poem: Her hair made bombast on the pillow. " Aspect (76) S-
  D 79-80, p. 28.

DORMAN, Peter John
"Valediction. " CarlMis (18:2) Sum 80, p. 34.

DORMAN, Sonya
"A Late Walk. " CropD (2/3) Aut-Wint 80, p. 15.
"Memory's Forest. " BaratR (8:1) Sum 80, p. 5.
"The River Merchant's Daughter, Updated. " CharR (6:1) Spr 80,
    p. 13.
"Summer Night. " Im (7:1) 80, p. 10.
"To Praise Dust" (for Carl Woods). EnPas (10) 80, p. 7.
"Writing Fiction. " Im (7:1) 80, p. 10.

DORSET, Gerald
"Surprise Party. " Tele (16) 80, p. 59.
"Sweet Insurgency. " Tele (16) 80, p. 60.

DORSETT, Robert
"The Death of Boethius. " Poetry (137:2) N 80, p. 95.

DORSETT, Thomas
"Peak Congregations. " Wind (38) 80, p. 24.

DOTY, M. R.
"Days of Dust" (w. Renata Treitel). Nimrod (24:1) Aut-Wint 80,
    p. 108.
"Family Photographs. " Aspen (9) Spr 80, p. 40.
"Glass Piano. " Outbr (4/5) Aut 79-Spr 80, p. 42.
"Imagining My Father's Death. " Durak (5) 80, p. 12.
"In a Hotel on Main Street. " Aspen (9) Spr 80, p. 41.
"Let's. " Tendril (7/8) Spr-Sum 80, p. 21.
"A Memorandum of Ten Voyages in the Staary Void. " Kayak
    (54) S 80, pp. 31-44.
"The Pruning Bill of Pierre Riviere. " Aspen (9) Spr 80, p. 39.
"Rains of Birds. " Agni (12) 80, p. 86.
"Sam, ". PoetryNW (21:3) Aut 80, p. 8.
"Showers of Fishes. " Agni (12) 80, p. 84.
"Werewolves' Fruit. " Outbr (4/5) Aut 79-Spr 80, p. 38.
"Whenever I Talk. " Outbr (4/5) Aut 79-Spr 80, p. 44.

DOUGLAS, Gilean
"Inscription in a Book. " Poem (38) Mr 80, p. 11.
"The Pattern Set. " Poem (38) Mr 80, p. 12.
"Where Freedom Is. " Poem (38) Mr 80, p. 13.

DOUSKEY, Franz
"Block Island. " PoNow (27) 80, p. 29.
"Flying Over Iowa. " PoNow (27) 80, p. 29.

DOVE, Richard
"The Cry's Outing" (tr. of Ernst Meister). ChiR (32:1) Sum 80,
    p. 105.

DOVE, Rita
"The Abduction. " VirQR (56:2) Spr 80, p. 276.

"Five Elephants. " Nat (230:8) 1 Mr 80, p. 253.
"The House Slave. " VirQR (56:2) Spr 80, p. 275.

DOW, Philip
"Drunk Last Night With Friends, I Go to Work Anyway. " PoNow
(27) 80, p. 26.
"Hot Day in Early Spring. " PoNow (27) 80, p. 27.

DOWNS, Stuart
"In Praise of Stone Walls. " SmF (11/12) Spr-Aut 80, p. 40.
"Like the Diamond Print Did. " SmF (11/12) Spr-Aut 80, p. 39.

DOWNS, Virginia
"Farewell to Plumed Horses. " CropD (1) Spr 80, p. 21.
"From the 8th Street Market. " CropD (1) Spr 80, p. 21.

DOXEY, W. S.
"Good Mornin', God, in Dixie. " PoetC (12:1) 80, p. 4.
"Mead Hall. " Poem (40) N 80, p. 19.
"Our Turn. " PoetC (12:1) 80, p. 2.
"The White Lie. " Poem (40) N 80, p. 20.

DOYLE, James
"The Ordination. " Bound (8:2) Wint 80, p. 317.
"The Skull. " Bound (8:2) Wint 80, p. 318.

DOYLE, Mike
"Noon Hour on Granville. " ConcPo (12:2) Aut 79, p. 83.

DRABIK, Grazyna
"atlantis" (tr. of Wislawa Szemborska w. Sharon Olds). Kayak
(55) Ja 81, p. 56.
"chance meeting" (tr. of Wislawa Szemborska w. Sharon Olds).
Kayak (55) Ja 81, p. 57.
"Chess" (tr. of Jacek Bierezin w. Austin Flint). PoNow (28)
80, p. 45.
"From an Expedition Which Did Not Take Place" (tr. of Wislawa
Szymborska w. Austin Flint). CharR (6:2) Aut 80, p. 52.
"Incantation" (tr. of Czeslaw Milosz w. Austin Flint). PoetryE
(3) 80, p. 56.
"Lot's Wife" (tr. of Wislawa Szymborska w. Austin Flint).
CharR (6:2) Aut 80, p. 51.
"Psalm" (tr. of Wislawa Szymborska w. Austin Flint). CharR
(6:2) Aut 80, p. 53.
"the two apes of breughel" (tr. of Wislawa Szemborska w.
Sharon Olds). Kayak (55) Ja 81, p. 57.
"words" (tr. of Wislawa Szemborska w. Sharon Olds). Kayak
(55) Ja 81, p. 58.

DRAGEL, Cheryl
"Deja-vu. " HangL (37) Spr 80, p. 66.

DRAKE, Albert
"Before Dawn. " CropD (2/3) Aut-Wint 80, p. 20.

DRAKE, Barbara
"Northern Lights and Crazy Ladies. " StoneC (7:3) D 80, p. 56.
"Up in the Mountains. " StoneC (7:3) D 80, p. 59.

DRAKOPOULOS, Anne
"That Country. " EngJ (69:5) My 80, p. 53.

DRESSEL, Jon
"From the Head of the Gadarene Pig Farmer's Association. "
    WebR (5:1) Wint 80, p. 13.
"A Real Trouper. " WebR (5:1) Wint 80, p. 10.

DREW, George
"Theodore Whyland. " AntR (38:2) Spr 80, p. 180.

DREYER, Luanne
"Vocational Goal. " Tele (16) 80, p. 115.

DREYER, Marsha Gabriela
"Months Have Passed, My Daughter" (tr. of Gioconda Belli).
    Cond (6) 80, p. 167.
"The Mother" (tr. of Gioconda Belli w. Electa Arenal). Cond
    (6) 80, p. 165.
"We Shall Beget Children" (tr. of Gioconda Belli w. Electa
    Arenal). Cond (6) 80, p. 169.
"We Were Three" (tr. of Claribel Alegria w. Electa Arenal).
    Cond (6) 80, p. 161.

DRINNAN, Marjorie
"Untitled: I will pick up your tears. " PottPort (2) 80-81, p. 41.

DRISCOLL, Jack
"Freeze. " CalQ (16/17) 80, p. 63.
"Keeping the Bears Awake. " CalQ (16/17) 80, p. 64.
"Refusing to Give Blood. " OhioR (25) 80, pp. 65-78.
"The Snare. " PoetryNW (21:2) Sum 80, p. 22.
"Undressing for Winter. " CarlMis (18:2) Sum 80, p. 170.

DRURY, John
"Scavenger on the Waterfront. " AntR (38:3) Sum 80, p. 336.
"Side Panels: Adam and Eve. " Poetry (136:5) Ag 80, p. 274.
"Winter Night. " CarolQ (32:1) Wint 80, p. 65.

DUBELYEW, Didi Susan
"Dribble Diseases. " Tele (16) 80, p. 48.
"Odes for the Offspring. " Tele (16) 80, p. 48.
"Who Needs Exercise???" Tele (16) 80, p. 49.

DUBIE, Norman
"Nine Black Poppies for Chac. " AmerPoR (9:1) Ja-F 80, p. 27.
"Parish. " NewYorker (56:42) 8 D 80, p. 56.
"The Pennacesse Leper Colony for Women. Cape Cod. 1922. "
    Tendril (9) 80, p. 51.

"Pictures at an Exhibition" (for J). <u>Poetry</u> (136:4) Jl 80, p. 203.

DUBNOV, E.
'There were only six months between Anna and me. " <u>MassR</u>
(21:3) Aut 80, p. 594.

DUBOIS, Louise
"ormbunkarna vid mina fötter. " <u>PortR</u> (26) 80, p. 378.

DUDIS, Ellen Kirvin
"Teething Season. " <u>LittleM</u> (12:3/4) 80, p. 34.

DUEMER, Joseph
"Cure for Insomnia. " <u>PoetryNW</u> (21:1) Sum 80, p. 20.
"Rules of Order" (for Don Devereux). <u>PoetryNW</u> (21:2) Sum 80,
    p. 19.

DUFFY, Maureen Nevin
"Spaces. " <u>US1</u> (12/13) Aut-Wint 80, p. 1.

DUGAN, Alan
"Apollo. " <u>PortR</u> (26) 80, p. 443.

DUGAN, Lawrence
"The Communicants. " <u>SouthernR</u> (16:2) Spr 80, p. 414.
"A Prayer for the Future. " <u>SouthernPR</u> (20:2) Aut 80, p. 34.
"Spy Wednesday. " <u>SouthernR</u> (16:2) Spr 80, p. 413.

DUGGAN, Devon
"Orange Leaves Are Escaping. " <u>EnPas</u> (10) 80, p. 9.

DUMITRESCU, Geo
"Adventures in Heaven" (tr. by author). <u>PortR</u> (26) 80, p. 321.
"Aventură în cer. " <u>PortR</u> (26) 80, p. 320.
"Dancing" (tr. by author). <u>PortR</u> (26) 80, p. 319.
"Dans!" <u>PortR</u> (26) 80, p. 318.
"Madrigal răsturnat. " <u>PortR</u> (26) 80, p. 323.
"Reversed Madrigal" (tr. by author). <u>PortR</u> (26) 80, p. 325.

DUNCAN, Robert
"Something Is Moving. " <u>Bound</u> (8:2) Wint 80, p. 45.

DUNHAM, Vera
"The Great Confrontation" (tr. of Andrei Voznesensky w. Wil-
    liam Jay Smith). <u>Atl</u> (245:4) Ap 80, p. 117.

DUNLOP, Lane
"Deep in each other's arms, ". <u>PoNow</u> (26) 80, p. 15.
'I am in some foreign subway with you with bare wooden seats. "
    <u>PoNow</u> (26) 80, p. 15.

DUNN, Douglas
"Between Bus-stop and Home" (to Pauel and Helena) (tr. of

Piotr Sommer). PortR (26) 80, p. 297.
"St. Kilda's Parliament: 1879-1979. " NewYorker (56:6) 31 Mr
80, p. 42.
"Two Gestures" (tr. of Piotr Sommer). PortR (26) 80, p. 295.
"Washing the Coins. " NewYorker (56:12) 12 My 80, p. 75.
"When" (tr. of Piotr Sommer). PortR (26) 80, p. 299.

DUNN, Ethel
"The Bull-Leaper. " Wind (38) 80, p. 25.

DUNN, Robert
"Envoys. " Nat (231:7) 13 S 80, p. 226.

DUNN, Stephen
"As It Moves. " PoetryNW (21:2) Sum 80, p. 4.
"The Bad Angels. " PoetryNW (21:2) Sum 80, p. 3.
"Because We Are Not Taken Seriously. " GeoR (34:1) Spr 80, p.
181.
"Expectations. " WatT (1) Aut 80, p. 74.
"The House of Solitude. " PraS (54:2) Sum 80, p. 21.
"I Come Home Wanting to Touch Everyone. " NewL (46:3) Spr
80, p. 88.
"The Inexpressible. " NoAmR (265:1) Mr 80, p. 57.
"The Inhabitants. " WatT (1) Aut 80, p. 75.
"A Little Squalor, Please. " PoetryNW (21:2) Sum 80, p. 5.
"Midnight. " DacTerr (17) 80, p. 23.
"My Brother's Work. " MassR (21:4) Wint 80, p. 786.
"The Photograph Album. " PoNow (26) 80, p. 40.
"That Saturday Without a Car. " NewYorker (56:22) 21 Jl 80, p.
36.
"Waiting With Two Members of a Motorcycle Gang for My Child
to Be Born" (for Andrea). DacTerr (17) 80, p. 24.

DUNNE, Carol
"Afterlife. " Tendril (7/8) Spr-Sum 80, p. 24.
"Billy Magic. " SouthernPR (20:1) Spr 80, p. 57.
"Hatches. " Poem (40) N 80, p. 7.
"Lost at Juniper Springs. " Poem (40) N 80, p. 5.
"Nights at Sparr. " Tendril (7/8) Spr-Sum 80, p. 26.
"Nursing the Hide. " Tendril (7/8) Spr-Sum 80, p. 27.
"Provender. " SouthernHR (14:2) Spr 80, p. 153.
"Removing the Dog-Dead Possum. " HiramPoR (27) Aut-Wint 80,
p. 14.
"Removing the Dog-Dead Possum. " Tendril (7/8) Spr-Sum 80,
p. 25.
"The Silent Stevedore. " Tendril (7/8) Spr-Sum 80, p. 22.
"The Surfing Boys at Sarasota. " SouthernHR (14:2) Spr 80, p.
128.
"Upon the Death of the Neighborhood Caitiff. " SoCaR (13:1) Aut
80, p. 75.
"Woman in the Country. " Poem (40) N 80, p. 6.

DUNNING, Stephen
"Cocking His Ear to the Traffic. " CharR (6:2) Aut 80, p. 43.

"Just after midnight. " NewL (47:1) Aut 80, p. 60.
"Pips. " GRR (11:1) 80, p. 40.
"Players Begin to Warm Up. " CharR (6:2) Aut 80, p. 43.
"Then Shut Out His Face. " PikeF (3) Wint 80, p. 7.
"There are moments a man. " NewL (47:1) Aut 80, p. 59.
"You, Brother. " PikeF (3) Wint 80, p. 7.

DuPLESSIS, Rachel Blau
    "Megaliths. " Montra (7) 80, p. 199.
    "Selvedge. " Montra (7) 80, p. 33.

DUPREE, Edison
    "Hypothesis. " BelPoJ (31:2) Wint 80-81, p. 17.
    "The Sunbather. " BelPoJ (31:2) Wint 80-81, p. 17.

DuPRIEST, Travis
    "The Day Before Death. " Aspen (9) Spr 80, p. 68.

DUPUIS, Gilbert
    "Ecrire. " Os (10) Spr 80, p. 26.

DURAK, Carol
    "Day Moon. " StoneC (7:2) My 80, p. 12.
    "Night. " StoneC (7:2) My 80, p. 15.
    "Returning. " StoneC (7:2) My 80, p. 13.
    "That Moment of Loon. " StoneC (7:2) My 80, p. 14.

DURANT, Harold J.
    "And I Wonder. " PottPort (2) 80-81, p. 4.

DURCAN, Paul
    "The Death by Heroin of Sid Vicious. " Ploughs (6:1) 80, p. 105.
    "Granny Tree in the Sky. " Ploughs (6:1) 80, p. 110.
    "Sally. " Ploughs (6:1) 80, p. 109.
    "Send a Message to Mary but Don't Bother If You Have an Im-
        portant Television Programme to Watch. " Ploughs (6:1) 80,
        p. 106.
    "Veronica Shee from the Town of Tralee. " Ploughs (6:1) 80, p.
        108.

D'URFEY, Thomas
    from Pills to Purge Melancholy: "The Hyde Park Frolic. "
        Playb (27:8) Ag 80, p. 161.

DUVAL, Quinton
    "Hayride" (In Memoriam, Andrew Grossbardt). NewL (46:4) Sum
        80, p. 65.
    "Scared. " PoNow (29) 80, p. 7.

DWYER, David
    "After the War. " Agni (12) 80, p. 74.

DWYER, Frank
    "Holiday in Moonachie. " BelPoJ (30:3) Spr 80, p. 4.

"In the Washington Zoo. " LitR (23:3) Spr 80, p. 383.
"Old Man. " CentR (24:4) Aut 80, p. 456.

DWYER, Timothy
    from the Balkans, '55: "Formulas of the Trip" (tr. of Tomas
        Tranströmer). Field (23) Aut 80, p. 8.
    "Isolated Swedish Houses" (tr. of Tomas Transtömer). Field
        (23) Aut 80, p. 6.

DYBEK, Stuart
    "Clothespins. " PoNow (28) 80, p. 23.
    "The Estrangement of Luis Morone. " VirQR (56:4) Aut 80, p.
        683.
    "Furniture. " PoNow (27) 80, p. 30.
    "Kid. " MinnR (NS 15) Aut 80, p. 8.
    "Lover. " MinnR (NS 15) Aut 80, p. 9.
    "Moving Out/Iowa City. " PoNow (27) 80, p. 30.
    "My Father's Fights. " PoNow (28) 80, p. 23.
    "Rebellion of the Hanged. " MinnR (NS 15) Aut 80, p. 10.
    "Three Windows. " MinnR (NS 15) Aut 80, p. 10.
    "Traveling Salesman. " PoNow (28) 80, p. 23.

DYE, Aaron
    "Car Pool. " CapeR (16:1) Wint 80, p. 22.

DYER, Dan
    "The Insomniac Awakens Frightened from a Dream of Flight. "
        CutB (15) Aut/Wint 80, p. 32.

DYER, Robert
    "Smoking Mirror. " Focus (14:86) Ap 80, p. 18.

DYER, T. A.
    "Autumn Laying In. " CreamCR (5:2) Spr 80, p. 45.
    "Lake County Poem" (for Liz). CreamCR (5:2) Spr 80, p. 46.

DYGERT, Ann
    "Jake and the Hired Girl. " PoNow (29) 80, p. 8.
    "Swimmer. " PoNow (29) 80, p. 8.

EADES, Joan
    "Heat Wave. " PoNow (29) 80, p. 8.

EADY, Cornelius
    "Bluto in a White Suit. " PoNow (29) 80, p. 21.
    "The Idiot Falls in Love. " PoNow (29) 80, p. 21.
    "The Victors. " PoNow (29) 80, p. 21.

EARLEY, Bernie
    "Miami Winter. " CalQ (16/17) 80, p. 57.

EASON, Alethea
    "The Sleep Watchers. " Wind (38) 80, p. 26.

EASTMAN, Donald
"Gloss. " Poem (39) Jl 80, p. 22.
"My Son in Morning. " Poem (39) Jl 80, p. 23.
"The Mythic Provision. " Poem (39) Jl 80, p. 21.
"The Night Visitors. " Poem (39) Jl 80, p. 20.

EATON, Charles Edward
"Affluence at Eau Claire. " Poem (40) N 80, p. 1.
"The Amputee. " SouthernPR (20:2) Aut 80, p. 19.
"Anatomy of an Explosion. " SouthernR (16:1) Wint 80, p. 162.
"Articulation of the Ruby Bracelet. " Salm (50/51) Aut 80-Wint
    81, p. 50.
"Black Umbrella. " PoNow (26) 80, p. 37.
"Bodies of Water. " Salm (50/51) Aut 80-Wint 81, p. 52.
"The Brass Bed. " PoNow (27) 80, p. 26.
"Chocolate Cake. " KanQ (12:1) Wint 80, p. 55.
"The Climatron. " Poem (40) N 80, p. 3.
"The Courtship. " SouthernR (16:1) Wint 80, p. 163.
"Don Juan in Autumn. " MidwQ (21:2) Wint 80, p. 256.
"The Finger Bowl. " Salm (50/51) Aut 80-Wint 81, p. 49.
"Idyll of Isolato. " Agni (12) 80, p. 107.
"Iron Lung. " SouthernPR (20:2) Aut 80, p. 18.
"June Issue With Swan Dive. " SouthernHR (14:3) Sum 80, p. 259.
"The Latter-Day Crisis of Crusoe. " MidwQ (21:2) Wint 80, p.
    255.
"Loose Mountain Lake. " Poem (38) Mr 80, p. 42.
"The Oasis. " Poem (38) Mr 80, p. 41.
"Praying Mantis. " ColEng (41:8) Ap 80, p. 885.
"Rest Homes. " Poem (40) N 80, p. 2.
"Sumptuous Siesta. " PoNow (27) 80, p. 6.
"Water Polo. " PoNow (27) 80, p. 26.
"Water Spider. " CapeR (16:1) Wint 80, p. 6.
"White Lace. " Poem (38) Mr 80, p. 43.

EBERHART, Richard
"Prayer to the God of Harm, the Song of the Poet" (for Rex-
    roth). Ark (14) 80, p. 184.
"Sea Storm. " AmerPoR (9:2) Mr-Ap 80, p. 7.
"Time's Clickings. " VirQR (56:1) Wint 80, p. 66.
"To Alpha Dryden Eberhart November 26, 1977, on being seventy-
    five. " Tendril (9) 80, p. 52.
"The Year" (for Rexroth). Ark (14) 80, p. 182.

EBERLY, David
"Last Call. " HangL (38) Aut 80, p. 18.

ECKERT-JUDD, Inge
"Letter to the Other Continent" (tr. of Hilde Domin). DenQ (15:
    1) Spr 80, p. 85.
"On Reading Pablo Neruda" (tr. of Hilde Domin). DenQ (15:1)
    Spr 80, p. 83.
"Question" (tr. of Hilde Domin). DenQ (15:1) Spr 80, p. 84.
"Salva Nos" (tr. of Hilde Domin). DenQ (15:1) Spr 80, p. 82.

ECONOMOU, George
"Breaklight. " Confr (20) Spr-Sum 80, p. 119.

EDELMAN, Ane
"The Trees, Deciduous" (to my brother). PoetryNW (21:2) Sum
80, p. 28.

EDMONDSON, Bill
"Hollywood" (for Peg Entwhistle). CalQ (16/17) 80, p. 117.

EDSON, Russell
"The Asexual. " Durak (4) 80, p. 15.
"The Condomizations. " Durak (4) 80, p. 14.
"The Great Amateur. " PoNow (28) 80, p. 36.
"Inside an Old Woman. " PoNow (26) 80, p. 14.
"The Man Who Fell in Love. " PoNow (28) 80, p. 36.
"The Old Woman's Mouth. " PoNow (28) 80, p. 36.
"Pigeons. " Tendril (9) 80, p. 53.
"The Unworkable. " PoNow (26) 80, p. 14.
"Why a Farmer Is Going to Have Sex with His Cow. " PoNow
(28) 80, p. 36.

EDWARDS, Anthony Wm.
"Love's Poem. " PikeF (3) Wint 80, p. 28.

EDWARDS, Eric
"Gentle Creature. " BosUJ (26:3) 80, p. 167.

EGEMO, Constance
"My Father in the Nursing Home. " DacTerr (17) 80, p. 25.

EGGERS, Paul
"Old Douglass Coming Out of Westport, Again. " Tendril (7/8)
Spr-Sum 80, p. 28.

EHRHART, W. D.
"Companions. " Northeast (3:8) Wint 80, p. 52.
"The Eruption of Mount St. Helens. " Sam (101) 80, p. 62.
"Matters of the Heart" (for Tom McGrath and James Cooney).
Sam (102) 80, p. 56.
The Poems of W. D. Ehrhart. Sam (93) 80. Entire issue.
"To You in Virginia. " Wind (37) 80, p. 12.
"Waking Alone in Darkness. " Sam (92) 80, p. 2.

EHRLICH, Shelley
"Potato. " SoDakR (18:2) Sum 80, p. 15.

EICHWALD, Richard
"Organ Recital" (for Wallace Stevens). SewanR (88:2) Spr 80, p.
178.
"Three Went Out a Sower. " SewanR (88:2) Spr 80, p. 179.

EIELSON, Jorge Eduardo
"Forum Romano" (tr. by Gerd and Miriam Joel). NewOR (7:3)

80, p. 262.
"Spring in the Villa Adriana" (tr. by Gerd and Miriam Joel).
NewOR (7:3) 80, p. 247.

EINZIG, Barbara
"Imposition" (for Vladyslaw C.).   CreamCR (5:2) Spr 80, p. 43.

EKSTRÖM, Margareta
Ord till Johanna on morgonen: "När du vaknar vet du inte me
bestämd het. " PortR (26) 80, p. 370.

ELDER, Karl
"On Seeing Footage of the 1975 Shooting of 106 Elephants. "
PoNow (26) 80, p. 32.

ELDRIDGE, Sheridan Wolf
"God and Me. " CEACritic (43:1) N 80, p. 39.
"I'm Learning. " CEACritic (43:1) N 80, p. 39.
"My Brother Billy Died Today. " CEACritic (43:1) N 80, p. 39.
"To Billy. " CEACritic (43:1) N 80, p. 39.
"To You, Jane. " CEACritic (43:1) N 80, p. 39.

ELGORRIAGA, José
from Between the Carnation and the Sword: (7, 11) (tr. of
Rafael Alberti w. Martin Paul). AmerPoR (9:5) S-O 80,
p. 34.
from Vertical Poetry: (6, 8) (tr. of Roberto Juarroz w. Martin
Paul). AmerPoR (9:5) S-O 80, p. 34.

ELIOT, Eileen
"a small inheritance. " PikeF (3) Wint 80, p. 7.

ELIZONDO, Salvador
"The Graphographer" (to Octavio Paz) (tr. by Bruce P. Rogers).
NewOR (7:3) 80, p. 303.

ELLEDGE, Jim
"Ambush. " Wind (38) 80, p. 69.
"Klondike. " PikeF (3) Wint 80, p. 3.

ELLENBOGEN, George
"The Renewal. " LitR (23:3) Spr 80, p. 393.

ELLIOTT, George P.
"Some who hourly hear afresh. " Poetry (136:4) Jl 80.   Inside
front cover.

ELLIOTT, Harley
"Older. " PoNow (26) 80, p. 42.
"Sometimes This Movie. " HiramPoR (27) Aut-Wint 80, p. 15.
"The Voice in the Heart of America" (for Steven).   HiramPoR
(27) Aut-Wint 80, p. 16.

ELLIOTT, William
  "Temperance Is Only a State of the Mind in Taconite Harbor. "
    PoetC (12:3) 80, p. 5.
  "Temperance River: Thursday. " PoetC (12:3) 80, p. 6.
  "Two Songs for a Rose" (tr. of Hakushu Kitahara). EnPas (10)
    80, p. 14.

ELLIOTT, William D.
  "Street. " Pan (21) 80, p. 17.

ELLIOTT, William I.
  "Menstruation" (tr. of Tanikawa Shuntarō). PortR (26) 80, p.
    245.

ELLIS, Craig
  "Postcard. " Aspect (76) S-D 79-80, p. 41.
  "take: New Moon, Venus, Sun in Virgo. " Aspect (76) S-D 79-
    80, p. 42.

ELLIS, Mary Lynn H.
  "This. " EngJ (69:5) My 80, p. 51.

ELLIS, R. Joseph
  "Memory Bomb. " Sam (98) 80, p. 33.

ELLIS, Rebecca
  "Accident. " PikeF (3) Wint 80, p. 10.

ELLIS, Ron
  "Dead Air. " PoetryNW (21:2) Sum 80, p. 31.

ELLISON, Jessie T.
  "the fishing trip. " WindO (37) Aut-Wint 80, p. 20.
  "One Woman. " WindO (36) Spr-Sum 80, p. 37.
  "Two of a Kind. " StoneC (7:2) My 80, p. 17.
  "Walk Across the Bridge. " WindO (37) Aut-Wint 80; on calendar.

ELLZEY, Steve
  "Caretaker. " CalQ (16/17) 80, p. 62.
  "Peeping Rose. " PoNow (29) 80, p. 9.

ELMAN, Richard
  "Memo. " Nat (231:22) 27 D 80, p. 710.

ELSBERG, John
  "Letters. " CropD (1) Spr 80, p. 18.
  "Park Fragments: Autumn. " Vis (1) 79.
  "Reflections. " Vis (1) 79.

ELSEY, David
  "Watering the Lawn. " SmPd (48) Wint 80, p. 10.

ELTETO, Louis J.
  "Jewish Cemetery in Prague" (for Paul Celan) (tr. of Erich

Arendt). PortR (26) 80, p. 146.
"Night" (tr. of Sándor Kányádi). PortR (26) 80, p. 170.
"They Took Me Along" (tr. of Paul Wiens). PortR (26) 80, p.
    143.
"Why Cry..." (tr. of László Benjámin). PortR (26) 80, p. 175.

ELUARD, Paul
    "L'amour la poesie" (tr. by Fred Cogswell). PottPort (2) 80-81,
    p. 41.

ELYTIS, Odysseus
    from Axion Esti: "Ode VI" (tr. by Kimon Friar). Durak (4)
    80, p. 45.
    "Body of Summer" (tr. by Edward Morin, Jana Hesser and Lefteris
    Pavlides). CharR (6:2) Aut 80, p. 49.
    "Drinking the Corinthian Sun" (tr. by Edward Morin, Jana Hesser
    and Lefteris Pavlides). CharR (6:2) Aut 80, p. 50.
    "Gift of a Silver Poem" (tr. by Kimon Friar). Durak (4) 80, p.
    44.
    from Maria Nephele: Twelve Poems (tr. by Athan Anagnostop-
    oulos). ParisR (78) Sum 80, pp. 62-78.
    "No Longer Do I Know the Night" (tr. by Edward Morin, Jane
    Hesser and Lefteris Pavlides). CharR (6:2) Aut 80, p. 50.
    "psalm and mosaic for a springtime in athens" (tr. by Nanos
    Valaoritis). Kayak (55) Ja 81, p. 20.

EMANS, Elaine V.
    "Cat, Leaping Over Marigolds. " KanQ (12:4) Aut 80, p. 110.
    "Father Recalled as a Dinner Companion. " FourQt (29:4) Sum
    80, p. 33.
    "Haloes. " GRR (11:1) 80, p. 32.
    "Mother as Student of Physiology. " KanQ (12:1) Wint 80, p. 20.
    "The Undreamed. " KanQ (12:1) Wint 80, p. 20.
    "Villanelle for Prairie Dogs. " MichQR (19:2) Spr 80, p. 214.

EMANUEL, Lynn
    "Dracula. " PraS (54:2) Sum 80, p. 81.
    "What I Know About the End of the Second World War. " PraS
    (54:2) Sum 80, p. 81.

EMBLEN, D. L.
    "Toward a Father's Funeral" (for Jim and Mignon). Epoch (29:
    3) Spr-Sum 80, p. 242.

EMERSON, Dorothy
    "Down Sleep's Dark Bank We Sink. " YaleR (70:1) Aut 80, p.
    103.
    "Lake Ainslee. " YaleR (70:1) Aut 80, p. 103.

EMERSON, Ralph Waldo
    "Concord Hymn. " Sam (103) 80, p. 10.

EMERUWA, Leatrice W.
    "East 105th and Euclid Street Peddler's Song. " Pig (7) My 80,

p. 63.
"For What-Sa-Name. " Pig (7) My 80, p. 78.
"Rage. " Pig (7) My 80, p. 77.

EMRICK, Ernestine Hoff
"One Worship. " ChrC (97:15) 23 Ap 80, p. 461.

ENGELS, John
"The Extinguishment. " Columbia (4) Spr-Sum 80, pp. 22-27.
"Fall Change. " PoNow (26) 80, p. 31.
"The Harbor. " GeoR (34:1) Spr 80, p. 14.
"In Late March. " NewL (47:1) Aut 80, p. 35.
"Night Sky, Earth Tremor. " NewL (47:1) Aut 80, p. 34.
"Partridge. " Antaeus (39) Aut 80, p. 68.
"Shark. " Antaeus (39) Aut 80, p. 66.

ENGLE, Ed Jr.
"Another Way. " PoNow (29) 80, p. 9.

ENGLISH, Maurice
"Copernicus, Darwin, Freud. " Poetry (136:5) Ag 80, p. 264.

ENGMAN, John
"The Brother. " PoetryNW (21:3) Aut 80, p. 29.
"From an Apartment on the Third Floor. " PoetryNW (21:3) Aut
80, p. 30.

ENSLIN, Theodore
from Axes: (24). Montra (7) 80, p. 30.
"Still Life and Opening: Los Organos, 1/28/80. " NewL (47:1)
Aut 80, p. 19.
"Stone-Tentative. " NewL (47:1) Aut 80, p. 18.

ENTREKIN, Charles
"Line Drawing #3: Self Portrait. " US1 (12/13) Aut-Wint 80,
p. 3.

ENZENSBERGER, Hans Magnus
"Blindly" (tr. by John N. Miller). CharR (6:2) Aut 80, p. 54.
"Camera Obscura" (tr. by Nicholas Kolumban). CutB (15) Aut/
Wint 80, p. 16.
"difficult work" (for theodor w. adorno) (tr. by Michael Mund-
henk). MinnR (NS 15) Aut 80, p. 11.
"Identity Check. " ParisR (77) Wint-Spr 80, p. 37.
"Notice of Loss. " ParisR (77) Wint-Spr 80, p. 36.
from The Sinking of the Titanic: "Third Canto. " NewYRB (27:5)
3 Ap 80, p. 15.

EPSTEIN, Elaine
"The First Sadness. " VirQR (56:2) Spr 80, p. 266.
"Luck. " VirQR (56:2) Spr 80, p. 267.
"Rothko at the Guggenheim. " MissouriR (3:3) Sum 80, p. 26.
"Thaw. " MissouriR (3:3) Sum 80, p. 27.

"Waiting for an Answer. " <u>MissouriR</u> (3:3) Sum 80, p. 25.

EPSTEIN, John
  "Love Poem. " <u>Wind</u> (37) 80, p. 13.

ERB, Elke
  "In the Picture" (tr. by Craig Federhen). <u>Field</u> (22) Spr 80, p.
    12.
  "Sheep's Wool Is Left Hanging" (tr. by Craig Federhen). <u>Field</u>
    (22) Spr 80, p. 11.

ERFORD, Esther
  "I Shall Call You Ceres. " <u>Wind</u> (36) 80, p. 13.
  "The Man from the Auburn <u>Wood</u>. " <u>Wind</u> (36) 80, p. 13.
  "A Small Song Diminishing. " <u>Wind</u> (36) 80, p. 14.

ERON, Don
  "The Price of Admission. " <u>OhioR</u> (24) 80, p. 90.

ESCUDERO, Betina
  "Nocturne of Saint Ildefonso" (tr. of Octavio Paz). <u>CutB</u> (14)
    Spr /Sum 80, pp. 18-27.

ESHLEMAN, Clayton
  "Cato's Altars. " <u>Pequod</u> (11) 80, p. 84.
  "Elegy on the Eternal Bum in the Heart of Bohemia" (tr. of
    Milan Exner w. Jan Benda). <u>Montra</u> (7) 80, pp. 115-121.
  "Hades in Manganese" (for James <u>Hillman</u>). <u>Montra</u> (7) 80, pp.
    63-69.
  from Hades in Manganese: "The Lich Gate. " <u>Bachy</u> (17) Spr
    80, p. 18.
  from Hades in Manganese: "Mother's Comb. " <u>Bachy</u> (17) Spr
    80, p. 19.
  from Hades in Manganese: "Ramapithecus" (for Bernard Bador).
    <u>Bachy</u> (17) Spr 80, p. 20.
  from Hades in Manganese: "Self-Portrait. " <u>Bachy</u> (17) Spr 80,
    p. 19.
  "Master Hanus to His Blindness. " <u>Pequod</u> (11) 80, p. 78.
  "Silence Raving. " <u>Pequod</u> (11) 80, p. 83.
  "The Thoroughbreds" (tr. of Aimé Césaire w. Annette Smith).
    <u>Montra</u> (7) 80, pp. 99-113.
  "The Tourist. " <u>Pequod</u> (11) 80, p. 81.

ESPELAND, Pamela Lee
  "The Goose Invited All the Pigs" (tr. of Halfdan Rasmussen w.
    Marilyn Nelson Waniek). <u>CarlMis</u> (18:2) Sum 80, p. 5.
  "Little Cloud" (tr. of Halfdan Rasmussen w. Marilyn Nelson
    Waniek). <u>CarlMis</u> (18:2) Sum 80, p. 5.
  "Poor Old Blue Monday" (tr. of Halfdan Rasmussen w. Marilyn
    Nelson Waniek). <u>CarlMis</u> (18:2) Sum 80, p. 6.
  "The Winter's Cold in Norway" (tr. of Halfdan Rasmussen w.
    Marilyn Nelson Waniek). <u>CarlMis</u> (18:2) Sum 80, p. 5.

ESPINO, Federico Licsi Jr.
"Bionic Adam" (tr. by author). PortR (26) 80, p. 290.
"Bionikong Adan. " PortR (26) 80, p. 290.
"Inbitasyon. " PortR (26) 80, p. 289.
"Innocence" (tr. by author). PortR (26) 80, p. 291.
"Invitation" (tr. by author). PortR (26) 80, p. 289.
"Kawalang-malay. " PortR (26) 80, p. 291.
"Pre-mortem" (tr. by author). PortR (26) 80, p. 292.

ESPMARK, Kjell
"Brevid hennes bänk står bänken. " PortR (26) 80, p. 365.
"Isoleringsrummet är all diskretion. " PortR (26) 80, p. 366.

ESPOSITO, Nancy
"Hypothesis. " Thrpny (3) Aut 80, p. 23.
"A Rare Wine of Good Vintage. " NoAmR (265:2) Je 80, p. 14.
"Shapeshifting. " Nat (231:2) 12 Jl 80, p. 58.

ESPRIU, Salvador
"Book of the Dead" (tr. by Meg Bogin). AmerPoR (9:3) My-Je
    80, p. 39.
"Don't You Hear the Sound the Hoe Makes?" (tr. by Meg Bogin).
    AmerPoR (9:3) My-Je 80, p. 39.
"Here the Voyage Ends" (tr. by Meg Bogin). AmerPoR (9:3)
    My-Je 80, p. 39.
"Old Brueghel Told It Thus" (tr. by Meg Bogin). AmerPoR (9:3)
    My-Je 80, p. 39.
"Remember Us" (tr. by Meg Bogin). AmerPoR (9:3) My-Je 80,
    p. 40.
"Song of Afternoon Arriving" (tr. by Meg Bogin). AmerPoR (9:3)
    My-Je 80, p. 40.
"Song of Triumphant Night" (tr. by Meg Bogin). AmerPoR (9:3)
    My-Je 80, p. 39.

ESRIG, Mark
"The Real Touch" (for Ariel). ConcPo (13:1) Spr 80, p. 59.

ESTEY, Richard
"Dark lamp enclosed with ants" (tr. of Salah Stétié). PortR (26)
    80, p. 256.
"Of all things the son, the untorn" (tr. of Salah Stétié). PortR
    (26) 80, p. 255.
"The red of the red woman" (tr. of Salah Stétié). PortR (26)
    80, p. 258.

ETTER, Dave
"Boom Boom on B Street. " PoNow (28) 80, p. 15.
"Ellen Opdycke: The Fall. " PoNow (26) 80, p. 23.
"Fat Girl. " Im (7:1) 80, p. 8.
"Getting at the Truth. " MidwQ (21:2) Wint 80, p. 254.
"Grass Roots. " MidwQ (21:2) Wint 80, p. 253.
"Home Cooking. " CharR (6:2) Aut 80, p. 32.
"Homesick in a River Town (1964). " MidwQ (21:3) Spr 80, p.

347.
"Joe Pennington and Joe Pennington, Junior. " Im (7:1) 80, p. 8.
"Junior Ives: Barn Burner. " PoNow (26) 80, p. 23.
"The Last Show in Tijuana. " Im (7:1) 80, p. 8.
"The Last Summer of Eustacia Hawthorne. " CharR (6:2) Aut 80,
    p. 32.
"Logan's Creek. " PoNow (27) 80, p. 13.
"Murder. " PoNow (26) 80, p. 41.
"Poem on My Father's Eightieth Birthday. " DacTerr (17) 80, p.
    26.
"Pregnant. " PoNow (26) 80, p. 4.
"Statement. " PoNow (27) 80, p. 24.
"The Time of Day. " PoNow (27) 80, p. 24.
"Worms. " PoNow (27) 80, p. 24.
"Zachary Grant: Guilt. " PoNow (26) 80, p. 23.

EUGSTER, Carla
"Behind the Curtain. " Sam (86) 79, p. 28.
"The Circuit Court Judge. " Sam (86) 79, p. 30.
"Erica. " Sam (86) 79, p. 30.
Peter and the Guru. Sam (85) 79. Entire issue.
"Upon Visiting an Old Labor Union Friend. " Sam (98) 80, p. 51.

EULBERG, Sister Mary Thomas
Two Haiku. PikeF (3) Wint 80, p. 8.

EVANS, David Allan
"Billy Pablick. " PoNow (28) 80, p. 31.
"Halloween. " SoDakR (18:2) Sum 80, p. 14.
"Ice Fishing. " PoNow (27) 80, p. 18.
"Minnesota" (for David and Dan). KanQ (12:1) Wint 80, p. 44.
"Old Man and His Cat. " SoDakR (18:2) Sum 80, p. 13.
"A Part of the Game" (for David). KanQ (12:1) Wint 80, p. 45.
"The Story of Lava. " DacTerr (17) 80, p. 27.
"A Winter Morning. " PoNow (26) 80, p. 34.

EVANS, David E.
"Reunion. " EngJ (69:5) My 80, p. 46.

EVARTS, Prescott Jr.
"Brownsville Rock. " KanQ (12:3) Sum 80, p. 132.
"Housekeeping. " KanQ (12:1) Wint 80, p. 18.

EVERSON, William
"Steelhead. " Ark (14) 80, p. 185.

EWART, Gavin
"Thrust and Riposte" (tr. of Eugenio Montale). Stand (21:2) 80,
    p. 4.

EWART, Ronald William
"The Voyage In" (tr. of Raymond Tschumi). PortR (26) 80, p.
    383.

EXNER, Milan
"Elegie o vecnem tulakovi v srdci cech. "   Montra (7) 80, pp.
114-120.

F., E. W.
"Denial" (tr. of G. N. B.).   BosUJ (26:3) 80, p. 159.

FAGAN, Kathy
"Daughter. "   Poetry (135:6) Mr 80, p. 329.

FAHEY, W. A.
"The Owl. "   Confr (20) Spr-Sum 80, p. 58.

FAINLIGHT, Ruth
"Passenger. "   Hudson (33:4) Wint 80, p. 559.

FAIR, Ronald
"The Domestic. "   BlackALF (14:4) Wint 80, p. 173.

FAIZ, Faiz Ahmed
"The Day Death Comes" (tr. by Naomi Lazard).   CutB (14) Spr /
Sum 80, p. 12.

FALKENBERG, Betty
"Post Mortem" (tr. of Georg Heym).   PoNow (28) 80, p. 45.

FALLEUR, Barbara
"Lesson One. "   StoneC (7:3) D 80, p. 46.
"The Miracle of Skin. "   StoneC (7:3) D 80, p. 47.

FANDEL, John
"Driving Home Through Night Fog. "   Poetry (136:3) Je 80, p.
141.
"Passing. "   HiramPoR (27) Aut-Wint 80, p. 17.

FANNING, Charles
"A Member of the Chorus. "   Tendril (7/8) Spr-Sum 80, p. 30.

FARBER, Norma
"Hush!"   PoNow (26) 80, p. 18.
"What, No Tree for Mary?"   Confr (20) Spr-Sum 80, p. 181.

FAREWELL, Patricia
"At the Diner. "   NewL (47:1) Aut 80, p. 7.
"A Confession. "   NewL (47:1) Aut 80, p. 6.
"Nostalgia. "   PartR (47:1) 80, p. 129.

FARINELLA, Salvatore
"Orgy Room. "   PoNow (27) 80, p. 24.
"Queer Dancing. "   PoNow (27) 80, p. 24.
"Tonight. "   PoNow (27) 80, p. 24.

FARNSWORTH, Robert
"Groceries. "   PoetryNW (21:3) Aut 80, p. 26.

"A Man Mistaken for Pretty Boy Floyd. " PoetryNW (21:3) Aut
    80, p. 27.
"Meditation That Must Conclude on an Atlantic Beach. " OhioR
    (25) 80, p. 59.
"Novella. " Shen (31:2) 80, p. 34.
"The Whale" (for my sister). AmerPoR (9:1) Ja-F 80, p. 47.

FARRANT, Elizabeth
    "All Charades. " PoetC (12:3) 80, p. 21.
    "Endangered Species. " PoetC (12:2) 80, p. 39.

FARROKHZAD, Forugh
    "Question" (tr. by Jascha Kessler and Amin Banani). CutB (14)
        Spr /Sum 80, p. 104.

FASEL, Ida
    "Industrial. " Vis (4) 80.

FAUCHER, Real
    Fires and Crucifixions. Sam (88) 80.   Entire issue.
    "Growing Up. " Sam (98) 80, p. 18.

FAULKNER, Leigh
    "Houdini Rat. " ConcPo (12:2) Aut 79, p. 71.
    "Rat Cancels an Engagement at the Community Hall. " ConcPo
        (12:2) Aut 79, p. 70.
    "Rat's Love Song. " ConcPo (12:2) Aut 79, p. 69.

FAY, Julie
    "Places" (for Carl Otis). PoNow (29) 80, p. 9.

FAY, Steve
    "Chemistry of the Prairie State. " Northeast (3:8) Wint 80, p.
        29.
    "How to See a Wildflower. " Northeast (3:8) Wint 80, p. 30.
    "One Morning the Country Boy Loses a Stomach for Commuting. "
        Northeast (3:8) Wint 80, p. 30.
    "Preparing the Garden. " PoNow (29) 80, p. 9.

FEDERHEN, Craig
    "Sheep's Wool Is Left Hanging" (tr. of Elke Erb). Field (22)
        Spr 80, p. 11.
    "In the Picture" (tr. of Elke Erb). Field (22) Spr 80, p. 12.

FEDERMAN, Raymond
    "L'envers du loin. " Os (10) Spr 80, p. 14.

FEDO, David
    "Camping at Thunder Bay. " SoDakR (18:2) Sum 80, p. 11.
    "Carrots. " Comm (107:5) 14 Mr 80, p. 154.
    "Carrots. " SoDakR (18:2) Sum 80, p. 12.

FEDULLO, Mich
    "The Echoing Green. " WatT (1) Aut 80, p. 82.

"Travelling from Pennsylvania to Arizona. " WatT (1) Aut 80, p. 80.

FEELA, David J.
"Cut. " Outbr (4/5) Aut 79-Spr 80, p. 18.

FEENEY, Mary
"Cliff" (tr. of Jean Follain). Durak (5) 80, p. 55.
"Rejection of Peace" (tr. of Jean Follain). Durak (5) 80, p. 54.

FEENY, Thomas
"Los Rojas. " CapeR (16:1) Wint 80, p. 46.
"The Lover's Visit. " CapeR (16:1) Wint 80, p. 47.
"Rats and Traps. " CapeR (15:2) Sum 80, p. 46.

FEHLER, Gene
"A Response to Frost. " Outbr (4/5) Aut 79-Spr 80, p. 83.

FEINBERG, Anat
"The Panhandle of Galilee" (tr. of Moshe Dor). Stand (21:4) 80,
    p. 9.

FEIRSTEIN, Frederick
"Spring. " SouthwR (65:2) Spr 80, p. 196.

FELDMAN, Alan
"Mother. " Tendril (7/8) Spr-Sum 80, p. 34.
"The Personals. " Tendril (9) 80, p. 54.
"Snow in May. " Tendril (7/8) Spr-Sum 80, p. 36.
"Talking. " Tendril (7/8) Spr-Sum 80, p. 32.

FELDMAN, Irving
"The Bathers. " Poetry (137:1) O 80, pp. 1-5.
"The Drowned Man. " NewRep (183:23) 6 D 80, p. 28.
"Eberheim. " NewRep (182:9) 1 Mr 80, p. 26.
"The Eel" (tr. of Guillaume Apollinaire). ModernPS (10:1) 80,
    p. 1.
"Progress. " Poetry (137:1) O 80, p. 6.
"The Renegade. " Confr (20) Spr-Sum 80, p. 87.

FELDMAN, Ruth
"Alarm. " PoNow (26) 80, p. 23.
"At the Registry of Motor Vehicles. " PoNow (26) 80, p. 29.
"Blind Man's Buff. " PoNow (26) 80, p. 23.
"Dead Woman in Apulia" (tr. of Vittorio Bodini w. Brian Swann).
    AmerPoR (9:6) N-D 80, p. 7.
"Delos. " PoNow (26) 80, p. 23.
"The Eaves" (tr. of Rocco Scotellaro w. Brian Swann). PoNow
    (27) 80, p. 46.
"Moonmad. " PoNow (26) 80, p. 29.
"Now That I've Lost You" (tr. of Rocco Scotellaro w. Brian
    Swann). PoNow (28) 80, p. 46.
"Portici: April First" (tr. of Rocco Scotellaro w. Brian Swann).

PoNow (27) 80, p. 46.
"Sibling." Tendril (7/8) Spr-Sum 80, p. 38.
"Speaking of Butterflies." PoNow (26) 80, p. 23.
"Stazzema Series" (tr. of Vittorio Bodini w. Brian Swann).
     AmerPoR (9:6) N-D 80, p. 6.
"Study for the Sanfelice Woman in Jail" (tr. of Vittorio Bodini
     w. Brian Swann). AmerPoR (9:6) N-D 80, p. 7.
"Via de angelis" (tr. of Vittorio Bodini w. Brian Swann).
     AmerPoR (9:6) N-D 80, p. 8.

FELDSTEIN, Kate Mele
"Touring the Camps." Pan (21) 80, p. 10.

FELL, Mary
"Moonshee." Pan (21) 80, p. 57.

FEREN, David
"After Christmas." Mouth (2:4) My 80, p. 17.
"Neptune's Jest." KanQ (12:4) Aut 80, p. 46.

FERGUSON, Ken
"One of Them." PottPort (2) 80-81, p. 36.

FERICANO, Paul
"Period Piece." PoNow (29) 80, p. 10.

FERLINGHETTI, Lawrence
"At Kenneth Rexroth's." Ark (14) 80, p. 188.
"Seeing A Woman As In A Painting By Berthe Morisot." Os
     (10) Spr 80, p. 17.

FERNANDEZ, Daniel
"Trade Route to Bethlehem." ChrC (97:42) 24 D 80, p. 1265.

FERNANDEZ, Eva
"Singing." PoetryNW (21:1) Spr 80, p. 45.

FERRARELLI, Rina
"Going Back" (tr. of Salvatore Quasimodo). WebR (5:1) Wint 80,
     p. 16.
"I was seven when." PoNow (29) 80, p. 11.

FERRY, David
"La Farandola dei Fanciolli." NewRep (183:15) 11 O 80, p. 24.

FESSLER, Warren
"Net Gain." SoCaR (12:2) Spr 80, p. 46.

FICOWSKI, Jerzy
"Do Jeruszalaim." PortR (26) 80, p. 300.
"Wnie bowziecie Miriam z ulicy zima 1942." PortR (26) 80, p.
     302.

FIEDLER, Leslie
  "A Prayer Before Departure. " <u>Poetry</u> (137:2) N 80, p. 78.

FIELD, Greg
  "A Kansas City Song. " <u>Focus</u> (14:86) Ap 80, p. 34.
  "My Father Was Born in the Bell of a Horn. " <u>DacTerr</u> (17) 80,
    p. 29.
  "The Sax Man Is Waiting to Play. " <u>Focus</u> (14:86) Ap 80, p. 34.

FIELD, Matt
  "Cain. " <u>Pan</u> (21) 80, p. 49.

FIELDER, William
  "Duel" (tr. of Cemal Sureya w. Oscan Yalim and Dionis Coffin
    Riggs). <u>DenQ</u> (15:2) Sum 80, p. 87.
  "San" (tr. of Cemal Sureya w. Oscan Yalim and Dionis Coffin
    Riggs). <u>DenQ</u> (15:2) Sum 80, p. 86.

FIFER, Elizabeth
  "Couture Comes Alive. " <u>StoneC</u> (7:1) F 80, p. 13.

FIFER, Ken
  "After Fire. " <u>NewL</u> (46:4) Sum 80, p. 101.
  "Each Day Reminds Me of an Island. " <u>NewL</u> (46:4) Sum 80, p.
    100.
  "The Lehigh Gap. " <u>NewL</u> (46:4) Sum 80, p. 100.
  "No Strings. " <u>NewL</u> (46:4) Sum 80, p. 100.
  "Strong Waters. " <u>NewL</u> (46:4) Sum 80, p. 101.

FINALE, Frank
  "Aunt Jemima. " <u>PoNow</u> (29) 80, p. 10.
  "The Hornets. " <u>PoNow</u> (29) 80, p. 10.
  "Kenny. " <u>PoNow</u> (29) 80, p. 10.
  "Mother. " <u>PoNow</u> (29) 80, p. 10.

FINCH, Casey
  "Horses. " <u>QW</u> (11) Aut-Wint 80-81, p. 93.
  "Wolves. " <u>QW</u> (11) Aut-Wint 80-81, p. 92.

FINCH, Roger
  "Duo Concertante. " <u>BelPoJ</u> (31:1) Aut 80, p. 19.
  "The Jar. " <u>Poem</u> (40) N 80, p. 31.
  "Rude Awakening. " <u>Poem</u> (40) N 80, p. 32.
  "Verb Pattern 24B. " <u>WindO</u> (37) Aut-Wint 80, p. 16.

FINCKE, Gary
  "The Cat That Will Not Leave Me. " <u>SouthernPR</u> (20:1) Spr 80,
    p. 9.
  "The Defense of Jean Grenier. " <u>HiramPoR</u> (27) Aut-Wint 80, p.
    18.
  "Falling Asleep at the Wheel. " <u>HiramPoR</u> (27) Aut-Wint 80, p.
    19.
  "The Girl Who Breathes Through a Hole in Her Neck. " <u>Poetry</u>

(136:2) My 80, p. 92.
"Tennis Elbow. " StoneC (7:1) F 80, p. 31.
"Threadbare. " SouthernPR (20:1) Spr 80, p. 10.

FINEGAN, Elizabeth A.
"Her Again. " HiramPoR (28) Spr-Sum 80, p. 16.

FINERAN, Mary C.
"Night Train. " CarolQ (32:2) Spr-Sum 80, p. 34.

FINK, Jon-Stephen
"The Calm: Part I. " Bachy (17) Spr 80, pp. 34-42.

FINKEL, Donald
"Building a Head. " PoNow (28) 80, p. 6.
"The Frame Carver. " PoNow (27) 80, p. 4.
"Hitting the Road. " PoNow (28) 80, p. 6.
"Memorandum. " PoNow (28) 80, p. 6.
"Savoring the Salt. " PoNow (28) 80, p. 6.

FINKELSTEIN, Norman
"The Dolls. " Wind (38) 80, p. 27.

FINLEY, C. Stephen
"As in a Fable. " Wind (38) 80, p. 30.
"From the Flood. " CarolQ (32:1) Wint 80, p. 63.
"No One Disturbs Me. " Wind (38) 80, p. 29.
"One Returning from a Country of Rabbits. " Wind (38) 80, p. 28.
"Twilight, Below Bucks Elbow Mountain at Crozet School. " StoneC (7:1) F 80, p. 19.
"Under Vega. " SmF (11 /12) Spr-Aut 80, p. 41.

FINLEY, Michael
"The Audience. " KanQ (12:4) Aut 80, p. 45.
"The New Country. " StoneC (7:1) F 80, p. 36.

FINNE, Diderik
"Clouds and Moss. " KanQ (12:3) Sum 80, p. 122.
"The Phantom of the Opera. " KanQ (12:3) Sum 80, p. 122.

FIORE, Peter
"The Leader of the Deed Was a Woman. " PoNow (29) 80, p. 11.

FIRESTONE, Laya
"Crow, Straight Flier. " Focus (14:86) Ap 80, p. 31.
"Last Night" (for A. A.). Focus (14:86) Ap 80, p. 31.
"The Son She Loved" (for N. L.). Focus (14:86) Ap 80, p. 31.
"The Watch. " Focus (14:86) Ap 80, p. 31.

FISCHER, Aaron
"Elegy" (for my grandmother). Antaeus (39) Aut 80, p. 77.

FISHER, David
"A Child's Christmas Without Dylan Thomas. " NewL (47:1) Aut
    80, p. 17.
"Mycaenae. " NewL (47:1) Aut 80, p. 16.

FISHER, David L.
"Homer. " MassR (21:3) Aut 80, p. 502.

FISHER, Gary
"the espresso machine. " Kayak (55) Ja 81, p. 19.

FISHER, Harrison
"The Lives of a Bengal Lancer. " CreamCR (5:2) Spr 80, p. 72.
"Punk Nuns. " CarolQ (32:1) Wint 80, p. 90.

FISHMAN, Charles
"Leonardo. " HolCrit (17:1) F 80, p. 15.
"Skin Hunger" (for Anne-Ruth Baehr). StoneC (7:1) F 80, p. 30.
"Slowly Homeward. " SouthernPR (20:2) Aut 80, p. 27.
"This Is Where I Live. " Confr (20) Spr-Sum 80, p. 127.

FITE, L. C.
"Stein Song. " Poem (38) Mr 80, p. 48.

FITZGERALD, Gerald P.
"Waking in Traffic. " BosUJ (26:3) 80, p. 110.

FITZGERALD, Jeanne
"The Case for Love. " BelPoJ (31:1) Aut 80, p. 21.
"Catechism. " BelPoJ (31:1) Aut 80, p. 21.
"The Pine Stand. " BelPoJ (31:1) Aut 80, p. 22.
"Second Childhood. " BelPoJ (31:1) Aut 80, p. 23.

FITZGERALD, Lauren
"at 7:30. " Nimrod (24:1) Aut-Wint 80, p. 20.

FITZGERALD, Robert
from the Aeneid II: (3-56) (translation). NewYRB (27:1) 7 F 80,
    p. 24.
"The Storm" (tr. of Virgil). Poetry (136:1) Ap 80, p. 1.

FITZPATRICK, Martin J.
"Domino Men. " PikeF (3) Wint 80, p. 28.

FITZPATRICK, Vincent
"Blue Collar Guy. " Mouth (2:4) My 80, p. 41.
"The Boy Rimbaud. " Mouth (2:4) My 80, p. 10.
"Pershing Square. " Mouth (2:4) My 80, p. 24.

FLANAGAN, Robert
"Semi-Private Mirages. " CropD (1) Spr 80, p. 21.
"Trucker. " PoNow (28) 80, p. 43.
"Wire. " CropD (1) Spr 80, p. 20.

FLANDERS, Jane
"Afterlife. " PoNow (26) 80, p. 8.
"The Butter Road." Comm (107:5) 14 Mr 80, p. 154.
"Ice Age. " LitR (23:3) Spr 80, p. 395.
"In the Dark." LitR (23:3) Spr 80, p. 395.
"That Recent Invention, the Wheel. " Shen (31:1) 79, p. 92.

FLANNER, Hildegarde
"Card of Thanks: One More New Year's Eve. " Salm (50/51)
    Aut 80-Wint 81, p. 28.
"The Name. " Salm (50/51) Aut 80-Wint 81, p. 30.
"Phone Booth Song. " Salm (50/51) Aut 80-Wint 81, p. 29.

FLANTZ, Richard
"Lord of the World" (tr. of Be'eri Hazak). PortR (26) 80, p.
    209.

FLAVIN, Jack
"Bucolics: The First Frost. " MidwQ (21:4) Sum 80, p. 435.
"The Kirlian Effect. " MidwQ (21:4) Sum 80, p. 437.
"1932. " MidwQ (21:2) Wint 80, p. 259.
"Three Bucolics. " MidwQ (21:4) Sum 80, p. 438.

FLEMING, Deborah
"Gleann na locha. " HiramPoR (27) Aut-Wint 80, p. 20.

FLEMING, Gerald
"Let Go: Once. " WebR (5:2) Aut 80, p. 51.
"Widow. " PortR (26) 80, p. 429.

FLEMING, Ray
"At the Land's End. " MidwQ (21:4) Sum 80, p. 442.
"Basketball Jones. " LitR (23:3) Spr 80, p. 397.
"Good for the Soul. " LitR (23:3) Spr 80, p. 396.

FLETCHER, Joyce Fay
"Afro-American Daughter. " Obs (5:1/2) Spr-Sum 79, p. 120.
"The Winos. " Obs (5:1/2) Spr-Sum 79, p. 120.
"Winter. " Obs (5:1/2) Spr-Sum 79, p. 122.

FLEU, Richard
"Indoors. " StoneC (7:2) My 80, p. 11.

FLINT, Austin
"Chess" (tr. of Jacek Bierezin w. Grazyna Drabik). PoNow
    (28) 80, p. 45.
"From an Expedition Which Did Not Take Place" (tr. of Wislawa
    Szymborska w. Grazyna Drabik). CharR (6:2) Aut 80, p.
    52.
"Incantation" (tr. of Czeslaw Milosz w. Grazyna Drabik).
    PoetryE (3) 80, p. 56.
"Lot's Wife" (tr. of Wislawa Szymborska w. Grazyna Drabik).
    CharR (6:2) Aut 80, p. 51.

"Psalm" (tr. of Wislawa Szymborska w. Grazyna Drabik).
CharR (6:2) Aut 80, p. 53.

FLINT, Roland
"Heads of the Children. " DacTerr (17) 80, p. 31.
"A Poem Called George, Sometimes. " DacTerr (17) 80, p. 30.

FLOOK, Maria
"The Crippled Heart. " AntR (38:2) Spr 80, p. 173.
"Imaginary Photograph of Myself Holding a Pumpkin. " AmerPoR
(9:5) S-O 80, p. 12.
"Monsters. " AntR (38:2) Spr 80, p. 174.

FLORY, Sheldon
"New Year. " PoNow (29) 80, p. 22.
"Portents. " PoNow (29) 80, p. 22.
"Wyoming, Summers, 1940s. " PoNow (29) 80, p. 22.

FODOR, András
"Field Hospital, 1945" (tr. by Jascha Kessler). LitR (23:3) Spr
80, p. 346.
"Your Body's Bread" (tr. by Jascha Kessler). LitR (23:3) Spr
80, p. 347.

FOERSTER, Richard
"Passings. " Epoch (29:2) Wint 80, p. 126.

FOLEY, Kathy
"Alice Ordered Me to Throw Up" (w. Jim Brodey). Tele (16)
80, p. 69.
"For Chester Burnette" (w. Jim Brodey). Tele (16) 80, p. 70.
"Numb Skull" (w. Jim Brodey). Tele (16) 80, p. 69.

FOLEY, M. J.
"Epitaph to Adam, the Orang Utan Defunct in the Dublin Zoo. "
Poem (40) N 80, p. 49.
"An Gaisc'ioch. " Poem (40) N 80, pp. 44-48.
"Michelangelo's 'David.'" Poem (40) N 80, p. 50.

FOLKESTAD, Marilyn
"Hoodoos. " PoetryNW (21:3) Aut 80, p. 45.
"It's Called a Moving Sale. " PoetryNW (21:3) Aut 80, p. 47.

FOLLAIN, Jean
"Cliff" (tr. by Mary Feeney). Durak (5) 80, p. 55.
from Present Day: "The Machine" (tr. by David Gascoyne).
Stand (21:2) 80, p. 69.
from Present Day: "Separations" (tr. by David Gascoyne).
Stand (21:2) 80, p. 68.
from Present Day: 'Women With Dark Circles Round Their
Eyes" (tr. by David Gascoyne). Stand (21:2) 80, p. 69.
"Rejection of Peace" (tr. by Mary Feeney). Durak (5) 80, p. 54.

FORCHE, Carolyn
"As Children Together. " AmerPoR (9:2) Mr-Ap 80, p. 6.
"City Walk-Up, Winter 1969. " Pequod (11) 80, p. 88.
"The Colonel. " Pequod (11) 80, p. 92.
"Endurance. " AmerPoR (9:2) Mr-Ap 80, p. 7.
"Joseph. " Pequod (11) 80, p. 90.
"Return" (for Josephine Crum). AmerPoR (9:5) S-O 80, p. 10.
"Reunion. " Tendril (9) 80, p. 55.

FOREST, Leonard
"as in florence... " (tr. by H. Paratte). PottPort (2) 80-81, p.
    42.
"beckoning... " (tr. by H. Paratte). PottPort (2) 80-81, p. 47.

FORSTROM, Martha
"Crossing by Coney Island Ferry. " Wind (38) 80, p. 31.

FORT, Charles
"Coloratura. " Pan (21) 80, p. 28.
"Grandfather. " Pan (21) 80, p. 28.

FOSTER, John L.
"The Leiden Hymns XX" (translation). BelPoJ (31:2) Wint 80-81,
    p. 9.

FOSTER, Ruel E.
"A Late Encounter with Five Fillies. " Poem (40) N 80, p. 34.
"Uncle Elgin to the Dark Tower Came. " Poem (40) N 80, p.
    36.

FOWLER, Adrian
"Artemis. " PottPort (2) 80-81, p. 5.

FOWLIE, Wallace
"The Word's Misdeed" (tr. of Alain Bosquet). PortR (26) 80,
    p. 140.

FOX, Connie
"Lautremontlight. " Tele (16) 80, p. 21.

FOX, Mary F.
"Forever. " Tele (16) 80, p. 58.
"Lament. " Tele (16) 80, p. 58.

frá HAMRI, Porsteinn
"Gesturinn. " PortR (26) 80, p. 186.

FRANCIS, Pat-Therese
"First Snow. " Wind (36) 80, p. 15.
"The Urge to Travel. " Tendril (7/8) Spr-Sum 80, p. 39.

FRANCIS, Robert
"After the age of birds the age. " NewL (46:4) Sum 80, p. 47.

FRANK, Bernhard
"Japanese Cup Painting. " PikeF (3) Wint 80, p. 8.
"Oncoming Headlights. " PikeF (3) Wint 80, p. 10.
"3 Reflections on Spring Dust. " PikeF (3) Wint 80, p. 30.

FRANZONE, Lina B.
"Giraffa. " PortR (26) 80, p. 212.
"Petali di Stelle. " PortR (26) 80, p. 214.

FRASE, Brigitte
"Coming Home to Chicago and Leaving. " Prima (5) 79, p. 84.
"Homage to My Clown Master" (for Theodore Roethke). Prima
    (5) 79, p. 82.
"What It Depends On. " Prima (5) 79, p. 82.

FRASER, C. E.
"Phantom. " PottPort (2) 80-81, p. 41.

FRASER, Raymond
"Once I Saw. " PottPort (2) 80-81, p. 50.
"Salvation. " PottPort (2) 80-81, p. 36.
"When I Was Working. " PottPort (2) 80-81, p. 21.

FRATE, Frank
"Investigation of Her Grey Soar(w)ing. " Sam (98) 80, p. 54.
"Investigation of the Man Without. " Sam (92) 80, p. 29.

FRAZEE, Jim
"The Glass Dolphin. " AmerPoR (9:6) N-D 80, p. 47.
"The Glass Dolphin. " SouthernPR (20:1) Spr 80, p. 15.

FRAZIER, Hood
"Father, How I Love You. " PoetC (12:3) 80, p. 12.
"How to Make Magic. " PoetC (12:3) 80, p. 11.

FREEMAN, Gaail
"In the Afternoon. " LitR (23:3) Spr 80, p. 381.

FREIVALDS, Karlis
"Amos and the Devil. " Vis (3) 80.
"Jazz Town Night" (for Lucia). Vis (1) 79.
"A Presence in Things Being Born of Earth. " Vis (1) 79.
"Symphony. " Vis (1) 79.
"We Are Bringing Music to Irene's. " Vis (2) 80.
"When I Heard Them.... " Vis (1) 79.

FREMONT, Jean
"You Can't Take It With You" (tr. of Raymond Quinot). PortR
    (26) 80, p. 44.

FRENCH, A.
"One Day" (tr. of Jaroslav Seifert). PortR (26) 80, p. 69.

FRENCH, Gary
  "The Ghost. "   HangL (37) Spr 80, p. 7.

FRIAR, Kimon
  from Axion Esti: "Ode VI" (tr. of Odysseus Elýtis).   Durak (4)
    80, p. 45.
  "Belfry" (tr. of Yánnis Ritsos w. Kostas Myrsiades).   Durak (5)
    80, pp. 34-44.
  "The Burial That Never Happened" (to Táso) (tr. of Yánnis
    Kondos).   Durak (4) 80, p. 50.
  "Chamber Music" (tr. of Nícos Phocás).   PortR (26) 80, p. 162.
  "Chamber Music" (tr. of Yánnis Kondós).   PortR (26) 80, p. 163.
  "Cold Light" (tr. of Naná Isaia).   PortR (26) 80, p. 159.
  "The Diver" (tr. of Nikos Phocas).   PoNow (27) 80, p. 44.
  "Episode" (tr. of Násos Vayenás).   PortR (26) 80, p. 166.
  "The Five" (tr. of Yannis Ritsos w. Kostas Myrsiades).   BelPoJ
    (30:4) Sum 80, p. 39.
  "Gift of a Silver Poem" (tr. of Odysseus Elýtis).   Durak (4) 80,
    p. 44.
  "Irresolute" (tr. of Yannis Ritsos w. Kostas Myrsiades).   Field
    (22) Spr 80, p. 79.
  "The Journey" (tr. of Yannis Ritsos w. Kostas Myrsiades).
    Field (22) Spr 80, p. 78.
  Nine Poems (tr. of Miltos Sahtouris).   Kayak (54) S 80, pp. 5-9.
  "Remembrance" (tr. of Yánnis Rítsos).   PortR (26) 80, p. 157.
  "Sea Stroke" (tr. of Yannis Ritsos w. Kostas Myrsiades).   Field
    (22) Spr 80, p. 77.
  "Silent Agreement" (tr. of Yánnis Rítsos).   PortR (26) 80, p.
    155.
  "Small Confession" (tr. of Yánnis Rítsos).   PortR (26) 80, p.
    156.
  "This Darkness" (tr. of Yannis Ritsos w. Kostas Myrsiades).
    Field (22) Spr 80, p. 81.
  "The Triumph of Constant Loss" (to Andonis Fostieris) (tr. of
    Katerína Angeláki-Roóke).   PortR (26) 80, p. 165.
  Twelve poems (tr. of Yánnis Ritsos w. Kostas Myrsiades).
    Durak (4) 80, pp. 55-62.
  "Upside Down" (tr. of Yannis Kondos).   PoNow (26) 80, p. 46.
  "White" (tr. of Yannis Ritsos w. Kostas Myrsiades).   Field (22)
    Spr 80, p. 80.
  "The Women" (tr. of Jenny Mastoraki).   PoNow (28) 80, p. 46.

FRIDAY, Will
  "Jon's Song: A Poem in Memory of Jon Walz. "   Wind (37) 80,
    p. 14.

FRIEBERT, Stuart
  "Another One for Dad. "   SoCaR (13:1) Aut 80, p. 71.
  "Assault" (tr. of Miroslav Holub w. Dana Ha'bova').   MalR (55)
    Jl 80, p. 134.
  "At Home" (tr. of Miroslav Holub w. Dana Habova).   PoNow (27)
    80, p. 46.
  "Before There Were Wonder Drugs or On Serious Childhood Ill-

ness. " PoetryNW (21:1) Spr 80, p. 34.
"Death of a Sparrow" (tr. of Miroslav Holub w. Dana Habova).
OntR (12) Spr-Sum 80, p. 54.
"Elegy" (tr. of Bernd Jentzsch). Field (22) Spr 80, p. 15.
"Elsewhere (tr. of Miroslav Holub). Durak (4) 80, p. 9.
"Getting Snowed In" (tr. of Karl Krolow). CarlMis (18:2) Sum
80, p. 47.
"Goat Song. " PoNow (27) 80, p. 42.
"Gradually" (tr. of Karl Krolow). CutB (14) Spr /Sum 80, p. 55.
"Keys for an Unwritten Poem" (tr. of Giovanni Raboni w. Vinio
Rossi). CutB (14) Spr /Sum 80, p. 50.
"The Love of Life" (tr. of Karl Krolow). Durak (4) 80, p. 48.
"MaMa" (tr. of Miroslav Holub w. Dana Ha'bova'). MalR (55)
Jl 80, p. 133.
"Margaret Flinders a. k. a. Polly Flinders. " MinnR (NS 15) Aut
80, p. 18.
"The Minotaur's Thoughts on Poetry" (tr. of Miroslav Holub).
Durak (4) 80, p. 5.
"Mr. Cogito's Contribution to Mayerling's Tragedy" (tr. of
Zbigniew Herbert). PoNow (28) 80, p. 46.
"More on Kites" (for LJ). QW (11) Aut-Wint 80-81, p. 117.
"Museum Visit. " CentR (24:3) Sum 80, p. 306.
"My Father by the Sea. " QW (11) Aut-Wint 80-81, p. 116.
"On Being Perfect. " SoCaR (13:1) Aut 80, p. 71.
"On the Dog Angel" (tr. of Miroslav Holub w. Dana Hábová).
OntR (12) Spr-Sum 80, p. 55.
"On the Origin of Poor Digestion" (tr. of Miroslav Holub w.
Dana Habova). Durak (4) 80, p. 8.
"On the Origin of Six P. M. " (tr. of Miroslav Holub). Durak (4)
80, p. 6.
"On the Origin of a Festive Morning" (tr. of Miroslav Holub w.
Dana Ha'bova'). MalR (55) Jl 80, p. 136.
"Once the Food Goes. " Durak (5) 80, p. 10.
"One Time" (tr. of Giovanni Rossi w. Vinio Rossi). CutB (14)
Spr /Sum 80, p. 52.
"Schoolbooks" (tr. of Luis Suardiaz). CarlMis (18:2) Sum 80, p.
97.
"A Special Performance for Statues" (tr. of Miroslav Holub).
Field (23) Aut 80, p. 31.
"Time for Bed. " PoetryNW (21:1) Spr 80, p. 33.
"Together. " Durak (4) 80, p. 10.
"Tunisian Excursion. " PoNow (27) 80, p. 31.
"Two Men" (tr. of Bernd Jentzsch). Field (22) Spr 80, p. 15.
"We Steal Away" (tr. of Karl Krolow). Durak (4) 80, p. 49.
"We will put on one of our heads, " (tr. of Miroslav Holub w.
Dana Ha'bova'). MalR (55) Jl 80, p. 131.
"Woman's Song" (tr. of Giovanni Raboni w. Vinio Rossi). CutB
(14) Spr /Sum 80, p. 51.
"Young King Cole. " Durak (5) 80, p. 11.

FRIEDMAN, Dorothy
"The Buccaneer. " HangL (38) Aut 80, p. 19.

FRIEDMAN, Jeff
'The Mannikin. " Poetry (136:6) S 80, p. 339.
"The Record-Breaking Heat Wave. " Poetry (136:6) S 80, p. 335.

FRIEDMANN, Elizabeth
"Shooting the cone. " Tele (16) 80, p. 84.

FRIEL, James P.
"The Divinity of Birds. " KanQ (12:1) Wint 80, p. 56.
"Revolutionary. " ChrC (97:3) 23 Ja 80, p. 63.

FRIEND, Robert
"The monasteries lift gold domes" (tr. of Yocheved Bat-Miriam).
PortR (26) 80, p. 201.

FRIMAN, Alice
"The Reckoning. " GeoR (34:2) Sum 80, p. 331.

FRINGELI, Dieter
"die hoffnungen. " PortR (26) 80, p. 384.

FROSCH, Thomas
"Flounder. " BelPoJ (31:2) Wint 80-81, p. 22.

FROST, Carol
"Aubade of an Early Homo Sapiens. " CharR (6:1) Spr 80, p. 12.
"Autumn Apology. " Pequod (11) 80, p. 66.
"Birthday. " NoAmR (265:4) D 80, p. 58.
"The Cemetery Is Empty. " Bits (11) 80.
"Death in Winter. " AmerPoR (9:3) My-Je 80, p. 10.
"The Fairy Tale. " AmerPoR (9:3) My-Je 80, p. 10.
"The Fairy Tale. " CharR (6:1) Spr 80, p. 12.
"Getting It Right. " MassR (21:2) Sum 80, p. 254.
"The Homemade Piano. " Pequod (11) 80, p. 65.

FROST, Kenneth
"Fat. " Confr (20) Spr-Sum 80, p. 155.

FROST, Richard
"The Horror Show. " PoNow (28) 80, p. 13.

FROST, Robert
"happiness. " Sam (86) 79, p. 31.

FROUDE, J. A.
"Rochester Assizes. " NewL (47:1) Aut 80, p. 12.

FRUMKIN, Gene
"The Kid Who Drew Horses. " CharR (6:2) Aut 80, p. 38.
"The Metaphysics of Paper. " CharR (6:2) Aut 80, p. 37.
"The Trouble With Lying. " CharR (6:2) Aut 80, p. 37.

FRY, Pauline J.
"Looking East. " Wind (36) 80, p. 10.

FUERTES, Gloria
"The Day When Peace Takes Hold" (tr. by Philip Levine and
Ada Long). PoetryE (1) 80, p. 87.
"Farmer" (tr. by Philip Levine and Ada Long). PoetryE (1) 80,
p. 86.
"Here I Am Exposed Like Everybody" (tr. by Philip Levine and
Ada Long). PoetryE (1) 80, p. 84.
"I Think Table and Say Chair" (tr. by L. H. Laurence and E.
G. Laurence). CutB (14) Spr/Sum 80, p. 107.
"My Neighbor" (tr. by Dorothy Scott Loos). PoNow (26) 80, p.
45.
"Prayer" (tr. by Philip Levine and Ada Long). PoetryE (1) 80,
p. 82.
"You'll Get Yours" (tr. by Philip Levine and Ada Long).
PoetryE (1) 80, p. 85.

FUKAYABU, Kiowara no
"Bedlam Heart" (tr. by Graeme Wilson). DenQ (15:3) Aut 80,
p. 81.

FULKER, Tina
"Alone. " Vis (3) 80.
"Daddy. " Vis (1) 79.
"Decree-Nisi. " Vis (1) 79.
"Drive Home from the Country. " Vis (3) 80.
"Green. " Vis (3) 80.
"I Want You. " Vis (2) 80.
"Isolation. " Vis (4) 80.
"Mother. " Vis (1) 79.
"Rape. " Vis (4) 80.
"Song for No Singer. " Vis (1) 79.
"Sunday. " Vis (3) 80.
"Take a Slow Dance. " Vis (4) 80.
"Towards the End. " Vis (2) 80.

FULLER, William
"Corrective Portraiture. " Kayak (53) My 80, p. 59. found
poem.
"Death by Drowning. " Poem (39) Jl 80, p. 6.
"Memories Stronger than Whiskey. " HiramPoR (28) Spr-Sum 80,
p. 17.
"The Old Princess Byelokonski Speaks to Sartre in Paris. "
PraS (54:3) Aut 80, p. 49.
"Outposts. " Wind (36) 80, p. 17.
"Sun Spots. " Poem (39) Jl 80, p. 5.

FULTON, Alice
"Bad Actor. " Aspen (10) Wint 80, p. 32.
"Diminuendo. " Aspen (10) Wint 80, p. 31.

FULTON, Robin
"Beside Her Desk Is the Desk" (tr. of Kjell Espmark). PortR
(26) 80, p. 365.

"Fable" (tr. of Östen Sjöstrand). PortR (26) 80, p. 373.
"It's All Discretion in the Isolation Ward" (tr. of Kjell Esp-
   mark). PortR (26) 80, p. 367.
"My loneliness" (tr. of Gunnar Harding). PortR (26) 80, p.
   359.
"Who stops his hands swimming?" (tr. of Gunnar Harding).
   PortR (26) 80, p. 357.

FUQUA, Carolyn Wilford
"In the Dentist's Chair. " Wind (37) 80, p. 10.
"Sweet Peas. " Wind (37) 80, p. 4.

FURNESS, R. S.
"Night" (tr. of Georg Trakl w. David McDuff and Jon Silkin).
   Stand (21:2) 80, p. 19.

FYMAN, Cliff
"Guided. " Tele (16) 80, p. 74.
"Philippine Feds. " Tele (16) 80, p. 75.

GABOUDIKIAN, Silva
"Far Away from Armenia: To a Foreigner. " PortR (26) 80, p.
   20.

GADOL, Charles
"Walks. " StoneC (7:3) D 80, p. 22.

GAGE, Deborah Ann
"K. " SoCaR (12:2) Spr 80, p. 15.

GAGNON, Madeleine
"Matrie" (à Jean Antonin Billard). Os (11) 80, pp. 3-11.

GAIK, Frank
"Rich Radice, a Chicago Kid Who Visited Each Summer. "
   CreamCR (5:1) Wint 79, p. 107.

GAIL, Hermann
"Auch ich könnte mir Benzin. " PortR (26) 80, p. 25.
"Ein Zwerg tänzelt auf der Folterbank. " PortR (26) 80, p. 28.
"Wein. " PortR (26) 80, p. 26.

GALE, Susan
"If They'd Let Me. " Sam (102) 80, p. 65.

GALLAGHER, Tess
"Bird-Window-Flying. " Tendril (9) 80, p. 56.
"Crepes Flambeau. " OP (29) Spr 80, p. 40.
"Four Dancers at an Irish Wedding. " BaratR (8:1) Sum 80, p.
   55.
"Harmless Streets. " BaratR (8:1) Sum 80, p. 53.
"High Octane Near Mountain Grove (1970). " MidwQ (21:3) Spr
   80, p. 348.

"Kisses with Good Threats. " OP (29) Spr 80, p. 42.
"My Mother Remembers That She Was Beautiful. " BaratR (8:1)
    Sum 80, p. 52.
"Second Sleep. " OP (29) Spr 80, p. 36.
"The Shirts. " OP (29) Spr 80, p. 38.
"Tableau Vivant. " NewYorker (56:38) 10 N 80, p. 58.
"Willingly. " Atl (246:4) O 80, p. 70.
"Woman-Enough. " StoneC (7:3) D 80, p. 71.

GALT, Tom
"Man and Dog. " StoneC (7:1) F 80, p. 29.

GALVIN, Brendan
"Edge. " Ascent (5:3) 80, p. 39.
"A Few Words from the Weeds. " Ascent (5:2) 80, p. 49.
"Insomniad. " GeoR (34:1) Spr 80, p. 81.
"Just in Case You're Wondering Who You Are. " Ascent (5:2) 80,
    p. 48.
"The Old Trip by Dream Train. " Tendril (9) 80, p. 57.
"Saying Her Name. " GeoR (34:3) Aut 80, p. 510.
"Shoveling Out. " Ascent (5:2) 80, p. 47.

GALVIN, James
"As If. " WatT (1) Aut 80, p. 10.
"Cache la Poudre. " Antaeus (36) Wint 80, p. 81.
"Hermits. " WatT (1) Aut 80, p. 8.
"Navigation. " Antaeus (36) Wint 80, p. 83.
"Not Lost but Gone. " ParisR (78) Sum 80, p. 125.
"Old Men on the Courthouse Lawn, Murray, Kentucky. " Antaeus
    (39) Aut 80, p. 71.
"Sadness. " ParisR (78) Sum 80, p. 123.
"To See the Stars in Daylight. " Field (23) Aut 80, p. 35.

GALVIN, Martin
"Home Remedies. " SmPd (49) Spr 80, p. 22.
"An Irish Dinner. " Comm (107:5) 14 Mr 80, p. 154.
"Legacy. " CapeR (15:2) Sum 80, p. 32.

GANTZ, Jeffrey
"Anniversary" (tr. of Eugenio Montale). StoneC (7:1) F 80, p.
    5.
"Berlinerblau. " StoneC (7:3) D 80, p. 7.
"Ezekiel Saw the Wheel" (tr. of Eugenio Montale). StoneC (7:1)
    F 80, p. 7.
"We Gather Together. " StoneC (7:3) D 80, p. 7.

GARDNER, Geoffrey
"Shutting a Book in the Woods. " Ark (14) 80, p. 189.

GARDNER, Sandra
"Milk Tooth. " Prima (5) 79, p. 10.

GARDNER, Stephen
"The Carpenter's Real Anguish. " HolCrit (17:3) Je 80, p. 12.

GARDNER, Virginia
"The Slaughter. "   Shen (31:2) 80, p. 22.

GARENTS, Vahakn
"My Swallow. "   PortR (26) 80, p. 17.

GARMHAUSEN, Jim
"Big Scene. " Tele (16) 80, p. 35.
"Karma. " Tele (16) 80, p. 35.

GARMON, John
"A Husband All Day. "   Comm (107:11) 6 Je 80, p. 340.

GARRISON, David
"Adolescence" (tr. of Vicente Aleixandre).   DenQ (15:3) Aut 80,
    p. 16.
"At Last" (tr. of Vicente Aleixandre).   DenQ (15:3) Aut 80, p.
    14.
"Face Behind the Glass (The Old Man's Gaze)" (tr. of Vicente
    Aleixandre).   DenQ (15:3) Aut 80, p. 17.

GARRISON, Joseph
"Cheering the Garden. "   PoetryNW (21:1) Spr 80, p. 42.

GARTH, Douglas
"The Rampart. "   BelPoJ (31:1) Aut 80, p. 31.

GARTON, Victoria
"Prairie Hallelujah. "   SoDakR (18:3) Aut 80, p. 12.
"The Taunt. "   SoDakR (18:3) Aut 80, p. 11.
"Victim of Sadism Receives Letters. "   Focus (14:86) Ap 80, p.
    16.
"With Intimacy the Myth. "   ConcPo (13:2) Aut 80, p. 40.

GASCOYNE, David
from Present Day: "The Machine" (tr. of Jean Follain).   Stand
    (21:2) 80, p. 69.
from Present Day: "Separations" (tr. of Jean Follain).   Stand
    (21:2) 80, p. 68.
from Present Day: "Women With Dark Circles Round Their
    Eyes" (tr. of Jean Follain).   Stand (21:2) 80, p. 69.

GASPER, Jillane Allison
"Taco Stud. "   PoNow (29) 80, p. 11.

GASS, Fred
"Mth 101 McGuffy Auditorium Dec. 21, 7:30 P. M. "   HiramPoR
    (27) Aut-Wint 80, p. 22.
"News Photo of Rector With Varsity Athletes. "   HiramPoR (27)
    Aut-Wint 80, p. 21.

GASS, William H.
"On Being Photographed. "   WebR (5:2) Aut 80, p. 16.

GATTI-TAYLOR, Marisa
"Letter to My Father" (tr. of Eros Alesi w. Jan Pallister).
EnPas (11) 80, pp. 4-10.

GAUER, Jim
"The Visit. " Poetry (136:3) Je 80, p. 154.
"What the Fire Conceals from Itself" (for Gaston Bachelard).
Poetry (136:3) Je 80, p. 152.

GAULDIN, Sara Saper
"Old Argonaut. " SouthwR (65:3) Sum 80, p. 290.

GAVRONSKY, Serge
"We belong to the movement within us. " NewOR (7:2) 80, p.
150.

GEBHARD, Christine
"Boggle. " AntR (38:3) Sum 80, p. 338.

GEIER, Joan Austin
"The Rat. " HiramPoR (28) Spr-Sum 80, p. 18.

GENEGA, Paul
"Ragweed. " KanQ (12:2) Spr 80, p. 16.

GENSLER, Kinereth
"Learning, With Archeologists. " Ploughs (6:2) 80, p. 100.

GENTILE, Karlene
"Night Fishing. " Focus (14:86) Ap 80, p. 33.
"Wooing. " Focus (14:86) Ap 80, p. 33.

GENTLEMAN, Dorothy Corbett
"Light Up the Screen. " Wind (37) 80, p. 21.

GEORGE, Anne
"Emily Your Name. " EngJ (69:5) My 80, p. 47.

GEORGE, Donna
"The Flirt. " HangL (38) Aut 80, p. 66.
"A Happily Ever After. " HangL (38) Aut 80, p. 65.

GEORGE, Emery
"Brazilian Rain Forest" (tr. of Gyula Illyes). PoNow (28) 80,
p. 46.
"Childhood" (for Dezso Baroti) (tr. of Miklos Radnoti). QW
(10) Wint-Spr 80, p. 77.
"Dusk on the Bank and the Tugboat Cries" (tr. of Miklos Rad-
noti). PoetryE (1) 80, p. 74.
"Evening in the Garden" (tr. of Miklos Radnoti). Columbia (4)
Spr-Sum 80, p. 28.
"Forgiveness" (tr. of Miklós Radnóti). PartR (47:4) 80, p. 609.
"Goats" (tr. of Miklos Radnoti). Columbia (4) Spr-Sum 80, p.

31.
"Into a Contemporary's Passport" (for the Szeged Youth Arts
College, for the community of educators, for my friends)
(tr. of Miklos Radnoti). QW (10) Wint-Spr 80, p. 78.
"May Truth" (tr. of Miklós Radnóti). PartR (47:4) 80, p. 609.
"Punctual Poem About Dusk" (tr. of Miklos Radnoti). Columbia
(4) Spr-Sum 80, p. 29.
"Salute the Day!" (tr. of Emery George). PoetryE (1) 80, p.
75.
"Variation on Sadness" (tr. of Miklós Radnóti). PartR (47:4) 80,
p. 608.

GEORGE, Stefan
"The Talking Head" (tr. by Peter Viereck). PoNow (28) 80, p.
44.

GEORGE, Tom
"Carol Champion. " CreamCR (5:2) Spr 80, p. 47.

GERACI, Francine
"You'd Hardly Think So. " MalR (54) Ap 80, p. 98.

GERARD, Jim
"Night of the Dreaming Moon. " Poem (39) Jl 80, p. 18.

GERBER, Dan
"Adagios. " PoNow (28) 80, p. 16.
"Below Emigrant. " PoNow (28) 80, p. 16.
Eight poems. PoNow (28) 80, pp. 16-23.
"Nights of Love. " PoNow (28) 80, p. 16.

GERBERICK, Marlene Ekola
"The Farm Sauna. " CarlMis (18:2) Sum 80, p. 174.

GERGELY, Agnes
"Nászéjszaka. " PortR (26) 80, p. 172.

GERMANACOS, N. C.
Fourteen poems. Bound (8:3) Spr 80, pp. 208-213.

GERNES, Sonia
"The Priest and the Glass Eye. " GRR (11:1) 80, p. 39.

GERRY, David
"Twig's Break" (for Mark). BelPoJ (30:4) Sum 80, p. 2.

GHAI, Gail
"Night Vision. " MalR (54) Ap 80, p. 42.
"Six Divine Circles. " MalR (54) Ap 80, p. 40.
"Somewhere in the Story. " MalR (54) Ap 80, p. 43.
"This Manner of Flattery. " MalR (54) Ap 80, p. 41.

GHISELIN, Brewster
"Apocalypse. " Poetry (135:6) Mr 80, p. 327.

"Equinox. " Poetry (135:6) Mr 80, p. 325.

GIANOLI, Paul
    "Midwestern Man. " Focus (14:86) Ap 80, p. 22.
    "Woman of Snow. " Focus (14:86) Ap 80, p. 22.

GIBB, Robert
    "Autumn on Isle Au Haut. " MissouriR (3:3) Sum 80, p. 20.
    "The Hunter Gracchus. " SmF (11/12) Spr-Aut 80, p. 49.
    "In This Syndrome. " WindO (37) Aut-Wint 80, p. 7.
    "The Last Photograph. " HiramPoR (27) Aut-Wint 80, p. 25.
    "The Long-Eared Owl. " EnPas (11) 80, p. 31.
    "The Objects of Desire. " HiramPoR (27) Aut-Wint 80, p. 23.
    "The Runner. " Wind (36) 80, p. 19.
    "Running Before the Storm. " WindO (37) Aut-Wint 80, p. 8.
    "Running the Autumn to Ground. " EnPas (11) 80, p. 32.
    "Ships in Ice Off Ten Pound Island, Glouster. " Wind (36) 80,
        p. 18.
    "The Spider. " WindO (37) Aut-Wint 80, p. 9.
    "Walking on the Pond. " NewL (47:1) Aut 80, p. 107.

GIBBONS, Reginald
    from Artifacts of an Earlier Self: "The Dream. " OntR (12)
        Spr-Sum 80, p. 27.
    "At Noon. " ParisR (77) Wint-Spr 80, p. 45.
    "Breath. " AmerPoR (9:6) N-D 80, p. 33.
    "The Cedar River" (for Mark Haverland). ParisR (77) Wint-Spr
        80, p. 44.
    "Michael's Room. " Hudson (33:2) Sum 80, p. 250.
    "The Ruined Motel. " AmerPoR (9:6) N-D 80, p. 33.
    "We Say. " AmerPoR (9:6) N-D 80, p. 33.

GIBBS, Barbara
    "The Lawnmower. " NewYorker (56:12) 12 My 80, p. 46.

GIBSON, Becky Gould
    "Denial. " Poem (40) N 80, p. 42.
    "Expecting. " Poem (40) N 80, p. 38.
    "Man in Satin. " Poem (40) N 80, p. 40.
    "November Sonnet. " Poem (40) N 80, p. 43.

GIBSON, Grace
    "From the Bottom of the Gorge. " CapeR (16:1) Wint 80, p. 1.

GIBSON, John R.
    "Anniversary. " Mouth (2:5) O 80, p. 10.
    "It's All Done With Mirrors. " Mouth (2:5) O 80, p. 11.
    "Sunday Afternoon. " Mouth (2:5) O 80, p. 12.

GIBSON, Keiko Matsui
    "The Self Approaches Zero" (tr. by Morgan Gibson). Ark (14)
        80, p. 191.

GIBSON, Margaret
"The Inheritance. " Poetry (137:1) O 80, p. 9.
"Journey. " MinnR (NS 15) Aut 80, p. 27.
"Long Walks in the Afternoon. " MichQR (19:1) Wint 80, p. 91.

GIBSON, Morgan
"The Self Approaches Zero" (tr. of Keiko Matsui Gibson). Ark
    (14) 80, p. 191.
"Slowly Becoming Chinese" (for Kenneth Rexroth and Carol
    Tinker). Ark (14) 80, p. 197.
"Staying in the Brook. " Ark (14) 80, p. 193.
"Waiting for Lao Tzu. " Ark (14) 80, p. 195.

GIDLOW, Elsa
"The Common Root: Concerning Goats, Bees, Man--. " Ark
    (14) 80, pp. 198-203.

GIFFORD, Peggy E.
"Summer Dance--Shaker Heights, 1965. " AntR (38:1) Wint 80,
    p. 55.

GILBERT, Celia
"The Constellation. " Hudson (33:4) Wint 80, p. 556.
"The Empire of the Senses. " Hudson (33:4) Wint 80, p. 555.
"Eurydice's Song. " ParisR (77) Wint-Spr 80, p. 38.
"In Memoriam: J. B. " Hudson (33:4) Wint 80, p. 557.
"Journey. " Poetry (136:2) My 80, p. 73.
"Nature. " Ploughs (6:2) 80, p. 82.
"Portrait of My Mother on Her Wedding Day. " Ploughs (6:2) 80,
    p. 84.
"The Still Lifes of Giorgio Morandi. " GeoR (34:3) Aut 80, p.
    592.

GILBERT, Chris
"Any Good Throat. " VirQR (56:3) Sum 80, p. 503.
"Marking Time" (for freda robertson). BlackALF (14:3) Aut 80,
    p. 124.
"Saxophone. " VirQR (56:3) Sum 80, p. 502.

GILBERT, El
from The Book of Nashville: "The Noise of Death. " BlackALF
    (14:4) Wint 80, p. 176.

GILBERT, Jack
"Being There. " AmerPoR (9:4) Jl-Ag 80, p. 48.
"Elephant Hunt in Guadalajara. " AmerPoR (9:4) Jl-Ag 80, p. 48.
"The Lives of Famous Men. " AmerPoR (9:4) Jl-Ag 80, p. 48.
"More Than Fifty. " AmerPoR (9:4) Jl-Ag 80, p. 48.
"Pewter. " AmerPoR (9:4) Jl-Ag 80, p. 48.
"Remembering My Wife. " AmerPoR (9:4) Jl-Ag 80, p. 48.

GILBERT, Sandra M.
"Accident. " Field (23) Aut 80, p. 12.

"Bad News. " PoNow (26) 80, p. 24.
"In the Fourth World. " PoNow (26) 80, p. 24.
"Jackson Heights. " Thrpny (2) Sum 80, p. 23.
"The Last Poem About the Snow Queen. " Field (23) Aut 80, p. 10.
"Low Tide. " PoetryNW (21:1) Spr 80, p. 9.
"The Mothers at Seventy. " Poetry (136:4) Jl 80, p. 196.
"My Grandmother in Paris. " Poetry (135:4) Ja 80, p. 204.
"New Year's Eve. " PoetryNW (21:1) Spr 80, p. 8.
"The Parachutist's Wife" (for Mark Linenthal and Frances Taffer). Field (23) Aut 80, p. 16.
"Pinocchio. " Field (23) Aut 80, p. 13.
"The Return of the Muse. " MassR (21:2) Sum 80, p. 291.
"Rissem. " Poetry (136:4) Jl 80, p. 191.
"The Summer Kitchen. " MassR (21:2) Sum 80, p. 289.
"Thinking About an Old Friend. " Poetry (136:4) Jl 80, p. 193.
"To a Man Who Advises Maturity. " Poetry (136:4) Jl 80, p. 195.
"Traffic Jam. " PoNow (26) 80, p. 24.

GILBOA, Amir
    "Cannons thundered far away" (tr. by Shirley Kaufman). Stand (21:4) 80, p. 8.
    Twelve poems (tr. by Jon Silkin, Natan Zach and Bat-Sheva Sheriff). Stand (21:4) 80, p. 4.

GILCHRIST, Ellen
    "The Calling. " PoNow (29) 80, p. 22.
    "The Land Surveyor's Daughter. " PoNow (29) 80, p. 22.
    "Summer. " CalQ (16/17) 80, p. 98.
    "The Widow Recalls Diving the Wall of Cayman. " CalQ (16/17) 80, p. 97.

GILDNER, Gary
    "All Hallows Eve in Kansas. " Shen (31:2) 80, p. 94.
    "Blue Like the Heavens. " NewL (46:3) Spr 80, p. 86.
    "Bourbon on a Sunday Afternoon. " PoNow (26) 80, p. 4.
    "Cinders. " Ark (14) 80, p. 204.
    "For My Father. " DacTerr (17) 80, p. 32.
    "Jabón. " Poetry (137:3) D 80, p. 146.
    "One Day in the Neighborhood. " PoNow (28) 80, p. 37.
    "Today They Are Roasting Rocky Norse. " Tendril (9) 80, p. 59.
    "Victory, Victory. " PoNow (27) 80, p. 14.

GILL, Arlen
    "Hotel Notre-Dame" (tr. of Blaise Cendrars w. Perry Oldham). WebR (5:1) Wint 80, p. 32.
    "Strangers' Inn" (tr. of Blaise Cendrars w. Perry Oldham). WebR (5:1) Wint 80, p. 36.

GILL, Evelyn P.
    "Running Girl Courts Blues. " GRR (11:1) 80, p. 44.
    "Today. " GRR (11:1) 80, p. 45.

GILL, John
"9/10/79. " HangL (38) Aut 80, p. 21.
"that's entertainment. " HangL (38) Aut 80, p. 20.

GIMELSON, Deborah
"Grandfather's Passage. " Nat (231:9) 27 S 80, p. 287.

GINSBERG, Allen
"I Lost You" (tr. of Angkarn Kalyanapongs). PortR (26) 80, p.
    400.

GISONNY, Anne
"The Woman Who Wears Perfume. " Pan (21) 80, p. 7.

GITLIN, Todd
"The Failure of Muscles to Form a Mask. " YaleR (70:1) Aut
    80, p. 104.

GIVEN, Gregory
"A Condition. " PartR (47:2) 80, p. 221.

GLANCY, Diane
from Amiel Haymaker: "Amiel. " Nimrod (24:1) Aut-Wint 80,
    p. 36.

GLANG, Gabriele
"Gift. " CropD (1) Spr 80, p. 12.
"On Changing One's Mind" (for Erin). CropD (1) Spr 80, p. 13.
"The Princess and the Pea. " CropD (1) Spr 80, p. 13.

GLASER, Elton
"Asters in October. " PoetryNW (21:1) Spr 80, p. 17.
"Delta Blues. " PoNow (29) 80, p. 23.
"Farmlife in Ohio. " PoNow (29) 80, p. 23.
"Hymn to the Left Hand. " CutB (15) Aut/Wint 80, p. 62.
"The Intangibles. " PoetryNW (21:1) Spr 80, p. 17.
"Interim Report. " PoetryNW (21:1) Spr 80, p. 16.
"Navigation by Night. " PoNow (29) 80, p. 23.
Peripheral Vision. Bits (Chapbook) 80. Entire issue.
"Vows. " ChiR (32:1) Sum 80, p. 100.
"Winter's Tale. " PoetryNW (21:1) Spr 80, p. 16.

GLASER, Michael S.
"Amira. " Poem (39) Jl 80, p. 54.

GLASS, Judith
"Love Poems. " Tele (16) 80, p. 90.

GLASS, Malcolm
"Acorn. " BelPoJ (31:2) Wint 80-81, p. 2.
"The Child. " BelPoJ (31:2) Wint 80-81, p. 4.
"Clean and Press. " PoetryNW (21:2) Sum 80, p. 41.
"Gar. " CharR (6:1) Spr 80, p. 22.

"The Hawk. " Im (6:2) 80, p. 10.
"Paying Attention. " BelPoJ (31:2) Wint 80-81, p. 3.
"Plague. " NewL (46:3) Spr 80, p. 50.
"Staying Ahead. " NewL (46:3) Spr 80, p. 52.
"Winter. " Im (6:2) 80, p. 10.

GLASSER, Jane Ellen
"The Blanket. " Hudson (33:3) Aut 80, p. 407.
"First Snow. " Hudson (33:3) Aut 80, p. 408.

GLAZE, Andrew
"The Fanatical You. " PoNow (26) 80, p. 12.

GLAZIER, Lyle
from Pilgrim from New England: "The guide Damyata. " Mouth
    (2:4) My 80, p. 40.

GLEASON, Madeline
"Why?" Ark (14) 80, p. 206.

GLEN, Emilie
"Cry. " Tele (16) 80, p. 110.
"Flower Kitchen. " Tele (16) 80, p. 110.

GLENN, Barbara
"Eurydice in Hell. " SouthernR (16:2) Spr 80, p. 419.
"On Reading the Old Captivity Narratives" (for J. L. W.).
    SouthernR (16:2) Spr 80, p. 418.

GLOVER, Jon
"The Painter and Science. " Stand (21:3) 80, p. 67.

GLOWNEY, John
"The Prized Horse. " BelPoJ (30:4) Sum 80, p. 33.

GLÜCK, Louise
"Consent. " Antaeus (37) Spr 80, p. 93.
"Dedication to Hunger. " Antaeus (37) Spr 80, pp. 94-98.
"First Goodbye. " Salm (50/51) Aut 80-Wint 81, p. 23.
"Hawk's Shadow. " Salm (50/51) Aut 80-Wint 81, p. 24.
"Lamentations. " Tendril (9) 80, p. 63.
"The Lincoln Relics. " Antaeus (37) Spr 80, p. 108.
"Night Piece. " Antaeus (37) Spr 80, p. 99.
"Palais des Arts. " Antaeus (37) Spr 80, p. 88.
"Porcelain Bowl. " Antaeus (37) Spr 80, p. 92.
"Tango. " Antaeus (37) Spr 80, p. 89.
"World Breaking Apart. " WatT (1) Aut 80, p. 1.

GOAD, Craig M.
"Making Way. " CapeR (16:1) Wint 80, p. 45.

GOEDICKE, Patricia
"The Disappearance. " Ascent (6:1) 80, p. 44.

"Etude. " NewL (46:4) Sum 80, p. 70.
"Illness as Metaphor" (for Susan Sontag). Harp (260:1556) Ja 80, p. 79.
"The Nine Tribes. " CharR (6:1) Spr 80, p. 16.
"One More Time. " AmerPoR (9:2) Mr-Ap 80, p. 28.
"This Moment. " NewL (47:1) Aut 80, p. 28.
"Well Furnished. " NewL (47:1) Aut 80, p. 29.

GÖRGEY, Gábor
"Fragments of Ten Poems" (tr. by Jascha Kessler). CutB (14) Spr/Sum 80, p. 53.

GOFF, Susan
"Mountain Springs. " CropD (1) Spr 80, p. 19.
"To the Mouse Under My Dryer. " CropD (1) Spr 80, p. 19.

GOLD, Herman
"Brothers. " WormR (77) 80, p. 29.
"Every Morning. " WormR (77) 80, p. 29.
"Heywood Broun. " WormR (77) 80, p. 29.
"Quandry. " WormR (77) 80, p. 29.
"Therapy. " WormR (77) 80, p. 29.

GOLDBARTH, Albert
"Balances. " CarolQ (32:3) Aut 80, p. 68.
"Closer. " Poetry (136:3) Je 80, p. 129.
"The Common Wall. " PraS (54:2) Sum 80, p. 17.
"Escapees. " Iowa (11:1) Wint 80, p. 120.
"For Hannah Spivack. " Bits (11) 80.
"Goat/Cat/Dog. " Poetry (136:3) Je 80, p. 127.
"Henry David's Song for the Dead. " PoetryNW (21:4) Wint 80-81, p. 29.
"His Daughter. " CarolQ (32:3) Aut 80, p. 71.
"In Delicate Times We Delicately Choose for Connotation. " OhioR (24) 80, p. 42.
"In 1865 she won second prize in the Bread Division at the local cattle show. " AmerPoR (9:2) Mr-Ap 80, p. 4.
"Inventing Home. " PraS (54:2) Sum 80, p. 16.
"J. W. " PoetryNW (21:4) Wint 80-81, p. 27.
"Keeping. " CutB (15) Aut/Wint 80, p. 49.
"Library Card in an Old Name. " NewRep (183:19) 8 N 80, p. 28.
"Limping Poem (1975). " MidwQ (21:3) Spr 80, p. 350.
"Lullabye: Don't See, Don't Know. " CharR (6:2) Aut 80, p. 14.
"... Marsilio Ficino. " CharR (6:2) Aut 80, p. 13.
"Matters. " BaratR (8:1) Sum 80, p. 18.
"The Musics. " NoAmR (265:1) Mr 80, p. 17.
"Over to Darkness. " AmerPoR (9:2) Mr-Ap 80, p. 3.
"The Part. " CutB (15) Aut/Wint 80, p. 7.
"Pencil. " CarolQ (32:1) Wint 80, pp. 32-41.
"Sara Wright. " PraS (54:2) Sum 80, p. 18.
"Seconds. " PoetryNW (21:4) Wint 80-81, p. 27.
"Small Difference. " Pequod (11) 80, p. 34.

"Some Lines. " CharR (6:2) Aut 80, p. 12.
"Sometimes, weeping. " FourQt (29:4) Sum 80, p. 20.
'The Song of My Father. " MissouriR (3:2) Wint 80, p. 34.
"Ssh. " Iowa (11:1) Wint 80, p. 121.
"The Story. " PoetryNW (21:2) Sum 80, p. 12.
"Thoreau/Who Directed Le Boucher/and Pope. " Poetry (136:3)
    Je 80, p. 131.
'Three Places. " AmerPoR (9:2) Mr-Ap 80, p. 4.
'The Tip. " BaratR (8:1) Sum 80, p. 19.
"Translation. " OhioR (24) 80, p. 43.
"Trying. " Iowa (11:1) Wint 80, p. 123.
'Wings. " Bits (11) 80.
'Witchita Burning. " CutB (15) Aut/Wint 80, p. 47.
"Yes, Now. " PoetryNW (21:4) Wint 80-81, p. 28.

GOLDBERG, Natalie
'The Farm. " CreamCR (5:1) Wint 79, p. 32.

GOLDEN, Darryl
'The Dance Hall Girl (to the Respectable Gentleman). " Wind (37)
    80, p. 15.
'The Neighbor. " Tele (16) 80, p. 100.
"Restless Tropic. " Tele (16) 80, p. 101.

GOLDEN, Gail Kadison
"Dolphins. " Outbr (4/5) Aut 79-Spr 80, p. 34.

GOLDENSOHN, Barry
"Becoming Real. " Salm (47/48) Wint-Spr 80, p. 54.
"Domestic Resurrection. " Salm (47/48) Wint-Spr 80, p. 55.
'The Haze of Recognition. " Salm (47/48) Wint-Spr 80, p. 53.
"Map of the World, Martin Frobisher, 1578. " NewRep (182:19)
    10 My 80, p. 30.

GOLDENSOHN, Lorrie
"Ambulance Call. " AmerPoR (9:4) Jl-Ag 80, p. 42.
"Bus Ride. " NewYorker (56:14) 26 My 80, p. 34.
"Farm Woman. " Poetry (135:4) Ja 80, p. 200.
"Gemini. " Poetry (135:4) Ja 80, p. 199.
"My Mother's Safety. " Poetry (135:4) Ja 80, p. 201.

GOLDIN, Judah
'Reading Faust. " AmerS (49:2) Spr 80, p. 210.

GOLDMAN, Michael
'The Acceptances. " PartR (47:1) 80, p. 130.

GOLDSBY, Marcie
'When You Are Eighty and I Am Thirty-Five. " CutB (15) Aut/
    Wint 80, p. 52.

GOLDWITZ, Susan
"After Leaving You and Oregon. " StoneC (7:1) F 80, p. 18.

"Life's Staff. " StoneC (7:1) F 80, p. 18.

GOLFFING, Francis
"Plain" (tr. of Johannes Bobrowski). PoNow (27) 80, p. 45.

GOM, Leona
"Wild Berries. " MalR (53) Ja 80, p. 51.

GOMEZ-CORREA, Enrique
"The Body That Emits Light and Heat Loses Weight" (tr. by
    Mary Crow). WebR (5:1) Wint 80, p. 37.

GONZALEZ, Angel
"I Look at My Hand" (tr. by Joel Hancock). CutB (14) Spr /Sum
    80, p. 13.

GOODENOUGH, J. B.
"Auntie Mandy. " HiramPoR (28) Spr-Sum 80, p. 19.
"Dream. " WebR (5:2) Aut 80, p. 57.
"Hex. " FourQt (30:1) Aut 80, p. 21.
"Kitchen Table Morning. " CapeR (15:2) Sum 80, p. 23.
"Lady of the Island. " HolCrit (17:5) D 80, p. 17.
"Map. " FourQt (29:2) Wint 80, p. 12.
"New England Heritage. " WebR (5:2) Aut 80, p. 56.
"To Market. " FourQt (30:1) Aut 80, p. 20.

GOODMAN, Deborah
"Bear Grass. " KanQ (12:3) Sum 80, p. 17.

GOODMAN, Diane
"When My Grandmother Died. " StoneC (7:3) D 80, p. 14.

GOODMAN, Miriam
"Staircase. " Aspect (76) S-D 79-80, p. 8.
"Trespass. " Aspect (76) S-D 79-80, p. 7.

GOODMAN, Ryah Tumarkin
"No One. " PoNow (27) 80, p. 17.

GORDETT, Marea
"Letter from Plum Island, 1890. " PoNow (29) 80, p. 11.
"Seasickness Is My Name. " PoetryNW (21:2) Sum 80, p. 26.

GORDON, Alan
"An Elevator Man's Autumn. " KanQ (12:3) Sum 80, p. 51.
"Mirrors" (for Lois). KanQ (12:3) Sum 80, p. 51.

GORDON, Coco
"Father That You Haven't Been Mine. " Bachy (17) Spr 80, p.
    96.
"A Girl Comes Into Life. " Bachy (17) Spr 80, p. 96.
"Return to the Winstead Road. " Im (7:1) 80, p. 4.
"Rooms. " Confr (20) Spr-Sum 80, p. 189.

"Where Departures Gather. " <u>Bachy</u> (17) Spr 80, p. 95.

GORDON, Howard Wm.
"Invalids. " <u>Obs</u> (5:1/2) Spr-Sum 79, p. 87.
"Taboo. " <u>Obs</u> (5:1/2) Spr-Sum 79, p. 87.

GORDON, Jaimy
"Brief Lives. " <u>OP</u> (30) Aut 80, p. 43.
"Exemplum on a Cockatiel. " <u>OP</u> (30) Aut 80, p. 44.
"The Getaway. " <u>OP</u> (30) Aut 80, p. 46.
"Stencil. " <u>OP</u> (30) Aut 80, p. 48.

GORDON, Kirpal Singh
"Letter to a Nun from Her Former Convent Sister" (for Pamela
      Stewart and Norman Dubie). <u>Wind</u> (36) 80, p. 21.
"Translations from the Sino-Russian War: The Runner.   1904. "
      <u>PoetryE</u> (1) 80, p. 61.

GORDON, Rebecca
"When I Was a Fat Woman. " <u>Cond</u> (6) 80, p. 56.

GORENBERG, Gershom
"Fish. " <u>CalQ</u> (16/17) 80, p. 133.

GOSSE, Peter
"Inventory, New Year 64. " <u>Stand</u> (21:1) 79-80, p. 48.

GOTTLIEB, Darcy
"If We Would Go Marrying Great Distances. " <u>Outbr</u> (4/5) Aut
      79-Spr 80, p. 23.
"Who of Those Coming After. " <u>Outbr</u> (4/5) Aut 79-Spr 80, p.
      24.

GOULD, Roberta
"Yes. " <u>PoNow</u> (27) 80, p. 47.

GOUMAS, Yannis
"Past the Tollgate. " <u>MalR</u> (54) Ap 80, p. 39.
"Solicitude. " <u>MalR</u> (54) Ap 80, p. 38.

GOZZANO, Guido
"Invernale. " <u>Poetry</u> (136:1) Ap 80, p. 10.
"Ketty" (tr. by Michael Palma). <u>Poetry</u> (136:1) Ap 80, p. 17.
"Totò merúmeni" (tr. by Michael Palma). <u>Poetry</u> (136:1) Ap 80,
      p. 14.

GRABILL, James
"Dry Heat. " <u>PoNow</u> (26) 80, p. 30.

GRABMAN, Richard
"Hitchhiking Riddle. " <u>WindO</u> (36) Spr-Sum 80, p. 29.
"Mourning Dove. " <u>WindO</u> (36) Spr-Sum 80, p. 29.

GRACEY, Dorothy
"Crumbs from the Table." SoCaR (13:1) Aut 80, p. 87.

GRAHAM, Chael
"Closed Lips." PoNow (29) 80, p. 11.

GRAHAM, David
"Clay." SouthernPR (20:2) Aut 80, p. 38.
"Dusk." Poetry (136:2) My 80, p. 89.
"Landscape of Domestic Life." GeoR (34:1) Spr 80, p. 161.
"What Is Coming." Pan (21) 80, p. 3.

GRAHAM, Jorie
"Coaltrains Crossing the Wyoming Prairie." Agni (13) 80, p.
    103.
"For My Father Looking for My Uncle." Nat (230:13) 5 Ap 80,
    p. 413.
"A Garden for Saint Jerome." PoetryNW (21:1) Spr 80, p. 7.
"Love Letter." Agni (13) 80, p. 104.
"Mind." WatT (1) Aut 80, p. 46.
"On Why I Would Betray You." Antaeus (36) Wint 80, p. 87.
"The Slow Sounding and Eventual Re-Emergence of." WatT (1)
    Aut 80, p. 44.
"Syntax." WatT (1) Aut 80, p. 42.
"Timothy." PoetryNW (21:1) Spr 80, p. 6.
"A Trojan Horse." PoetryNW (21:1) Spr 80, p. 5.

GRAHAM, Robin
"Cattle in the Rain" (tr. of Bonus Zimuya). Stand (21:1) 79-80,
    p. 51.
"My Home" (tr. of Bonus Zimuya). Stand (21:1) 79-80, p. 50.
"No Songs" (tr. of Bonus Zimuya). Stand (21:1) 79-80, p. 52.

GRAHAM, Taylor
"Aguilar." CropD (2/3) Aut-Wint 80, p. 13.
"Another Song for Natalie, Blind." CropD (1) Spr 80, p. 17.
"Letter Home." CropD (1) Spr 80, p. 17.
"What the Thief Left." CropD (2/3) Aut-Wint 80, p. 21.

GRAHAM, Tom
"Untitled: On intensely tactile days." PottPort (2) 80-81, p. 11.

GRAHAM, W. S.
"From Gigha Young." MalR (55) Jl 80, p. 46.
"Look at the Children." MalR (55) Jl 80, p. 47.

GRAPES, Jack
"A Burning." Bachy (16) Wint 80, p. 73.
"Nearing the Point." Bachy (16) Wint 80, p. 71.
"To Write a Poem." Bachy (16) Wint 80, p. 72.
"Trees, Coffee, and the Eyes of the Deer." Bachy (16) Wint 80,
    p. 69.
"Which Cup, Which Eye." Bachy (16) Wint 80, p. 71.

GRAVES, Robert
"Advent of Summer. " BosUJ (26:3) 80, p. 21.

GRAY, Alice Wirth
"A Present for Poor Monsieur Proust. " Poetry (136:2) My 80,
    p. 82.
"Zoo Prepares to Adopt Metric System. " Poetry (136:2) My 80,
    p. 83.

GRAY, Lee
"Generations. " Vis (1) 79.

GRAY, Patrick Worth
"Body. " WebR (5:1) Wint 80, p. 64.
"Circumnavigation. " KanQ (12:4) Aut 80, p. 45.
"Disappearances" (for Jocelynn). Annex (2) 79, pp. 16-35.
"Dusk in Lynnville, Alabama. " PoNow (27) 80, p. 19.
"Fear. " WormR (78) 80, p. 45.
"Fifteen. " ChrC (97:21) 4-11 Je 80, p. 635.
"Hands. " Wind (36) 80, p. 23.
"Labor Day. " Wind (36) 80, p. 23.
"The Longest Journey. " StoneC (7:1) F 80, p. 45.
"Poplars. " ChrC (97:30) 1 O 80, p. 911.
"Position Classifier. " WormR (78) 80, p. 46.
"Tables. " ConcPo (13:2) Aut 80, p. 64.
"Telephone Call. " MalR (54) Ap 80, p. 132.
"Today We Studied the Farmer, Dad. " WormR (78) 80, p. 46.
"Vowels. " WormR (78) 80, p. 47.

GRAY, Robert H.
"Voices. " StoneC (7:1) F 80, p. 9.

GRAZIANO, Frank
"Homage to Emmylou Harris. " BelPoJ (30:4) Sum 80, pp. 10-
    14.

GREACEN, Robert
"Birthday. " GRR (11:1) 80, p. 25.
"Father and Son. " GRR (11:1) 80, p. 24.
"A Poet Dying. " GRR (11:1) 80, p. 23.

GREELEY, Lee Lawrence
"White-Fishing. " EngJ (69:5) My 80, p. 57.

GREEN, Bob
"Indian Fighter. " LittleBR (1:1) Aut 80, p. 77.

GREEN, George
"Noli me tangere. " EnPas (10) 80, p. 21.

GREEN, George Dawes
"Breezy's kill. " Poem (39) Jl 80, p. 15.

GREENBAUM, Jessica
"Pantoum About Civilisation. " LittleM (12:3/4) 80, p. 30.
"The Rude Awakening of Steven Steven Stephen. " LittleM (12:3/4)
    80, p. 32.

GREENBERG, Barbara L.
"The Death of the Autobiographer. " PoNow (28) 80, p. 17.
"Hungry Again. " PraS (54:2) Sum 80, p. 20.
"Judge Kroll. " NowestR (18:3) 80, p. 97.

GREENBERG, Davetta
"I Can Count on It. " AmerPoR (9:2) Mr-Ap 80, p. 14.
"The Pictures You Have Left for Me. " AmerPoR (9:2) Mr-Ap
    80, p. 14.

GREENE, Jeffrey
"Moving Into Position. " WatT (1) Aut 80, p. 52.
"With One Shot. " WatT (1) Aut 80, p. 51.
"Yards. " WatT (1) Aut 80, p. 50.

GREENWALD, Martha
"At the Moscow Symphony. " EngJ (69:5) My 80, p. 56.

GREENWAY, William
"I Am Young. " LitR (23:3) Spr 80, p. 408.
"Things I Cannot Possibly Take Care of. " LitR (23:3) Spr 80, p.
    409.

GREGER, Debora
"Book of Hours. " AmerPoR (9:4) Jl-Ag 80, p. 12.
"Calibrations. " Nat (230:13) 5 Ap 80, p. 407.
"Compline. " GeoR (34:2) Sum 80, p. 272.
"The Invention of Routine. " PoNow (29) 80, p. 23.
"Long Divisions. " Antaeus (39) Aut 80, p. 73.
"A Moment's Architecture. " NoAmR (265:4) D 80, p. 47.
"Object Lessons. " Nat (230:12) 29 Mr 80, p. 380.
"Patches of Sky. " PoNow (29) 80, p. 23.
"Precipitation. " NewYorker (56:43) 15 D 80, p. 42.

GREGERSON, Linda
"Frame. " Poetry (136:2) My 80, p. 78.
"The Three-Legged Dog at the Heart of Our Home. " Poetry
    (136:2) My 80, p. 76.
"Wife. " Poetry (136:2) My 80, p. 77.

GREGG, Linda
"The Defeated. " Tendril (9) 80, p. 65.
"A Game Called Fear. " NewYorker (56:19) 30 Je 80, p. 40.
"Growing Up. " PoetryE (3) 80, p. 30.
"Staying On. " PoetryE (3) 80, p. 31.

GREGOR, Arthur
"Detours. " PoNow (28) 80, p. 17.

"On Demise. " PoNow (26) 80, p. 20.

GREGORY, Carolyn Holmes
"For Georgia O'Keefe. " Prima (5) 79, p. 81.

GREGORY, Clyde
"the dance. " CreamCR (5:2) Spr 80, p. 24.
"Moving by Touch. " BelPoJ (30:3) Spr 80, p. 30.

GREGORY, Cynde
"he spoke through me. " Prima (5) 79, p. 7.

GREY, Lucinda
"Speech. " SouthernPR (20:1) Spr 80, p. 26.

GREY, Robert W.
"Ruins. " Wind (38) 80, p. 32.

GRIECO, Joseph
"After a rain. " CapeR (15:2) Sum 80, p. 9.

GRIFFIN, Jeffery J.
"Getting Strong Now" (for J.W.). BlackALF (14:4) Wint 80, p.
    174.
"In Minutes When. " BlackALF (14:4) Wint 80, p. 174.

GRIFFIN, Jonathan
Eleven Poems. Montra (7) 80, pp. 137-146.
"Peace" (tr. of Casimiro de Brito). PortR (26) 80, p. 309.
"Telegram: No Special Category" (for Egito Goncalves) (tr. of
    António Ramos Rusa). PortR (26) 80, p. 315.

GRIFFITH, David
"Father's Map. " PoetryNW (21:3) Aut 80, p. 11.
"Mother's Map. " PoetryNW (21:3) Aut 80, p. 12.

GRIFFITH, Jonathan
"For the Suicides. " CapeR (16:1) Wint 80, p. 37.

GRIFFITH, Lois Elaine
"Chica. " Cond (6) 80, p. 106.
"Howard Beach. " Cond (6) 80, p. 108.

GRIGSBY, Gordon
"Obsidian Knife. " Vis (4) 80.

GRIMES, Nikki
"May" (for Mae Jackson). Obs (5:1/2) Spr-Sum 79, p. 88.
"Pyramids. " Obs (5:1/2) Spr-Sum 79, p. 88.
"We, the Poets. " Obs (5:1/2) Spr-Sum 79, p. 88.

GRIMSHAW, James A. Jr.
"Elk-Spotting in Church Park: An Eschatology" (for Robert Penn

Warren). SouthernR (16:4) Aut 80, p. 937.

GRIMSSON, Stefan Hordur
"Síodegi. " PortR (26) 80, p. 177.
"Vetrardagur. " PortR (26) 80, p. 178.
"Winter Day" (tr. by Alan Boucher). Vis (2) 80.

GRINDE, Olav
"Letter to Light" (tr. of Rolf Jacobsen). CutB (14) Spr /Sum 80,
    p. 106.

GRONOWICZ, Antoni
"The Blind Man of Himself. " CropD (2 /3) Aut-Wint 80, p. 37.
"Village Sketch. " CropD (2 /3) Aut-Wint 80, p. 27.

GROSHOLZ, Emily
"Conversations in Athens. " Tele (16) 80, p. 120.
"In Medias Res. " Iowa (10:4) Aut 79, p. 39.

GROSS, Suzanne
"The Woman and the Waterhorse. " BelPoJ (31:2) Wint 80-81,
    p. 18.

GROSSBARDT, Andrew
"Bluefishing. " AmerS (49:2) Spr 80, p. 235.
Eight poems. QW (10) Wint-Spr 80, pp. 7-14.
"In the High Country. " AmerS (49:2) Spr 80, p. 234.

GROSSMAN, Florence
"Sewing Box. " Poetry (136:2) My 80, p. 86.
"Summer Weekend. " PoNow (28) 80, p. 47.
"Tree. " Poetry (136:2) My 80, p. 87.

GROSSMAN, Martin
"Summer Night: Ontario. " PoNow (28) 80, p. 20.

GROSSMAN, Richard
"Boy. " DacTerr (17) 80, p. 35.
"Calm. " ChiR (31:3) Wint 80, p. 92.
"Caution. " Wind (36) 80, p. 25.
"Closeness. " AndR (7:1) Spr 80, p. 60.
"Detail. " ChiR (31:3) Wint 80, p. 94.
"Disease. " LitR (23:3) Spr 80, p. 339.
"Elephant. " CarolQ (32:1) Wint 80, p. 75.
"Flow. " Wind (36) 80, p. 26.
"Immortality. " LitR (23:3) Spr 80, p. 339.
"in praise of our last heroes. " Kayak (55) Ja 81, p. 24.
"Incest. " PoNow (26) 80, p. 18.
"Island of Liberty. " PoNow (26) 80, p. 18.
"Pain. " Wind (36) 80, p. 25.
"Paranoia. " Im (7:1) 80, p. 5.
"Relativity. " LitR (23:3) Spr 80, p. 340.
"Shyness. " AndR (7:1) Spr 80, p. 60.

"Spring. " Wind (36) 80, p. 26.
"2 Daughters. " PoNow (26) 80, p. 18.
"Waking. " Im (7:1) 80, p. 5.
"Weariness. " ChiR (31:3) Wint 80, p. 93.

GROSZ, Joseph
"Wedding Night" (tr. of Agnes Gergely). PortR (26) 80, p. 173.

GROVER-ROGOFF, Jay
"Snow as a way of life. " Stand (21:3) 80, p. 68.

GRUTZMACHER, Harold M.
"Knowledge. " BallSUF (21:1) Wint 80, p. 14.

GUERNSEY, Bruce
"Back Road. " Poetry (135:4) Ja 80, p. 209.

GUGGENHEIM, Herbert S.
"Among the Waves. " BelPoJ (31:1) Aut 80, p. 11.

GUILFORD, Chuck
"In an Alien Craft. " KanQ (12:3) Sum 80, p. 139.

GUILLEVIC, Eugene
from Inclus: Twenty-three poems (tr. by Samuel Danon).
   MalR (54) Ap 80, pp. 50-60.

GULLANS, Charles
"Moscow Suburban Nights. " MichQR (19:2) Spr 80, p. 229.

GULLING, Dennis
"Notes from the Native Son. " Wind (36) 80, p. 28.

GUNDY, Jeff
"C. W. Meets a Feminist pome and is Liberated. " PikeF (3)
   Wint 80, p. 11.
"C. W. Vows to Say Goodbye to the Goddess and Hello to the
   Muse. " PikeF (3) Wint 80, p. 11.

GUNN, Thom
"As Expected. " Thrpny (1) Wint-Spr 80, p. 3.
"Crystal. " MichQR (19:1) Wint 80, p. 25.
"Painkillers. " MichQR (19:1) Wint 80, p. 26.

GUNNARS, Kristjana
"Ilya. " ConcPo (12:2) Aut 79, p. 15.
"Patricia. " ConcPo (12:2) Aut 79, p. 16.

GURLEY, George H. Jr.
"Home Movies. " Focus (14:86) Ap 80, p. 36.
"Manhunt. " Focus (14:86) Ap 80, p. 36.
"Morning News in the State of Kansas. " PoetryNW (21:3) Aut
   80, p. 42.

"The Question. " PoetryNW (21:3) Aut 80, p. 41.
"Stool Pigeon. " Focus (14:86) Ap 80, p. 36.
"A Theory of Spectator Sports. " PoetryNW (21:3) Aut 80, p. 39.

GUSS, David
   "God at the Foot of the Mountain. " CreamCR (5:2) Spr 80, p.
   42.

GUSTAFSSON, Lars
   "Sonnet 1: The Desert at Rio Grande" (tr. by Philip Martin).
   CarlMis (18:2) Sum 80, p. 34.

GUSTAVSON, Jeffrey
   "Letter to Martha. " Agni (13) 80, p. 93.

GUSTIN, Lawrence W.
   "Bump On. " CreamCR (5:2) Spr 80, p. 61.
   "dark sky-shawls. " CreamCR (5:2) Spr 80, p. 63.

GUTENKAUF, Wendy
   "Baba. " EngJ (69:5) My 80, p. 60.

GUTIERREZ, Victor
   "The Last Bastion" (for the writers of AKWP). Sam (92) 80, p.
   23.

GWYNN, R. S.
   "The Land of Cocaine" (tr. of Anonymous, 13th c. France).
   Playb (27:6) Je 80, p. 181.

HAAVIKKO, Paavo
   "Ei viini tule humalaan, juomalla, ei syksy. " PortR (26) 80,
   p. 132.

HABERMAN, Daniel
   "Sea Chantey. " SunM (9/10) Sum 80, p. 31.

HABOVA, Dana
   "Assault" (tr. of Miroslav Holub w. Stuart Friebert). MalR (55)
   Jl 80, p. 134.
   "At Home" (tr. of Miroslav Holub w. Stuart Friebert). PoNow
   (27) 80, p. 46.
   "Death of a Sparrow" (tr. of Miroslav Holub w. Stuart Friebert).
   OntR (12) Spr-Sum 80, p. 54.
   "MaMa" (tr. of Miroslav Holub w. Stuart Friebert). MalR (55)
   Jl 80, p. 133.
   "On the Dog Angel" (tr. of Miroslav Holub w. Stuart Friebert).
   OntR (12) Spr-Sum 80, p. 55.
   "On the Origin of a Festive Morning" (tr. of Miroslav Holub w.
   Stuart Friebert). MalR (55) Jl 80, p. 136.
   "On the Origin of Poor Digestion" (tr. of Miroslav Holub w.
   Stuart Friebert). Durak (4) 80, p. 8.
   "We will put on one of our heads, " (tr. of Miroslav Holub w.

Stuart Friebert). MalR (55) Jl 80, p. 131.

HACKER, Marilyn
"Burnham Beeches. " Poetry (136:3) Je 80, p. 134.
"Canzone. " Shen (31:1) 79, p. 38.
"La Fontaine de Vaucluse" (for Marie Ponsot). Tendril (9) 80,
    p. 66.
"Little Green-Eyed Suite. " OP (29) Spr 80, p. 49.
"A Man With Sons" (for David Batterham). Poetry (136:3) Je
    80, p. 135.
"Return. " AmerPoR (9:3) My-Je 80, p. 31.
"Some of the Boys. " AmerPoR (9:3) My-Je 80, p. 31.
"La Vie de Chateau. " AmerPoR (9:3) My-Je 80, p. 31.

HADAS, Rachel
"First Date in the Turkish Bath. " Thrpny (3) Aut 80, p. 21.

HAGEDORN, Jessica
"The Woman Who Thought She Was More Than a Samba. " Ark
    (14) 80, pp. 207-211.

HAGLAND, Nan ER
"On the 3:55 to Grand Central. " SmPd (50) Aut 80, p. 19.

HAHN, Robert
"Never Be as Fast as I Have Been. " PoNow (28) 80, p. 33.
"The Nicolsons at Home: In the Garden. " PoNow (26) 80, p.
    13.

HAHN, Steve
"A July Storm: Johnson, Nemaha County, Nebraska. " KanQ
    (12:1) Wint 80, p. 106.
"Tearing Out the Plaster. " KanQ (12:1) Wint 80, p. 107.

HAINES, John
"Deserted Cabin. " Tendril (9) 80, p. 69.
"Lament of the Builders. " Durak (5) 80, p. 52.
"The Night People. " Durak (5) 80, p. 53.
"Rain Country. " Ark (14) 80, p. 212.

HAINING, James
"Journal. " SouthwR (65:1) Wint 80, p. 71.

HAISLIP, John
"Auden at Seal Rock. " ConcPo (13:2) Aut 80, p. 93.
"Joyce at Seal Rock. " ConcPo (13:2) Aut 80, p. 93.

HAJNAL, Anna
"Evening" (tr. by Juliette Victor-Rood and András Török).
    DenQ (15:1) Spr 80, p. 75.

HALE, Frances
"Father. " Poem (40) N 80, p. 16.

"Metaphor. "   Poem (40) N 80, p. 18.
"Moving On. "   CentR (24:2) Spr 80, p. 185.

HALE, Robert
"The Origin of Evil. "   ChrC (97:8) 5 Mr 80, p. 256.

HALEY, Vanessa
"At the Smithsonian. "   Poetry (136:2) My 80, p. 71.
"Dead Horses. "   Poetry (136:2) My 80, p. 70.
"Excuses. "   SmPd (48) Wint 80, p. 21.

HALL, David
"Mother Nature Is a Sadist. "   Sam (86) 79, p. 38.
"Recluse. "   Sam (86) 79, p. 40.
"Whore's Prayer. "   Sam (86) 79, p. 39.

HALL, Donald
"Q Cart Man. "   Tendril (9) 80, p. 70.

HALL, Gail
"Circling. "   Pan (21) 80, p. 51.
"Turning. "   Pan (21) 80, p. 52.

HALL, James Baker
"Notes Toward a Politics for the Future. "   Hudson (33:3) Aut 80,
    p. 403.

HALL, Jim
"Back Then. "   PoNow (26) 80, p. 14.
"Sorting the Photos. "   Poetry (135:5) F 80, p. 281.

HALL, Marty
"Letter to Sebastian from North Carolina. "   Pan (21) 80, p. 55.
"Postcard from Kentucky. "   Wind (38) 80, p. 17.

HALL, Thelma R.
"Child of the World. "   Poem (39) Jl 80, p. 17.
"Spring Ritual. "   Poem (39) Jl 80, p. 16.

HALL, William Keith
"Summer House. "   HolCrit (17:4) O 80, p. 11.

HALLEY, Anne
"Lullabye. "   AmerPoR (9:2) Mr-Ap 80, p. 28.

HALLIDAY, Mark
"Key to the Highway. "   NewRep (182:11) 15 Mr 80, p. 34.
"The Students. "   NewRep (183:20) 15 N 80, p. 24.
"Texas Material. "   Ploughs (6:2) 80, p. 135.

HALMAN, Talat Sait
"All Things Side by Side" (tr. of Melih Cevdat Anday w. Brian
    Swann).   PoNow (26) 80, p. 46.

HALPERIN 156

"In Those Small Lakes" (tr. of Melih Cevdat Anday w. Brian
  Swann). PoNow (26) 80, p. 46.
"Lycian Women" (tr. of Melih Cevdat Anday w. Brian Swann).
  PoNow (26) 80, p. 46.
"Open Window" (tr. of Melih Cevdat Anday w. Brian Swann).
  CharR (6:2) Aut 80, p. 55.

HALPERIN, Mark
  "Autumn. " VirQR (56:4) Aut 80, p. 681.
  "Franz Jages Hater's Epistemology. " Tendril (9) 80, p. 71.
  "The Man Who Loved Darkness. " CarolQ (32:1) Wint 80, p. 59.
  "The Old Neighborhood" (for Bruce Cohen). PoNow (26) 80, p.
    15.
  "Percipi. " Epoch (29:3) Spr-Sum 80, p. 240.
  "Wessex. " Shen (31:2) 80, p. 77.

HALPERN, Daniel
  "Dead Fish. " Iowa (11:1) Wint 80, p. 129.
  "The End of Vigil. " Poetry (136:5) Ag 80, p. 271.
  "For Cats. " MissouriR (3:3) Sum 80, p. 7.
  "Late. " Poetry (135:6) Mr 80, p. 335.
  "Night Food. " MissouriR (3:3) Sum 80, p. 8.
  "No Letters. " WatT (1) Aut 80, p. 83.
  "Portoncini Dei Morti. " Harp (261:1564) S 80, p. 89.
  "Return. " Tendril (9) 80, p. 72.
  "Return" (for Ellen). Poetry (135:6) Mr 80, p. 333.
  "Summer Constellations. " Poetry (136:5) Ag 80, p. 269.
  "The Storm. " Poetry (136:5) Ag 80, p. 267.
  "This Place. " GeoR (34:3) Aut 80, p. 638.
  "Under Darkness. " Iowa (10:4) Aut 79, p. 29.

HAMBLIN, Robert W.
  "Autumn at Woodland Hills Country Club. " CapeR (15:2) Sum
    80, p. 49.
  "San Francisco: August 1977. " CapeR (15:2) Sum 80, p. 48.

HAMBURGER, Michael
  "Besides Me" (tr. of Marin Sorescu). Stand (21:3) 80, p. 52.
  "Carbon Paper" (tr. of Marin Sorescu). Poetry (136:1) Ap 80,
    p. 27.
  "A Film of the Comedian Chaplin" (tr. of Bertolt Brecht).
    BosUJ (26:3) 80, p. 170.
  "The Greenhouse" (tr. of Bertolt Brecht). BosUJ (26:3) 80, p.
    169.
  "In the Second Year of My Flight" (tr. of Bertolt Brecht).
    BosUJ (26:3) 80, p. 170.
  "The Mask of Evil" (tr. of Bertolt Brecht). BosUJ (26:3) 80,
    p. 169.
  "Nature Poems" (tr. of Bertolt Brecht). BosUJ (26:3) 80, p.
    168.
  "Poisons" (tr. of Marin Sorescu). Poetry (136:1) Ap 80, p. 25.
  "Question" (tr. of Marin Sorescu). Poetry (136:1) Ap 80, p. 29.
  "Seneca" (tr. of Marin Sorescu). Poetry (136:1) Ap 80, p. 28.

"Shakespeare" (tr. of Marin Sorescu). Poetry (136:1) Ap 80,
   p. 27.
"The Shopper" (tr. of Bertolt Brecht). BosUJ (26:3) 80, p. 171.
"The Thieves" (tr. of Marin Sorescu). Stand (21:3) 80, p. 53.
"The World's One Hope" (tr. of Bertolt Brecht). BosUJ (26:3)
   80, p. 172.

HAMILL, Sam
"The Egg. " ThRiPo (15/16) 80, p. 30.
"To Kenneth Rexroth. " Ark (14) 80, p. 214.

HAMILTON, Carol
"Butlers and Bakers and We. " ChrC (97:11) 26 Mr 80, p. 349.
"Dissection of the Eye of a Cow, Related in Its Workings to Our
   Own. " SmPd (48) Wint 80, p. 24.
"Red Land. " SoDakR (18:2) Sum 80, p. 5.

HAMILTON-LaCOSTE, Elisabeth
"Dream" (tr. of Blanca Varela). CutB (14) Spr/Sum 80, p. 33.
"Family Secret" (tr. of Blanca Varela). CutB (14) Spr/Sum 80,
   p. 34.
"Finding" (tr. of Blanca Varela). CutB (14) Spr/Sum 80, p. 32.
"First Dance" (tr. of Blanca Varela). CutB (14) Spr/Sum 80,
   p. 31.
"On the Order of Things" (to Octavio Paz) (tr. of Blanca Varela).
   CutB (14) Spr/Sum 80, p. 28.
from Out of Time: (I, II, III, IV) (tr. of Blanca Varela). CutB
   (14) Spr/Sum 80, p. 35.

HAMMER, Patrick Jr.
"Extension. " StoneC (7:1) F 80, p. 33.
"Nightbirds. " StoneC (7:1) F 80, p. 33.

HAMMIAL, Philip
"Once Upon a Short Sweet Time. " Tele (16) 80, p. 111.
"Verily. " Tele (16) 80, p. 111.

HAMMOND, Karla M.
"For C. S. G. " Prima (5) 79, p. 59.
"The Three-Legged Foal. " SmPd (49) Spr 80, p. 7.

HAN Yong-un
"Silence of My Lover" (tr. by Cho Wun-che and David James).
   WindO (36) Spr-Sum 80, p. 32.

HANCOCK, Joel
"I Look at My Hand" (tr. of Angel González). CutB (14) Spr/
   Sum 80, p. 13.

HANDY, Nixeon Civille
"George Is Important. " EnPas (11) 80, p. 17.
"Hometown Parade 1930. " Wind (36) 80, p. 30.

HANNERS, La Verne
"Little Old Ladies, Oil, and Bears." BallSUF (21:1) Wint 80, p. 58.

HANSEN, Jon
"Away on My Brother's Birthday" (tr. of Su-Tung'po). ChiR (31: 4) Spr 80, p. 158.
"Bearer's Song" (tr. of Tao Ch'ien). ChiR (31:4) Spr 80, p. 160.
"Driving from Batavia to Bergen." PoNow (28) 80, p. 47.
from Nineteen Ancient Songs: "Thoughts of Returning Home" (tr. of Anonymous). ChiR (31:4) Spr 80, p. 159.

HANSEN, Tom
"A Candle for Paul." DacTerr (17) 80, p. 36.
"Father's Head." DacTerr (17) 80, p. 37.
"In the Wide-Awake Dark." BallSUF (21:1) Wint 80, p. 56.
"A Man Marooned on a Desert Island Talks to His Feet." BallSUF (21:1) Wint 80, p. 77.

HANSON, Howard G.
"Let Journeys Be Made." ArizQ (36:4) Wint 80, p. 329.
"To Artemis." BallSUF (21:1) Wint 80, p. 73.
"You Are Penates." ArizQ (36:1) Spr 80, p. 20.

HANZLICEK, C. G.
from The One Song: (1, 4, 9, 10, 14). PoNow (27) 80, p. 16.

HANZLIK, Josef
"Lampa." PortR (26) 80, p. 70.

HARALSON, Carol
"Doors" (w. Charlotte Stewart). Nimrod (24:1) Aut-Wint 80, p. 102.
"Doors II" (w. Charlotte Stewart). Nimrod (24:1) Aut-Wint 80, p. 103.
"Reaching Across" (w. Charlotte Stewart). Nimrod (24:1) Aut-Wint 80, p. 104.

HARASYM, Sally
"Capable Wings." PottPort (2) 80-81, p. 50.

HARDER, Uffe
"Dagene synker igennem mig." PortR (26) 80, p. 96.

HARDING, Gunnar
"Den som hindrar hans händer från att simma." PortR (26) 80, p. 356.
"Min ensamhet." PortR (26) 80, p. 358.

HARFORD, Irina
"Bittersweet." Ark (14) 80, p. 233.

HARINGTON, Donald
"The Villanelle. " NewL (46:3) Spr 80, p. 84.

HARMON, William
"Eldorado. " CarolQ (32:2) Spr-Sum 80, p. 66.
"He-Who-May-Say (Invocations and Palinodes Together Through-
    out and Simultaneously). " Agni (13) 80, p. 28.
"Messages Left on Engineers' Desks. " Agni (13) 80, p. 30.
"A Poet in a Landscape of Language. " Kayak (54) S 80, p. 20.
"Rime. " CarolQ (32:2) Spr-Sum 80, p. 67.

HARMSTON, Dick
"After Reading an Entry in My Grandmother's Journal Concerning
    the Big Spring in Vintah Canyon. " EngJ (69:5) My 80, p.
    53.

HARPER, Elizabeth
"Indian Giver. " PottPort (2) 80-81, p. 33.

HARPER, Michael S.
"Bird of Paradise. " CarlMis (18:3) Wint 80, p. 235.
"Going to the Territory: Icons of Geography of the Word: A
    Meditation on the Life and Times of Ralph Waldo Ellison. "
    CarlMis (18:3) Wint 80, p. 6.
"Hemp. " CarlMis (18:3) Wint 80, p. 105.
"Nathan's Cadenza. " CarlMis (18:3) Wint 80, p. 106.
"Richard Yarde's Blues. " CarlMis (18:3) Wint 80, p. 109.
"Secretary. " CarlMis (18:3) Wint 80, p. 110.
"Stepto's Veil. " CarlMis (18:3) Wint 80, p. 108.

HARRIMAN, Barbara
"helping someone to escape. " Kayak (55) Ja 81, p. 27.
"waiting in line. " Kayak (55) Ja 81, p. 29.
"your room our room my room. " Kayak (55) Ja 81, p. 28.

HARRIS, Jana
"Lady in a Hundred Dollar Car One Night on the Side of the
    Road. " Cond (6) 80, p. 53.

HARRIS, John S.
"Jack's Fork" (for David Schlamb). WebR (5:2) Aut 80, p. 53.

HARRIS, Joseph
"Autumn Inventory. " Wind (36) 80, p. 10.
"Haiku 19. " Wind (36) 80, p. 54.

HARRIS, Laura
"Fears. " CropD (1) Spr 80, p. 10.

HARRIS, Marie
"Angelus. " Os (11) 80, p. 16.
"Woods. " Os (11) 80, p. 15.

HARRIS, Melanie Gause
"The Metal Rape. " SoCaR (13:1) Aut 80, p. 77.

HARRIS, Michael
"Accounting Again: Zero. " StoneC (7:1) F 80, p. 20.
"Barn Swallow. " Atl (246:2) Ag 80, p. 67.

HARRIS, Peter
"A Doo Without a Wop" (for the Temptin Temptations). Obs
(5:1 /2) Spr-Sum 79, p. 89.

HARRIS, William J.
"Is This About the Jack Kerouac?" PoNow (28) 80, p. 39.

HARRISON, Keith
"Street Crossing" (tr. of Tomas Tranströmer). CarlMis (18:2)
Sum 80, p. 47.
"Summer Poem" (for Dorothy). CarlMis (18:2) Sum 80, p. 98.

HARRISON, Stanley R.
"Settling. " SouthwR (65:1) Wint 80, p. 27.

HARRISON, Steve
"B. F. Skinner. " SouthernHR (14:3) Sum 80, p. 222.

HARRISON, Tony
"Lines to My Grandfathers. " Stand (21:3) 80, p. 4.

HARSHMAN, Marc
"The Barn. " QW (11) Aut-Wint 80-81, p. 114.
"The Easter Woods. " PoNow (29) 80, p. 13.
"Poem: If I could tell you the stars knew. " PoNow (29) 80, p.
12.
"Reading Back. " PoNow (29) 80, p. 13.
"Someplace to Start. " PoNow (29) 80, p. 12.

HART, Joanne
"My Father Fishes. " DacTerr (17) 80, p. 38.

HART, Kevin
"My Children. " NewL (46:3) Spr 80, p. 13.
"Stockyard Creek. " NewL (46:3) Spr 80, p. 12.

HARTNETT, D. W.
"The Picture. " GRR (11:1) 80, p. 42.

HARVEY, Gayle Elen
"sitting shiva for a married lover. " Prima (5) 79, p. 21.

HARVEY, Helen Bohlen
"Beyond Bread. " Poem (39) Jl 80, p. 10.
"Chrysalis and Crystal. " Poem (39) Jl 80, p. 8.
"Night Route. " Poem (39) Jl 80, p. 9.

"Soliloquy: East Meets West. " Poem (39) Jl 80, p. 7.

HARVILL, JoAnn
"Death of a Namesake in the First Year. " SouthernPR (20:1)
Spr 80, p. 42.

HARWOOD, Gwen
"Return of the Native. " NewL (46:3) Spr 80, p. 32.

HASAN, Rabiul
"Summer Evenings in the Mississippi Delta. " Im (7:1) 80, p. 8.

HASHMI, Alamgir
"A Find from the Dead-Letter Office. " ModernPS (10:1) 80, p.
40.
"Keeping Awake Over Finnegan. " ChiR (31:3) Wint 80, p. 69.
"Vietnamese Girl Crossing the Street in Zurich. " ModernPS
(10:1) 80, p. 39.

HASKINS, Lola
"Changing the Speed Limit. " SouthernPR (20:2) Aut 80, p. 8.
"Employment. " BelPoJ (31:2) Wint 80-81, p. 36.
"I Am Someone. " CalQ (16/17) 80, p. 148.

HASLEY, Louis
"Arabesque. " FourQt (29:3) Spr 80, p. 14.

HASS, Robert
"The Feast. " PoNow (26) 80, p. 24.
"Old Dominion. " PoNow (26) 80, p. 24.
"The Origin of Cities. " Tendril (9) 80, p. 73.

HASSE, Margaret
"The Graveyard Shift. " DacTerr (17) 80, p. 40.

HASSELSTROM, Linda M.
"Poem for N'de, Too Late. " Northeast (3:8) Wint 80, p. 47.
"Rancher: 1864-1928. " MidwQ (21:2) Wint 80, p. 241.

HATHAWAY, James
"Explaining the Ways of God to Victor. " Agni (12) 80, p. 111.
"Frog Baseball. " Agni (12) 80, p. 112.

HATHAWAY, Jeanine
"In Random Fields of Impulse and Repose. " GeoR (34:1) Spr 80,
p. 40.
"Reconnaissance. " Northeast (3:8) Wint 80, p. 24.

HATHAWAY, Lodine Brown
"Old Band Leader. " ChrC (97:26) 13-20 Ag 80, p. 794.

HATHAWAY, William
"L'Art pour L'Art. " CharR (6:1) Spr 80, p. 25.

"Coloring Margarine. " Columbia (4) Spr-Sum 80, p. 87.
"Crawfishing. " PoNow (28) 80, p. 15.
"The Initiation. " PoNow (27) 80, p. 41.
"Time in the Woods" (for Fred Benton). CimR (52) Jl 80, p. 46.
"Two Friends. " NewOR (7:2) 80, p. 134.

HATTERSLEY, Michael
"Consensus. " StoneC (7:2) My 80, p. 7.
"Key West in July with a Nod. " Tele (16) 80, p. 113.
"The Specimen. " StoneC (7:2) My 80, p. 6.

HAUCK, Chris
"Relic. " BelPoJ (31:2) Wint 80-81, p. 1.

HAUK, Barbara
"Taxidermy. " BelPoJ (31:2) Wint 80-81, p. 25.

HAUPTMAN, Robert
"Phases" (tr. of Christine Busta). CutB (14) Spr /Sum 80, p. 62.

HAWKINS, Hunt
"Fifteen Hungry Cheerleaders. " PoetryNW (21:4) Wint 80-81, p. 24.

HAWKINS, Thomas
"The Fisherman. " KanQ (12:3) Sum 80, p. 124.

HAWKSWORTH, Marjorie
"Gramp. " HiramPoR (27) Aut-Wint 80, p. 26.
"Hallowe'en. " CarlMis (18:2) Sum 80, p. 49.
"In What Far Land?" BallSUF (21:1) Wint 80, p. 75.
"Prior to the Judgement. " BallSUF (21:1) Wint 80, p. 61.

HAY, John
"Comb Jelly. " MassR (21:2) Sum 80, p. 232.
"Music by the Waters. " MassR (21:2) Sum 80, p. 231.
"The Storm. " MassR (21:2) Sum 80, p. 231.

HAYDEN, Robert
"The Dogwood Trees" (for Robert Slagle). MichQR (19:1) Wint 80, p. 93.
"Double Feature. " MichQR (19:1) Wint 80, p. 92.
"Oh, not with statues' rhetoric. " Poetry (136:2) My 80, Inside front cover.

HAYES, Diana
"Crossing. " MalR (54) Ap 80, p. 100.

HAYN, Annette
"Disappearance 2. " Wind (38) 80, p. 34.
"Young Girl Sleeping Late. " Wind (38) 80, p. 34.

HAYNES, Douglas
"Winter" (tr. of Pierre Reverdy w. Anne Waldman).   Ark (14)
80, p. 394.

HAZAK, Be'erl
"Lord of the World. "   PortR (26) 80, p. 208.

HAZO, Samuel
"Leafing. "   Hudson (33:1) Spr 80, p. 59.
"Maps for a Son Are Drawn as You Go. "   AmerS (49:1) Wint 79-
80, p. 34.
"sexes. "   Hudson (33:1) Spr 80, p. 58.

HEAD, Gwen
"A Gift of Dragon Combs. "   WatT (1) Aut 80, p. 53.
"To Let Go. "   Nimrod (24:1) Aut-Wint 80, p. 93.
"Wildflowers. "   AntR (38:1) Wint 80, p. 64.

HEALY, Eloise Klein
"Out in the World of Strangers. "   HangL (38) Aut 80, p. 25.

HEANEY, Seamus
from Sweeny Astray: (17, 18, 19, 20, 21, 22, 23).   Ploughs
(6:1) 80, pp. 111-117.

HEARN, Bonnie
"Eating the Poems. "   Pig (7) My 80, p. 93.

HEARST, James
"Castrating the Pigs. "   PoNow (28) 80, p. 34.
"Cerebral Palsy. "   WindO (36) Spr-Sum 80, p. 35.
"Consider a Poem. "   StoneC (7:1) F 80, p. 16.
"An in Between Time. "   PoNow (28) 80, p. 34.
"It Might Be True. "   EngJ (69:9) D 80, p. 65.
"Lack of Seed Power. "   Harp (261:1566) N 80, p. 70.
"Something Given. "   PoNow (28) 80, p. 42.
"Something Given. "   StoneC (7:1) F 80, p. 17.
"The Way the Light Shines. "   PoNow (27) 80, p. 6.
"Weather Words. "   PoNow (28) 80, p. 34.

HECHT, Anthony
"Cape Cod Lullaby" (tr. of Joseph Brodsky).   Columbia (4) Spr-
Sum 80, pp. 36-49.
"The Transparent Man. "   NewEngR (3:2) Wint 80, p. 158.

HECHT, Susan
"Night Steamer Leaving Greece. "   Pig (7) My 80, p. 60.

HEDIN, Robert
"Fishing Off Green's Point at the Start of Spring. "   Ark (14) 80,
p. 236.
"Letter Home. "   DacTerr (17) 80, p. 41.
"The Shrine of Tanit. "   KanQ (12:3) Sum 80, p. 104.

'The Wreck of the Great Northern. " PoNow (26) 80, p. 41.

HEFFERNAN, Michael
"Afternoon with Angels" (for Dave Smith). CarolQ (32:2) Spr-
Sum 80, p. 20.
"Kathy Dancing. " CarolQ (32:1) Wint 80, p. 72.

HEFFERNAN, Thomas
"Easter. " SouthernPR (20:2) Aut 80, p. 35.

HEGI, Ursula
"She tends the fire. " PoetryNW (21:2) Sum 80, p. 35.

HEIDE, Christopher
"Another of Those Jobs Nobody Wants. " PottPort (1) 79-80, p.
19.
"At the Salt Water Lake. " PottPort (1) 79-80, p. 15.
"Everyone Will Have to Live in Mobile Homes. " PottPort (1)
79-80, p. 19.
'The Test of the Day. " PottPort (1) 79-80, p. 15.

HEILBRONN, Monica
"Writing. " PoetC (12:1) 80, p. 16.

HEILPRIN, Marilyn
'Word Dance. " Vis (2) 80.

HEINEMAN, W. F.
'The Change. " StoneC (7:3) D 80, p. 12.

HEINRICH, Peggy
"Ellen at 20. " NewRena (13) Aut 80, p. 72.

HELLER, Michael
"Being at Easthampton: A Sequence. " Pequod (11) 80, p. 20.
'In a Dark Time, on His Grandfather. " Harp (261:1566) N 80,
p. 88.
'In the Builded Place. " Bound (8:3) Spr 80, p. 164.
'With a Telescope in the Sangre de Cristos. " Bound (8:3) Spr
80, p. 166.

HEMAN, Bob
"Charm Against Demons. " Tele (16) 80, p. 76.
"Getting Wet. " HangL (38) Aut 80, p. 26.
"Music. " HangL (38) Aut 80, p. 27.
"Music. " Tele (16) 80, p. 76.
'The Old Woodcut. " HangL (38) Aut 80, p. 26.

HEMENWAY, Phillip
"Homage to John Clare. " Tendril (7/8) Spr-Sum 80, p. 40.

HENDERSON, Archibald
'Nakedness. " PoNow (28) 80, p. 15.

HENDERSON, David
"Third Eye/World. " BlackALF (14:3) Aut 80, p. 111.

HENDERSON, Jock Jr.
"The Martyr and the Army. " Comm (107:14) 1 Ag 80, p. 439.
"The Proof of the Haunted Tool. " Comm (107:14) 1 Ag 80, p.
    439.
"Rat Brain Scan Check Points. " Comm (107:14) 1 Ag 80, p.
    438.

HENIGHAN, Tom
"Animal Pictures. " Sam (92) 80, p. 22.

HENLEY, Lloyd
"Dawn of the Eighties. " CharR (6:2) Aut 80, p. 20.
"Honeysuckle. " CapeR (15:2) Sum 80, p. 35.
"Man of Gardens. " CapeR (15:2) Sum 80, p. 34.

HENN, Sister Mary Ann
"Clouds. " Wind (38) 80, p. 36.
"Could a Heaven Be More Perfect?" Wind (38) 80, p. 37.
"Did You Know That I Knew?" Wind (38) 80, p. 36.
"Faw-ther. " Wind (38) 80, p. 36.

HENNEDY, Hugh
"Seeing Moving Things. " BallSUF (21:1) Wint 80, p. 3.
"Wind After Snow. " BelPoJ (31:1) Aut 80, p. 3.

HENNEN, Tom
"Farm on a Winter Morning. " DacTerr (17) 80, p. 42.
"I Think of Bread and Water and the Roots of a Tree All Wet. "
    NewL (47:1) Aut 80, p. 108.

HENRY, Michael
"Color Chart. " Sam (92) 80, p. 70.
"Summer Fallow. " Sam (102) 80, p. 2.

HENRY, Sarah
"Valentine. " SmPd (50) Aut 80, p. 10.

HENSHAW, Tyler
"Measuring Time. " Im (6:2) 80, p. 3.

HENSON, David
"The Mother of the Boy Who Went Blind from Staring at the
    Solar Eclipse Complains to the Psychologist. " PoNow (29)
    80, p. 13.

HENSON, Lance
"Indians With Umbrellas. " StoneC (7:3) D 80, p. 68.
"On the Mescalero Reservation. " StoneC (7:3) D 80, p. 67.
"Song in Summer. " StoneC (7:3) D 80, p. 68.

HEPBURN, Robert
"A Newsman's Prayer. " Sam (92) 80, p. 26.

HERBERT, Zbigniew
"Mr. Cogito's Contribution to Mayerling's Tragedy" (tr. by Stuart Friebert). PoNow (28) 80, p. 46.

HERMAN, Ira
"Small Tragedies in Civilized Places. " PoNow (29) 80, p. 14.

HERMANS, Theo
"Night Sounds" (tr. of Paul van Ostaijen). ChiR (32:1) Sum 80, p. 107.
"Ulysses" (tr. of Hugo Claus). PortR (26) 80, p. 272.

HERMSEN, Terry
"August. " Outbr (4/5) Aut 79-Spr 80, p. 25.
"Back Entrance. " Outbr (4/5) Aut 79-Spr 80, p. 26.

HERNANDEZ, Miguel
"Like the Bull" (tr. by Willis Barnstone). ChiR (31:4) Spr 80, p. 148.

HERNTON, Calvin
"Hands. " BlackALF (14:3) Aut 80, p. 112.

HERPORT, Susan Hall
"Faded Photos. " MalR (54) Ap 80, p. 123.

HERR, Joy E.
"My Death in Ann Arbor. " CapeR (16:1) Wint 80, p. 7.

HERRON, Elizabeth
"The Bridge. " PikeF (3) Wint 80, p. 27.
"The Wild Weeds. " PikeF (3) Wint 80, p. 27.

HERRSTROM, David
"Chainsaw. " US1 (12/13) Aut-Wint 80, p. 9.
"Learning the Assay. " US1 (12/13) Aut-Wint 80, p. 8.
"Pig. " US1 (12/13) Aut-Wint 80, p. 9.

HERSHMAN, M. F.
"Avian. " BelPoJ (31:1) Aut 80, p. 12.
"The Hold. " BelPoJ (31:1) Aut 80, p. 13.

HERSHON, Jed
"Saturday at the Catskills, 1975. " HangL (37) Spr 80, p. 56.

HERSHON, Robert
"Cats and Dogs" (for Jean Stewart). HangL (37) Spr 80, p. 18.
"The Doctor Who Wanted. " PoNow (26) 80, p. 29.
"Friends of Friends. " PoNow (28) 80, p. 24.
"Here's a Surprise. " PoNow (28) 80, p. 6.

"It. " PoetryNW (21:4) Wint 80-81, p. 32.
"Obit Enclosed. " PoNow (28) 80, p. 24.
"Popularity. " HangL (37) Spr 80, p. 21.
"Preoccupation. " PoNow (27) 80, p. 20.
"Tin Cans. " PoNow (28) 80, p. 24.
"A Walk: Dead and Closed. " HangL (37) Spr 80, p. 22.
"The Wrong Way to Remsen Street" (for Carol Baum). HangL
   (37) Spr 80, p. 20.

HERZELE, Margarethe
   "März mondnacht. " PortR (26) 80, p. 36.
   "Mutter chaos. " PortR (26) 80, p. 37.

HESS, Linda
   from Bijak: "Padas" (tr. of Kabir w. Shukdev Singh). MalR
      (54) Ap 80, pp. 79-85.
   from Bijak: "Sakhis" (tr. of Kabir w. Shukdev Singh). MalR
      (54) Ap 80, p. 86.

HESS, Walter
   "Before Sleep. " AmerPoR (9:3) My-Je 80, p. 32.
   "Daughter. " AmerPoR (9:3) My-Je 80, p. 32.
   "Overlook. " AmerPoR (9:3) My-Je 80, p. 32.
   "Poem: The old hag says. " AmerPoR (9:3) My-Je 80, p. 32.

HESSELBEIN, John
   "Fingers. " SmPd (50) Aut 80, p. 11.

HESSER, Jana
   "Body of Summer" (tr. of Odysseus Elytis w. Edward Morin
      and Lefteris Pavlides). CharR (6:2) Aut 80, p. 49.
   "Drinking the Corinthian Sun" (tr. of Odysseus Elytis w. Edward
      Morin and Lefteris Pavlides). CharR (6:2) Aut 80, p. 50.
   "No Longer Do I Know the Night" (tr. of Odysseus Elytis w.
      Edward Morin and Lefteris Pavlides). CharR (6:2) Aut 80,
      p. 50.

HESTER, M. L.
   "Closet. " StoneC (7:3) D 80, p. 10.
   "Daisy. " Wind (36) 80, p. 31.
   "The Editor of Dreams. " PoNow (29) 80, p. 46.
   "The Employee of the All-Nite Doughnut Shop. " Wind (36) 80,
      p. 31.
   "International Motherhood Assoc. " LitR (23:3) Spr 80, p. 350.
   "The Last American Man With Class. " LitR (23:3) Spr 80, p.
      350.
   "The Meditations of O. C. MacClean: Killing Possum. " LitR
      (23:3) Spr 80, p. 351.
   "The Poet Confounds a Physician. " Spirit (5:1 /2) Aut-Wint 79-
      80, p. 35.

HEWITT, Christopher
   "Mourning. " EnPas (11) 80, p. 13.

HEWITT, Geof
"Blocks. " NewL (47:1) Aut 80, p. 26.
"Graywater Washing. " NewL (47:1) Aut 80, p. 26.
"Vantage" (for H. C.). NewL (46:4) Sum 80, p. 98.
"Vision 2. " NewL (47:1) Aut 80, p. 27.
"Vision 3. " NewL (47:1) Aut 80, p. 27.

HEY, Phil
"Choice. " PoNow (26) 80, p. 9.
"Elsie's Cafe in Aurelia Iowa. " PoNow (26) 80, p. 9.
"The Hoop. " PoNow (28) 80, p. 24.
"Mason Jar. " PoNow (28) 80, p. 18.
"Reorganizing the Stars: Mickey Mantle, Willie Mays, the Big
    Apple. " PoNow (28) 80, p. 24.
"Tractor. " PoNow (28) 80, p. 18.

HEYD, Michael
"The Shadow Cat. " Outbr (4/5) Aut 79-Spr 80, p. 22.

HEYEN, William
"The Child. " CropD (1) Spr 80, p. 9.
"Redwings. " Tendril (9) 80, p. 74.
"Spring Song for William Wordsworth. " Bits (11) 80.
"This Night. " Harp (261:1566) N 80, p. 70.

HEYM, Georg
"The Blind Men" (tr. by Peter Viereck). PoNow (26) 80, p. 45.
"Post Mortem" (tr. by Betty Falkenberg). PoNow (28) 80, p. 45.

HEYNEN, Jim
"The Barn. " SouthernPR (20:2) Aut 80, p. 48.
"Falling Out of Love. " ConcPo (13:2) Aut 80, p. 18.
"How to Start an Epic. " ConcPo (13:2) Aut 80, p. 18.
"Morning Chores. " Tendril (9) 80, p. 75.

HIBBARD, Scott G.
"The Fisherman's Permission. " CutB (15) Aut/Wint 80, p. 53.

HICKEY, Mark
"It Is Enough. " CreamCR (5:2) Spr 80, p. 70.
"Post Card. " StoneC (7:2) My 80, p. 29.
"The Road Along the Thumb and Forefinger. " CapeR (15:2) Sum
    80, p. 4.
"A Sailing Sonnet. " StoneC (7:2) My 80, p. 29.

HIGGINS, Frank
"Starting from Ellis Island. " DacTerr (17) 80, p. 43.

HIGGINS, Sr. Anne D. C.
"The Space Window at the Washington Cathedral. " Comm (107:7)
    11 Ap 80, p. 212.

HIKARU, Hida
"Before Farewell" (for Staffan Berg). Ark (14) 80, p. 239.

"A Snowy Heron Was Dead. " Ark (14) 80, p. 238.

HIKMET, Nazim
Ten poems (tr. by Randy Blasing and Mutlu Konuk). PoetryE
(3) 80, pp. 6-18.

HILBERRY, Conrad
"Christmas, Mexico. " Poetry (137:3) D 80, p. 148.
"The Expatriate. " Poetry (136:6) S 80, p. 326.
"The Moon Seen as a Slice of Pineapple. " Poetry (136:6) S 80,
p. 325.
"Nuestra Señora de la salud. " Poetry (136:5) S 80, p. 327.

HILD, Harold
"The Subtle Bear. " KanQ (12:1) Wint 80, p. 139.

HILDEBIDLE, John
"The County. " PoetryNW (21:1) Spr 80, p. 27.
"For Harriet Quimby, Aviatrix: July 1, 1912. " BelPoJ (30:3)
Spr 80, p. 23.
"The Supplication of Dorothy Bradford. " Aspect (76) S-D 79-80,
p. 49.
"To Speak of the Fear That Is Autumn. " SouthernPR (20:1) Spr
80, p. 19.

HILL, James E. Jr.
"Algebraic Expression. " PikeF (3) Wint 80, p. 28.
"Phase 1. " PikeF (3) Wint 80, p. 28.

HILL, Jeanne Foster
"The Feather in the Hall. " AmerPoR (9:3) My-Je 80, p. 36.
"Looking at a Map and a Mountain. " AmerPoR (9:3) My-Je 80,
p. 36.
"Written While Preparing the Pot Roast on an October Day in
Buffalo. " AmerPoR (9:3) My-Je 80, p. 36.

HILL, Nellie
"Soup on a Cold Day. " CentR (24:1) Wint 80, p. 80.

HILL, Robert W.
"The Braidlike Structure of Things. " SouthernR (16:1) Wint 80,
p. 157.
"The Work, the Rest. " SouthernR (16:1) Wint 80, p. 158.

HILL, Roberta
"Midwinter Stars. " Nat (231:11) 11 O 80, p. 356.

HILL, Russell
"The Eel River. " NowestR (18:3) 80, p. 62.

HILL, William D.
"Battery. " EngJ (69:5) My 80, p. 55.

HILLEBRAND, Robert
"Being Alone. " KanQ (12:1) Wint 80, p. 133.

HILLMAN, Brenda
"Aubade" (for my mother). PraS (54:3) Aut 80, p. 81.
"Cameo. " Thrpny (3) Aut 80, p. 15.
"February. " PraS (54:3) Aut 80, p. 82.
"Tending the Fire. " WatT (1) Aut 80, p. 12.
"The Wrench. " Thrpny (1) Wint-Spr 80, p. 16.

HILSINGER, Serena Sue
"Triptych of Gossips" (for L. E. B. and C. H. E.). BelPoJ (31:1)
    Aut 80, p. 41.

HILTON, David
"Big C Suite" (for "Tommy" Hilton). MinnR (NS 15) Aut 80, pp.
    12-17.
"Dusk, Early March. " PoNow (26) 80, p. 30.
"A Night in 762. " PoNow (27) 80, p. 9.

HILTON, William C.
"Decay. " BallSUF (21:1) Wint 80, p. 53.
"Rest-House: Manila, '45. " PoetryNW (21:3) Aut 80, p. 43.

HIND, Steven
"After Oklahoma" (for Cliff). MidwQ (21:4) Sum 80, p. 445.
"The Day Hoppy Fell Off the Train" (for Jim). MidwQ (21:4)
    Sum 80, p. 443.
"Horsecatcher" (for J. H. M.). MidwQ (21:4) Sum 80, p. 444.

HINDLEY, Norman
"Getaway. " StoneC (7:3) D 80, p. 51.
"Letter to Massasoit from William Blackstone at School in Eng-
    land. " StoneC (7:3) D 80, p. 50.
"Wood Butcher" (for my father). PoNow (29) 80, p. 45.

HINDS, Jeanette
"Mortification. " ChrC (97:13) 9 Ap 80, p. 405.

HINRICHSEN, Dennis
"Elegy Spoken to a Tree. " YaleR (69:3) Spr 80, p. 444.
"Elegy Spoken to My Grandfather. " SlowLR (4) 80, p. 4.
"To a Ghost. " SlowLR (4) 80, p. 6.

HINTZ, Lisa
"the dank. " EngJ (69:5) My 80, p. 54.

HIONIS, Argyris
"Decadence" (to Fondas Kondylis). Spirit (5:1 /2) Aut-Wint 79-
    80, p. 32.

HIRSCH, Edward
"Dance You Monster to My Soft Song!" Bound (8:2) Wint 80, p.

325.
"Dusk: Elegy for the Dark Sun. " YaleR (70:2) Wint 81, p. 260.
"Factories. " PartR (47:2) 80, p. 227.
"For the Sleepwalkers. " Poetry (137:3) D 80, p. 151.
"Regret. " NewYorker (56:7) 7 Ap 80, p. 129.
"A Valentine from Rimbaud. " Bound (8:2) Wint 80, p. 324.

HIRSCH, Linda Blaker
"Though the leaves fade. " CropD (2/3) Aut-Wint 80, p. 21.

HIRSCHFIELD, Ted
"A. M. -P. M. " CapeR (15:2) Sum 80, p. 27.
"Housekeeping. " CapeR (15:2) Sum 80, p. 26.
"Vacuum Cleaner. " CapeR (15:2) Sum 80, p. 24.

HISSONS, Dora Sherwood
"Spider. " BelPoJ (31:1) Aut 80, p. 3.

HITCHCOCK, George
"Antoni Gaudi. " PoetryE (1) 80, p. 63.
"Burning It Down. " Ark (14) 80, p. 241.
"Definitions. " Ark (14) 80, p. 240.
"Transformations. " PoetryE (1) 80, p. 64.
"When I Came Back to Dancing Misery. " Tendril (9) 80, p. 76.

HJALMARSSON, Johann
"From the Circus" (tr. by Alan Boucher). Vis (2) 80.

HJORTSHOJ, Keith
"Voices. " HangL (37) Spr 80, p. 23.

HOAG, Ronald Wesley
"Deer Hunting. " Aspen (10) Wint 80, p. 54.

HODGE, Jan D.
"Isometrics. " Bits (11) 80.

HODGE, Marion
"True Child. " HolCrit (17:2) Ap 80, p. 18.

HODGEN, John
"Crazy Woman Putting on Lipstick. " BelPoJ (30:4) Sum 80, p.
    23.
"Two Silos. " EngJ (69:5) My 80, p. 52.

HODGES, Elizabeth
"Birthday. " Aspect (76) S-D 79-80, p. 27.
"Blue Ridge. " NoAmR (265:1) Mr 80, p. 27.
"Business Trips. " HolCrit (17:4) O 80, p. 11.

HODGES, Karen
"Father M. , On Wearing the Collar. " BelPoJ (31:1) Aut 80, p.
    17.

"Gauntlet Run. " BelPoJ (31:1) Aut 80, p. 16.
"Nature Loves to Hide. " BelPoJ (31:1) Aut 80, p. 14.
"Venus 1979. " BelPoJ (31:1) Aut 80, p. 15.

HOEFT, Robert D.
"Emily Dickinson in an Eighteen Wheeler. " Pan (21) 80, p. 48.
"He Who Lights Last. " Pan (21) 80, p. 47.
"On the Importance of Form (the Icicle). " CropD (2 /3) Aut-
    Wint 80, p. 39.

HOEY, Allen
"Jacklighting. " CutB (15) Aut/Wint 80, p. 46.
'Terms of Endearment. " Tendril (7/8) Spr-Sum 80, p. 41.
"The Visionary Runner. " Tele (16) 80, p. 119.

HOFER, Mariann
"At Hart Crane's Memorial in Garrettsville, Ohio. " PoNow (29)
    80, p. 14.

HOFFMAN, Daniel
from Brotherly Love: (30, 31, 33, 34, 35, 37, 38, 39). Hudson
    (33:3) Aut 80, pp. 358-370.
from Brotherly Love: "To the Maker of 'A Peaceable Kingdom. '"
    GeoR (34:4) Wint 80, p. 813.
"High Society. " Hudson (33:1) Spr 80, p. 9.
"On the Industrial Highway. " Tendril (9) 80, p. 77.

HOFFMAN, Henry A.
"My Great Sixth Power Grandfather. " KanQ (12:3) Sum 80, p.
    72.

HOFFMAN, Jill
"Mother-of-Pearl. " PartR (47:1) 80, p. 128.
"Regret. " PartR (47:1) 80, p. 128.

HOFMANNSTHAL, Hugo von
"Experience" (tr. by John N. Miller). WebR (5:2) Aut 80, p.
    20.

HOFSTADTER, Marc
from Un feu va devant nous: "A Voice" (tr. of Yves Bonnefoy).
    Bound (8:2) Wint 80, p. 276.
from Un feu va devant nous: "Evening Speech" (tr. of Yves
    Bonnefoy). Bound (8:2) Wint 80, p. 278.
from Un feu va devant nous: "The Bedroom" (tr. of Yves
    Bonnefoy). Bound (8:2) Wint 80, p. 274.
from Un feu va devant nous: "The Light, Changed" (tr. of
    Yves Bonnefoy). Bound (8:2) Wint 80, p. 277.
from Un feu va devant nous: "The Myrtle" (tr. of Yves Bonne-
    foy). Bound (8:2) Wint 80, p. 275.

HOGAN, Linda
"Fear of the Dark. " DenQ (14:4) Wint 80, p. 4.

"The Floating World. " DenQ (14:4) Wint 80, p. 3.
"Guarding Sleep" (for my daughter, Sandra). DenQ (14:4) Wint
    80, p. 6.
"Morning. " SmPd (48) Wint 80, p. 22.
from Oneida: "Mr. Noyes Initiates the Silk Girl into Sex. "
    Ark (14) 80, p. 244.
from Oneida: "Museum in the Mansion House. " Ark (14) 80,
    p. 245.
from Oneida: "The Women Quilting. " Ark (14) 80, p. 242.
"Small Life. " DenQ (14:4) Wint 80, p. 8.
"Window in Stone. " SmPd (48) Wint 80, p. 23.
"Woman Gardening. " DenQ (14:4) Wint 80, p. 9.

HOGAN, Michael
"the condor. " Kayak (55) Ja 81, p. 52.

HOGUE, Cynthia
"Interior. " QW (10) Wint-Spr 80, p. 90.

HOHENSTEIN, Anne
"Horizon" (tr. of Vicente Huidobro). EnPas (10) 80, p. 15.

HOLAN, Vladimir
"Death" (tr. by Kaca Polackova-Henly). Nat (230:20) 24 My 80,
    p. 633.
"Smrt. " PortR (26) 80, p. 76.

HOLBERN, Bryan K.
"Adversity. " Wind (37) 80, p. 18.
"Apathy. " Wind (37) 80, p. 18.

HOLDEN, Jonathan
"At the Dump" (to Claude). QW (11) Aut-Wint 80-81, p. 54.
"Carp. " PoNow (27) 80, p. 18.
"Cleaning the Flue. " ModernPS (10:1) 80, p. 41.
"First Snow. " Iowa (11:1) Wint 80, p. 113.
"God. " KanQ (12:1) Wint 80, p. 7.
"In the Denver Museum: A Diorama. " ModernPS (10:1) 80, p.
    43.
"Looking for Shooting Stars. " MissouriR (3:2) Wint 80, p. 18.
"One-Ring Circus. " Poetry (136:4) Jl 80, p. 197.
"The Ordinary Deja Vu of a Rainy Morning. " Iowa (11:1) Wint
    80, p. 111.
"The Secret. " VirQR (56:3) Sum 80, p. 506.
"Turning Off the Light. " PraS (54:4) Wint 80-81, p. 65.
"Washing My Son. " KanQ (12:1) Wint 80, p. 8.
"Wetter. " Aspen (9) Spr 80, p. 64.

HOLLAMAN, Keith
"Arm in Arm" (tr. of Benjamin Péret). Durak (4) 80, p. 12.
"One Move One Less" (tr. of Benjamin Péret). Durak (4) 80,
    p. 13.

HOLLAND, Barbara A.
"Dial-an-Oracle. " NewRena (12) Spr 80, p. 71.

HOLLAND, John
"Antipodes. " Agni (12) 80, p. 36.

HOLLANDER, Jean
"Picksites II. " Poem (40) N 80, p. 29.
"Severing. " Poem (40) N 80, p. 30.

HOLLANDER, John
"The Boat. " WebR (5:1) Wint 80, p. 50.
"Figures of Speech. Figures of Thought. Figures of Earth and
    Water. " WebR (5:1) Wint 80, p. 50.
"Morning in the Islands. " NewRep (182:14) 5 Ap 80, p. 29.

HOLLEY, Margaret
"Coming Home. " Northeast (3:8) Wint 80, p. 38.
"Cypresses. " Northeast (3:8) Wint 80, p. 36.
"Great Aunt Beth. " Northeast (3:8) Wint 80, p. 37.
"The Man Under the Bed. " Northeast (3:8) Wint 80, p. 35.
"The Red Leaves. " Northeast (3:8) Wint 80, p. 36.
"Your Woods. " Prima (5) 79, p. 10.

HOLLIS, Angela
"Fishing at Port Townsend. " PoetryNW (21:2) Sum 80, p. 20.

HOLLO, Anselm
"July 31, Andraz" (tr. of Tomaž Salamun). NewL (47:1) Aut
    80, p. 55.
"Night" (tr. of Tomaž Salamun). NewL (47:1) Aut 80, p. 56.
"Nile" (tr. of Tomaž Salamun). NewL (47:1) Aut 80, p. 54.
"Proverbs" (tr. of Tomaž Salamun). NewL (47:1) Aut 80, p.
    55.
"Vacation Time" (tr. of Tomaž Salamun). NewL (47:1) Aut 80,
    p. 53.
"What Is What" (tr. of Tomaž Salamun). NewL (47:1) Aut 80,
    p. 54.

HOLLOWAY, John
"The Source. " Stand (21:2) 80, p. 59.

HOLMAN, Bob
"Unity. " Tele (16) 80, p. 5.

HOLSCHER, Rory
"Fever Meditation. " BelPoJ (31:2) Wint 80, p. 13.
"Open Statement. " ColEng (42:4) D 80, p. 367.
"Taughannock Falls. " BelPoJ (31:2) Wint 80-81, p. 12.

HOLUB, Miroslav
"Assault" (tr. by Dana Ha'bova' and Stuart Friebert). MalR (55)
    Jl 80, p. 134.

"At Home" (tr. by Dana Habova and Stuart Friebert). <u>PoNow</u>
    (27) 80, p. 46.
"Death of a Sparrow" (tr. by Dana Hábová and Stuart Friebert).
    <u>OntR</u> (12) Spr-Sum 80, p. 54.
"Doma." <u>PortR</u> (26) 80, p. 65.
"Elsewhere" (tr. by Stuart Friebert and author). <u>Durak</u> (4) 80,
    p. 9.
"Experimental Animals" (tr. by Daniel Simko). <u>Durak</u> (5) 80,
    p. 8.
"MaMa" (tr. by Dana Ha'bova' and Stuart Friebert). <u>MalR</u> (55)
    Jl 80, p. 133.
"The Minotaur's Thoughts on Poetry" (tr. by author and Stuart
    Friebert). <u>Durak</u> (4) 80, p. 5.
"On the Dog Angel" (tr. by Dana Hábová and Stuart Friebert).
    <u>OntR</u> (12) Spr-Sum 80, p. 55.
"On the Origin of a Festive Morning" (tr. by Dana Ha'bova' and
    Stuart Friebert). <u>MalR</u> (55) Jl 80, p. 136.
"On the Origin of Poor Digestion" (tr. by Dana Habova and
    Stuart Friebert). <u>Durak</u> (4) 80, p. 8.
"On the Origin of Six P. M." (tr. by author and Stuart Friebert).
    <u>Durak</u> (4) 80, p. 6.
"A Special Performance for Statues" (tr. by author and Stuart
    Friebert). <u>Field</u> (23) Aut 80, p. 31.
"We will put on one of our heads, " (tr. by Dana Ha'bova and
    Stuart Friebert). <u>MalR</u> (55) Jl 80, p. 131.

HOLZMAN, Michael
    "At the Anthropology Museum. " <u>Bound</u> (8:2) Wint 80, p. 132.
    "Billy. " <u>Bound</u> (8:2) Wint 80, p. 135.
    "The Pigs of Chapultepec Park. " <u>Bound</u> (8:2) Wint 80, p. 133.
    "The Souvenir Shop at Teotihuacan. " <u>Bound</u> (8:2) Wint 80, p.
        136.
    "Zócalo, Not Zona Rosa. " <u>Bound</u> (8:2) Wint 80, p. 134.

HOMER, Art
    "A Child's Fear of Numbers. " <u>CharR</u> (6:2) Aut 80, p. 27.

HONECKER, George J.
    "The Man Who Studies Roses. " <u>Nimrod</u> (24:1) Aut-Wint 80, pp.
        45-58.
    "Poem in Which I Discover the True Meaning of My Birth. "
        <u>SunM</u> (9/10) Sum 80, p. 128.

HONGO, Garrett Karou
    "On the Duck" (for Mark Lundsten). <u>Bachy</u> (16) Wint 80, p. 81.
    "Washizu's Final Soliloquy" (for Lawrence Raab). <u>Bachy</u> (16)
        Wint 80, p. 82.
    "Yellow Light. " <u>NewYorker</u> (56:33) 6 O 80, p. 64.

HONIG, Edwin
    from Divan del Tamarit: "Casida of the Boy Wounded by Water"
        (tr. of Garcia Lorca). <u>BosUJ</u> (26:3) 80, p. 148.
    from Divan del Tamarit: "Casida of the Branches" (tr. of

Garcia Lorca). BosUJ (26:3) 80, p. 147.
from Divan del Tamarit: "Gacela of Love Unforeseen" (tr. of
Garcia Lorca). BosUJ (26:3) 80, p. 144.
from Divan del Tamarit: "Gacela of Love's Memory" (tr. of
Garcia Lorca). BosUJ (26:3) 80, p. 146.
from Divan del Tamarit: "Gacela of Miraculous Love" (tr. of
Garcia Lorca). BosUJ (26:3) 80, p. 143.
from Divan del Tamarit: "Gacela of the Escape" (tr. of Garcia
Lorca). BosUJ (26:3) 80, p. 145.
"Night Island." PoNow (26) 80, p. 4.
"Partida. " PoNow (27) 80, p. 3.
Twelve poems. PoNow (28) 80, pp. 2, 38.

HOOD, Ernest A.
"Three Love Songs Sung to Michael. " Mouth (2:5) O 80, p. 20.

HOOPER, Patricia
"In Summer. " PoNow (27) 80, p. 30.
"Milk. " SouthernPR (20:2) Aut 80, p. 10.
"Poem for a Child Seen Only at Nightfall. " PoNow (27) 80, p.
30.

HOOVER, Paul
"Concerning the The. " PartR (47:4) 80, p. 616.
"Ode to the Minor Premise." ChiR (32:1) Sum 80, p. 31.

HOOVER, Robert
"Sound. " Wind (38) 80, p. 38.

HOPE, A. D.
"Salabhanjika. " NewL (46:3) Spr 80, p. 29.

HOPE, Marsha
"To whoever planted the bomb in the Holy City Hardware. "
Stand (21:4) 80, p. 37.

HOPES, David
"Bird bones. " PoetryNW (21:1) Spr 80, p. 38.
"For One Whose Birthday Was the Feast of Saint James. "
KanQ (12:1) Wint 80, p. 17.
"The Hairdresser. " KanQ (12:1) Wint 80, p. 18.
"October. " PoetryNW (21:1) Spr 80, p. 40.

HOPKINS, Ruth
"Literary Birth. " Wind (37) 80, p. 59.

HOPKINS, Steven
"Adrienne. " Northeast (3:8) Wint 80, p. 48.

HOPPER, Paul Thorfinn
"The Water Under the Grass" (tr. of Paul la Cour). Vis (3) 80.

HORNE, Lewis
"Open Field. " CapeR (15:2) Sum 80, p. 36.

"Winter Nights. " SouthernHR (14:3) Sum 80, p. 247.

HORSTING, Eric
  "Brevity. " PoNow (26) 80, p. 47.
  "Crushes. " Agni (13) 80, p. 88.

HORTON, Barbara
  "Winter. " Prima (5) 79, p. 42.

HORTON, Mark
  "Conquest. " Poem (38) Mr 80, p. 57.

HORVATH, John
  "Clouds. " UTR (6:3/4) 80, p. 22.
  "Triptych. " UTR (6:3/4) 80, p. 24.

HORVATH, Lou
  "cobweb strophes. " Tele (16) 80, p. 98.

HORWOOD, Harold
  "Beside the Tracks. " PottPort (2) 80-81, p. 47.
  "Green and Pleasant Land. " PottPort (2) 80-81, p. 5.
  "In Flanders Fields. " PottPort (2) 80-81, p. 11.
  "Journalist's Night Thoughts. " PottPort (1) 79-80, p. 28.
  "Recessional. " PottPort (1) 79-80, p. 20.

HOTHAM, Gary
  Five Haiku. Northeast (3:8) Wint 80, p. 32.
  Three Haiku. WindO (36) Spr-Sum 80, p. 4.

HOUCHIN, Ron
  "Investigations of a Young Dog. " CalQ (16/17) 80, p. 122.

HOUSER, Preston L.
  "Haiku. " WindO (36) Spr-Sum 80, p. 5.

HOUSTON, Peyton
  "Clearing the Distances. " OP (30) Aut 80, p. 56.

HOUY, Julie
  "Dancing at the Park. " PoNow (29) 80, p. 14.
  "What's Your Line?" PoNow (29) 80, p. 14.

HOVDE, A. J.
  "Squirrel. " HolCrit (17:1) F 80, p. 15.

HOWARD, Ben
  "Re-visiting the Cloister. " PraS (54:2) Sum 80, p. 62.
  "The Wood Splitter" (for William Underhill). PraS (54:2) Sum
    80, p. 61.

HOWARD, Jim
  "Boy Trash Picker. " NewL (46:3) Spr 80, p. 119.

HOWARD, Mary
  "Namesake, 1881. " PoetC (12:1) 80, p. 14.

HOWARD, Richard
  "Attic Red-Figure Calix, Revelling in Progress, Circa 510
      B. C. " YaleR (70:2) Wint 81, p. 263.
  "On Hearing Your Lover Is Going to the Baths Tonight. "
      NewRep (182:21) 24 My 80, p. 30.

HOWELL, Christopher
  "Liberty and Ten Years of Return" (for the Veterans). AntR (38:
      3) Sum 80, p. 337.
  "Ling Wei on the North Road. " CalQ (16/17) 80, p. 120.
  "Ling Wei's Small Song for His Home Valley. " CalQ (16/17) 80,
      p. 118.
  "Ling Wei's Song Upon Waking" (for the Longs). CalQ (16/17)
      80, p. 119.
  "On the Back of the Note I Left You When I Went Out I Have
      Written This Ode. " Iowa (10:4) Aut 79, p. 22.
  "The Pitcher's Pride. " Iowa (11:1) Wint 80, p. 128.

HOY, Nancy
  "Social Worker. " EngJ (69:5) My 80, p. 58.

HOY, Ruby
  "Hands Are the Ancestors of Words. " GRR (11:1) 80, p. 33.
  "Rituals. " GRR (11:1) 80, p. 34.

HOYT, Cynthia
  "Call the Hour. " Harp (260:1556) Ja 80, p. 27.

HOYT, Don A.
  "Genesis Repeated. " Wind (38) 80, p. 39.

HSIU Ou-yang
  Ten Tz'u (tr. by Jerome P. Seaton). LitR (23:4) Sum 80, p.
      498.

HUCHEL, Peter
  "Children in Autumn" (tr. by Rich Ives). CharR (6:1) Spr 80,
      p. 37.
  "Greek Morning" (tr. by Rich Ives). CharR (6:1) Spr 80, p. 32.
  "House Near Olmitello" (tr. by Rich Ives). QW (11) Aut-Wint
      80-81, p. 39.
  "In Brittany" (tr. by Rich Ives). CutB (14) Spr/Sum 80, p. 60.
  "Landscape Beyond Warsaw" (tr. by Rich Ives). QW (11) Aut-
      Wint 80-81, p. 37.
  "Military Cemetery" (tr. by Rich Ives). QW (11) Aut-Wint 80-
      81, p. 38.
  "Momtschil" (tr. by Rich Ives). QW (11) Aut-Wint 80-81, p. 42.
  "Thrace" (tr. by Rich Ives). CutB (14) Spr/Sum 80, p. 61.
  "Verona" (tr. by Rich Ives). QW (11) Aut-Wint 80-81, p. 41.
  "Winter Psalm" (for Hans Mayer) (tr. by Rich Ives). QW (11)

Aut-Wint 80-81, p. 43.
"Winter Quarters" (tr. by Rich Ives). QW (11) Aut-Wint 80-81,
    p. 40.

HUDDLE, David
    "Delivering the Times, 1952-1955. " PoNow (27) 80, p. 25.
    "Mrs. Green. " PoNow (27) 80, p. 25.
    "What Pig Clemons Told My Mother. " PoNow (27) 80, p. 25.

HUDGINS, Andrew
    "Awaiting Winter Visitors: Jonathan Edwards, 1749. "
        NewYorker (56:5) 24 Mr 80, p. 46.
    "The Bog of the Fathers. " AmerPoR (9:5) S-O 80, p. 47.
    "Broad Daylight" (for Silas). Confr (20) Spr-Sum 80, p. 28.
    "Cats and Egypt. " SouthernHR (14:2) Spr 80, p. 143.
    "A Plague of Frogs. " PoNow (29) 80, p. 15.
    "The Stoker's Sunday Morning. " Hudson (33:3) Aut 80, p. 406.
    "Tamar. " SouthernHR (14:2) Spr 80, p. 142.
    "To My Brother, on His Baptism. " SouthernR (16:4) Aut 80, p.
        936.

HUDSON, Marc
    "George Vancouver's Death Dream. " HiramPoR (28) Spr-Sum
        80, p. 20.

HUDSPITH, Vicki
    "Chattwick Island. " Tele (16) 80, p. 30.
    "The Facade of a New Iran. " SunM (9/10) Sum 80, pp. 109-
        114.
    "Special Characteristics. " Tele (16) 80, p. 29.

HUERTA, Efrain
    "Dawn After a Single Star" (tr. by James Normington). PoNow
        (27) 80, p. 44.

HUEY, Mark
    "Nightmare" (for Maude). CharR (6:2) Aut 80, p. 29.

HUGHES, Austin
    "Meriwether Lewis at Grinder's Inn. " FourQt (29:3) Spr 80, p.
        3.
    "Thomas Say at New Harmony. " FourQt (29:3) Spr 80, p. 4.
    "To-Kah-Na's Spirit-Quest. " FourQt (29:3) Spr 80, p. 5.

HUGHES, Dorothy
    "Falling in Love. " MassR (21:3) Aut 80, p. 486.
    "Strawberries. " MassR (21:1) Spr 80, p. 176.

HUGHES, Langston
    "A House in Taos. " ConcPo (13:2) Aut 80, p. 53.

HUGHES, Richard
    "He Had the Look. " CapeR (16:1) Wint 80, p. 18.

"I Like the Rain Here. " CapeR (16:1) Wint 80, p. 19.
"They Throw Words. " CapeR (16:1) Wint 80, p. 19.
"What Opens Her Eyes. " CapeR (16:1) Wint 80, p. 18.

HUGHES, Riley
"At the Grave of Dylan Thomas, Laugharne. " FourQt (29:4)
    Sum 80, p. 32.

HUGHES, Ted
"Do Not Pick Up the Telephone. " Ploughs (6:1) 80, p. 86.
"A Dove. " Ploughs (6:1) 80, p. 85.
"Lily. " Ploughs (6:1) 80, p. 84.
from Lumb's Remains: "A primrose petal's edge. " BosUJ (26:3)
    80, p. 59.
from Lumb's Remains: "calves harshly parted from their ma-
    mas. " BosUJ (26:3) 80, p. 59.
from Lumb's Remains: "The dead man lies, marching here and
    there. " BosUJ (26:3) 80, p. 58.
from Lumb's Remains: "The night wind, muscled with rain. "
    BosUJ (26:3) 80, p. 58.
"You Hated Spain. " Ploughs (6:1) 80, p. 82.

HUGO, Richard
"The Braes" (for Sorley and Renee MacLean). AmerPoR (9:3)
    My-Je 80, p. 18.
"Carloway Broch. " Field (22) Spr 80, p. 22.
"Glen Uig. " Tendril (9) 80, p. 78.
"Last Words to James Wright. " GeoR (34:3) Aut 80, p. 556.
"St. John's Chapel. " AmerPoR (9:3) My-Je 80, p. 18.
"The Standing Stones of Callanish. " Nat (230:11) 22 Mr 80, p.
    346.
"Tony. " ConcPo (13:2) Aut 80, p. 85.
"Trumpan. " AmerPoR (9:3) My-Je 80, p. 18.

HUIDOBRO, Vicente
"Horizon" (tr. by Anne Hohenstein). EnPas (10) 80, p. 15.

HUMES, Harry
"Flocking. " BelPoJ (31:2) Wint 80-81, p. 6.
"Gun Dream. " Pan (21) 80, p. 8.
"The Master of Dirt. " HolCrit (17:3) Je 80, p. 15.
"robbing the pillars. " Kayak (53) My 80, p. 29.
"Stalling for Time. " HiramPoR (28) Spr-Sum 80, p. 23.
"Studying the Light. " Pan (21) 80, p. 8.
"Winter Stream. " Pan (21) 80, p. 9.

HUMFLEET, Melanie
"Blossom Thinning. " WindO (36) Spr-Sum 80, p. 16.

HUMMA, John
"Afternoon Difficulty. " SoCaR (13:1) Aut 80, p. 48.

HUMMER, T. R.
"Coming Back: False Dawn. " WestHR (34:4) Aut 80, p. 314.

"Heat and Pressure. " SouthernR (16:1) Wint 80, p. 173.
"The Man Who Beat the Game at Johnny's Truck Stop" (for
    Bruce Weigl). CimR (50) Ja 80, p. 42.
"Mountains Through a Restaurant Window. " ThRiPo (15/16) 80,
    p. 32.
"The Naming. " CimR (50) Ja 80, p. 27.
"The Rural Carrier Discovers That Love Is Everywhere. "
    Comm (107:11) 6 Je 80, p. 340.
"Shadow in the Air. " NoAmR (265:1) Mr 80, p. 27.

HUMMER, Terry
    "The Beating. " QW (11) Aut-Wint 80-81, p. 87.

HUNT, William
    "Beginning at the Beginning. " GeoR (34:2) Sum 80, p. 269.
    "A Darkening Outing at Sea. " NewL (46:4) Sum 80, p. 106.
    "Grandfather in the Room of Night. " MassR (21:4) Wint 80, p.
        737.
    "She Who Holds Us Also Carries the Bell. " NewL (46:4) Sum
        80, p. 107.

HUNTINGTON, Cynthia
    "No One. " VirQR (56:2) Spr 80, p. 262.

HUNTLEY, Daniel
    "Clearing Brush on Goat Mountain. " Wind (36) 80, p. 33.

HUQ, Sanaul
    "Jibon-shilpi. " PortR (26) 80, p. 39.

HUSSEIN, Salah Jama
    "Another Handcuff. " Obs (5:1/2) Spr-Sum 79, p. 111.
    "The Road" (for Yusuf). Obs (5:1/2) Spr-Sum 79, p. 110.

HUSSEY, Anne
    "Indian Summer, 1927. " SouthernR (16:1) Wint 80, p. 151.

HUTCHINSON, Joseph
    "Remedies. " PoNow (29) 80, p. 15.

HUTCHISON, Joseph
    "After a Glib Essay on James Wright. " Northeast (3:8) Wint
        80, p. 26.
    "After Harvest. " Im (6:2) 80, p. 5.
    "Allegiance. " Im (6:2) 80, p. 5.
    "An Animal Death. " Im (6:2) 80, p. 5.
    "Milkweed on a Windy Spring Day. " Im (6:2) 80, p. 5.

HYLAND, L. Rae
    "Seam. " Pig (7) My 80, p. 73.

IBACH, Howard
    "Listening to you. " UTR (6:3/4) 80, p. 27.

IBUR, Jane Ellen
"2 Riddles. " WebR (5:2) Aut 80, p. 78.

IGNATOW, David
"Kaddish. " Nat (231:17) 22 N 80, p. 550.
"Last Words. " MissouriR (4:1) Aut 80, p. 11.
"Lying Quietly. " HangL (38) Aut 80, p. 28.
"My Own House. " Tendril (9) 80, p. 79.
"1905. " Nat (231:17) 22 N 80, p. 550.
"Plans. " PoNow (26) 80, p. 34.
"A white cloud is revealing itself to me as a sign of peace. "
   PoNow (26) 80, p. 14.

IKAN, Ron
"Hittites and Pomegranates. " PoNow (26) 80, p. 34.
"Nightgame. " PoNow (28) 80, p. 31.

ILCE, Ana
"Calle de Verano. " NowestR (18:3) 80, p. 68.

ILLYES, Gyula
"Afterward" (tr. by Jascha Kessler). CentR (24:2) Spr 80, p.
   186.
"Brazilian Rain Forest" (tr. by Emery George). PoNow (28)
   80, p. 46.
"Cannibal Future" (tr. by Jascha Kessler). CentR (24:2) Spr 80,
   p. 187.
"On an Infant" (tr. by Jascha Kessler). CentR (24:2) Spr 80, p.
   186.

INEZ, Colette
"Combing the Bones of Our Vows. " SouthernPR (20:1) Spr 80,
   p. 73.
"Courtier's Lament. " Nimrod (24:1) Aut-Wint 80, p. 81.
"Damsel Flies. " Confr (20) Spr-Sum 80, p. 41.
"In a Borderline Class of Her Own. " SouthernPR (20:1) Spr 80,
   p. 72.
"Pound Noted for Measures of Weight. " OhioR (25) 80, p. 102.
"Weight of Days. " PoNow (27) 80, p. 13.
"Woodrow Wilson. " MichQR (19:3) Sum 80, p. 324.

ING, Nancy C.
"Gazing at the Fog" (tr. of Lo Ching). PortR (26) 80, p. 389.
"Nameless" (tr. of Chung Tin-wen). PortR (26) 80, p. 387.

INWOOD, Paula
"friend to a companion piece" (for ellen). Nimrod (24:1) Aut-
   Wint 80, pp. 37-39.

IOANNOU, Susan
"The Celebration. " MalR (54) Ap 80, p. 44.

IOVINE, Julie V.
"Sun don't dazzle but leave me. " Tele (16) 80, p. 42.

IRELAND, Donna
"Sons" (tr. of Slav H. Karaslavov w. Kevin Ireland). PortR
   (26) 80, p. 54.

IRELAND, Kevin
"Sons" (tr. of Slav H. Karaslavov w. Donna Ireland). PortR
   (26) 80, p. 54.

IRIBARNE, Louis
"Campo di Fiori" (tr. of Czeslaw Milosz w. David Brooks).
   NewYRB (27:16) 23 O 80, p. 8.

IRION, Mary Jean
"A Mosaic of Peace. " ChrC (97:22) 18-25 Je 80, p. 668.
"Solar Eclipse. " NewEngR (3:2) Wint 80, p. 209.

IRVING, James
"Earth. " PottPort (1) 79-80, p. 35.
"Hawk Thoughts. " PottPort (1) 79-80, p. 26.
"A Song and Dance. " PottPort (1) 79-80, p. 23.

IRWIN, Mark
"Dandelions. " Antaeus (39) Aut 80, p. 75.
"Winter Ritual" (tr. of Nichita Stanescu w. Mariana Carpinisan).
   Iowa (10:4) Aut 79, p. 38.

ISAIA, Naná
"Cold Light. " PortR (26) 80, p. 158.

ISON, Tawnya M.
"Our Friendless Years. " Wind (37) 80, p. 19.

ISSENHUTH, Jean-Pierre
"Cage et Lanterne. " Os (10) Spr 80, p. 25.
"Etude de feuille. " Os (10) Spr 80, p. 25.

IVASK, Astrid
"Cikaga" (Ellenai). PortR (26) 80, p. 251.
"Poem: "Ka medniekam mednis tev janosauj mirklis. " PortR
   (26) 80, p. 252.
"The same steps lead down to the sea" (tr. of Ivar Ivask w.
   author). PortR (26) 80, p. 111.

IVASK, Ivar
"Needsamad sammud viivad mereranda. " PortR (26) 80, p. 111.

IVES, Rich
"Children in Autumn" (tr. of Peter Huchel). CharR (6:1) Spr
   80, p. 37.
"December Sonnet" (tr. of Georg Trakl). CutB (14) Spr/Sum
   80, p. 57.
"Flemish Dawn. " MalR (54) Ap 80, p. 142.
"Greek Morning" (tr. of Peter Huchel). CharR (6:1) Spr 80, p.

32.

"House Near Olmitello" (tr. of Peter Huchel). QW (11) Aut-
     Wint 80-81, p. 39.
"I Am Doing This for Both of Us. " MalR (54) Ap 80, p. 140.
"In Brittany" (tr. of Peter Huchel). CutB (14) Spr /Sum 80, p.
     60.
"Landscape Beyond Warsaw" (tr. of Peter Huchel). QW (11)
     Aut-Wint 80-81, p. 37.
"Memory, a Small Brown Bird. " VirQR (56:2) Spr 80, p. 265.
"Military Cemetery" (tr. of Peter Huchel). QW (11) Aut-Wint
     80-81, p. 38.
"Momtschil" (tr. of Peter Huchel). QW (11) Aut-Wint 80-81, p.
     42.
"Radiant Autumn" (tr. of Georg Trakl). CutB (14) Spr /Sum 80,
     p. 58.
"Thrace" (tr. of Peter Huchel). CutB (14) Spr /Sum 80, p. 61.
"Verona" (tr. of Peter Huchel). QW (11) Aut-Wint 80-81, p. 41.
"Whispered in the Afternoon" (tr. of Georg Trakl). CutB (14)
     Spr /Sum 80, p. 59.
"Winter Psalm" (for Hans Mayer) (tr. of Peter Huchel). QW
     (11) Aut-Wint 80-81, p. 43.
"Winter Quarters" (tr. of Peter Huchel). QW (11) Aut-Wint 80-
     81, p. 40.

IVIE, Kelly
    "Gull Lake Reunion. " Poetry (136:2) My 80, p. 88.

JACK, Cardigan
    "The Immigrant No. IV. " LittleM (12:3 /4) 80, p. 76.

JACKSON, Angela
    "The Bloom Amid Alabaster Still. " Obs (5:3) Wint 79, p. 90.
    "Divination. " Obs (5:3) Wint 79, p. 88.
    "Invocation. " Obs (5:3) Wint 79, p. 87.
    "One Kitchen" (for Angeline and Alcie). Obs (5:3) Wint 80, p.
       88.
    "(untitled): who would trade. " Obs (5:3) Wint 79, p. 91.
    "Wares for the Man Wherever the Song Is. " Obs (5:3) Wint 79,
       p. 92.

JACKSON, Glenn F.
    "Crow Flight. " Wind (38) 80, p. 40.

JACKSON, Haywood
    "Coaching Is a Satisfying Job, Especially Now They've Let the
       Girls Play Too. " Sam (86) 79, p. 54.
    "Drunk in Delphi. " KanQ (12:3) Sum 80, p. 92.
    "Fellow Travelers. " Sam (101) 80, p. 67.
    "First Day on the Job: 7:55 A. M. " Sam (102) 80, p. 54.
    "Hephaestos as Midwife, Physician and Lover. " CropD (2 /3)
       Aut-Wint 80, p. 36.
    "If I Am Marcello Mastroianni, Can You Be Lina Wertmuller?"
       Focus (14:88) S 80, p. 31.

"Ursa Major, Hair Down. " SouthernPR (20:1) Spr 80, p. 64.
"Views of Spring, from a Chevy Pickup. " Sam (102) 80, p. 55.

JACKSON, Richard
"The Puzzle. " QW (11) Aut-Wint 80-81, p. 22.
"To Lisa at the Asylum. " Salm (47/48) Wint-Spr 80, p. 59.

JACOBS, Lucky
"The Bridges: Storm Coming. " Wind (36) 80, p. 34.
"Sacrifice Bunt. " PoNow (28) 80, p. 31.

JACOBS, Maria
"Ferrari. " MalR (54) Ap 80, p. 126.
"Song of the Intruder. " MalR (54) Ap 80, p. 127.
"Space/Time Complements. " MalR (54) Ap 80, p. 124.

JACOBS, Nyssa
"Reincarnation. " PikeF (3) Wint 80, p. 23.

JACOBS, Sondra Dunner
"Woman, Your Eyes Say It All. " StoneC (7:2) My 80, p. 16.

JACOBSEN, Josephine
"Border. " Poetry (135:4) Ja 80, p. 196.
"Elective Affinities. " PoNow (26) 80, p. 8.
"How We Learn. " NewL (46:4) Sum 80, p. 103.
"A Motel in Troy, N.Y." Poetry (137:2) N 80, p. 66.
"The Nightwatchman. " Poetry (137:2) N 80, p. 67.
"Pondicherry Blues (for voice and snaredrum). " PoNow (26) 80,
    p. 8.

JACOBSEN, Rolf
"Letter to Light" (tr. by Olav Grinde). CutB (14) Spr/Sum 80,
    p. 106.

JACOBSON, Dale
"One Long Day. " PoNow (29) 80, p. 15.

JACOBY, Jay
"Ars est longa, auditus brevis. " Tele (16) 80, p. 99.
"Song of the Chastised Gourmet. " Tele (16) 80, p. 99.

JACOX, Lynn C.
"The Dream. " SouthernPR (20:2) Aut 80, p. 53.

JAEGER, Sharon Ann
"Keeping the Lowest of Profiles. " StoneC (7:2) My 80, p. 30.
"A Nightmare of Jacob's. " StoneC (7:2) My 80, p. 31.

JAFFE, Dan
"Eden" (adaptation of Lev Mak). Focus (14:86) Ap 80, p. 32.
"Poem for a Bar Mitzva. " DacTerr (17) 80, p. 44.
"Red Square" (adaptation of Lev Mak). Focus (14:86) Ap 80,
    p. 32.

JAHNS, T. R.
  "The Breakdown of Natural Order. " SouthwR (65:4) Aut 80, p.
    373.
  "Standing in Kansas. " PoNow (28) 80, p. 19.

JAMES, David
  "The Great Furniture Store Dream. " Aspen (10) Wint 80, p. 14.
  "Insomnia. " DenQ (15:2) Sum 80, p. 89.
  "Living in the Back Country. " Aspen (10) Wint 80, p. 13.
  "Silence of My Lover" (tr. of Han Yong-un w. Cho Wun-che).
    WindO (36) Spr-Sum 80, p. 32.

JAMES, Sibyl
  "A Letter Back. " Tendril (7/8) Spr-Sum 80, p. 42.
  "New Saws. " Pig (7) My 80, p. 24.
  "A Paean to Peonies. " LittleM (12:3/4) 80, p. 83.
  "Rock and Roll. " MichQR (19:4/20:1) Aut-Wint 80-81, p. 701.
  "Shine and a Hair Cut" (for Nick Licata). Pig (7) My 80, p. 56.
  "Strangers on a Train. " Tendril (7/8) Spr-Sum 80, p. 43.

JAMISON, Barbara
  "Death in Zihuatenejo. " CalQ (16/17) 80, p. 66.

JAMISON, Stephen
  "The Jack's Eye. " AmerPoR (9:3) My-Je 80, p. 45.

JAMMES, Francis
  "There's a Simple-Minded... " (for Stephane Mallarme) (tr. by
    Antony Oldknow). CutB (15) Aut/Wint 80, p. 58.

JANES, Percy
  "John Canuck: A Portrait of Success. " PottPort (2) 80-81, p.
    27.
  "Rest in Truth. " PottPort (2) 80-81, p. 25.

JANEVSKI, Slavko
  "Ballad for the Stone. " PortR (26) 80, p. 470.
  "Bridge. " PortR (26) 80, p. 468.

JANKIEWICZ, Henry
  "the aged. " Kayak (53) My 80, p. 43.
  "the letter. " Kayak (53) My 80, p. 42.
  "the light behind us. " Kayak (53) My 80, p. 41.

JANOVER, Helene
  "what is the life of the ghost?" Ark (14) 80, p. 246.

JANOWITZ, Phyllis
  "Although I Am Taking Courses in the Language. " Ploughs (6:2)
    80, p. 31.
  "The Apple Tree and Mrs. Lucky Enter Winter Together. "
    Ploughs (6:2) 80, p. 33.
  "Calliope. " Pig (7) My 80, p. 89.

"Case. " NewYorker (56:25) 11 Ag 80, p. 36.
"Squeaky Nursery Tunes. " Pig (7) My 80, p. 14.
"Visiting Rites. " Ploughs (6:2) 80, p. 35.

JANOWS, Jill
"Declaration. " Tendril (7/8) Spr-Sum 80, p. 46.
"The Red Flowers. " Tendril (7/8) Spr-Sum 80, p. 45.
"War Widows. " Tendril (7/8) Spr-Sum 80, p. 44.

JAQUISH, Karen I.
"Nightspells. " CapeR (15:2) Sum 80, p. 28.

JARMAN, Mark
"Ascension of the Red Madonna" (for Michael Kane).   Field (22)
    Spr 80, p. 71.
"Bees at the Tide Line. " WatT (1) Aut 80, p. 78.
"Down and Up Again. " Durak (4) 80, p. 16.
"Growing Quiet. " ThRiPo (15/16) 80, p. 33.
"House of Gold. " Field (22) Spr 80, p. 72.
"labors of the months. " Kayak (53) My 80, p. 8.

JASON, Philip K.
"Farm Auction: Accident, Maryland. " Outbr (4/5) Aut 79-Spr
    80, p. 19.

JASTRUN, Mieczyslaw
"Encirclement" (tr. by Benjamin Sher).   NewOR (7:2) 80, p. 113.
"Ruins of the Cathedral of St. John" (tr. by Benjamin Sher).
    NewOR (7:2) 80, p. 112.

JAUSS, David
"Which Is True?" (tr. of Antonio Machado).   WebR (5:1) Wint
    80, p. 17.

JELLEMA, Rod
"Ancestors. " PoNow (27) 80, p. 25.
"Conduction. " PoNow (27) 80, p. 25.
"Head Down. " PoNow (27) 80, p. 25.
"Randall Jarrell (1914-1965). " PoNow (27) 80, p. 25.

JENDRZEJCZYK, L. M.
"Hiroshima Walk. " ChrC (97:25) 30 Jl-6 Ag 80, p. 759.

JENKINS, Jay
"Big Sur. " Bachy (16) Wint 80, p. 101.
"Californicus Oakus Doakus. " Bachy (16) Wint 80, p. 100.
"A Good Creek Walker's Like a Dancer. " Bachy (16) Wint 80,
    p. 101.
"Lepus Californicus. " Bachy (16) Wint 80, p. 100.
"Lizard. " Bachy (16) Wint 80, p. 101.
"Long Beach. " Bachy (16) Wint 80, p. 101.

JENKINS, Louis
"A Drive in the Country on the First Fall Day. " PoNow (28)

80, p. 37.
"Twins. " AmerPoR (9:3) My-Je 80, p. 35.
"The Ukrainian Easter Egg. " AmerPoR (9:3) My-Je 80, p. 34.
"Violence on Television. " AmerPoR (9:3) My-Je 80, p. 34.

JENNINGS, Kate
"Sunday Afternoon in November. " SouthernPR (20:1) Spr 80, p.
20.

JENSEN, Doris B.
"Leah. " Comm (107:11) 6 Je 80, p. 340.

JENSEN, Laura
"Gravel. " Field (23) Aut 80, p. 68.
"A Horse Is Named Sardine. " AmerPoR (9:1) Ja-F 80, p. 18.
"Household. " Tendril (9) 80, p. 80.
"Kitchen. " Field (23) Aut 80, p. 66.
"Memory. " NewYorker (56:3) 10 Mr 80, p. 142.
"The Woman. " Field (23) Aut 80, p. 69.

JENTZSCH, Bernd
"Elegy" (tr. by Stuart Friebert). Field (22) Spr 80, p. 16.
"Two Men" (tr. by Stuart Friebert). Field (22) Spr 80, p. 15.

JEPPESON, Ron
"August 1, 1971. " PottPort (1) 79-80, p. 11.
"Frigid Country. " PottPort (1) 79-80, p. 47.
"Isolation. " PottPort (1) 79-80, p. 48.
"November 24, 1970. " PottPort (1) 79-80, p. 46.
"The Private Sinners. " PottPort (1) 79-80, p. 48.

JERGA, Ladislav
"East Berlin. " Wind (37) 80, p. 20.

JEROME, Judson
"Crop Dust. " CropD (2/3) Aut-Wint 80, p. 58.
"The Negress in the Closet. " CropD (1) Spr 80, p. 21.

JESSE, Mildred
"Tipping the Scale. " PoetryNW (21:2) Sum 80, p. 41.

JESSYE, Eva
"To Grandmother Penny Jessye. " LittleBR (1:1) Aut 80, p. 22.

JOEL, Gerd
"Forum Romano" (tr. of Jorge Eduardo Eielson w. Miriam
Gerd). NewOR (7:3) 80, p. 262.
"Spring in the Villa Adriana" (tr. of Jorge Eduardo Eielson w.
Miriam Joel). NewOR (7:3) 80, p. 247.

JOEL, Miriam
"Forum Romano" (tr. of Jorge Eduardo Eielson w. Gerd Joel).
NewOR (7:3) 80, p. 262.

"Spring in the Villa Adriana" (tr. of Jorge Eduardo Eielson w.
Gerd Joel). NewOR (7:3) 80, p. 247.

JOHANSEN, Karin
"Blue Night on the Hills" (tr. of Jorgen Gustava Brandt).
PortR (26) 80, p. 99.

JOHANSONS, Pāvils
"Mazā dzelzcelstacijā uz laukiem. " PortR (26) 80, p. 253.

JOHNSON, Bernard
"The Pilgrim's Return" (tr. of Miodrag Pavlović). PortR (26)
80, p. 477.

JOHNSON, David
"Allowance. " BelPoJ (30:3) Spr 80, p. 20.
"Waking. " BelPoJ (30:3) Spr 80, p. 21.

JOHNSON, Denis
"In a Light of Other Lives. " AmerPoR (9:1) Ja-F 80, p. 40.
"White, White Collars. " AmerPoR (9:1) Ja-F 80, p. 40.
"You. " AmerPoR (9:1) Ja-F 80, p. 40.

JOHNSON, Don
"The Children's Hour. " Poetry (136:2) My 80, p. 94.
"The Children's Hour. " Tendril (9) 80, p. 81.
"Late Afternoon at Waimea Bay" (for Daniel). QW (10) Wint-Spr
80, p. 112.

JOHNSON, Halvard
"Killing Time. " HangL (37) Spr 80, p. 24.

JOHNSON, Hank
"As You Hold This. " CarlMis (18:2) Sum 80, p. 172.

JOHNSON, Joan
"Elegy for the Girl Who Died in the Dump at Ford's Gulch. "
Poem (39) Jl 80, p. 44.

JOHNSON, Joe
"Harlem. " BlackALF (14:3) Aut 80, p. 113.

JOHNSON, Karen
"Albatross. " Tendril (7/8) Spr-Sum 80, p. 47.
"From the Third Panel of Bosch's 'The Millennium': A Con-
tinuing Story. " Tendril (7/8) Spr-Sum 80, p. 48.
"Persephone. " PraS (54:1) Spr 80, p. 54.
"Prometheus: The True Story. " Tendril (7/8) Spr-Sum 80, p.
49.

JOHNSON, Kathleen Jeffrie
"The Lost Child. " Vis (2) 80.

JOHNSON, Kristopher
"Fawn. " Hudson (33:2) Sum 80, p. 248.
"Therapy. " Hudson (33:2) Sum 80, p. 247.

JOHNSON, Paul
"Because. " Focus (14:86) Ap 80, p. 16.
"Game. " Focus (14:86) Ap 80, p. 16.
"Let Her Travel Far. " Focus (14:86) Ap 80, p. 16.
"Parent's Day. " Focus (14:86) Ap 80, p. 16.

JOHNSON, Peter M.
"An Excerpt from a Journal Sewn into the Jacket Pocket of a
     Recluse. " PoetryNW (21:1) Spr 80, p. 41.
"Vespers. " Pan (21) 80, p. 60.

JOHNSON, Rita
"Heritage. " Wind (37) 80, p. 21.

JOHNSON, Robin
"Knock, Come Lightly. " CarlMis (18:2) Sum 80, p. 171.

JOHNSON, Tom
"Becoming Is Perfection. " SouthernR (16:1) Wint 80, p. 168.
"The Emperor's Garden. " SouthernR (16:1) Wint 80, p. 169.
"Vermeer. " Poetry (135:5) F 80, p. 265.

JOHNSRUD, Steve
"Two Spheres. " AntR (38:3) Sum 80, p. 335.

JOHNSTON, Caryl
"In Isaac's Age. " LitR (23:3) Spr 80, p. 389.

JOINER, Lawrence
"Honeysuckle. " Poem (39) Jl 80, p. 26.
"Rules. " Poem (39) Jl 80, p. 24.

JONAS, Janelle
"In the Shadows. " HangL (37) Spr 80, p. 59.
"Orange Peels Float. " HangL (37) Spr 80, p. 60.

JONDORF, W. Robert
"Choptank. " SouthernR (16:2) Spr 80, p. 407.
"Dolphins at Bethany Beach. " SouthernR (16:2) Spr 80, p. 406.

JONES, Andrew McCord
"Mistress of Lackworth. " Wind (37) 80, p. 6.

JONES, Elizabeth
"Aphrodisiac. " PottPort (1) 79-80, p. 12.
"Dice. " PottPort (2) 80-81, p. 19.
"Easter Diversion. " PottPort (1) 79-80, p. 35.
"How Summer Comes to Nova Scotia. " PottPort (1) 79-80, p.
     36.

"Nude on the Dartmouth Ferry. " PottPort (1) 79-80, p. 37.
"Valentine. " PottPort (2) 80, p. 36.

JONES, Patricia
"Dedicated to Lori Sharpe. " Obs (5:1/2) Spr-Sum 79, p. 115.
"Eagle Rock. " Obs (5:1/2) Spr-Sum 79, p. 113.
"It Must Be Her Heartbreak Talking" (for Camille and Regina).
    Obs (5:1/2) Spr-Sum 79, p. 116.
"LP. " Obs (5:1/2) Spr-Sum 79, p. 115.
"Poem Written Rosh Hashanah" (for Ted Greenwald). Obs (5:1/2)
    Spr-Sum 79, p. 118.
"The Woman Who Loved Musicians. " Obs (5:1/2) Spr-Sum 79,
    p. 117.

JONES, Paul
"The Find. " OhioR (24) 80, p. 44.
"History of the Islands. " SouthernPR (20:2) Aut 80, p. 36.
"Sister-With-No-Hands. " SouthernPR (20:1) Spr 80, p. 52.

JONES, Robert
"One Not to Be Trusted Grieves for John Lennon. " ChrC (97:43)
    31 D 80, p. 1287.
"The Preacher Reflects, However Briefly, Upon the State of His
    Craft. " ChrC (97:18) 14 My 80, p. 540.
"These Days. " ChrC (97:6) 20 F 80, p. 199.

JONES, Ronald B.
"Untitled: You hated the neighborhood. " PikeF (3) Wint 80, p.
    21.

JOSEPH, Catherine
"A Case Study. " Aspect (76) S-D 79-80, p. 21.

JOSEPH, Lawrence
"Is It You?" Comm (107:23) 19 D 80, p. 726.
"The Phoenix Has Come to a Mountain in Lebanon. " PoetryE
    (3) 80, p. 37.
from Shouting at No One: "Do What You Can. " OntR (13) Aut-
    Wint 80-81, p. 37.
from Shouting at No One: "Driving Again. " OntR (13) Aut-Wint
    80-81, p. 39.
"Then. " Stand (21:3) 80, p. 60.

JOSEPHS, Allen
"Childhood and Death" (tr. of Federico Garcia Lorca). VirQR
    (56:1) Wint 80, p. 63.

JOSHUA, Raynell "Frostie"
"I Look Like This Because.... " PikeF (3) Wint 80, p. 28.

JOYCE, William
"A Xmas Poem. " Agni (12) 80, p. 34.
"The Joggers. " WestHR (34:4) Aut 80, p. 365.

JOZSEF, Attila
"Islands Crop Up" (tr. by Nicholas Kolumban). CutB (15) Aut/
Wint 80, p. 38.
"A Vision" (tr. by John Batki). PoNow (26) 80, p. 45.

JUARROZ, Roberto
from Vertical Poetry: (6, 8) (tr. by Martin Paul and José El-
gorriaga). AmerPoR (9:5) S-O 80, p. 34.

JUDA, Joseph
"She." Tele (16) 80, p. 103.

JUDSON, John
"Hiroshima." PikeF (3) Wint 80, p. 8.
"Psalm in May." SmF (11/12) Spr-Aut 80, p. 58.
"Spring Psalm." SmF (11/12) Spr-Aut 80, p. 57.

JUSTICE, Donald
"The Insomnia of Tremayne." NewYorker (56:8) 14 Ap 80, p.
54.
"Thinking About the Past." Tendril (9) 80, p. 82.

JUUD, Pilual
"I Was Full of Air as an Old Bullfrog." CutB (14) Spr/Sum 80,
p. 108. An improvisation.

KABIR
from Bijak: "Padas" (tr. by Linda Hess and Shukdev Singh).
MalR (54) Ap 80, pp. 79-85.
from Bijak: "Sakhis" (tr. by Linda Hess and Shukdev Singh).
MalR (54) Ap 80, p. 86.

KACHINSKE, Timothy
"Heavenly Star" (tr. of Benedek Kiss). Stand (21:3) 80, p. 64.

KAHLAU, Heinz
"What Else?" Stand (21:1) 79-80, p. 48.

KAHLER, Maude E.
"Antique Shop in a Barn." CropD (2/3) Aut-Wint 80, p. 20.

KAHN, Paul
"The Award" (for Norman Fischer). Tele (16) 80, p. 33.
"O-she-li-ni (Extraordinary)." Tele (16) 80, p. 32.

KALLSEN, T. J.
"Breakfast Recipe." KanQ (12:2) Spr 80, p. 74.
"Evel Knievel Is Sanctified." PoNow (29) 80, p. 15.

KALYANAPONGS, Angkarn
"I Lost You." PortR (26) 80, p. 399.
"Scoop Up the Sea." PortR (26) 80, p. 397.

KAMEEN, Paul
"Locus #12. " SoCaR (13:1) Aut 80, p. 90.
"Memorabilia. " KanQ (12:3) Sum 80, p. 85.

KANDEL, Lenore
"American Dreams. " Ark (14) 80, p. 248.

KANE, Katherine
"Meditation on an Age. " VirQR (56:3) Sum 80, p. 509.
"To Henry VIII's Ghost. " VirQR (56:3) Sum 80, p. 508.
"Tryst. " VirQR (56:3) Sum 80, p. 510.

KANE, T. Paul
"Sassetta on St. Francis. " Shen (31:2) 80, p. 31.

KANFER, Allen
"The Ape and the Man of Imagination. " LitR (23:3) Spr 80, p.
    378.
"The Aster, the Weed, and the Game" (for Ethan). SoCaR (13:1)
    Aut 80, p. 89.

KANGAS, J. R.
"Letter in March" (for C. R.). SoCaR (13:1) Aut 80, p. 91.

KANIA, Karin
"Consciousness. " CentR (24:4) Aut 80, p. 457.

KANYADI, Sándor
"A ház elött egész éjszaka (reminiszcencia). " PortR (26) 80, p.
    168.

KAPLAN, Edward
"Litany on 6th Avenue. " StoneC (7:1) F 80, p. 24.

KAPLAN, Rebbekka
"Warning to the Man Who Breaks Glasses. " Im (6:2) 80, p. 4.

KARASLAVOV, Slav H.
"Sons. " PortR (26) 80, p. 53.

KARATHANOS, Patricia Hager
"Uptown at the Bar. " CapeR (15:2) Sum 80, p. 17.

KARNISH, Marlam
"Russian Novel. " EngJ (69:5) My 80, p. 46.

KARP, Vickie
"Endless Greetings. " NewYorker (56:19) 30 Je 80, p. 34.
"The Neighborhood Environmental Center. " NewYorker (55:47)
    7 Ja 80, p. 34.

KARR, Mary
"From the 99th Floor. " Aspen (9) Spr 80, p. 56.

"Goon Squad" (for Robert Long). Aspen (9) Spr 80, p. 57.
"Insomnia." Aspen (9) Spr 80, p. 58.

KASCHNITZ, Marie Luise
"Can't Forget" (tr. by Lisel Mueller). Poetry (136:6) S 80, p. 345.
"Hiroshima." Poetry (136:6) S 80, p. 342.
"A Map of Sicily" (tr. by Lisel Mueller). Poetry (136:6) S 80, p. 344.
"My Curiosity" (tr. by Lisel Mueller). Poetry (136:6) S 80, p. 346.
"Toward Evening" (tr. by Lisel Mueller). Poetry (136:6) S 80, p. 345.

KATCHADOURIAN, Stina
"the ferns at my feet" (tr. of Louise Dubois). PortR (26) 80, p. 379.
"Influence of Beings" (tr. of Eva Runefelt). PortR (26) 80, p. 363.
"Listen to what you don't hear" (tr. of Ingrid Sjöstrand). PortR (26) 80, p. 369.
"Love Poem (Rome)" (tr. of Eva Runefelt). PortR (26) 80, p. 361.
from The Love Story of the Century: "An alcoholic's wife" (tr. of Märta Tikkanen). PortR (26) 80, p. 117.
from The Love Story of the Century: "I love you so immensely" (tr. of Märta Tikkanen). PortR (26) 80, p. 124.
from The Love Story of the Century: "Love and love--" (tr. of Märta Tikkanen). PortR (26) 80, p. 123.
from The Love Story of the Century: "You're asking me" (tr. of Märta Tikkanen). PortR (26) 80, p. 121.

KATES, J.
"Trying to Follow Instructions." Outbr (4/5) Aut 79-Spr 80, p. 17.
"Winters" (for R. W.). Outbr (4/5) Aut 79-Wint 80, p. 16.

KATO, Eileen
"Fever" (tr. of Sean O. Riordan). DenQ (15:2) Sum 80, p. 88.

KATROVAS, Richard
"Bloomfield, Inc." PoetryE (3) 80, p. 32.
"The Blue Candle." Columbia (5) Aut-Wint 80, p. 63.
"Children of the Palms." PoetryE (3) 80, p. 34.
"Elegy for My Mother." Columbia (5) Aut-Wint 80, p. 64.

KATZ, Menke
"On God's Children." Confr (20) Spr-Sum 80, p. 96.

KATZ, Steve
from Journalism: "Napanoch Correctional Facility." Bound (8:2) Wint 80, pp. 256-273.

KAUFFMAN, Janet
"The End of March. " PoNow (26) 80, p. 34.

KAUFMAN, Lisa
"Private Duty" (for Rose). NewL (47:1) Aut 80, p. 58.

KAUFMAN, Shirley
"Cannons thundered far away" (tr. of Amir Gilboa). Stand (21:4)
    80, p. 8.
"Déjà Vu. " Field (22) Spr 80, p. 73.
"Relics. " Stand (21:4) 80, p. 8.

KAUFMAN, Stuart
"Murdered Friends on Lexington Avenue. " AmerPoR (9:6) N-D
    80, p. 16.
"The Ultimate Cigar. " AmerPoR (9:6) N-D 80, p. 16.

KAVANAGH, Patrick
"Lines Written on a Seat on the Grand Canal, Dublin, 'Erected
    to the Memory of Mrs. Dermot O'Brien. '" PoetryE (1) 80,
    p. 73.

KAY, John
"Who Asked for It. " Wind (36) 80, p. 35.

KEARNEY, Lawrence
"Dead on His Feet in Lackawanna. " MissouriR (3:2) Wint 80, p.
    29.
"The Emperor's Old Clothes. " VirQR (56:1) Wint 80, p. 72.
"Jacob and the Angel. " ParisR (77) Wint-Spr 80, p. 33.
"Mother, Alone in the Attic. " MissouriR (3:2) Wint 80, p. 26.

KEATS, John
"Where Be You Going, You Devon Maid?" Playb (27:3) Mr 80,
    p. 165.

KEELER, Marian
"The Art Historian. " CalQ (16/17) 80, p. 102.
"Hood Ornament. " CalQ (16/17) 80, p. 101.

KEELEY, Edmund
"Caique" (tr. of Angelos Sikelianos w. Philip Sherrard). Pequod
    (11) 80, p. 38.
"On a Ray of Winter Light" (tr. of George Seferis w. Philip
    Sherrard). Columbia (4) Spr-Sum 80, p. 33.
"On Stage" (tr. of George Seferis w. Philip Sherrard). GeoR
    (34:2) Sum 80, p. 357.
"Sparta" (tr. of Angelos Sikelianos w. Philip Sherrard). Pequod
    (11) 80, p. 39.
"Summer Solstice" (tr. of George Seferis w. Philip Sherrard).
    Antaeus (36) Wint 80, pp. 44-51.

KEEN, Suzanne
"Virginia's Song. " EngJ (69:5) My 80, p. 54.

KEENAN, Deborah
"A Poem About White Flowers. " DacTerr (17) 80, p. 45.

KEFFER, Leslie
"Olga Orozco" (tr. of Olga Orozco). PortR (26) 80, p. 15.

KEITH, Jeff
"Summer Lonely. " Mouth (2:4) My 80, p. 46.

KEIZER, Garret
"The Bather. " Poem (39) Jl 80, p. 4.
"The Tourist. " Poem (39) Jl 80, p. 3.

KELLER, David
"Circling the Site. " Pequod (11) 80, p. 86.
"February Afternoon. " US1 (12/13) Aut-Wint 80, p. 17.
"In a Void" (tr. of Eugenio Montale w. Donald Sheehan). CutB
    (14) Spr/Sum 80, p. 96.
"Repartee" (tr. of Eugenio Montale w. Donald Sheehan). CutB
    (14) Spr/Sum 80, p. 97.
"A Visit Down-River. " US1 (12/13) Aut-Wint 80, p. 9.

KELLER, Madeleine
"For Neil Welliver. " Tele (16) 80, p. 18.
"Water" (for Karen McCready). Tele (16) 80, p. 19.

KELLNHAUSER, John T.
"Leningrad 1966: Alexei. " Mouth (2:5) O 80, p. 22.
"Oslo 1966: Andy. " Mouth (2:5) O 80, p. 23.
"Wien 1967: Karl. " Mouth (2:5) O 80, p. 24.
"Wisconsin 1963: Richard. " Mouth (2:5) O 80, p. 25.

KELLY, Dave
"Consenting Adults. " PoNow (28) 80, p. 29.
"I Am Afraid. " PoNow (28) 80, p. 25.
"One Summer Afternoon. " PoNow (28) 80, p. 25.
"The Reader. " PoNow (28) 80, p. 25.
"Separate Bundles. " PoNow (28) 80, p. 29.
"Sparring with God. " PoNow (28) 80, p. 29.

KELLY, David J.
"A Prayer for Nightwander. " Poem (39) Jl 80, p. 19.

KELLY, J. Patrick
"The Small Birds. " Ascent (5:2) 80, p. 31.

KELLY, M. L.
"Sentimental Journey. " CapeR (15:2) Sum 80, p. 44.
"White Sheet. " CapeR (15:2) Sum 80, p. 43.

KELLY, Robert
"a taut medley of deep strings. " Ark (14) 80, pp. 255-260.

KEMF, Elizabeth
"Before the Dive. " HolCrit (17:1) F 80, p. 14.

KEMPHER, Ruth Moon
from The Prattsburg Correspondence: "Letter V to C. , Friday
    Morning, May 28. " WindO (37) Aut-Wint 80, p. 5.
"Work in Progress: Cassandra Meanwhile Vacuums. " HiramPoR
    (27) Aut-Wint 80, p. 27.

KENGEI, The Monk
"Foolish Women" (tr. by Graeme Wilson). DenQ (15:3) Aut 80,
    p. 82.

KENISON, Gloria
Twelve poems. WormR (80) 80, p. 137.

KENNEDY, David C.
"The Bayman. " PottPort (2) 80-81, p. 49.
"Litany of the Saints. " PottPort (2) 80-81, p. 10.
"A Long Time Ago on Bell Island. " PottPort (2) 80-81, p. 27.
"Once I Saw the Perfect Woman. " PottPort (2) 80-81, p. 51.

KENNEDY, Terry
"Evil Ode" (tr. of Alicja Patey-Grabowska). DenQ (15:1) Spr 80,
    p. 81.

KENNEDY, X. J.
"Aphasia" (for C. F.). OP (29) Spr 80, p. 25.
"Epitaph for a Tennis Champ. " PoNow (28) 80, p. 33.
"In a Dry Season. " PoNow (26) 80, p. 5.
"Ode. " Tendril (9) 80, p. 83.
"On an Editor. " Bits (11) 80.
"To an Unpopular Novelist. " OP (29) Spr 80, p. 25.
"To Dorothy on Her Exclusion from the Guinness Book of World
    Records. " Atl (246:2) Ag 80, p. 62.
"To Mercury. " OP (29) Spr 80, p. 24.

KENNEY, Richard
"Misrule. " CarolQ (32:2) Spr-Sum 80, pp. 5-17.

KENT, Debra
"Bloodspot. " Pan (21) 80, p. 16.

KENT, Margaret
"The Injustice. " SouthernPR (20:2) Aut 80, p. 23.
"Lost Signals. " Poetry (137:1) O 80, p. 23.
"Translation: From Words. " SouthernPR (20:2) Aut 80, p. 24.
"Watching the Island" (for David). Poetry (137:1) O 80, p. 25.

KENT, Richard
"A Birthday Hum. " Field (22) Spr 80, p. 5.

KENYON, Jane
"The Bat. " Ploughs (6:2) 80, p. 16.

"The Bearer Pool in December. " NewRep (182:14) 5 Ap 80, p. 34.

"Bright Sun After Heavy Snow. " NewRep (183:18) 1 N 80, p. 26.

"February: Thinking of Flowers. " NewL (47:1) Aut 80, p. 24.

"Indolence in Early Winter. " NewL (47:1) Aut 80, p. 23.

"Summer 1890, Near the Gulf. " Ploughs (6:2) 80, p. 15.

"Things. " NewRep (183:26) 27 D 80, p. 38.

KEPPLER, Joseph F.
"That Bad. " PoNow (29) 80, p. 15.

KERLEY, Gary
"Finding Harbor. " Wind (36) 80, p. 36.

KERSCHE, Peter
"Now" (tr. of Edvard Kocbek w. Herbert Kuhner). MalR (53) Ja 80, p. 28.

"Pontus" (tr. of Edvard Kocbek w. Herbert Kocbek). MalR (53) Ja 80, p. 27.

"Primary Numbers" (tr. of Edvard Kocbek w. Herbert Kuhner). MalR (53) Ja 80, p. 26.

KERTESZ, Louise
"Songs for Settling In. " NewOR (7:1) 80, p. 16.

KESSLER, Jascha
"Afterward" (tr. of Gyula Illyes). CentR (24:2) Spr 80, p. 186.

"Cannibal Future" (tr. of Gyula Illyes). CentR (24:2) Spr 80, p. 187.

"Field Hospital, 1945" (tr. of András Fodor). LitR (23:3) Spr 80, p. 346.

"On an Infant" (tr. of Gyula Illyes). CentR (24:2) Spr 80, p. 186.

"Question" (tr. of Forugh Farrokhzad w. Amin Banani). CutB (14) Spr /Sum 80, p. 104.

"Requiem" (tr. of Otto Orbán). CutB (14) Spr /Sum 80, p. 15.

"Twenty Eight Years" (tr. of Miklós Radnóti). NewL (47:1) Aut 80, p. 56.

"Your Body's Bread" (tr. of András Fodor). LitR (23:3) Spr 80, p. 347.

KESSLER, Stephen
"Fool Serenade. " Bachy (17) Spr 80, p. 97.

"Grief and Then Some. " Bachy (17) Spr 80, p. 97.

"In the Grain. " Ark (14) 80, p. 263.

"Manhood. " Ark (14) 80, p. 261.

"Phrenology. " Bachy (17) Spr 80, p. 98.

KEVORKIAN, Karen
"January Birthdays" (for Robin). Prima (5) 79, p. 9.

KEYSER, Paul
"The Fishermen. " CalQ (16 /17) 80, p. 152.

'The River Merchant's Reply. " CalQ (16/17) 80, p. 153.

KHERDIAN, David
'Histories. " DacTerr (17) 80, p. 47.

KICKNOSWAY, Faye
from Janie: "An eye, a viscous eye, with the sight stopped and nothing in the. " Tendril (9) 80, p. 84.

KIKEL, Rudy
"Address to My Old Crowd. " Mouth (2:5) O 80, p. 4-8.
"Cox and Hoyle. " Mouth (2:5) O 80, p. 2.
"Sitting Tight. " Mouth (2:4) My 80, p. 6.
"Your Gingivectomy. " Mouth (2:4) My 80, p. 37.

KILBANE, Kate
"After the Accident. " Columbia (5) Aut-Wint 80, p. 55.

KILGORE, James C.
"The Full Price. " BlackALF (14:3) Aut 80, p. 125.
"Gambian Magic. " BlackALF (14:3) Aut 80, p. 124.
"Gourmet Day. " BlackALF (14:3) Aut 80, p. 125.
'No Hiding Place. " BlackALF (14:3) Aut 80, p. 125.
"No Ordinary Beginning. " Obs (5:3) Wint 79, p. 86.

KILINA, Patricia
"The Parchment of Memory" (tr. of Wadym Lesytch). PortR (26) 80, p. 417.

KIMM, Robert E.
"Song of Myself. " Pan (21) 80, p. 39.

KIMMEL, Lawrence W.
"Bound in its snake skin. " NewL (46:4) Sum 80, p. 48.

KING, Cynthia
"Fan Mail. " Prima (5) 79, p. 55.

KING, James F.
"Pedagogy. " StoneC (7:3) D 80, p. 22.

KINGERY, Margaret
"Heroic Journalism. " Sam (101) 80, p. 16.

KINNELL, Galway
"Angling, a Day. " AmerPoR (9:2) Mr-Ap 80, p. 26.
"The Apple. " MissouriR (3:2) Wint 80, p. 7.
"Cemetery Angels. " Atl (245:3) Mr 80, p. 86.
"Daybreak. " NewYorker (55:51) 4 F 80, p. 34.
"Flying Home. " NewYRB (27:12) 17 Jl 80, p. 26.
"The Gray Heron. " NewYorker (55:51) 4 F 80, p. 34.
"Les Invalides. " NewRep (182:7) 16 F 80, p. 28.
"The Last Hiding Places of Snow. " AmerPoR (9:2) Mr-Ap 80,

p. 24.
"On the Tennis Court at Night. " AmerPoR (9:2) Mr-Ap 80, p.
    27.
"The Sadness of Brothers. " AmerPoR (9:2) Mr-Ap 80, p. 25.

KINNICK, B. Jo.
"Charles Has a Good Ear. " EngJ (69:5) My 80, p. 45.

KINZIE, Mary
"Des Knaben Wunderhorn. " Salm (50/51) Aut 80-Wint 81, p. 31.
"Designation. " Pequod (11) 80, pp. 54-58.
"From Grace the Mind a Drop of Manna Dew. " SouthernR (16:3)
    Sum 80, p. 605.
"Heroic Statue in a Garden Run Wild. " Salm (50/51) Aut 80-
    Wint 81, p. 32.
"Marriage Table. " Pequod (11) 80, p. 59.
"Negatives" (for William Hunt). Salm (50/51) Aut 80-Wint 81,
    p. 33.
"Novum Organum. " Poetry (136:5) Ag 80, p. 285.
"Parting Inscription. " SouthernR (16:3) Sum 80, p. 607.
"Reading During Marriage. " NewRep (183:9) 30 Ag 80, p. 30.
"Resurrection. " SouthernR (16:3) Sum 80, p. 604.
"Their Story. " Poetry (136:5) Ag 80, p. 283.

KIRBY, David
"Either Way. " CreamCR (5:1) Wint 79, p. 105.
"The Last Good Kiss. " SouthernPR (20:1) Spr 80, p. 76.

KIRCHNER, Eddie
"Hitch-Hiking. " PikeF (3) Wint 80, p. 28.

KIRK, Kevin
"Parachuters. " EngJ (69:5) My 80, p. 54.

KIRKLAND, Will
"Giacomo Casanova Accepts the Office of Librarian Which Is Of-
    fered to Him, in Bohemia, by the Count of Waldstein" (tr.
    of Antonio Colinas w. Francisco Sanz). PortR (26) 80, p.
    344.

KIRSCH, Sarah
"The Dshwari Cloister Ruins" (tr. by Elizabeth Weber). CutB
    (14) Spr/Sum 80, p. 41.
"The Night Spreads Out Its Fingers" (tr. by Elizabeth Weber).
    CutB (14) Spr/Sum 80, p. 40.
from Rückenwind and Zaubersprüche: Ten poems. Bound (8:3)
    Spr 80, pp. 190-196.
"Summons Chant" (tr. by Elizabeth Weber). CutB (14) Spr/Sum
    80, p. 39.

KIRSCHEN, Mark
Seventeen Poems. Montra (7) 80, pp. 163-190.

KIRWAN, A.
"Around Midnight. " Pan (21) 80, p. 30.

KISHKAN, Theresa
"Ice-Age. " OntR (12) Spr-Sum 80, p. 59.
"A Shadow of Antlers" (for Ann York). OntR (12) Spr-Sum 80,
    p. 61.

KISS, Benedek
"Heavenly Star" (tr. by Timothy Kachinske). Stand (21:3) 80, p.
    64.

KISTLER, Terrance
"Letter to Frances. " Harp (261:1562) Jl 80, p. 37.
"Woman Mask. " Harp (261:1562) Jl 80, p. 16.

KISTLER, William
"Note from a Prussian Colonel: 1940. " Nimrod (24:1) Aut-Wint
    80, p. 35.
"Sketch of Two. " Nimrod (24:1) Aut-Wint 80, p. 34.

KITAHARA, Hakushu
"Two Songs for a Rose" (tr. by William Elliott). EnPas (10)
    80, p. 14.

KITCHEN, Judith
"Spring Puddle. " PoetryNW (21:4) Wint 80-81, p. 19.
"Tomboy. " PoNow (29) 80, p. 16.

KIZER, Carolyn
"After Basho. " OP (29) Spr 80, p. 29.
"Reading Your Poems in Your House While You Are Away" (for
    Richard Shelton). OP (29) Spr 80, p. 26.
"Threatening Letter. " OP (29) Spr 80, p. 28.

KLAPPERT, Peter
"Estienne. " Tendril (9) 80, p. 85.
"Grandfather Philip. " CreamCR (5:1) Wint 79, p. 7.
"Hard Measures. " CreamCR (5:1) Wint 79, p. 9.
"Infectious Scotoma. " CropD (1) Spr 80, p. 8.
"Laughter in the Peroration. " CropD (2/3) Aut-Wint 80, p. 41.
"The Mole's Eye. " CropD (1) Spr 80, p. 8.
"Satan Who Is Most Noisy When He Whispers. " Agni (12) 80,
    pp. 24-29.

KLAUCK, D. L.
"Chew Mail Pouch. " GeoR (34:1) Spr 80, p. 144.

KLECK, Judith
"Songs for Whidbey. " SouthernPR (20:2) Aut 80, p. 46.

KLEE, Paul
"Embrace. " NewL (46:4) Sum 80, p. 54.

KLEIN, Jim
"Her Husband." WormR (78) 80, p. 50.
"The Lady from the Rape Squad." WormR (78) 80, p. 50.

KLEIN, Melanie
"The Cat from Outer Space." PikeF (3) Wint 80, p. 18.

KLEINZAHLER, August
Ten poems. Montra (7) 80, pp. 122-131.

KLEMM, Wilhelm
"Clearing Station" (tr. by David McDuff). Stand (21:2) 80, p. 21.

KLIEWER, Warren
"Intestate" (for Michael Lewis). KanQ (12:4) Aut 80, p. 121.

KLINE, Wayne
"Lapless." CropD (1) Spr 80, p. 19.
"The Worms." CropD (1) Spr 80, p. 19.

KLOEFKORN, William
from Honeymoon: "For one thing, Doris says." PoNow (28)
    80, p. 14.
from Honeymoon: (42). DacTerr (17) 80, p. 48.
from Honeymoon: "I buy Doris a rug." PoNow (28) 80, p. 14.
from Honeymoon: "We are watching the sun go down beyond the
    Falls." PoNow (28) 80, p. 14.
"The Loose Dog." PoNow (28) 80, p. 25.
"Out-and-Down Pattern." Spirit (5:1/2) Aut-Wint 79-80, p. 6.
"Pioneer Courtship." PoNow (28) 80, p. 25.
"Unplanting the Tree." PoNow (28) 80, p. 25.

KNAPP, William
"From Melville's Study." NewYorker (56:15) 2 Je 80, p. 44.

KNIGHT, Arthur Winfield
"The Breakdown." CropD (2/3) Aut-Wint 80, p. 34.
"Under Cover." PoNow (27) 80, p. 35.

KNIGHT, Elizabeth A.
"A Young Woman in Love With an Old Man." DacTerr (17) 80,
    p. 49.

KNIGHT, Ethridge
"Vigo County." NewL (46:4) Sum 80, p. 49.

KNOEPFLE, John
"Abstractions of the man." Focus (14:86) Ap 80, p. 12.
"Each depositor." Focus (14:86) Ap 80, p. 12.
"He plays for himself." Focus (14:86) Ap 80, p. 12.
"He says if he hums." Focus (14:86) Ap 80, p. 12.
"a man his time I." DacTerr (17) 80, p. 50.
"Rain drying up in the fields." Focus (14:86) Ap 80, p. 12.

"Snow shadowing blue. " Focus (14:86) Ap 80, p. 12.

KNOLL, Michael
"Eating the Darkness. " AmerPoR (9:6) N-D 80, p. 36.
"Elegy for the Rest of the World." AmerPoR (9:6) N-D 80, p. 36.

KNOTT, Bill
"Street corner. " Tendril (9) 80, p. 89.

KNOX, Caroline
"The Cavendish Club. " Poetry (137:3) D 80, p. 152.
"Nancy Drew. " Poetry (137:3) D 80, p. 155.
"Sol Invictus. " Poetry (137:3) D 80, p. 156.

KOCBEK, Edvard
"Man and His Neighbor. " PortR (26) 80, p. 482.
"Melody" (tr. by Herbert Kuhner and Ina Jun Broda). MalR (53) Ja 80, p. 29.
"Now" (tr. by Herbert Kuhner and Peter Kersche). MalR (53) Ja 80, p. 28.
"Pontus" (tr. by Herbert Kuhner and Peter Kersche). MalR (53) Ja 80, p. 27.
"Primary Numbers" (tr. by Herbert Kuhner and Peter Kersche). MalR (53) Ja 80, p. 26.
"The Tongue. " PortR (26) 80, p. 484.

KOCH, Michael
"Landscape with Two Tombs and an Assyrian Dog" (tr. of Federico Garcia Lorca). Durak (5) 80, p. 18.
"Norm and Paradise of Blacks" (tr. of Federico Garcia Lorca). Durak (5) 80, p. 19.

KOCH, Tom
"That Was the Year That Was. " Playb (27:1) Ja 80, pp. 226-7.
"To a Country Music Star. " Playb (27:12) D 80, p. 202.
"To a Gay Liberation Leader. " Playb (27:12) D 80, p. 203.
"To Dan Rather. " Playb (27:12) D 80, p. 203.
"To Fidel Castro. " Playb (27:12) D 80, p. 202.
"To the National Football League. " Playb (27:12) D 80, p. 203.

KOENIG, Robert L.
"Isolation Ward. " HiramPoR (27) Aut-Wint 80, p. 29.

KOERTGE, Ronald
"Abandoned Shoe Locates Owner in Los Angeles. " PoNow (26) 80, p. 35.
"The Breast Report. " Wind (36) 80, p. 37.
"Clothes Make the Man. " PoNow (26) 80, p. 35.
"Functions of Body Hair. " WormR (80) 80, p. 158.
"Genuine Success Story. " WormR (80) 80, p. 158.
"Inventing Everyday Hems: Sunglasses. " WormR (80) 80, p. 160.

"June Poem. " WormR (80) 80, p. 160.
"Lassie's Wedding Night. " WormR (80) 80, p. 159.
"Last Minute Change of Plans. " WormR (77) 80, p. 3.
"Night Games. " WormR (77) 80, p. 4.
"Perils of Misspelling. " PoNow (28) 80, p. 42.
"The Poet's Genealogy: A Fragment. " WormR (80) 80, p. 161.
"Pronouncing My Name. " WormR (77) 80, p. 2.
"The Seven Dwarfs, Each on His Deathbed, Remember Snow
      White. " WormR (77) 80, p. 2.
"Sidekicks. " WormR (77) 80, p. 1.
"The Ski Mask Bandit. " PoNow (28) 80, p. 29.
"Slipper Sox. " WormR (80) 80, p. 159.
"The Virgin, the Dynamo and the IBM 300. " WormR (77) 80, p.
      4.
"The Women's Movement. " Wind (36) 80, p. 37.

KOETHE, John
"The Guarded Optimist. " ParisR (78) Sum 80, p. 112.
"The Little Boy. " CreamCR (5:2) Spr 80, p. 7.
"Malignant Calm. " ParisR (78) Sum 80, p. 111.
"Picture of Little Letters. " ParisR (78) Sum 80, p. 113.
"A Refrain. " ParisR (78) Sum 80, p. 110.

KOHL, Susan
"The Bound Foot of a Chinese Lady. " PikeF (3) Wint 80, p. 26.

KOHLBERG, Madonna
"He Looked at Me. " Spirit (5:1/2) Aut-Wint 79-80, p. 27.

KOHLER, Sandra
"Leaving. " PoNow (27) 80, p. 34.
"Nobody Cares. " PoNow (29) 80, p. 16.

KOLB, Elene Margot
"Slow Season. " PoNow (29) 80, p. 15.

KOLIAS, Helen
"Beneath the Forgetfulness. " CarolQ (32:3) Aut 80, p. 24.
"Copy" (tr. of Yannis Ritsos). WebR (5:2) Aut 80, p. 44.
"A Drop of Water" (tr. of Yannis Ritsos). WebR (5:2) Aut 80,
      p. 44.
"An Insignificant Chronicle of Love" (tr. of Yannis Ritsos).
      CarolQ (32:3) Aut 80, p. 23.
"Signs" (tr. of Yannis Ritsos). WebR (5:2) Aut 80, p. 45.
"Without Counter-Balance. " WebR (5:2) Aut 80, p. 45.

KOLUMBAN, Nicholas
"The Blood of the Walsung House" (tr. of Otto Orban). CharR
      (6:1) Spr 80, p. 39.
"Camera Obscura" (tr. of Hans Magnus Enzenberger). CutB (15)
      Aut/Wint 80, p. 16.
"Islands Crop Up" (tr. of Attila Jozsef). CutB (15) Aut/Wint 80,
      p. 38.

"The Letter" (tr. of Otto Orban).   CharR (6:1) Spr 80, p. 38.

KOMACHI, Ono no
"Anguish" (tr. by Graeme Wilson).   DenQ (15:3) Aut 80, p. 84.

KOMUNYAKAA, Yusef
"Passion of a Body Painting. " Pan (21) 80, p. 58.
"Passion of Cicadas. " Pan (21) 80, p. 58.

KONDOS, Yánnis
"The Burial That Never Happened" (to Táso) (tr. by Kimon
    Friar). Durak (4) 80, p. 50.
"Chamber Music. " PortR (26) 80, p. 163.
"Upside Down" (tr. by Kimon Friar). PoNow (26) 80, p. 46.

KONESKI, Blazhe
"Among the Trees. " PortR (26) 80, p. 474.
"Revenge. " PortR (26) 80, p. 472.

KONUK, Mutlu
Ten poems (tr. of Nazim Hikmet w. Randy Blasing).   PoetryE
    (3) 80, pp. 6-18.

KOONTZ, Tom
"Scene for Langston: White Frame House with White Shingles in
    a Late November Sunshine. " WindO (36) Spr-Sum 80, p. 30.

KOOPMAN, Mireya Urquida
"Another Station. " UTR (6:3/4) 80, p. 35.
"Cochabamba, Always. " UTR (6:3/4) 80, p. 32.
"Cocoa Beach in the Atlantic. " UTR (6:3/4) 80, p. 37.
"The Lonely Jogger at Jacksonville Beach. " UTR (6:3/4) 80, p.
    36.
"A Requiem for a Man. " UTR (6:3/4) 80, p. 31.
"Tejados Rojos. " UTR (6:3/4) 80, p. 34.
"The Year of the Child and After. " UTR (6:3/4) 80, p. 33.

KOOSER, Ted
"A Box of Old Keys. " CropD (2/3) Aut-Wint 80, p. 30.
"Father. " PraS (54:4) Wint 80-81, p. 22.
"Mrs. Jones: (1974). " MidwQ (21:3) Spr 80, p. 351.
"Night Piece. " CropD (2/3) Aut-Wint 80, p. 19.
"A Summer Night. " ThRiPo (15/16) 80, p. 34.
"A Winter Morning. " PoNow (26) 80, p. 31.
"Within the Realm of Possibility. " PoNow (28) 80, p. 41.

KORNBLUM, Allan
"Remembering I'm Jewish. " Spirit (5:1/2) Aut-Wint 79-80, p.
    28.

KOSTELANETZ, Richard
"Recall-Epigraphs" (w. Beth Biegler).   Im (7:1) 80, p. 6.
"Stringfour. " Os (11) 80, p. 12.

KOTARO, Takamura
"Learning by Touch" (tr. by Graeme Wilson). WestHR (34:4)
Aut 80, p. 334.

KOTESKI, Jovan
"Bricklayer" (tr. by Bryce Conrad). CharR (6:1) Spr 80, p. 30.
"Fatigue" (tr. by Bryce Conrad). CharR (6:1) Spr 80, p. 30.
"Lust" (tr. by Bryce Conrad). CharR (6:1) Spr 80, p. 30.
"Melancholy" (tr. by Bryce Conrad). CharR (6:1) Spr 80, p. 31.
"Prisovjani" (tr. by Bryce Conrad). CharR (6:1) Spr 80, p. 32.
"Sisters" (tr. by Bryce Conrad). CharR (6:1) Spr 80, p. 31.
"Village Poverty" (tr. by Bryce Conrad). CharR (6:1) Spr 80,
p. 31.
"Walk" (tr. by Bryce Conrad). CutB (14) Spr /Sum 80, p. 56.

KOTTLER, Dorian Brooks
"List" (for my father). DacTerr (17) 80, p. 51.

KOVACS, Steven
"Razglednica" (tr. of Miklós Radnóti). DenQ (15:1) Spr 80, p.
79.

KRAMER, Aaron
"Called In. " Vis (4) 80.
"Primal Street. " Vis (3) 80.
"The Voice of San Miguel. " Vis (3) 80.

KRAMER, Larry
"Iowa. " PoNow (28) 80, p. 19.

KRAMER, Lawrence
"Another River. " Iowa (10:4) Aut 79, p. 32.

KRANZ, Judith
"Bear Creek Cemetery. " Wind (36) 80, p. 48.
"a curious thing. " SmPd (50) Aut 80, p. 9.

KRAPF, Norbert
"Memory of" (tr. of Katrine Von Hutten). Stand (21:3) 80, p. 15.
"Statement of Place" (tr. of Katrine Von Hutten). Stand (21:3)
80, p. 15.
"Waking in Europe. " PoNow (27) 80, p. 33.
"When I Was Little" (tr. of Katrine Von Hutten). Stand (21:3)
80, p. 14.

KRAUJIETE, Aina
"The Bride" (tr. by Inara Cedrins). PoNow (27) 80, p. 45.
"In the Field" (tr. by Inara Cedrins). PoNow (27) 80, p. 45.

KRAUSS, Janet
"At Home in My Yard in Connecticut After a Visit to Massachu-
setts. " ColEng (42:1) S 80, p. 61.

KRESH, David
"From Krzywcz. " KanQ (12:1) Wint 80, p. 54.

KRETZ, Thomas
"Glouster Gazing. " LitR (23:3) Spr 80, p. 380.
"The Kiosk. " ChrC (97:1) 2-9 Ja 80, p. 17.
"Travelers' Warnings. " Tele (16) 80, p. 79.
"Two Brothers Before Luke Divided. " ChrC (97:26) 13-20 Ag
    80, p. 783.

KRIEGER, Ted
"The Death of a Grain Train. " Sam (86) 79, p. 18.

KRIEL, Margot
"The moon in a liqueur glass. " Prima (5) 79, p. 48.
"Summer lot. " Prima (5) 79, p. 24.

KRIESEL, Michael
"Faint Tan. " Sam (92) 80, p. 56.
"Note. " Sam (86) 79, p. 36.

KROETSCH, Robert
"Sketches of a Lemon. " MalR (54) Ap 80, p. 46.

KROGFUS, Miles
"Sun Photographs. " Poetry (136:2) My 80, p. 90.

KROK, Peter
"The Lightning Bug. " FourQt (29:3) Spr 80, p. 23.

KROLL, Ernest
"China Station (San Francisco). " ConcPo (13:2) Aut 80, p. 87.
"Cinquecentennial. " LitR (23:3) Spr 80, p. 356.
"Hallelujah. " PoNow (26) 80, p. 15.
"The Magnet. " KanQ (12:3) Sum 80, p. 140.
"Pig. " KanQ (12:2) Spr 80, p. 77.
"Ponderosa. " SouthwR (65:2) Spr 80, p. 175.
"Springhouse in Snake Time. " BallSUF (21:2) Spr 80, p. 2.
"Telephone Lineman. " ChrC (97:7) 27 F 80, p. 229.

KROLL, Judith
"Life Under the Czar. " LittleM (12:3/4) 80, p. 80.
"Loving Someone Else. " NewYorker (55:53) 18 F 80, p. 41.

KROLOW, Karl
"basta" (tr. by Felix Pollak). Kayak (53) My 80, p. 50.
"Fingers" (tr. by Paul Morris). Pequod (11) 80, p. 52.
"Getting Snowed In" (tr. by Stuart Friebert). CarlMis (18:2)
    Sum 80, p. 47.
"Gradually" (tr. by Stuart Friebert). CutB (14) Spr/Sum 80, p.
    55.
"A Hot Day" (tr. by John N. Miller). CharR (6:2) Aut 80, p.
    55.

"I advance the clock" (tr. by Felix Pollak). Kayak (53) My 80,
    p. 50.
"I will walk along the river" (tr. by Felix Pollak). Kayak (53)
    My 80, p. 48.
"The Love of Life" (tr. by Stuart Friebert). Durak (4) 80, p.
    48.
"Portrait of a Hand" (tr. by Paul Morris). Pequod (11) 80, p.
    52.
"rain" (tr. by Felix Pollak). Kayak (53) My 80, p. 49.
"some things remain" (tr. by Felix Pollak). Kayak (53) My 80,
    p. 49.
"We Steal Away" (tr. by Stuart Friebert). Durak (4) 80, p. 49.

KRUCHKOW, Diane
    "(found poem): The two-headed garter snake. " Aspect (76) S-D
    79-80, p. 21.

KRUSOE, James
    "The Fox-Boy. " PoNow (26) 80, p. 25.
    "The Legacy. " PoNow (26) 80, p. 25.
    "The Lost Continent. " PoNow (26) 80, p. 25.

KRYSL, Marilyn
    "Leda. " Field (22) Spr 80, p. 6.
    "Persephone, to Demeter. " LittleM (12:3/4) 80, p. 22.
    "Sestina Against Matrimony. " LittleM (12:3/4) 80, p. 18.
    "Sestina:". LittleM (12:3/4) 80, p. 20.
    "Voice Box. " Field (22) Spr 80, p. 8.

KUBY, Lolette
    "Craftsmen. " HiramPoR (27) Aut-Wint 80, p. 30.

KUHNER, Herbert
    "The bridge points northwest" (tr. of Johann A. Boeck). PortR
    (26) 80, p. 30.
    "A dwarf hops on the rack" (tr. of Hermann Gail). PortR (26)
    80, p. 29.
    "I too could inject gasoline" (tr. of Hermann Gail). PortR (26)
    80, p. 25.
    "I've Divided" (tr. of Walther Nowotny). PortR (26) 80, p. 31.
    "March Moon Night" (tr. of Margarethe Herzele). PortR (26)
    80, p. 36.
    "Melody" (tr. of Edvard Kocbek w. Ina Jun Broda). MalR (53)
    Ja 80, p. 29.
    "Mother Chaos" (tr. of Margarethe Herzele). PortR (26) 80, p.
    37.
    "Now" (tr. of Edvard Kocbek w. Peter Kersche). MalR (53) Ja
    80, p. 28.
    "Pontus" (tr. of Edvard Kocbek w. Peter Kersche). MalR (53)
    Ja 80, p. 27.
    "Primary Numbers" (tr. of Edvard Kocbek w. Peter Kersche).
    MalR (53) Ja 80, p. 26.
    "Vienna" (tr. of Hermann Gail). PortR (26) 80, p. 27.

KUIC, Ranka
"Life" (tr. of Milos Crnjanski). PortR (26) 80, p. 481.

KULKARNI, Venkatesh Srinivas
"Onyx or a Version of the Beauty and the Fish. " BallSUF (21:1)
Wint 80, pp. 16-30.

KUMIN, Judith
"Being in Love" (tr. of William Cliff w. Maxine Kumin). PoNow
(26) 80, p. 44.
"This morning lying in bed some English memories" (tr. of Wil-
liam Cliff w. Maxine Kumin). PoNow (26) 80, p. 44.

KUMIN, Maxine
"Being in Love" (tr. of William Cliff w. Judith Kumin). PoNow
(26) 80, p. 44.
"Continuum: A Love Poem. " Atl (246:3) S 80, p. 69.
"Halfway. " Tendril (9) 80, p. 90.
"The Incest Dream. " OntR (12) Spr-Sum 80, p. 50.
"Never. " OntR (12) Spr-Sum 80, p. 47.
"Peeling Fence Posts. " OntR (12) Spr-Sum 80, p. 44.
"Relearning the Language of April. " OntR (12) Spr-Sum 80, p.
45.
"Spending the Night. " OntR (12) Spr-Sum 80, p. 48.
"Stopped Time in Blue and Yellow. " OntR (12) Spr-Sum 80, p.
46.
"This morning lying in bed some English memories" (tr. of Wil-
liam Cliff w. Judith Kumin). PoNow (26) 80, p. 44.
"An Unfinished Story. " OntR (12) Spr-Sum 80, p. 49.

KUNENE, Mazisi
"Ihubo liko Biko. " PortR (26) 80, p. 494.
"Inkondlo enqagedwanga. " PortR (26) 80, p. 493.
"Inkondlo ngemkosi embili. " PortR (26) 80, p. 496.
"Kwakulukhuni ukuzalwa kwakho, Mtanami. " PortR (26) 80, p.
498.
"Lessons in Duality" (tr. by author). PortR (26) 80, p. 497.
"The Second Birth of the Great Shaka of the Zulus" (tr. by au-
thor). PortR (26) 80, p. 499.
"Steve Biko's Anthem" (tr. by author). PortR (26) 80, p. 495.
"Unfinished epic" (tr. by author). PortR (26) 80, p. 493.

KUNNAS, Kirsi
"Tänään. " PortR (26) 80, p. 134.

KUNZE, Reiner
"Answer. " Stand (21:1) 79-80, p. 48.
"Reasons for Taking Care of the Car" (tr. by Peter Spycher).
Field (22) Spr 80, p. 13.
"Refuge Even Behind Refuge" (for Peter Huchel) (tr. by Peter
Spycher). Field (22) Spr 80, p. 14.
"Refuge Even Beyond the Refuge" (for Peter Huchel) (tr. by
C. E. Thalenberg). Spirit (5:1 /2) Aut-Wint 79-80, p. 19.

KURAS, Pat M.
"Cheating Poem. " Mouth (2:5) O 80, p. 19.
"I fail to notice your blushing with. " Mouth (2:4) My 80, p. 17.
"Rules for Ex-Lovers. " Mouth (2:5) O 80, p. 18.

KUSATAO, Nakamura
"Haiku" (tr. by Janine Beichman). DenQ (15:1) Spr 80, p. 47.

KUZMA, Greg
"Breasts. " OhioR (25) 80, p. 26.
"Poems for My Brother. " Hudson (33:3) Aut 80, pp. 383-390.
"The Weight. " CropD (2/3) Aut-Wint 80, p. 30.
"You (1974). " MidwQ (21:3) Spr 80, p. 352.

KWON, Il Song
"The Apocalypse" (tr. by author). PortR (26) 80, p. 247.

KWON, Paula
"March. " AndR (7:1) Spr 80, p. 69.

KYCKALHAHN-WILKINS, Christine
"Coffee Cup. " Northeast (3:8) Wint 80, p. 54.

L., A.
"Ivette-1955. " CropD (2/3) Aut-Wint 80, p. 35.

LABARE, Martie
"The End of Tragedy" (for Robin Hirsch). Tele (16) 80, p. 106.
"Flying West and Then. " Tele (16) 80, p. 104.
"July Rainbows" (for Paul Violi). Tele (16) 80, p. 105.
"Lake Louise. " Tele (16) 80, p. 104.
"Poem: South. " Tele (16) 80, p. 105.

LaBOMBARD, Joan
"Gold. " PoetryNW (21:4) Wint 80-81, p. 14.

LACEY, Walter
"Skydiver. " Sam (102) 80, p. 49.

LaFARGE, Sheila
"The Action: continuities. " PortR (26) 80, p. 82.
"The Action: symmetries" (tr. of Inger Christensen). PortR
    (26) 80, p. 85.
"The Scene: transitivities" (tr. of Inger Christensen). PortR
    (26) 80, p. 81.
"The Text: extensions" (tr. of Inger Christensen). PortR (26)
    80, p. 79.
"The Text: integrities" (tr. of Inger Christensen). PortR (26)
    80, p. 83.
"The Text: universalities" (tr. of Inger Christensen). PortR
    (26) 80, p. 84.

LaFLEUR, William
"The Day the Ocean Came to Newark. " US1 (12/13) Aut-Wint

80, p. 12.

LAIBMAN, David
"On Morality." NewWR (48:6) N-D 80, p. 5.

LAKE, Paul
"Fields." SoCaR (12:2) Spr 80, p. 16.
"A Hawk." ConcPo (13:1) Spr 80, p. 46.
"South of the City." Thrpny (3) Aut 80, p. 15.
"The Temple." Wind (37) 80, p. 22.

LAMB, Elizabeth Searle
"Haiku." WindO (37) Aut-Wint 80. on calendar.

LAMBERT, Diane
"Crisp, heart-cutting whites." HangL (37) Spr 80, p. 61.

LAMDEN, Susan
"The First Farm." CalQ (16/17) 80, p. 151.
"Indian Caves." CalQ (16/17) 80, p. 150.

LAMKIN, Kurt
"black wind." BlackALF (14:4) Wint 80, p. 175.

LAMPORT, Felicia
"President Zia of Pakistan Dismisses US Aid Offer as 'Peanuts.'"
NewRep (182:5) 2 F 80, p. 20.

LAMPSON, David
"Fugitive Pieces." Bachy (16) Wint 80, p. 114.

LANCASTER, Beverly
"a collection of epigrams." WindO (37) Aut-Wint 80, p. 15.

LANDAU, Julie
"Ancient Style Poem" (tr. of Li Po). DenQ (15:1) Spr 80, p. 94.
"Li Ting Yen" (tr. of Chang Sheng). DenQ (15:1) Spr 80, p. 95.

LANDGRAF, Susan
"Hat Poem for Ricky." Pig (7) My 80, p. 74.
"The Truth of Lines." Tendril (7/8) Spr-Sum 80, p. 50.

LANE, Erskine
"Poems by Saigyo (1118-1190)." Ark (14) 80, p. 264.

LANE, John
"The Homecoming of Osceola." StoneC (7:3) D 80, p. 38.
"Leaving, or the Poor and the Snow" (for David Romtvedt).
StoneC (7:3) D 80, p. 41.

LANE, Mary
"Webs." Tele (16) 80, p. 93.

LANE, Mervin
"Spring Count. " CharR (6:2) Aut 80, p. 42.

LANE, William
"Pickins, W. Va. " PoNow (27) 80, p. 19.

LANG, Jon
"Poem for My Generation. " BelPoJ (30:4) Sum 80, p. 22.

LANG, Susanna
"Two Colors" (tr. of Yves Bonnefoy). Nimrod (24:1) Aut-Wint
    80, pp. 31-33.
"Wetlands. " Nimrod (24:1) Aut-Wint 80, p. 31.

LANGE, Art
"Sonnet for the Season. " SunM (9/10) Sum 80, p. 166.

LANGTON, Charles
"It Will Come In. " AntR (38:1) Wint 80, p. 63.
"Our Life, Then Our Lives" (for Mary). AntR (38:2) Spr 80, p.
    176.

LANGTON, Daniel J.
"Expecting. " KanQ (12:1) Wint 80, p. 94.
"Monotonio. " Im (7:1) 80, p. 9.

LANHAM, Tib
"Leaves. " Poem (39) Jl 80, p. 59.
"Wait!" Poem (39) Jl 80, p. 60.

LANIER, Doris
"Flamenco. " Im (6:2) 80, p. 4.
"Opus 10. " Im (6:2) 80, p. 4.
"Opus 11. " LitR (23:3) Spr 80, p. 345.

LANNON, Sharon
"Fencing. " EngJ (69:5) My 80, p. 54.

LAPE, Sue
"Tigress. " Wind (37) 80, p. 39.

LAPIDUS, Jacqueline
"Parc Montsouris. " HangL (38) Aut 80, p. 30.
"Tortoise. " HangL (38) Aut 80, p. 31.

LAPINGTON, S. C.
"The Foal. " Stand (21:1) 79-80, p. 4.
"A Reedbunting. " Stand (21:1) 79-80, p. 4.
"A Robin. " Stand (21:1) 79-80, p. 4.

LAPPIN, Linda
"meditation. " Kayak (53) My 80, p. 7.
"the miracle of the hand. " Kayak (53) My 80, p. 6.

"the miracle of the voice. " Kayak (54) S 80, p. 19.

LARDAS, Konstantinos
  "Your Arms. " FourQt (30:1) Aut 80, p. 19.

LARGENT, Christopher
  "City. " Wind (36) 80, p. 4.

LARKIN, Joan
  "Blood" (for Kate). Cond (6) 80, p. 52.

LARRISSY, Edward
  "The Other Side of You. " GRR (11:2/3) 80, p. 51.
  "Still With Your Eyes. " GRR (11:2/3) 80, p. 52.

LARSON, Jeanne
  "Bus Out of Nashville: A Letter to My Husband. " QW (10) Wint-
    Spr 80, p. 79.

LARSON, Rich
  "December 21st" (for Wanwadee). CapeR (16:1) Wint 80, p. 29.

LaRUE, James
  "The Cage. " PikeF (3) Wint 80, p. 3.

LaSALLE, Peter
  "Basement Flat, Fourth Street. " BallSUF (21:1) Wint 80, p. 71.
  "Rent-a-Car. " CimR (53) O 80, p. 21.

LASKEY, Karen
  "Sending No Postcards Home. " LittleBR (1:1) Aut 80, p. 58.

LAST, Jim
  "Night. " Wind (36) 80, p. 3.

LATEEF, Nora L.
  "The Blind Spot. " HangL (37) Spr 80, p. 62.

LATHAN, George
  "Black Woman, Black Woman. " NewRena (12) Spr 80, p. 53.

LATTA, John
  "For Meriopi Ypsilantis. " Epoch (29:3) Spr-Sum 80, pp. 272-
    279.
  "Poem (En forme d'une lettre). " OhioR (25) 80, p. 100.

LATTIMORE, David
  "Our house? No it's the. " NewL (46:4) Sum 80, p. 50.

LATTIMORE, Richmond
  "Disadvantages. " Ark (14) 80, p. 271.
  "The Elite. " PoetryNW (21:3) Aut 80, p. 3.
  "Form and Actuality. " PoetryNW (21:3) Aut 80, p. 4.

"Medea to the Women of Corinth. " Ark (14) 80, p. 269.
"Winter Return. " PoetryNW (21:3) Aut 80, p. 3.

LAUGHLIN, James
"It Does Me Good. " Ark (14) 80, p. 272.
"The Person. " Poetry (136:3) Je 80, p. 157.

LAURENCE, E. G.
"I Think Table and Say Chair" (tr. of Gloria Fuertes w. L. H.
Laurence). CutB (14) Spr/Sum 80, p. 107.

LAURENCE, L. H.
"I Think Table and Say Chair" (tr. of Gloria Fuertes w. E. G.
Laurence). CutB (14) Spr/Sum 80, p. 107.

LAUTERBACH, Ann
"Here and There" (for Hector Leonardi). AmerPoR (9:3) My-Je
80, p. 46.
"Not Bored, Not Ill at Ease or Cold. " Harp (261:1564) S 80, p.
58.
"Saint Lucia. " Pequod (11) 80, p. 17.

LAUTERMILCH, Steven
"Breathing, You Invisible Poem" (tr. of Rainer Maria Rilke).
WestHR (34:1) Wint 80, p. 84.
"Fever. " CentR (24:3) Sum 80, p. 302.
"The Grief" (tr. of Rainer Maria Rilke). NewOR (7:2) 80, p.
122.
"Oh, This Is the Beast" (tr. of Rainer Maria Rilke). WestHR
(34:1) Wint 80, p. 83.
"Solitary" (tr. of Rainer Maria Rilke). WestHR (34:1) Wint 80,
p. 81.
"The Woman Beside the Road. " CentR (24:3) Sum 80, p.
302.

LAWDER, Donald
"Cribbage With My Father. " BelPoJ (30:4) Sum 80, p. 43.

LAWLER, Patrick
"Odd, the Bride Stripped Bare by Her Bachelors. " Epoch (29:2)
Wint 80, p. 112.

LAWLESS, Gary
"for Steve, his river. " Ark (14) 80, p. 273.

LAWNER, Lynne
"Dark Craving. " GeoR (34:3) Aut 80, p. 558.

LAWRENCE, Allen
"Logging Road on French Mountain. " GRR (11:1) 80, p. 21.
"Side Entrance to the Hospital. " GRR (11:1) 80, p. 22.

LAWRENCE, D. H.
"God, but it is good to have died and been trodden out. "   Bachy
(16) Wint 80, p. 11.

LAWRY, Mercedes
"Blackcloth. " StoneC (7:2) My 80, p. 17.
"Bicycle Blues. " Wind (38) 80, p. 53.
"Triangle. " Wind (38) 80, p. 64.

LAWSON, Christopher
"Living in the Moors. " Wind (38) 80, p. 35.

LAWSON, David
"Hub City on the Verge of Spring. " PoetC (12:1) 80, p. 24.

LAWSON, Sir Wilfred
"Queen Bath-Sheba. " Playb (27:12) D 80, p. 248.

LAZARD, Naomi
"The Day Death Comes" (tr. of Faiz Ahmed Faiz).   CutB (14)
Spr /Sum 80, p. 12.

LAZER, Hank
"Decision. " PoNow (26) 80, p. 15.
"The Gaunt One Dreamed.... " Bound (8:2) Wint 80, p. 320.
"The History of His Laugh. " WormR (77) 80, p. 5.
"It So Happens. " Bound (8:2) Wint 80, p. 319.
"Psychology of the Washer" (for Les Pearlstein).   WormR (77)
80, p. 5.
"The Rules. " WebR (5:2) Aut 80, p. 47.
"The Story of Ruddy's Life. " WebR (5:2) Aut 80, p. 47.
"This One. " PoetryE (1) 80, p. 69.
"Twelve Years Old. " WebR (5:2) Aut 80, p. 49.
"Types and Opposites of Flight. " Bound (8:2) Wint 80, p. 321.
"The Well. " Bound (8:2) Wint 80, p. 323.

LEA, Sydney
"Accident. " NewYorker (56:18) 23 Je 80, p. 36.
"A Dream Near Water. " MassR (21:2) Sum 80, p. 271.
"Drooge's Barn. " SewanR (88:1) Wint 80, p. 22.
"Father's Game. " SewanR (88:1) Wint 80, p. 24.
"The Floating Candles" (for my brother Mahlon).   NewYorker
(56:26) 18 Ag 80, p. 38.
"Her Watches: In a Dry Time. " SewanR (88:1) Wint 80, p. 21.
"A Natural Shame. " NewRep (182:24) 14 Je 80, p. 35.
"Searches for a Friend" (for Dave Smith).   QW (10) Wint-Spr
80, p. 69.
"Searching the Drowned Man: The Third Day. " Ascent (5:2) 80,
p. 29.
"The Urge to Appropriate. " SouthernR (16:1) Wint 80, p. 130.
"Wandering the City. " SouthernR (16:1) Wint 80, p. 129.

LEACH, Chester R.
  "The Victim Anticipates a History. " HiramPoR (27) Aut-Wint 80,
     p. 31.

LEACH, Linda
  "Full Moons. " CentR (24:3) Sum 80, p. 305.

LEALE, B. C.
  "For Sale and Wanted. " Kayak (53) My 80, p. 26.
  "Fractured Landscapes. " Kayak (53) My 80, p. 26.
  "Where Is Your Headache?" Kayak (53) My 80, p. 26.

LEAMON, Marlene
  "Break a Leg. " PoetryNW (21:2) Sum 80, p. 40.

LEARY, Paris
  "Gaudeamus Igitur. " Poetry (135:5) F 80, p. 285.
  "May 1865. " MinnR (NS 15) Aut 80, p. 28.
  "Oxford Commination. " Poetry (135:5) F 80, p. 283.

LECHNER, Laura A.
  "Holding Up. " HangL (38) Aut 80, p. 29.

LEDWELL, Frank J.
  "Ever to Confess You're Bored Means You Have No Inner Re-
     sources.... " PottPort (1) 79-80, p. 15.

LEE, Mary Hope
  "Chicago (Winter 78). " Cond (6) 80, p. 68.

LEE, Tom
  "Little Willie. " Wind (38) 80, p. 41.
  "Valley of Shadows. " Wind (38) 80, p. 41.

LEEDY, David
  "Port Blakely Cemetery. " Comm (107:20) 7 N 80, p. 628.

LEET, Judith
  "On Participating in Four Forms of Planetary Motion. " Poetry
     (137:3) D 80, p. 163.
  "The Play of the Mind. " Poetry (137:3) D 80, p. 165.
  "Returning Lewis to His Freedom. " Poetry (137:3) D 80, p. 168.
  "Sum. " Poetry (137:3) D 80, p. 162.

LEFCOWITZ, Barbara F.
  "Disappointment. " Vis (1) 79.
  "Legacy. " Vis (1) 79.
  "Synchrony: A Sestina. " CropD (1) Spr 80, p. 15.
  "Winter Solstice Plus One Plus. " KanQ (12:3) Sum 80, p. 88.

LEFFEL, Lawrence
  "Decoys. " Im (6:2) 80, p. 11.
  "Magellan. " Im (7:1) 80, p. 9.

LEFFLER, Merrill
"A Short History. " Vis (1) 79.
"Springtime Near Munich. " Vis (3) 80.
"Take Hold. " Vis (1) 79.

LEGARE, Huguette
"Les dents de notre vide culturel. " PottPort (1) 79-80, p. 37.
"J'aime mon émotion. " PottPort (1) 79-80, p. 34.
"Tout un village de capitaines. " PottPort (1) 79-80, p. 37.

LEHMAN, David
"In Praise of A. R. Ammons. " Poetry (136:3) Je 80, p. 148.
"Towards the Vanishing Point. " SunM (9/10) Sum 80, p. 133.
"A Serious Kiss" (for Stephanie). SunM (9/10) Sum 80, p. 136.

LEHMAN, John
"Del's Supper Club. " CreamCR (5:2) Spr 80, p. 64.
"Hardware. " CreamCR (5:1) Wint 79, p. 109.

LEHRMAN, J.
"I'll always remember the night. " PoNow (26) 80, p. 37.

LEIBLEIN, Adelle
"Poem: you know when to come into the circle of her eyes. "
    Tendril (7/8) Spr-Sum 80, p. 52.

LEIGHT, Peter
"Frame. " MassR (21:4) Wint 80, p. 721.
"Leaving Aiolia. " PartR (47:4) 80, p. 613.

LEITHAUSER, Brad
"Angel. " NewRep (182:19) 17 My 80, p. 30.
"11 Astronomical Riddles, with Answers Supplied. " NewEngR
    (3:2) Wint 80, p. 263.

LeMASTER, J. R.
"Destiny of a Poet" (tr. of Claude Vigée w. Kenneth Lawrence
    Beaudoin). WebR (5:2) Aut 80, p. 77.
"Michael's Tomb" (tr. of Claude Vigée w. Kenneth Lawrence
    Beaudoin). WebR (5:2) Aut 80, p. 76.

LEMM, Richard
"Leaks. " PottPort (2) 80-81, p. 32.

LEPORE, Dominick
"Pages" (tr. of Gigi Dessi). DenQ (15:1) Spr 80, p. 88.
"Reward" (tr. of Gigi Dessi). DenQ (15:1) Spr 80, p. 89.

LERNER, Linda
"The Clean Break. " ColEng (42:2) O 80, p. 152.

LESNIAK, Rose
"Your Thinking and Mine. " Prima (5) 79, p. 56.

LESS, Sam
"The Dream. " Mouth (2:4) My 80, p. 18.
"Driving Through Golden, New Mexico. " Mouth (2:4) My 80, p.
18.

LESSER, Rika
"La Defunta. " AmerPoR (9:4) Jl-Ag 80, p. 13.
"Etruscan Things. " MassR (21:1) Spr 80, pp. 39-44.
from Etruscan Things: "Calchas Haruspex. " AmerPoR (9:5) S-
O 80, p. 24.
from Etruscan Things: "Canopic Jar. " AmerPoR (9:5) S-O 80,
p. 22.
from Etruscan Things: "From Vetulonia. " AmerPoR (9:5) S-O
80, p. 24.
from Etruscan Things: "Hut Urn. " AmerPoR (9:5) S-O 80, p.
22.
from Etruscan Things: "La Banditaccia, 1979. " AmerPoR (9:5)
S-O 80, p. 22.
from Etruscan Things: "The Mummy Speaks. " AmerPoR (9:5)
S-O 80, p. 23.
from Etruscan Things: "Vortex. " AmerPoR (9:5) S-O 80, p. 23.
"Graves of the Hetaerae" (tr. of Rainer Maria Rilke).
AmerPoR (9:5) S-O 80, p. 26.
"Guardiana Della Sepoltura. " AmerPoR (9:4) Jl-Ag 80, p. 13.
"Inside the Rose" (tr. of Rainer Maria Rilke). AmerPoR (9:5)
S-O 80, p. 26.
"Of Woman Born. " Shen (31:2) 80, p. 32.
"Orpheus. Eurydice. Hermes" (tr. of Rainer Maria Rilke).
AmerPoR (9:5) S-O 80, p. 25.
"Requiem for a Friend" (tr. of Rainer Maria Rilke). AmerPoR
(9:5) S-O 80, p. 27.
"The Sonnets to Orpheus I, 2" (tr. of Rainer Maria Rilke).
AmerPoR (9:5) S-O 80, p. 27.
"Wild Rosebush" (tr. of Rainer Maria Rilke). AmerPoR (9:5)
S-O 80, p. 27.

LESSING, Karin
Nine poems. Montra (7) 80, pp. 5-15.

LESYTCH, Wadym
from Illusions, (II). PortR (26) 80, p. 414.
"The Parchment of Memory. " PortR (26) 80, p. 416.

LEVANT, Jonathan
"The Forest. " Wind (38) 80, p. 43.

LEVCHEV, Lyubomir
"Starway. " PortR (26) 80, p. 50.

LEVENDOSKY, Charles
"the boys pock highway signs. " Bits (11) 80.

LEVERING, Donald
"Below Yacquina Head Lighthouse. " Wind (37) 80, p. 40.

"Toolroom Under a Stairwell" (for John Haines). Wind (37) 80, p. 41.

LEVERTOV, Denise
"An Arrival. " Ark (14) 80, p. 274.
"The 90th Year" (for Lore Segal). BosUJ (26:3) 80, p. 69.
from a sequence in progress: "Eros, O Eros, hail. " Ark (14) 80, p. 276.

LEVI, Steven
"IV. " CropD (1) Spr 80, p. 14.
"V. " CropD (1) Spr 80, p. 14.

LEVI, Tom Mergentime
"Just Visiting. " Wind (38) 80, p. 44.

LEVIN, J.
"The Heat in Harvard Yard. " WormR (77) 80, p. 31.
"To Complete the Circle. " WormR (77) 80, p. 30.

LEVIN, Phillis
"The Paperweight. " VirQR (56:3) Sum 80, p. 505.

LEVINE, Anne-Marie
"Portrait of an Intellectual. " PoNow (29) 80, p. 16.

LEVINE, Ellen
"For My Birthday. " MinnR (NS 15) Aut 80, p. 32.
"Goldfish. " Tendril (7/8) Spr-Sum 80, p. 51.
"Muir Woods. " Prima (5) 79, p. 48.
"Poetry Reading" (for Leslie Norris). Poem (38) Mr 80, p. 52.
"Sweet Basil. " Poem (38) Mr 80, p. 51.
"When My Father Appears. " BelPoJ (30:3) Spr 80, p. 13.

LEVINE, Miriam
"In the Flesh. " Aspect (76) S-D 79-80, p. 50.

LEVINE, Philip
"Day by Day. " PoetryE (3) 80, p. 24.
"The Day When Peace Takes Hold" (tr. of Gloria Fuertes w. Ada Long). PoetryE (1) 80, p. 87.
"The Doctor of Starlight. " MichQR (19:3) Sum 80, p. 299.
"Farmer" (tr. of Gloria Fuertes w. Ada Long). PoetryE (1) 80, p. 86.
"For a Song. " ConcPo (13:2) Aut 80, p. 94.
"Genius. " PoetryE (3) 80, p. 26.
"Get Up. " NewYorker (56:10) 28 Ap 80, p. 128.
"Having Been Asked 'What Is a Man?' I Answer. " Poetry (136: 6) S 80, p. 313.
"Here I Am Exposed Like Everybody" (tr. of Gloria Fuertes w. Ada Long). PoetryE (1) 80, p. 84.
"Keep Talking. " Poetry (136:6) S 80, p. 311.
"Left on the Shore. " PoNow (26) 80, p. 25.

"Letters. " Antaeus (38) Sum 80, p. 156.
"Milkweed. " PoNow (26) 80, p. 25.
"My Angel. " Antaeus (38) Sum 80, p. 160.
"The Myth. " Poetry (136:6) S 80, p. 319.
"Never Before. " NewYorker (56:39) 17 N 80, p. 52.
"News of the World. " Antaeus (38) Sum 80, p. 158.
"One. " Poetry (136:6) S 80, p. 317.
"The One I Am. " MichQR (19:3) Sum 80, p. 301.
"Paraguay. " Antaeus (38) Sum 80, p. 162.
"Prayer" (tr. of Gloria Fuertes w. Ada Long). PoetryE (1) 80,
    p. 82.
"The Radio. " Poetry (136:6) S 80, p. 315.
"Rain. " PoetryE (3) 80, p. 25.
"Rain Downriver. " NewYorker (56:1) 25 F 80, p. 50.
"She's Not Gone. " ParisR (77) Wint-Spr 80, p. 114.
"Steel. " NewYorker (56:45) 29 D 80, p. 40.
"The Voice. " Tendril (9) 80, p. 91.
"You'll Get Yours" (tr. of Gloria Fuertes w. Ada Long). Po-
    etryE (1) 80, p. 85.

LEVIS, Larry
"Blue Stones" (for my son, Nicholas). Field (23) Aut 80, p. 71.
"Blue Stones" (for my son, Nicholas). Tendril (9) 80, p. 93.
"Picking Grapes in an Abandoned Vineyard. " NewYorker (56:38)
    10 N 80, p. 52.
"The Spirit Says, You Are Nothing. " Aspen (10) Wint 80, p. 9.
"To a Wall of Flame in a Steel Mill, Syracuse, New York,
    1969. " Poetry (136:3) Je 80, p. 137.
"To a Woman Glancing Up From the River. " Poetry (136:3) Je
    80, p. 139.
"To My Ghost Reflected in the Auxvasse River. " Aspen (10)
    Wint 80, p. 7.

LEVITIN, Alexis
"Portrait of a Woman" (tr. of Eugenio de Andrade). PoNow (28)
    80, p. 44.

LEVITT, Annabel
"Lucy's Boudoir" (for the count). Tele (16) 80, p. 12.
"the races. " Tele (16) 80, p. 14.

LEVY, Robert J.
"cases. " Kayak (53) My 80, p. 5.
"The Fool. " PraS (54:4) Wint 80-81, p. 11.
"give us this day, our daily bread. " Kayak (53) My 80, p. 3.
"The Healing. " PraS (54:4) Wint 80-81, p. 11.
"Late One Night. " PoNow (29) 80, p. 16.
"six forms of affection in search of an other. " Kayak (53) My
    80, p. 4.

LEWANDOWSKI, Stephen
"Hard frozen January &. " HangL (38) Aut 80, p. 32.
"Klipnockie. " PoNow (29) 80, p. 24.

"The Old Man. " DacTerr (17) 80, p. 52.
"Sauerkraut Festival, Phelps, NY. " PoNow (29) 80, p. 24.
"Second Coming by Bus. " HangL (38) Aut 80, p. 34.
"Seneca Castle, NY. " PoNow (26) 80, p. 19.
"Sucker Brook. " PoNow (29) 80, p. 24.
"Tug Hill. " HangL (38) Aut 80, p. 33.

LEWIS, Janet
from the Swans: "Song of the Enchanted Swans Who Once Were
    Princes. " Thrpny (1) Wint-Spr 80, p. 13.
"Words for a Song. " NewRep (183:12) 20 S 80, p. 30.

LEWIS, Kathy Pierce
"Goodbye San Diego, Goodbye Mother. " Vis (2) 80.
"Janus at Dawn. " Vis (3) 80.
"The Mouse. " Vis (1) 79.

LEWIS, Robert W.
"The Bury. " DacTerr (17) 80, p. 54.

LEWIS, Roger
"Fire Eater. " CropD (2/3) Aut-Wint 80, p. 23.
"Piranha Serrasalmus nattereri. " CropD (1) Spr 80, p. 18.

LEY, Murray Hickey
"Easter. " Comm (107:7) 11 Ap 80, p. 212.

LIBBEY, Elizabeth
"Practicing Parts. " BaratR (8:1) Sum 80, p. 41.
"The Woman of Two Groves. " BaratR (8:1) Sum 80, p. 42.

LIDDY, James
"How Mother Came Home. " NewEngR (3:2) Wint 80, p. 234.
"John 13:23, Dante, Paradise XXV. 113. " CreamCR (5:1) Wint 79,
    p. 19.

LIEBERMAN, Jean Clark
"Inheritance. " BelPoJ (31:1) Aut 80, p. 39.

LIEBERMAN, Laurence
"Blue Heron. " Nat (230:10) 15 Mr 80, p. 314.
"Bone Dance. " CharR (6:2) Aut 80, p. 7.
"The Clouds. " CharR (6:2) Aut 80, p. 5.
"God's Measurements. " Tendril (9) 80, p. 95.
"The Kofukuji Arsonists. " PartR (47:1) 80, p. 121.
"Lament for the Doomed Minnows. " AmerPoR (9:6) N-D 80, p.
    46.
"On the Life That Waits" (for James Wright). CharR (6:2) Aut
    80, p. 6.
"The Protectors: Oak and Stone. " AmerPoR (9:6) N-D 80, p.
    45.
"Psychodrama: Tokyo Mime Film. " AmerPoR (9:6) N-D 80, p.
    45.
"The Roof Tableau of Kashikojima. " AmerPoR (9:6) N-D 80, p.

44.
"Two Songs of Leave-Taking." QW (10) Wint-Spr 80, p. 122.
"Wreckage of the Pagoda Moons." SewanR (88:1) Wint 80, p. 26.

LIETZ, Robert
"Analysis of a Particular Design." SoDakR (18:3) Aut 80, p. 20.
"At Park and East Division." CharR (6:1) Spr 80, p. 27.
"Family Homes." CarolQ (32:2) Spr-Sum 80, p. 51.
"In a Construction Ditch." SoDakR (18:3) Aut 80, p. 22.
"Making Home." CharR (6:1) Spr 80, p. 26.
"The Man Who Moves Twice" (for Philip Booth). CarolQ (32:3)
    Aut 80, p. 44.
"Poem After Seeing a Photograph of the Turin Shroud" (for Bob
    Herz). MassR (21:4) Wint 80, p. 695.
"The River Man." Confr (20) Spr-Sum 80, p. 108.
"Woman's Matters." CarolQ (32:3) Aut 80, p. 46.

LIFSHIN, Lyn
"After a Day We Stay in Bed Till the Sun Is Close to Setting."
    NoAmR (265:1) Mr 80, p. 23.
"After the Water." LittleM (12:3/4) 80, p. 87.
"All Night Boogie." Os (10) Spr 80, p. 21.
"All the Night the Night Has Been." CalQ (16/17) 80, p. 59.
"ABC Newsman Bill Stewart Murdered." WindO (36) Spr-Sum 80,
    p. 19.
"August 2 Racetrack at 7 AM." WindO (36) Spr-Sum 80, p. 18.
"The Blue Thursday the Sorry Comma Letter Fold." PoNow (27)
    80, p. 11.
"Condom Tuesday." WormR (77) 80, p. 16.
"Co op City Reading." PoNow (27) 80, p. 11.
"Coughing at Night." CreamCR (5:1) Wint 79, p. 31.
"Eating Glass." Pig (7) My 80, p. 38.
"Everytime I Tried to Tell You the Words Just Come Out Wrong
    So I'll Have to Say I Love You in a Song." Wind (37) 80,
    p. 25.
"Georgia O'Keefe." WormR (77) 80, p. 15.
"The Glass Man Comes on to Me in a Restaurant." Vis (1) 79.
"Graceland Cemetery." PoNow (26) 80, p. 36.
"He Counts on His Fingers." SouthernHR (14:3) Sum 80, p. 246.
"Hearing the News." Wind (37) 80, p. 26.
"He's Too Striking Like a Floodlight at the Window Near Your
    Bed at 3 AM." Prima (5) 79, p. 54.
"Hiding Out." Wind (37) 80, p. 24.
"Howland House." Vis (2) 80.
"In the Room Where You Think the Door Is Somewhere Different."
    Vis (4) 80.
"The It's All Done With Mirrors Madonna." CropD (1) Spr 80,
    p. 16.
"Jackson Garden Union College Schenectady." PoNow (26) 80, p.
    36.
"Jealousy." Wind (37) 80, p. 24.
"Lania." Vis (1) 79.
"Lasagna Madonna." NewL (46:3) Spr 80, p. 121.

"Light Footsteps a Coach Full of People Laughing Duane Mansion
    Duanesburg. " PoNow (26) 80, p. 36.
"Loudon Cottage Cherry Hill Lane Loudonville. " PoNow (26) 80,
    p. 36.
"Madonna. " WormR (78) 80, pp. 60-74.
"The Man Who Collects Corks. " Vis (2) 80.
"Manuscripts. " PoNow (27) 80, p. 11.
"May Rituals. " Vis (1) 79.
"Midwest. " CapeR (16:1) Wint 80, p. 36.
"Montreal. " US1 (12/13) Aut-Wint 80, p. 8.
"Moon Dust. " LittleM (12:3/4) 80, p. 85.
"My Mother Is Getting Old. " WindO (36) Spr-Sum 80, p. 17.
Nine poems. WormR (80) 80, p. 152.
"November. " CalQ (16/17) 80, p. 58.
"The Old Dog. " HangL (37) Spr 80, p. 26.
"Old Men Hotel Brenner. " CapeR (16:1) Wint 80, p. 35.
"Seeing My Mother's Friends and Relatives After My Parents'
    Divorce Split Whole Houses and Cities in Two. " HiramPoR
    (27) Aut-Wint 80, p. 32.
"Seminary Street. " Im (6:2) 80, p. 7.
"The Sex Offender in Chicago. " Im (6:2) 80, p. 7.
"She Said When Brought St. Francis's Bones. " Pig (7) My 80,
    p. 86.
"Solar Heat Madonna. " Pig (7) My 80, p. 92.
"Students. " CapeR (15:2) Sum 80, p. 19.
"These Hot Muggy Nights Middlebury. " HangL (37) Spr 80, p.
    25.
"Things You Can't Stand About Him. " WormR (77) 80, p. 16.
"This Is What You Have to Do So Just Do It. " Vis (2) 80.
"This Long Winter. " Wind (37) 80, p. 26.
"To Make a Poem That Glows Like Lamb Chops in the Oven. "
    NewL (46:3) Spr 80, p. 120.
"To the Person Who Picked Up My New Roll of Stamps the One
    Moment I Wasn't Looking. " WormR (77) 80, p. 16.
"Tuesday. " Pig (7) My 80, p. 38.
"When He Tried to Kiss Me It Was Like Someone Pressing Their
    Finger Inside Your Nose. " WormR (77) 80, p. 15.
"Where His Lips Were, Barbwire. " Vis (4) 80.
"White and Gold. " Wind (37) 80, p. 25.
"White Monday. " HangL (37) Spr 80, p. 28.
"You Got Into My Life Too Fast. " Vis (1) 79.

LIFSON, Martha Ronk
    "Columbus, Ohio, 1949. " HangL (38) Aut 80, p. 35.
    "A Female Ghost speaks to me and says. " HangL (38) Aut 80,
        p. 37.
    Fifteen Poems. Bachy (17) Spr 80, p. 106.
    "Sitting in Juan's restaurant all afternoon, La Paz. " HangL (38)
        Aut 80, p. 36.
    "Thinking about how one thing becomes another and vice versa. "
        ChiR (31:4) Spr 80, p. 100.

LIGHT, Joanne
    "When the Sky Is Filled With Wondrous Things. " PottPort (2)

80-81, p. 25.

LIGNELL, Kathleen
"Acadia. " BelPoJ (31:2) Wint 80-81, p. 28.
"The Woman Adrift Over San Francisco. " BelPoJ (31:2) Wint 80-
    81, p. 29.

LIHN, Enrique
"Figures of Speech" (tr. by Dave Oliphant).   NewOR (7:3) 80, p.
    218.
"Kafka" (tr. by David Unger).   PoNow (27) 80, p. 44.

LILLYWHITE, Harvey
"Passing Time. " SoDakR (18:3) Aut 80, p. 27.
"Ride to Chicago, 1932. " SoDakR (18:3) Aut 80, p. 26.

LIMAN, Claude
"Fixing My Watch in North-Western Ontario, November 10, 1976"
    (for the Edmund Fitzgerald).   ConcPo (12:2) Aut 79, p. 82.

LINDEMAN, Jack
"Hiatus. " SouthernPR (20:1) Spr 80, p. 69.

LINDEN, Gurli
"Det tar lång tid. " PortR (26) 80, p. 130.
"Under ditt hjärta. " PortR (26) 80, p. 128.

LINDHOLDT, Paul
"Young Man Sleeping Drunk. " PoNow (29) 80, p. 17.

LINDLEY, Frances
"Letter to a Dead Artist. " Atl (245:1) Ja 80, p. 32.

LINDNER, Carl
"After a Week of Jogging. " SouthwR (65:2) Spr 80, p. 154.
"The Only Game. " FourQt (29:3) Spr 80, p. 2.
"A Savage Something. " SouthernPR (20:1) Spr 80, p. 16.
"Shooting Baskets in a Dark Gymnasium. " BelPoJ (30:3) Spr 80,
    p. 19.
"Shooting Baskets in a Dark Gymnasium. " PoNow (29) 80, p. 45.

LINDO, Hugo
from Only the Voice: "Today you fall as a stone to water" (tr.
    by Elizabeth G. Miller).   NewOR (7:3) 80, p. 278.

LINDOP, Grevel
"In Europe Everything Has Been Painted. " GRR (11:2/3) 80, p.
    39.
"Russet Apples. " GRR (11:2/3) 80, p. 36.
"Snow. " GRR (11:2/3) 80, p. 38.
"The Traveller at Yazd. " GRR (11:2/3) 80, p. 37.

LINDSAY, Frannie
"Easter Sunday. " MalR (56) O 80, p. 58.

"Eve's Last Words. " MalR (56) O 80, p. 56.
"For the Sea Turtles. " MalR (56) O 80, p. 57.
"The Girl with the Cello. " StoneC (7:1) F 80, p. 12.
"The Horse We Lie Down In" (for Helen). Iowa (10:4) Aut 79,
    p. 30.
"Laura's Ghost. " Iowa (10:4) Aut 79, p. 31.
"Mes Sabots. " AntR (38:4) Aut 80, p. 471.
"Naming the Flowers. " Pan (21) 80, p. 19.

LINDSTROM, Naomi
    "The Word Is Still Lip" (tr. of Octavio Armand). NewOR (7:3)
        80, p. 293.
    "You Call" (tr. of Octavio Armand). NewOR (7:3) 80, p. 292.

LINEHAN, Don
    "Charlie Sweeney. " PottPort (2) 80-81, p. 46.

LINN, Robert
    "The Old Man. " HiramPoR (27) Aut-Wint 80, p. 33.

LINTHICUM, John
    "I Have Decided. " NewL (46:4) Sum 80, p. 66.

LIPMAN, Joel
    "General Store. " AmerPoR (9:3) My-Je 80, p. 32.
    "A Man Asks What I Need. " CreamCR (5:1) Wint 79, p. 14.
    "Mary and Kathy One Two Three and Four. " AmerPoR (9:3)
        My-Je 80, p. 33.
    "New Year. " AmerPoR (9:3) My-Je 80, p. 34.
    "Ride Out. " PoNow (29) 80, p. 17.
    from Sweet Home Chicago, part 2: "Got Helen. " AmerPoR (9:3)
        My-Je 80, p. 33.

LI, Po
    "Ancient Style Poem" (tr. by Julie Landau). DenQ (15:1) Spr 80,
        p. 94.

LIPSITZ, Lou
    "Calming Influence. " VirQR (56:4) Aut 80, p. 682.
    "Pettiness. " VirQR (56:4) Aut 80, p. 681.

LITTAUER, Andrew
    "Rock-Hoard" (for a Russian in England). SewanR (88:3) Sum 80,
        p. 361.
    "Umbilicus. " SewanR (88:3) Sum 80, p. 360.
    "Waking. " SewanR (88:3) Sum 80, p. 360.

LITTLE, Carl von Kienbusch
    "His Letters. " GeoR (34:3) Aut 80, p. 660.

LITTLE, Geraldine C.
    "For Venice, Sinking. " PoetryNW (21:1) Spr 80, p. 22.
    "One Kind of Bestiary. " PoetryNW (21:4) Wint 80-81, p. 20.

"Reversal. " PoNow (29) 80, p. 17.
"Thoughts from a Prone Position: Michelangelo, Sistine Chapel. "
    (23:3) Spr 80, p. 357.

LIU, Stephen Shu Ning
    "On Pali Lookout. " NowestR (18:3) 80, p. 103.

LLEWELLYN, Alun
    "Lizard. " PortR (26) 80, p. 196.
    "Taliesin: The Essence of All Things. " PortR (26) 80, p. 195.

LLOYD, David
    "Abraham. " Poem (38) Mr 80, p. 17.

LLOYD, Michael Gordon
    "Requiem for Pier Paolo Pasolini" (tr. of Eugénio de Andrade
    w. Mário Cláudio). PortR (26) 80, p. 311.

LLOYD, Seth
    "some fun games. " HangL (37) Spr 80, p. 63.
    "Two girls screaming. " HangL (37) Spr 80, p. 64.

LO Ching
    "Gazing at the Fog. " PortR (26) 80, p. 388.

LOCHHEAD, Liz
    "Fourth of July Fireworks. " GRR (11:2/3) 80, p. 22.
    "The Furies. " GRR (11:2/3) 80, p. 19.
    "My Rival's House. " GRR (11:2/3) 80, p. 17.

LOCKE, Duane
    "Apologia pro vita sua. " UTR (6:3/4) 80, p. 38.
    "A Couple from New Jersey Comes to Retire in Florida. " UTR
    (6:3/4) 80, p. 40.
    "A Cypress Pond in a State Park. " UTR (6:3/4) 80, p. 41.
    "An Unfinished Lie. " UTR (6:3/4) 80, p. 42.
    "The Wrecked Boat. " UTR (6:3/4) 80, p. 39.

LOCKLIN, Gerald
    "After the Final. " WormR (77) 80, p. 34.
    "Anglo-French Ingenuity. " WormR (78) 80, p. 82.
    "another light goes out. " WormR (80) 80, p. 139.
    "cabernet nostalgia. " WormR (80) 80, p. 141.
    "Charity Begins at Home. " PoNow (26) 80, p. 43.
    "Decadent. " WormR (78) 80, p. 81.
    "The Fall Classic. " PoNow (28) 80, p. 32.
    "Father of Lies. " WormR (78) 80, p. 82.
    "The Fetishist Reviewer. " PoNow (26) 80, p. 43.
    "The Humanities Office Building. " PoNow (26) 80, p. 43.
    "i do belong to the American Federation of Labor!" WormR
    (80) 80, p. 142.
    "John Wayne. " WormR (77) 80, p. 33.
    "Letters and Science. " WormR (77) 80, p. 37.

"a man who served two masters, and then some. " WormR (80)
    80, p. 138.
"Marie. " WormR (77) 80, p. 34.
"My Aunt Bea. " WormR (78) 80, p. 80.
"my brother. " WormR (80) 80, p. 141.
"Retracted Traction. " WormR (77) 80, p. 33.
"reverse psychology rules all. " WormR (80) 80, p. 138.
"Think Tiny and Carry a Big Stick. " WormR (77) 80, p. 37.
"Verbum Sap Sat. " PoNow (26) 80, p. 43.
"the veterans. " WormR (80) 80, p. 140.
"You Can Even Move It to a Sitz-Bath. " WormR (77) 80, p. 36.

LOCKWOOD, Margo
    "Black Dog. " NewRep (183:25) 20 D 80, p. 30.
    "Expressway Driving. " Ploughs (6:2) 80, p. 70.
    "Health. " Ploughs (6:2) 80, p. 71.
    "Oxford Street Museum. " Ploughs (6:2) 80, p. 66.
    "Wind Flowers. " Ploughs (6:2) 80, p. 69.
    "Yellow Day Like a Still Life. " Ploughs (6:2) 80, p. 68.

LOEB, Karen
    "Catching the Drift. " Pig (7) My 80, p. 20.

LOGAN, John
    "Travelling" (for P. T.). OhioR (24) 80, p. 54.

LOGAN, William
    "Blue Yacht. " NoAmR (265:4) D 80, p. 19.
    "The Entrance to Winter. " MissouriR (3:3) Sum 80, p. 22.
    "Protective Colors. " GeoR (34:2) Sum 80, p. 373.
    "Sealife. " QW (10) Wint-Spr 80, p. 35.
    "Sheep. " SewanR (88:3) Sum 80, p. 354.
    "Summer Island. " SewanR (88:3) Sum 80, p. 355.

LOGUE, Mary
    "Fathers and Daughters. " DacTerr (17) 80, p. 55.

LOMAS, Herbert
    "(Late Summer)" (tr. of Lassi Nummi). PortR (26) 80, p. 135.
    "This Afternoon" (tr. of Kirsi Kunnas). PortR (26) 80, p. 134.

LOMBARDY, Anthony
    "A Letter Home. " NewYorker (56:31) 22 S 80, p. 36.

LONDON, Jonathan
    "Silence in the Lonely House (Pesach, Night of Full Moon)"
        (for David Meltzer). MalR (56) O 80, p. 126.

LONG, Ada
    "The Day When Peace Takes Hold" (tr. of Gloria Fuertes w.
        Philip Levine). PoetryE (1) 80, p. 87.
    "Farmer" (tr. of Gloria Fuertes w. Philip Levine). PoetryE
        (1) 80, p. 86.

"Here I Am Exposed Like Everybody" (tr. of Gloria Fuertes w. Philip Levine). <u>PoetryE</u> (1) 80, p. 84.
"Prayer" (tr. of Gloria Fuertes w. Philip Levine). <u>PoetryE</u> (1) 80, p. 82.
"You'll Get Yours" (tr. of Gloria Fuertes w. Philip Levine). <u>PoetryE</u> (1) 80, p. 85.

LONG, Robert
"burning out." <u>Kayak</u> (55) Ja 81, p. 60.
"Debts." <u>NewYorker</u> (56:36) 27 O 80, p. 177.
"First Day of Spring." <u>NewYorker</u> (56:6) 31 Mr 80, p. 36.
"Poem: Someone you loved is dead." <u>Poetry</u> (136:5) Ag 80, p. 288.
"Saying One Thing" (for Daisy Jacobs). <u>Poetry</u> (136:5) Ag 80, p. 289.
from The Sonnets: (15, 17, 18). <u>SunM</u> (9/10) Sum 80, p. 167.
"Thruway" (for Mary Karr). <u>Poetry</u> (136:5) Ag 80, p. 287.
"water" (for Heather McHugh). <u>Kayak</u> (55) Ja 81, p. 59.
"What It Is" (for Krys Powell). <u>Poetry</u> (136:5) Ag 80, p. 286.

LOOS, Gloria Scott
"My Neighbor" (tr. of Gloria Fuertes). <u>PoNow</u> (26) 80, p. 45.

LOPES, Michael
"Teaching Is Easy Money." <u>AndR</u> (7:1) Spr 80, p. 22.

LORCA, Federico Garcia
"Childhood and Death" (tr. by Allen Josephs). <u>VirQR</u> (56:1) Wint 80, p. 63.
from Divan del Tamarit: "Casida of the Boy Wounded by Water" (tr. by Edwin Honig). <u>BosUJ</u> (26:3) 80, p. 148.
from Divan del Tamarit: "Casida of the Branches" (tr. by Edwin Honig). <u>BosUJ</u> (26:3) 80, p. 147.
from Divan del Tamarit: "Gacela of Love Unforeseen" (tr. by Edwin Honig). <u>BosUJ</u> (26:3) 80, p. 144.
from Divan del Tamarit: "Gacela of Love's Memory" (tr. by Edwin Honig). <u>BosUJ</u> (26:3) 80, p. 146.
from Divan del Tamarit: "Gacela of Miraculous Love" (tr. by Edwin Honig). <u>BosUJ</u> (26:3) 80, p. 143.
from Divan del Tamarit: "Gacela of the Escape" (tr. by Edwin Honig). <u>BosUJ</u> (26:3) 80, p. 145.
"The Goring and Death" (tr. by David K. Loughran). <u>CutB</u> (14) Spr/Sum 80, p. 64.
"Landscape with Two Tombs and an Assyrian Dog" (tr. by Michael Koch). <u>Durak</u> (5) 80, p. 18.
"Norm and Paradise of Blacks" (tr. by Michael Koch). <u>Durak</u> (5) 80, p. 19.

LORD, Gigi
"The Green Eye Rolled Go-Go to the Fist." <u>Im</u> (7:1) 80, p. 9.

LORR, Katharine
"Ablutions." <u>Vis</u> (3) 80.

"Caesarian. " Vis (2) 80.
"Lying In. " Vis (2) 80.
"Sonogram. " Vis (4) 80.

LOTT, Clarinda Harriss
"Body My House. " Vis (1) 79.
"Echo. " Vis (3) 80.
"The Hang of It. " Vis (1) 79.
"Late September Running Poem. " CarlMis (18:2) Sum 80, p.
    157.
"Mad Maud Decides Not to Become a Nun. " CarlMis (18:2) Sum
    80, p. 158.
"Mermaid Song. " Vis (1) 79.
"Quarks. " Vis (2) 80.

LOUGHRAN, David K.
"The Goring and Death" (tr. of Federico Garcia Lorca). CutB
    (14) Spr/Sum 80, p. 64.

LOUIS, Adrian C.
"For Alice at the State School. " SmPd (50) Aut 80, p. 18.

LOUTHAN, Robert
"New to the Urban Life. " MassR (21:2) Sum 80, p. 332.
"One Thing About High School. " PoNow (29) 80, p. 24.
"The Signal" (for Michael Ryan). PoNow (29) 80, p. 24.
"What Hurt My Hands. " PoNow (29) 80, p. 24.
"When the Broadcast Ends. " ParisR (78) Sum 80, p. 190.

LOVELL, Barbara
"When You Go. " SouthernPR (20:1) Spr 80, p. 25.

LOW, Denise
"June 29. " KanQ (12:1) Wint 80, p. 110.
"Tuttle Creek Catch. " CapeR (15:2) Sum 80, p. 7.

LOWENSTEIN, Robert
"Upwind. " Wind (37) 80, p. 27.

LOWERY, Mike
"Bonnie Beach, 8th Grade Cheerleader. " PoNow (29) 80, p. 25.
"Siege Perilous. " PoNow (29) 80, p. 25.
"Sir Gawain and the Green Night. " CapeR (16:1) Wint 80, p. 20.
"Welfare Refuge. " PoNow (29) 80, p. 25.
"The Wild Blue Yonder. " PoNow (29) 80, p. 25.

LOWRY, Betty
"Explaining the Person in the Tower. " ColEng (41:5) Ja 80, p.
    551.
"Fishing Cat Story. " ColEng (41:5) Ja 80, p. 550.

LUBOWE, Stephen
"The Surrogate. " CapeR (16:1) Wint 80, p. 44.

LUCINA, Sister Mary
  "At Night Listening to the Erie. " Im (7:1) 80, p. 11.
  "Circling Through Silence. " Wind (37) 80, p. 28.
  "Fog. " Wind (37) 80, p. 29.
  "Holes" (for Brian). Wind (37) 80, p. 28.
  "Your Star, Your Word. " Im (7:1) 80, p. 11.

LUCY, Seán
  "Thanking Henry for His Voices. " WindO (36) Spr-Sum 80, p. 6.

LUDVIGSON, Susan
  "Breasts. " OhioR (25) 80, p. 62.
  "Burials. " SouthernPR (20:1) Spr 80, p. 47.
  "Good Child. " OP (29) Spr 80, p. 30.
  "The Kiss. " OP (29) Spr 80, p. 31.
  "Little Women. " OhioR (25) 80, p. 63.
  "Margaret. " OP (29) Spr 80, p. 32.
  "Tiwi Woman. " GeoR (34:3) Aut 80, p. 518.
  "The Widow. " Poetry (136:3) Je 80, p. 142.

LUECKE, Janemarie
  "The Barn. " Outbr (4/5) Aut 79-Spr 80, p. 84.
  "The Cream Separator. " Outbr (4/5) Aut 79-Spr 80, p. 86.

LUHRMANN, Tom
  "Beyond Belief. " GeoR (34:2) Sum 80, p. 332.
  "Destinations. " VirQR (56:4) Aut 80, p. 674.
  "Edge of the Summer. " VirQR (56:4) Aut 80, p. 673.
  "South Wheelock. " VirQR (56:4) Aut 80, p. 673.
  "Tulip Trees. " VirQR (56:4) Aut 80, p. 676.

LULL, Janis
  "A Narrative of Cat and Mouse. " LittleM (12:3/4) 80, p. 75.
  "Woman with Two Daughters. " LittleM (12:3/4) 80, p. 74.

LUNDKVIST, Artur
  "The Baker" (tr. by Diana Wormuth). OntR (12) Spr-Sum 80, p. 23.
  "Furioso" (tr. by Diana Wormuth). OntR (12) Spr-Sum 80, p. 25.
  "Mill Memory" (tr. by Diana Wormuth). OntR (12) Spr-Sum 80, p. 24.
  "Stairway" (tr. by William Jay Smith and Leif Sjoberg). PoetryE (3) 80, p. 57.
  "Temples" (tr. by Diana Wormuth). OntR (12) Spr-Sum 80, p. 21.

LUSK, Daniel
  "Insomnia. " DacTerr (17) 80, p. 56.
  "Lichen. " NewRena (13) Aut 80, p. 76.
  "Plasterers. " NewRena (13) Aut 80, p. 77.

LUTHER, Susan
  "Two Views of Howard's Chapel. " Poem (40) N 80, p. 8.

LUX, Thomas
"After a Few Whiffs of Another World. " Poetry (137:2) 80, p.
    159.
"The Dark Comes on in Cubes, in Blocks. " Field (22) Spr 80,
    p. 59.
"Graveyard by the Sea. " Tendril (9) 80, p. 99.
"His Job Is Honest and Simple: Keeping. " Field (22) Spr 80,
    p. 58.
"His Spine Curved Just Enough. " Poetry (137:3) D 80, p. 161.
"History and Abstraction. " AmerPoR (9:3) My-Je 80, p. 37.
"It's the Little Towns I Like. " Poetry (137:3) D 80, p. 160.
"Lament City. " AmerPoR (9:3) My-Je 80, p. 37.
"Like a Wide Anvil from the Moon the Light. " Field (22) Spr
    80, p. 60.
"The Night So Bright a Squirrel Reads. " Poetry (137:3) D 80,
    p. 158.
"Our Kisses Being Durable" (for Jean Kilbourne). AmerPoR (9:3)
    My-Je 80, p. 37.
"There Were Some Summers. " Field (22) Spr 80, p. 57.

LYLES, Peggy Willis
"Following the Dots. " KanQ (12:1) Wint 80, p. 121.
"Haiku. " WindO (37) Aut-Wint 80.   on calendar.
"Plainsong in a Charleston Garden. " CapeR (16:1) Wint 80, p.
    49.
"Talisman of the Dowager Queen. " CapeR (16:1) Wint 80, p. 48.
Two Haiku. WindO (36) Spr-Sum 80, p. 5.
"Wake of the Turtle, Wake of the Tugboat. " CapeR (15:2) Sum
    80, p. 8.

LYNSKEY, Edward
"Chipped Impressions. " CropD (2/3) Aut-Wint 80, p. 39.

LYONS, Richard J.
"Apology. " PoetC (12:1) 80, p. 20.
"Courtroom Artist. " PoetC (12:2) 80, p. 20.
"Double Identity. " DacTerr (17) 80, p. 58.
"Watching the Deaf Boy Play the Piano. " CarlMis (18:2) Sum
    80, p. 35.

McAFEE, Thomas
"Anorexia Nervosa. " Focus (14:86) Ap 80, p. 13.
"At Home, Far Away Inside. " Focus (14:86) Ap 80, p. 13.
"For Mary Lou Williams, at Piano, at the Hickory House. "
    Focus (14:86) Ap 80, p. 13.
"If There Is a Perchance. " OhioR (24) 80, p. 89.
"Missouri River. " Focus (14:86) Ap 80, p. 13.
"Question for a Medieval Mystic. " Focus (14:86) Ap 80, p. 13.
"Zone of Quiet Desperation. " Focus (14:86) Ap 80, p. 13.

McALEAVEY, David
"Can-opener. " Ascent (5:3) 80, p. 52.

McALLISTER, Bruce
"Party." SouthwR (65:4) Aut 80, p. 383.

McALLISTER, Catherine
"Circle." Sam (98) 80, p. 16.
"Night Line." Sam (98) 80, p. 25.

McANALLY-KNIGHT, Mary
"Haiku # 3." Prima (5) 79, p. 45.

McAULEY, James J.
"Succubus." PoetryNW (21:3) Aut 80, p. 18.

MacBETH, George
"A Gift." AmerPoR (9:1) Ja-F 80, p. 39.
"The Truth." AmerPoR (9:1) Ja-F 80, p. 39.
"Two Days After." AmerPoR (9:1) Ja-F 80, p. 39.

McBRIDE, Mekeel
"Katelizabeth, Saint of Unpardonable Sorrow." Aspect (76) S-D
    79-80, p. 19.
"Marking, Again, the Perimeter of Solitude." Aspect (76) S-D
    79-80, p. 15.
"The Pharmacist Goes Cloud Bathing" (for Richard Daly).
    Aspect (76) S-D 79-80, p. 16.
"This Quiet Place." LittleM (12:3/4) 80, p. 78.
"The Will to Live." Tendril (9) 80, p. 101.

McCABE, Brian
"Enter a Fifth Man, Crying." GRR (11:2/3) 80, p. 85.
"The Imaginary Thief." GRR (11:2/3) 80, p. 84.
"The Ulterior Man." GRR (11:2/3) 80, p. 86.

MacCAIG, Norman
"Balances." Ploughs (6:1) 80, p. 91.
"Enough." Ploughs (6:1) 80, p. 92.
"In memoriam." Ploughs (6:1) 80, p. 89.
"Real life Christmas card." Ploughs (6:1) 80, p. 90.
"To create what?" Ploughs (6:1) 80, p. 93.
"Toad." Ploughs (6:1) 80, p. 88.

McCALLUM, Paddy
"Low Tide at Oyster Bay." MalR (54) Ap 80, p. 37.

McCANN, Clark
from The Whales: "The Cry." Bachy (16) Wint 80, p. 36.
from The Whales: "Dolphins." Bachy (16) Wint 80, p. 36.
from The Whales: "Noah and the Whales." Bachy (16) Wint 80,
    p. 36.
from The Whales: "The Whiteness of the Whale." Bachy (16)
    Wint 80, p. 34.
from The Whales: "Whale Songs." Bachy (16) Wint 80, p. 34.

McCANN, Janet
"At the End of Winter. " Pig (7) My 80, p. 16.
"August. " StoneC (7:1) F 80, p. 8.
"Case Study for Diagnosis. " Pig (7) My 80, p. 13.
"Children in the Park. " CapeR (16:1) Wint 80, p. 8.
"The Dream. " CimR (53) O 80, p. 13.
"On the Roof. " CapeR (16:1) Wint 80, p. 9.
"Passing It On. " Poem (39) Jl 80, p. 57.
"Poem for My Daughter. " PoetC (12:3) 80, p. 26.
"Poem With Alternate Lines Missing. " Pig (7) My 80, p. 51.
"Sending for Things. " Poem (39) Jl 80, p. 58.

McCARRISTON, Linda
"Barn Fire" (for Mike). OhioR (25) 80, p. 98.
"Birthday Girl: 1950" (for my mother). OhioR (25) 80, p. 99.
"Spring. " PoNow (29) 80, p. 31.

McCARTHY, Gerald
"Note in a Bottle. " NewL (46:4) Sum 80, p. 108.
"Riding Fence. " NewL (46:4) Sum 80, p. 109.

McCARTHY, Thomas
"An Irish Writer's Diary. " GRR (11:2/3) 80, p. 115.
"Listening to Novelists. " GRR (11:2/3) 80, p. 114.
"Old Boke, the Coachman. " GRR (11:2/3) 80, p. 113.

McCARTIN, James
"My Mother. " NewL (47:1) Aut 80, p. 8.
"The Prendergast. " NewL (47:1) Aut 80, p. 9.

McCLANE, Kenneth A.
"At November's Turn. " Wind (37) 80, p. 30.
"Harlem. " Wind (37) 80, p. 32.
"Meditation. " FourQt (29:3) Spr 80, p. 28.
"Mother's Song" (for Genevieve). Wind (37) 80, p. 31.
"One Shall Forever Lone Among Trees. " Wind (37) 80, p. 30.
"Spring Hill. " CapeR (15:2) Sum 80, p. 2.
"Swampfire. " Wind (37) 80, p. 32.

McCLATCHY, J. D.
"Ravel: Noble and Sentimental Waltzes. " Shen (31:2) 80, p. 96.
"A Winter Without Snow. " NewRep (182:10) 8 Mr 80, p. 28.

McCLOSKEY, Mark
"The Alpha Islands. " PoNow (27) 80, p. 9.
"I Liked Your Lover Better than You. " PoetryNW (21:4) Wint
    80-81, p. 18.
"The Principal's New House. " PoNow (26) 80, p. 9.

McCLURE, Michael
"Black Paper Silhouettes at Disneyland. " PoNow (26) 80, p. 5.
"Memories from Childhood. " LittleBR (1:1) Aut 80, p. 19.
"Memories from Childhood. " PoNow (26) 80, p. 5.

McCOLL, Michael
  "Dog Shakes Me. " KanQ (12:3) Sum 80, p. 50.
  "Electric Stars. " PoNow (29) 80, p. 18.
  "Quietly Burning. " KanQ (12:3) Sum 80, p. 49.

McCOMBS, Judith
  from After the Surveyor's Death: "Fragment. " Nimrod (24:1)
    Aut-Wint 80, p. 24.
  from After the Surveyor's Death: "In the Year of Your Death. "
    Nimrod (24:1) Aut-Wint 80, p. 21.
  from After the Surveyor's Death: "The Headstone & the Bearer. "
    Nimrod (24:1) Aut-Wint 80, pp. 24-25.
  from After the Surveyor's Death: "The Inheritor. " Nimrod (24:
    1) Aut-Wint 80, p. 22.

McCORQUODALE, Robin
  "Dinner Party. " Wind (37) 80, p. 37.
  "Poem from a Basement. " SoCaR (13:1) Aut 80, p. 88.
  "Twentieth Birthday. " Wind (37) 80, p. 37.

McCRORIE, Edward
  "Under Story. " BelPoJ (30:4) Sum 80, p. 36.

McCULLOUGH, Ken
  "Buckley Interviews Borges" (for Ray Di Palma). HiramPoR
    (27) Aut-Wint 80, p. 35.
  "In the Summer of the Year One. " SoCaR (13:1) Aut 80, p. 14.
  "The Wanderer Laughs at First. " HiramPoR (27) Aut-Wint 80,
    p. 34.

McCULLY, Hilton
  "Gloire a cheud mhaduinn. " PottPort (2) 80-81, p. 32.

McCUNE, Kate
  "Because We Must Finally Love Our Parents We Come to Love
    Our Hometowns Too. " PoetryNW (21:2) Sum 80, p. 44.

McCURDY, Harold
  "The Chapel at Vence. " SewanR (88:2) Spr 80, p. 180.
  "Near the Hospital Landing Pad. " ChrC (97:15) 23 Ap 80, p.
    466.
  "Petition. " ChrC (97:12) 2 Ap 80, p. 364.

McCURRY, Jim
  "For ABC. " Bound (8:2) Wint 80, p. 122.
  "The Intention" (for ABC). Bound (8:2) Wint 80, p. 123.

McDERMOTT, John
  "The Riverview. " US1 (12/13) Aut-Wint 80, p. 15.

McDONALD, Agnes
  "Arrival and Beyond. " SouthernPR (20:2) Aut 80, p. 17.
  "Seeing You Off. " SouthernPR (20:1) Spr 80, p. 24.

McDONALD, Anne
"Acrostic with a Palette and Seven Brushes. " PoetryNW (21:3)
    Aut 80, p. 22.
"The Middle of the Movie: Last Year at Marienbad. " Pan (21)
    80, p. 29.

McDONALD, Barry
"Chicken Red. " KanQ (12:2) Spr 80, p. 36.

MacDONALD, Bernell
"Shoulders. " Pan (21) 80, p. 53.

MACDONALD, Cynthia
"January 1980. " AmerPoR (9:6) N-D 80, p. 13.

McDONALD, Roger
"Apis Mellifica. " NewL (46:3) Spr 80, p. 27.
"The husband. " NewL (46:3) Spr 80, p. 26.

MacDONALD, Sylvia F.
"The Lover's Promise. " PottPort (1) 79-80, p. 21.
"Running Away. " PottPort (1) 79-80, p. 25.
"Untitled: if there was a way. " PottPort (1) 79-80, p. 27.

McDONALD, Walter
"The Fan. " PoNow (28) 80, p. 32.
"Giving Time. " NewOR (7:1) 80, p. 41.
"Living in Daughter's House. " Ascent (5:3) 80, p. 14.
"Netting Bats Near Orizaba" (to Dilford). CutB (15) Aut/Wint
    80, p. 56.
"Reading to Daughter" (for Glenn). CimR (53) O 80, p. 14.
"Tornado Alley. " HiramPoR (28) Spr-Sum 80, p. 24.

McDOWELL, Robert
"Hold Your Breath. " NewEngR (3:2) Wint 80, p. 266.
"sahara. " Kayak (54) S 80, p. 27.

McDUFF, David
"Clearing Station" (tr. of Wilhelm Klemm). Stand (21:2) 80, p.
    21.
"Italy" (tr. of Giuseppe Ungaretti w. Jon Silkin). Stand (21:2)
    80, p. 6.
"The Kite" (tr. of Aleksandr Blok w. Jon Silkin). Stand (21:2)
    80, p. 8.
"Night" (tr. of Georg Trakl w. Jon Silkin and R. S. Furness).
    Stand (21:2) 80, p. 19.
"Strophes" (tr. of Joseph Brodsky). Stand (21:1) 79-80, p. 5.
"Trumpets" (tr. of Georg Trakl w. Jon Silkin). Stand (21:2)
    80, p. 20.
"A white low sun" (tr. of Marina Tsvetayeva w. Jon Silkin).
    Stand (21:2) 80, p. 7.

MACEDO, Helder
"Vesperal. " PortR (26) 80, p. 306.

McELHINNY, Lisa
"crazy man on main street. " Wind (38) 80, p. 61.

McELROY, Colleen J.
"Dreams of Johnson Grass. " SouthernPR (20:1) Spr 80, p. 11.
"From Blue Waters. " SouthernPR (20:1) Spr 80, p. 13.

McEUEN, James
"The Debt. " PoetryNW (21:4) Wint 80-81, p. 37.

McFADDEN, David
from Night of Endless Radiance: (I, II, III, IV, V). MalR (55)
Jl 80, pp. 138-143.

McFARLAND, Ron
"Frost Warning. " Poem (38) Mr 80, p. 7.
"A Multitude of Birds. " Poem (38) Mr 80, p. 8.
"Playing Soccer on the Fourth of July. " CapeR (15:2) Sum 80,
p. 21.
"There's Something Suspicious. " Poem (38) Mr 80, p. 10.
"The Trivial Life. " Poem (38) Mr 80, p. 9.

McFEE, Michael
"At Play. " WestHR (34:2) Spr 80, p. 157.
"Hatteras. " Nat (230:19) 17 My 80, p. 601.
"homiletic homonyms. " Kayak (54) S 80, p. 22.
"Silo Letter in the Dead of a Warm Winter. " MassR (21:4) Wint
80, p. 692.
"Summer Bald. " SmF (11/12) Spr-Aut 80, p. 38.

McGRATH, Thomas
"All the Dead Soldiers. " PoNow (28) 80, p. 26.
"At the Motel de dieu: Rediscovery After Absence" (for Slim).
PoNow (28) 80, p. 4.
"In Silence and Solitude. " PoNow (28) 80, p. 26.
"Love Song. " PoNow (28) 80, p. 26.
"Prophecy. " MinnR (NS 15) Aut 80, p. 6.
"Proposal. " MinnR (NS 15) Aut 80, p. 6.
"Spanish Fandango. " MinnR (NS 15) Aut 80, p. 5.
"Trinc. " Ark (14) 80, pp. 277-283.

McGUCKIAN, Medbh
"Choosing. " GRR (11:2/3) 80, p. 54.
"The Grand Mountain Hotel. " GRR (11:2/3) 80, p. 55.
"Phases. " GRR (11:2/3) 80, p. 54.

MACHADO, Antonio
"Which Is True?" (tr. by David Jauss). WebR (5:1) Wint
80, p. 17.

McHUGH, Heather
"Form. " NewYorker (56:37) 3 N 80, p. 180.
"Retired School-Teacher. " Tendril (9) 80, p. 102.

237   McILWAIN

McILWAIN, Sandy
"Chopping Wood Beside the Harbor, January." OhioR (24) 80, p.
22.
"Everything Looks Ordinary." Shen (31:1) 79, p. 90.
"So Much Depends." Shen (31:1) 79, p. 89.

McKAIN, David
"Iron Deer." ModernPS (10:1) 80, p. 37.

MacKAY, Brent
"Ariadne." Montra (7) 80, p. 136.
"Autumn." Montra (7) 80, p. 132.
"Dining Out in Southern France." Montra (7) 80, p. 133.
"Expeditionary." Montra (7) 80, p. 135.
"Noche." Montra (7) 80, p. 134.

MacKAY, Kathryn E.
"The Worry." MalR (53) Ja 80, p. 62.

McKAY, Matthew
"Full Moon." CalQ (16/17) 80, p. 65.
"The Mention of Iwo Jima Prolongs Our Interview." Wind (37)
80, p. 33.

McKAY, Mireille
"Je m'en souviens." ConcPo (12:2) Aut 79, p. 85.

McKEE, Carolyn
"Mean Streets." CropD (2/3) Aut-Wint 80, p. 32.

McKEE, Louis
"Chill Factor." CapeR (16:1) Wint 80, p. 13.
"Entering the Bower." PikeF (3) Wint 80, p. 3.
"Schuylkill County." CapeR (16:1) Wint 80, p. 12.
"Schuylkill County." FourQt (30:1) Aut 80, p. 29.

MACKENZIE, Ginny
"Skipstone." Ploughs (6:2) 80, p. 127.
"To Louis-Auguste Cezanne." Pequod (11) 80, p. 70.
"The West Branch." Pequod (11) 80, p. 71.

McKENZIE-PORTER, Patricia
"A Hundred Times." PottPort (1) 79-80, p. 7.
"Kikimora." PottPort (2) 80-81, p. 47.
"October Among the LaHane Islands." PottPort (1) 79-80, p. 48.
"Sable Fog." PottPort (2) 80-81, p. 51.

McKEOWN, Tom
"Against Winter." PoNow (26) 80, p. 31.
"awakening in Kiev." Kayak (53) My 80, p. 17.
"The Difficult Morning." CreamCR (5:2) Spr 80, p. 21.
"evening in moscow." Kayak (53) My 80, p. 18.
"invitation of the mirrors." Kayak (53) My 80, p. 16.

"Portrait of an Unknown Woman, Pushkin Museum, Moscow. "
  CreamCR (5:2) Spr 80, p. 23.
"Thrown Back. " CreamCR (5:2) Spr 80, p. 22.

McKERNAN, John
  "Family Portrait in Color. " WormR (78) 80, p. 78.
  "The Narrative of the Window. " Aspen (9) Spr 80, p. 83.
  "Now in India. " Tele (16) 80, p. 73.
  "On Loving Omaha Nebraska. " WormR (78) 80, p. 77.
  "The Star Was Hidden Behind a Day Old Cloud. " VirQR (56:4)
    Aut 80, p. 678.
  from Thirty Three Poems: "Part One of Poem # 19. " Mouth
    (2:5) O 80. Front cover.
  "White Thread. " VirQR (56:4) Aut 80, p. 677.

MACKEY, John J.
  "Where Have All the Hippies Gone?" EngJ (69:5) My 80, p. 46.

McKILLOP, Carolyn J.
  "Untitled: Early fingers of the dawn. " PottPort (1) 79-80, p.
    19.

McKINNEY, Irene
  "For Women Who Have Been Patient All Their Lives. "
    SouthernPR (20:1) Spr 80, p. 27.
  "the only portrait of emily dickinson. " Kayak (53) My 80, p. 19.
  "To His Wife. " QW (11) Aut 80, p. 89.

MacKINNON, Alasdair
  "Evening" (tr. of Ciril Zlobec). PortR (26) 80, p. 487.
  "From the cycle: The Melancholy of the Second Echelon" (tr. of
    Veno Taufer). PortR (26) 80, p. 491.
  "Man and His Neighbor" (tr. of Edvard Kocbek). PortR (26) 80,
    p. 483.
  "The Silent Grindbeetle" (tr. of Dane Zajc). PortR (26) 80, p.
    489.
  "The Tongue" (tr. of Edvard Kocbek). PortR (26) 80, p. 485.

MACKLIN, Elizabeth
  "Leaving One of the State Parks After a Family Outing. " Poetry
    (135:4) Ja 80, p. 207.
  "The Unruly Thoughts of the Dog Trainer's Lover. " NewYorker
    (56:7) 7 Ap 80, p. 48.
  "A Woman Kneeling in the Big City. " NewYorker (56:14) 26 My
    80, p. 42.

McLAUGHLIN, Dorothy
  "An Arctic Invasion. " CapeR (16:1) Wint 80, p. 24.

McLAUGHLIN, Mark
  "Doolb. " HangL (37) Spr 80, p. 65.

McLAUGHLIN, Nancy
  "Poem About a Horse. " PoetryNW (21:4) Wint 80-81, p. 30.

McLAUGHLIN, William
"Early Study in Anthropology. " PoetryNW (21:4) Wint 80-81, p.
  22.

MacLEAN, Catharin
"At the Windsor Commercial Hotel. " PottPort (2) 80-81, p. 12.

MacLEAN, Kenneth
"From All the Public Places. " ConcPo (13:1) Spr 80, p. 53.

MacLEAN-FIELD, Crystal
"The Lilac-Blue Ceramic. " DacTerr (17) 80, p. 28.

MacLEISH, Archibald
"Birth of Eventually Venus. " Poetry (137:2) N 80, p. 64.
"Poem Dedicated to the Advancement of Aviation. ... " Poetry
  (137:2) N 80, p. 65.
"Poem: Who of us all have seen. " Poetry (137:2) N 80, p. 64.
"Project for an Aesthetic Sub-Title: Moonlight of a Man. "
  Poetry (137:2) N 80, p. 65.
"Vernissage. " Poetry (137:2) N 80, p. 63.

MacLEOD, Alistair
"On This of February's Cold. " PottPort (2) 80-81, p. 49.

McLEOD, Stephen
"Love, Like the Forest, Decays. " PoetryE (3) 80, p. 23.

MacLOW, Jackson
"Satires from a Physics Textbook. " SunM (9/10) Sum 80, p.
  217.

McMAHAN, Michael
"American Dream Sequence, II. " WindO (36) Spr-Sum 80, p. 21.
"Sundays in the Winter of the Middle Class. " WindO (36) Spr-
  Sum 80, p. 22.
"There Are Worse Things Than Having an American Poet for a
  Lover. " WindO (36) Spr-Sum 80, p. 23.

McMAHN, Michael
"The Grasses of Kezar Marsh. " SmPd (50) Aut 80, p. 20.

McMAHON, Lynne
"Branches and China. " MissouriR (3:3) Sum 80, p. 24.

McMAHON, Michael Beirne
"The Auction. " CropD (2/3) Aut-Wint 80, p. 25.
"Shovel Pass. " CropD (2/3) Aut-Wint 80, p. 25.

McMANIS, Jack
"1980 Poet Speaks to Crumbling Picture of Baudelaire. " ChrC
  (97:19) 21 My 80, p. 573.

McMICHAEL, James
from Four Good Things: "No sleep for either of us on the flight
to. " ParisR (77) Wint-Spr 80, pp. 26-30.

MacMORRAN, Tom
"Awakened by a Storm in April. " Wind (36) 80, p. 40.
"Homecoming. " Wind (36) 80, p. 39.

McMULLEN, Rosemary
"Evening Milking. " Outbr (4/5) Aut 79-Spr 80, p. 61.
"The Outpost in Winter. " Outbr (4/5) Aut 79-Spr 80, p. 62.

McNAIR, Wesley
"The Bald Spot. " Poetry (136:5) Ag 80, p. 292.
"The Poetic License. " Poetry (136:5) Ag 80, p. 294.

McNARIE, Alan
"The Baying. " Wind (36) 80, p. 44.

McNASPY, C. J.
"Stained Glass" (tr. of Toshijuki Doi). NewOR (7:1) 80, p. 56.

McNIECE, James
"Conversations With My Dead Friend. " StoneC (7:1) F 80, p. 26.

McNULTY, Tim
"I Consider Once More the Walls. " HangL (38) Aut 80, p. 42.
"Ode to the Goddess on the Morning of First Spring Light. "
    HangL (38) Aut 80, p. 43.
"Planting Seedlings Across the Canal from Trident. " HangL (38)
    Aut 80, p. 40.
"Two Puddle Sutra. " HangL (38) Aut 80, p. 41.
"With the Moon. " Ark (14) 80, p. 284.

McPHERON, Judith
"In the Swaying Field. " StoneC (7:1) F 80, p. 32.
"In the Swaying Field. " StoneC (7:2) My 80, p. 41.
"Watching for Water. " Pig (7) My 80, p. 34.
"Water. " Harp (261:1562) Jl 80, p. 31.

McPHERSON, Sandra
"Alleys. " AmerPoR (9:6) N-D 80, p. 14.
"Black Soap. " Poetry (135:5) F 80, p. 255.
"Debut. " Poetry (135:5) F 80, p. 253.
"The Delicacy" (for M. H.). AmerPoR (9:1) Ja-F 80, p. 29.
"The Firefly. " Antaeus (38) Sum 80, p. 89.
"For Elizabeth Bishop. " AmerPoR (9:6) N-D 80, p. 14.
"Haze. " Poetry (135:5) F 80, p. 251.
"His Body. " Tendril (9) 80, p. 103.
"If the Cardinals Were Like Us. " Antaeus (38) Sum 80, p. 87.
"In the Deceased Woman's Blossoming Yard. " Iowa (10:4) Aut
    80, p. 28.
"The Jet Engine" (for Gwen Head). Poetry (135:5) F 80, p. 249.

"Lullaby. " Poetry (135:5) F 80, p. 252.
"Man in an Old Myth. " Antaeus (39) Aut 80, p. 64.
"The Spa of the Posthumous. " Iowa (10:4) Aut 79, p. 27.
"Unexplained Absences. " WatT (1) Aut 80, p. 76.
"The Wheel. " ConcPo (13:2) Aut 80, p. 17.

McPHILLIAMY, Therese
   "A Response to a Picture of a Cambodian Refugee on the Front
      Page of the New York Times School Weekly, October 29,
      1979. " EngJ (69:5) My 80, p. 48.

McQUILKIN, Rennie
   "Baptism. " PoetryNW (21:3) Aut 80, p. 9.
   "Cat. " LitR (23:3) Spr 80, p. 390.
   "Earthquake. " PoetC (12:3) 80, p. 16.
   "Her Own Ministrone. " PoetC (12:2) 80, p. 35.
   "Luna Moth" (for Naomi). HiramPoR (27) Aut-Wint 80, p. 38.
   "A Real Scene in the Atheneum. " PoetC (12:2) 80, p. 36.
   "Spring Song. " HiramPoR (27) Aut-Wint 80, p. 37.
   "The Steam, the Steam. " PoetryNW (21:3) Aut 80, p. 10.
   "The Uprising. " PoetC (12:3) 80, p. 14.

MADDEN, David
   "The World's One Breathing. " PortR (26) 80, p. 437.

MADDEN, Patrick
   from The Songs of Asian Jack: "A Dream. " AntR (38:3) Sum
      80, p. 342.
   from The Songs of Asian Jack: "A Nightmare. " AntR (38:3)
      Sum 80, p. 343.
   from The Songs of Asian Jack: "Betty Slips Her Cham. "
      AntR (38:3) Sum 80, p. 342.
   from The Songs of Asian Jack: "Dawn. " AntR (38:3) Sum 80,
      p. 344.
   from The Songs of Asian Jack: "Dockside. " AntR (38:3) Sum
      80, p. 340.
   from The Songs of Asian Jack: "Feeling for the Change. "
      AntR (38:3) Sum 80, p. 343.
   from The Songs of Asian Jack: "Jack and the Fever. " AntR
      (38:3) Sum 80, p. 341.

MADDOX, Everette
   "The New Odor" (for Ralph). PoNow (29) 80, p. 17.

MADINGOANE, Ingoapele
   "did you know?" PortR (26) 80, p. 332.

MAGEE, Wes
   "Sheep, Buried. " BelPoJ (30:4) Sum 80, p. 1.

MAGER, Don
   "Canto Faggoto" (for JP). Mouth (2:5) O 80, p. 27.
   "Migrations and Exiles. " Mouth (2:4) My 80, p. 19.

"10 March 1778, Valley Forge: Lieutenant Enslin Is Drummed
from the Army. " Mouth (2:4) My 80, p. 9.
"1327: The Chronicler of Neath Abbey in Wales. " Mouth (2:5)
O 80, p. 34.

MAGISTRALE, T.
"Hey, Bukowski. " PikeF (3) Wint 80, p. 11.
"A Poet's Place. " PikeF (3) Wint 80, p. 11.

MAGNUSSON, Sigurdur A.
"Africa" (tr. of Hannes Sigfússon). PortR (26) 80, p. 181.
"Afternoon: 1968" (tr. of Stefán Hörour Grimsson). PortR (26)
80, p. 177.
"Barn týnist. " PortR (26) 80, p. 184.
"A Child Lost" (tr. by author). PortR (26) 80, p. 185.
"I ask. I hear" (tr. of Jón Oskar). PortR (26) 80, p. 183.
"Marie Antoinette" (tr. of Hannes Pétursson). PortR (26) 80,
p. 189.
"The Visitor" (tr. of Porsteinn frá Hamri). PortR (26) 80, p.
187.
"Winterday" (tr. of Stefán Hörour Grimsson). PortR (26) 80, p.
179.

MAGORIAN, James
"Apathy Award. " PikeF (3) Wint 80, p. 8.

MAHAPATRA, Jayanta
"The Morning of the Dead Fish. " SewanR (88:3) Sum 80, p. 356.
"The Quality of Ruins. " SewanR (88:3) Sum 80, p. 357.

MAHNKE, John
"Bauble and Anchor. " Durak (5) 80, p. 56.
"Last Halloween of Anonymity. " QW (10) Wint-Spr 80, p. 114.
"Sizeable Thing. " QW (10) Wint-Spr 80, p. 113.

MAHON, Derek
"Rathlin Island. " Ploughs (6:1) 80, p. 130.
"The World Is Everything That Is the Case. " Ploughs (6:1) 80,
p. 129.

MAHONEY, Lizabeth Fairclough
"My occupation. " UTR (6:3/4) 80, p. 43.
"We shall enter upon a trackless memory. " UTR (6:3/4) 80, p.
44.

MAIA, Circe
"Wet Grapes... " (tr. by Patsy Boyer and Mary Crow). CutB
(14) Spr/Sum 80, p. 101.
"A Wind Will Come from the South" (tr. by Patsy Boyer and
Mary Crow). CutB (14) Spr/Sum 80, p. 103.

MAIER, Carol
"Possible Love Poem to the Usurer" (tr. of Octavio Armand).

NewOR (7:2) 80, p. 101.

MAILMAN, Leo
"Green Trees. " WormR (78) 80, p. 53.
"In between. " Wind (38) 80, p. 46.
"Job City. " WormR (77) 80, pp. 17-28.
"The Literary Bookstore. " WormR (78) 80, p. 53.
"The Odyssey Revisited. " Wind (38) 80, p. 46.
"Route 60: Winter, Spring, Tying, Danforth, Tate and York. "
    Wind (38) 80, p. 45.

MAINO, Jeannette
"Disillusion. " KanQ (12:1) Wint 80, p. 166.

MAISEL, Carolyn
"Falling to Grace. " NoAmR (265:3) S 80, p. 63.
"Going North. " NoAmR (265:3) S 80, p. 63.

MAK, Lev
"Eden" (adapted by Dan Jaffe). Focus (14:86) Ap 80, p. 32.
"Red Square" (adapted by Dan Jaffe). Focus (14:86) Ap 80, p.
    32.

MAKUCK, Peter
"Back Roads by Night. " BelPoJ (31:2) Wint 80-81, p. 31.
"Meat. " BelPoJ (31:2) Wint 80-81, p. 32.
"Racing. " PoNow (29) 80, p. 18.
"Running. " PoNow (29) 80, p. 18.

MALANGA, Gerard
"To the Melody of the Southern Country. " Ark (14) 80, p. 285.

MALE, Belkis Cuza
"Mujer brava que casó con Dios. " PortR (26) 80, p. 59.

MALEC, Emily Keller
"My Mother Was Christmas. " CapeR (16:1) Wint 80, p. 32.

MALLARME, Stéphane
"Cantique de Saint Jean. " SouthernR (16:2) Spr 80, p. 440.
"A Tomb for Anatole" (tr. by Paul Auster). ParisR (78) Sum
    80, pp. 136-148.

MALONEY, John Owen
"For William Carlos Williams. " Poetry (137:1) O 80, p. 30.
"Laura-by-the-Sea. " Poetry (137:1) O 80, p. 28.
"Loose Ladder. " Poetry (137:1) O 80, p. 36.
"Raining Towards Aries. " Poetry (137:1) O 80, p. 32.
"Water. " Poetry (137:1) O 80, p. 34.

MALONEY, Linda
"There Is a Woman at My Door, Pounding. " Pan (21) 80, p. 46.

MALPEZZI, Frances M.
"Spring. In Arkansas. " BallSUF (21:1) Wint 80, p. 12.

MALTMAN, Kim
"Branch Lines. " MalR (53) Ja 80, p. 30.

MANDELSTAM, Osip
"The Abbé" (tr. by Robert Tracy). NewOR (7:1) 80, p. 35.
"Charlie Chaplin" (tr. by Robert Tracy). LitR (23:3) Spr 80, p.
  386.
"Kamehb. " Poetry (136:1) Ap 80, p. 21.
from Stone: "Petersburg Stanzas" (for N. Gumilyov) (tr. by
  Robert Tracy). LitR (23:3) Spr 80, p. 385.
from Stone: (6, 44, 78) (tr. by Robert Tracy). Poetry (136:1)
  Ap 80, p. 21.

MANESS, Sandra
"The Subjunctive Mood. " PoetryNW (21:2) Sum 80, p. 18.

MANGAN, Gerald
"Hallowe'en and the Liffey. " GRR (11:2/3) 80, p. 79.
"Last. " GRR (11:2/3) 80, p. 83.

MANN, Charlotte
"The Neophyte. " ChrC (97:20) 28 My 80, p. 605.

MANTEUFFEL, Jonathan D.
"The Glass. " PoNow (29) 80, p. 18.

MARANO, Russell
"Appalachian Landscape. " Wind (36) 80, p. 42.
"Moon Changes. " KanQ (12:1) Wint 80, p. 109.

MARCELLO, Leo Luke
"Gumbo Shop. " WindO (37) Aut-Wint 80, p. 3.
"Once as I was peeling one. " WindO (37) Aut-Wint 80, p. 4.

MARCUS, Morton
"Some Words for Hard Times. " Durak (5) 80, p. 16.

MARGGRAFF, Roberta
"Crossfire. " EngJ (69:5) My 80, p. 61.

MARGOLIS, Gary
"The Stable. " ConcPo (13:2) Aut 80, p. 86.

MARIAH, Paul
"Variations from the Japanese" (for Kenneth Rexroth). Ark (14)
  80, p. 286.

MARIANI, Paul
"Crossing Cocytus. " Agni (13) 80, pp. 117-123.

MARION, Jeff Daniel
"J. D. M. " DacTerr (17) 80, p. 60.

MARK, E. M.
"in a scheme. " PoNow (29) 80, p. 18.

MARKS, S. J.
"Clouded Sky" (tr. of Miklos Radnoti w. Steven Polgar and
    Stephen Berg). PoetryE (1) 80, p. 76.
"A Letter to My Wife" (tr. of Miklos Radnoti w. Steven Polgar
    and Stephen Berg). PoetryE (1) 80, p. 78.

MARKUM, Ann
"Trees. " Pig (7) My 80, p. 8.

MAROHL, J.
"Heaven. " UTR (6:3/4) 80, p. 46.
"Rain. " UTR (6:3/4) 80, p. 47.
"Wind. " UTR (6:3/4) 80, p. 45.

MARSDEN, Carolyn
"A Painter, His Model and a Woman Looking at Hats. " CutB
    (15) Aut/Wint 80, p. 5.
"What You Wanted. " MissouriR (3:3) Sum 80, p. 15.

MARSHALL, Caroline
"How We Go On. " PoNow (29) 80, p. 25.
"September Weather. " PoNow (29) 80, p. 25.

MARSHALL, Donald
"Dog Days. " CimR (52) Jl 80, p. 48.

MARSHALL, S. Mervette
"Engrossed in Love of Life. " Obs (5:1/2) Spr-Sum 79, p. 93.
"Talking With Myself. " Obs (5:1/2) Spr-Sum 79, p. 93.
"Today I Saw Mervin. " Obs (5:1/2) Spr-Sum 79, p. 92.

MARTEAU, Robert
from Vigie: "Appareille ô beauté je te fais une aire" (tr. by
    Louis Simpson). AmerPoR (9:1) Ja-F 80, p. 44.
from Vigie: "Il est minuit" (tr. by Louis Simpson). AmerPoR
    (9:1) Ja-F 80, p. 44.
from Vigie: "Innommé toujours est le monde" (tr. by Louis
    Simpson). AmerPoR (9:1) Ja-F 80, p. 44.
from Vigie: "Trop de poètes font feu de tout" (tr. by Louis
    Simpson). AmerPoR (9:1) Ja-F 80, p. 44.

MARTIN, Charles Casey
"Culls. " AntR (38:1) Wint 80, p. 56.
"Midnight Lunchbreak. " AntR (38:1) Wint 80, p. 58.
"Two Men in Butternuts Bargaining Silently Over a Wrecked
    Pickup. " PoetryNW (21:3) Aut 80, p. 24.

MARTIN, Connie
"Chubb. " PoNow (29) 80, p. 18.

MARTIN, D. Roger
... May Tend to Incriminate Me. Sam (94) 80. Entire issue.
"The Nuclear Age Comes to Centerville. " Sam (98) 80, p. 19.

MARTIN, Jim
"Daddy's Land. " CreamCR (5:2) Spr 80, p. 88.
"Ludie Jenkins. " CreamCR (5:1) Wint 79, p. 115.

MARTIN, Melvin
"Aspiration: To a Constructive View. " NewRena (12) Spr 80, p.
51.
"The Road to School. " NewRena (12) Spr 80, p. 52.
"Spring's Last Semester. " NewRena (13) Aut 80, p. 81.

MARTIN, Philip
"Lake-Walk, Sweden" (for Lars). CarlMis (18:2) Sum 80, p. 48.
"Sonnet 1: The Desert at Rio Grande" (tr. of Lars Gustafsson).
CarlMis (18:2) Sum 80, p. 34.

MARTINEZ, Dionisio D.
"The Wife of the Man. " SouthernPR (20:1) Spr 80, p. 41.

MARTINEZ, Lillian B.
"Believe It!" NewWR (48:3) My-Je 80, p. 4.
"Let's Talk. " NewWR (48:3) My-Je 80, p. 5.

MARTINSON, Harry
"The Ball of Fluff" (tr. by W. H. Auden and Leif Sjoberg).
PoetryE (1) 80, p. 37.
"The Butterfly" (tr. by W. H. Auden and Leif Sjoberg).
PoetryE (1) 80, p. 36.
"The Cock Reads the Field" (tr. by William Jay Smith and Leif
Sjoberg). PoetryE (1) 80, p. 38.
"The Swan" (tr. by W. H. Auden and Leif Sjoberg). PoetryE
(1) 80, p. 35.

MARTY, Miriam
"In August" (to Dad). SouthernPR (20:1) Spr 80, p. 44.

MASON, David James
"The Inlaid Chair. " KanQ (12:3) Sum 80, p. 140.

MASON-BROWNE, Nicholas
"Peace River Country. " MalR (53) Ja 80, p. 107.

MASTORAKI, Jenny
"The Women" (tr. by Kimon Friar). PoNow (28) 80, p. 46.

MATEVSKI, Mateja
"rock. " PortR (26) 80, p. 466.

MATHE, Sylvie
"Verb and Matter" (tr. of Jean Tardieu). PortR (26) 80, p. 139.

MATHESON, William H.
"(232)" (tr. of Maurice Scève). WebR (5:1) Wint 80, p. 18.

MATHIS, Cleopatra
"As You Stalk the Sleep of My Forgetting. " Pequod (11) 80, p. 41.
"Aunt Drucilla's Pasture. " US1 (12/13) Aut-Wint 80, p. 20.
"Bathing With Alexandra. " StoneC (7:3) D 80, p. 76.
"The Bats. " SouthernR (16:2) Spr 80, p. 426.
"Birthday Letter from Rockport. " StoneC (7:3) D 80, p. 73.
"Bittersweet Nightshade. " SouthernR (16:2) Spr 80, p. 427.
"For Allison, on the Obscenity of Flowers. " SouthernR (16:2) Spr 80, p. 428.
"Making Bread While You Die in the Next House" (for Grotchy). SouthernR (16:2) Spr 80, p. 425.
"Out of the Season of Sleep. " StoneC (7:3) D 80, p. 74.
"A Place of Another Name. " Pequod (11) 80, p. 40.
"Riding on Empty. " PoNow (29) 80, p. 26.
"Sea Walk. " StoneC (7:3) D 80, p. 75.
"Snow. " PoNow (29) 80, p. 26.
"You Go Home, 1968. " US1 (12/13) Aut-Wint 80, p. 20.
"Your Mother Takes Us Back to Liberty. " US1 (12/13) Aut-Wint 80, p. 20.

MATKOWSKI, Bette
"To My Father. " HiramPoR (27) Aut-Wint 80, p. 39.

MATSON, Clive
"Angled beams of sunlight, pink roses in a vase. " HangL (38) Aut 80, p. 38.
"Feint and Jab. " HangL (38) Aut 80, p. 39.
"I want my experience shared!" HangL (38) Aut 80, p. 38.
"I want to make fists in your hair, trace your lips. " HangL (38) Aut 80, p. 38.
"Moon rises over water, tilting its horns. " HangL (38) Aut 80, p. 38.
"Overnight, love's transformed me: seeped my flesh. " HangL (38) Aut 80, p. 38.
"Pre-emptive Strike. " US1 (12/13) Aut-Wint 80, p. 4.
"This first night I don't sleep, I doze and wake. " HangL (38) Aut 80, p. 38.

MATTESON, Fredric
"Mouth to Mouth. " KanQ (12:1) Wint 80, p. 46.

MATTHAEI, Marcella
"Momentarily across the black of your hair. " Ark (14) 80, p. 288.
"To Kenneth. " Ark (14) 80, p. 289.

MATTHEWS, Jack
"It. " Poetry (137:2) N 80, p. 69.
"An Old Sportswriter Celebrates His Fiftieth Anniversary of
    Covering the Yale-Dartmouth Game. " NewRep (183:17) 25
    O 80, p. 36.
"Things. " Poetry (137:2) N 80, p. 68.
"The World's Oldest Authority on Keats. " Poetry (137:2) N 80,
    p. 70.

MATTHEWS, William
"Averted Eyes. " OhioR (25) 80, p. 96.
"Clean Slate. " PoNow (28) 80, p. 6.
"Cows Grazing at Sunrise. " Antaeus (36) Wint 80, p. 84.
"December Forecasts in Seattle. " GeoR (34:4) Wint 80, p. 838.
"The Dedication of My First Book. " Tendril (7/8) Spr-Sum 80,
    p. 53.
"Funeral Homes. " Antaeus (36) Wint 80, p. 85.
"Housework. " NewYorker (56:36) 27 O 80, p. 49.
"A Late Movie. " Tendril (9) 80, p. 100.
"Maude (Paphiopedelum X Maudiae). " Tendril (7/8) Spr-Sum 80,
    p. 54.
"New. " Atl (245:6) Je 80, p. 67.
"A Roadside Near Ithaca. " PoNow (28) 80, p. 26.
"Room Tone. " Durak (5) 80, p. 9.
"Spring Snow. " PoNow (28) 80, p. 26.

MATTHIAS, John
from Northern Summer: "I: The Castle. " Salm (50/51) Aut 80-
    Wint 81, p. 43.
from Northern Summer: "II: Pied-a-Terre. " Salm (50/51) Aut
    80-Wint 81, p. 45.
from Northern Summer: "III: The Mine. " Salm (50/51) Aut
    80-Wint 81, p. 47.

MATTISON, Alice
"Breastfeeding. " ParisR (77) Wint-Spr 80, p. 112.
"Cool Day in July. " Ploughs (6:2) 80, p. 129.

MAURA, Sister S. S. N. D.
"After Christmas. " ChrC (97:2) 16 Ja 80, p. 44.
"Back Porch Fundamentalist. " ChrC (97:18) 14 My 80, p. 552.
"Woman's Liberation. " SouthernHR (14:2) Spr 80, p. 127.

MAXFIELD, John E.
"Solitude. " KanQ (12:1) Wint 80, p. 62.

MAXSON, Gloria
"Curriculum. " ChrC (97:35) 5 N 80, p. 1061.
"Glorobots. " ChrC (97:19) 21 My 80, p. 576.
"The Old Chief Muses at the Feast. " ChrC (97:38) 26 N 80, p.
    1148.
"Sophisticate. " ChrC (97:3) 23 Ja 80, .p. 67.

MAXSON, H. A.
"Apples" (for my wife, Doreen). CimR (50) Ja 80, p. 12.
"Floaters. " QW (10) Wint-Spr 80, p. 88.
"Is a Dance" (for my daughter, Corrie). CimR (50) Ja 80, p.
    63.
"The Snow Angels. " CharR (6:2) Aut 80, p. 11.
"Two Owls. " CimR (50) Ja 80, p. 26.
"Waking in the New House. " WindO (36) Spr-Sum 80, p. 36.
"When We Need to Say That One of Those We Love Is Dead. "
    CharR (6:2) Aut 80, p. 10.

MAXTON, Hugh
"At Hardisty's Farm" (for John and Hermione). GRR (11:2/3)
    80, p. 25.
"Survivors of Pavilion. " GRR (11:2/3) 80, pp. 29-35.

MAXWELL, Anne
"poem for John Logan. " FourQt (30:1) Aut 80, p. 30.

MAXWELL, Margo
"Millinery Number: February 15, 1916. " Ascent (5:3) 80, p. 49.
"Vanity Number: November 15, 1917. " Ascent (5:3) 80, p. 50.
"When the Lady Nefor, She Whom the King Knows, Wakes. "
    ChiR (31:3) Wint 80, pp. 70-75.

MAYES, Frances
"Cycle. " CalQ (16/17) 80, p. 158.

MAYFIELD, Carl
"Song. " PoetryNW (21:4) Wint 80-81, p. 29.

MAYHALL, Jane
"Trip. " NewRena (12) Spr 80, p. 70.

MAYHEW, Jonathan
"Poem: There is no need to invent imaginary. " CalQ (16/17)
    80, p. 123.

MAYO, E. L.
"This Wind. " NewL (46:3) Spr 80, p. 89.
"We Still Must Follow. " NewL (46:3) Spr 80, p. 89.

MAZEIKA, Stanley
"The Teacher. " Sam (102) 80, p. 66.

MAZUR, Gail
"Longfellow Park, August" (for Lloyd). Ploughs (6:2) 80, p. 72.
"Next Door. " Ploughs (6:2) 80, p. 74.

MAZZOCCO, Robert
"Egypt. " NewYorker (56:42) 8 D 80, p. 50.

MEAD, Philip
"The Chinese Graves in Beechworth Cemetery. " NewL (46:3)

Spr 80, p. 6.

MEADOR, Roy
"Capturing the Ocean as Decoration. " SoDakR (18:2) Sum 80, p. 6.
"Ten Thousand Things. " SoDakR (18:2) Sum 80, p. 6.

MEADS, Kathy
"Filming the Everyday. " Tendril (7/8) Spr-Sum 80, p. 55.
"Time Warp. " Wind (36) 80, p. 45.

MEHREN, Stein
"Sne. " PortR (26) 80, p. 280.

MEHROTRA, Arvind Krishna
"after maluk. " Kayak (54) S 80, p. 12.

MEIRI, Alexandra
"Tel-Aviv Beach, Winter '74" (tr. of Raquel Chalfi). AmerPoR
(9:5) S-O 80, p. 33.

MEISSNER, William
"Adolescence. " CalQ (16/17) 80, p. 154.
"Climbing into My Father's Skin. " PoetryNW (21:2) Sum 80, p. 21.
"Death of the Vampire. " PoNow (29) 80, p. 26.
"Hometown Widow. " MidwQ (21:4) Sum 80, p. 446.
"Lake Winter: The Ice Walkers. " SouthernPR (20:2) Aut 80, p. 55.
"The Lip Collector. " PoNow (26) 80, p. 41.
"My Father's Closet. " MidwQ (21:4) Sum 80, p. 448.
"Returning to Find It. " MidwQ (21:4) Sum 80, p. 447.
"The Slaughterhouse Boys. " PoNow (26) 80, p. 12.
"The Teacher Who Ate Dittos. " ColEng (42:1) S 80, p. 59.
"The UFO in Iowa. " PoNow (29) 80, p. 26.

MEISTER, Ernst
"The Cry's Outing" (tr. by Richard Dove). ChiR (32:1) Sum 80,
p. 105.

MELHEM, D. H.
"I can sit quietly with Kant. " Outbr (4/5) Aut 79-Spr 80, p. 91.

MELLOTT, Leland
"My Cousin, Home from Mexico Anacortes, Washington. "
BallSUF (21:1) Wint 80, p. 68.

MELNYCZUK, Askold
"Dogs" (adapted from Gregory Skovoroda). Agni (13) 80, p. 76.
"Eagle and Magpie" (adapted from Gregory Skovoroda). Agni (13)
80, p. 77.
"Owl and Thrush" (adapted from Gregory Skovoroda). Agni (13)
80, p. 78.

MELONE, Deborah
"The Ravine. " Aspect (76) S-D 79-80, p. 14.

MELTZER, David
"O bride and queen. " Ark (14) 80, p. 290.

MENASHE, Samuel
"Scissors. " Thrpny (1) Wint-Spr 80, p. 11.

MENDONSA, Andy
")In stereotype(. " SmPd (49) Spr 80, p. 19.

MENEBROKER, Ann
"Chain Letter 1980. " WormR (78) 80, p. 56.
"Growing Up. " WormR (78) 80, p. 57.
"John. " WormR (78) 80, p. 57.

MENEGHETTI, Cristina
"te necesito. " PortR (26) 80, p. 445.

MENNELL, Sally Bryer
"Belladonna. " MalR (54) Ap 80, p. 143.

MEREDITH, Joseph
"The Cold. " KanQ (12:3) Sum 80, p. 87.
"Midnight, Walking the Wakeful Daughter" (for Emily). KanQ
     (12:3) Sum 80, p. 86.

MEREDITH, William
"Examples of Created Systems" (for Robert Penn Warren).
     Tendril (9) 80, p. 104.
"Ideogram. " AmerPoR (9:5) S-O 80, p. 48.
"John and Anne. " AmerPoR (9:5) S-O 80, p. 47.
"Memoirs. " NewYorker (56:17) 16 Je 80, p. 40.
"My Mother's Life. " Poetry (136:4) Jl 80, p. 187.
"The Revenant. " Poetry (136:4) Jl 80, p. 188.
"Stages. " Poetry (136:4) Jl 80, p. 190.
"Trelawny's Dream. " NewRep (183:16) 18 O 80, p. 28.
"Two Masks Unearthed in Bulgaria" (for Kolyo Sevov). AmerPoR
     (9:5) S-O 80, p. 47.
"Winter on the River. " NewYorker (56:30) 15 S 80, p. 44.

MERRIAM, Eve
from Tales from the Television Woods: "Big Joe's Happiness
     Hour. " PoNow (28) 80, p. 11.
from Tales from the Television Woods: "Brief Pause. " PoNow
     (28) 80, p. 11.

MERRILL, James
"Concerning Plato. " Antaeus (36) Wint 80, p. 166.
"Developers at Crystal River. " YaleR (70:1) Aut 80, p. 100.
"Page from the Koran. " Tendril (9) 80, p. 105.
"The Pier: Under Pisces. " NewYorker (56:21) 14 Jl 80, p. 28.

MERRILL, Lee
"Woodpiles Low. " Northeast (3:8) Wint 80, p. 25.

MERRIN, Jeredith
"Lisa, Reading" (for Randall Jarrell). PoetryNW (21:2) Sum 80,
   p. 43.
"The Most Beautiful Animal. " PoetryNW (21:2) Sum 80, p. 42.

MERWIN, W. S.
"Going from the Green Window. " Field (23) Aut 80, p. 5.
"James" (in memory of James Wright). NewYorker (56:9) 21 Ap
   80, p. 40.
"A Pause by the Water. " NewYorker (56:16) 9 Je 80, p. 42.
"Sun and Rain. " Ark (14) 80, p. 291.
"To Dana for Her Birthday. " Tendril (9) 80, p. 106.

MESCHERY, Tom
"Giant's Fourth Complaint. " PoetryNW (21:4) Wint 80-81, p. 31.

MESMER, Sharon
"The Nordic Skull in Double Exposure. " Tele (16) 80, p. 107.

MESSERLI, Doug
"Days on Glass. " Tele (16) 80, p. 26.
"Some Distance. " Tele (16) 80, p. 26.

MESSING, Robin
"Botanic Gardens I. " Tele (16) 80, p. 61.
"Botanic Gardens II. " Tele (16) 80, p. 62.
"Underneath. " Tele (16) 80, p. 63.

METRAS, Gary
"After the Disaster. " Sam (86) 79, p. 27.
"The Night Watch. " PikeF (3) Wint 80, p. 26.
"The Subcommittee on Poetry Control. " Sam (101) 80, p. 65.
The Yearnings. Sam (87) 80. Entire issue.

METZ, Jerred
"Angels in the House. " Focus (14:86) Ap 80, p. 16.
"Her True Body. " Focus (14:86) Ap 80, p. 17.
"Speak Like Rain. " Focus (14:86) Ap 80, p. 17.

METZ, Roberta
"Bones. " SouthernPR (20:1) Spr 80, p. 29.
"Demons. " PoNow (27) 80, p. 43.
"Exactly. " PoNow (27) 80, p. 43.
"Sea Changes. " KanQ (12:1) Wint 80, p. 158.
"Skin-Deep. " CentR (24:4) Aut 80, p. 455.
"Sweet Nothings. " SouthernPR (20:1) Spr 80, p. 30.
"Trees. " KanQ (12:1) Wint 80, p. 158.

MICHAELIS, Hanny
"Het bladerloze licht. " PortR (26) 80, p. 273.

"Wie bij daglicht. " PortR (26) 80, p. 274.

MICHAUX, Henri
"Individual Concerns" (tr. by Claudette Snodgrass and Jo Ann Monks). NewOR (7:2) 80, p. 149.

MICHELSON, Richard
"For Miss B., My Eighth Grade English Teacher Who Asked: 'How Do You Expect to Write Poetry When You Don't Even Know How to Behave!'" SmPd (48) Wint 80, p. 15. (also (49) Spr 80, p. 32).
"Proud Parents. " SmPd (48) Wint 80, p. 14.

MICKA, Mary Virginia
"Old River Town. " SouthernPR (20:2) Aut 80, p. 32.

MICKELBERRY, William
"SR 232. " SouthernPR (20:2) Aut 80, p. 39.

MIDDLEBROOK, Diane
"Four Episodes in a Contagion of Dreams. " SouthernR (16:2) Spr 80, p. 416.

MIDDLETON, Christopher
"Idiocy of Rural Life" (for Kofi Awoonor). BosUJ (26:3) 80, p. 101.

MIDDLETON, David
"Burial Urn: An Inscription. " SouthernR (16:2) Spr 80, p. 438.
"Epistle: On Receiving a Book. " SouthernR (16:2) Spr 80, p. 437.
"God the Father. " SouthernR (16:2) Spr 80, p. 439.
"Midwinter Stars. " SouthernR (16:2) Spr 80, p. 439.
"Oro. " SouthernR (16:2) Spr 80, p. 438.
"Reading in Solitude. " SouthernR (16:2) Spr 80, p. 437.

MIHAILOVIC, Vasa D.
"Everybody Will Write Poetry" (tr. of Branto Miljković w. Charles David Wright). PortR (26) 80, p. 478.

MIHOPOULOS, Effie
"Peruvian Festival. " Pig (7) My 80, p. 9.

MIKLITSCH, Robert
"Pastourelle: The Pleasures of Evening. " Shen (31:2) 80, p. 79.

MILBURN, Michael
"Departures. " PraS (54:1) Spr 80, p. 77.

MILES, Josephine
"Breakfast. " PoNow (27) 80, p. 23.
"Brim. " Ark (14) 80, p. 292.
"The Mark. " CalQ (16/17) 80, p. 103.

"Moving In. " PoNow (27) 80, p. 23.
"Travelers. " PoNow (27) 80, p. 23.

MILES, Richard
"The Garden at Dawn. " NewYorker (56:6) 31 Mr 80, p. 91.

MILES, Ron
"pas de deux. " MalR (53) Ja 80, p. 132.

MILJKOVIC, Branko
"Everybody Will Write Poetry. " PortR (26) 80, p. 478.

MILLER, A. McA.
"Words for John Ruskin. " BelPoJ (30:3) Spr 80, p. 26.

MILLER, Arthur
"Degas Invented Her. " Agni (13) 80, p. 106.

MILLER, Carl
"Three Pictures of a Cormorant. " HiramPoR (27) Aut-Wint 80,
    p. 40.
"A Toad Sketched in Ballpoint. " BallSUF (21:1) Wint 80, p. 13.

MILLER, Carol
"The Grandmother: Re-entry. " Confr (20) Spr-Sum 80, p. 188.

MILLER, E. Ethelbert
"Bringing Back the Draft. " BlackALF (14:3) Aut 80, p. 123.
"The Last Days of Bo Willie" (for jerry ward). BlackALF (14:3)
    Aut 80, p. 122.
"Sweet Honey in the Rock" (for bernice reagon). BlackALF (14:3)
    Aut 80, p. 123.

MILLER, Elizabeth G.
from Only the Voice: "Today you fall as a stone to water. "
    (tr. of Hugo Lindo). NewOR (7:3) 80, p. 278.

MILLER, Errol
"Where the Sea Wolf Howls. " Wind (37) 80, p. 34.

MILLER, J. L.
"Bread and Butter Pickles. " PoNow (27) 80, p. 34.
"Consider Lilies. " BallSUF (21:1) Wint 80, p. 70.
"On the Effect of Grace. " BallSUF (21:1) Wint 80, p. 70.
"Vision of John Chapman, Aged Ten. " BallSUF (21:1) Wint 80,
    p. 15.
"Your Cloud-Like Hair, My Dear. " BallSUF (21:1) Wint 80, p.
    70.

MILLER, Jane
"The I Will If You Will. " Agni (13) 80, p. 36.
"Immense Virgin Girls. " WatT (1) Aut 80, p. 14.
"Seven O'Clock Train. " Pequod (11) 80, p. 53.

MILLER, Jim Wayne
"Country Dark. " GRR (11:1) 80, p. 10.
Eight poems. SmF (11/12) Spr-Aut 80, pp. 16-26.
"For Richard Chase. " GRR (11:1) 80, p. 5.
"Jim Worley Fries Trout on South Squalla. " GRR (11:1) 80, p.
    6.
"A Log. " GRR (11:1) 80, p. 10.
"Tracks. " GRR (11:1) 80, p. 8.

MILLER, John N.
"Archaic Torso of Apollo" (tr. of Rainer Maria Rilke). WebR
    (5:2) Aut 80, p. 18.
"Blindly" (tr. of Magnus Enzensberger). CharR (6:2) Aut 80, p.
    54.
"Daphne and Friend. " PikeF (3) Wint 80, p. 7.
"Experience" (tr. of Hugo von Hofmannsthal). WebR (5:2) Aut
    80, p. 20.
"Gifts. " SouthernHR (14:4) Aut 80, p. 338.
"A Hot Day" (tr. of Karl Krolou). CharR (6:2) Aut 80, p. 55.
"The Knight" (tr. of Rainer Maria Rilke). WebR (5:2) Aut 80,
    p. 19.

MILLER, Joren
"El Morocco. " Wind (36) 80, p. 46.
"Encounter. " Wind (36) 80, p. 47.
"Grandad's Return. " Wind (36) 80, p. 47.

MILLER, Rita A.
"August Night. " SouthernPR (20:1) Spr 80, p. 43.

MILLER, Sara
"Symptoms. " CutB (15) Aut/Wint 80, p. 37.
"Taps for John Paul Jones. " CutB (15) Aut/Wint 80, p. 35.

MILLER, Vassar
"An Essay in Criticism by Way of Rebuttal. " NewL (47:1) Aut
    80, p. 78.
"Elegy for a Dog. " PoNow (26) 80, p. 40.
"Late Start. " NewL (47:1) Aut 80, p. 78.
"Lullaby for My Mother. " NewL (47:1) Aut 80, p. 77.
"On Finding an Old Snapshot. " NewL (47:1) Aut 80, p. 76.
"So Far. " Confr (20) Spr-Sum 80, p. 88.
"Too Much Company. " PoNow (28) 80, p. 16.
"Unalterable. " NewL (47:1) Aut 80, p. 77.
"A Wasted Life. " PoNow (26) 80, p. 34.

MILLETT, John
"House poem. " SmPd (48) Wint 80, p. 29.
"An Old Man Prays Alone in the Cathedral of the Sacre Coeur at
    St. Germain Des Prés. " StoneC (7:3) D 80, p. 15.

MILLIER, Warren C.
"A Work of Art Has No Need of Others. " StoneC (7:3) D 80, p.
    23.

MILLIKEN, Patrick
"The Bus from Here to There. " PraS (54:3) Aut 80, p. 65.
"I Am Teaching Myself the Music of Poetry. " PraS (54:3) Aut
    80, p. 66.
"Standing at the Edge of a Cliff Overlooking Trees. " OhioR (24)
    80, p. 92.

MILLS, George
"Hour. " StoneC (7:3) D 80, p. 16.
"Nameless. " StoneC (7:3) D 80, p. 16.

MILLS, Michael C.
"Michaelangelo's Pieta. " QW (10) Wint-Spr 80, p. 113.

MILLS, Ralph J. Jr.
"Brief Thaw. " Poem (38) Mr 80, p. 34.
"Gone" (for my father). DacTerr (17) 80, p. 61.
"Late Moon" (for Stephen Berg). Poem (38) Mr 80, p. 32.
"Only. " NewEngR (3:2) Wint 80, p. 268.
"Poem: The sky's blue varnish gleams. " Poem (38) Mr 80, p.
    33.
"Some Kind of Voice" (for Al Poulin). Poem (38) Mr 80, p. 29.
"Yellow. " Poem (38) Mr 80, p. 30.

MILLS, Sparling
"Child of Ten. " PottPort (2) 80-81, p. 27.
"The Facts of Life. " PottPort (1) 79-80, p. 27.

MILLS, William
"Arctic Circle. " QW (10) Wint-Spr 80, p. 36.
"Leaving Szentendre. " QW (10) Wint-Spr 80, p. 37.

MILNER, Ian
"Death" (tr. of Vladimír Holan). PortR (26) 80, p. 76.
"The Lamp" (tr. of Josef Hanzlik). PortR (26) 80, p. 72.

MILNER, Philip
"Doc Pavy. " PottPort (1) 79-80, p. 39.
"Eldon 'Nub' Griffin. " PottPort (2) 80-81, p. 12.
"Prof. Allison B. Carney. " PottPort (2) 80-81, p. 5.

MILOSZ, Czeslaw
"Campo di Fiori" (tr. by David Brooks and Louis Iribarne).
    NewYRB (27:16) 23 O 80, p. 8.
"Incantation" (tr. by Grazyna Drabik and Austin Flint). PoetryE
    (3) 80, p. 56.

MILTON, John R.
"Prelude to Postlude. " DacTerr (17) 80, p. 62.

MINER, K.
"Oranges in Cellophane. " WindO (37) Aut-Wint 80, p. 11.
"The Second Bus. " WindO (37) Aut-Wint 80, p. 11.

MINER, Virginia Scott
"Elegy for Former Students." Focus (14:86) Ap 80, p. 29.
"Festival of the Redeemer." WindO (36) Spr-Sum 80, p. 42.
"Of Death." Focus (14:86) Ap 80, p. 29.

MINKLER, Marvin A.
"Summer Storm." SmPd (50) Aut 80, p. 28.

MINOR, James
"Farewell." SoDakR (18:2) Sum 80, p. 9.
"Poem for My Brother." SoDakR (18:2) Sum 80, p. 10.
"Reflection at My Grandfather's Funeral." DacTerr (17) 80, p.
   63.

MINTON, Helena
"Geishas." AndR (7:1) Spr 80, p. 40.
"Two Views of Plymouth." Im (7:1) 80, p. 12.

MINTY, Judith
"Letters to My Daughters 16." BaratR (8:1) Sum 80, p. 30.
"Letters to My Daughters 17." BaratR (8:1) Sum 80, p. 34.

MIRANDA, Gary
"Field Trip" (for Barbara Beauchamp and Susan Raymo).
   AmerPoR (9:1) Ja-F 80, p. 38.
"The Gambler" (for Stephen Dunn). PoetryNW (21:2) Sum 80, p.
   32.
"Premonition." Aspect (76) S-D 79-80, p. 25.
"Salmon Ladder at the Government Locks, Seattle" (for Pat
   Thenell). Poetry (135:4) Ja 80, p. 202.
"The Spider-Web Suns Reflections on a Child's Drawings."
   AmerPoR (9:1) Ja-F 80, p. 38.
"Still Lifes: Hoh Rain Forest." Poetry (135:4) Ja 80, p. 203.

MIRON, Gaston
"Art Poétique" (tr. by Louis Simpson). AmerPoR (9:1) Ja-F 80,
   p. 45.
from Courtepointes: "Il fait un temps fou" (tr. by Louis Simp-
   son). AmerPoR (9:1) Ja-F 80, p. 45.
"La Pauvreté Anthropos" (tr. by Louis Simpson). AmerPoR (9:1)
   Ja-F 80, p. 46.
"Rue Saint-Christophe" (tr. by Louis Simpson). AmerPoR (9:1)
   Ja-F 80, p. 45.

MIRSKIN, Jerry
"Compatible Beliefs." StoneC (7:3) D 80, p. 61.
"The Exception." StoneC (7:3) D 80, p. 62.
"In the Feeling." StoneC (7:3) D 80, p. 61.
"One Less." StoneC (7:3) D 80, p. 62.

MISHKIN, Julia
"Black and White." PoetryNW (21:1) Spr 80, p. 37.
"Letter With No Signature." PoetryNW (21:1) Spr 80, p. 37.

"9/21/78." Poetry (136:3) Je 80, p. 151.
"Something Like Lust." Poetry (136:3) Je 80, p. 150.
"This Country." Poetry (136:3) Je 80, p. 149.

MISHLER, Bill
"Poem from a Single Room Apartment in Hagersten, 1970" (tr.
of Lars Noren). PoetryE (3) 80, p. 61.

MITCHELL, Roger
"Cinderella." Poetry (137:3) D 80, p. 149.
"The girls in the Hounslow Chinese Take-Away make gestures
like angry." CreamCR (5:1) Wint 79, p. 52.
"You never think of it that way then." CreamCR (5:1) Wint 79,
p. 53.

MITCHELL, Stephen
"Now it is time that gods came walking out" (tr. of Rainer
Maria Rilke). Thrpny (3) Aut 80, p. 3.

MITCHELL, Susan
"The Picture Over Our Bed." PoNow (29) 80, p. 46.

MITCHELL, Thomas
"Nantucket Revisited." NewEngR (3:2) Wint 80, p. 260.
"Seven Years of Snow." NewEngR (3:2) Wint 80, p. 261.

MITSUNE, Oshikoshi no
"White Chrysanthemum" (tr. by Graeme Wilson). DenQ (15:3)
Aut 80, p. 83.

MIZEJEWSKI, Linda
"The Moon Over Norfolk, Virginia." QW (11) Aut-Wint 80, p.
19.

MOCARSKI, Timothy P.
"City." ArizQ (36:1) Spr 80, p. 96.

MODEE, Steven A.
"Post-Sputnik Panic." EngJ (69:5) My 80, p. 56.

MOE, Keith
"Thinking We Get Away." BelPoJ (30:3) Spr 80, p. 5.

MOFFETT, Judith
"All Saints Day." PraS (54:2) Sum 80, p. 23.
"From the Audobon Report (October)." PraS (54:2) Sum 80, p.
22.
from Variations on a Theme: "Leaf Lesson." Poetry (136:5)
Ag 80, p. 273.

MOFFI, Larry
"Above a Dry Pool." AntR (38:3) Sum 80, p. 347.
"Manners." OhioR (24) 80, p. 52.

"Notes for a Lecture. " OhioR (24) 80, p. 53.

MOKICHI, Saito
"Graveyard" (tr. by Graeme Wilson). WestHR (34:4) Aut 80, p. 334.

MOLOFSKY, Merie
"For Lee. " Pig (7) My 80, p. 87.

MONAGHAN, E. A.
"Upon Reading Ashberry. " UTR (6:3/4) 80, p. 48.

MONETTE, Paul
"Changing Places" (to Nick). SouthwR (65:2) Spr 80, p. 176.

MONGEAU, David P.
"Mayhew by the Lake. " ThRiPo (15/16) 80, p. 35.

MONKS, JoAnn
"Individual Concerns" (tr. of Henri Michaux w. Claudette Snod-
grass). NewOR (7:2) 80, p. 149.

MONROE, Jonathan
"At Palavas. " PoNow (29) 80, p. 31.

MONTAGUE, John
"The Black Lake" (after Gerard Dillon). Ploughs (6:1) 80, p. 42.
"The Leap. " MalR (55) Jl 80, p. 8.
"Springs. " Ploughs (6:1) 80, p. 43.
"Turnhole. " Ploughs (6:1) 80, p. 40.
"The Well Dreams. " Ploughs (6:1) 80, p. 37.

MONTALBETTI, Mario
"My (Love Poem)" (tr. by Maureen Ahern). NewOR (7:3) 80,
p. 255.

MONTALE, Eugenio
from La bufera e altro: "Anniversario. " StoneC (7:1) F 80, p.
5.
from La bufera e altro: "Ezekiel Saw the Wheel. " StoneC (7:1)
F 80, p. 6.
"La frangia dei capelli.... " WatT (1) Aut 80, p. 86.
"In a Void" (tr. by David Keller and Donald Sheehan). CutB (14)
Spr/Sum 80, p. 96.
"Repartee" (tr. by David Keller and Donald Sheehan). CutB (14)
Spr/Sum 80, p. 97.
"Serenata Indiana. " WatT (1) Aut 80, p. 88.
"Three Private Madrigals" (tr. by Vinio Rossi and David Young).
Field (23) Aut 80, p. 41.
"Thrust and Riposte" (tr. by Gavin Ewart). Stand (21:2) 80, p.
4.
"Il tuo volo. " WatT (1) Aut 80, p. 84.

MONTESI, A. J.
"Crazy Kate. " HiramPoR (28) Spr-Sum 80, p. 25.

MOODY, Roger
"Leaving the City. " Wind (37) 80, p. 39.
"Their Tails Ugly as Their Shirts. " CreamCR (5:2) Spr 80, p. 74.
"To Dana Who Never Wrote Unless I Did. " CreamCR (5:2) Spr 80, p. 75.

MOODY, Shirley
"Nursery Webs. " SouthernPR (20:2) Aut 80, p. 17.

MOORE, Barbara
"Among Barlach's Wooden Sculpture. " SouthernHR (14:2) Spr 80, p. 154.
"For Luke Moore. " SouthernHR (14:2) Spr 80, p. 144.
"Homemade Machine. " DenQ (15:2) Sum 80, p. 62.
"Parable of the Cicada. " DenQ (15:2) Sum 80, p. 60.

MOORE, Elizabeth
"Witness. " CarolQ (32:1) Wint 80, p. 94.

MOORE, Honor
"First Time: 1950. " Shen (31:2) 80, p. 76.

MOORE, James
"All the Raised Arms. " AmerPoR (9:3) My-Je 80, p. 10.
"Here, Too, There Is a Paradise. " AmerPoR (9:3) My-Je 80, p. 11.
"Rothko. " ParisR (78) Sum 80, p. 200.
"The Weak Light. " ParisR (78) Sum 80, p. 199.

MOORE, Rosalie
"Rainstorm After Reading Einstein. " AmerPoR (9:4) Jl-Ag 80, p. 42.

MOORE, Todd
"The Hatfields Pose. " PoNow (27) 80, p. 42.

MOORE, Tom
"Suspicions of Water. " ColEng (41:8) Ap 80, p. 884.

MOORHEAD, Andrea
"Buffalo Harbor. " Os (10) Spr 80, p. 12.
"Christus Cycle. " Os (11) 80, pp. 18-29.
"stone and fire. " Os (10) Spr 80, p. 13.
"your name. " Os (10) Spr 80, p. 11.

MOOS, Michael
"The Archer. " DacTerr (17) 80, p. 64.

MOOSE, Martin H.
"The Dead Crow. " MalR (54) Ap 80, p. 64.
"Listening. " MalR (54) Ap 80, p. 62.
"The Room. " MalR (54) Ap 80, p. 63.

MORAES, Dom
"To be lord and master in your own house" (tr. of Nathan Zach).
    PortR (26) 80, p. 210.
'To the ridge like the first rain" (tr. of T. Carmi). PortR (26)
    80, p. 206.

MORCK, Sidsel
"Den sterkeste. " PortR (26) 80, p. 279.

MORGAN, Frederick
"Alexander. " AmerS (49:4) Aut 80, p. 448.
"The Choice. " NewRep (183:21) 22 N 80, p. 30.
"Song. " OntR (13) Aut-Wint 80-81, p. 32.

MORGAN, John
"America. " ThRiPo (15/16) 80, p. 36.
'Her Ecstasy. " Poetry (136:5) Ag 80, p. 282.

MORGAN, Robert
"Ancient. " SmF (11/12) Spr-Aut 80, p. 29.
"The Aster. " SmF (11/12) Spr-Aut 80, p. 33.
"Bats. " SmF (11/12) Spr-Aut 80, p. 32.
"Bonus. " PoNow (28) 80, p. 16.
"Cave of Statues. " WatT (1) Aut 80, p. 7.
"Cleaning Off the Cemetery. " VirQR (56:4) Aut 80, p. 668.
"Goiter. " WatT (1) Aut 80, p. 6.
"Hay Scuttle. " VirQR (56:4) Aut 80, p. 670.
"Log Fires. " SmF (11/12) Spr-Aut 80, p. 27.
"Manure Pile. " VirQR (56:4) Aut 80, p. 669.
"Mirror Farming. " Tendril (9) 80, p. 107.
"Potato Hole. " SmF (11/12) Spr-Aut 80, p. 28.
"Slop Bucket. " SmF (11/12) Spr-Aut 80, p. 31.
'Timber Sled. " SmF (11/12) Spr-Aut 80, p. 30.

MORGAN, Seth
"These Days. " Wind (37) 80, p. 18.

MORIN, Edward
"Body of Summer" (tr. of Odysseus Elytis w. Jana Hesser and
    Lefteris Pavlides). CharR (6:2) Aut 80, p. 49.
"Drinking the Corinthian Sun" (tr. of Odysseus Elytis w. Jana
    Hesser and Lefteris Pavlides). CharR (6:2) Aut 80, p. 50.
"Filling Station. " MichQR (19:4/20:1) Aut-Wint 80-81, p. 749.
"Forecasting the Economy. " Confr (20) Spr-Sum 80, p. 92.
"No Longer Do I Know the Night" (tr. of Odysseus Elytis w.
    Jana Hesser and Lefteris Pavlides). CharR (6:2) Aut 80,
    p. 50.
"You, Landlady. " PoNow (27) 80, p. 14.

MORISON, Ted
"Endure. " Poem (38) Mr 80, p. 2.
"Omen. " Poem (38) Mr 80, p. 1.

MORITZ, A. F.
"Triumph of Epicurus. " PraS (54:4) Wint 80-81, p. 8.

MORLEY, Hilda
"Louse Point, August 1978. " Pequod (11) 80, p. 62.
"My Favorite Words: Moving. " Pequod (11) 80, p. 61.
"Your Yellow, Your Red, Mondrian. " Pequod (11) 80, p. 60.

MORRIS, Herbert
"The Body of a Man. " Salm (47/48) Wint-Spr 80, p. 63.
"Daguerreotypie der Niagara Falls. " Shen (31:1) 79, pp. 59-64.
"Havana. " NewEngR (3:2) Wint 80, p. 235.
"Two in Fields. " Agni (12) 80, p. 76.

MORRIS, John N.
"The Examined Life. " NewYorker (55:50) 28 Ja 80, p. 38.

MORRIS, Mary
"To the Tiger Who Sleeps at the Foot of My Bed. " KanQ (12:1)
    Wint 80, p. 30.

MORRIS, Mervyn
"She. " PortR (26) 80, p. 231.

MORRIS, Paul
"Fingers" (tr. of Karl Krolow). Pequod (11) 80, p. 52.
"In Venice" (tr. of Georg Trakl). DenQ (15:1) Spr 80, p. 87.
"Portrait of a Hand" (tr. of Karl Krolow). Pequod (11) 80, p.
    51.
"Sonja" (tr. of Georg Trakl). Pequod (11) 80, p. 50.
"To the Boy Elis" (tr. of Georg Trakl). DenQ (15:1) Spr 80, p.
    86.

MORRIS, William L.
"Polar Dawn. " ChiR (31:3) Wint 80, p. 35.

MORRISON, Douglas
"Summer Dream. " StoneC (7:3) D 80, p. 19.
"Winter Portrait: Reflections, South of Barnegat. " StoneC (7:3)
    D 80, p. 18.

MORRISON, Theodore
"A Scale of Losses. " MassR (21:4) Wint 80, p. 768.

MORRISSEY, Michael
"Reflections in a Green City. " PortR (26) 80, p. 276.

MORT, Jo-Ann
"A Jew's First Battle. " Stand (21:2) 80, p. 58.

MORTON, Bruce
"High Plains Harvest. " KanQ (12:1) Wint 80, p. 107.
"Summers. " KanQ (12:1) Wint 80, p. 108.

MORTON, Grace
"Kalpa. " PraS (54:4) Wint 80-81, p. 25.

MORTON, W. C.
"Dafney's Lamentation. " SouthernPR (20:1) Spr 80, p. 60.
"Onyx. " SouthernPR (20:1) Spr 80, p. 61.

MOSBY, George Jr.
"blues for a young boy: prison poem. " HangL (37) Spr 80, p.
    29.
"the dumb wife. " HangL (37) Spr 80, p. 30.
"the escape to freedom-land. " HangL (37) Spr 80, p. 31.
"the field #2. " CropD (1) Spr 80, p. 10.
"Prison Rain. " CropD (2/3) Aut-Wint 80, p. 23.
"since we're parted. " CropD (1) Spr 80, p. 10.
"Tracy Melissa: Down in the Oaks. " CropD (2/3) Aut-Wint 80,
    p. 23.

MOSES, Robert J.
"The Academic Man. " EngJ (69:5) My 80, p. 44.

MOSES, W. R.
"The Color of Monday. " PoNow (26) 80, p. 10.
"Mode of Knowing. " QW (11) Aut-Wint 80-81, p. 111.
"Monster: Lake Henry. " PoNow (28) 80, p. 20.
"What It Comes to. " PoNow (26) 80, p. 10.

MOSS, Howard
"The Long Island Night. " Tendril (9) 80, p. 108.
"Mentioning These Things. " NewYorker (56:28) 1 S 80, p. 26.
"The Seasons in New York. " NewYorker (56:35) 20 O 80, p. 56.

MOSS, Stanley
"For Margaret. " NewYorker (56:24) 4 Ag 80, p. 38.
"Lenin, Gorky and I. " VirQR (56:3) Sum 80, p. 501.
"Letter to the Butterflies. " VirQR (56:3) Sum 80, p. 499.

MOTE, John A.
"Prayer of an Aging Jogger. " ChrC (97:12) 2 Ap 80, p. 370.

MOTT, Michael
"Chimborazo. " SouthernPR (20:2) Aut 80, p. 57.
"Homestead. " Iowa (11:1) Wint 80, pp. 115-119.

MOUL, Keith
"Farther Than a Mile. " Wind (36) 80, p. 68.

MOULTON, Donalee
"For the Nite. " PottPort (1) 79-80, p. 36.

"For Dawn Rae: For the Future." PottPort (1) 79-80, p. 36.
"I Remember When." PottPort (1) 79-80, p. 35.

MOULTON-BARRETT, Donalee
"In the Garden." PottPort (2) 80-81, p. 11.

MOUW, Gudrun
"At the Mission Museum." CimR (52) Jl 80, p. 29.

MUELLER, Lisel
"About Still Life." MissouriR (3:2) Wint 80, p. 9.
"The Blind Leading the Blind." Tendril (9) 80, p. 109.
"Can't Forget" (tr. of Marie Luise Kaschnitz). Poetry (136:6)
  S 80, p. 345.
"Hiroshima" (tr. of Marie Luise Kaschnitz). Poetry (136:6) S
  80, p. 343.
"A Map of Sicily" (tr. of Marie Luise Kaschnitz). Poetry (136:6)
  S 80, p. 344.
"My Curiosity" (tr. of Marie Luise Kaschnitz). Poetry (136:6)
  S 80, p. 346.
"The Old Song and Dance." MissouriR (3:2) Wint 80, p. 10.
"Taxco." PoNow (27) 80, p. 31.
"Toward Evening" (tr. of Marie Luise Kaschnitz). Poetry (136:6)
  S 80, p. 345.

MULAC, Jim
"Letter to Carl." Spirit (5:1/2) Aut-Wint 79-80, p. 9.

MULDOON, Paul
"The Avenue." Ploughs (6:1) 80, p. 10.
"Cuba." Ploughs (6:1) 80, p. 9.
"Holy Thursday." Ploughs (6:1) 80, p. 14.
"Immrama." Ploughs (6:1) 80, p. 13.
"Promises, Promises." Ploughs (6:1) 80, p. 11.

MULHEARN, Kathryn
"Rape Manual." Prima (5) 79, p. 28.
"Three Visits." Prima (5) 79, p. 27.

MULLEN, Harryette
"Momma Sayings." OP (29) Spr 80, p. 14.
"The Night We Slept on the Beach." OP (29) Spr 80, p. 10.
"Painting Myself a New Mirror." OP (29) Spr 80, p. 12.
"Saturday Afternoon, When Chores Are Done." OP (29) Spr 80,
  p. 16.

MULLER, Erik
"Detour." EnPas (11) 80, p. 26.

MULRANE, Scott H.
"The Largest Industry in France." PoNow (29) 80, p. 31.

MUNDHENK, Michael
"difficult work" (for theodor w. adorno) (tr. of Hans Magnus

Enzensberger). MinnR (NS 15) Aut 80, p. 11.

MUNESADA, Yoshimine no
"Pathway" (tr. by Graeme Wilson). DenQ (15:3) Aut 80, p. 80.

MUÑOZ, Jorge Bravo
"Bogotá. " PortR (26) 80, p. 56.

MURATORI, Fred
"Adam's Meditation on His New Fall Wardrobe. " SouthernHR
(14:3) Sum 80, p. 210.
"The Maestro. " PoNow (29) 80, p. 31.
"The Real Muse. " HolCrit (17:3) Je 80, p. 14.

MURAWSKI, Elisabeth
"Drawn to Completion. " CarolQ (32:3) Aut 80, p. 85.
"First the Small Houses. " CarolQ (32:1) Wint 80, p. 96.
"Kind. " CarolQ (32:3) Aut 80, p. 83.
"One Hour Out of Baltimore. " CarolQ (32:1) Wint 80, p. 97.
"Setting Out. " SouthernPR (20:2) Aut 80, p. 14.
"To Reconstruct a Mine. " CarolQ (32:3) Aut 80, p. 84.
"The Way. " ChrC (97:3) 23 Ja 80, p. 72.
"The Woodcutter. " PoetC (12:3) 80, p. 25.

MURPHY, Aidan
"Bad Spell. " GRR (11:2/3) 80, p. 99.
"Intimate Strangers. " GRR (11:2/3) 80, p. 101.
"Memorial Albert Camus. " GRR (11:2/3) 80, p. 98.
"1 per-cent. " GRR (11:2/3) 80, p. 100.

MURPHY, George E. Jr.
"Experience. " PoetC (12:1) 80, p. 10.
"For the Girl Who Must Sleep With Her Father. " PoetC (12:3)
80, p. 2.
"October. " PoetC (12:3) 80, p. 4.
"Plum Harbor" (for my daughter). PoetC (12:1) 80, p. 8.
"Silence. " PoetC (12:2) 80, p. 12.
"Silence (later). " PoetC (12:2) 80, p. 12.
"Stars. " PoetC (12:2) 80, p. 16.

MURPHY, Peter E.
"Before You Eat. " Comm (107:5) 14 Mr 80, p. 154.

MURPHY, Rich
"The Carpenter. " Tele (16) 80, p. 114.
"Rouge City. " Tele (16) 80, p. 114.

MURRAY, G. E.
"What the Waters Hold. " Ascent (6:1) 80, pp. 7-12.

MURRAY, Les A.
"The Doorman. " NewYorker (56:34) 13 O 80, p. 46.
"Telling the cousins. " NewL (46:3) Spr 80, p. 21.

MURRAY, Philip
"The Kiss." AmerS (49:4) Aut 80, p. 488.
"On the Death of Steele's Father." Poetry (135:5) Jl 80, p. 264.

MUSGRAVE, Susan
"Day After Day." ThRiPo (15/16) 80, p. 38.
"Second Sight." ThRiPo (15/16) 80, p. 40.
"You Are on Some Road." ThRiPo (15/16) 80, p. 39.

MUSKE, Carol
"Census." Antaeus (39) Aut 80, p. 69.
"Dulce lignum, dulces clavos." Field (23) Aut 80, p. 75.
"Golden Retriever." NewYorker (56:35) 20 O 80, p. 52.
"The Invention of Cuisine." Tendril (9) 80, p. 110.
"Worry" (for Sister Jeanne d'arc). Field (23) Aut 80, p. 76.

MYCUE, Edward
"Choices." PoNow (27) 80, p. 17.
"My Ugly Recent Past." Im (6:2) 80, p. 12.
"Where the Wind Begins." Im (7:1) 80, p. 12.

MYERS, Doug
"The Dense Color of the Biologist's Room." CutB (15) Aut/Wint
    80, p. 34.

MYERS, Jack
"Elsewhere." MissouriR (3:3) Sum 80, p. 30.
"Lightweight." NoAmR (265:1) Mr 80, p. 39.
"Living Inside a Dot." QW (10) Wint-Spr 80, p. 75.
"The Lover Meets His Desire." QW (10) Wint-Spr 80, p. 76.
"Mockingbird, Copy This." OhioR (24) 80, p. 39.
"Telepathic Note to Poet Friends." VirQR (56:2) Spr 80, p. 263.
"Winging It." Tendril (9) 80, p. 111.

MYERS, Joan Rohr
"Planting Tulips." CapeR (15:2) Sum 80, p. 50.
"Potatoes." SouthernHR (14:4) Aut 80, p. 338.

MYERS, Valjoan
"the morning edge of a dream." EngJ (69:5) My 80, p. 44.

MYRSIADES, Kostas
"Belfry" (tr. of Yannis Ritsos w. Kimon Friar). Durak (5) 80,
    pp. 34-44.
"The Five" (tr. of Yannis Ritsos w. Kimon Friar). BelPoJ (30:
    4) Sum 80, p. 39.
"Irresolute" (tr. of Yannis Ritsos w. Kimon Friar). Field (22)
    Spr 80, p. 79.
"The Journey" (tr. of Yannis Ritsos w. Kimon Friar). Field
    (22) Spr 80, p. 78.
"Sea Stroke" (tr. of Yannis Ritsos w. Kimon Friar). Field (22)
    Spr 80, p. 77.
"This Darkness" (tr. of Yannis Ritsos w. Kimon Friar). Field

(22) Spr 80, p. 81.
Twelve poems (tr. of Yannis Ritsos w. Kimon Friar). <u>Durak</u>
    (4) 80, pp. 55-62.
"White" (tr. of Yannis Ritsos w. Kimon Friar). <u>Field</u> (22) Spr
    80, p. 80.
from The World Is One: "Doubtful Encounters" (tr. of Yannis
    Ritsos). <u>Durak</u> (5) 80, p. 45.
from The World Is One: "Encounters" (tr. of Yannis Ritsos).
    <u>Durak</u> (5) 80, p. 48.
from The World Is One: "Freedom of Travel" (tr. of Yannis
    Ritsos). <u>Durak</u> (5) 80, p. 46.
from The World Is One: "Vatican Museum" (tr. of Yannis Rit-
    sos). <u>Durak</u> (5) 80, p. 47.

MYRVAAGNES, Naomi
    "Biography. " <u>AndR</u> (7:1) Spr 80, p. 75.

NADEL, Alan
    "Feeding the Stranger's Fire. " <u>GeoR</u> (34:3) Aut 80, p. 636.
    "What Jackson Pollock Must Have Known. " <u>Shen</u> (31:1) 79, p. 40.

NAESS, Kate
    "Ghosts" (tr. by Nadia Christensen). <u>PoNow</u> (26) 80, p. 45.

NAGLE, Alice Connelly
    "Do you suppose. " <u>SmPd</u> (48) Wint 80, p. 25.
    "It /day to day, one day. " <u>Wind</u> (36) 80, p. 49.
    "presuming. " <u>Wind</u> (36) 80, p. 50.

NAGOURNEY, Peter
    "Poem: You save shells from the sea. " <u>SouthernHR</u> (14:1) Wint
    80, p. 30.

NAIDEN, James
    "Minneapolis Sonnet #61. " <u>Wind</u> (37) 80, p. 35.
    "Minneapolis Sonnet #68. " <u>Wind</u> (37) 80, p. 35.

NAKAGAWA, Onsey
    "Fireworks. " <u>WindO</u> (37) Aut-Wint 80. on calendar.

NAMEROFF, Rochelle
    "Scarlet O'Hara. " <u>Tele</u> (16) 80, p. 54.

NANFITO, Bryanne
    "Cold Blooded Murder. " <u>Tele</u> (16) 80, p. 118.
    "Eyes. " <u>Tele</u> (16) 80, p. 116.
    "The House That Jack Built. " <u>SmPd</u> (48) Wint 80, p. 28.
    "Street Talk. " <u>Tele</u> (16) 80, p. 117.
    "1030 South Main Street. " <u>SmPd</u> (48) Wint 80, p. 27.

NAPORA, Joe
    "This Fine Call Is the Result of Many Years of Field Testing by
    Men Who Have Made a Fine Art of Calling Turkeys. " <u>Kayak</u>
    (53) My 80. back cover. found poem.

NARGI, Gary
"1975. " Wind (38) 80, p. 51.

NARIHIRA, Ariwara no
"Last Poem" (tr. by Graeme Wilson). DenQ (15:3) Aut 80, p.
   85.

NASH, Valery
"Son-in-Law. " Wind (38) 80, p. 48.

NASIO, Brenda
"For Love of Mother. " StoneC (7:1) F 80, p. 25.

NASSER, Vicki Paski
"Theatre of the Absurd. " KanQ (12:4) Aut 80, p. 6.

NATHAN, Leonard
"Altamira. " MassR (21:4) Wint 80, p. 662.
"Keeping the Faith. " ThRiPo (15/16) 80, p. 42.
"Leavings. " PraS (54:2) Sum 80, p. 63.
"The Old Chiefs. " PoNow (27) 80, p. 38.
"Sick Leave. " Bits (11) 80.
"Sleeping in the Old Room. " PoNow (26) 80, p. 16.
"A Very Forgiving Person. " PraS (54:2) Sum 80, p. 64.
"Waiting Room Only. " Salm (47/48) Wint-Spr 80, p. 56.

NATHAN, Norman
"chinese screen 3. " MalR (53) Ja 80, p. 46.
"chinese screen 5. " MalR (53) Ja 80, p. 47.
"chinese screen 6. " MalR (53) Ja 80, p. 48.
"chinese screen 7. " MalR (53) Ja 80, p. 49.
"chinese screen 8. " MalR (53) Ja 80, p. 50.
"Continuous Feature. " KanQ (12:4) Aut 80, p. 62.

NAVARRE, Jane Piirto
"December Snow. " PoNow (29) 80, p. 32.
"Working the Concession Stand for the Band Boosters. " PoNow
   (29) 80, p. 32.

NECKER, Robert
"Dance. " StoneC (7:1) F 80, p. 30.
"A Day Off for the Numbered Man. " US1 (12/13) Aut-Wint 80,
   p. 13.

NEELD, Judith
"Love. " Pig (7) My 80, p. 68.
"Summer Island. " SouthwR (65:3) Sum 80, p. 310.

NELMS, Sheryl L.
"Dragon Fly Wing. " GRR (11:1) 80, p. 41.
"Texas Ice Storm. " PoetC (12:3) 80, p. 28.
"yellow-headed blackbird. " SmPd (49) Spr 80, p. 19.

NELSON, Friederike Kolbl
"Mother." Prima (5) 79, p. 16.

NELSON, Howard
"If My Wife Dies." NewL (46:4) Sum 80, p. 51.
"September 19, 1819: John Keats." BelPoJ (30:4) Sum 80, p. 34.
"Story Heard by a Coal Stove." Outbr (4/5) Aut 79-Spr 80, p. 56.
"Winter Night, Cold Spell." CarolQ (32:1) Wint 80, p. 58.

NELSON, Paul
"Universal Donor." GeoR (34:3) Aut 80, p. 589.

NELSON, Rodney
"Father to Son." DacTerr (17) 80, p. 65.

NEMEROV, Howard
"Acorn, Yom Kippur." NewRep (182:1/2) 5-12 Ja 80, p. 38.
"The Author to His Body on Their Fifteenth Birthday." NewRep (182:12) 22 Mr 80, p. 30.
"Insomnia I." Salm (50/51) Aut 80-Wint 81, p. 17.
"Insomnia II." Salm (50/51) Aut 80-Wint 81, p. 18.
"The Tapestry." Tendril (9) 80, p. 113.

NEPO, Mark
"Arroyo." Antaeus (38) Sum 80, p. 92.
"Endgame." PortR (26) 80, p. 443.
"Oh My Voice, Over and Over the Wind." KanQ (12:3) Sum 80, p. 30.

NERUDA, Pablo
"At Last There Is No One" (tr. by Alastair Reid). NewYorker (56:27) 25 Ag 80, p. 35.
"Exile" (tr. by Alastair Reid). NewYorker (56:27) 25 Ag 80, p. 34.
"Father" (tr. by Alastair Reid). NewYorker (56:27) 25 Ag 80, p. 34.
"The River Born in the Cordilleras" (tr. by Alastair Reid). NewYorker (56:27) 25 Ag 80, p. 34.
"Sex" (tr. by Alastair Reid). NewYorker (56:31) 22 S 80, p. 56.
"To Silvestre Revueltas of Mexico, in His Death" (tr. by Harry Thomas). MichQR (19:1) Wint 80, p. 89.

NESSE, Åse-Marie
"Marc Chagall." PortR (26) 80, p. 283.
"Odyssevs." PortR (26) 80, p. 282.

NETO, Maria Amélia
from The Silence of Amon: (VIII) (tr. by author). PortR (26) 80, p. 313.
O silencio de Amon: (VIII). PortR (26) 80, p. 312.

NEW, Lucia
"Havana, Winter 1979." Vis (1) 79.

NEWBROUGH, Ross
"Flame thrower." PoNow (29) 80, p. 32.
"The Lesson." PoNow (29) 80, p. 33.
"Missouri, 1955." PikeF (3) Wint 80, p. 10.

NEWBY, Richard L.
"The Day Mavor Bundy's Old Mare Died: Monody for Lost Poets. "
  BallSUF (21:1) Wint 80, p. 65.

NEWMAN, Felice
"Prisoner's Testimony After Burial." LittleM (12:3/4) 80, p. 57.

NEWMAN, Jerry
"Anne Sexton." CreamCR (5:2) Spr 80, p. 41.

NEWMAN, P. B.
"Bean and Egret." Im (6:2) 80, p. 5.
"Big Men." PoNow (29) 80, p. 32.
"The Light of the Red Horse." Columbia (4) Spr-Sum 80, p. 84.
"Survival in a Flood-Zone." SouthernPR (20:1) Spr 80, p. 49.

NEWMAN, Wade
"Lot's Wife." CarolQ (32:2) Spr-Sum 80, p. 55.
"Sylvia Plath." SouthernPR (20:1) Spr 80, p. 39.

NEZAHUALCOYOTL (Hungry Coyote)
"Lone Mind" (tr. by John Ceely). Tele (16) 80, p. 15.
"Never" (tr. by John Ceely). Tele (16) 80, p. 16.
"Stand Up" (tr. by John Ceely). Tele (16) 80, p. 17.

NICK, Dagmar
"Above the Harbor of Lindos" (tr. by Jim Barnes). DenQ (14:4)
  Wint 80, p. 127.
Zeugnis und Zeichen. CharR (Supp) 80. Entire issue.

NICKENS, Thomas G.
"Pacified." Wind (37) 80, p. 36.

NICKERSON, Shelia
"Platform." Bits (11) 80.

NI CUILLEANAIN, Eiléan
"A l'usage de M. et Mme. Van Gramberen." Ploughs (6:1) 80,
  p. 162.
"As if suddenly reincarnated." Ploughs (6:1) 80, p. 160.
"Like One Borne Away in a Dance and Veiled." Ploughs (6:1)
  80, p. 161.

NIDITCH, B. Z.
"Cello Playing." CapeR (15:2) Sum 80, p. 18.

"Lamentation. " Os (11) 80, p. 14.
"Playing Beethoven. " Os (11) 80, p. 13.
"Song of Not So Long Ago. " Im (7:1) 80, p. 9.
"The Wagon Bed. " Im (7:1) 80, p. 9.

NIFLIS, Michael
"A Federal Sexton Speaks. " Comm (107:20) 7 N 80, p. 628.
"Leonidas' Thermopylae. " PartR (47:4) 80, p. 610.

NIJMEIJER, Peter
"How to Start a Wine-Cellar" (tr. of Habakuk II de Balker).
    PortR (26) 80, p. 269.
"Lovesick Robot" (tr. of Willem M. Roggeman). PortR (26) 80,
    p. 48.
"Poem for Ulrike Meinhof" (tr. of Willem M. Roggeman).
    PortR (26) 80, p. 46.
"Tautology of the Subject" (tr. of K. Schippers). PortR (26) 80,
    p. 271.
"Two thirds air" (tr. of Eddy Van Vliet). PortR (26) 80, p. 270.

NILSEN, Richard
"Wyatt Earp. " PoNow (29) 80, p. 33.

NIMMO, Kurt
"Cathode Consciousness. " Sam (98) 80, p. 38.
Midnight Shift in Detroit. Sam (83) 79. Entire issue.

NIMS, John Frederick
"The Young Ionia. " Tendril (9) 80, p. 114.

NIMTZ, Steven
"Like Water, Like Stone. " EnPas (10) 80, p. 18.

NIST, John
"The Art of Loving" (tr. of Manuel Bandeira). AmerPoR (9:6)
    N-D 80, p. 35.
"Akhilleus. " Poem (38) Mr 80, pp. 21-25.
"Cripple at the Ballet. " SouthernHR (14:3) Sum 80, p. 234.
"Villanelle. " NewL (47:1) Aut 80, p. 52.
"The Virgin Mary" (tr. of Manuel Bandeira). AmerPoR (9:6)
    N-D 80, p. 35.

NITCHIE, Donald
"Framing. " StoneC (7:3) D 80, p. 8.
"Hands. " StoneC (7:3) D 80, p. 9.

NITCHIE, George W.
"Cohasset: Sea and Surf in February. " Shen (31:1) 79, p. 37.
"Death of a Zebra. " Shen (31:1) 79, p. 36.
"Interim Report from a Sabbatical Leave. " Shen (31:1) 79, p.
    36.

NITZSCHE, Jane Chance
"Sentry. " SouthernHR (14:1) Wint 80, p. 69.

"Shopping." Prima (5) 79, p. 8.

NIXON, Colin
"On a Great Classic." ChrC (97:36) 12 N 80, p. 1084.
"Unable to Symbolize." ChrC (97:28) 10-17 S 80, p. 848.

NOBLE, Charles
"At One in the Morning." MalR (56) O 80, p. 154.

NOCERINO, Kathryn
"Shazam!" PoNow (29) 80, p. 27.
"Stuffed." PoNow (29) 80, p. 27.

NOLAN, James
"Angel Eggs." PoNow (26) 80, p. 10.
"Blood Salad." PoNow (26) 80, p. 10.

NOLL, Bink
"Emptying the Birthplace." SouthernPR (20:2) Aut 80, p. 30.
"The New Bed." BelPoJ (31:1) Aut 80, p. 24.
"The Walkways." BelPoJ (31:1) Aut 80, p. 25.

NORDAN, Lewis
"He Fishes With His Father's Ghost." SouthernHR (14:2) Spr 80,
    p. 126.

NORDBARANDT, Henrik
"Idyl." PortR (26) 80, p. 89.
"Kroge." PortR (26) 80, p. 86.
"Lille essay om sproget." PortR (26) 80, p. 88.

NORDHAUS, Jean
"Communism and Capitalism." CropD (1) Spr 80, p. 9.
"Migrations." CentR (24:1) Wint 80, p. 81.
"September." CropD (1) Spr 80, p. 9.
"Yahrzeit Candle." KanQ (12:1) Wint 80, p. 60.

NOREN, Lars
from Diary: (1, 2, 4, 5, 6) (tr. by Lennart Bruce). PoetryE
    (3) 80, p. 63.
from Order: (May 9) (tr. by Lennart Bruce). PoetryE (3) 80,
    p. 62.
"Poem from a Single Room Apartment in Hagersten, 1970" (tr.
    by Bill Mishler). PoetryE (3) 80, p. 61.

NORMINGTON, James
"Astronomy" (tr. of Juan Jose Arreola). PoNow (28) 80, p. 44.
"Dawn After a Single Star" (tr. of Efrain Huerta). PoNow (27)
    80, p. 44.

NORRIS, Gunilla Brodde
"The Gray Angel." Pig (7) My 80, p. 39.
"The Old Doll as Muse." SouthernPR (20:2) Aut 80, p. 45.

"September Rain. " SouthernPR (20:2) Aut 80, p. 44.

NORRIS, Leslie
"Ponies. " Atl (245:5) My 80, p. 79.

NORSE, Harold
from Life and Death in Plaza Real: "Bullets. " Ark (14) 80, p.
298.
from Life and Death in Plaza Real: "G. O. D. " Ark (14) 80, p.
302.
from Life and Death in Plaza Real: "The Barcelona Girls and
Boys. " Ark (14) 80, p. 300.

NORTH, Gloria
20th Century Man. Sam (84) 79. Entire issue.

NORTH, Michael
"Samurai Movie. " AntR (38:1) Wint 80, p. 67.
"The Steady Days. " AntR (38:1) Wint 80, p. 66.

NORTH, Susan
"The Fiddler's Bitch. " BelPoJ (30:3) Spr 80, p. 22.
"Passage. " PraS (54:1) Spr 80, p. 40.

NORTHUP, Harry E.
Ten Poems. Bachy (17) Spr 80, pp. 111-117.

NORTON, Camille
"Felicani of Milk Street. " Aspect (76) S-D 79-80, p. 36.
from Harrisburg Poem: (2). Aspect (76) S-D 79-80, p. 37.
"The Pursuit of Longing. " Cond (6) 80, pp. 151-158.

NOVAK, Helga M.
"Margarete with the Trunk" (tr. by Allen H. Chappel). NewOR
(7:1) 80, p. 59.

NOVAK, Michael Paul
"The Numismatist. " Focus (14:88) S 80, p. 31.

NOVEMBER, Sharyn
"At the Fish Hatchery. " PortR (26) 80, p. 438.
"Avedon Photographs 1: Dorian Leigh, 1947. " StoneC (7:2) My
80, p. 20.
"Avedon Photographs 2: Dorian Leigh, 1949. " StoneC (7:2) My
80, p. 21.
"Christmas. " Poetry (137:3) D 80, p. 133.

NOWLAN, Alden
"The Inflatable Woman. " PottPort (2) 80-81, p. 25.
"Stinky Billy. " PottPort (2) 80-81, p. 39.

NOWOTNY, Walther
'Ich Habe. " PortR (26) 80, p. 31.

NUMMI, Lassi
"Loppukesä." <u>PortR</u> (26) 80, p. 135.

NUSSBAUM, Elaine
"Warriors." <u>Wind</u> (36) 80, p. 36.

NUSSBAUM, Laureen
"Just Imagine" (tr. of Gerald Bisinger). <u>PortR</u> (26) 80, p. 34.

NYE, Naomi
"Canada." <u>EnPas</u> (10) 80, p. 6.
"Chula." <u>EnPas</u> (10) 80, p. 4.
"What She Knew." <u>EnPas</u> (10) 80, p. 5.

NYHART, Nina
"Poem for G. L. B." <u>Ploughs</u> (6:2) 80, p. 125.
"Sleeping Alone." <u>Ploughs</u> (6:2) 80, p. 126.

OATES, Joyce Carol
"The Ebony Casket." <u>Harp</u> (260:1559) Ap 80, p. 118.
"F---" (for Robert Phillips). <u>MichQR</u> (19:4/20:1) Aut-Wint 80-
    81, p. 617.
"Jesus, Heal Me." <u>NewRep</u> (182:4) 26 Ja 80, p. 26.
"Portrait: Woman with a Girl's Face." <u>SouthernR</u> (16:2) Spr 80,
    p. 402.
"Prelude." <u>SouthernR</u> (16:2) Spr 80, p. 401.
"Things Run Down." <u>Nat</u> (231:9) 27 S 80, p. 292.

O'BLENIS, Edward
"Haiku." <u>WindO</u> (37) Aut-Wint 80. on calendar.
"One Line Haiku." <u>WindO</u> (37) Aut-Wint 80. on calendar.

O'CONNELL, Richard
"Morning After." <u>Ark</u> (14) 80, p. 303.
"The Relay." <u>Ark</u> (14) 80, p. 303.

O'CONNOR, Mark
"Wing." <u>NewL</u> (46:3) Spr 80, p. 34.

O'CONNOR, Michael Patrick
"An Eclogue from the East." <u>Mouth</u> (2:5) O 80, p. 9.
"Striking the Air." <u>Mouth</u> (2:5) O 80, p. 10.

ODAM, Joyce
"Life-Wish." <u>KanQ</u> (12:4) Aut 80, p. 132.

ODEN, Gloria
"Girl on a Dolphin." <u>Ark</u> (14) 80, p. 304.

ODOM, Douglas
"All of the Things She Does Not Look Like Doing." <u>Sam</u> (86)
    79, p. 55.
"Rocks Off." <u>Sam</u> (86) 79, p. 55.
"The Woman and the Dog." <u>Sam</u> (86) 79, p. 55.

O'DONNELL, Norah E.
"Winter: 1974." CreamCR (5:2) Spr 80, p. 85.

O'GRADY, Desmond
"FoFo." Ploughs (6:1) 80, p. 127.
"Cavafy in Alexandria." Ploughs (6:1) 80, p. 128.

O'HEHIR, Diana
"abandoning our religion." Kayak (53) My 80, p. 31.
"Again." Field (23) Aut 80, p. 33.
"The Artists Model." CalQ (16/17) 80, p. 55.
"Buried Alive Together." PoetryNW (21:1) Spr 80, p. 43.
"the city is pulled out to sea." Kayak (53) My 80, p. 32.
"Empty." PoetryNW (21:1) Spr 80, p. 44.
"ghosts." Kayak (53) My 80, p. 33.
"Gift." PoetryNW (21:1) Spr 80, p. 44.
"Meet Me." PoNow (28) 80, p. 9.
"Offspring." PoNow (28) 80, p. 9.
"our chance." Kayak (53) My 80, p. 30.
"The Plumber's Apprentice." CalQ (16/17) 80, p. 56.
"Questions and Answers." Field (23) Aut 80, p. 32.
"Recognition." Poetry (136:4) Jl 80, p. 201.
"Seasonal Change." Poetry (136:4) Jl 80, p. 200.
"Sleeping Pill." ParisR (77) Wint-Spr 80, p. 102.
"Suitor." Field (23) Aut 80, p. 34.
"34,000 Feet." CalQ (16/17) 80, p. 54.
"When You Die." Poetry (136:4) Jl 80, p. 199.

OIJER, Bruno K.
"Blue Cup of Snow." Tele (16) 80, p. 24.

O'KEEFE, Richard R.
"The Paperweight." Aspen (10) Wint 80, p. 81.

OKTENBERG, Adrian
"Homage to Lady Murasaki." NewL (47:1) Aut 80, p. 15.
"Six O'Clock News, July 4, 1979." NewL (47:1) Aut 80, p. 13.

OLDENBURG, Patty Mucha
"They're building a new roof." Tele (16) 80, p. 68.
"Time to dream and suddenly the pressure is off." Tele (16) 80,
    p. 68.

OLDER, Julia
"Looking Alike in the Dark." Prima (5) 79, p. 68.

OLDHAM, Perry
"Hotel Notre-Dame" (tr. of Blaise Cendrars w. Arlen Gill).
    WebR (5:1) Wint 80, p. 32.
"Strangers' Inn" (tr. of Blaise Cendrars w. Arlen Gill). WebR
    (5:1) Wint 80, p. 36.

OLDKNOW, Antony
"The Chair." Nat (230:12) 29 Mr 80, p. 376.

"The Doge." Sam (86) 79, p. 2.
"In the Dark Cafe." CreamCR (5:1) Wint 79, p. 29.
"There's a Simple-Minded..." (for Stephane Mallarme) (tr. of
     Francis Jammes). CutB (15) Aut/Wint 80, p. 58.

OLDS, Sharon
"Afternoon on the Vineyard." PoNow (28) 80, p. 41.
"Armor." Poetry (136:4) Jl 80, p. 210.
"atlantis" (tr. of Wislawa Szemborska w. Grazyna Drabik).
     Kayak (55) Ja 81, p. 56.
"Bestiary." PoetryNW (21:2) Sum 80, p. 33.
"chance meeting" (tr. of Wislawa Szemborska w. Grazyna
     Drabik). Kayak (55) Ja 81, p. 57.
"The Child Dead of Hunger in Yerevan." SouthernHR (14:1) Wint
     80, p. 19.
"the conoisseuse of slugs." Kayak (53) My 80, p. 58.
"the derelict." Kayak (53) My 80, p. 57.
"Electra on the Mother and Father." SouthernHR (14:1) Wint 80,
     p. 19.
"fate." Kayak (53) My 80, p. 57.
"The Fear of Oneself." Poetry (136:4) Jl 80, p. 209.
"For My Daughter." MassR (21:4) Wint 80, p. 653.
"The Gentlemen in the U-Boats." NewL (46:4) Sum 80, p. 67.
"I Could Not Tell (for Muriel Rukeyser)." SouthernHR (14:1)
     Wint 80, p. 18.
"Infinite Bliss." PoNow (29) 80, p. 27.
"Medical Students." KanQ (12:1) Wint 80, p. 131.
"Monarchs." Atl (245:3) Mr 80, p. 48.
"Monarchs." PoNow (29) 80, p. 27.
"Mother and Child." SouthernHR (14:1) Wint 80, p. 18.
"My Father Snoring." NewRep (182:5) 2 F 80, p. 28.
"of all the dead that have come to me, this once." Kayak (55)
     Ja 81, p. 6.
"Reunion." Pan (21) 80, p. 44.
"the two apes of breughel" (tr. of Wislawa Szemborska w. Grazy-
     na Drabik). Kayak (55) Ja 81, p. 57.
"The Unjustly Punished Child." PoNow (29) 80, p. 27.
"words" (tr. of Wislawa Szemborska w. Grazyna Drabik). Kayak
     (55) Ja 81, p. 58.
"The Young Partisans." Pequod (11) 80, p. 16.

O'LEARY, Tomas
"Weeds (1975)." MidwQ (21:3) Spr 80, p. 354.

OLES, Carole
"A Collage: The National Standard." Poetry (136:5) Ag 80, p.
     276.
"Conditional." PraS (54:2) Sum 80, p. 27.
"The Dream Carrying Furniture." PoetryNW (21:4) Wint 80-81,
     p. 25.
"Francestown Suite" (for Jabez Holmes). Tendril (9) 80, p. 116.
"Handedness, a Right Handed View." PraS (54:2) Sum 80, p. 25.
"I Will Draw You in Three Lines." Poetry (136:5) Ag 80, p. 278.

"In Nashville. " Poetry (136:5) Ag 80, p. 279.
"Life in the Soil. " PraS (54:2) Sum 80, p. 26.
"Poem Found in an Ensign's Journal. " Aspect (76) S-D 79-80,
    p. 39.
"Poem in Search of Different Endings. " PraS (54:2) Sum 80, p.
    29.
"Reading Father. " Tendril (7/8) Spr-Sum 80, p. 56.
"Shore-Walking. " Agni (13) 80, p. 91.
"Stonecarver" (for Father). Ploughs (6:2) 80, p. 106.
"Stonecarver, Restoring. " PraS (54:2) Sum 80, p. 28.
"Stonecarver's Wife. " Ploughs (6:2) 80, p. 104.
"Women Near Sea. " Nimrod (24:1) Aut-Wint 80, p. 66.

OLIPHANT, Dave
    "Figures of Speech" (tr. of Enrique Lihn). NewOR (7:3) 80, p.
    218.

OLIVER, Louis "Little Coon"
    "Ensaba Hutsie. " StoneC (7:3) D 80, p. 70.
    "Many Many Moons, No Rain. " StoneC (7:3) D 80, p. 69.

OLIVER, Mary
    "American Primitive. " ThRiPo (15/16) 80, p. 19.
    "At Blackwater Pond. " ThRiPo (15/16) 80, p. 21.
    "Cold Poem. " WestHR (34:2) Spr 80, p. 138.
    "Crossing the Swamp. " Atl (245:5) My 80, p. 56.
    "Fall Song. " PoetryNW (21:2) Sum 80, p. 27.
    "In the Provincelands. " Bits (11) 80.
    "The Kitten. " AmerS (49:2) Spr 80, p. 247.
    "The Lost Children. " ThRiPo (15/16) 80, p. 16.
    "Morning at Great Pond. " ThRiPo (15/16) 80, p. 22.
    "Night. " Bits (11) 80.
    "An Old Whorehouse. " ThRiPo (15/16) 80, p. 23.
    "The Rabbit. " ThRiPo (15/16) 80, p. 24.
    "Rules for the Dance (1967). " MidwQ (21:3) Spr 80, p. 356.
    "The Snakes. " ThRiPo (15/16) 80, p. 25.
    "Storm. " WestHR (34:4) Aut 80, p. 351.

OLIVER, Michael Brian
    "Approaching Midsummer. " PottPort (2) 80-81, p. 20.

OLIVER, Raymond
    "The Focus. " Thrpny (3) Aut 80, p. 8.
    "Reverie, Interrupted by a Letter (Feb. 6, 1618). " Thrpny (2)
    Sum 80, p. 11.

OLIVEROS, Chuck
    "Elegy. " CapeR (15:2) Sum 80, p. 41.

OLSEN, William
    "Addressing His Dead Wife, Kansas, 1916. " NewOR (7:2) 80, p.
    168.
    "On an Imagined Arrival Somewhere in the Midwest. " PoetC
    (12:2) 80, p. 31.

OLSON, Andrew
"Dreaming of Melons." PraS (54:1) Spr 80, p. 17.

OLSON, Elder
"In Despair He Orders a New Typewriter." AmerS (49:3) Sum
      80, p. 334.
"Merry Christmas!" NewL (46:3) Spr 80, p. 85.
"Volcán de Agua" (for James E. Miller Jr.). Poetry (136:4) Jl
      80, p. 211.

OLSON, Kirby
"New Orleans Scene." Tele (16) 80, p. 115.

OLSON, Toby
"My Moon Girl." NewL (46:4) Sum 80, p. 23.
"Tide Trail." NewL (46:4) Sum 80, p. 24.
"Two Trips." NewL (46:4) Sum 80, p. 26.

O'MALLEY, Sister Emanuela
"Corn Harvest." KanQ (12:2) Spr 80, p. 77.
"False Prophet." KanQ (12:2) Spr 80, p. 78.

ONDAATJE, Michael
"The Hour of Cowdust." Stand (21:1) 79-80, p. 31.

OPPEN, Mary
"As the River Flows." Montra (7) 80, p. 17.
"Conversation." Montra (7) 80, p. 18.
"Homesick." Montra (7) 80, p. 19.
"Is There a Woman Who Knows Her Own Way." Montra (7) 80,
      p. 22.
"Mother and Daughter and the Sea." Montra (7) 80, p. 16.
"Muse." Montra (7) 80, p. 20.
"The Pearl." Montra (7) 80, p. 21.
Poems and Transpositions. Montra (Supplement) 80. Entire is-
      sue.

OPPENHEIMER, Joel
"Flowers." Harp (261:1564) S 80, p. 83.

ORANGE, Wendy
"Letter to Michael." Aspect (76) S-D 79-80, p. 23.
"Welcoming You." Aspect (76) S-D 79-80, p. 22.

ORBAN, Ottó
"The Blood of the Walsung House" (tr. by Nicholas Kolumban).
      CharR (6:1) Spr 80, p. 39.
"The Letter" (tr. by Nicholas Kolumban). CharR (6:1) Spr 80,
      p. 38.
"Requiem" (tr. by Jascha Kessler). CutB (14) Spr/Sum 80, p.
      15.

ORESICK, Peter
"After the Movement." SlowLR (4) 80, p. 35.

"Jump. " PoetryNW (21:3) Aut 80, p. 23.
"May Songs. " SlowLR (4) 80, p. 33.

ORFALEA, Greg
"A Gift You Must Lose. " AntR (38:4) Aut 80, p. 467.
"Head Down. " AntR (38:4) Aut 80, p. 466.

ORIEL-PETERSON, Anne
"Cocktail Party. " Vis (4) 80.
"The Invisible Boundaries. " Vis (1) 79.
"Tower of Babel. " Vis (3) 80.

ORLEN, Steve
"The Aga Khan. " Tendril (9) 80, p. 117.
"All That We Try to Do. " Ploughs (6:2) 80, p. 90.
"March 15, 1979" (for M. H. O.) Ploughs (6:2) 80, p. 93.
"Recompense. " Ploughs (6:2) 80, p. 95.

ORLOCK, C.
"Ninth Month. " SoDakR (18:2) Sum 80, p. 21.
"Packing. " SoDakR (18:2) Sum 80, p. 21.

O'ROURKE, David
"Confrontation. " MalR (54) Ap 80, p. 128.
"For Your Inferiority Complex. " MalR (54) Ap 80, p. 129.

OROZCO, Olga
"Olga Orozco. " PortR (26) 80, p. 14.

ORR, Ed
"The Penitent Magdalen of Georges de la Tour. " SouthernHR
    (14:3) Sum 80, p. 208.

ORR, Gregory
"An Abandoned, Overgrown Cemetery in the Pasture Near Our
    House. " Antaeus (38) Sum 80, p. 93.
"Child's Song. " Atl (246:5) N 80, p. 91.
"Friday Lunchbreak. " Tendril (9) 80, p. 118.
"The Guns. " ParisR (77) Wint-Spr 80, p. 99.
"Hospital Albert Schweitzer. " NewYorker (56:2) 3 Mr 80, p. 42.
"Indian Summer. " ParisR (77) Wint-Spr 80, p. 101.
"A Last Address to My Ghosts. " ParisR (77) Wint-Spr 80, p.
    100.
"Murderer's Songs. " ParisR (77) Wint-Spr 80, p. 98.
"On the Lawn. " Nat (231:11) 11 O 80, p. 350.
Salt Wings. PoetryE (2) 80. Entire issue.
"Two Sonnets About Keats. " Pequod (11) 80, p. 10.
"Virginia Backyard; July. " Antaeus (38) Sum 80, p. 94.

ORTBLAD, Dennis
"North African Lotus Eating. " KanQ (12:1) Wint 80, p. 150.

ORTEN, Jiri
"Elegy Number Seven" (tr. by Lyn Coffin). DenQ (15:1) Spr 80,

p. 76.

ORTH, Ghita
"Acrophobia. " Poem (39) Jl 80, p. 56.
"Translation. " Poem (39) Jl 80, p. 55.

ORTIZ, Simon J.
"Lunch. " DenQ (14:4) Wint 80, p. 20.
"Sunday. " DenQ (14:4) Wint 80, p. 19.

ORTOLANI, Al
"Grandmother. " LittleBR (1:1) Aut 80, p. 20.

OSAKI, Mark
"Old Man Thinking of Small Breasts. " GeoR (34:3) Aut 80, p.
616.

OSBEY, Brenda Marie
Eight Poems. Obs (5:1/2) Spr-Sum 79, p. 79.

OSERS, Ewald
"Home" (tr. of Miroslav Holub). PortR (26) 80, p. 65.
from The Plague Column: "What's all this talk of grey hair" (tr.
of Jaroslav Seifert). PortR (26) 80, p. 67.
from Those Who Have Prohibited Themselves: "There are some
who no longer wish to be" (tr. of Jan Skácel). PortR (26)
80, p. 75.
"Visitors" (tr. of Jan Skácel). PortR (26) 80, p. 74.

OSKAR, Jon
"Autumn" (tr. by Alan Boucher). Vis (4) 80.
"Eg spyr. Eg heyri. " PortR (26) 80, p. 182.
"Search" (tr. by Alan Boucher). Vis (2) 80.

OSTRIKER, Alicia
"Anecdote With Flowers, 1919. " AmerPoR (9:5) S-O 80, p. 35.
"The Blood. " PoNow (27) 80, p. 10.
"The Change. " Poetry (136:5) Ag 80, p. 261.
"In the Dust. " Poetry (136:5) Ag 80, p. 263.
"Old Men. " PoNow (27) 80, p. 10.
"Two Writers. " US1 (12/13) Aut-Wint 80, p. 14.
"A Woman Walking in the Suburbs. " US1 (12/13) Aut-Wint 80, p.
14.

OSTROM, Hans
"Sierra City.   September. " CalQ (16/17) 80, p. 100.

O'SULLIVAN, Garrett
In the Name of The Father The Son and The Holy Spirit. UTR
(6:2) 80.   Entire issue.

OTT, Tom
"A Wake. " FourQt (30:1) Aut 80, p. 36.

OVERTON, Ron
"Miss Conklin. " PoNow (29) 80, p. 28.
"Moon Shot. " PoNow (29) 80, p. 28.
"The Watch. " PoNow (29) 80, p. 28.

OWEN, Eileen
"Song for Autumn. " PoetryNW (21:3) Aut 80, p. 32.

OWEN, Maureen
"for Emily (Dickinson). " OP (30) Aut 80, p. 42.
"Frogs Ringing Gongs in a Skull. " OP (30) Aut 80, p. 40.
"Goodbye September. " OP (30) Aut 80, p. 41.

OWEN, Sue
"deception. " Kayak (53) My 80, p. 12.
"Nothing. " PoNow (28) 80, p. 47.
"The Owl. " Nat (230:9) 8 Mr 80, p. 284.
"superstition. " Kayak (53) My 80, p. 13.

OWER, John
"Christmas Card for Dark Paper. " Wind (37) 80, p. 42.
"The Secretaries. " Wind (37) 80, p. 42.

ÖZTUNA, Güner
"Devinimler. " PortR (26) 80, p. 402.
"Incidents" (tr. by author). PortR (26) 80, p. 406.

PACK, Robert
"The Kiss. " Poetry (135:6) Mr 80, p. 319.
"The Kiss" (for Kevin). Tendril (9) 80, p. 119.
"Looking at a Mountain Range--While Listening to a Mozart Piano
    Concert. " Poetry (135:6) Mr 80, p. 317.

PACKARD, William
"After the Class. " CropD (2/3) Aut-Wint 80, p. 33.

PADDOCK, Harold
"Annual Report. " PottPort (2) 80-81, p. 52.
"Ash Vale. " PottPort (2) 80-81, p. 28.

PADILLA, Heberto
"Houses" (tr. by Alastair Reid). NewYRB (27:13) 14 Ag 80, p.
    21.
"Note" (tr. by Alastair Reid). NewYRB (27:13) 14 Ag 80, p. 21.

PAFF, Eric W.
"On Sitting Up Late, Watching Kittens. " BallSUF (21:2) Spr 80,
    p. 53.

PAGE, B. Sanford
"All Songs. " BallSUF (21:2) Spr 80, p. 47.

PAGE, Geoff
"The catacomb. " NewL (46:3) Spr 80, p. 8.

"Coloratura. " NewL (46:3) Spr 80, p. 8.

PAGE, William
"Arthritis. " Poem (40) N 80, p. 27.
"Dark Fire. " Im (7:1) 80, p. 3.
"Painlessly Out of Ourselves. " SouthwR (65:3) Sum 80, p. 246.
"Souvenir. " PoNow (29) 80, p. 33.
"Speaking of the Past. " Poem (40) N 80, p. 28.

PAINTER, Pamela
"The Farm. " LitR (23:3) Spr 80, p. 391.
"Suicide Note. " LitR (23:3) Spr 80, p. 392.

PALEN, John
"Dividend. " GRR (11:1) 80, p. 48.
"For My Father. " WindO (36) Spr-Sum 80, p. 45.
"Meditation on Kubik's Second Symphony. " WindO (36) Spr-Sum
    80, p. 45.
"Self Portrait with Cameras. " GRR (11:1) 80, p. 46.
"To Carol. " GRR (11:1) 80, p. 47.

PALENZONA, Francesco
"Giraffe" (tr. of Lina B. Franzone). PortR (26) 80, p. 213.
"Star Petals" (tr. of Lina B. Franzone). PortR (26) 80, p. 214.

PALEY, Morton
"Theodore Roethke. " CalQ (16/17) 80, p. 126.

PALLISTER, Jan
"Letter to My Father" (tr. of Eros Alesi w. Marisa Gath-Tay-
    lor). EnPas (11) 80, pp. 4-10.

PALMA, Michael
"Ketty" (tr. of Guido Guzzano). Poetry (136:1) Ap 80, p. 17.
"Totò merúmeni" (tr. of Guido Gozzano). Poetry (136:1) Ap 80,
    p. 14.
"A Wintry Scene" (tr. of Guido Gozzano). Poetry (136:1) Ap 80,
    p. 11.

PALMER, Leslie
"Monkey Island, Now Let's See the Allegories. " Tele (16) 80,
    p. 31.

PALMER, William
"The Baby Is Mostly Yours I Tell Her. " PoNow (29) 80, p. 33.
"The Spaces Between Rings. " PoNow (29) 80, p. 33.

PANKEY, Eric
"Cain. " CharR (6:2) Aut 80, p. 28.
"Ceremony. " CharR (6:2) Aut 80, p. 28.
"Renaming the Evening. " CapeR (15:2) Sum 80, p. 10.

PANTAZON, James
"Crowded. " CreamCR (5:1) Wint 79, p. 49.

PAPE, Greg
"The Circle of the Year. " <u>PoNow</u> (28) 80, p. 9.

PAPENHAUSEN, Carol
"Album. " <u>WebR</u> (5:1) Wint 80, p. 58.

PARADIS, Philip
"Instructions for Living a Paper-Boy's Life. " <u>QW</u> (10) Wint-Spr
    80, p. 35.
"Rejection Letter. " <u>PoNow</u> (29) 80, p. 33.

PARATTE, Henri
"as in florence... " (tr. of Leonard Forest).   <u>PottPort</u> (2) 80, p.
    42.
"Au premier temps de la valse de l'eau.... " <u>PottPort</u> (1) 79-80,
    p. 12.
"Au second temps de la valse de l'eau.... " <u>PottPort</u> (1) 79-80,
    p. 12.
"Au troisieme temps.... " <u>PottPort</u> (1) 79-80, p. 12.
"beckoning... " (tr. of Leonard Forest). <u>PottPort</u> (2) 80-81, p.
    47.
"Future of a Country" (tr. of Phil Comeau). <u>PottPort</u> (2) 80, p.
    36.
"Untitled: Sometimes. " <u>PottPort</u> (1) 79-80, p. 29.
"Winterella. " <u>PottPort</u> (1) 79-80, p. 29.

PARINI, Jay
"As Would Seem Alone. " <u>SouthernR</u> (16:1) Wint 80, p. 133.
"Heartland Lake. " <u>SewanR</u> (88:4) Aut 80, p. 555.
"High Gannet. " <u>SewanR</u> (88:4) Aut 80, p. 554.
"The Hunters. " <u>YaleR</u> (70:1) Aut 80, p. 102.
"Ice Fishing. " <u>SewanR</u> (88:4) Aut 80, p. 555.
"In the Meadow. " <u>VirQR</u> (56:4) Aut 80, p. 671.
"Naming the Losses" (for Luke). Hudson (33:2) Sum 80, p. 228.
"Near Aberdeen. " <u>NewYorker</u> (55:50) 28 Ja 80, p. 101.
"1913. " <u>Hudson</u> (33:2) Sum 80, p. 227.
"Snake Hill. " <u>SouthernR</u> (16:1) Wint 80, p. 132.
"The Water Season. " <u>YaleR</u> (70:1) Aut 80, p. 101.
"Winter of the Dog. " <u>VirQR</u> (56:4) Aut 80, p. 672.
"Working the Face. " <u>SouthernR</u> (16:1) Wint 80, p. 134.

PARISH, Barbara Shirk
"Kansas Memoirs. " <u>PraS</u> (54:4) Wint 80-81, p. 40.
"Traveling Middle Class. " <u>SmPd</u> (49) Spr 80, p. 8.

PARKER, Naomi
"On Hearing Hugo" (for Peter Balakian). <u>Wind</u> (38) 80, p. 50.

PARLATORE, Anselm
"Coitus. " <u>AmerPoR</u> (9:3) My-Je 80, p. 38.
"Cunnilingus. " <u>AmerPoR</u> (9:3) My-Je 80, p. 38.
"Foreplay. " <u>AmerPoR</u> (9:3) My-Je 80, p. 38.
"Memory. " <u>AmerPoR</u> (9:3) My-Je 80, p. 38.
"Post-Coital Depression. " <u>AmerPoR</u> (9:3) My-Je 80, p. 38.

PARNOK, Sophia
Eight poems (tr. by Rima Shore). Cond (6) 80, p. 171.

PARRATT, Anne
"The Family Law Bill." PortR (26) 80, p. 22.
"My Sister." PortR (26) 80, p. 23.

PARRIS, Peggy
"Damn You Queen Elizabeth." Kayak (55) Ja 81, p. 12.
"How to Forget." Kayak (55) Ja 81, p. 13.
"London Descending." EnPas (10) 80, p. 11.
"Paris 1920." Kayak (55) Ja 81, p. 14.
"Ransom Note." Kayak (55) Ja 81, p. 16.
"To the Lady Who Fainted in the Luncheonette." Tendril (7/8)
    Spr-Sum 80, p. 57.

PASS, John
"An Apprehension." MalR (55) Jl 80, p. 145.

PASTAN, Linda
"A. M." GeoR (34:4) Wint 80, p. 827.
"Ethics." Tendril (9) 80, p. 121.
"Helen Bids Farewell to Her Daughter Hermione." Poetry (137:2)
    N 80, p. 77.
"Hippolyte at Breakfast." Poetry (137:2) N 80, p. 76.
"The Japanese Way." NewEngR (3:2) Wint 80, p. 170.
"Meditation by the Stove." Ploughs (6:2) 80, p. 48.
"P. M." GeoR (34:4) Wint 80, p. 826.
"Returning." Ploughs (6:2) 80, p. 47.
"What We Look at Last." MissouriR (4:1) Aut 80, p. 19.
"While You Slept." PoNow (27) 80, p. 5.
"Who Is It Accuses Us?" Harp (260:1560) My 80, p. 94.

PASTERNAK, Boris
"The Stars in Summer" (tr. by Mark Rudman and Bohdan Boy-
    chuk). PoNow (27) 80, p. 45.

PASTOR, Ricardo
from Cantico Traspasado: "Just Before Nothing, and Soon After
    Smoke" (tr. of Oscar Cerruto). GRR (11:1) 80, p. 27.
from Cantico Traspasado: "Surreptitious Person" (tr. of Oscar
    Cerruto). GRR (11:1) 80, p. 31.
from Cantico Traspasado: "Those Who End in the Night" (tr. of
    Oscar Cerruto). GRR (11:1) 80, p. 29.

PASTORI, Luis
"La Otra Magia." PortR (26) 80, p. 449.

PATEY-GRABOWSKA, Alicja
"Evil Ode" (tr. by Terry Kennedy). DenQ (15:1) Spr 80, p. 81.

PATNAIK, Deba P.
from Katak: (I, II, III, IV, V, VI). NewL (46:3) Spr 80, p. 116.

PATT, Richard
   "Maybe" (tr. of Osvaldo Ramous). NewOR (7:1) 80, p. 25.

PATTERSON, Raymond R.
   "What is it like." NewL (46:4) Sum 80, p. 52.

PATTON, Patti
   "December." StoneC (7:2) My 80, p. 8.
   "A Line." StoneC (7:2) My 80, p. 9.

PAUL, James
   "Abraham Wonders." ParisR (78) Sum 80, p. 196.
   "After the Explosion of the Year." PoetryNW (21:1) Spr 80, p.
      46.
   "Feet, a Sermon." Poetry (136:5) Ag 80, p. 280.
   "The Nine." ParisR (78) Sum 80, p. 195.
   "W. S. Paul." PoetryNW (21:1) Spr 80, p. 45.
   "The Water Tower." Poetry (136:5) Ag 80, p. 281.

PAUL, Jay S.
   "Fifteen Years Gone." StoneC (7:1) F 80, p. 35.

PAUL, Martin
   from Between the Carnation and the Sword: (7, 11) (tr. of
      Rafael Alberti w. José Elgorriaga). AmerPoR (9:5) S-O 80,
      p. 34.
   from Vertical Poetry: (6, 8) (tr. of Roberto Juarroz w. José
      Elgorriaga). AmerPoR (9:5) S-O 80, p. 34.

PAULIN, Tom
   "Ceremony on the Border." GRR (11:2/3) 80, p. 50.
   "Desert martin." GRR (11:2/3) 80, p. 49.

PAU-LLOSA, Ricardo
   "The Bell." BelPoJ (30:3) Spr 80, p. 15.
   "Conquistador." PoetC (12:2) 80, p. 26.
   "Gorilla: Meditations on a Zoologist." BelPoJ (30:3) Spr 80, p.
      16.
   "Icarus and Ariadne." BelPoJ (30:3) Spr 80, p. 16.
   "The Iceberg." BelPoJ (30:3) Spr 80, p. 17.

PAULY, Susan Mae
   "Cell Hall D." Prima (5) 79, p. 25.

PAVESE, Cesare
   "Death Agony" (tr. by William Arrowsmith). BosUJ (26:3) 80,
      p. 35.
   "Deola Thinking" (tr. by William Arrowsmith). BosUJ (26:3) 80,
      p. 34.
   "Morning" (tr. by William Arrowsmith). BosUJ (26:3) 80, p. 33.
   "The Old Drunk" (tr. by William Arrowsmith). BosUJ (26:3) 80,
      p. 38.
   "Sultry hands" (tr. by William Arrowsmith). BosUJ (26:3) 80,

p. 36.
"Women in Love" (tr. by William Arrowsmith). BosUJ (26:3)
80, p. 37.

PAVLICH, Walter
"Revisiting the Field. " PoNow (29) 80, p. 47.

PAVLIDES, Lefteris
"Body of Summer" (tr. of Odysseus Elytis w. Edward Morin and
Jana Hesser). CharR (6:2) Aut 80, p. 49.
"Drinking the Corinthian Sun" (tr. of Odysseus Elytis w. Edward
Morin and Jana Hesser). CharR (6:2) Aut 80, p. 50.
"No Longer Do I Know the Night" (tr. of Odysseus Elytis w.
Edward Morin and Jana Hesser). CharR (6:2) Aut 80, p.
50.

PAVLOVIC, Miodrag
"The Pilgrim's Return. " PortR (26) 80, p. 476.

PAVLOVSKI, Radovan
"Lightning's Widow. " PortR (26) 80, p. 464.
"Primal Lightning. " PortR (26) 80, p. 462.
"Two Roosters: Red and Black" (tr. by Bryce Conrad). CharR
(6:2) Aut 80, p. 56.
"The Youth Who Sleeps at Noon" (tr. by Bryce Conrad). CharR
(6:2) Aut 80, p. 57.

PAWLOWSKI, Robert
"A Drama of Significant Events. " SouthernHR (14:2) Spr 80, p.
140.
"Suicide. " SoCaR (13:1) Aut 80, p. 62.

PAYACK, Peter
"Possible Explanation for the Misunderstanding. " AndR (7:1)
Spr 80, p. 68.

PAYNE, John Burnett
"The Pansy of Sodom. " Mouth (2:5) O 80, p. 38.

PAYNE, Nina
"Lines for the Fisherman. " MassR (21:4) Wint 80, p. 783.
"Two Grandmothers" (for A. S.). MassR (21:4) Wint 80, p. 782.

PAZ, Octavio
from A Draft of Shadows: "Homage to Claudius Ptolemy" (tr. by
Eliot Weinberger). Ark (14) 80, p. 307.
from A Draft of Shadows: "In Defense of Pyrrho" (for Julian)
(tr. by Eliot Weinberger). Ark (14) 80, p. 308.
"Nocturne of Saint Ildefonso" (tr. by Betina Escudero). CutB
(14) Spr/Sum 80, pp. 18-27.

PEACOCK, Molly
"The Life of Leon Bonvin. " SouthernR (16:2) Spr 80, p. 420.

PEARLSON, Fredda S.
  "Nourishing the Darkness (fire sounds). " CentR (24:2) Spr 80, p.
    187.
  "Once Again the Light (first sounds). " CentR (24:2) Spr 80, p.
    188.
  "Traveling Light (space sounds). " CentR (24:2) Spr 80, p. 188.

PEARSON, Stephen
  "The Migration. " Stand (21:3) 80, p. 26.

PEASE, Deborah
  "Flight in Its True Aspect. " BelPoJ (31:1) Aut 80, p. 6.
  "Hard of Hearing. " LittleM (12:3/4) 80, p. 68.

PEASE, Roland
  "Tennis Together. " PoNow (28) 80, p. 32.

PECK, Gail
  "Last Granny Poem. " Wind (38) 80, p. 51.

PECK, John
  from Graduals: "The Altar. " Salm (50/51) Aut 80-Wint 81, p.
    19.
  from Graduals: "The Dream of Arthur. " Salm (50/51) Aut 80-
    Wint 81, p. 20.
  from Hours Near the Crossing: "A scrawl of vine across. "
    Pequod (11) 80, p. 3.
  "The Welder. " NewRep (182:3) 19 Ja 80, p. 38.

PECKENPAUGH, Angela
  "Begin With Music. " Pan (21) 80, p. 59.
  "Not a Clean Division. " CreamCR (5:1) Wint 79, p. 113.
  "Wake Up Charm for the Drugged Bride. " Wind (38) 80, p. 52.

PEDRICK, Jean
  "Patrick. " Aspect (76) S-D 79-80, p. 45.

PEHRSON, Peter
  "Lyrics for Clerks of Chic (Part Two). " Mouth (2:4) My 80, p.
    42.

PELLETIER, Cathie
  "The Wait. " NowestR (18:3) 80, p. 71.

PENNA, Sandro
  "The day I gave over to the earth" (tr. by W. S. DiPiero).
    PoNow (26) 80, p. 44.
  "False Spring" (tr. by W. S. DiPiero). PoNow (27) 80, p. 46.
  "The Father's Tomb" (tr. by W. S. DiPiero). PoNow (27) 80,
    p. 46.
  "In the city he looked almost" (tr. by W. S. DiPiero). PoNow
    (26) 80, p. 44.
  "School" (tr. by W. S. DiPiero). PoNow (27) 80, p. 46.

"September moon on the dark valley" (tr. by W. S. DiPiero).
PoNow (26) 80, p. 44.
"Tell me, you great dreaming trees" (tr. by W. S. DiPiero).
PoNow (26) 80, p. 44.
"Woman in a Streetcar" (tr. by W. S. DiPiero).   PoNow (27) 80,
p. 46.

PENNANT, Edmund
"Hold My Hand. " SewanR (88:4) Aut 80, p. 549.
"Negative. " SewanR (88:4) Aut 80, p. 548.

PENNER, Judith
"D. W. " PottPort (1) 79-80, p. 29.
"Untitled: I take my little boat--a shallop, say. " PottPort (1)
79-80, p. 22.
"Untitled: So much happens because I'm here. " PottPort (2) 80-
81, p. 21.

PENZAVECCHIA, James
"The River. " LittleM (12:3/4) 80, p. 33.

PERCHIK, Simon
"*:1 clam only the rim, its water. " Focus (14:88) S 80, p. 31.

PEREIRA, Sam
"Our Father of Hotels. " MissouriR (3:2) Wint 80, p. 31.

PERET, Benjamin
"Arm in Arm" (tr. by Keith Hollaman).   Durak (4) 80, p. 12.
"Badly Shaven" (tr. by Keith Hollaman).   Field (23) Aut 80, p.
27.
"Hello" (tr. by Keith Hollamen).   Field (23) Aut 80, p. 30.
"Nebulous" (tr. by Keith Hollaman).   Field (23) Aut 80, p. 29.
"One More One Less" (tr. by Keith Hollaman).   Durak (4) 80, p.
13.

PEREZ-DIOTIMA, Leigh
"Counterpoints. " BelPoJ (30:3) Spr 80, p. 24.
"Lake Walk at New Year's. " BelPoJ (30:3) Spr 80, p. 25.
"20th Century Amazon Poem. " BelPoJ (30:3) Spr 80, p. 24.

PERKINS, D. N.
"Bellyflopper. " HiramPoR (28) Spr-Sum 80, p. 27.
"Deep Currents. " GRR (11:1) 80, p. 20.
"I Went Sledding on the Moon. " PraS (54:3) Aut 80, p. 63.
"The November Road. " PraS (54:3) Aut 80, p. 62.
"Orpheus Wondering. " PraS (54:3) Aut 80, p. 61.
"Serpent. " HiramPoR (28) Spr-Sum 80, p. 27.

PERKINS, James Ashbrook
"Beckford Paley and His Underwoods. " GRR (11:1) 80, p. 64.

PERLIS, Alan
"The Man Who Ate Himself. " CarolQ (32:1) Wint 80, p. 73.

PERREAULT, George
"Hunger." SmPd (50) Aut 80, p. 31.

PERRICONE, Christopher
"A Pirate of Illusion on Canal Street." CalQ (16/17) 80, p. 160.

PERRIN, Byron
"events to be considered ... where banana leaves die in." Tele
(16) 80, p. 125.

PERRON, Lee
"We Pause to Look at 8 Falls." PoNow (26) 80, p. 43.

PERRY, Georgette
"On Reading the Cloud of Unknowing." SouthernHR (14:4) Aut 80,
p. 316.

PESEROFF, Joyce
"Approaching Absolute Zero." Tendril (9) 80, p. 122.
"Feeding the Fire." Ploughs (6:2) 80, p. 77.
"My Parent's House." Aspect (76) S-D 79-80, p. 27.
"The Red Rocker." Ploughs (6:2) 80, p. 76.
"While Reading John Clare at the Summer House." NewRep (182:
8) 23 F 80, p. 28.

PESKETT, William
"From Belfast to Suffolk." GRR (11:2/3) 80, p. 102.
"A Man and a Girl." GRR (11:2/3) 80, p. 103.
"Mouse." GRR (11:2/3) 80, p. 103.

PETERFREUND, Stuart
"A Counting." PoNow (28) 80, p. 43.

PETERS, Robert
Fifteen poems. PoNow (26) 80, p. 2, 38.
"Snapshots with Buck, Model-A Ford, and Kitchen." PoNow (27)
80, p. 40.

PETERSON, Geoff
"Big Sky." StoneC (7:2) My 80, p. 10.
"Tokyo Rose." Aspen (10) Wint 80, p. 55.

PETERSON, Jim
"Flat Tires." PoNow (29) 80, p. 34.
"Keys." SouthernPR (20:1) Spr 80, p. 71.
"The Water." CharR (6:2) Aut 80, p. 31.

PETERSON, Robert
"leaving taos." Kayak (53) My 80, p. 15.

PETH, Richard
"Breakfast." PoNow (29) 80, p. 34.

PETIC, Zorika
"gift. " Wind (38) 80, p. 11.

PETRIE, Paul
"Accident. " AmerS (49:2) Spr 80, p. 248.
"Feeding the Birds. " CentR (24:4) Aut 80, p. 453.
"The Room. " LitR (23:3) Spr 80, p. 344.
"The Stone. " LitR (23:3) Spr 80, p. 343.

PETROSKY, Tony
"The Other Life" (for Wilfredo Chiesa). GeoR (34:4) Wint 80, p.
  828.

PETTEE, Dan
"Lady. " CapeR (15:2) Sum 80, p. 38.

PETURSSON, Hannes
"Marie Antoinette. " PortR (26) 80, p. 188.

PEVEAR, Richard
"Picture and Book Remain. " Agni (13) 80, p. 38.
"Untitled: September mornings. " Agni (13) 80, p. 39.
"Untitled: The blue sky stung with stiff needles. " Agni (13) 80,
  p. 40.

PFEIFER, Mike
"Girl in the White Blouse. " CarolQ (32:1) Wint 80, p. 95.

PFINGSTON, Roger
"After the Blizzard. " Northeast (3:8) Wint 80, p. 23.
"Archivally Processed. " SlowLR (4) 80, p. 65.
"Poachers. " PoNow (27) 80, p. 20.
"The Soft Spot. " Northeast (3:8) Wint 80, p. 23.
"The White Mask. " SlowLR (4) 80, p. 66.

PHELAN, Mary M.
"At the Artificial Eye Office. " WebR (3:2) Aut 80, p. 79.

PHELPS, Dean
"Echoes. " NewL (47:1) Aut 80, p. 25.
"Two Days in Inishmore. " NewL (47:1) Aut 80, p. 24.

PHILBRICK, Stephen
"Leaving Here. " PoNow (26) 80, p. 13.
"No Father. " PoNow (28) 80, p. 17.
"To the Gray Man Who Gave Me a Ride on the Gray Day That
  My Father Died. " PoNow (27) 80, p. 39.

PHILIPOV, Vladimir
"Starway" (tr. of Lyubomir Levchev). PortR (26) 80, p. 51.

PHILIPPOU, Niki Ladaki
"The Virgin of the Steps" (tr. by author). PortR (26) 80, p. 62.

PHILLIPS, Dennis
"The Frontier: Part Five." <u>Bachy</u> (16) Wint 80, pp. 135-149.
"The Frontier: Part Five: Frontier, II--Conclusion." <u>Bachy</u>
    (17) Spr 80, pp. 70-78.

PHILLIPS, Dorrie
"Revival at the Laundromat." <u>PottPort</u> (1) 79-80, p. 23.
"3 A.M." <u>PottPort</u> (2) 80-81, p. 31.

PHILLIPS, Frances
"Breaking in New." <u>HangL</u> (37) Spr 80, p. 46.
"Harmonica." <u>HangL</u> (37) Spr 80, p. 45.
"Praire." <u>HangL</u> (37) Spr 80, p. 49.

PHILLIPS, Frank H.
"Desiderate." <u>StoneC</u> (7:1) F 80, p. 31.

PHILLIPS, Lisa
"Evening Song." <u>UTR</u> (6:3/4) 80, p. 52.
"Stormy Evening." <u>UTR</u> (6:3/4) 80, p. 53.

PHILLIPS, Louis
"Even the Beautiful Can Be Crazy." <u>PoetC</u> (12:1) 80, p. 30.
"I Don't Know What I Want to Do, but I Know I Don't Want to
    Do It." <u>KanQ</u> (12:1) Wint 80, p. 110.
"The Poster of the Mexican Dance Company." <u>Confr</u> (20) Spr-
    Sum 80, p. 40.

PHILLIPS, Max
"The Burning Girl." <u>PartR</u> (47:2) 80, p. 230.
"Variations on a Watercolor by Amy Jones." <u>PartR</u> (47:1) 80,
    p. 124.

PHILLIPS, Patricia
"An Educator's Wasteland." <u>EngJ</u> (69:5) My 80, p. 49.

PHILLIPS, Robert
"The Fenceless Gate" (for Michael Benedikt). <u>PoNow</u> (28) 80,
    p. 37.
"A Letter to Auden." <u>Shen</u> (31:2) 80, p. 13.
"Middle Age: A Nocturne." <u>NewYorker</u> (56:23) 28 Jl 80, p. 82.
"Milton Avery's "Sea Grasses and Blue Sea." <u>Shen</u> (31:2) 80, p.
    12.
"Once." <u>Hudson</u> (33:2) Sum 80, p. 223.
"Running on Empty." <u>Hudson</u> (33:2) Sum 80, p. 226.
"Snap. Crackle. Pop." <u>Hudson</u> (33:2) Sum 80, p. 224.
"Vertical and Horizontal." <u>Hudson</u> (33:2) Sum 80, p. 225.

PHOCAS, Nikos
"Chamber Music." <u>PortR</u> (26) 80, p. 162.
"The Diver" (tr. by Kimon Friar). <u>PoNow</u> (27) 80, p. 44.

PICANO, Felice
"Gym Shorts." <u>PoNow</u> (26) 80, p. 26.

"The Hanged Man. " PoNow (26) 80, p. 26.
"Words for Conrad Aiken. " PoNow (26) 80, p. 26.

PICKETT, Thomas P.
  "Egg Poem. " SoCaR (13:1) Aut 80, p. 73.
  "Hunting the End. " SoCaR (13:1) Aut 80, p. 72.

PICKETT, Tom
  "At the Grave" (for Lewis Cole). Sam (101) 80, p. 61.

PIERCE, D. C.
  "Stonehammer. " MalR (53) Ja 80, pp. 94-100.

PIERCE, Edith Lovejoy
  "The Mill Wheel. " ChrC (97:28) 10-17 S 80, p. 837.
  "On the Shooting of Archbishop Romero. " ChrC (97:14) 16 Ap
    80, p. 437.

PIERCY, Marge
  "Cutting the Grapes Free. " OP (29) Spr 80, p. 22.
  "Dirty Poem. " Aspect (76) S-D 79-80, p. 52.
  "In Memoriam Walter and Lillian Lowenfels. " Ark (14) 80, p.
    309.
  "The Man Who Is Leaving. " OP (30) Aut 80, p. 50.
  "The Moon Is Always Female. " OP (29) Spr 80, p. 18.
  "Neurotic in July. " Ark (14) 80, p. 311.
  "Night Fight. " Tendril (9) 80, p. 123.
  "Ragged Ending. " Ploughs (6:2) 80, p. 101.
  "Snow, Snow. " OP (30) Aut 80, p. 55.
  "Three Losers' Poems" (for I. W.). OP (30) Aut 80, p. 52.
  "Touch. " PoNow (26) 80, p. 6.
  "Two Peach Trees. " PoNow (26) 80, p. 6.
  "Waking Every Night at 3 A. M. " OP (30) Aut 80, p. 49.
  "When a friend dies. " PoNow (28) 80, p. 27.
  "Will we work together?" PoNow (28) 80, p. 27.
  "The world comes back, like an old cat. " Aspect (76) S-D 79-80,
    p. 51.
  "Wrong Monday. " Aspect (76) S-D 79-80, p. 52.

PIERSON, Philip
  "Blues for St. Christopher. " QW (10) Wint-Spr 80, p. 32.

PIJEWSKI, John
  "Babcia. " CentR (24:2) Spr 80, p. 190.
  "The Labor Camp. " CentR (24:2) Spr 80, p. 189.

PILBEAM, Allen
  "Mary, Picking Daisies. " PikeF (3) Wint 80, p. 28.

PILLIN, William
  "All of My Cities. " Durak (4) 80, p. 42.
  "Black Rain. " Durak (4) 80, p. 38.
  "The Blue Candle. " Durak (4) 80, p. 40.

"Canzone for My Grandmother. " Durak (4) 80, p. 39.
"Diminuendo. " Durak (4) 80, p. 37.
"History. " Durak (4) 80, p. 41.
"Holy Beggars. " Durak (4) 80, p. 36.
Twelve poems. Bachy (16) Wint 80, pp. 12-19.

PINKAVA, Václav
"Invocation. " PartR (47:1) 80, p. 118.
"A Memory. " PartR (47:1) 80, p. 118.
"Midnight Magic. " PartR (47:1) 80, p. 119.
"A Nostalgic Swim. " PartR (47:1) 80, p. 119.

PINSKER, Sanford
"At the Garage. " KanQ (12:1) Wint 80, p. 139.
"Figuring Out the Hopi. " ConcPo (13:2) Aut 80, p. 52.
"The Fulbright Poem at the End of the Mind. " CEACritic (43:1)
     N 80, p. 40.
"Night Hawks. " PoNow (27) 80, p. 35.
"On Hot, August Days. " PoNow (26) 80, p. 30.
"Shipping Costs. " CEACritic (43:1) N 80, p. 40.

PINSKY, Robert
"Dying. " Poetry (136:4) Jl 80, p. 206.
"The Living. " YaleR (70:1) Aut 80, p. 97.
"Ralegh's Prizes. " NewYorker (56:29) 8 S 80, p. 34.
"Tennis" (to Howard Wilcox). Tendril (9) 80, p. 124.

PISTORIUS, Nancy Sue
"Cockroach. " Pig (7) My 80, p. 54.

PITKIN, Anne
"July Evening, La Push, Washington" (for Emily and Paul).
     WatT (1) Aut 80, p. 48.

PITNER, Erin Clayton
"For a Friend Dying. " CapeR (16:1) Wint 80, p. 38.

PLANTIER, John
"He Carries Water Uphill. " StoneC (7:3) D 80, p. 21.
"Recording. " StoneC (7:3) D 80, p. 21.

PLIMPTON, Sarah
"Windows of blue. " DenQ (15:2) Sum 80, pp. 45-49.

PLUMLY, Stanley
"Chinese Tallow. " OhioR (25) 80, p. 32.
"Dark All Afternoon" (for Laura Jensen). Ploughs (6:2) 80, p.
     17.
"Fifth and 94th. " NewYorker (56:1) 25 F 80, p. 120.
"Ground Birds in Open Country. " AmerPoR (9:2) Mr-Ap 80, p.
     15.
"The Missionary Position. " NewYorker (56:15) 2 Je 80, p. 133.
"Snowing, Sometimes. " GeoR (34:4) Wint 80, p. 752.

"Summer Celestial." Tendril (9) 80, p. 127.
"Virginia Beach." AmerPoR (9:2) Mr-Ap 80, p. 15.

PLUMPP, Sterling D.
   "For Paul Robeson." Obs (5:3) Wint 79, p. 83.
   "For Richard Wright." Obs (5:3) Wint 79, p. 84.
   "I Hear the Shuffle of the People's Feet." Obs (5:3) Wint 79,
      pp. 75-82.
   "Time." BlackALF (14:4) Wint 80, p. 172.

POBO, Kenneth
   "Cricket Killings." CreamCR (5:1) Wint 79, p. 17.
   "Studio Apartment." CapeR (15:2) Sum 80, p. 16.
   "The Villa Park Argus." WindO (36) Spr-Sum 80, p. 39.

POLACKOVA-HENLEY, Kaca
   "Death" (tr. of Vladimir Holan). Nat (230:20) 24 My 80, p.
      633.

POLAN, James
   "Dialogue before a Wall of Masks at the Museum" (w. Michelle
      Zeff). Nimrod (24:1) Aut-Wint 80, p. 107.

POLETTE, Keith
   "Cinders and Wings" (for Patty). Sam (92) 80, p. 60.

POLGAR, Steven
   "Clouded Sky" (tr. of Miklos Radnoti w. Stephen Berg and S. J.
      Marks). PoetryE (1) 80, p. 76.
   "A Letter to My Wife" (tr. of Miklos Radnoti w. Stephen Berg
      and S. J. Marks). PoetryE (1) 80, p. 78.
   "Waiting" (tr. of Sandor Csoori). AmerPoR (9:4) Jl-Ag 80, p.
      42.

POLING, Wm.
   "The Fat Magician Suffers Misfortune of an Indeterminate Na-
      ture." HiramPoR (28) Spr-Sum 80, p. 28.

POLK, Noel
   "Wreck." SouthernR (16:1) Wint 80, p. 164.

POLLAK, Felix
   "Astigmatism." BelPoJ (30:3) Spr 80, p. 9.
   "basta" (tr. of Karl Krolow). Kayak (53) My 80, p. 50.
   "The Counselor." NewL (46:4) Sum 80, p. 104.
   "Early to Bed." PoNow (26) 80, p. 35.
   "I advance the clock" (tr. of Karl Krolow). Kayak (53) My 80,
      p. 50.
   "I will walk along the river" (tr. of Karl Krolow). Kayak (53)
      My 80, p. 48.
   "The Man in the Blue Suit." BelPoJ (30:3) Spr 80, p. 10.
   "A Plea of Guilty." BelPoJ (30:3) Spr 80, p. 7.
   "rain" (tr. of Karl Krolow). Kayak (53) My 80, p. 49.

"scrabble. " Kayak (54) S 80, p. 23.
"some things remain" (tr. of Karl Krolow). Kayak (53) My 80,
      p. 49.

POLLENS, David
      "Clearing the Yard. " NewYorker (56:2) 3 Mr 80, p. 36.

POLLITT, Katha
      "Chinese Finches. " Shen (31:2) 80, p. 75.
      "Of the Scythians. " ParisR (78) Sum 80, p. 201.
      "Sea Grasses. " Poetry (137:1) O 80, p. 38.
      "Seal Rock. " ParisR (77) Wint-Spr 80, p. 42.
      "Wild Escapes. " ParisR (77) Wint-Spr 80, p. 43.
      "Woman Asleep on a Banana Leaf. " Nat (230:14) 12 Ap 80, p.
      442.

POLLOCK, David Scott
      "Back in the Armchair Again. " Vis (1) 79.
      "Praying Mantis. " Vis (1) 79.

PONGE, Francis
      "The End of Fall" (tr. by Robert Bly). OhioR (24) 80, p. 58.

PONSOT, Marie
      "For John Keats, on the sense of his biography. " OP (30) Aut
      80, p. 30.
      "Residual Paralysis" (for June Jordan). LittleM (12:3/4) 80, p.
      98.

POPE, Deborah
      "There Is Something. " OhioR (24) 80, p. 28.
      "The Victim Utters a Warning. " HiramPoR (28) Spr-Sum 80, p.
      29.

PORRITT, Ruth
      "Chicken. " CropD (2/3) Aut-Wint 80, p. 15.

PORTER, Anne
      "Four Poems in One. " Comm (107:20) 7 N 80, p. 628.

PORTER, Helen
      "Middle-Aged Radical at a Poetry Reading. " PottPort (2) 80-81,
      p. 10.

PORTER, Mary
      "The Grass Wouldn't Thaw. " EnPas (11) 80, p. 14.

POSNER, David
      "Egret. " NewYorker (56:5) 24 Mr 80, p. 42.

POSTER, Carol
      "L'éclipse" (tr. of Jacques Prévert). LitR (23:3) Spr 80, p.
      401.

"Excess. " Outbr (4/5) Aut 79-Spr 80, p. 88.
"Lazarus. " LitR (23:3) Spr 80, p. 355.
"Le lézard" (tr. of Jacques Prévert). LitR (23:3) Spr 80, p. 401.
"Limits. " Outbr (4/5) Aut 79-Spr 80, p. 89.
"Meanings. " Outbr (4/5) Aut 79-Spr 80, p. 90.

POWELL, Enid Levinger
"Pinwheel. " FourQt (29:4) Sum 80, p. 33.

POWELL, Joe
"Small Houses. " SouthernPR (20:2) Aut 80, p. 67.

POWELL, Mary
"The Astrologer. " Tele (16) 80, p. 72.
"Missing Person. " Tele (16) 80, p. 73.

POWELL, Nancy
"At Seabreeze Campground. " SouthernPR (20:1) Spr 80, p. 63.

POWER, Kevin
from Rückenwind and Zaubersprüche: Ten poems (tr. of Sarah Kirsch w. Helmbrecht Breinig). Bound (8:3) Spr 80, pp. 191-197.

POWERS, Jack
"Frontier. " Sam (98) 80, p. 49.
"Hobo, from Boston, West. " Sam (101) 80, p. 66.
"If I Had a Million. " Sam (98) 80, p. 48.
"Seven Turns of a Cylinder. " Sam (102) 80, p. 50.

POWERS, Jessica
"Cancer Patient. " Comm (107:12) 20 Je 80, p. 367.

POYNER, Ken
"Deciding on Children. " Wind (37) 80, p. 47.
"The First Murder of Ponce de Leon. " PoetC (12:3) 80, p. 20.
"Frankenstein. " PoNow (29) 80, p. 34.
"Humility. " CropD (2/3) Aut-Wint 80, p. 38.
"The Morticians' Convention. " CropD (2/3) Aut-Wint 80, p. 38.
"The Surrender. " PoetC (12:3) 80, p. 20.

PRADO, Holly
"After Struggling with the Mystery of It All. " Bachy (16) Wint 80, p. 75.
"By Seasonal Odor. " Bachy (16) Wint 80, p. 74.
"The Face It Will Have Later. " Bachy (16) Wint 80, p. 74.
"Nothing Is Closed Except All the Doors" (for the poems of H. D.). Bachy (16) Wint 80, p. 76.
"Shell. " Bachy (16) Wint 80, p. 76.
"The Wind the Question of What It Will Do Next. " Bachy (16) Wint 80, p. 76.

PRATT, Charles
"Approach. " HiramPoR (27) Aut-Wint 80, p. 41.
"Jonah. " LitR (23:3) Spr 80, p. 406.
"Leaves. " HiramPoR (27) Aut-Wint 80, p. 42.

PRATT, Minnie Bruce
"The Sound of One Fork. " Cond (6) 80, p. 22.

PRECIOUS, Jocelyn
"If. " Sam (101) 80, p. 31.

PRESTRIDGE, Sam
"Dawn. " SlowLR (4) 80, p. 78.
"Guitar Lesson" (for Nadell). SlowLR (4) 80, p. 76.
"Proving the Existence of Sorrow" (for Joycelyn). SlowR (4) 80,
    p. 77.
"A Walk After Work. " SlowLR (4) 80, p. 75.

PREVERT, Jacques
"L'éclipse" (tr. by Carol Poster). LitR (23:3) Spr 80, p. 401.
"Le lézard" (tr. by Carol Poster). LitR (23:3) Spr 80, p. 401.

PRICE, Alice
"Hawks Stay Alive" (w. Francine Ringold). Nimrod (24:1) Aut-
    Wint 80, p. 109.
"Landscape of the Dancer. " Comm (107:15) 29 Ag 80, p. 468.
"Spiritus" (w. Ann Weisman). Nimrod (24:1) Aut-Wint 80, p.
    110.

PRICE, Curmie
Nine Poems. Obs (5:1/2) Spr-Sum 79, pp. 123-129.

PRICE, Reynolds
"Two Mysteries. " OntR (13) Aut-Wint 80-81, pp. 27-31.

PRIVETT, Katharine
"Choosing. " CapeR (16:1) Wint 80, p. 17.
"Edith Piaf. " CapeR (15:2) Sum 80, p. 40.
"Eulogy for Alice Paul. " WebR (5:2) Aut 80, p. 81.
"The Sleepwalker. " CapeR (16:1) Wint 80, p. 16.
"Stonehenge and All That. " CapeR (16:1) Wint 80, p. 17.
"Through Stained Glass. " WebR (5:2) Aut 80, p. 80.

PROCTOR, James W.
"The Long Intimacy. " Wind (37) 80, p. 43.

PROTHO, Nancy
"Late Spring. " Shen (31:2) 80, p. 78.

PRUNTY, Wyatt
"Incision to a Dialogue. " SouthwR (65:3) Sum 80, p. 291.
"Seining the Blue. " Pequod (11) 80, p. 64.

PURDUM, Gene
  "The Entrepreneur." LitR (23:3) Spr 80, p. 388.

PURENS, Ilmars
  "Blue China. " Epoch (29:3) Spr-Sum 80, p. 241.

PUSHKIN, Aleksandr
  "Elegy" (tr. by Robley Wilson Jr.). CutB (14) Spr /Sum 80, p.
  100.

PUZISS, Marta
  "In the Egyptian Room. " Vis (4) 80.
  "Night Flying. " Vis (2) 80.
  "Solstice. " Vis (1) 79.
  'To My Father, Walking. " Vis (1) 79.

PYE, Deborah
  "Salvagings. " Tendril (7 /8) Spr-Sum 80, p. 58.

QUADERER, Hansjörg
  "Stein und Stein. " PortR (26) 80, p. 260.

QUARTEY, Rex
  "A Yoke of Curses. " PortR (26) 80, p. 150.

QUASIMODO, Salvatore
  "Going Back" (tr. by Rina Ferrarelli). WebR (5:1) Wint 80, p.
  16.

QUEEN, J.
  "The Part of the Bed You Sleep On. " PottPort (1) 79, p. 34.

QUERTERMOUS, Max
  "Penelope, Clytemnestra. " SouthernHR (14:2) Spr 80, p. 127.

QUICK, Joyce
  "Acceptance Address; A Dream. " PoetryNW (21:2) Sum 80, p.
  15.

QUINN, Eileen Moore
  "Lunacy. " SmPd (50) Aut 80, p. 16.

QUINN, Fran
  'The cataract. " NewL (46:4) Sum 80, p. 53.

QUINN, John
  "Things I Didn't Tell Madjid. " ThRiPo (15 /16) 80, p. 43.

QUINN, John Robert
  "Dandelion Wine. " PoNow (28) 80, p. 39.

QUINOT, Raymond
  "Vous ne l'emporterez pas avec vous. " PortR (26) 80, p. 43.

QUINTANA, Leroy V.
"Jose Mentiras Was Saying. " ConcPo (13:2) Aut 80, p. 95.
"Walking Backwards" (para Jeff Trujillo). ConcPo (13:2) Aut 80,
      p. 95.

QUIXLEY, Jim
"I Can't Stand It. " Mouth (2:4) My 80, p. 26.

RAAB, Lawrence
"Valediction. " AmerS (49:3) Sum 80, p. 368.

RABBITT, Thomas
"Cemetery Art. " Shen (31:1) 79, p. 35.
"Gargoyle. " Shen (31:1) 79, p. 35.
"Weathercock. " Shen (31:1) 79, p. 34.

RABONI, Giovanni
"Keys for an Unwritten Poem" (tr. by Vinio Rossi and Stuart
      Friebert). CutB (14) Spr /Sum 80, p. 50.
"One Time" (tr. by Vinio Rossi and Stuart Friebert). CutB (14)
      Spr /Sum 80, p. 52.
"Woman's Song" (tr. by Vinio Rossi and Stuart Friebert). CutB
      (14) Spr /Sum 80, p. 51.

RACHEL, Naomi
"after the suicide of a close friend" (for dale). Wind (38) 80,
      p. 54.
"elegy. " Wind (38) 80, p. 54.
"Its Echo. " Outbr (4 /5) Aut 79-Spr 80, p. 63.
"where they wait. " Wind (38) 80, p. 54.

RACINE, Jean
"Andromaque. " Poetry (136:1) Ap 80, p. 30.

RADIN, Doris
"Song. " Confr (20) Spr-Sum 80, p. 137.

RADNOTI, Miklós
"Childhood" (for Dezso Baroti) (tr. by Emery George). QW (10)
      Wint-Spr 80, p. 77.
"Clouded Sky" (tr. by Steven Polgar, Stephen Berg, and S. J.
      Marks). PoetryE (1) 80, p. 77.
"Dusk on the Bank and the Tugboat Cries" (tr. by Emery
      George). PoetryE (1) 80, p. 74.
"Evening in the Garden" (tr. by Emery George). Columbia (4)
      Spr-Sum 80, p. 28.
"Forgiveness" (tr. by Emery George). PartR (47:4) 80, p. 609.
"Goats" (tr. by Emery George). Columbia (4) Spr-Sum 80, p.
      31.
"Into a Contemporary's Passport" (for the Szeged Youth Arts
      College, for the community of educators, for my friends)
      (tr. by Emery George). QW (10) Wint-Spr 80, p. 78.
"A Letter to My Wife" (tr. by Steven Polgar, Stephen Berg, and

S. J. Marks). PoetryE (1) 80, p. 79.
"May Truth" (tr. by Emery George). PartR (47:4) 80, p. 609.
"Punctual Poem About Dusk" (tr. by Emery George). Columbia
    (4) Spr-Sum 80, p. 29.
"Razglednica" (tr. by Steven Kovács). DenQ (15:1) Spr 80, p.
    79.
"Salute the Day!" (tr. by Emery George). PoetryE (1) 80, p.
    75.
"Twenty eight Years" (tr. by Jascha Kessler). NewL (47:1) Aut
    80, p. 56.
"Variation on Sadness" (tr. by Emery George). PartR (47:4) 80,

RADTKE, Rosetta
"How Peter First Saw the Birds. " Northeast (3:8) Wint 80, p.
    27.
"Winter Room. " Northeast (3:8) Wint 80, p. 28.

RAE, Mildred Baird
"Disconcerte. " PottPort (1) 79-80, p. 21.

RAFFA, Joseph
"A Lovely Face Suggests Suicide. " Pan (21) 80, p. 54.

RAFFEL, Burton
"Girl: A Marine Portrait. " Pan (21) 80, p. 21.
"On Interpreting Milton. " Pan (21) 80, p. 23.
"Visiting America. " Pan (21) 80, p. 22.

RAHMANN, Pat
"Last Trip Together. " KanQ (12:3) Sum 80, p. 86.

RAIL, De Wayne
"Implications of August. " PoNow (26) 80, p. 30.

RAINE, Kathleen
"Short Poems. " Ark (14) 80, pp. 313-318.

RAISOR, Philip
"Basic Biology. " SouthernR (16:1) Wint 80, p. 172.
"Basic Physics. " SouthernR (16:1) Wint 80, p. 171.
"Demolition. " SouthernR (16:1) Wint 80, p. 170.

RAIZISS, Sonia
"Challenger at Sunset. " PoNow (27) 80, p. 8.
"fathers. " PoNow (26) 80, p. 26.
"first rooster. " PoNow (26) 80, p. 26.
"parents. " PoNow (26) 80, p. 26.

RAKOSI, Carl
"Manhattan" (for Rexroth). Ark (14) 80, pp. 319-325.

RALSTON, Miriam
"Notice Upon Your Arrival. " Wind (37) 80, p. 44.

RAMANUJAN, A. K.
  Fifteen poems. CarlMis (18:2) Sum 80, pp. 64, 117-123.

RAMKE, Bin
  "Parabolic. " GeoR (34:4) Wint 80, p. 734.
  "Projection: Milk and Memory. " GeoR (34:3) Aut 80, p. 658.
  "Rose Hill Shopping Center. " SouthernR (16:4) Aut 80, pp. 921-
     931.

RAMOUS, Osvaldo
  "Maybe" (tr. by Richard Patt). NewOR (7:1) 80, p. 25.

RAMSEY, Jarold
  "First Morning in Oregon. " PoNow (26) 80, p. 19.
  "Hunting Arrowheads. " WestHR (34:3) Sum 80, p. 233.
  "A Letter from Uganda, 1978. " PoetryNW (21:1) Spr 80, p. 31.
  "The Spring Witch. " ConcPo (13:2) Aut 80, p. 13.
  "Volo Ut Sis. " GeoR (34:2) Sum 80, p. 302.

RAMSEY, Paul
  "For Allen Tate. " MichQR (19:2) Spr 80, p. 227.
  "Spokesmen. " MichQR (19:2) Spr 80, p. 228.

RANAN, Wendy
  "Boundaries. " Aspect (76) S-D 79-80, p. 46.
  "Evolution. " Aspect (76) S-D 79-80, p. 46.

RANASINGHE, Anne
  "At What Dark Point. " PortR (26) 80, p. 350.
  "Comment on a Review of an Exhibition of Graphics from the
     G. D. R. " PortR (26) 80, p. 352.

RANDALL, Virginia
  "A Dead Man" (to Rafael Morales) (tr. of Vicente Aleixandre w.
     Maureen Ahern). DenQ (15:3) Aut 80, p. 18.
  "My Night" (tr. of Vicente Aleixandre w. Maureen Ahern).
     DenQ (15:3) Aut 80, p. 20.
  "No Star" (tr. of Vicente Aleixandre w. Maureen Ahern). DenQ
     (15:3) Aut 80, p. 19.

RANDICH, Jean
  "Heart Work. " NewL (46:3) Spr 80, p. 91.

RANKIN, Jennifer J.
  "Dinner with a Friend. " AmerPoR (9:2) Mr-Ap 80, p. 34.
  "October Poem. " AmerPoR (9:2) Mr-Ap 80, p. 35.
  "This Is How It Happens. " OntR (12) Spr-Sum 80, p. 51.

RANKIN, Paula
  "The Dream in Which the Bed Is an Automobile. " KanQ (12:1)
     Wint 80, p. 52.
  "For My Mother, Feeling Useless. " QW (10) Wint-Spr 80, p.
     29.

"Getaway Lines. " ThRiPo (15/16) 80, p. 44.
"The Hypochondriac. " PoNow (26) 80, p. 32.
"Tending. " QW (10) Wint-Spr 80, p. 31.
"Webs. " MissouriR (3:3) Sum 80, p. 31.
"The Woman Who Built Her House on the Sand. " NewOR (7:2)
    80, p. 141.
"Working Third Shift. " PoNow (26) 80, p. 32.

RANKIN, Robert J.
"as a child. " SmPd (49) Spr 80, p. 9.
"at the Y. " SmPd (49) Spr 80, p. 11.
"christmas morning. " SmPd (48) Wint 80, p. 13.
"coffee and buns. " SmPd (49) Spr 80, p. 12.
"Emmanuel dies at 31. " SmPd (49) Spr 80, p. 13.
"on the assembly line. " SmPd (49) Spr 80, p. 10.
"a stone speaks. " PikeF (3) Wint 80, p. 8.

RANNIT, Aleksis
"Maillol. " PortR (26) 80, p. 110.

RANSOM, Candice F.
"September Solstice. " CropD (1) Spr 80, p. 18.

RAPHAEL, Dan
"Lie Northerner. " Tele (16) 80, p. 36.
"men who live w/ marines. " Tele (16) 80, p. 37.

RAS, Barbara
"Fever. " CarlMis (18:2) Sum 80, p. 81.
"On the New Year" (for E. W. and P. J.). CarlMis (18:2) Sum
    80, p. 80.
"Passings. " CarlMis (18:2) Sum 80, p. 79.

RASMUSSEN, Halfdan
"The Goose Invited All the Pigs" (tr. by Marilyn Nelson Waniek
    w. Pamela Lee Espeland). CarlMis (18:2) Sum 80, p. 5.
"Little Cloud" (tr. by Marilyn Nelson Waniek w. Pamela Lee
    Espeland). CarlMis (18:2) Sum 80, p. 5.
"Poor Old Blue Monday" (tr. by Marilyn Nelson Waniek w.
    Pamela Lee Espeland). CarlMis (18:2) Sum 80, p. 6.
"The Winter's Cold in Norway" (tr. by Marilyn Nelson Waniek w.
    Pamela Lee Espeland). CarlMis (18:2) Sum 80, p. 5.

RASNIC, Ruth
"The Inner Land" (tr. of Moshe Dor). PortR (26) 80, p. 199.

RASOF, Henry
"An Apocrypha. " PartR (47:1) 80, p. 126.

RATH, Paula
"... For My Daughters. " BelPoJ (30:3) Spr 80, p. 14.

RATNER, Rochelle
"Lady Pinball 35. " Tele (16) 80, p. 34.

"Lady Pinball 43. " PoNow (28) 80, p. 7.
"Lady Pinball 50. " Tele (16) 80, p. 34.
"Lady Pinball 62: The Father." PoNow (28) 80, p. 7.
"A Someday Song for Sophia. " Tendril (9) 80, p. 129.

RATTI, John
    "Metaphor. " HangL (37) Spr 80, p. 52.
    "One Winter Night Many Years Ago. " HangL (37) Spr 80, p. 51.
    "White Turnips. " HangL (37) Spr 80, p. 50.

RAWLINS, Sue
    "I Put in for Transfer. " PoetryNW (21:4) Wint 80-81, p. 38.
    "The Witch Pretends No Magic. " PoetryNW (21:4) Wint 80-81,
        p. 39.

RAY, David
    "After Chiyo. " Ark (14) 80, p. 326.
    "The Barber. " PoNow (28) 80, p. 27.
    "Baskin's Wooden Angel. " Ascent (5:2) 80, p. 17.
    "The Bellini in the Corner. " CharR (6:1) Spr 80, p. 21.
    "Cozumel Harbor. " Ark (14) 80, p. 328.
    "De Mortuis. " Ark (14) 80, p. 329.
    "The Farm in Calabria. " PoNow (28) 80, p. 12.
    The Farm in Calabria. Spirit (5:1/2) Aut-Wint 79-80, pp. 39-
        64.
    "The Father of the Curious Child. " DacTerr (17) 80, p. 66.
    "In Tornado Country. " Harp (260:1557) F 80, p. 92.
    "The Last Class. " QW (11) Aut-Wint 80-81, p. 60.
    "The Matter of Social Life. " NewYorker (56:12) 12 My 80, p.
        141.
    "Notes to an Anthology" (for J. L.). PoNow (28) 80, p. 13.
    "An Old Woodcut. " CharR (6:1) Spr 80, p. 22.
    "Snapshots. " PoNow (28) 80, p. 27.
    "Take Me Back to Tulsa. " PoNow (28) 80, p. 27.
    "Thanks, Robert Frost. " Tendril (9) 80, p. 130.
    "The Tourists at Uxmal. " PoNow (27) 80, p. 33.
    "A Winter Scene. " MissouriR (4:1) Aut 80, p. 18.

RAY, Judy
    "The Belly Dance Class. " PoNow (29) 80, p. 28.
    "Flamingoes. " PoNow (29) 80, p. 28.
    "The Pebble Ring" (for David). PoNow (29) 80, p. 28.
    "Written on My Father's 86th Birthday." DacTerr (17) 80, p.
        67.

RAY, Robert Beverly
    "The Logic of August. " Poetry (136:5) Ag 80, p. 249.
    "Morning Music. " Poetry (136:5) Ag 80, p. 252.
    "Pronunciamientos from the Guest House. " Poetry (136:5) Ag
        80, p. 256.
    "Translations from an Imaginary Poet. " Poetry (136:5) Ag 80,
        p. 258.

RAY, Shrule
"The Gang of Saints. " Focus (14:88) S 80, p. 31.

RAZLER, Marion
"Pieces of a Country Childhood. " EngJ (69:5) My 80, p. 53.

REA, Susan Irene
"Hare's Hill Pond. " CalQ (16/17) 80, p. 127.
"Orchids. " FourQt (30:1) Aut 80, p. 19.

REA, Tom
"April. " PoNow (26) 80, p. 47.

READ, Elfreida
"Emily. " MalR (56) O 80, p. 138.

REARDON, Patrick
"A Certain Way. " CapeR (15:2) Sum 80, p. 20.
"Fly's Weight. " CapeR (15:2) Sum 80, p. 20.

RECTOR, Liam
"Laurence Harvey. " NewL (46:4) Sum 80, p. 97.
"My Drink Is Interrupted" (for James Haft). CreamCR (5:1)
      Wint 79, p. 116.
"Ralph Watches. " PoetryNW (21:1) Spr 80, p. 36.
"Saxophone. " Kayak (53) My 80, p. 46.

REDGROVE, Peter
"To the Postmaster General. " AmerS (49:3) Sum 80, p. 300.

REDMOND, Chris
"An Attempt at Flirting. " ConcPo (12:2) Aut 79, p. 72.

REED, Jeremy
"the abominable. " Kayak (55) Ja 81, p. 32.
"beyond the wall. " Kayak (55) Ja 81, p. 31.
"black opium. " Kayak (55) Ja 81, p. 30.
"Home. " Kayak (55) Ja 81, p. 33.
"A Moment's Hesitation. " PartR (47:2) 80, p. 220.

REED, John R.
"GM Tech Center. " MichQR (19:4/20:1) Aut-Wint 80-81, p. 703.
"Morning. " NewRena (13) Aut 80, p. 98.

REED, Thomas
"The Ant Polo Players. " Outbr (4/5) Aut 79-Spr 80, p. 73.
"The Indian. " Outbr (4/5) Aut 79-Spr 80, p. 74.
"The Snow-Wife. " Outbr (4/5) Aut 79-Spr 80, p. 72.

REED, Tom
"The Concealed Weapon. " Tele (16) 80, p. 109.

REES, William H. H.
"(e. g. , collecting baseball cards: the champions of '66. "

SmPd (50) Aut 80, p. 17.

REEVE, F. D.
"The Interment of Christ." AmerPoR (9:5) S-O 80, p. 35.
"A Pair of Gloves." YaleR (70:1) Aut 80, p. 99.
"The Tempest." AmerPoR (9:5) S-O 80, p. 35.
"View Over Soho, Lower Manhattan." AmerPoR (9:5) S-O 80,
     p. 35.

REIBSTEIN, Regina
"Mother and Child." CarlMis (18:2) Sum 80, p. 172.
"My Father Left." Wind (37) 80, p. 45.

REICH, Heather Tosteson
"Carl's Game." BelPoJ (30:3) Spr 80, p. 2.
"Cutting the Mustard." SmPd (48) Wint 80, p. 6.
"Flux." Wind (38) 80, p. 56.
"Marjoram Trusts in Percentages." SmPd (48) Wint 80, p. 6.
"Prudence Plays Skittles." BelPoJ (30:3) Spr 80, p. 3.
"Tarragon." SmPd (48) Wint 80, p. 5.

REID, Alastair
"At Last There Is No One" (tr. of Pablo Neruda). NewYorker
     (56:27) 25 Ag 80, p. 35.
"Exile" (tr. of Pablo Neruda). NewYorker (56:27) 25 Ag 80, p.
     34.
"Father" (tr. of Pablo Neruda). NewYorker (56:27) 25 Ag 80, p.
     34.
"Houses" (tr. of Heberto Padilla). NewYRB (27:13) 14 Ag 80,
     p. 21.
"Note" (tr. of Heberto Padilla). NewYRB (27:13) 14 Ag 80, p.
     21.
"The River Born in the Cordilleras" (tr. of Pablo Neruda).
     NewYorker (56:27) 25 Ag 80, p. 34.
"Sex" (tr. of Pablo Neruda). NewYorker (56:31) 22 S 80, p. 56.

REID, Colin
"Changeling." SewanR (88:4) Aut 80, p. 552.

REID, Monty
"Letter." MalR (54) Ap 80, p. 130.
"The Rock Tumbler." MalR (54) Ap 80, p. 131.

REID, P. C.
"&, ". WebR (5:1) Wint 80, p. 59.

REILLY, Robert T.
"Children, Don't Answer." ChrC (97:18) 14 My 80, p. 551.

REINERT, Nancy Hormel
"Gopher Snake." Poetry (136:2) My 80, p. 96.

REINHARDT, Alan
"The Sun Raven." CalQ (16/17) 80, p. 132.

REISS, James
"Trying Not to Feel Desperate." AmerPoR (9:3) My-Je 80, p. 10.

REITER, Thomas
"The Attic." CharR (6:2) Aut 80, p. 48.
"Following Through." QW (10) Wint-Spr 80, p. 87.
"Walking on Moss" (for my son). PoetryNW (21:3) Aut 80, p. 37.

RENBERG, Margareta
"Destruction" (tr. of Ingrid Clareus). PoetryE (3) 80, p. 67.
"The Disappointed" (tr. by Ingrid Clareus). PoetryE (3) 80, p. 71.
"The Foreign Café" (tr. by Ingrid Clareus). PoetryE (3) 80, p. 70.
"Hope" (tr. by Ingrid Clareus). PoetryE (3) 80, p. 66.
"An iceclear light" (tr. by Ingrid Clareus). PoetryE (3) 80, p. 69.
"Mine" (tr. by Ingrid Clareus). PoetryE (3) 80, p. 68.
"Saturated commotion" (tr. by Ingrid Clareus). PoetryE (3) 80, p. 72.

RENDLEMAN, Danny L.
"Canning." PoNow (27) 80, p. 23.
"Crow Agency." PoNow (27) 80, p. 23.
"Scout." PoNow (27) 80, p. 23.
"Winning at Poker." PoNow (27) 80, p. 23.

RENNER, Bruce
"Lengthening." CreamCR (5:2) Spr 80, p. 9.
"A Page for Dewey." CreamCR (5:2) Spr 80, p. 8.

RESS, Lisa
"Feeding the Animals in Winter." Outbr (4/5) Aut 79-Spr 80, p. 46.
"Taking Down the Barn." Outbr (4/5) Aut 79-Spr 80, p. 45.

RETALLACK, Joan
"Aerial Lemon: A Citrus Crown." Shen (31:1) 79, p. 83.
"Wittgenstein at the Movies." LittleM (12:3/4) 80, p. 10.

REVARD, Carter
"The Country's." DenQ (14:4) Wint 80, p. 48.
"Dancing with Dinosaurs." DenQ (14:4) Wint 80, p. 50.
"Foetal Research." CharR (6:2) Aut 80, p. 26.
Nonymosity. Sam (99) 80. Entire issue.
"Now" (for Oscar Howe). DenQ (14:4) Wint 80, p. 53.
"People from the Stars." Focus (14:86) Ap 80, p. 17.
"Stone Age." Focus (14:86) Ap 80, p. 17.

REVEAL, David
"Scrambled Eggs." PoNow (29) 80, p. 34.

REVERDY, Pierre
"Winter" (tr. by Anne Waldman and Douglas Haynes).   Ark (14)
    80, p. 394.

REVERE, Elizabeth
"If Someday. " CapeR (16:1) Wint 80, p. 30.
"Marie. " CapeR (16:1) Wint 80, p. 30.

REWAK, William J.
"Hibernation. " Wind (36) 80, p. 45.
"Quick Now, Here, Now, Always--. " KanQ (12:3) Sum 80, p.
    131.

REXROTH, Kenneth
"Chidori. " Ark (14) 80, p. 113.

RICE, Chris
"Mass Politics. " GRR (11:2/3) 80, p. 104.
"To Have Slept with You. " GRR (11:2/3) 80, p. 105.
"Watermark. " GRR (11:2/3) 80, p. 106.

RICHARDS, Melanie
"November Evening. " Pan (21) 80, p. 43.

RICHARDSON, Ron
"Oblique?" Tele (16) 80, p. 122.
"Walla Walla Blue (Penitentiary). " Tele (16) 80, p. 122.

RICHMOND, Steve
"Demons. " Bachy (16) Wint 80, pp. 122-131.
"Lament. " WormR (78) 80, p. 47.
Seven Gagaku. WormR (80) 80, p. 143.
"sunday morning poem birds making music. " WormR (80) 80,
    p. 146.
Three gagaku. WormR (78) 80, p. 47.

RICKEL, Boyer
"After Amichai. " Ploughs (6:2) 80, p. 116.
"For My Motherhood. " BelPoJ (31:2) Wint 80-81, p. 26.
"A Man at His Window. " Ploughs (6:2) 80, p. 115.

RIEL, Steven
"How to Dream. " Mouth (2:5) O 80, p. 35.

RIFBJERG, Klaus
"Langsom vals. " PortR (26) 80, p. 90.

RIGGS, Dionis Coffin
"Duel" (tr. of Cemal Sureya w. Oscan Yalim and William
    Fielder). DenQ (15:2) Sum 80, p. 87.
"San" (tr. of Cemal Sureya w. Oscan Yalim and William Field-
    er). DenQ (15:2) Sum 80, p. 86.

RIGSBEE, David
"Cleaning Vegetables. " SouthernPR (20:1) Spr 80, p. 70.
"Green Frogs. " CarolQ (32:2) Spr-Sum 80, p. 48.
"My Brother's Kitchen. " CarolQ (32:2) Spr-Sum 80, p. 46.

RILEY, Beau
"Crash Landing in Lower Manhattan. " Mouth (2:4) My 80, pp.
    27-36.

RILEY, Joanne M.
"Birth of Color. " SoDakR (18:3) Aut 80, p. 14.
"Fledgling. " ConcPo (13:2) Aut 80, p. 73.
"Plums. " ConcPo (13:2) Aut 80, p. 73.
"Seed Catalogue. " SoDakR (18:3) Aut 80, p. 16.
"Snow Child. " SoDakR (18:3) Aut 80, p. 15.

RILEY, Michael D.
"Macramé. " ArizQ (36:1) Spr 80, p. 69.

RILKE, Rainer Maria
"Archaic Torso of Apollo" (tr. by John N. Miller). WebR (5:2)
    Aut 80, p. 18.
"Atmen, du unsichtbares gedicht. " WestHR (34:1) Wint 80, p.
    83.
"Der Einsame. " WestHR (34:1) Wint 80, p. 81.
"Graves of the Hetaerae" (tr. by Rika Lesser). AmerPoR (9:5)
    S-O 80, p. 26.
"The Grief" (tr. by Steven Lautermilch). NewOR (7:2) 80, p.
    122.
"Inside the Rose" (tr. by Rika Lesser). AmerPoR (9:5) S-O 80,
    p. 26.
"The Knight" (tr. by John N. Miller). WebR (5:2) Aut 80, p. 19.
"The Neighbor" (tr. by Franz Wright). CutB (14) Spr/Sum 80,
    p. 38.
"Now it is time that gods came walking out" (tr. by Stephen
    Mitchell). Thrpny (3) Aut 80, p. 3.
"O Dieses ist das tier. " WestHR (34:1) Wint 80, p. 82.
"Orpheus. Eurydice. Hermes" (tr. by Rika Lesser).
    AmerPoR (9:5) S-O 80, p. 25.
"Requiem for a Friend" (tr. by Rika Lesser). AmerPoR (9:5)
    S-O 80, p. 27.
"The Sonnets to Orpheus I, 2" (tr. by Rika Lesser). AmerPoR
    (9:5) S-O 80, p. 27.
"Wild Rosebush" (tr. by Rika Lesser). AmerPoR (9:5) S-O 80,
    p. 27.

RIMBAUD, Arthur
"Vowels" (tr. by Bill Zavatsky). Durak (4) 80, p. 46.

RINALDI, Nicholas M.
"The Camel. " SouthernPR (20:1) Spr 80, p. 5.
"Hermann Göring: Last Word. " BallSUF (21:3) Sum 80, pp.
    37-42.

"A Vast Silence Arrives in the Sky in the Shape of a Phantom
    Battleship. " SouthernHR (14:3) Sum 80, p. 224.
"We Meet / We Part / We Meet Again. " SouthwR (65:4) Aut 80,
    p. 355.

RINGOLD, Francine
    "Hawks Stay Alive" (w. Alice Price). Nimrod (24:1) Aut-Wint
        80, p. 109.
    "How the Petals Seem the Same" (w. Anita Skeen). Nimrod (24:
        1) Aut-Wint 80, p. 105.
    "Summer Morning at Round Hill Farm" (w. Anita Skeen). Nim-
        rod (24:1) Aut-Wint 80, p. 106.

RIORDAIN, Sean O.
    "Fever" (tr. by Eileen Kato). DenQ (15:2) Sum 80, p. 88.

RIPPY, Bob
    "Harvesting Walnuts" (for Gary Snyder). HiramPoR (28) Spr-
        Sum 80, p. 30.

RITCHIE, Elisavietta
    "Cliff-Hanging. " Vis (4) 80.
    "Fart Divers. " Vis (4) 80.
    from Notes of a Balkan October: "By the Danube. " Vis (4) 80.
    from Notes of a Balkan October: "Gypsy Summer. " Vis (4) 80.
    "Shore Leave: Repulse Bay, Hong Kong. " PoNow (27) 80, p.
        33.

RITSOS, Yánnis
    "Belfry" (tr. by Kimon Friar and Kostas Myrsiades). Durak (5)
        80, pp. 34-44.
    "Beneath the Forgetfulness" (tr. by Helen Kolias). CarolQ (32:3)
        Aut 80, p. 24.
    "Copy" (tr. by Helen Kolias). WebR (5:2) Aut 80, p. 44.
    "A Drop of Water" (tr. by Helen Kolias). WebR (5:2) Aut 80,
        p. 44.
    "The Five" (tr. by Kimon Friar and Kostas Myrsiades). BelPoJ
        (30:4) Sum 80, p. 39.
    "An Insignificant Chronicle of Love" (tr. by Helen Kolias).
        CarolQ (32:3) Aut 80, p. 23.
    "Irresolute" (tr. by Kimon Friar and Kostas Myrsiades). Field
        (22) Spr 80, p. 79.
    "The Journey" (tr. by Kimon Friar and Kostas Myrsiades).
        Field (22) Spr 80, p. 78.
    "Remembrance. " PortR (26) 80, p. 157.
    "The Sandbar Debacle. " QW (11) Aut-Wint 80-81, p. 94.
    "Sea Stroke" (tr. by Kimon Friar and Kostas Myrsiades). Field
        (22) Spr 80, p. 77.
    "Signs" (tr. by Helen Kolias). WebR (5:2) Aut 80, p. 45.
    "Silent Agreement. " PortR (26) 80, p. 154.
    "Small Confession. " PortR (26) 80, p. 156.
    "This Darkness" (tr. by Kimon Friar and Kostas Myrsiades).
        Field (22) Spr 80, p. 81.

Twelve poems (tr. by Kimon Friar and Kostas Myrsiades).
   Durak (4) 80, pp. 55-62.
"White" (tr. by Kimon Friar and Kostas Myrsiades).   Field (22)
   Spr 80, p. 80.
"Without Counter-Balance" (tr. by Helen Kolias).   WebR (5:2)
   Aut 80, p. 45.
from The World Is One: "Doubtful Encounters" (tr. by Kostas
   Myrsiades).   Durak (5) 80, p. 45.
from The World Is One: "Encounters" (tr. by Kostas Myrsi-
   ades).   Durak (5) 80, p. 48.
from The World Is One: "Freedom of Travel" (tr. by Kostas
   Myrsiades).   Durak (5) 80, p. 46.
from The World Is One: "Vatican Museum" (tr. by Kostas
   Myrsiades).   Durak (5) 80, p. 47.

RIVERS, J. W.
"Admonitions of a Magyar Mother to Her Son Leaving on Cam-
   paign. " GRR (11:1) 80, p. 35.
"Fire. " PoetC (12:3) 80, p. 29.
"Going Home by Bike at Night. " HiramPoR (27) Aut-Wint 80,
   p. 43.
"Newcomer. " SouthernHR (14:2) Spr 80, p. 128.
"Storm. " PoetC (12:3) 80, p. 28.
"Wake. " SouthwR (65:2) Spr 80, p. 190.

ROBBINS, Anthony
"Dear Andy. " Wind (38) 80, p. 57.
"Good Friday. " Wind (38) 80, p. 58.

ROBBINS, Chris
"Rustling Against Walls. " Pig (7) My 80, p. 61.

ROBBINS, Doren
"Chicken Ranch Kitchen" (for Ben and Yetta Gurstain).   Ark (14)
   80, p. 332.
"The Dawn, the Deep Light. " Bachy (16) Wint 80, p. 132.
"The Hands of a Friend in the Hospital. " Bachy (16) Wint 80,
   p. 134.
"To My Friends. " Ark (14) 80, p. 330.
"Underneath All Her Waters. " Bachy (16) Wint 80, p. 133.
"The Vow. " Bachy (16) Wint 80, p. 134.

ROBBINS, Martin
"On a Pompeian Young Man's Head. " FourQt (30:1) Aut 80, p.
   11.
"On the Colorado River. " PoNow (26) 80, p. 19.

ROBBINS, Richard
"For My Grandfather. " CarolQ (32:2) Spr-Sum 80, p. 78.
"Li. " CarolQ (32:2) Spr-Sum 80, p. 79.

ROBBINS, Rick
"The Gift. " Nat (230:4) 2 F 80, p. 122.

ROBBINS, S. A.
  "Eyeball Soup. " PoNow (29) 80, p. 34.
  "Strawberries. " PoNow (29) 80, p. 35.

ROBBINS, Susannah
  "Seattle. " BelPoJ (30:3) Spr 80, p. 32.

ROBBINS, Tim
  "Jazz 42 Boundless" (for John S.). HangL (38) Aut 80, p. 67.

ROBERTS, Cynthia Day
  "Dreaming of an Old Lover. " Wind (37) 80, p. 46.
  "From the Carousel. " Wind (37) 80, p. 46.

ROBERTS, Dave
  "Threnody" (for Dick Conklin). StoneC (7:3) D 80, p. 4.

ROBERTS, George
  "Thanking My Father for Reading to Me. " DacTerr (17) 80, p.
    68.

ROBERTS, Hortense Roberta
  "My Sister. " BelPoJ (31:1) Aut 80, p. 31.

ROBERTS, Len
  "The Encouraging Sea. " QW (11) Aut-Wint 80-81, p. 112.
  "The Indians. " WorldO (14:3/4) Spr/Sum 80, p. 21.
  "Metal Rooster. " WindO (36) Spr-Sum 80, p. 20.
  "The Servant. " QW (11) Aut-Wint 80-81, p. 113.
  "Using Equations. " NowestR (18:3) 80, p. 98.
  "Warm Soda. " Wind (38) 80, p. 59.
  "Wind Over Land. " PoNow (29) 80, p. 35.
  "Writing a Poem Over My Father's Grave Without Knowing How
    It Will End. " WindO (36) Spr-Sum 80, p. 20.

ROBERTS, Teresa
  "For the purpose of labelling. " HangL (38) Aut 80, p. 68.
  "Frank at 10 Seen 8 Years Later. " HangL (38) Aut 80, p. 68.

ROBIN, Ralph
  "Directions. " Poetry (136:2) My 80, p. 97.

ROBINSON, David
  "The Barrel. " SouthernPR (20:2) Aut 80, p. 52.

ROBINSON, Frank K.
  "Haiku. " WindO (36) Spr-Sum 80, p. 4.

ROBINSON, G. F.
  "road. " UTR (6:3/4) 80, p. 54.

ROBINSON, James Miller
  "The Big Sweep. " Sam (86) 79, p. 64.

"The Empty Church. " CharR (6:2) Aut 80, p. 40.
"The Platter. " Poem (38) Mr 80, p. 16.
"The Return. " StoneC (7:2) My 80, p. 19.
"Through the Laundramat Window. " Poem (38) Mr 80, p. 14.
"The Vagabond. " CharR (6:2) Aut 80, p. 41.

ROBINSON, Lee M.
"On the Road. " Prima (5) 79, p. 57.

ROBINSON, Leonard Wallace
"In the Whale. " NewYorker (56:7) 7 Ap 80, p. 131.

ROBINSON, Peter
"The Counterpane. " GRR (11:2/3) 80, p. 110.
"Dirty Language. " GRR (11:2/3) 80, p. 111.
"Writing on the Quiet. " GRR (11:2/3) 80, p. 109.

ROBSON, Ros
"The Venus Trap. " Wind (37) 80, p. 48.

ROCHESTER, Earl of (John Wilmot)
"Grecian Kindness. " Playb (27:3) Mr 80, p. 165.

RODDEN, Daniel E.
"Follow These Instructions. " PikeF (3) Wint 80, p. 16.

RODITI, Edouard
"A Private Life. " Durak (5) 80, pp. 57-61.

RODNEY, Janet
"Letter from Homer, from Alashka" (w. Nathaniel Tarn). SunM
    (9/10) Sum 80, p. 28.

ROGERS, Bruce P.
"The Graphographer" (to Octavio Paz) (tr. of Salvador Elizondo).
    NewOR (7:3) 80, p. 303.

ROGERS, Del Marie
"The Underground River. " Epoch (29:3) Spr-Sum 80, p. 259.

ROGERS, Larry S.
"(Untitled): "Arkansas was our father. " Wind (37) 80, p. 49.

ROGERS, Mary Bee
"The Circle" (to my sister). Wind (37) 80, p. 50.
"Coffin. " Wind (37) 80, p. 50.
"25 Frauenthal Strasse" (for Sharon). Wind (37) 80, p. 51.

ROGERS, Pattiann
"Achieving Perspective. " Poetry (136:6) S 80, p. 332.
"By Hearing the Same Story Over and Over. " PoetryNW (21:4)
    Wint 80-81, p. 6.
"Concepts and Their Bodies (The Boy in the Field Alone). "

Poetry (136:6) S 80, p. 330.
"The Determinations of the Scene." Poetry (136:6) S 80, p. 333.
"The Rites of Passage." PoetryNW (21:4) Wint 80-81, p. 3.
"The Significance of Location." PoetryNW (21:4) Wint 80-81, p. 5.
"Suppose Your Father Was a Redbird." PoetryNW (21:4) Wint 80-81, p. 4.
ROGGEMAN, Willem M.
"Gedicht voor Ulrike Meinhof." PortR (26) 80, p. 45.
"De verliefde robot." PortR (26) 80, p. 47.

ROHDENBURG, F. D.
"Lines for Beth." Bound (8:2) Wint 80, p. 326.

ROHMAN, S.
"Games." StoneC (7:1) F 80, p. 22.

ROITER, Howard
"To Zygmunt Strawczynski (1908-1976), a Treblinka Survivor." ConcPo (13:1) Spr 80, p. 86.

ROLLINGS, Alane
"Holly." ThRiPo (15/16) 80, p. 45.
"The Landscape at Wit's End." Prima (5) 79, p. 69.

ROMAINE, Elaine
from Body Hoots: "evensong for the voice." Pig (7) My 80, p. 10.
from Body Hoots: "mouthful." Pig (7) My 80, p. 10.

ROMERO, Leo
"Celso's Father." DacTerr (17) 80, p. 70.

RONAN, Richard
"Seated Nude." AmerPoR (9:1) Ja-F 80, p. 28.

ROORDA, Randall
"Plein-Air Poetry." ConcPo (13:2) Aut 80, p. 35.

ROOT, Judith C.
"The Gerbil Who Got Away." HolCrit (17:3) Je 80, p. 13.

ROOT, William Pitt
"All at Once." NowestR (18:3) 80, p. 15.
"Bamboo and Ducks by a Rushing Stream." ConcPo (13:2) Aut 80, p. 88.
"Dancers on an Island with No Roads." Poetry (137:1) O 80, p. 40.
"Early News in Fog." PoNow (26) 80, p. 20.
"Eureka and the Shark." PoNow (26) 80, p. 20.
"Half Shift." Poetry (137:1) O 80, p. 39.
"In a Single Heartbeat of the Light." ConcPo (13:1) Spr 80, p. 54.

"In Another Country. " NewYorker (56:3) 10 Mr 80, p. 54.
"Night Swim" (for Rachel). Atl (246:2) Ag 80, p. 74.
"Out There" (for Charles Levendosky). Atl (245:1) Ja 80, p. 59.
"Parting the Waters. " QW (11) Aut-Wint 80-81, p. 20.
"Prologue for a Book of Songs. " CutB (15) Aut/Wint 80, p. 51.
"Rain, You Say. " QW (11) Aut-Wint 80-81, p. 21.
"Song. " Poetry (137:1) O 80, p. 41.
"Waiting for Rain by the River" (for Wendell Berry and Ed Mc-
   Lanahan). NowestR (18:3) 80, p. 17.
"Why I Like Painters. " Iowa (11:1) Wint 80, p. 126.
"Window Built for My Daughter at Summer Solstice. " NoAmR
   (265:1) Mr 80, p. 40.
"Wrapping Up After a Writers Conference. " PoetryNW (21:2)
   Sum 80, p. 13.

ROPER, Jim
   "When the Veil Lifted" (w. Ann Weisman). Nimrod (24:1) Aut-
   Wint 80, p. 106.

RORIE, Ed
   "The Plough and the Song. " SouthernPR (20:2) Aut 80, p. 44.

ROSA, António Ramos
   "Telegrama sem classificacão especial" (a Egito Goncalves).
   PortR (26) 80, p. 314.

ROSE, Lynne Carol
   "Easter Sunday. " GRR (11:1) 80, p. 12.
   "Reincarnation" (for Evelyn Thorne). GRR (11:1) 80, p. 15.

ROSE, Pat
   "Mice-O Man Meeks Calliope Horse. " Pig (7) My 80, p. 67.

ROSELIEP, Raymond
   Four Haiku. PikeF (3) Wint 80, p. 8.
   "Haiku. " WindO (37) Aut-Wint 80. on calendar.
   "Nocturne. " ChrC (97:40) 10 D 80, p. 1212.
   "One Afternoon. " ChrC (97:24) 16-23 Jl 80, p. 726.
   "Room 433. " ChrC (97:14) 16 Ap 80, p. 428.
   "Rosabel. " PoNow (27) 80, p. 7.
   "Tallith. " ChrC (97:8) 5 Mr 80, p. 252.
   Three Haiku. WindO (36) Spr-Sum 80, p. 3.
   "12. " PoNow (26) 80, p. 10.

ROSEN, Kenneth
   "Glitter. " PoNow (26) 80, p. 7.
   "Ozymandias. " ThRiPo (15/16) 80, p. 46.
   "Redwing. " Poetry (136:3) Je 80, p. 158.
   "Snapper. " ThRiPo (15/16) 80, p. 47.
   "Spring. " PoNow (26) 80, p. 6.

ROSEN, Michael J.
   "Calling into Question. " CarolQ (32:3) Aut 80, p. 20.

"The Fire Pond." NewYorker (56:23) 28 Jl 80, p. 38.
from Making Scenes: "November." Agni (13) 80, p. 85.
from Making Scenes: "November Again." Agni (13) 80, p. 86.
"Nowhere but Older." Shen (31:2) 80, p. 13.
"Poem for the Cutting of Nijinsky's Feet at His Death" (for
    Elizabeth Ann Shiblaq). Pan (21) 80, p. 41.
"The Woman in Ice." CarolQ (32:3) Aut 80, p. 21.

ROSENBERG, Chuck
"Consolation Prize." SunM (9/10) Sum 80, p. 118.

ROSENBERG, David
from Ecclesiastes: "I. (1:1)." Harp (260:1556) Ja 80, p. 68.
from Ecclesiastes: "II. (1:12)." Harp (260:1556) Ja 80, p. 68.
"In Our Beds of Doubt or Certainty." Hudson (33:4) Wint 80, pp.
    522-528.
JoB Speaks. UnmOx (21) Sum 80. Entire issue.

ROSENBERG, L. M.
"Valentine's Day at Johns Hopkins Hospital." NewL (47:1) Aut
    80, p. 106.

ROSENBERGER, Francis Coleman
"Are You Just Back for a Visit or Are You Going to Stay?"
    Poetry (135:4) Ja 80, p. 197.
"If He Must Forever Kill His Father." DacTerr (17) 80, p. 71.

ROSENBLUM, Martin J.
"Perhaps." CreamCR (5:2) Spr 80, p. 40.

ROSENFELD, Rita
...Bound Books. Sam (82) 79. Entire issue.

ROSENTHAL, Abby
"June Song." KanQ (12:1) Wint 80, p. 132.
"Losing Time and Growing Old in Traffic." KanQ (12:1) Wint
    80, p. 132.

ROSENTHAL, David
"Just Beyond the Window" (tr. of Marcelo Covian). PortR (26)
    80, p. 13.

ROSKOLENKO, Harry
"From Classical Journey." NewL (46:3) Spr 80, p. 45.
"Lyrical Implosion." NewL (46:3) Spr 80, p. 44.
"Old World, New World." NewL (46:3) Spr 80, p. 44.
"Pacific Coast Walkabout." Confr (20) Spr-Sum 80, p. 175.

ROSS, Carolyn
"Interval." AmerS (49:4) Aut 80, p. 512.
"This Spring." Northeast (3:8) Wint 80, p. 53.

ROSSI, Vino
"Keys for an Unwritten Poem" (tr. of Giovanni Raboni w. Stuart

Friebert). CutB (14) Spr /Sum 80, p. 50.
"One Time" (tr. of Giovanni Raboni w. Stuart Friebert). CutB
     (14) Spr /Sum 80, p. 52.
"Three Private Madrigals" (tr. of Eugenio Montale w. David
     Young). Field (23) Aut 80, p. 43.
"Woman's Song" (tr. of Giovanni Raboni w. Stuart Friebert).
     CutB (14) Spr /Sum 80, p. 51.

ROTELLA, Guy
"Somewhere Farm. " Tendril (7 /8) Spr-Sum 80, p. 59.

ROTH, Andrew Paul
"#2. " HiramPoR (28) Spr-Sum 80, p. 31.

ROTHENBERG, Jerome
"The Holy Words of Tristan Tzara. " Ark (14) 80, pp. 342-349.
"The Little Saint of Huautla" (for Maria Sabina). Bound (8:3)
     Spr 80, p. 141.
"A Poem in Yellow After Tristan Tzara. " PartR (47:4) 80, p.
     611.

ROTHFORK, John
"Ceremony. " ConcPo (13:2) Aut 80, p. 15.
"The Same Cowboy. " ConcPo (13:2) Aut 80, p. 14.
"Zen Phlogiston. " PikeF (3) Wint 80, p. 27.

ROTHMAN, David
"The Cattle Prod Variations. " PoNow (29) 80, p. 35.

ROUSE, Irene
"Barbed Wire" (to my father, Reed Munson). CropD (1) Spr 80,
     p. 11.
"Bridges. " CropD (1) Spr 80, p. 12.

RUARK, Gibbons
"His Mother's Lament for His English. " MidwQ (21:4) Sum 80,
     p. 449.
"His Undersong. " MidwQ (21:4) Sum 80, p. 449.
"Lament (1974). " MidwQ (21:3) Spr 80, p. 357.
"Words to Accompany a Wildflower from Edward Thomas's Hill-
     side. " PoetryNW (21:3) Aut 80, p. 36.

RUBIN, Larry
"Going Deeper into the Album. " SewanR (88:4) Aut 80, p. 553.
"Lines for a Poet, After Her Shock Treatments. " MalR (56) O
     80, p. 55.
"Lines for a Victorian Mother. " SouthernPR (20:2) Aut 80, p.
     29.
"Lines to a Physical Education Major, Stuck in an English
     Class. " PoNow (26) 80, p. 18.
"The Mother, Bewildered. " SouthernR (16:4) Aut 80, p. 932.
"A Note on the Dangers of Continental Drift. " SouthernHR (14:1)
     Wint 80, p. 68.

RUBIN, Stan Sanvel
"Lullaby. " PoetryNW (21:2) Sum 80, p. 30.

RUBINSTEIN, Geoffrey
"At the Grocery Store: Robert and Joshua. " WindO (36) Spr-
   Sum 80, p. 31.

RUCHERT, Wallace Jr.
"Skin Diving Off Oahu. " PoNow (28) 80, p. 33.

RUDD, Gail
"Nightmare. " DenQ (15:2) Sum 80, p. 76.
"The Sleep Horse. " DenQ (15:2) Sum 80, p. 78.

RUDMAN, Mark
"The Black Dove. " VirQR (56:3) Sum 80, p. 496.
"The Man in the Room. " ParisR (78) Sum 80, p. 117.
"The Stars in Summer" (tr. of Boris Pasternak w. Bohdan Boy-
   chuk). PoNow (27) 80, p. 45.

RUEFLE, Mary
"Torture. " CalQ (16/17) 80, p. 39.

RUENZEL, David
"A Case of Mental Illness. " Sam (86) 79, p. 41.
"The Killer's Confession. " SouthernPR (20:2) Aut 80, p. 21.

RUESCHER, Scott
"The Caption. " Nat (231:13) 25 O 80, p. 416.
"Midget White Picket Fences. " AntR (38:1) Wint 80, p. 62.
"The Tall Grass. " AntR (38:1) Wint 80, p. 60.

RUFF, John
"On a Train to Rome. " DacTerr (17) 80, p. 72.

RUFFIN, Paul
"Hotel Fire: New Orleans. " GeoR (34:2) Sum 80, p. 374.
"Lighting the Furnace Pilot. " CalQ (16/17) 80, p. 124.

RUFUS, Milan
"Death" (tr. by Daniel Simko). CutB (14) Spr/Sum 80, p. 11.
"To Go Home" (tr. by Daniel Simko). CutB (14) Spr/Sum 80,
   p. 8.

RUGGLES, Eugene
"Memorial Day, 1979. " NewYorker (56:25) 11 Ag 80, p. 30.

RUGO, Mariève
"Borders. " Tendril (9) 80, p. 131.
"Correspondence. " NewRena (12) Spr 80, p. 54.
"Limbo. " CarolQ (32:1) Wint 80, p. 91.
Twenty poems. Tendril (7/8) Spr-Sum 80, pp. 85-105.

RUKEYSER, Muriel
  "The Backside of the Academy. " Ark (14) 80, p. 350.
  "The changeable spirit finds itself out. " Poetry (136:2) My 80,
    Inside front cover.

RUNCIMAN, Lex
  "Grosbeaks. " CutB (15) Aut /Wint 80, p. 80.

RUNEFELT, Eva
  "Kärleksdikt (Rom). " PortR (26) 80, p. 360.
  "Väsensverkan. " PortR (26) 80, p. 362.

RUSS, Lawrence
  "The Burning-Ground" (to the Muse). VirQR (56:2) Spr 80, p.
    270.

RUSSELL, Carol Ann
  "News from All Directions. " OhioR (24) 80, p. 38.

RUSSELL, Norman H.
  "The Fog. " CharR (6:1) Spr 80, p. 9.
  "Green Treefrog. " CharR (6:1) Spr 80, p. 10.
  "In the Early Winter Night. " SlowLR (4) 80, p. 7.
  "Little Sleep This Night. " CharR (6:1) Spr 80, p. 9.
  "One Always May Choose. " SmPd (48) Wint 80, p. 11.
  "Prey to All Enemies. " SmPd (48) Wint 80, p. 12.
  "Singing the Song of Spring. " PoNow (28) 80, p. 8.
  "The Stream. " NowestR (18:3) 80, p. 67.
  "The Wind. " SlowLR (4) 80, p. 8.
  "The World Within the World. " CharR (6:1) Spr 80, p. 8.

RUSSELL, Peter
  "Ascent" (tr. of Carlo Biadene). MalR (55) Jl 80, p. 61.
  "Hope Gone Dead" (tr. of Carlo Biadene). MalR (55) Jl 80, p.
    63.
  "An Unknown God" (tr. of Carlo Biadene). MalR (55) Jl 80, p.
    62.

RUSSELL, R. Stephen
  "Somewhere inside me A moth burns. " NewL (46:4) Sum 80, p.
    55.

RUSSELL, Timothy
  "Day Without Rain. " PoNow (27) 80, p. 47.

RUTAN, Catherine
  Betrayals. OhioR (24) 80, pp. 59-72.

RUTSALA, Vern
  "Abandoned Poem" (to Paul Valéry). NewL (47:1) Aut 80, p. 111.
  "The Fears of the Poor. " Poetry (137:3) D 80, p. 131.
  "The Final Cut. " NewYorker (56:5) 24 Mr 80, p. 74.
  "Hospitality. " PoNow (28) 80, p. 5.

"Lines Begun in Dejection. " Iowa (11:1) Wint 80, p. 132.
"Little-Known Sports: Being Hopeless. " AmerPoR (9:5) S-O 80,
    p. 44.
"Little-Known Sports: Deliberate Misunderstanding. " AmerPoR
    (9:5) S-O 80, p. 44.
"Little-Known Sports: Getting Lost. " AmerPoR (9:5) S-O 80,
    p. 43.
"Little-Known Sports: Hating. " AmerPoR (9:5) S-O 80, p. 43.
"Little-Known Sports: Tedium. " AmerPoR (9:5) S-O 80, p. 43.
"Little-Known Sports: The Loneliness of the Long Distance
    Runner or, Keeping Your Mouth Shut. " AmerPoR (9:5) S-O
    80, p. 44.
"Living in the Past. " PoNow (28) 80, p. 5.
"Occupation. " Durak (4) 80, p. 11.
"Offering Consolation. " PoNow (26) 80, p. 15.
"On the Town. " Iowa (11:1) Wint 80, p. 131.
"On Time. " PoNow (26) 80, p. 15.
"Pictures of Herr Keuner. " NewL (47:1) Aut 80, p. 110.
"Prospectus for Visitors. " Poetry (137:3) D 80, p. 129.
"Ruined Cities and Tedious Ways: Pao Chao. " AmerPoR (9:5)
    S-O 80, p. 42.
"Skaters. " Poetry (137:3) D 80, p. 127.
"Something Like Spinks. " ThRiPo (15/16) 80, p. 50.
"This Poem Is a Tyrant. " PoetryNW (21:1) Spr 80, p. 11.
"What We Really Want. " PoNow (27) 80, p. 6.

RYAN, Dennis
"Bahamian Seaview. " Poem (38) Mr 80, p. 59.
"Walking with Senta. " Poem (38) Mr 80, p. 60.

RYAN, Margaret
"Four Glorious New Zinnias and Other Distinguished Award Win-
    ners. " Confr (20) Spr-Sum 80, p. 115.

RYAN, Michael
"An Apology to Patty. " NewRep (183:7) 16 Ag 80, p. 43.
"A Shape for It. " Poetry (135:5) F 80, p. 273.
"Where I'll Be Good. " Ploughs (6:2) 80, p. 24.
"Why. " Ploughs (6:2) 80, p. 20.

RYAN, R. M.
"Absent Minded. " CimR (53) O 80, p. 63.
"From the Dead of Winter. " CimR (53) O 80, p. 54.
"To Be Classical We Must. " CimR (53) O 80, p. 39.

RYDER, Sarah
"At the Shore. " PoNow (29) 80, p. 35.

RYERSON, Alice
"The Death Watchers. " Prima (5) 79, p. 22.

RZEPKA, Charles
"The Wedding. " Poem (39) Jl 80, p. 29.

SAARITSA, Pentti
"Lumi, Kummajainen, ".   PortR (26) 80, p. 136.

SABINES, Jaime
"I went to the pawnshop and told them" (tr. by Linda Scheer).
    PoNow (28) 80, p. 44.
"The television bothers me" (tr. by Linda Scheer).   PoNow (28)
    80, p. 44.

SACHIKO, Yoshihara
"The Cat" (tr. by John Solt and the author).   Ark (14) 80, p.
    404.
"Speaking of Bread" (tr. by John Solt w. author).   Ark (14) 80,
    p. 406.
"Sundown" (tr. by John Solt w. author).   Ark (14) 80, p. 407.

SACKS, Peter
"Kirkpatrick Playing Back. "   NewYorker (55:51) 4 F 80, p. 41.
"A Visit to the Hillstead Museum. "   NewRep (183:1/2) 5-12 Jl
    80, p. 26.

SADOFF, Ira
"February: Pemaquid Point. "   ParisR (77) Wint-Spr 80, p. 105.
"Intimacy at First Light: Bath, Maine Shipyard. "   Ploughs (6:2)
    80, p. 58.
"The Invasion of the Body Snatchers. "   Ploughs (6:2) 80, p. 56.
"January: First Light. "   NewYorker (55:49) 21 Ja 80, p. 36.
"Omaha of the Pacific. "   Ploughs (6:2) 80, p. 54.
"The Vacation in Miami: July, 1954. "   Ploughs (6:2) 80, p. 60.

SAFDIE, Joe
from Memories of Native Ground Part Three: The Public Mem-
    ory: "American Summer. "   Bachy (17) Spr 80, pp. 118-128.

SAGAN, Miriam
"Approximately for You. "   HangL (38) Aut 80, p. 44.
"Girl in the Mirror. "   Sam (92) 80, p. 57.

SAGEL, Jim
"entró abuelito pasando como una sombra. "   Os (10) Spr 80, p.
    20.
"Hands. "   DacTerr (17) 80, p. 73.

SAGOFF, Maurice
from Shrink Lits: "Rod McKuen's Listen to the Warm. "   Atl
    (245:5) My 80, p. 100.

SAHTOURIS, Miltos
Nine Poems (tr. by Kimon Friar).   Kayak (54) S 80, pp. 5-9.

SAIL, Lawrence
"Time Machines. "   Stand (21:4) 80, p. 48.

ST. JOHN, Becky
"Shifts. " Wind (37) 80, p. 52.

ST. JOHN, David
"Cantina. " VirQR (56:3) Sum 80, p. 511.
"Doubt. " Durak (5) 80, p. 13.
"Lavender. " Ploughs (6:2) 80, p. 45.
"The Mask. " Field (22) Spr 80, p. 10.
"Of the Remembered. " ParisR (77) Wint-Spr 80, pp. 167-178.
"Slow Blues for the Pilgrim. " Ploughs (6:2) 80, p. 43.
"Until the Sea Is Dead. " NewYorker (56:20) 7 Jl 80, p. 32.

SAISER, Marjorie
"Arcanum. " KanQ (12:3) Sum 80, p. 20.
"Saturday 6 October. " KanQ (12:3) Sum 80, p. 28.

SAJKOVIC, Olivera
"Celtic song of a meeting after death" (tr. from the Swedish).
    NewRena (12) Spr 80, p. 43.

SALAMUN, Tomaž
"July 31, Andraž" (tr. by author and Anselm Hollo). NewL (47:
    1) Aut 80, p. 55.
"Night" (tr. by author and Anselm Hollo). NewL (47:1) Aut 80,
    p. 56.
"Nile" (tr. by author and Anselm Hollo). NewL (47:1) Aut 80,
    p. 54.
"Proverbs" (tr. by author and Anselm Hollo). NewL (47:1) Aut
    80, p. 55.
"Vacation Time" (tr. by author and Anselm Hollo). NewL (47:1)
    Aut 80, p. 53.
"What Is What" (tr. by author and Anselm Hollo). NewL (47:1)
    Aut 80, p. 54.

SALERNO, Salvatore Jr.
"Signatures. " WebR (5:1) Wint 80, p. 56.

SALINAS, Luis Omar
"Darkness Under the Trees. " PoetryE (3) 80, p. 44.
"For Good Pablo. " PoetryE (1) 80, p. 57.
"In a Foggy Morning. " PoetryE (3) 80, p. 43.
"Late Evening Conversation with My Friend's Dog, Moses, After
    Watching Viscont's The Innocent. " PoetryE (3) 80, p. 45.
"Letter Too Late to Vallejo. " Columbia (5) Aut-Wint 80, p. 53.
"Many Things of Death. " NowestR (18:3) 80, p. 72.
"This May Morning. " PoetryE (3) 80, p. 42.

SALINGER, Wendy
"Cameron's Song: Cloudless Sulphur. " NewYorker (56:4) 17 Mr
    80, p. 38.
"The Disobedient Prophet. " PoetryE (1) 80, p. 68.
"Relief of Children. " VirQR (56:1) Wint 80, p. 73.
"Wind on the Moon. " VirQR (56:1) Wint 80, p. 76.

SALISBURY, Ralph
"Cyclones in Yellow Feathers: Adult Education Class. " Confr
(20) Spr-Sum 80, p. 107.
"Means Snow. " PoNow (27) 80, p. 15.

SALKEY, Andrew
"Boats in the Tops of Trees. " NewL (46:4) Sum 80, p. 112.
"A Recollection of Caribbea. " NewL (46:4) Sum 80, p. 113.
"Truth to Caribbea. " NewL (46:4) Sum 80, p. 113.

SALTER, Mary Jo
"Two Pigeons. " NewRep (183:14) 4 O 80, p. 30.

SALTMAN, Benjamin
"Cauliflower. " Bachy (17) Spr 80, p. 93.
"A Cool Place. " Bachy (17) Spr 80, p. 92.
"Forgiveness During a Walk on Prospect Street. " Bachy (17)
Spr 80, p. 94.
"Grass Where the Dead Walk Quietly. " Bachy (17) Spr 80, p. 93.
"Killing a Bird on the Road to Toledo. " Bachy (17) Spr 80, p.
94.
"Like Peaches. " Bachy (17) Spr 80, p. 92.

SALVAGGIO, Marc
"Turning Stones. " Nat (230:3) 26 Ja 80, p. 90.

SAMARAS, Nicholas
"The Hospital Visit. " Aspect (76) S-D 79-80, p. 48.

SAMUEL, Jean
"And We Shall Call the Body a Forest. " Bachy (16) Wint 80, p.
97.
"David Holds the Camera. " Bachy (16) Wint 80, p. 98.
"A Rose the White Silk of Her Neck. " Bachy (16) Wint 80, p.
99.

SAMUELSON, Janet
"First Story. " CentR (24:1) Wint 80, p. 79.
"A Trilogy of Celebration. " CentR (24:1) Wint 80, p. 79.

SANDEEN, Ernest
"Homo-Sapiens. " Epoch (29:2) Wint 80, p. 115.
"3 Poems. " Epoch (29:2) Wint 80, p. 114.

SANDERS, Mark
"Bladen, Nebraska. " KanQ (12:2) Spr 80, p. 90.
"Near the Tracks. " KanQ (12:2) Spr 80, p. 97.

SANER, Reg
"Circumnavigations of Air. " StoneC (7:3) D 80, p. 24.
"Heliophagy at Il Poderino. " PraS (54:3) Aut 80, p. 45.
"Historians of Air. " StoneC (7:3) D 80, p. 24.
"Vesuvian Postcard Morning. " PraS (54:3) Aut 80, p. 44.

SANFEDELE, Ann
"Epitaph for a Merchant Marine. " AmerPoR (9:3) My-Je 80, p.
    37.
"Gemini. " AmerPoR (9:3) My-Je 80, p. 38.
"Gramercy Park. " AmerPoR (9:3) My-Je 80, p. 38.
"The Part of Fortune. " AmerPoR (9:3) My-Je 80, p. 37.

SANTOS, Sherod
"After a Long Illness. " Poetry (137:1) O 80, p. 16.
"Kafka. " WatT (1) Aut 80, p. 55.
"On the Last Day of the World. " Poetry (137:1) O 80, p. 12.
"The Palace Hotel at 2 A. M. " WestHR (34:1) Wint 80, p. 40.
"Sirens in Bad Weather. " NewYorker (56:12) 12 My 80, p. 41.
"Three Fragments. " Poetry (137:1) O 80, p. 14.

SANZ, Francisco
"Giacomo Casanova Accepts the Office of Librarian Which Is Of-
    fered to Him, in Bohemia, by the Count of Waldstein" (tr.
    of Antonio Colinas w. Will Kirkland). PortR (26) 80, p.
    344.

SAPIA, Yvonne
"The Cave Divers. " SouthernPR (20:2) Aut 80, p. 54.
"North Florida Pastoral. " Confr (20) Spr-Sum 80, p. 27.

SAPIEYEVSKI, Anne
"Mozart at the Kennedy Center. " CropD (2 /3) Aut-Wint 80, p.
    26.
"Oboe Solo. " CropD (2 /3) Aut-Wint 80, p. 29.
"The Perfect Couple. " CropD (1) Spr 80, p. 17.
"Sleepsong for a Grown Woman. " CropD (1) Spr 80, p. 17.

SARGENT, Dana
"The Death of a Sleeping Church. " ChrC (97:6) 20 F 80, p. 189.
"Elegy for a Pair of Worn-out Sandals. " ChrC (97:32) 15 O 80,
    p. 968.
"The Marsh Hump. " PoNow (29) 80, p. 35.

SARGENT, Robert
"Lending the King of the Golden River to a Young Woman. "
    SouthernHR (14:4) Aut 80, p. 337.
"Looking for Oldness. " CimR (52) Jl 80, p. 64.
"Uncle John, About 1900. " CimR (52) Jl 80, p. 64.

SARRACINO, Carmine
"Killing the Flamingos. " EnPas (10) 80, p. 10.

SARRETT, Sylvia
"Again. " EngJ (69:7) O 80, p. 21.

SARTON, May
"Lady of the Lake. " PortR (26) 80, p. 439.

SARVIG, Ole
"Pupper. " PortR (26) 80, p. 97.

SATHERLEY, David
"For P. Jacquillard. " PottPort (2) 80-81, p. 52.
"Who Was that Masked Man." PottPort (2) 80-81, p. 18.

SAUL, George Brandon
"Considering Mountains. " ArizQ (36:2) Sum 80, p. 117.

SAULS, Roger
"Seminary. " CarolQ (32:2) Spr-Sum 80, p. 21.

SAUM, Karen
"That Sun Who's Mine. " BelPoJ (31:1) Aut 80, p. 10.

SAUNDERS, Geraldine
"Becky and the Rev. " US1 (12/13) Aut-Wint 80, p. 18.

SAVAGE, Ann Marie
"In a Night. " CapeR (15:2) Sum 80, p. 30.

SAVANT, John
"For the Parents of Jimmy Who Died Young. " SouthernR (16:2)
    Spr 80, p. 435.
"In the Time of the Rose" (for Sister Martin). SouthernR (16:2)
    Spr 80, p. 434.
"Three for Wallace Stevens. " SouthernR (16:2) Spr 80, p. 431.

SAVITT, Lynne
"Ellen's Brother. " PoNow (29) 80, p. 29.
"Lust in 28 Flavors" (for Guy). PoNow (29) 80, p. 29.
"May 1978. " Pig (7) My 80, p. 55.

SAVOIE, Paul
"Salamandre. " ConcPo (12:2) Aut 79, p. 25.

SAWATZKY, Sharon Blessum
"Anger and I. " BelPoJ (31:1) Aut 80, p. 33.

SAYLES, Carton
"Brocade. " CreamCR (5:1) Wint 79, p. 103.
"Vamoos, trapper." CreamCR (5:2) Spr 80, p. 86.

SCALAPINO, Leslie
"If I Go Out Anywhere. " Bachy (17) Spr 80, p. 79.

SCANNELL, Vernon
"Old Man in Winter. " AmerS (49:1) Wint 79-80, p. 36.

SCARPA, Vivien C.
"The Gamut. " Vis (3) 80.
"Reflections. " Vis (3) 80.

"Through Windows. " Vis (3) 80.

SCATES, Maxine
"Groceries for the Bomb. " PoNow (29) 80, p. 36.
"Neighbors, 1958. " PoNow (29) 80, p. 36.
"Violence. " PraS (54:1) Spr 80, p. 12.
"Working. " PraS (54:1) Spr 80, p. 13.

SCEVE, Maurice
"(232)" (tr. by William H. Matheson). WebR (5:1) Wint 80, p.
    18.

SCHAEFER, Ted
"The Last Mass of the Animals. " CharR (6:1) Spr 80, p. 15.
"The Shriners Parade Massacre. " Focus (14:86) Ap 80, p. 30.
"Stunned in Late Winter by the Flower Chamber of the Chicago
    Lincoln Park Conservatory. " WebR (5:2) Aut 80, p. 54.
"Tinnitus. " Focus (14:86) Ap 80, p. 30.
"Trucks Through the Neighborhood. " WebR (5:2) Aut 80, p. 55.

SCHAEFFER, Susan Fromberg
"Birthday. " OP (30) Aut 80, p. 33.
"The Doll. " ThRiPo (15/16) 80, p. 56.
"Flowers at Night. " OP (30) Aut 80, p. 34.
"Flowers at Night. " SoDakR (18:2) Sum 80, p. 17.
"Hearts and Flowers. " CentR (24:1) Wint 80, p. 85.
"The Leavetaking. " SouthernR (16:1) Wint 80, pp. 139-146.
"Leaving. " SoDakR (18:2) Sum 80, p. 19.
"Leaving Florida. " OP (30) Aut 80, p. 35.
"Maps. " PoNow (26) 80, p. 37.
"Monkeys at the City. " Confr (20) Spr-Sum 80, p. 68.
"The Monkey's Choice. " Confr (20) Spr-Sum 80, p. 69.
"The Odd Day. " CentR (24:1) Wint 80, p. 84.
"Revising. " DenQ (14:4) Wint 80, p. 126.
"Peace. " ColEng (42:1) S 80, p. 60.
"Rising. " SoDakR (18:2) Sum 80, p. 18.
"Sleeping Last. " OP (30) Aut 80, p. 38.
"That Day. " Tele (16) 80, p. 96.
"Twenty Years. " MichQR (19:3) Sum 80, p. 321.

SCHAFF, Emily W.
"Some of the Questions. " Pig (7) My 80, p. 79.

SCHARNHORST, Gary
"Sonnet in Subjunctive Mood. " BallSUF (21:1) Wint 80, p. 57.

SCHARTON, M. A.
"At the Medicine Wheel. " KanQ (12:1) Wint 80, p. 150.

SCHEDLER, Gilbert
"The Book of Common Prayer. " ChrC (97:40) 10 D 80, p. 1214.

SCHEELE, Roy
"By the Path. " SmF (11/12) Spr-Aut 80, p. 43.

"Changing the Flowers. " Comm (107:20) 7 N 80, p. 628.
"Five Above. " SmF (11/12) Spr-Aut 80, p. 45.
"Mountain Anemone. " SmF (11/12) Spr-Aut 80, p. 44.
"Stanchions. " SmF (11/12) Spr-Aut 80, p. 42.

SCHEER, Linda
"I went to the pawnshop and told them" (tr. of Juan Jose Arre-
    ola). PoNow (28) 80, p. 44.
"The television bothers me" (tr. of Juan Jose Arreola). PoNow
    (28) 80, p. 44.

SCHEIBLI, Silvia
"Hummingbird's Song. " UTR (6:3/4) 80, p. 55.
The Lantern's Dance in the Beehive. UTR (6:1) 80. Entire is-
    sue.
"Letter to Alan Britt About More Reports on the Slaughter of
    Dolphins. " UTR (6:3/4) 80, p. 56.

SCHELLING, Andrew
"The Bracelet. " ChiR (31:4) Spr 80, p. 147.

SCHENCK, Rebecca
"Ragged Robin. " SmF (11/12) Spr-Aut 80, p. 56.

SCHEVILL, James
"Agua, the Volcano Called 'Water. '" PoNow (27) 80, p. 32.
"At the Healer's Tomb. " PoNow (27) 80, p. 32.
"Colonial Church Bells. " PoNow (27) 80, p. 32.
"The First Heavy Rain of the Rainy Season. " PoNow (27) 80, p.
    32.
"High School Football Coach. " PoNow (26) 80, p. 40.
"Maria Confounded by Dolls. " PoNow (27) 80, p. 32.
"Nevada" (tr. of Luis Cernuda). PoNow (26) 80, p. 46.
"Roadblock. " PoNow (27) 80, p. 32.

SCHIFF, Jeff
"Apples" (for Michael Waters). CimR (53) O 80, p. 52.
"Finishing This Letter. " StoneC (7:3) D 80, p. 13.
"In a Field with Neumann Walking Passed. " CimR (53) O 80, p.
    64.
"The Layoff. " StoneC (7:3) D 80, p. 13.
"Revolution. " StoneC (7:3) D 80, p. 13.
"Winter Twilight. " OhioR (24) 80, p. 27.

SCHIPPERS, K.
"De tautologie van het object. " PortR (26) 80, p. 271.

SCHLESINGER, Ann Rae
"In the Afternoon. " HangL (37) Spr 80, p. 53.

SCHLOSS, David
"The Earthly Paradise. " PartR (47:4) 80, p. 607.
"Key West. " Antaeus (38) Sum 80, p. 90.

SCHLOSSER, Robert
"The Lynching Spirit Remained from 1904. " Sam (98) 80, p. 28.
"3293 (for Draft-Age Americans). " Sam (98) 80, p. 29.

SCHLUTER, Randall
"Message 800214. " Sam (98) 80, p. 30.

SCHMIDT, Michael R.
"Evening" (tr. of Helder Macedo). PortR (26) 80, p. 307.

SCHMITZ, Barbara
"(hats). " Tele (16) 80, p. 9.

SCHMITZ, Dennis
"Country Deaths. " Antaeus (38) Sum 80, p. 127.
"Cutting Out a Dress. " Tendril (9) 80, p. 132.
"Lucky Tiger. " Antaeus (38) Sum 80, p. 125.

SCHNACK, Asger
"Sproget for de tabte steder. " PortR (26) 80, p. 92.

SCHNACKENBERG, Gjertrud
"A Dream. " Ploughs (6:2) 80, p. 25.
"Holding a Raccoon's Jaw. " Ploughs (6:2) 80, p. 26.

SCHNEBERG, Willa
"Magic Rocks. " Aspect (76) S-D 79-80, p. 26.

SCHNEIDER, Nina
"Earth Science. " ParisR (78) Sum 80, p. 198.

SCHNELL, Hartmut
"About Separate Departures" (tr. of Rolf Dieter Brinkmann).
     NewL (46:4) Sum 80, p. 36.
"Mourning on the Clothesline in January" (tr. of Rolf Dieter
     Brinkmann). NewL (46:4) Sum 80, p. 36.
"Oh, Peaceful Noon" (tr. of Rolf Dieter Brinkmann). NewL (46:
     4) Sum 80, p. 35.
"Poem: Destroyed countryside with" (tr. of Rolf Dieter Brink-
     mann). NewL (46:4) Sum 80, p. 37.

SCHOEBERLEIN, Marion
"Woman on the Stairs of Summer. " StoneC (7:1) F 80, p. 14.

SCHOENBERGER, Nancy
"A Small Thing. " Poetry (137:3) D 80, p. 145.
"Train to Seattle. Christmas Morning. " Poetry (137:3) D 80,
     p. 143.

SCHOLL, Betsy
"Riding Hood. " VirQR (56:1) Wint 80, p. 70.

SCHOLNICK, Michael
"Let's Turn Here" (w. Tom Weigel). Tele (16) 80, p. 37.

SCHOR, Sandra
"The Practical Life" (for Marie Ponsot). <u>PraS</u> (54:1) Spr 80,
    p. 42.

SCHORR, Mark
"Figures Implied in the Painting" (for Elaine S. R. and Morris
    R.). <u>ParisR</u> (78) Sum 80, p. 114.
"A Walk Through the School of the Mind. " <u>AndR</u> (7:1) Spr 80,
    p. 11.

SCHOTT, Carol
"After Eleven Years, This One's for You. " <u>PikeF</u> (3) Wint 80,
    p. 36.
"Mr. and Mrs. Kurmford. " <u>PikeF</u> (3) Wint 80, p. 36.
"Nebraska. " <u>KanQ</u> (12:2) Spr 80, p. 74.

SCHOTT, John
"The Poem Cries Out of Its Dark Envelope. " <u>HiramPoR</u> (28)
    Spr-Sum 80, p. 32.

SCHOTT, Penelope Scambly
"The Choraliers. " <u>Outbr</u> (4/5) Aut 79-Spr 80, p. 99.
"Digging. " <u>LitR</u> (23:3) Spr 80, p. 410.

SCHRAMM, Darrell G. H.
"Break of Night. " <u>Mouth</u> (2:4) My 80, p. 43.
"Horse Trough. " <u>CropD</u> (2/3) Aut-Wint 80, p. 27.

SCHREIBER, Ron
"Panacea. " <u>Mouth</u> (2:5) D 80, p. 33.

SCHULER, Robert
"Helixes. " <u>DacTerr</u> (17) 80, p. 74.

SCHULER, Ruth Wildes
"Episode #163-1979. " <u>Sam</u> (92) 80, p. 25.
"The Ides of March, 1980. " <u>Sam</u> (98) 80, p. 52.
"May Aunt Sarah Rest in Peace. " <u>Tele</u> (16) 80, p. 92.
"When Madness Leads the Blind. " <u>Sam</u> (92) 80, p. 24.

SCHULMAN, Grace
"Inventory" (tr. of T. Carmi). <u>Nat</u> (231:22) 27 D 80, p. 712.
"Story" (tr. of T. Carmi). <u>Nat</u> (230:14) 12 Ap 80, p. 438.
"Sutton Hoo Ship Burial. " <u>AmerPoR</u> (9:3) My-Je 80, p. 47.

SCHULTZ, Al
"Winter Night/Looking from the Back Door. " <u>DacTerr</u> (17) 80,
    p. 76.

SCHUYLER, James
"Song. " <u>NewYorker</u> (55:47) 7 Ja 80, p. 48.

SCHWARTZ, Hillel
"The Earl Brothers, Taxidermy. " <u>Tendril</u> (7/8) Spr-Sum 80,

p. 61.
"Getting On. " MalR (53) Ja 80, p. 43.
"Guido Riccio da Fogliano" (for J. L.).   SouthernHR (14:4) Aut
    80, p. 310.
"Kingsley Billiards. " Tendril (7/8) Spr-Sum 80, p. 60.
"Second Growth. " Pan (21) 80, p. 56.

SCHWARTZ, Howard
"Blessing of the Firstborn. " Focus (14:86) Ap 80, p. 27.
"The Eve Root. " Focus (14:86) Ap 80, p. 27.
"Iscah. " Focus (14:86) Ap 80, p. 27.

SCHWARTZ, Jeffrey
"The Lady in the Window of the Island Hotel. " Aspect (76) S-D
    79-80, p. 20.
"The Marsh. " Agni (12) 80, p. 105.
"The Wedding Picture" (for T and J).   LittleM (12:3/4) 80, p.
    72.

SCHWARTZ, Lloyd
"The Recital. " Ploughs (6:2) 80, p. 138.

SCHWARTZ, Selwyn S.
"Pilgrimage" (tr. by author).   PortR (26) 80, p. 458.

SCOTELLARO, Rocco
"Blind Man. " WormR (77) 80, p. 11.
"By the Parallel Bars in the Park. " WormR (77) 80, p. 9.
"The City Is Killing Me. " MinnR (NS 15) Aut 80, p. 21.
"The Eaves" (tr. by Ruth Feldman and Brian Swann).   PoNow
    (27) 80, p. 46.
"14 Years Together and Otherwise. " WormR (77) 80, p. 10.
"I Love You, But. " WormR (77) 80, p. 12.
"I'm Getting to Know Her. " WormR (77) 80, p. 11.
"Looking for a Clear Picture. " Tele (16) 80, p. 84.
"My 9 Yr. Old Daughter on a Bad Day. " WormR (77) 80, p. 9.
"Nature Poem" (for California).   Tele (16) 80, p. 83.
"Now That I've Lost You" (tr. by Ruth Feldman and Brian
    Swann).   PoNow (28) 80, p. 46.
"Portici: April First" (tr. by Ruth Feldman and Brian Swann).
    PoNow (27) 80, p. 46.

SCOTT, Claudia
"The Gardener in Autumn. " Cond (6) 80, p. 25.
"The Rock Comes Up Out of the Ground. " Cond (6) 80, p. 24.

SCOTT, Dennis
"Letters to My Son: 7. " PortR (26) 80, p. 230.
"Printsong. " PortR (26) 80, p. 227.
"Variations on a Theme. " PortR (26) 80, p. 228.

SCOTT, Herbert
"The Meeting. " DacTerr (17) 80, p. 75.
"Night Walking. " VirQR (56:3) Sum 80, p. 507.

SCOTT, Louise
"Sounds and Seasons. " Wind (38) 80, p. 60.
"Stonehenge. " Wind (38) 80, p. 60.

SCUDDER, Alice
"You Used to Wear Those High Topped Tennis Shoes. " Ploughs
(6:2) 80, p. 123.

SCULLY, James
May Day. MinnR (NS 14) Spr 80. Entire issue.
"Nature Study. " NewYorker (56:40) 24 N 80, p. 52.

SEABURG, Alan
"Black Stars and Time. " CapeR (16:1) Wint 80, p. 40.
"The Larger Hope. " Comm (107:7) 11 Ap 80, p. 212.
"The Miracle. " CapeR (16:1) Wint 80, p. 41.
"The Passing Bell. " CapeR (16:1) Wint 80, p. 42.
"The Sweet Sorrow. " CapeR (16:1) Wint 80, p. 43.
"Teacher, What Shall We Do. " Comm (107:7) 11 Ap 80, p. 212.

SEARS, Peter
"By the Pond. " PoNow (26) 80, p. 34.

SEATON, Esta
"Black Holes. " Wind (38) 80, p. 62.

SEATON, Jerome P.
Ten Tz'u (tr. of Ou-yang Hsiu). LitR (23:4) Sum 80, p. 498.

SEAVER, Kirsten A.
"Marc Chagall" (tr. of Åse-Marie Nesse). PortR (26) 80, p.
283.
"Odysseus" (tr. of Åse-Marie Nesse). PortR (26) 80, p. 282.
"The Strongest" (tr. of Sidsel Morck). PortR (26) 80, p. 279.

SEBENTHALL, R. E.
"The Serpent's Corner. " Prima (5) 79, p. 60.

SECREST, Margaret
"Epitaph for Eva. " Sam (98) 80, p. 55.

SEELY, Clinton
"Banalata Sen (banalatā sena)" (tr. of Jibanananda Das). LitR
(23:3) Spr 80, p. 369.
"Beggar (bhikhirī)" (tr. of Jibanananda Das). LitR (23:3) Spr
80, p. 374.
"Blue Skies (nīlimā)" (tr. of Jibanananda Das). LitR (23:3) Spr
80, p. 375.
"In Camp (kyāmpe)" (tr. of Jibanananda Das). LitR (23:3) Spr
80, p. 370.
"In Fields Fertile and Fallow (khete prāntare)" (tr. of Jibananan-
da Das). LitR (23:3) Spr 80, p. 376.
"Naked Lonely Hand (nagna nirjana hāta)" (tr. of Jibanananda

Das). LitR (23:3) Spr 80, p. 373.

SEESE, Ethel Gray
"Flight. " Wind (37) 80, p. 51.
"To an Elm. " Wind (37) 80, p. 17.

SEFERIS, George
"On a Ray of Winter Light" (tr. by Edmund Keeley and Philip
    Sherrard). Columbia (4) Spr-Sum 80, p. 33.
"On Stage" (tr. by Edmund Keeley and Philip Sherrard). GeoR
    (34:2) Sum 80, p. 357.
"Summer Solstice" (tr. by Edmund Keeley and Philip Sherrard).
    Antaeus (36) Wint 80, pp. 44-51.

SEIDMAN, Hugh
"The Artist. " Aspen (9) Spr 80, p. 59.
"Eurydice. " Poetry (136:5) Ag 80, p. 290.

SEIFERT, Edward
"Light the Divider. " ChrC (97:1) 2-9 Ja 80, p. 16.

SEIFERT, Jaroslav
"Až jednou. " PortR (26) 80, p. 68.
"Morový sloup. " PortR (26) 80, p. 66.

SEILER, Christiane
"Confusion" (tr. by Constance Urdang). WebR (5:2) Aut 80, p.
    41.
"A Dish of Fragments, or Ostracism" (tr. by Constance Urdang).
    WebR (5:2) Aut 80, p. 40.
"Ninety-Four" (tr. by Constance Urdang). WebR (5:2) Aut 80, p.
    39.
"Street-car Solace, or Framed by a Hood" (tr. by Constance
    Urdang). WebR (5:2) Aut 80, p. 38.
"The Tapeworm" (tr by Constance Urdang). WebR (5:2) Aut 80,
    p. 42.

SELLENT, Joan
"Lineage" (tr. of Anton Carrera). PortR (26) 80, p. 346.

SELLERS, Bettie
"Earth Colors. " Poem (39) Jl 80, p. 1.
"Seasoned Travelers. " Poem (39) Jl 80, p. 2.
"There Was a Place We Could Have Met. " SouthernPR (20:1) Spr
    80, p. 65.

SELTZER, Joanne
"Wedding Ring. " Prima (5) 79, p. 68.

SEMONES, Charles
"Wedding Before Palm Sunday. " Wind (36) 80, p. 51.

SENEVIRATNE, Gamini
"Death, Like a Horse. " PortR (26) 80, p. 349.

SETH, Vikram
"Divali. " Thrpny (2) Sum 80, p. 17.

SETTERBERG, Ruth
"Spring Litany. " Wind (37) 80, p. 38.

SEXTON, Anne
"The Evil Seekers. " BosUJ (26:3) 80, p. 189.
"The Fallen Angels. " BosUJ (26:3) 80, p. 191.
"Welcome Morning. " BosUJ (26:3) 80, p. 190.

SEYFRIED, Robin
"Dancing Attendance. " PoetryNW (21:2) Sum 80, p. 46.
"Same Dream, Three Endings. " PoetryNW (21:2) Sum 80, p. 45.

SHABO, Gary
"Poem: Maybe it spends the day inside of shoes. " PoNow (27)
    80, p. 47.

SHAFARZEK, Susan E.
"In My Mother's House. " PoNow (29) 80, p. 36.

SHAFER, Margaret
"Elegy for an Eastern Cat. " StoneC (7:3) D 80, p. 5.
"In Hanna. " ChiR (32:1) Sum 80, p. 10.
"Photograph: Train. " ChiR (32:1) Sum 80, p. 8.

SHAKA, Nattt Moziah
"love poem /song regarding weymouth falls" (for Shelley).
    PottPort (2) 80-81, p. 32.

SHANDLEY, Doreen
"Snape Marshes. " Stand (21:2) 80, p. 57.

SHANLEY, Helen
"I Scared Myself. " CreamCR (5:1) Wint 79, p. 50.

SHANTIRIS, Kita
"Malignance. " CarlMis (18:2) Sum 80, p. 96.

SHAPCOTT, Thomas
"Absences. " NewL (46:3) Spr 80, p. 14.

SHAPIRO, Alan
"The Names" (for Kenneth Fields and Nora Cain). SouthernR
    (16:2) Spr 80, p. 404.

SHAPIRO, Harvey
"A Jerusalem Notebook. " Poetry (136:4) Jl 80, p. 214.

SHAVER, Shelley
"Bereaved. " AmerPoR (9:2) Mr-Ap 80, p. 36.

SHAW, Catherine
"Meditation on a Typo. " LittleM (12:3/4) 80, p. 29.

SHAW, Robert B.
"Out Back in the Evening. " ParisR (78) Sum 80, p. 197.

SHAW, Stephen
"Dickens/Magrite. " PoetC (12:2) 80, p. 28.
"Eclipse. " PoetC (12:1) 80, p. 22.

SHAW, William
"The Poet as Upstart Crow. " WindO (37) Aut-Wint 80, p. 13.

SHECK, Laurie
"Ronald. " PoNow (28) 80, p. 37.
"The Vanilla Flower. " PoetryNW (21:1) Spr 80, p. 24.

SHECTMAN, Robin
"The Visitor. " CalQ (16/17) 80, p. 129.

SHEEHAN, Donald
"In a Void" (tr. of Eugenio Montale w. David Keller). CutB (14)
     Spr/Sum 80, p. 96.
"Repartee" (tr. of Eugenio Montale w. David Keller). CutB (14)
     Spr/Sum 80, p. 97.

SHEEHY, Donald G.
"Ice. " Wind (36) 80, p. 55.

SHEETS, Dan
"It Happened One Night.... " Spirit (5:1/2) Aut-Wint 79-80, p.
     25.

SHEFFIELD, Anne
"McKenzie Bridge. " PoNow (29) 80, p. 36.

SHEINBERG, Maddy
"Blue Chrysanthemum. " CentR (24:3) Sum 80, p. 304.
"Books Speak in the Dark. " CentR (24:3) Sum 80, p. 304.

SHELNUTT, Eve
"Mother, almost dead by hanging. " SlowLR (4) 80, p. 49.
"To the Man Carrying in One Claw a Scaling Knife. " SlowLR (4)
     80, p. 50.
"The Women of Andrea del Sarto. " SlowLR (4) 80, p. 48.

SHELTON, Richard
"The Boojum Tree. " PoNow (26) 80, p. 27.
"Celebration in Sonora. " PoetryE (3) 80, p. 40.
"Face. " Tendril (9) 80, p. 133.
"In the Beginning Was the Word. " Harp (261:1565) O 80, p. 62.
"Pain. " PoNow (26) 80, p. 27.
"Promises. " Harp (261:1565) O 80, p. 63.

"Reaching for the Gun." PoNow (26) 80, p. 27.
"Snow." PoetryE (1) 80, p. 56.
"Song of the Hogan." Harp (261:1565) O 80, p. 63.
"Territorial Rights." NewYorker (56:6) 31 Mr 80, p. 111.
"To You." Harp (261:1565) O 80, p. 62.
"The Whole Truth." PoetryE (1) 80, p. 54.

SHENG, Chang
   "Li Ting Yen" (tr. by Julie Landau). DenQ (15:1) Spr 80, p. 95.

SHEPHERD, Dona
   "Sadness." PikeF (3) Wint 80, p. 16.

SHEPHERD, J. Barrie
   "...And the Life Everlasting." ChrC (97:12) 2 Ap 80, p. 373.
   "Days of Ashes." ChrC (97:6) 20 F 80, p. 197.
   "Fashioning." ChrC (97:31) 8 O 80, p. 942.
   "Haven." ChrC (97:43) 31 D 80, p. 1291.
   "In Passing." ChrC (97:1) 2-9 Ja 80, p. 11.
   "Mid-Lent Crisis." ChrC (97:10) 19 Mr 80, p. 315.
   "Over the River." ChrC (97:38) 26 N 80, p. 1159.
   "The View from Easter." ChrC (97:13) 9 Ap 80, p. 403.
   "What's Cooking, Explorer?" ChrC (97:41) 17 D 80, p. 1238.

SHEPHERD, Neil
   "The Double Bed." PoNow (27) 80, p. 47.

SHER, Benjamin
   "Encirclement" (tr. of Mieczyslaw Jastrun). NewOR (7:2) 80, p.
      113.
   "Exit from a Movie Theater" (tr. of Wislawa Szymborska).
      NewOR (7:2) 80, p. 110.
   "Homecoming" (tr. of Wislawa Szymborska). NewOR (7:2) 80, p.
      111.
   "Ruins of the Cathedral of St. John" (tr. of Mieczyslaw Jastrun).
      NewOR (7:2) 80, p. 112.

SHER, Steven
   "Feasting on Two Coasts." Tele (16) 80, p. 23.

SHERBURNE, James C.
   "Blue." HiramPoR (27) Aut-Wint 80, p. 45.
   "Cord Burning." HiramPoR (28) Spr-Sum 80, p. 34.
   "March 23." SoDakR (18:3) Aut 80, p. 17.
   "Old Screws." HiramPoR (28) Spr-Sum 80, p. 33.
   "Pipestream." HiramPoR (27) Aut-Wint 80, p. 44.

SHERIFF, Bat-Sheva
   Twelve poems (tr. of Amir Gilboa w. Jon Silkin and Natan
      Zach). Stand (21:4) 80, p. 4.

SHERMAN, Joseph
   "My Immigrants." PottPort (1) 79-80, p. 6.

SHERRARD, Philip
"Caique" (tr. of Angelos Sikelianos w. Edmund Keeley). Pequod
(11) 80, p. 38.
"On a Ray of Winter Light" (tr. of George Seferis w. Edmund
Keeley). Columbia (4) Spr-Sum 80, p. 33.
"On Stage" (tr. of George Seferis w. Edmund Keeley). GeoR
(34:2) Sum 80, p. 357.
"Sparta" (tr. of Angelos Sikelianos w. Edmund Keeley). Pequod
(11) 80, p. 39.
"Summer Solstice" (tr. of George Seferis w. Edmund Keeley).
Antaeus (36) Wint 80, pp. 44-51.

SHERRY, James
from Lazy Sonnets: "Praising Laziness." SunM (9/10) Sum 80,
p. 170.
from Lazy Sonnets: "Sloth." SunM (9/10) Sum 80, p. 172.
from Lazy Sonnets: "Symbiosis." SunM (9/10) Sum 80, p. 171.
"To Repair Inadequacies." PartR (47:2) 80, p. 218.

SHERWIN, Judith Johnson
"The Ghost That Walks (1974)" (for Max). MidwQ (21:3) Spr 80,
p. 358.
from Impossible Loves: "Sussel Attempts the Seduction/Of His
Plate Glass Fish." PartR (47:2) 80, pp. 214-15.
"Lovely Leo, Roaring Leo." AmerPoR (9:3) My-Je 80, p. 35.
"The Worth." AmerPoR (9:3) My-Je 80, p. 35.

SHERWOOD, Martha
"Day by Day by." Prima (5) 79, p. 13.

SHERWOOD, Nancy
"I've Listened to Too Much Radio Music." PottPort (1) 79-80,
p. 18.

SHEVIN, David
"Dear Joan." Tele (16) 80, p. 56.
"Expedition." Tele (16) 80, p. 56.
"1 x 11 76." Tele (16) 80, p. 57.

SHIDELER, Ross
"Reply to Richard Hugo re: the past." CimR (52) Jl 80, p. 30.

SHIELDS, James W.
"Cetacean Dialogue." StoneC (7:3) D 80, p. 11.

SHIFFERT, Edith
"After the Vacancy of Darkness." Ark (14) 80, p. 353.

SHIKI, Masaoka
"Haiku" (tr. by Janine Beichman). DenQ (15:1) Spr 80, p. 47.

SHIPLEY, Betty
from Called Up Yonder: "Perfect Attendance." Sam (101) 80,
p. 18.

SHIRLEY, Aleda
"Wife." CarolQ (32:1) Wint 80, p. 78.

SHIRLEY, Philip
"Avoiding Boredom from Montgomery to Tuscaloosa." Wind (38)
    80, p. 63.
"Jug Fishing the Alabama River, 1971." Wind (38) 80, p. 63.

SHISLER, Barbara Esch
"Green of the Way." StoneC (7:2) My 80, p. 28.

SHOLL, Betsy
"Elegy." PoetryNW (21:4) Wint 80-81, p. 15.

SHORB, Michael
"The Execution of Thomas More (1535)." Comm (107:23) 19 D
    80, p. 716.

SHORE, Jane
"Anthony." Ploughs (6:2) 80, p. 18.
"Persian Miniature." Tendril (9) 80, p. 134.

SHORE, Rima
Eight poems (tr. of Sophia Parnok). Cond (6) 80, p. 171.

SHORT, Frank
"Winding Through Softwoods." PoNow (27) 80, p. 37.

SHORT, Gary
"In Nevada in Winter." PoNow (29) 80, p. 37.
"Two Poems About Wells, Nevada." PoNow (28) 80, p. 19.

SHOWSTACK, Randy
"Caribbeans Dance." Aspect (76) S-D 79-80, p. 35.

SHRIVER, Peggy L.
"Anno Domini." ChrC (97:42) 24 D 80, p. 1265.

SHULLENBERGER, Bill
"Spring Equinox." Pan (21) 80, p. 61.

SHUMACHER, Peggy
"The Apple." Agni (13) 80, p. 107.

SHUMWAY, Mary
"The Naming." Im (7:1) 80, p. 11.

SHUNTARO, Tanikawa
"Menstruation." PortR (26) 80, p. 244.

SHURIN, Aaron
"Raving # 25, Vernal Equinox." HangL (38) Aut 80, p. 45.

SHUTTLEWORTH, Paul
"Black Cinders. " SouthwR (65:2) Spr 80, p. 127.
"Mow. " DacTerr (17) 80, p. 77.

SIEGEL, Robert
"The Florist's Daughter. " MidwQ (21:2) Wint 80, p. 257.
"Muskie. " BaratR (8:1) Sum 80, p. 6.
"Rinsed with Gold, Endless, Walking the Fields. " BaratR (8:1)
    Sum 80, p. 7.
"Spastic. " MidwQ (21:2) Wint 80, p. 258.

SIETSEMA, John
"Parody. " EngJ (69:5) My 80, p. 54.

SIGFUSSON, Hannes
"Afríka. " PortR (26) 80, p. 180.

SIKELIANOS, Angelos
"Caique" (tr. by Edmund Keeley and Philip Sherrard). Pequod
    (11) 80, p. 38.
"Sparta" (tr. by Edmund Keeley and Philip Sherrard). Pequod
    (11) 80, p. 39.

SILBERT, Layle
"Good Night. " PoNow (29) 80, p. 37.

SILESKY, Barry
"Birches. " Northeast (3:8) Wint 80, p. 34.

SILK, Bobbie Bayliss
"Petrified Wood. " PikeF (3) Wint 80, p. 3.

SILK, Dennis
"Traces of Mr. C. " Stand (21:4) 80, p. 22.

SILKIN, Jon
"The Cathedral Chair. " MassR (21:1) Spr 80, p. 80.
"Italy" (tr. of Giuseppe Ungareth w. David McDuff). Stand (21:2)
    80, p. 6.
"The kite" (tr. of Aleksandr Blok w. David McDuff). Stand (21:2)
    80, p. 8.
"A Man, a Woman, and a Fan. " SewanR (88:1) Wint 80, p. 29.
"Meaning Something. " SouthernR (16:2) Spr 80, p. 396.
"Night" (tr. of Georg Trakl w. David McDuff and R. S. Furness).
    Stand (21:2) 80, p. 19.
"Trumpets" (tr. of Georg Trakl w. David McDuff). Stand (21:2)
    80, p. 20.
Twelve poems (tr. of Amir Gilboa w. Natan Zach and Bat-Sheva
    Sheriff). Stand (21:4) 80, p. 4.
"A white low sun" (tr. of Marina Tsvetayeva w. David McDuff).
    Stand (21:2) 80, p. 7.

SILVA, Gary
"Angels. " PoetC (12:2) 80, p. 24.

"Derailment. " PoetC (12:1) 80, p. 26.
"Something About a Friendship" (for B).   PoetC (12:2) 80, p. 23.

SILVA, Jeff
   "Inkling of Wings. " Pan (21) 80, p. 26.

SILVA, Lakshmi de
   "Tangalle. " PortR (26) 80, p. 348.

SILVER-LILLYWHITE, Eileen
   "All That Autumn. " MissouriR (3:3) Sum 80, p. 19.
   "Franklin, Massachusetts. " KanQ (12:3) Sum 80, p. 132.
   "Slow Dance. " CutB (15) Aut/Wint 80, p. 11.

SILVERMAN, Stuart
   "What Else?" CropD (2/3) Aut-Wint 80, p. 31.

SILVERSTEIN, Shel
   "California C's. " Playb (27:11) N 80, p. 169.
   "Paintin' Her Fingernails. " Playb (27:2) F 80, p. 132.
   "Uncle Don 'Who Read Us the Sunday Funnies on the Radio. ' "
      Playb (27:3) Mr 80, pp. 115-117.

SIMBECK, Rob
   "The Cruets Clatter. " Epoch (29:2) Wint 80, p. 136.

SIMIC, Charles
   "Apocrypha. " Antaeus (38) Sum 80, p. 48.
   "Butcher Shop. " Tendril (9) 80, p. 135.
   "Ditty. " Antaeus (38) Sum 80, p. 51.
   "History Book. " Durak (5) 80, p. 15.
   "Like Whippoorwills. " Antaeus (38) Sum 80, p. 53.
   "Morning Classes. " Durak (5) 80, p. 14.
   "My Widow. " Antaeus (38) Sum 80, p. 49.
   "Primer. " Antaeus (38) Sum 80, p. 52.
   "Relations. " Antaeus (38) Sum 80, p. 50.
   "A Theory. " Antaeus (38) Sum 80, p. 47.
   "The Tomb of Stéphan Mallarmé. " GeoR (34:3) Aut 80, p. 590.

SIMKO, Daniel
   "About Love" (tr. of Stefan Strážay). CutB (14) Spr/Sum 80, p.
      10.
   "Death" (tr. of Milan Rufus). CutB (14) Spr/Sum 80, p. 11.
   "Experimental Animals" (tr. of Miroslav Holub). Durak (5) 80,
      p. 8.
   "The Shrubbery Is Darkening" (tr. of Stefan Strážay). CutB (14)
      Spr/Sum 80, p. 9.
   "To Go Home" (tr. of Milan Rufus). CutB (14) Spr/Sum 80, p.
      8.

SIMMERMAN, Jim
   "Cartoon. " CarolQ (32:2) Spr-Sum 80, p. 54.
   "Long Bones. " CarolQ (32:2) Spr-Sum 80, p. 52.

"My Parents Send Me a Ring from the Bahamas. " Columbia (5)
     Aut-Wint 80, p. 54.
"Sex. " Aspen (10) Wint 80, p. 46.
"Winter, Your Father's House. " OP (30) Aut 80, pp. 24-29.

SIMMONS, James
     "The Baggage and the Toff. " Ploughs (6:1) 80, p. 45.
     "The First Goodbye Letter. " Ploughs (6:1) 80, p. 51.
     "Mr Cordelia. " Ploughs (6:1) 80, p. 48.

SIMON, Greg
     "For a Russian Poet: Cherdyn, June, 1934. " NewYorker (56:13)
          19 My 80, p. 136.
     "Second Childhood. " NewRep (183:4) 26 Jl 80, p. 37.

SIMON, John Oliver
     "Bridgeport, California. " PoNow (26) 80, p. 19.

SIMPSON, Grace Pow
     "Finding Our Voices. " SmPd (50) Aut 80, p. 23.

SIMPSON, Louis
     "Art Poétique" (tr. of Gaston Miron). AmerPoR (9:1) Ja-F 80,
          p. 45.
     "Back in the States. " GeoR (34:2) Sum 80, p. 321.
     from Courte pointes: "Il fait un temps fou" (tr. of Gaston
          Miron). AmerPoR (9:1) Ja-F 80, p. 45.
     "An Irish Poet. " PoetryE (1) 80, p. 72.
     "La Pauvreté Anthropos" (tr. of Gaston Miron). AmerPoR (9:1)
          Ja-F 80, p. 46.
     "A River Running By. " GeoR (34:2) Sum 80, p. 320.
     "Rue Saint-Christophe" (tr. of Gaston Miron). AmerPoR (9:1)
          Ja-F 80, p. 45.
     from Vigie: "Appareille ô beauté je te fais une aire" (tr. of
          Robert Marteau). AmerPoR (9:1) Ja-F 80, p. 44.
     from Vigie: "Il est minuit" (tr. of Robert Marteau). AmerPoR
          (9:1) Ja-F 80, p. 44.
     from Vigie: "Innommé toujours est le monde" (tr. of Robert
          Marteau). AmerPoR (9:1) Ja-F 80, p. 44.
     from Vigie: "Trop de poètes font feu de tout" (tr. of Robert
          Marteau). AmerPoR (9:1) Ja-F 80, p. 44.
     "Why Do You Write About Russia?" OhioR (24) 80, p. 6.

SIMPSON, Mark
     "Coming Clear. " CreamCR (5:2) Spr 80, p. 90.

SIMPSON, Peter L.
     "Another Trip. " Focus (14:86) Ap 80, p. 32.
     "Behind our eyes. " Focus (14:86) Ap 80, p. 32.
     "In Memory of Robinson Jeffers. " Focus (14:86) Ap 80, p. 32.
     "New Poem. " Focus (14:86) Ap 80, p. 32.

SINGER, D. K.
     "For Irving Layton. " ConcPo (12:2) Aut 79, p. 44.

SINGH, Shukdev
from Bijak: "Padas" (tr. of Kabir w. Linda Hess). MalR (54)
Ap 80, pp. 79-85.
from Bijak: "Sakhis" (tr. of Kabir w. Linda Hess). MalR (54)
Ap 80, p. 86.

SINISGALLI, Leonardo
"I Know Now Not to Complain" (tr. by W. S. DiPiero). NewOR
(7:2) 80, p. 121.

SIOTIS, Dinos
"Black Days Are Coming." PortR (26) 80, p. 160.

SIROWITZ, Hal
"Father Fingers." BelPoJ (30:3) Spr 80, p. 1.
"Untitled: When the lights dimmed inside." SmPd (50) Aut 80,
p. 10.

SISSON, Jonathan
"Movable Type." ParisR (77) Wint-Spr 80, p. 113.

SIVARAKSA, Sulah
"Scoop Up the Sea" (tr. of Angkarn Kalyanapongs). PortR (26)
80, p. 398.

SJÖBERG, Leif
"The Ball of Fluff" (tr. of Harry Martinson w. W. H. Auden).
PoetryE (1) 80, p. 37.
"The Butterfly" (tr. of Harry Martinson w. W. H. Auden).
PoetryE (1) 80, p. 36.
"The Cock Reads the Field" (tr. of Harry Martinson w. William
Jay Smith). PoetryE (1) 80, p. 38.
"On the Outermost Edge" (tr. of Osten Sjostrand w. William Jay
Smith). PoetryE (1) 80, p. 43.
"On the Outermost Edge" (tr. of Östen Sjöstrand w. William Jay
Smith). PortR (26) 80, p. 376.
"Stairway" (tr. of Artur Lundkvist w. William Jay Smith).
PoetryE (3) 80, p. 57.
"The Swan" (tr. of Harry Martinson w. W. H. Auden). PoetryE
(1) 80, p. 35.

SJÖSTRAND, Ingrid
"Hör vad du inte hör." PortR (26) 80, p. 368.

SJÖSTRAND, Östen
"Favola." PortR (26) 80, p. 372.
"On the Outermost Edge" (tr. by William Jay Smith and Leif
Sjoberg). PoetryE (1) 80, p. 43.
"Vid havets yttersta gräns." PortR (26) 80, p. 374.

SKACEL, Jan
"Návstevy." PortR (26) 80, p. 74.
"Ti Kterí zakázali sami sebe." PortR (26) 80, p. 75.

SKEEN, Anita
  "How the Petals Seem the Same" (w. Francine Ringold).   Nimrod
      (24:1) Aut-Wint 80, p. 105.
  "Summer Morning at Round Hill Farm" (w. Francine Ringold).
      Nimrod (24:1) Aut-Wint 80, p. 106.

SKELTON, Robin
  "the good reason. " Kayak (54) S 80, p. 24.
  "Leavings. " OntR (13) Aut-Wint 80-81, p. 33.
  "Locality. " PoetryNW (21:4) Wint 80-81, p. 12.
  "Our Place and Theirs. " OntR (13) Aut-Wint 80-81, p. 34.
  "Sanctuary. " PoetryNW (21:4) Wint 80-81, p. 11.
  "A Seat in the Movies. " ConcPo (13:2) Aut 80, p. 74.
  "a walk on sunday. " Kayak (54) S 80, p. 25.
  "Why Should the Novelists Have All the Fun?" Kayak (54) S 80,
      p. 26.

SKINNER, Jeffrey
  "Her Side. " Poetry (136:2) My 80, p. 80.
  "His Side. " Poetry (136:2) My 80, p. 79.
  "To the Miller's Daughter. " BelPoJ (31:2) Wint 80-81, p. 10.

SKINNER, Knute
  "The Cow. " Tendril (9) 80, p. 136.
  "The News. " PortR (26) 80, p. 435.

SKLAR, Susan
  "Eight Hundred Years. " Pan (21) 80, p. 1.
  "Our Wedding. " Pan (21) 80, p. 1.

SKLAREW, Myra
  "Insomnia. " Vis (1) 79.
  "Twenty-Four Hours. " Vis (1) 79.

SKLOOT, Floyd
  "Probationary Period. " SlowLR (4) 80, p. 21.
  "Relocation. " SlowLR (4) 80, p. 19.

SKOVORODA, Gregory
  "Dogs" (adapted by Askold Melnyczuk). Agni (13) 80, p. 76.
  "Eagle and Magpie" (adapted by Askold Melnyczuk). Agni (13)
      80, p. 77.
  "Owl and Thrush" (adapted by Askold Melnyczuk). Agni (13) 80,
      p. 78.

SKOYLES, John
  "Excuse for a Love Poem. " Agni (13) 80, p. 33.
  "If You Have an Enemy. " GeoR (34:2) Sum 80, p. 292.

SKRAMSTAD, Susan
  "Behavior Chart. " Prima (5) 79, p. 16.

SLAGEL, Jim
  "Read a poem to a computer tonight. " EngJ (69:5) My 80,

front cover.

SLATE, Ron
"The Confession with No Sound." ThRiPo (15/16) 80, p. 52.
"Epithalamium." PoetryNW (21:1) Spr 80, p. 35.
"The Late Ferry." PoNow (29) 80, p. 37.
"The Penguins." PoetryNW (21:1) Spr 80, p. 35.
"The Snow Queen." ThRiPo (15/16) 80, p. 54.

SLAYTON, Ann
"Imitation." PoNow (29) 80, p. 37.

SLEIGH, Thomas R.
"The Invalid." LittleM (12:3/4) 80, p. 66.
"On Holiday." PartR (47:2) 80, p. 213.

SLESINGER, Warren
"Mistake, Mistress, Mistrust." HiramPoR (27) Aut-Wint 80, p.
46.

SLOAN, Benjamin
"The Milkman and the Housewife." CreamCR (5:1) Wint 79, p.
20.

SMALLEY, Joan
"From the Editor re: Bait." Aspen (10) Wint 80, p. 12.

SMALLWOOD, Randy
"The Deceived/The Damned." Wind (36) 80, pp. 56-61.

SMETZER, Michael
"Animals Hunting." KanQ (12:2) Spr 80, p. 43.

SMILLIE, Bill
"The Sacrificial Fly." PoNow (29) 80, p. 38.

SMITH, Annette
"The Thoroughbreds" (tr. of Aimé Césaire w. Clayton Eshleman).
Montra (7) 80, pp. 99-113.

SMITH, Arthur
"Lullaby." GeoR (34:4) Wint 80, p. 870.
"Nap." NewYorker (56:39) 17 N 80, p. 62.
"Summoned: A Baptism." NoAmR (265:4) D 80, p. 51.

SMITH, Bruce
"Winter and Spring. Things I Forgot to Tell Thean Logan Before
She Left." Poetry (135:5) F 80, p. 270.

SMITH, Dave
"The Abused (Hansel and Gretel)." QW (10) Wint-Spr 80, p. 43.
"Against Lawyers." WestHR (34:2) Spr 80, p. 116.
"Blue Spruce." OntR (13) Aut-Wint 80-81, pp. 61-72.

"Building Houses." QW (10) Wint-Spr 80, p. 41.
"Cleaning a Fish." NewYorker (56:10) 28 Ap 80, p. 42.
"Continuing Snow." QW (10) Wint-Spr 80, p. 40.
"Discovering Obscenities on Her Wall, I Pray." QW (10) Wint-
    Spr 80, p. 44.
"Dream Flight." NewYorker (55:52) 11 F 80, p. 36.
"Drudge." Tendril (7/8) Spr-Sum 80, p. 63.
"Elegy in an Abandoned Boatyard." NewYorker (56:40) 24 N 80,
    p. 44.
"Going Out at Dawn in the Country of Our Kin." ParisR (77)
    Wint-Spr 80, p. 108.
"Homage to Edgar Allan Poe." AmerPoR (9:4) Jl-Ag 80, p. 32.
"Mud Holes." NewYorker (56:24) 4 Ag 80, p. 30.
"The Perspective and Limits of Snapshots." Tendril (9) 80, p.
    137.
"A Place in the Forest." Poetry (135:6) Mr 80, p. 315.
"The Pornography Box." PraS (54:4) Wint 80-81, pp. 47-51.
"Sax Man." ParisR (77) Wint-Spr 80, p. 109.
"The Soft Belly of the World." Poetry (135:6) Mr 80, p. 313.
"The Song of Wine (1975)." MidwQ (21:3) Spr 80, p. 359.
"Tide Pools." Poetry (135:6) Mr 80, p. 311.
"To Celia, Before the Yachts." PraS (54:4) Wint 80-81, p. 43.
"The Traveling Photographer: Circa 1880" (to A. G.). PraS
    (54:4) Wint 80-81, pp. 52-56.
"Two Songs for the Round of the Year." WestHR (34:3) Sum 80,
    p. 251.
"Under a White Shawl of Pine." AmerS (49:3) Sum 80, p. 370.
"Waking Under Spruce with My Love." ParisR (77) Wint-Spr 80,
    p. 107.
"The Water Horse." PraS (54:4) Wint 80-81, p. 44.
"Your Christmas Present." NewYorker (56:44) 22 D 80, p. 40.

SMITH, David Thrall
    "Ice Music." StoneC (7:1) F 80, p. 8.

SMITH, Douglas C.
    "Average All American." SmPd (50) Aut 80, p. 29.
    "From the Balcony." ConcPo (12:2) Aut 79, p. 84.

SMITH, Gary
    "Holly Springs." BlackALF (14:4) Wint 80, p. 177.

SMITH, Harry
    "On Earth's Children." Confr (20) Spr-Sum 80, p. 97.

SMITH, Iain Crichton
    "Autumn." Stand (21:3) 80, p. 66.
    "The Boat People." Ploughs (6:1) 80, p. 96.
    "Clann Nighean an Sgadain." PortR (26) 80, p. 328.
    from The Folk Songs and Folklore of South Uist: "Did you see
        the modest girl?" Ploughs (6:1) 80, p. 95.
    from the Gaelic of Sorley Maclean: "Springtide." Ploughs (6:1)
        80, p. 94.

"The Herring Girls" (tr. by author). PortR (26) 80, p. 329.
"Running Repairs. " Stand (21:3) 80, p. 66.

SMITH, Jack E. Jr.
"Afternoon. " Wind (38) 80, p. 65.
"Dauphin County Pennsylvania, 1979" (for John Meehan). Wind
(38) 80, p. 66.
"Dining in the Station at 'The Old Express. " Wind (38) 80, p.
66.
"Elegy for Miss Grace Kerr. " Wind (38) 80, p. 65.

SMITH, Jared
"Entering the Room of the Late Poet. " PartR (47:2) 80, p. 223.
"For a Friend from the Old Country. " Wind (38) 80, p. 68.

SMITH, Jordan
"The Vampire. " Agni (12) 80, p. 30.
"Vine Valley. " Agni (12) 80, p. 31.

SMITH, Kay
"Evolution. " PottPort (2) 80-81, p. 41.

SMITH, Ken
"Hunéus the Shoemaker. " Stand (21:3) 80, p. 5.

SMITH, Le Roy Jr.
"Earth as Made. " Comm (107:23) 19 D 80, p. 716.
"Puritan Antiphons. " Comm (107:7) 11 Ap 80, p. 212.

SMITH, Marcel
"Center Green Human" (tr. of Alfredo Barrera Vasquez). CutB
(14) Spr /Sum 80, p. 109.

SMITH, Margaret
"Arbitrate. " BosUJ (26:3) 80, p. 45.
"Tantrum of Bones." BosUJ (26:3) 80, p. 43.

SMITH, Mark E.
"Inheritance. " LitR (23:3) Spr 80, p. 348.

SMITH, Mary Lonnberg
"A Moment's Attention. " HiramPoR (27) Aut-Wint 80, p. 47.
"Walk of the Chicken. " HiramPoR (27) Aut-Wint 80, p. 48.

SMITH, Newton
"Out of Place. " SouthernPR (20:2) Aut 80, p. 26.

SMITH, R. T.
"Andrew Wyeth's 'Adam.'" SlowLR (4) 80, p. 68.
"Andrew Wyeth's 'Seed Corn.'" SlowLR (4) 80, p. 69.
"Curing Shed" (for Jim Applewhite). HiramPoR (28) Spr-Sum 80,
p. 35.
"For Jennie at 15. " Tendril (7/8) Spr-Sum 80, p. 64.

"Intruder. " ConcPo (13:1) Spr 80, p. 74.
"Outings. " SlowLR (4) 80, p. 70.
"Poem for David Janssen. " BallSUF (21:2) Spr 80, p. 79.

SMITH, Stephen E.
"Bushnell Hamp Tells About the Friday Night Fight Down at
Shorty's Tavern. " PoetryNW (21:4) Wint 80-81, p. 44.
"Cricket Poem. " PoNow (29) 80, p. 38.
"The Death of Carmen Miranda. " SouthernPR (20:1) Spr 80, p.
53.
"From Florida. " CapeR (15:2) Sum 80, p. 31.
"How Fat Baskin Cole Eat Hisself Out of a Wife. " PoetryNW
(21:4) Wint 80-81, p. 43.
"How the River Took Daughtry McLamb. " PoetryNW (21:4) Wint
80-81, p. 41.
"Leroy Pinrawes Tells How in Detroit a Porno Movie Was Some-
thing Like Love. " PoetryNW (21:4) Wint 80-81, p. 46.
"Taint. " PoetryNW (21:4) Wint 80-81, p. 42.

SMITH, Tom
"Journeys of the Dead. " EnPas (11) 80, p. 19.
"Taking the Sun. " EnPas (11) 80, p. 21.
"Why Birds Sing. " VirQR (56:4) Aut 80, p. 680.

SMITH, Vivian
"Still Life. " NewL (46:3) Spr 80, p. 20.
"Twenty Years of Sydney. " NewL (46:3) Spr 80, p. 20.

SMITH, William Jay
"The Cock Reads the Field" (tr. of Harry Martinson w. Leif
Sjoberg). PoetryE (1) 80, p. 38.
"The Great Confrontation" (tr. of Andrei Voznesensky w. Vera
Dunham). Atl (245:4) Ap 80, p. 117.
"On the Outermost Edge" (tr. of Östen Sjöstrand w. Leif Sjo-
berg). PoetryE (1) 80, p. 43.
"On the Outermost Edge" (tr. of Östen Sjöstrand w. Leif Sjö-
berg). PortR (26) 80, p. 376.
"Stairway" (tr. of Artur Lundkvist w. Leif Sjoberg). PoetryE
(3) 80, p. 57.
"The Tall Poets. " SouthernR (16:2) Spr 80, pp. 391-395.

SMYKLO, Pat
"Japanese Boy in Internment Camp. " CalQ (16/17) 80, p. 125.

SMYTH, Paul
"A Photograph of Two Survivors. " EnPas (11) 80, p. 27.

SNELLER, Del
"My Feet on Your Sky. " StoneC (7:2) My 80, p. 26.

SNEYD, Steve
"At the Thirteenth Hour. " PortR (26) 80, p. 106.

SNIKERE, Velta
"Small Railway Station in the Country" (tr. of Pāvils Johansons).
PortR (26) 80, p. 253.

SNIVELY, Susan
"Fable." Thrpny (2) Sum 80, p. 3.
"The Invisible Man" (for Claude Rains). Thrpny (3) Aut 80, p.
10.

SNODGRASS, Claudette
"Individual Concerns" (tr. of Henri Michaux w. JoAnn Monks).
NewOR (7:2) 80, p. 149.

SNODGRASS, W. D.
"The Children." Salm (50/51) Aut 80-Wint 81, p. 25.
"Version 'B' Magda Goebbels." Salm (50/51) Aut 80-Wint 81,
p. 26.

SNOTHERLY, Mary C.
"Drought." SouthernPR (20:2) Aut 80, p. 62.

SNOW, Karen
"Retirement." BelPoJ (30:4) Sum 80, pp. 16-21.

SNYDER, Bob
"Billy Greenhorn's Tragedy." MinnR (NS 15) Aut 80, p. 26.
"Satori on Summer Street." BelPoJ (31:2) Wint 80-81, p. 34.

SNYDER, Gary
"Smokey the Bear Sutra." WindO (36) Spr-Sum 80, p. 8.

SOBIN, Anthony
"The Dream of the Moth." BelPoJ (30:4) Sum 80, p. 26.
"Driving Home to See the Folks." PoetryNW (21:2) Sum 80, p.
16.
"Fear of the Telephone." BelPoJ (30:4) Sum 80, p. 27.

SOBIN, Gustaf
"Bronze an Exercise in Style." Montra (7) 80, p. 52.
"The Cheval Glass." Montra (7) 80, p. 51.
"Flowering Cherries." Montra (7) 80, p. 49.
"Journey Book: Mexico" (tr. of Beatrice Caracciolo w. Eliot
Weinberger). Montra (7) 80, pp. 78-83.
"Lagoon: Reliquiae." Montra (7) 80, p. 58.
"Leis Esparentaus." Montra (7) 80, p. 46.
"Spring: An Extravagance." Montra (7) 80, p. 48.
"Violets." Montra (7) 80, p. 55.

SOCOLOW, Elizabeth
"House Cleaning." US1 (12/13) Aut-Wint 80, p. 4.
"Lover in the Kitchen." US1 (12/13) Aut-Wint 80, p. 4.
"Six Months Without Being Able to Listen to Bluegrass or Bach."
US1 (12/13) Aut-Wint 80, p. 4.

SOLDO, John J.
"Sonnet 20: Phyllis: phullon, leaf, foliage." Wind (38) 80, p. 39.

SOLOWEY, E.
"In Dissonance." Os (10) Spr 80, p. 24.
"Thorn Tree." Os (10) Spr 80, p. 23.

SOLT, John
"The Cat" (tr. of Yoshihara Sachiko). Ark (14) 80, p. 404.
"Love Poems for Sachiko." Ark (14) 80, p. 355.
from Manyoshu: (1, 2). Ark (14) 80, p. 357.
"A Saying of Confucius." Ark (14) 80, p. 361.
"Speaking of Bread" (tr. of Yoshihara Sachiko). Ark (14) 80, p. 406.
"Sundown" (tr. of Yoshihara Sachiko). Ark (14) 80, p. 407.

SOMERVILLE, Jane
"A Beau Language Without a Drop of Blood." CapeR (16:1) Wint 80, p. 11.
"Denials." CapeR (16:1) Wint 80, p. 10.
"Miss Gwendolyn Brooks." Aspen (10) Wint 80, p. 33.

SOMMER, Jason
"Coal." NewRep (182:22) 31 My 80, p. 26.
"Wedding Photographs." NewRep (183:3) 19 Jl 80, p. 34.

SOMMER, Piotr
"Dwa gesty." PortR (26) 80, p. 295.
"Kiedy." PortR (26) 80, p. 298.
"Miedzy przystankiem a domen" (Paulowi i Helenie). PoNow (26) 80, p. 296.

SONDE, Susan
"Sunlight Leaves This." Vis (2) 80.

SONIAT, Katherine
"Weathering." CharR (6:2) Aut 80, p. 30.

SONNE, Jorgen
"Kammerkantate i moll." PortR (26) 80, p. 94.
"Shanty." PortR (26) 80, p. 93.

SONNEVI, Goran
"Clarity" (tr. by Robert Bly). PoetryE (1) 80, p. 19.
from The Impossible: (85, 87, 93, 182) (tr. by Lennart Bruce). PoetryE (1) 80, p. 20.

SOOS, R. Jr.
"with wings on." Wind (38) 80, p. 70.

SORESCU, Marin
"Besides Me" (tr. by Michael Hamburger). Stand (21:3) 80, p. 52.

"Carbon Paper" (tr. by Michael Hamburger).   Poetry (136:1) Ap 80, p. 26.
"Otrǎvuri. " Poetry (136:1) Ap 80, p. 24.
"Question" (tr. by Michael Hamburger).   Poetry (136:1) Ap 80, p. 29.
"Seneca" (tr. by Michael Hamburger).   Poetry (136:1) Ap 80, p. 28.
"Shakespeare" (tr. by Michael Hamburger).   Poetry (136:1) Ap 80, p. 27.
"The Thieves" (tr. by Michael Hamburger).   Stand (21:3) 80, p. 53.

SORRELLS, Helen
"The Lost Child. " KanQ (12:2) Spr 80, p. 55.
"Mind Can Be Called to Supper. " Wind (36) 80, p. 62.
"November. " Wind (36) 80, p. 62.
"Tomorrow There May Be Winter. " Wind (36) 80, p. 63.
"The Woman from France. " SouthernPR (20:1) Spr 80, p. 36.

SOSSAMAN, Stephen
"A Veteran Attends a July Fourth Barbeque. " CentR (24:3) Sum 80, p. 308.
"A Viet Cong Sapper Dies. " CentR (24:3) Sum 80, p. 307.

SOTO, Gary
"The Ashes. " Poetry (135:6) Mr 80, p. 331.
"Beto. " Thrpny (1) Wint-Spr 80, p. 8.
"Sueño. " Poetry (136:6) S 80, p. 340.
"Towards It. " Poetry (136:6) S 80, p. 341.
"The Widow Perez. " Poetry (135:6) Mr 80, p. 332.

SOURS, John Appling
"Dinner on the Terrace by the Canal. " HolCrit (17:4) O 80, p. 19.

SOUTH, G. Robin
"Summer Night-Rain. " PottPort (2) 80-81, p. 37.

SOUTH, Karen
"The Eye. " WebR (5:1) Wint 80, p. 55.
"Keeping the Moments of Sand. " WebR (5:1) Wint 80, p. 54.

SOUTHWICK, Marcia
"The Night Won't Save Anyone. " Poetry (135:5) F 80, p. 267.
"No Such Thing. " Antaeus (37) Spr 80, p. 59.
"The Vanishing Street. " GeoR (34:3) Aut 80, p. 614.

SOWELL, Kathleen
"Me-Mama. " SmPd (48) Wint 80, p. 7.
"Whole Wheat. " SmPd (50) Aut 80, p. 11.

SPACKS, Barry
"Babies. " GeoR (34:2) Sum 80, p. 396.

"Intersection. " Atl (246:4) O 80, p. 98.
"Judges in Summer. " Poetry (136:6) S 80, p. 329.
"The Poetry Bug. " Poetry (136:6) S 80, p. 328.
"Six Small Songs for a Silver Flute. " Tendril (9) 80, p. 138.
"Thinking of Peas" (for Tanya Berry). CalQ (16/17) 80, p. 135.

SPAULDING, John
   "Stones. " SouthernPR (20:2) Aut 80, p. 61.

SPEAKES, Richard
   "Hannah's Travel. " Iowa (10:4) Aut 79, pp. 16-21.

SPEAR, Cindy
   "March 21st. " PottPort (2) 80-81, p. 42.

SPEAR, Gary
   "Cutting Apples. " StoneC (7:3) D 80, p. 53.
   "The Lady and the Harp. " StoneC (7:3) D 80, p. 54.
   "II. " StoneC (7:3) D 80, p. 55.

SPEAR, Roberta
   "Dust" (for Elizabeth Cotton). MissouriR (3:2) Wint 80, p. 17.

SPEECE, Merry
   Detail from an American Landscape. Bits (Chapbook) 80. En-
      tire issue.

SPEER, Laurel
   "The Bedraggled Bird. " Sam (102) 80, p. 45.
   "Bob Wasn't There. " CropD (2/3) Aut-Wint 80, p. 17.
   "Branwell Be Well. " PoNow (29) 80, p. 29.
   "Don't Dress Your Cat in an Apron. " LittleM (12:3/4) 80, p.
      100.
   "E. E. Said It Better. " CropD (2/3) Aut-Wint 80, p. 17.
   "Last Holdout in Vermont. " Sam (92) 80, p. 37.
   "Many Fought and Did Not Die. " Tele (16) 80, p. 121.
   "The Millionth Page Turn. " CapeR (16:1) Wint 80, p. 15.
   "Old Enemies at a Meeting of the Minds. " Tele (16) 80, p. 121.
   "One Day in the Life of Memorizing. " CapeR (16:1) Wint 80, p.
      14.
   "Shirley Grossman and the Cross Country Team. " PoNow (29)
      80, p. 29.
   "Watching My Talent Fade. " HolCrit (17:5) D 80, p. 16.
   "White Elephants. " PoNow (29) 80, p. 29.

SPINGARN, Lawrence P.
   "Bore-Hunting in Pasadena. " MalR (53) Ja 80, p. 44.
   "The Croquet Players: Dusk. " PoNow (27) 80, p. 27.
   "The Dog's Funeral. " PoNow (27) 80, p. 27.
   "In the Verdugos. " PoNow (27) 80, p. 35.
   "The Locker Room. " PoNow (27) 80, p. 27.
   "Position at Noon. " PoNow (27) 80, p. 35.
   "Sirocco. " PoNow (27) 80, p. 27.

SPIRES, Elizabeth
"Blame." Ploughs (6:2) 80, p. 30.
"Blue Nude." Ploughs (6:2) 80, p. 28.
"Boardwalk." Poetry (136:6) S 80, p. 321.
"Catchpenny Road." Poetry (136:6) S 80, p. 323.
"Instructions for the Sleeper." PartR (47:4) 80, p. 606.
"Tequila." NewYorker (56:31) 22 S 80, p. 44.

SPIVACK, Kathleen
"Approaching the Canvas." Tendril (9) 80, p. 140.
"As Animals." MichQR (19:4/20:1) Aut-Wint 80-81, p. 667.
"the bakery." Kayak (53) My 80, p. 52.
"Daphne." PartR (47:2) 80, p. 219.
"Marble." PoNow (26) 80, p. 37.
"Meditation." MassR (21:3) Aut 80, p. 548.
"meeting a woman friend." Kayak (53) My 80, p. 53.
"Sleeping Next to You in North Dakota." MassR (21:3) Aut 80,
    p. 549.
"you." Kayak (53) My 80, p. 51.

SPRAGUE, Stuart
"Convention Wrap-Up." ChrC (97:5) 6-13 F 80, p. 125.

SPYCHER, Peter
"Reasons for Taking Care of the Car" (tr. of Reiner Kunze).
    Field (22) Spr 80, p. 13.
"Refuge Even Behind Refuge" (for Peter Huchel) (tr. of Reiner
    Kunze). Field (22) Spr 80, p. 14.

STACH, Carl
"A Poem Obliquely About Bruegel's Icarus." BelPoJ (30:4) Sum
    80, p. 15.

STAFFORD, Kim Robert
"Being the Last to Leave." ThRiPo (15/16) 80, p. 57.
"The Family Gathered Here." ThRiPo (15/16) 80, p. 58.
"It Begins With Ashes." CarolQ (32:2) Spr-Sum 80, p. 33.
"John Clare." Nat (230:6) 16 F 80, p. 186.
"A Lesson in Architecture." VirQR (56:1) Wint 80, p. 69.
"Letter to Phil Sisters Star Route October." CarolQ (32:3) Aut
    80, p. 81.
"Mr. Epp's Garden in Aurora." VirQR (56:1) Wint 80, p. 68.
"Picnic." KanQ (12:3) Sum 80, p. 28.
"Putting Hand-Set Type Away" (for printers and travelers).
    SmF (11/12) Spr-Aut 80, p. 59.
"Salamander." KanQ (12:3) Sum 80, p. 29.
"The Surface." ThRiPo (15/16) 80, p. 59.
"Waiting to Be Born." ThRiPo (15/16) 80, p. 60.

STAFFORD, William
"Answerers." Tendril (9) 80, p. 141.
"At Max Wickert's Place." Pequod (11) 80, p. 7.
"Being an American." PoNow (27) 80, p. 7.

"Coming Back to Kansas. " LittleBR (1:1) Aut 80, p. 38.
"Confessions of an Individual. " PoNow (28) 80, p. 7.
"Elms in Winter. " SoDakR (18:4) Wint 81, p. 81.
"Everything Twice. " Atl (245:6) Je 80, p. 76.
"For Later. " AmerPoR (9:1) Ja-F 80, p. 16.
"Grandmother. " SoDakR (18:4) Wint 81, p. 81.
"Help from History. " AmerS (49:3) Sum 80, p. 356.
"Historical Facts. " DacTerr (17) 80, p. 78.
"In a Corner. " MichQR (19:2) Spr 80, p. 156.
"A Last Service. " MichQR (19:2) Spr 80, p. 158.
"Learning a Word While Climbing. " Poetry (135:4) Ja 80, p.
     191.
"Living Out Here. " SoDakR (18:4) Wint 81, p. 84.
"The Long Lens. " AmerPoR (9:1) Ja-F 80, p. 16.
"Looking Across the River. " Poetry (135:4) Ja 80, p. 188.
"A Memorial for My Mother. " LittleBR (1:1) Aut 80, p. 39.
"A Message from Space. " Pequod (11) 80, p. 5.
"Missionary Meadowlark. " LittleBR (1:1) Aut 80, p. 40.
Nine poems. Field (22) Spr 80, pp. 27-46.
"One of My Letters. " ParisR (77) Wint-Spr 80, p. 104.
"One of the Many Dreams of Childhood. " DacTerr (17) 80, p.
     79.
"Places. " SoDakR (18:4) Wint 81, p. 82.
"Remembering. " MichQR (19:2) Spr 80, p. 157.
"Remembering Mountain Men. " ConcPo (13:2) Aut 80, p. 4.
"Renegade. " ConcPo (13:2) Aut 80, p. 4.
"A Return to Garden City. " LittleBR (1:1) Aut 80, p. 40.
"The Room. " Nat (230:3) 26 Ja 80, p. 93.
"Ruby Was Her Name. " ParisR (77) Wint-Spr 80, p. 103.
"Saving Things. " LittleBR (1:1) Aut 80, p. 37.
"Sending These Messages. " Poetry (135:4) Ja 80, p. 187.
"Serving with Gideon. " AmerPoR (9:3) My-Je 80, p. 12.
"Survivor" (for Kenneth Rexroth and our generation). Ark (14)
     80, p. 262.
"A Tentative Welcome to Readers. " Poetry (135:4) Ja 80, p.
     191.
"These Hands. " Nat (230:1) 5-12 Ja 80, p. 22.
"Things Not in the Story. " Pequod (11) 80, p. 6.
"Things the Wind Says. " SoDakR (18:4) Wint 81, p. 83.
"This Year. " Tendril (7 /8) Spr-Sum 80, p. 65.
"A Walk in September. " NewL (46:4) Sum 80, p. 56.
"A War-Monument Speech for July 4 (1973). " MidwQ (21:3) Spr
     80, p. 361.
"Watching Her Go. " Poetry (135:4) Ja 80, p. 190.
"With Neighbors One Afternoon. " Poetry (135:4) Ja 80, p. 189.

STAGG, Barry
"Into My Procrustean Bed. " PottPort (2) 80-81, p. 39.
"Will You Have Changed When You Come Home?" PottPort (2)
     80-81, p. 26.

STALL, Lindon
"Song of Saint John" (tr. of Stéphane Mallarmé). SouthernR
     (16:2) Spr 80, p. 441.

STALLMAN, R. W.
"At the Carnival. " SouthernR (16:1) Wint 80, p. 175.
"The Solar Snake. " SouthernR (16:1) Wint 80, p. 174.

STAMBLER, Peter
"Ex Centris: To Olaf in the Wilderness. " Shen (31:2) 80, p. 19.
"From Olaf, to Henrik in Rome. " Shen (31:2) 80, p. 16.

STANDING, Sue
"Mostly Departures" (for L.). Ploughs (6:2) 80, p. 27.
"Observatory Hill. " Nat (230:18) 10 My 80, p. 567.

STANESCU, Nichita
"Winter Ritual" (tr. by Mariana Carpinisan and Mark Irwin).
Iowa (10:4) Aut 79, p. 38.

STANFORD, Ann
"The Center of the Garden. " Ark (14) 80, p. 365.
"Dreaming the Garden. " Ark (14) 80, p. 363.
"Garden Poems: 1, 2, 3, 4, 5. " SouthernR (16:2) Spr 80, pp.
385-390.

STANLEY, Nancy
"August 7, 1978. " EngJ (69:5) My 80, p. 58.

STANTON, Joseph
"Kapiolani's Banyans. " SmPd (48) Wint 80, p. 26.

STANTON, Maura
"Alcestis" (for Stanley Kunitz). Tendril (9) 80, p. 142.
"The Dimestore Clerk. " PoNow (28) 80, p. 41.
"Elegy for the Whole World (1974). " MidwQ (21:3) Spr 80, p.
362.
"The Lion's Eyebrows. " AmerPoR (9:5) S-O 80, p. 3.

STAP, Don
"Full Moon" (for Sandra). PoetryNW (21:3) Aut 80, p. 33.
"What Will You Remember?" QW (10) Wint-Spr 80, p. 94.

STARBUCK, George
"The Spell Against Spelling. " Atl (245:2) F 80, p. 92.

STARK, David
"Night Sky. " CimR (52) Jl 80, p. 13.
"On Learning of the Pickling of California Bandit Joaquin Mur-
rieta's Head in One Gallon of Whiskey--July, 1853. " PoNow
(29) 80, p. 38.
"Whale Watch--St. Lawrence Island, Alaska" (for my brother).
CarolQ (32:2) Spr-Sum 80, p. 88.

STEELE, Dona
"Poem: She kept her surrealistic features under wraps. " Pan
(21) 80, p. 40.

STEFANILE, Selma
I Know a Wise Bird (for Felix). Sparrow (40) 80. Entire issue.

STEFFEN, Timothy W.
"A Person in Hiding." Mouth (2:4) My 80, p. 8.

STEFFLER, John
"In Class." PottPort (2) 80-81, p. 9.
"My Father's Lunch." PottPort (2) 80-81, p. 11.
"Parent Problem." PottPort (2) 80-81, p. 49.

STEHMAN, John
"Sheet Metal Screws." PartR (47:2) 80, p. 222.

STEIN, Paul
"The Humors." OhioR (25) 80, p. 81.

STEINARR, Steinn
"Atlantis" (tr. by Alan Boucher). Vis (2) 80.

STEINBERG, Alan L.
"Intensive Care" (for Charles). Poem (38) Mr 80, p. 45.
"The Old Woman Across the Way." Poem (38) Mr 80, p. 47.
Three Haikus About Western Man. Poem (38) Mr 80, p. 46.

STEINBERGH, Judith
"Disoriented." Tendril (7/8) Spr-Sum 80, p. 70.
"Ending." Tendril (7/8) Spr-Sum 80, p. 67.
"Forecast." Tendril (7/8) Spr-Sum 80, p. 67.
"If There Were No Phone." Tendril (7/8) Spr-Sum 80, p. 68.
"Options." Tendril (7/8) Spr-Sum 80, p. 66.

STEINGASS, David
"Bed." PoNow (28) 80, p. 42.

STEINKE, Russell
"Gas Station." CharR (6:2) Aut 80, p. 24.

STEINMAN, Lisa M.
"Language Without Geography." Epoch (29:3) Spr-Sum 80, p. 238.

STEPANCHEV, Stephen
"Hawk." PoNow (27) 80, p. 18.
"Leaving the Hospital." PoNow (27) 80, p. 18.
"Loving Them." PoNow (26) 80, p. 5.
"Waiting." PoNow (27) 80, p. 18.

STEPHENS, Michael
"Knives." ParisR (78) Sum 80, p. 194.

STEPHENSON, Shelby
"All the Dead Goats." PoNow (29) 80, p. 30.

'Coming Out. " Comm (107:5) 14 Mr 80, p. 142.
"Holding On. " SouthernPR (20:1) Spr 80, p. 48.
"My Recurring Dream. " PoNow (29) 80, p. 30.
"When January Is Cold. " PoNow (29) 80, p. 30.

STERN, Gerald
"Acacia. " Poetry (136:3) Je 80, p. 146.
"The Angel Poem. " AmerPoR (9:4) Jl-Ag 80, p. 15.
"Cow Worship. " PoetryE (3) 80, p. 27.
"Days of 1978. " MissouriR (3:2) Wint 80, p. 39.
"A Hundred Years from Now. " AmerPoR (9:4) Jl-Ag 80, p. 17.
"In Carpenter's Woods. " Tendril (9) 80, p. 143.
"June Fourth. " Poetry (136:3) Je 80, p. 145.
"The Poem of Liberation. " AmerPoR (9:4) Jl-Ag 80, p. 16.
"The Roar. " NewYorker (56:41) 1 D 80, p. 50.
"The Rose Warehouse. " MissouriR (3:2) Wint 80, p. 38.
"These Birds. " PoetryE (3) 80, p. 28.
"Thinking About Shelley. " Poetry (136:3) Je 80, p. 144.
"Visiting Florida Again. " PoetryE (3) 80, p. 29.
"Your Animal. " AmerPoR (9:4) Jl-Ag 80, p. 16.

STERN, Robert
"(untitled): "where is the galaxy of love. " Wind (36) 80, p. 20.

STERNBERG, Ricardo
"Flamenco. " Nat (231:20) 13 D 80, p. 648.

STERRETT, Jane
'Wanting to Bleed. " PoetryNW (21:3) Aut 80, p. 19.

STETIE, Salah
"De toutes choses le fils, le violon.... " PortR (26) 80, p. 255.
"Obscure lampe enserrée de fourmis. " PortR (26) 80, p. 256.
"Le rouge de la femme rouge. " PortR (26) 80, p. 257.

STETLER, Charles
"Sign of the Times. " WormR (77) 80, p. 8.
"To John Garfield, for Whom the Postman Only Rang Once. "
   WormR (77) 80, p. 7.

STEURY, Tim
"Boar Fight. " SouthernPR (20:2) Aut 80, p. 40.

STEVENS, Alex
"An 80-Years Self, Portrait. " NewYorker (56:7) 7 Ap 80, p. 119.
'In Scorching Time. " GeoR (34:1) Spr 80, p. 110.
'Rouge et noir. " NewYorker (56:10) 28 Ap 80, p. 136.

STEVENS, Shirley S.
"The Carpenter's Rood. " ChrC (97:42) 24 D 80, p. 1265.

STEVENSON, Anne
"Lockkeeper's Island. " MichQR (19:3) Sum 80, p. 322.

STEVER, Margo
"News of Franconia. " CropD (1) Spr 80, p. 13.

STEWARD, D. E.
"Twenty Seven Days. " Bachy (17) Spr 80, pp. 27-33.

STEWART, Charlotte
"Doors" (w. Carol Haralson). Nimrod (24:1) Aut-Wint 80, p.
   102.
"Doors II" (w. Carol Haralson). Nimrod (24:1) Aut-Wint 80, p.
   103.
"Reaching Across" (w. Carol Haralson). Nimrod (24:1) Aut-Wint
   80, p. 104.

STEWART, Dolores
"Awake at 4:00 A. M. " Tendril (7/8) Spr-Sum 80, p. 71.

STEWART, Douglas
"Images from the Mountains" (for David Campbell). NewL (46:3)
   Spr 80, p. 22.

STEWART, Frank
"Night Character" (tr. of Dino Campana). CutB (14) Spr/Sum
   80, p. 17.

STEWART, H. K.
"Living Along the Done. " QW (11) Aut-Wint 80-81, p. 99.

STEWART, Pamela
from The One and the Other: Nine poems. AmerPoR (9:6) N-D
   80, p. 3.

STEWART, Robert
"Boss Told Me. " Focus (14:86) Ap 80, p. 35.
"A Flow Behind the Walls. " Focus (14:86) Ap 80, p. 35.
"View. " NewL (46:4) Sum 80, p. 57.
"The Weatherman Says He's Sorry. " Focus (14:86) Ap 80, p. 35.
"What It Takes to Be a Plumber" (to my father). DacTerr (17)
   80, p. 80.

STEWART, Susan
"In the Exact Middle of the Night. " PoNow (29) 80, p. 39.
"My Ear to the Chest of the World. " PoNow (29) 80, p. 39.
"The White Houses. " PoNow (29) 80, p. 39.

STILES, Ward
"The Day of the Child. " SouthwR (65:2) Spr 80, p. 155.

STILL, James
"Visitor. " Wind (38) 80, p. 70.

STILWELL, Elizabeth
"Costumed. " BallSUF (21:1) Wint 80, p. 60.
"Endangered Species. " BallSUF (21:1) Wint 80, p. 76.

STIX, Judith Saul
"Word Studies: Bursts. " Ascent (6:1) 80, p. 31.

STOCK, Bud
"Clytie. " CapeR (16:1) Wint 80, p. 31.
"Olea. " CapeR (16:1) Wint 80, p. 31.

STOCKDALE, John C.
"Of a Childhood Filled with Wars. " PottPort (2) 80-81, p. 10.

STOCKWELL, Brenda S.
"Easter Flood. " SouthernPR (20:1) Spr 80, p. 23.

STOKES, Terry
"Before Sleep. " ParisR (78) Sum 80, p. 119.
"Nobody Makes Better Bebop-a-lula Than You. " Bits (11) 80.

STOKESBURY, Leon
"This Other. " QW (10) Wint-Spr 80, p. 93.

STOLOFF, Carolyn
"Among the Shod. " NewL (46:4) Sum 80, p. 58.

STONE, Carole
"At a Lunch Counter in Downtown Easton. " BelPoJ (30:3) Spr
     80, p. 11.
"My Father's Chauffeur. " SouthernPR (20:1) Spr 80, p. 58.
"Old Man at Nightfall. " FourQt (30:1) Aut 80, p. 35.

STONE, Joan
"Side Yard. " PoetryNW (21:3) Aut 80, p. 20.

STONE, John
"Even Though. " AmerS (49:3) Sum 80, p. 336.
"How I'd Have It. " AmerS (49:2) Spr 80, p. 226.
"The Truck. " AmerS (49:4) Aut 80, p. 464.

STONE, Ruth
"Liebeslied. " CalQ (16/17) 80, p. 32.
"Orange Poem Praising Brown. " CalQ (16/17) 80, p. 31.
"Where I Came From. " CalQ (16/17) 80, p. 34.
"Why Kid Yourself. " CalQ (16/17) 80, p. 35.
"Women Laughing. " CalQ (16/17) 80, p. 33.

STONE, Sandra
"Game. " PoetryNW (21:2) Sum 80, p. 31.
"Listening to the Muffled Breath of Lake Geneva. " PortR (26)
     80, p. 433.

STORACE, Pat
"After a Chorus from the Bacchae. " SunM (9/10) Sum 80, p.
     204.

STORK, Gerry
"Just the Same." NewL (47:1) Aut 80, p. 32.
"Moment" (for David). NewL (47:1) Aut 80, p. 33.

STORNI, Alfonsina
"I Will Sleep" (tr. by Vinnie-Marie D'Ambrosio). CutB (14)
    Spr /Sum 80, p. 99.

STOTT, Dorothy
"Last Time of Saying. " MalR (54) Ap 80, p. 149.

STOUT, Liz
"Waiting. " PoNow (26) 80, p. 47.

STOUT, Robert Joe
"The Company Insurance Clerk Explains the Dental Plan. "
    StoneC (7:2) My 80, p. 24.
"A Father Describes His Married Daughter. " Sam (86) 79, p.
    31.
"Gopher. " StoneC (7:2) My 80, p. 25.
"The Hate in Us. " WindO (36) Spr-Sum 80, p. 43.
"Return. " FourQt (29:2) Wint 80, p. 18.

STOUTENBURG, Adrien
"fact versus fancy and vice versa. " Kayak (53) My 80, p. 34.
"Schopenhauer and the Orangutan. " PoetryNW (21:1) Spr 80, p.
    51.
"storm's eye. " Kayak (53) My 80, p. 35.

STOWELL, Phyllis
"In the Colorless Hour. " SouthwR (65:4) Aut 80, p. 415.

STOYER, Tracy
"To Her Brash Suitor. " EngJ (69:5) My 80, p. 60.

STRAHAN, B. R.
"Dark Waters. " Vis (4) 80.
"Discoveries of Light. " Vis (1) 79.
"Exile-in-Winter. " Vis (2) 80.
"Last Door. " Vis (3) 80.
"The Modern Poet Thinks. " Vis (1) 79.
"Note Found in a Pocket. " Vis (3) 80.
"Spring Peepers. " Vis (3) 80.

STRAND, Mark
"Elegy for My Father. " Tendril (9) 80, pp. 144-148.
"The Gift. " ParisR (77) Wint-Spr 80, p. 31.
"My Mother on an Evening in Late Summer. " NewYorker (56:23)
    28 Jl 80, p. 34.
"Night in Hackett's Cove. " NewRep (183:5 /6) 2-9 Ag 80, p. 32.
"An Ox Looks at Man" (tr. of Carlos Drummond de Andrade).
    NewYorker (56:30) 15 S 80, p. 50.

STRATTON, Bert
"The Yellow Pages." Tele (16) 80, p. 97.

STRAZAY, Stefan
"About Love" (tr. by Daniel Simko). CutB (14) Spr/Sum 80, p. 10.
"The Shrubbery Is Darkening" (tr. by Daniel Simko). CutB (14) Spr/Sum 80, p. 9.

STRICKLIN, Robert
"Credo." BallSUF (21:1) Wint 80, p. 53.

STRINGER, David H.
"History Class." EngJ (69:5) My 80, p. 58.

STRONG, Eithne
"Diameter." PortR (26) 80, p. 192.
"Unions." PortR (26) 80, p. 193.

STRONGIN, Lynn
"Mailbox Flowers." Pan (21) 80, p. 4.

STRUTHERS, Ann
"Old Women at Church." NewL (46:4) Sum 80, p. 64.
"Prester John." PoetC (12:1) 80, p. 12.

STRYK, Dan
"Confessions of a Black Sheep on a Farm." Confr (20) Spr-Sum 80, p. 87.
"Drought." PoNow (29) 80, p. 39.
"Mosquitos." Wind (36) 80, p. 50.
"Nighttrain." QW (10) Wint-Spr 80, p. 115.

STRYK, Lucien
"Cherries." Tendril (9) 80, p. 149.
"Storm." NewL (46:4) Sum 80, p. 59.

STUART, Dabney
"Begging on North Main." SouthernR (16:1) Wint 80, p. 124.
"A Chance Encounter." SouthernR (16:1) Wint 80, p. 126.
"Histories." SouthernR (16:1) Wint 80, p. 125.
"The Opposite Field." Tendril (7/8) Spr-Sum 80, pp. 73-77.
"The Opposite Field" (to my brother). Tendril (9) 80, pp. 150-154.
"Patrimony." Tendril (7/8) Spr-Sum 80, p. 72.

STUART, Floyd C.
"Balloon." Poem (40) N 80, p. 57.
"Hedgehog." CimR (52) Jl 80, p. 63.
"How Spring Comes." Poem (40) N 80, p. 54.
"In Deep Woods." Poem (40) N 80, p. 56.
"Love's Country." SouthernPR (20:2) Aut 80, p. 63.

STUCK, Nancy Jo
    "X--The Unknown Quantity. " Wind (36) 80, p. 35.

SUARDIAZ, Luis
    "Schoolbooks" (tr. by Stuart Friebert). CarlMis (18:2) Sum 80,
        p. 97.

SUBLETT, Dyan
    "Still Life: Interiors" (for Gwen Gugell). OhioR (25) 80, p. 22.

SUDDICK, Tom
    "ee cummings at Coney Island. " Sam (101) 80, p. 19.
    "What Do You Want from Life?" Sam (101) 80, p. 19.

SUDERMAN, Elmer F.
    "Old Windmill. " Wind (38) 80, p. 21.
    "Places Too Small for Maps. " KanQ (12:2) Spr 80, p. 44.

SUGIOKA, Stephanie
    "After Reading the Tale of the Genji. " BelPoJ (31:2) Wint 80-81,
        p. 5.

SULLIVAN, Chuck
    "Being Chosen. " CarolQ (32:1) Wint 80, p. 61.

SULLIVAN, Francis
    "Allegories: For When You Fill with Death. " Pan (21) 80, p.
        34.
    "Narratives for Osip Mandelstam. " Pan (21) 80, p. 36.
    "Prayer Before an Icon. " Pan (21) 80, p. 33.
    "Rothko Chapel, Houston. " Pan (21) 80, p. 31.

SUMMERS, Cat
    "Heartland. " PottPort (2) 80-81, p. 5.

SUMMERS, Hollis
    "The Intersection. " PoNow (27) 80, p. 5.
    "On Sharing Miracles. " PoNow (27) 80, p. 5.

SUMMERS, Mad Anthony
    "If Only. " Sam (98) 80, p. 26.

SUREYA, Cemal
    "Duel" (tr. by Oscan Yalim, William Fielder and Dionis Coffin
        Riggs). DenQ (15:2) Sum 80, p. 87.
    "San" (tr. by Oscan Yalim, William Fielder and Dionis Coffin
        Riggs). DenQ (15:2) Sum 80, p. 86.

SUSSMAN, S. W.
    "April's Fools. " Pan (21) 80, p. 25.

SUTHERLAND, Elizabeth
    "I Would Like to Die Fucking. " Ark (14) 80, p. 368.

"Poem for Kenneth. " Ark (14) 80, p. 366.

SUTHERLAND, Fraser
"After the Sad Movie. " PottPort (2) 80-81, p. 41.
"From an Imaginary Folksong. " PottPort (1) 79-80, p. 21.
'Return to Cold Comfort Farm. " PottPort (1) 79-80, p. 28.

SUTHERLAND-SMITH, James
"Bachelor. " GRR (11:2/3) 80, p. 46.
"A Journey by Mandeville. " GRR (11:2/3) 80, p. 44.
"The Seasons. " GRR (11:2/3) 80, p. 40.

SUTTER, Barton
"Shoe Shop. " Poetry (135:5) F 80, p. 261.
"Static. " Poetry (135:5) F 80, p. 263.

SUTTON, Catherine
"Photography Exhibit: 'New York, 1890-1910. '" PoetC (12:2) 80,
    p. 40.

SU-TUNG'P-O
"Away on My Brother's Birthday" (tr. by Jon Hansen). ChiR
    (31:4) Spr 80, p. 158.

SUWA Yu
"A Copy Book of Yanaka. " Ark (14) 80, p. 369.
"Tomorrow. " Vis (4) 80.

SVEHLA, John
"Chicago Bloom Clouds. " Wind (38) 80, p. 23.

SVOBODA, Alva
"Easy Green Proof. " Tele (16) 80, p. 77.

SVOBODA, Robert J.
"After Tennyson. " SmPd (48) Wint 80, p. 8.
"Mating Call on 4. " SmPd (48) Wint 80, p. 8.
"Old Hat. " SmPd (48) Wint 80, p. 7.
"A Pessimist Is Born. " SmPd (48) Wint 80, p. 8.

SVOBODA, Terese
"Arbor Day. " PoNow (29) 80, p. 46.
"Barking Dogs. " VirQR (56:2) Spr 80, p. 273.
'Never the moth's token. " ParisR (78) Sum 80, p. 193.
"No Season for It. " NewEngR (3:2) Wint 80, p. 238.
"Planet X. " PoNow (26) 80, p. 47.
"Sonnet. " NewL (47:1) Aut 80, p. 103.
"This country. " NewL (47:1) Aut 80, p. 102.
"This Is What I Have. " VirQR (56:2) Spr 80, p. 272.
'Wheatfield. " NewEngR (3:2) Wint 80, p. 237.
'Wood Cut. " NewL (47:1) Aut 80, p. 102.

SWAN, Jon
"Conjuring Blues in the Surf at Nantucket. " NewYorker (56:29)

8 S 80, p. 38.

SWANGER, David
"A Miner Describes His Death. " CharR (6:2) Aut 80, p. 30.
"Missed Connective" (for Deborah). NewL (46:4) Sum 80, p.
  110.
"Rowing in Turns. " Tendril (9) 80, p. 155.
"To My Brother and Sister. " NewL (46:4) Sum 80, p. 111.

SWANN, Brian
"All Things Side by Side" (tr. of Melih Cevdat Anday w. Talat
  Halman). PoNow (26) 80, p. 46.
"Captains. " PoNow (27) 80, p. 31.
"Dead Woman in Apulia" (tr. of Vittorio Bodini w. Ruth Feld-
  man). AmerPoR (9:6) N-D 80, p. 7.
"Description. " ParisR (78) Sum 80, p. 191.
"The Eaves" (tr. of Rocco Scotellaro w. Ruth Feldman). PoNow
  (27) 80, p. 46.
"In This Country. " MinnR (NS 15) Aut 80, p. 23.
"In Those Small Lakes" (tr. of Melih Cevdat Anday w. Talat
  Halman). PoNow (26) 80, p. 46.
"Lycian Women" (tr. of Melih Cevdat Anday w. Talat Holman).
  PoNow (26) 80, p. 46.
"moon of ripening berries. " Kayak (55) Ja 81, p. 3.
"Murder. " NewOR (7:1) 80, p. 66.
"Now That I've Lost You" (tr. of Rocco Scotellaro w. Ruth Feld-
  man). PoNow (28) 80, p. 46.
"Open Window" (tr. of Melih Cevdet Anday w. Talat Sait Hal-
  man). CharR (6:2) Aut 80, p. 55.
"Portici: April First" (tr. of Rocco Scotellaro w. Ruth Feldman).
  PoNow (27) 80, p. 46.
"Second Hand. " WebR (5:1) Wint 80, p. 15.
"Stazzema Series" (tr. of Vittorio Bodini w. Ruth Feldman).
  AmerPoR (9:6) N-D 80, p. 6.
"Study for the Sanfelice Woman Jail" (tr. of Vittorio Bodini w.
  Ruth Feldman). AmerPoR (9:6) N-D 80, p. 7.
"Via de angelis" (tr. of Vittorio Bodini w. Ruth Feldman).
  AmerPoR (9:6) N-D 80, p. 8.

SWANSON, John
"Among the Trees" (tr. of Blazhe Koneski). PortR (26) 80, p.
  475.
"Ballad for the Stone" (tr. of Slavko Janevski). PortR (26) 80,
  p. 471.
"Bridge" (tr. of Slavko Janevski). PortR (26) 80, p. 469.
"Lightning's Widow" (tr. of Radovan Pavlovski). PortR (26) 80,
  p. 465.
"Primal Lightning" (tr. of Radovan Pavlovski). PortR (26) 80,
  p. 463.
"Revenge" (tr. of Blazhe Koneski). PortR (26) 80, p. 473.
"rock" (tr. of Mateja Matevski). PortR (26) 80, p. 467.

SWANSON, Stephen O.
"Consider the Lilies. " ChrC (97:12) 2 Ap 80, p. 370.

SWANSTON, Sarah
"Condiments. " EngJ (69:5) My 80, p. 57.

SWARTS, Helene
"Grazing. " ChrC (97:26) 13-20 Ag 80, p. 789.
"In the Fall. " ChrC (97:31) 8 O 80, p. 933.

SWARTS, William
"The Workbench. " Outbr (4/5) Aut 79-Spr 80, p. 71.

SWARTZ, David
"The Mass of Maple. " PikeF (3) Wint 80, p. 3.

SWEENEY, Matthew
"After the Silence. " GRR (11:1) 80, p. 19.
"Hunters. " GRR (11:1) 80, p. 18.
"Singing. " GRR (11:1) 80, p. 17.
"The Television Creature Speaks. " GRR (11:2/3) 80, p. 107.

SWENSON, Cole
"Funeral. " PoNow (29) 80, p. 39.
"Please. " AmerPoR (9:6) N-D 80, p. 36.

SWENSON, Eric
"Embarking" (tr. of Fatho Amoi). PortR (26) 80, p. 217.
"The Local Market" (tr. of Jean Dodo). PortR (26) 80, p. 219.
"To Poets" (tr. of Bernard B. Dadié). PortR (26) 80, p. 222.

SWENSON, Karen
"Graduation. " PortR (26) 80, p. 441.
"The House of Winter. " DenQ (15:2) Sum 80, p. 74.
"The Man Who Candled. " Aspen (10) Wint 80, p. 50.
"Selling Her Engagement Ring. " PraS (54:2) Sum 80, p. 15.
"The Snow Queen's Mirror. " DenQ (15:2) Sum 80, p. 73.

SWENSON, May
"Blood Test. " Poetry (137:2) N 80, p. 98.
"A Day Like Rousseau's Dream. " Poetry (137:2) N 80, p. 96.
"Dummy, 51, to Go to Museum Ventriloquist Dead at 75. "
    Poetry (137:2) N 80, p. 99.
"Saguaros Above Tucson. " Poetry (137:2) N 80, p. 100.

SWIFT, Joan
"Charms Against Bears. " AntR (38:4) Aut 80, p. 463.
"The Horses at Hanagita. " AntR (38:4) Aut 80, p. 464.
"Night Flying" (for Henry). AntR (38:4) Aut 80, p. 465.

SWILKY, Jody
"Floating. " NoAmR (265:3) S 80, p. 23.
"Nothing but Image. " MissouriR (3:3) Sum 80, p. 13.
"A Small Gathering. " GeoR (34:3) Aut 80, p. 613.

SWISS, Thomas
"February. " LitR (23:3) Spr 80, p. 405.

"Letter from Des Moines. " LitR (23:3) Spr 80, p. 403.
"The Young Couple. " LitR (23:3) Spr 80, p. 404.

SWOPE, Brenda
"On Refusing to Be Dead. " CentR (24:1) Wint 80, p. 83.
"Playing the Trumpet Blue" (for s. b.). CentR (24:1) Wint 80, p. 82.

SWOPE, Mary
"Putting Away the Boat. " StoneC (7:2) My 80, p. 26.

SYLVESTER, Janet
"Managing the Composition" (for Mary). Agni (13) 80, p. 108.

SZERLIP, Barbara
"Of Material. " Ark (14) 80, p. 372.
"Of Poetry. " Ark (14) 80, p. 370.

SZYMBORSKA, Wislawa
"atlantis" (tr. by Girazyna Drabik and Sharon Olds). Kayak (55) Ja 81, p. 57.
"chance meeting" (tr. by Girazyna Drabik and Sharon Olds). Kayak (55) Ja 81, p. 57.
"Exit from a Movie Theater" (tr. by Benjamin Sher). NewOR (7:2) 80, p. 110.
"From an Expedition Which Did Not Take Place" (tr. by Austin Flint and Grazyna Drabik). CharR (6:2) Aut 80, p. 52.
"Homecoming" (tr. by Benjamin Sher). NewOR (7:2) 80, p. 111.
"Lot's Wife" (tr. by Austin Flint and Grazyna Drabik). CharR (6:2) Aut 80, p. 51.
"Psalm" (tr. by Austin Flint and Grazyna Drabik). CharR (6:2) Aut 80, p. 53.
"the two apes of breughel" (tr. by Grazyna Drabik and Sharon Olds). Kayak (55) Ja 81, p. 57.
"words" (tr. by Grazyna Drabik and Sharon Olds). Kayak (55) Ja 81, p. 58.

TAGGART, John
"Not This Not That. " ChiR (31:3) Wint 80, pp. 76-91.

TAGLIABUE, John
"Archilochos. " NewL (46:3) Spr 80, p. 118.
"Leonardo's Anatomical Drawings from the Windsor Castle Collection on Exhibit in the Palazzo Vecchio. " Aspen (10) Wint 80, p. 28.
"Privilege. " NewL (46:4) Sum 80, p. 60.
"Reunion. " PoNow (27) 80, p. 8.
"Swaying in Poetic Rhythm. " PoNow (27) 80, p. 8.
Three poems from a greek journal: (1, 2, 3). Kayak (53) My 80, p. 36.
"To Start a Legend. " Bound (8:2) Wint 80, p. 327.

TAKUJI, Ote
"Blue Fox" (tr. by Graeme Wilson). WestHR (34:4) Aut 80, p. 335.

TALARICO, Ross
"Chain Reaction. " QW (10) Wint-Spr 80, p. 76.
"Halloween" (for Joseph). PoetryNW (21:3) Aut 80, p. 14.
"Mary Leakey's Poem. " Iowa (11:1) Wint 80, p. 125.

TALL, Deborah
"Manhunt. " Pequod (11) 80, p. 11.
"Steps. " Pequod (11) 80, p. 13.

TAMBUZI
"My Caseworker. " NewRena (13) Aut 80, p. 80.
"The Phone Call. " NewRena (13) Aut 80, p. 78.

TAMEN, Pedro
"Regando lentamente as floresdoriso. " PortR (26) 80, p. 305.
"Slowly Watering the Flowers of Laughter" (tr. by author).
    PortR (26) 80, p. 305.

T'AO Ch'ien
"Bearer's Song" (tr. by Jon Hansen). ChiR (31:4) Spr 80, p.
    160.

TAPSCOTT, Stephen
"In Fairfield, Connecticut. " AmerPoR (9:6) N-D 80, p. 5.
"It Has Happened. " AmerPoR (9:6) N-D 80, p. 6.
"Leaving Plainfield. " Epoch (29:3) Spr-Sum 80, p. 260.
"Oats. " ParisR (77) Wint-Spr 80, p. 40.

TARACHOW, Michael
"Close To. " Northeast (3:8) Wint 80, p. 31.
"Looking for Landmarks. " Northeast (3:8) Wint 80, p. 31.

TARDIEU, Jean
"Verbe et matière. " PortR (26) 80, p. 138.

TARN, Nathaniel
"Letter from Homer, from Alashka" (w. Janet Rodney). SunM
    (9/10) Sum 80, p. 28.
"Palenque. " Montra (7) 80, pp. 71-77.

TARNAWSKY, Yuriy
"He Died in a Barbershop" (tr. by author). PortR (26) 80, p.
    411.

TARTAGLIONE, Marlene
"The Climb. " Wind (36) 80, p. 64.

TARTAR, Helen
"Brushing, June 1979: A Diptych. " Tele (16) 80, p. 91.
"First Day in California: August 6, 1979. " Tele (16) 80, p. 92.

TATE, James
"Alive Son of Awake, Wonder of the Age. " Durak (5) 80, p. 5.

"Blue Spill. "   Ploughs (6:2) 80, p. 38.
"Five Years Old. "   Ploughs (6:2) 80, p. 39.
"Homage to Bob. "   Durak (5) 80, p. 6.
"If It Would All Please Hurry. " AmerPoR (9:1) Ja-F 80, p. 9.
"Land of Little Sticks, 1945. " AmerPoR (9:1) Ja-F 80, p. 8.
from The Lost Pilot: "Aunt Edna (1967). " MidwQ (21:3) Spr 80,
    p. 363.
"Nobody's Business. " Tendril (9) 80, p. 156.
"On the Shores of Lake Disappointment. " Durak (5) 80, p. 7.
"Paint 'Til You Faint. " Ploughs (6:2) 80, p. 41.
"Riven Doggeries. " PoNow (27) 80, p. 27.
"Sloops in the Bay. " NewL (46:4) Sum 80, p. 61.
"Sloops in the Bay. " PoNow (27) 80, p. 27.
"A Wedding. " LittleBR (1:1) Aut 80, p. 16.
"The Wild Cheese. " Ploughs (6:2) 80, p. 40.
"You Already Said That. " PoNow (27) 80, p. 27.

TATSUJI, Miyoshi
    "My Cat" (tr. by Graeme Wilson).   WestHR (34:4) Aut 80, p.
    336.

TAUFER, Veno
    From the cycle: "The Melancholy of the Second Echelon. "
    PortR (26) 80, p. 490.

TAYLOR, Alexander
    "Chamber Cantata; minor mode" (tr. of Jorgen Sonne w. author).
        PortR (26) 80, p. 95.
    "Chrysalises" (tr. of Ole Sarvig w. author).   PortR (26) 80, p.
        97.
    "The Days Sink Through Me" (tr. of Uffe Harder w. author).
        PortR (26) 80, p. 96.
    "Hooks" (tr. of Henrik Nordbrandt).   PortR (26) 80, p. 87.
    "Idyl" (tr. of Henrik Nordbrandt).   PortR (26) 80, p. 89.
    "Language for the Lost Places" (tr. of Asger Schnack w. author).
        PortR (26) 80, p. 92.
    "Little Essay on Language" (tr. of Henrik Nordbrandt).   PortR
        (26) 80, p. 88.
    "Shanty" (tr. of Jorgen Sonne w. author).   PortR (26) 80, p. 93.
    "Slow Waltz" (tr. of Klaus Rifbjerg).   PortR (26) 80, p. 91.

TAYLOR, Bruce Edward
    "Strophe. " NewOR (7:2) 80, p. 184.

TAYLOR, Charles
    "Game" (for Ursula Le Guin).   CropD (2/3) Aut-Wint 80, p. 19.

TAYLOR, Davis
    "Afterwards. " MinnR (NS 15) Aut 80, p. 29.

TAYLOR, Henry
    "The Aging Professor Considers His Rectitude" (for Quentin Vest).
        WestHR (34:1) Wint 80, p. 37.

"Desperado Gets Himself Together." BelPoJ (31:1) Aut 80, p. 34.
"Projectile Point, Circa 2500 B.C." SouthernPR (20:2) Aut 80, p. 60.
"Shapes, Vanishings." WestHR (34:3) Sum 80, p. 254.

TAYLOR, I. P.
"Mallard." GRR (11:2/3) 80, p. 11.
"Nature Study." GRR (11:2/3) 80, p. 10.
"Years." GRR (11:2/3) 80, p. 12.

TAYLOR, John
"Medical Note." SouthwR (65:3) Sum 80, p. 284.
"Trying to Make a Joyful Noise." PoetryNW (21:2) Sum 80, p. 47.

TAYLOR, Laurie
"Anaesthesia." SouthernPR (20:1) Spr 80, p. 22.
"Chickens." Sam (102) 80, p. 31.
"Early Thaw." CapeR (15:2) Sum 80, p. 1.
"The Fish Pond." CapeR (16:1) Wint 80, p. 7.
"They Say I Have Your Eyes." DacTerr (17) 80, p. 81.

TAYLOR, Wm. E.
"Christ!" UTR (6:3/4) 80, p. 58.
"Count Down." UTR (6:3/4) 80, p. 60.
"Message to the Almighty Impossible." UTR (6:3/4) 80, p. 62.
"Treachery, though you hold the rank of bird colonel." UTR (6:3/4) 80, p. 57.
"Two Responses to the Atom Bomb." UTR (6:3/4) 80, p. 59.

TELLO, Jaime
"The Other Magic" (tr. of Luis Pastori). PortR (26) 80, p. 452.
"The Woman We Did Not See" (tr. of Fernando Paz Castillo). PortR (26) 80, p. 455.

TENBRINK, Carole L.
"The City." CapeR (15:2) Sum 80, p. 15.

TERASAKI, Etsuko
"The Summer Moon" (tr. of Bashō). CutB (14) Spr/Sum 80, p. 91.

TERRILL, Kathryn
"My Spanish Hair." PoetryNW (21:1) Spr 80, p. 3.
"Wristwatch." PoetryNW (21:1) Spr 80, p. 4.

TERRILL, Richard
"At the Lake: To a Brother Before Marriage." NoAmR (265:4) D 80, p. 33.
"From." NoAmR (265:3) S 80, p. 7.

TERRIS, Virginia R.
"I start chewing my nails and soon I have swallowed my entire

hand. " PoNow (26) 80, p. 15.

TERVO, Heather J.
"Tribute. " EngJ (69:5) My 80, p. 58.

THALENBERG, C. E.
"Refuge Even Beyond the Refuge" (for Peter Huchel) (tr. of
   Reiner Kunze). Spirit (5:1/2) Aut-Wint 79-80, p. 19.

THALMAN, Mark
"Reading with an Interpreter for the Deaf. " Bits (11) 80.

THARP, Roland
"The Ageing Friends. " PraS (54:1) Spr 80, p. 39.
"Carpenters, Waterfall, Stream, Sea. " PraS (54:1) Spr 80, p.
   36.
"Sack-of-Bones. " PraS (54:1) Spr 80, p. 37.
"Two Incantations of Ill Will. " PraS (54:1) Spr 80, p. 38.

THELEN, Stephan
"Stone and Stone" (tr. of Hansjörg Quaderer). PortR (26) 80, p.
   261.

THEOBALDY, Jurgen
"Words you can't erase. " NewL (46:4) Sum 80, p. 38.

THIERS, Naomi
"Therapy" (for Dawn). CropD (2/3) Aut-Wint 80, p. 24.

THOMAS, D. M.
"Protest. " AmerS (49:4) Aut 80, p. 510.
"Smile. " AmerS (49:1) Wint 79-80, p. 51.

THOMAS, Gail
"South African Song. " BelPoJ (30:4) Sum 80, p. 4.

THOMAS, Harry
"To Silvestre Revueltas of Mexico, in His Death" (tr. of Pablo
   Neruda). MichQR (19:1) Wint 80, p. 89.

THOMAS, Janet
"5:50 Home. " Ark (14) 80, p. 379.
"Fort Worden--Monday Evening. " Ark (14) 80, p. 382.

THOMAS, Jim
"Antagonist. " KanQ (12:1) Wint 80, p. 149.
"Naming a Pigeon. " CapeR (15:2) Sum 80, p. 42.
"Poem as Waterline. " KanQ (12:1) Wint 80, p. 149.

THOMAS, John
"Alba. " Bachy (16) Wint 80, p. 29.
"Apologia. " Bachy (16) Wint 80, p. 31.
"Great Zen Master. " Bachy (16) Wint 80, p. 27.

"Minor Classics. " Bachy (16) Wint 80, p. 29.
"My Bird. " Bachy (16) Wint 80, p. 28.
"Pan: A Sequel. " Bachy (16) Wint 80, p. 29.
"Wabi. " Bachy (16) Wint 80, p. 27.

THOMAS, Lorenzo
"Wheeling" (for Clement & Lewis). BlackALF (14:3) Aut 80, p.
   109.

THOMAS, Maurice
"Above Fredericksburg, Virginia" (for Osborne Thomas). Poem
   (39) Jl 80, p. 37.
"The Dead Are Denied Flesh That They May Not Weep. " Poem
   (39) Jl 80, p. 38.
"Garner's House. " Poem (39) Jl 80, p. 35.
"Getting Out of the Red House. " Poem (39) Jl 80, p. 33.
"Pond Spirit. " Poem (39) Jl 80, p. 34.
"Side Trip" (for Tress Stanifer). Poem (39) Jl 80, p. 36.

THOMAS, R. S.
"Boom. " LittleR (13/14) 80, p. 3. Issue devoted to R. S.
   Thomas.
"Citizen. " LittleR (13/14) 80, p. 3. Issue devoted to R. S.
   Thomas.
"History. " LittleR (13/14) 80, p. 4. Issue devoted to R. S.
   Thomas.
"St. John 8. " LittleR (13/14) 80, p. 4. Issue devoted to R. S.
   Thomas.

THOMPSON, Agnes
"In Favor Of. " KanQ (12:3) Sum 80, p. 124.

THOMPSON, Gary
"The Book. " BelPoJ (31:2) Wint 80-81, p. 35.

THOMPSON, Hilary
"Skinny Dipping at Easter. " PottPort (2) 80-81, p. 27.

THOMPSON, Joanna
"Funeral. " AmerS (49:1) Wint 79-80, p. 104.

THOMPSON, Nance E.
"After a Poetry Reading. " Sam (102) 80, p. 14.
"The Last Room. " Sam (101) 80, p. 56.
"Robot Masturbates. " Sam (92) 80, p. 45.
"To Child of Four Years. " Sam (101) 80, p. 57.

THOMPSON, Phil
"Embers. " PottPort (2) 80-81, p. 9.
"Into Their Hearts. " PottPort (1) 79-80, p. 47.
"Lures. " PottPort (1) 79-80, p. 44.
"Pathfinder. " PottPort (1) 79-80, p. 47.
"Pawn to Queen-Three. " PottPort (2) 80-81, p. 33.

THOMPSON, Phyllis
"Eurydice." Tendril (9) 80, p. 157.
"History" (for Frank Anderson, M. D.). SlowLR (4) 80, p. 51.
"The Wind of Manoa. " SlowLR (4) 80, p. 53.

THOMSON, Barbara E.
"Poem: In autumn seeing wild asters through her eyes. "
    BelPoJ (31:1) Aut 80, p. 33.

THOMSON, Sharon
"Boiling." Poetry (135:6) Mr 80, p. 322.
"The Family Tree. " Poetry (135:6) Mr 80, p. 321.
"Meditation. " Poetry (135:6) Mr 80, p. 322.

THORNBURG, Thomas R.
"Homage to Catullus. " BallSUF (21:1) Wint 80, p. 31.

THORNE, Evelyn
"For Georgia O'Keefe. " Wind (37) 80, p. 53.
"Forms from Asia. " Wind (37) 80, p. 53.
"Garden at 5 Oclock. " GRR (11:1) 80, p. 16.
"Waif of Time. " GRR (11:1) 80, p. 14.

THORPE, Dwayne
"The Gathering. " MichQR (19:1) Wint 80, p. 116.
"Sunflower Harvest. " MichQR (19:1) Wint 80, p. 115.

THRONE, Marilyn
"October's Child. " Outbr (4/5) Aut 79-Spr 80, p. 5.
"Small Sounds of a Summer's Night. " Outbr (4/5) Aut 79-Spr
    80, p. 4.
"A Study in Fog. " Outbr (4/5) Aut 79-Spr 80, p. 8.
"Towns of Ohio. " Outbr (4/5) Aut 79-Spr 80, p. 3.
"What She Wished. " Outbr (4/5) Aut 79-Spr 80, p. 7.
"What Used to Count. " Outbr (4/5) Aut 79-Wint 80, p. 6.

THURSTON, Harry
"Clouds Flying Before the Eye" (for my grandparents Hilda and
    Jeremiah Reede). PottPort (1) 79-80, p. 26.
"Mooring. " PottPort (1) 79-80, p. 20.
"Sanctuary" (for Joseph Basaraba). PottPort (1) 79-80, p. 22.
"Spent Light. " PottPort (1) 79-80, p. 25.

TICK, Edward
"The Dying Child. " WindO (37) Aut-Wint 80. on calendar.

TIEMANN, William H.
"After-Christmas Chore. " ChrC (97:42) 24 D 80, p. 1267.

TIKKANEN, Marta
"ur Århundradets Kärlekssaga: 'Du frågar mej. '" PortR (26)
    80, p. 120.
"ur Århundradets Kärlekssaga: 'En alkoholisthustru. '" PortR

(26) 80, p. 114.
"ur Arhundradets Kärlekssaga: 'Jag älskar dej så oerhört. '"
   PortR (26) 80, p. 124.
"ur Arhundradets Kärlekssaga: 'Kärleken och Kärleken. '"
   PortR (26) 80, p. 122.

TILLETT, L. A. H.
   "Concept Two-Oh. " Wind (36) 80, p. 17.

TILLINGHAST, David
   "The Whippoorwill. " SouthernR (16:1) Wint 80, p. 166.
   "Women Hoping for Rain. " SouthernR (16:1) Wint 80, p. 167.

TILLINGHAST, Richard
   "Aspens and a Photograph. " MissouriR (3:2) Wint 80, p. 15.
   "Blue (after Mallarmé). " PartR (47:2) 80, pp. 225-26.

TIMMERMAN, W. T.
   "I Told My Friend Those Are Sacred. " Wind (37) 80, p. 55.

TINKER, Carol
   "The Well Field" (for my husband, Kenneth Rexroth). Ark (14)
      80, p. 127.

TINSLEY, Bonnie
   "Crazy Alice #2. " WindO (36) Spr-Sum 80, p. 28.

TIPTON, David
   "For Robert Lowell" (tr. of Antonio Cisneros w. Maureen
      Ahern). NewOR (7:3) 80, p. 240.
   "The House at Punta Nero (that Empire)" (tr. of Antonio Cis-
      neros). NewOR (7:3) 80, p. 241.
   "King Lear" (tr. of Antonio Cisneros). NewOR (7:3) 80, p. 239.
   "Return Visit to London (Ars Poetica 2)" (tr. of Antonio Cis-
      neros). NewOR (7:3) 80, p. 237.

TISERA, Mary
   "Bead Fern. " StoneC (7:1) F 80, p. 15.

TISHMAN, Arthur Ezra
   "She Waits for Winter. " Poem (39) Jl 80, p. 40.
   "Villanelle. " Poem (39) Jl 80, p. 39.

TJALSMA, H. W.
   "To Maillol's model" (tr. of Aleksis Rannit). PortR (26) 80, p.
      110.

TODD, Ruthven
   "Doctrine of Signatures. " Stand (21:2) 80, p. 48.
   "Monotropia Uniflora. " Stand (21:2) 80, p. 47.
   "The Wall and the Elementals" (for Joellen). Stand (21:2) 80,
      p. 49.

TODD, Theodora
"Sleeping Together. " CutB (15) Aut /Wint 80, p. 83.

TÖRÖK, András
"Evening" (tr. of Anna Hajnal w. Juliette Victor-Rood). DenQ
(15:1) Spr 80, p. 75.

TOLEGIAN, Aram
"Far Away from Armenia: To a Foreigner" (tr. of Silva Gaboud-
ikian). PortR (26) 80, p. 20.
"My Swallow" (tr. of Vahakan Garents). PortR (26) 80, p. 18.

TOMLINSON, Charles
"Giovanni Diodati" (tr. of Attilio Berblucci). Stand (21:3) 80, p.
75.

TOMLINSON, Kerry
"the other woman. " Ark (14) 80, p. 383.
"photographer. " Ark (14) 80, p. 384.

TOMLINSON, Rawdon
"Despondency. " HolCrit (17:3) Je 80, p. 14.
"It. " PoetryNW (21:3) Aut 80, p. 21.
"On the Cliffs, Drinking Autumn Good-bye. " SoDakR (18:2) Sum
80, p. 8.

TOMONORI, Ki no
"Contentment" (tr. by Graeme Wilson). DenQ (15:3) Aut 80, p.
82.

TOMPKINS, Elise
"Four Lectures by Robert Lowell. " NewRep (183:13) 27 S 80, p.
28.

TOMSHANY, Tom
"If We Let You. " Sam (102) 80, p. 67.

TOMSKY, James
"In This Bright Day. " DacTerr (17) 80, p. 82.

TONGUE, Margaret
"At Saugatuck. " BelPoJ (31:1) Aut 80, p. 38.
"Endangered Species. " BelPoJ (31:1) Aut 80, p. 37.

TOOL, Dennis
"Riddles" (tr. of Maurice Carême). CarlMis (18:2) Sum 80, p.
106.

TOOMBS, Ann
"Poem Inspired by Flight. " EngJ (69:5) My 80, p. 44.

TORGERSEN, Eric
"Blue Racer. " PoNow (27) 80, p. 43.

"Blue Racer Two." PoNow (27) 80, p. 43.

TORNES, Beth
"Church." Durak (4) 80, p. 54.

TORRESON, Rodney
"Dream." PoNow (29) 80, p. 40.
"Dreams and the Evening News." PoNow (29) 80, p. 40.

TOURE, Askia Muhammad
"Cornrow 3." BlackALF (14:3) Aut 80, p. 109.

TOWLE, Parker
"After Bruegel's Hunters in the Snow." StoneC (7:1) F 80, p. 21.

TRACHTENBERG, Paul
"Short Changes for Loretta." Bachy (17) Spr 80, pp. 135-141.

TRACY, Robert
"The Abbé" (tr. of Osip Mandelstam). NewOR (7:1) 80, p. 35.
"Charlie Chaplin" (tr. of Osip Mandelstam). LitR (23:3) Spr 80, p. 386.
from Stone: "Petersburg Stanzas" (for N. Gumilyov) (tr. of Osip Mandelstam). LitR (23:3) Spr 80, p. 385.
from Stone: (6, 44, 78) (tr. of Osip Mandelstam). Poetry (136:1) Ap 80, p. 21.

TRAKL, Georg
"December Sonnet" (tr. by Rich Ives). CutB (14) Spr /Sum 80, p. 57.
"In Venice" (tr. by Paul Morris). DenQ (15:1) Spr 80, p. 87.
"Night" (tr. by David McDuff, Jon Silkin and R. S. Furness). Stand (21:2) 80, p. 19.
"Radiant Autumn" (tr. by Rich Ives). CutB (14) Spr /Sum 80, p. 58.
"Sonja" (tr. by Paul Morris). Pequod (11) 80, p. 50.
"To the Boy Elis" (tr. by Paul Morris). DenQ (15:1) Spr 80, p. 86.
"Trumpets" (tr. by David McDuff and Jon Silkin). Stand (21:2) 80, p. 20.
"Whispered in the Afternoon" (tr. by Rich Ives). CutB (14) Spr / Sum 80, p. 59.

TRAMMELL, Robert
from Lovers /Killers: "All Old Lovers Forgotten." SouthwR (65:3) Sum 80, p. 285.
from Lovers /Killers: "Transformation #2." SouthwR (65:3) Sum 80, p. 285.
from Lovers /Killers: "Winter." SouthwR (65:3) Sum 80, p. 286.

TRAMWAY, Ariei
"My Last Trip to Chicago." Pig (7) My 80, p. 6.

TRANSTRÖMER, Tomas
    from the Balkans, '55: "Formulas of the Trip" (tr. by Timothy
      Dwyer). Field (23) Aut 80, p. 9.
    "Below Freezing" (tr. by Robert Bly). PoetryE (1) 80, p. 7.
    "Icelandic Hurricane. " Pequod (11) 80, p. 2.
    "Isolated Swedish Houses" (tr. by Timothy Dwyer). Field (23)
      Aut 80, p. 6.
    "Street Crossing" (tr. by Keith Harrison). CarlMis (18:2) Sum
      80, p. 47.
    "Street Crossing" (tr. by Robert Bly). PoetryE (1) 80, p. 8.

TRAWICK, Leonard
    "Feeling for Fish. " Poetry (136:3) Je 80, p. 156.
    "Gingerbread. " PoNow (27) 80, p. 15.
    "Psyches. " Poetry (136:3) Je 80, p. 155.

TRAXLER, Patricia
    "The Glasscutters. " HangL (37) Spr 80, p. 54.
    "Number Seven Love. " PoNow (28) 80, p. 40.
    "The Roomer." HangL (37) Spr 80, p. 55.
    "Waking in Nice. " MalR (53) Ja 80, p. 92.

TRECHOCK, Mark
    "Bicycling Near Blooming Prairie, Minnesota. " CreamCR (5:1)
      Wint 79, p. 114.
    "The Church in a Changing World. " ChrC (97:39) 3 D 80, p.
      1187.

TREECE, Malra
    "A Matter of Priorities. " CapeR (15:2) Sum 80, p. 47.

TREGEBOV, Rhea
    "Tango Moderno. " CarolQ (32:3) Aut 80, p. 82.

TREITEL, Margot
    "American Scene: A Grant Wood Triptych. " CutB (15) Aut /Wint
      80, p. 12.
    "Daily Life. " WindO (36) Spr-Sum 80, p. 15.
    "From a Room on Jane Street. " StoneC (7:3) D 80, p. 20.
    "Here in the Tropics. " Tendril (7/8) Spr-Sum 80, p. 79.
    "I Enter the Steambath. " Northeast (3:8) Wint 80, p. 67.
    "Landscape with Variations. " Northeast (3:8) Wint 80, p. 65.
    "The Moral Equivalent of War." Northeast (3:8) Wint 80, p. 66.
    "The Moral of the Story. " WindO (36) Spr-Sum 80, p. 13.
    "Re-enacting the Battle Scene. " PraS (54:1) Spr 80, p. 46.
    "Sestina with Boat and Feeling. " HolCrit (17:4) O 80, p. 10.
    "Shifting Persona. " WindO (36) Spr-Sum 80, p. 13.
    "Speaking in a Dead Language. " PraS (54:1) Spr 80, p. 45.
    "Stock Characters. " WindO (36) Spr-Sum 80, p. 15.
    "What Remains.... " CentR (24:4) Aut 80, p. 457.
    "Wiping the Slate Clean. " WindO (36) Spr-Sum 80, p. 14.

TREITEL, Renata
    "Days of Dust" (w. Mark Doty). Nimrod (24:1) Aut-Wint 80, p.

108.
"In a strange land." Nimrod (24:1) Aut-Wint 80, p. 63.
"Take This Candle." Nimrod (24:1) Aut-Wint 80, p. 65.

TRELAWNY, Victor
"All Over Hallow's Eve." PortR (26) 80, p. 436.
"Not Here." Iowa (10:4) Aut 80, p. 23.

TREMBLAY, Gail
"Crow Voices." DenQ (14:4) Wint 80, p. 118.
"Gathering Basket Grass." DenQ (14:4) Wint 80, p. 113.
"Grandfather Dancing" (for Peter Ernest). DenQ (14:4) Wint 80,
    p. 114.
"Night Gives Old Woman the Word." DenQ (14:4) Wint 80, p.
    116.

TREPFER, Karen
"Clamming." StoneC (7:3) D 80, p. 64.
"Weather." StoneC (7:3) D 80, p. 63.

TRETHEWEY, Eric
"Antecedents." NoAmR (265:2) Je 80, p. 5.
"Her Swing" (for Natasha). PraS (54:3) Aut 80, p. 48.
"Lost." SouthernHR (14:4) Aut 80, p. 336.

TRIMBLE, Mary
"Interior, with Ashes." Ascent (6:1) 80, p. 40.

TRINIDAD, David
"The Boy." Bachy (16) Wint 80, p. 95.
"Delphi." Bachy (16) Wint 80, p. 92.
"In Praise of Him." Bachy (16) Wint 80, p. 96.
"The Sphinx." Bachy (16) Wint 80, p. 94.
"Thebes." Bachy (16) Wint 80, p. 93.
"Wedding Night." Bachy (16) Wint 80, p. 93.

TRITEL, Barbara
"Crow's Feet." CalQ (16/17) 80, p. 41.
"Picking Cherries." CalQ (16/17) 80, p. 40.

TROW, Lisa
"The Nightwatch." CimR (53) O 80, p. 22.

TROWBRIDGE, William
"Agnolo in Plague Time." PraS (54:2) Sum 80, p. 74.
"Drumming Behind You in the High School Band." PoNow (29)
    80, p. 40.
"Excalibur." HiramPoR (27) Aut-Wint 80, p. 49.
"In Memoriam: Gorgeous George." PoetC (12:2) 80, p. 17.
"Traveling in Spring." PoNow (29) 80, p. 40.

TROYANOVICH, Steve
"For Kenneth Patchen." WormR (78) 80, p. 58.

"St. Juke." WormR (78) 80, p. 58.

TRUDELL, Dennis
    "Green Tomatoes." GeoR (34:2) Sum 80, p. 290.
    "Sing and Dance." GeoR (34:2) Sum 80, p. 291.

TRUESDALE, C. W.
    "Avocados." MinnR (NS 15) Aut 80, p. 30.

TSCHUMI, Raymond
    "Le voyage intérieur." PortR (26) 80, p. 382.

TSURAYUKI, Ki no
    "Mirror Weather" (tr. by Graeme Wilson). DenQ (15:3) Aut 80,
        p. 85.

TSVETAEVA, Marina
    "The Crevice" (tr. by Liza Tucker). Pequod (11) 80, p. 75.
    "Dis-tance; Versts, Miles" (tr. by Liza Tucker). Pequod (11)
        80, p. 77.
    "Hamlet's Dialogue with His Conscience" (tr. by Liza Tucker).
        Pequod (11) 80, p. 74.
    "Insomnia Has Enveloped My Eyes" (tr. by Liza Tucker).
        Pequod (11) 80, p. 72.
    "The Letter" (tr. by Liza Tucker). Pequod (11) 80, p. 76.
    "A white low sun" (tr. by David McDuff and Jon Silkin). Stand
        (21:2) 80, p. 7.

TUCKER, Liza
    "The Crevice" (tr. of Marina Tsvetaeva). Pequod (11) 80, p.
        75.
    "Dis-tance; Versts, Miles" (tr. of Marina Tsvetaeva). Pequod
        (11) 80, p. 77.
    "Hamlet's Dialogue with His Conscience" (tr. of Marina Tsveta-
        eva). Pequod (11) 80, p. 74.
    "Insomnia Has Enveloped My Eyes" (tr. of Marina Tsvetaeva).
        Pequod (11) 80, p. 72.
    "The Letter" (tr. of Marina Tsvetaeva). Pequod (11) 80, p. 76.

TULLOS, Sue
    "Persephone in Autumn." ArizQ (36:3) Aut 80, p. 239.

TULLOSS, Rod
    "No foot disturbed a foot." US1 (12/13) Aut-Wint 80, p. 2.
    "Reading Tranströmer at Bear Mountain Inn." US1 (12/13) Aut-
        Wint 80, p. 2.

TURCO, Lewis
    "A Dainty Sum." PoetryNW (21:3) Aut 80, p. 31.
    "Three Poems for Emily." OntR (13) Aut-Wint 80-81, p. 35.

TURNER, Alberta T.
    "Daughter, Daughter." PoNow (26) 80, p. 27.

"Emilio, Romero, Father, Chester, Ted--. " PoNow (26) 80, p.
    27.
"Long Lowing. " PoNow (26) 80, p. 27.
"Making Old Bones. " PoNow (26) 80, p. 16.
"Midden (1973). " MidwQ (21:3) Spr 80, p. 364.

TURNER, Alison
    from For My Father, the Birdwatcher: "For My Father, the
        Birdwatcher. " Nimrod (24:1) Aut-Wint 80, pp. 42-43.
    from For My Father, the Birdwatcher: "Pearl Harbor Comes
        Over the Radio. " Nimrod (24:1) Aut-Wint 80, p. 41.
    from For My Father, the Birdwatcher: "Wartime: Nantucket. "
        Nimrod (24:1) Aut-Wint 80, pp. 41-42.

TURNER, Edith
    "Se-ami. " Prima (5) 79, p. 5.

TUTHILL, Stacy
    "Moon Grammar. " Vis (3) 80.

TUTTLE, Lynn
    "Obituary. " Pig (7) My 80, p. 11.

TWICHELL, Chase
    "Near Solon, Iowa. " PoNow (27) 80, p. 19.
    "Three Dreams of Disaster. " PraS (54:4) Wint 80-81, p. 94.
    "Your Eightieth. " PraS (54:4) Wint 80-81, p. 93.

TYLER, Kathy
    "Hay-Rick Time. " PottPort (1) 79-80, p. 7.
    "Jerry O'Brien. " PottPort (1) 79-80, p. 20.
    "The Ultimate Freedom. " PottPort (1) 79-80, p. 15.
    "Untitled: As she digs to plant dahlia bulbs. " PottPort (1) 79-
        80, p. 22.

TYSH, George
    "A Little Memory. " HangL (38) Aut 80, p. 48.

UHER, L.
    "For Gertrude Who Dances. " SoDakR (18:2) Sum 80, p. 8.
    "Willow Island, Summer. " SoDakR (18:2) Sum 80, p. 7.

ULMER, James
    "The Apple Thief. " QW (11) Aut-Wint 80-81, p. 95.
    "Tornado Watch. " PoetryNW (21:3) Aut 80, p. 16.

UMAVIJANI, Montri
    from Sketches for Purgatory: (1, 3, 6, 12, 28, 30, 44, 45, 46,
        47, 52). Ark (14) 80, p. 385.

UMBREIT, Paula
    "Cliffbound. " ConcPo (13:2) Aut 80, p. 16.

UNDERWOOD, Corinne
"Trying to Look Serene in a Full Lotus." Focus (14:86) Ap 80,
    p. 29.

UNGARETTI, Giuseppe
"Italy" (tr. by David McDuff and Jon Silkin). Stand (21:2) 80, p.
    6.

UNGER, Barbara
"Geological Faults." Nat (230:18) 10 My 80, p. 570.

UNGER, David
"Kafka" (tr. of Enrique Lihn). PoNow (27) 80, p. 44.
"My Daughter's Abortion." PoNow (29) 80, p. 41.
"Waiting Alone" (tr. of Luis Cernuda). PoNow (28) 80, p. 44.

UNTERECKER, John
"Cold's Three Visits." ThRiPo (15/16) 80, p. 62.
"Hawaii, near Apua Point." SouthernR (16:2) Spr 80, p. 430.
"Interval." PoNow (26) 80, p. 9.
"The Muse." NewL (46:4) Sum 80, p. 40.
"Navigator." NewEngR (3:2) Wint 80, p. 172.
"Not Swimming Below the Cliffs: Oahu." PoetryNW (21:2) Sum
    80, p. 34.
"Portrait." Tendril (9) 80, p. 160.
"The Red Coat." Tendril (7/8) Spr-Sum 80, p. 80.

UPDIKE, John
"The Melancholy of Storm Windows." BosUJ (26:3) 80, p. 95.
"Poisoned in Nassau." BosUJ (26:3) 80, p. 96.
"Sleepless in Scarsdale." BosUJ (26:3) 80, p. 97.
"Taste." AmerPoR (9:1) Ja-F 80, p. 20.
"Wordly Monk's Song." Bits (11) 80.

UPSHAW, Reagan
"After Basil Bunting." SunM (9/10) Sum 80, p. 190.

UPTON, Lee
"In the Rudolf Nureyev Dream." Salm (47/48) Wint-Spr 80, p.
    61.

URDANG, Constance
"Alone" (for Catalina de Erazu). Ascent (5:3) 80, p. 38.
"Baked Potatoes." PoNow (27) 80, p. 7.
"Confusion" (tr. of Christiane Seiler). WebR (5:2) Aut 80, p. 41.
"A Dish of Fragments, or Ostracism" (tr. of Christiane Seiler).
    WebR (5:2) Aut 80, p. 40.
"Grapes." PoNow (27) 80, p. 7.
"His Sleep." Shen (31:1) 79, p. 41.
"Ninety-Four" (tr. of Christiane Seiler). WebR (5:2) Aut 80, p.
    39.
"Snow." PoNow (27) 80, p. 7.
"Streetcar-Solace or Framed by a Hood" (tr. of Christiane

Seiler). WebR (5:2) Aut 80, p. 38.
"Summertime." PoNow (28) 80, p. 17.
"The Tapeworm" (tr. of Christiane Seiler). WebR (5:2) Aut 80,
    p. 42.

UROSEVIC, Vlada
"Clumsy Amusements." StoneC (7:3) D 80, p. 28.
"Inner Abyss." StoneC (7:3) D 80, p. 26.

URQUHART, Jane
"Migrations." MalR (53) Ja 80, p. 60.

URTECHO, Alvaro
"Lazaro." NowestR (18:3) 80, p. 70.

USCHUK, Pamela
"Opening the Winter Blossom." CutB (15) Aut/Wint 80, p. 9.

VACHON, Christine
"I Rode His Shoulders." HangL (37) Spr 80, p. 67.
"When I Was a Child." HangL (37) Spr 80, p. 68.

VAETH, Kim
"A Flute in the Middle of the Night." OP (30) Aut 80, p. 22.
"Look." OP (30) Aut 80, p. 20.
"The Selfishness of Sleep." OP (30) Aut 80, p. 21.

VALAORITIS, Nanos
"psalm and mosaic for a springtime in athens" (tr. of Odysseus
    Elytis). Kayak (55) Ja 81, p. 20.

VALENTA, Helen
"A Chinese Girl Speaks to Her Chosen Husband." CentR (24:4)
    Aut 80, p. 454.
"Endings." CentR (24:4) Aut 80, p. 454.
"19th-Century Concerns." LitR (23:3) Spr 80, p. 342.
"A Young Girl Reads the Great Russian Authors." LitR (23:3)
    Spr 80, p. 341.

VALENTINE, Jean
"The Imagination School." AmerPoR (9:1) Ja-F 80, p. 3.
"Love and Work: Freud Dying." AmerPoR (9:1) Ja-F 80, p. 3.
"Mandelstam." AmerPoR (9:1) Ja-F 80, p. 3.
"Turn" (for F. and P.L.). AmerPoR (9:1) Ja-F 80, p. 3.

Van BRUNT, H. L.
"Cerberus." NewL (46:3) Spr 80, p. 123.
"The Clearing There." PoNow (27) 80, p. 37.
"Elbows." OhioR (24) 80, p. 93.
"Hic Jacet." Wind (36) 80, p. 66.
"In the Distance." NewL (46:3) Spr 80, p. 123.
"Lumiere." Harp (260:1557) F 80, p. 92.
"Lying Out in the Rain." GeoR (34:1) Spr 80, p. 127.

"Motels, Hotels, and Other People's Houses. " NewL (46:3) Spr
    80, p. 122.
"Romance. " SouthernPR (20:1) Spr 80, p. 32.
"Rookery. " Wind (36) 80, p. 66.
"Skunk Cabbage (at Yaddo). " PoNow (27) 80, p. 37.
"Windsurfing in Oyster Harbors. " SoDakR (18:1) Spr 80, p. 29.

VANCIL, Pat
    "Search. " Wind (37) 80, p. 56.

VANDERSEE, Charles
    "As Your Photographer. " SouthernPR (20:1) Spr 80, p. 31.
    "Stories. " PoetryE (1) 80, p. 66.
    "Tantra. " AmerPoR (9:6) N-D 80, p. 8.

VANGELISTI, Paul
    "An Elegance for Doda. " Ark (14) 80, p. 389.
    "Homage to M. " Ark (14) 80, p. 390.

Van HOUTEN, Lois
    "At the Center of the Wound /Is the Navel. " StoneC (7:2) My 80,
        p. 27.

Van OSTAIJEN, Paul
    "Night Sounds" (tr. by The Hermans). ChiR (32:1) Sum 80, p.
        107.

Van VLIET, Eddy
    "Twee derden lucht. " PortR (26) 80, p. 270.

Van WALLEGHEN, Michael
    "Fun at Crystal Lake. " SouthernR (16:2) Spr 80, p. 399.
    "Mistakes. " Ascent (5:3) 80, p. 36.
    "The Sibyl at Snug Harbor. " SouthernR (16:2) Spr 80, p. 398.

Van WINCKEL, Nance
    "Lost in Riverview Trailercourt. " PoetryNW (21:1) Spr 80, p.
        28.
    "Lowell Reservoir. " PoNow (27) 80, p. 42.
    "New Love. " PoetryNW (21:1) Spr 80, p. 30.
    "Turning 27 with My Own Nose" (for Tycho Brahe). AntR (38:2)
        Spr 80, p. 178.
    "When You Are Gone. " KanQ (12:1) Wint 80, p. 77.

VARELA, Blanca
    "Dream" (tr. by Elisabeth Hamilton-La Coste). CutB (14) Spr /
        Sum 80, p. 33.
    "Family Secret" (tr. by Elisabeth Hamilton-La Coste). CutB (14)
        Spr /Sum 80, p. 34.
    "Finding" (tr. by Elisabeth Hamilton-La Coste). CutB (14) Spr /
        Sum 80, p. 32.
    "First Dance" (tr. by Elisabeth Hamilton-La Coste). CutB (14)
        Spr /Sum 80, p. 31.

"On the Order of Things" (to Octavio Paz) (tr. by Elisabeth
  Hamilton-La Coste). CutB (14) Spr/Sum 80, p. 28.
from Out of Time: (I, II, III, IV) (tr. by Elisabeth Hamilton-La
  Coste). CutB (14) Spr/Sum 80, p. 35.
"Story" (tr. by Maureen Ahern). NewOR (7:3) 80, p. 291.
"Vals del Angelus II." PortR (26) 80, p. 286.

VARGO, Beth Copeland
  "Migraine." SouthernPR (20:1) Spr 80, p. 21.

VAS DIAS, Robert
  "The Blooms." Stand (21:1) 79-80, p. 23.
  "The Glass." Stand (21:1) 79-80, p. 22.

VASQUEZ, Alfredo Barrera
  "Center Green Human" (tr. by Marcel Smith). CutB (14) Spr/
  Sum 80, p. 109.

VASSYLKIVSKY, Eugenia
  from Illusions, (II) (tr. of Wadym Lesytch). PortR (26) 80, p.
  415.

VAUGHAN, Kathy
  "A Fist Clenched with Life." PottPort (2) 80-81, p. 21.
  "i am she is you/we are." PottPort (2) 80-81, p. 10.

VAYENAS, Násos
  "Episode." PortR (26) 80, p. 166.

VECCHIO, Gloria del
  "Large Drawing of a River Island." US1 (12/13) Aut-Wint 80, p.
  5.

VEINBERG, Jon
  "Arts and Crafts at the Rehabilitation Center." CharR (6:1) Spr
  80, p. 14.
  "An Old Photograph." Thrpny (2) Sum 80, p. 13.

VENCLOVA, Tomas
  "Eilerastis apie atminti." PortR (26) 80, p. 263.
  "Sustok, sustok. Suyra sakinys." PortR (26) 80, p. 265.

VENN, George
  "Blue Hour: Grandview Cemetery." PoetryNW (21:1) Spr 80, p.
  52.
  "Fable." PoetryNW (21:1) Spr 80, p. 54.
  "The Trail to School." PoetryNW (21:1) Spr 80, p. 55.
  "Voice from Another Wilderness." PoetryNW (21:1) Spr 80, p.
  53.

VENNES, Raymond
  "Le coeur des hommes et des choses." PottPort (2) 80-81, p.
  20.

"Je me cherche un pays. " PottPort (2) 80-81, p. 33.

VENTSIAS, Roberta
  "The Bridegroom's Dream. " CharR (6:2) Aut 80, p. 38.
  "Facing Surgery. " CharR (6:2) Aut 80, p. 39.
  "Points of Reference. " ColEng (41:5) Ja 80, p. 549.

VENUTI, Lawrence
  "Noon Glare" (tr. of Milo de Angelis). ChiR (32:1) Sum 80, p.
    106.

VERASTEGUI, Enrique
  "If You Stay in My Country" (tr. by Maureen Ahern). NewOR
    (7:3) 80, p. 297.

VERDERY, Daniel
  "Shifts of Avatar. " SewanR (88:2) Spr 80, p. 181.

VERNON, John
  "Caterpillars. " AmerPoR (9:2) Mr-Ap 80, p. 48.
  "Dragonfly. " VirQR (56:4) Aut 80, p. 670.
  "Each. " VirQR (56:4) Aut 80, p. 671.

VERNON, William
  "Animal Adjustment. " Sam (101) 80, p. 36.
  "Bats. " Im (7:1) 80, p. 5.
  "Land of Sinkholes. " Sam (102) 80, p. 44.
  To a Friend.... Sam (97) 80. Entire issue.

VIANT, William
  "Family of the Artist. " StoneC (7:2) My 80, p. 16.

VICTOR, David A.
  "The Creek. " SoDakR (18:3) Aut 80, p. 13.

VICTOR-ROOD, Juliette
  "Evening" (tr. of Anna Hajnal w. András Torok). DenQ (15:1)
    Spr 80, p. 75.

VIEL, Lyndon
  "Heretic. " ChrC (97:21) 4-11 Je 80, p. 638.

VIERECK, Peter
  "The Blind Men" (tr. of Georg Heym). PoNow (26) 80, p. 45.
  "Revolution: The Halfgod Daydream. " PoNow (26) 80, p. 17.
  "The Talking Head" (tr. of Stefan George). PoNow (28) 80, p.
    44.

VIGEE, Claude
  "Destiny of a Poet" (tr. by J. R. LeMaster and Kenneth Law-
    rence Beaudoin). WebR (5:2) Aut 80, p. 77.
  "Michael's Tomb" (tr. by J. R. LeMaster and Kenneth Law-
    rence Beaudoin). WebR (5:2) Aut 80, p. 76.

VILLARRUBIA, Jan
"Hors D'Oeuvres." DacTerr (17) 80, p. 83.
"Night Rides in Haiti." LitR (23:3) Spr 80, p. 349.

VINZ, Mark
"Late Show." SmF (11/12) Spr-Aut 80, p. 48.
"Late Summer Song." PoNow (26) 80, p. 31.
"Office Hours." PoNow (27) 80, p. 41.
"Snow Dance, Snow Dream." SmF (11/12) Spr-Aut 80, p. 47.

VIOLI, Paul
"Concordance." SunM (9/10) Sum 80, p. 137.

VIRGIL
"The Storm" (tr. by Robert Fitzgerald). Poetry (136:1) Ap 80,
   p. 1.

VIVIAN, Tim
"The Night of Amos Kroeger" (to Ian Seaton). WebR (5:1) Wint
   80, p. 51.

VLASOPOLOS, Anca
"The Trapped Bird." SmPd (49) Spr 80, p. 5.

VLIET, R. G.
"Jet Plane." Poetry (135:4) Ja 80, p. 193.
"Mrs. McElroy." Poetry (135:4) Ja 80, p. 192.
"Penny Ballad of Elvious Ricks." Poetry (135:4) Ja 80, p. 194.
"Samuel Palmer." PoNow (26) 80, p. 7.
"Song, Crystal Radio Song." PoNow (26) 80, p. 7.

VOGELSANG, Arthur
"Correspondents." Ascent (5:3) 80, p. 20.

VOIGT, Ellen Bryant
"Year's End." OhioR (25) 80, p. 64.

VOLBORTH, J. Ivaloo
"From Harney Peak." DenQ (14:4) Wint 80, p. 82.
"In the Lodge." DenQ (14:4) Wint 80, p. 78.
"Song for Grandmother." DenQ (14:4) Wint 80, p. 83.
"Sweet Medicine." DenQ (14:4) Wint 80, p. 80.
"Vihio Images." DenQ (14:4) Wint 80, p. 81.
"Woman Ascending" (for Robin). DenQ (14:4) Wint 80, p. 79.

VOLK, Craig
"Voice-of-the-Cloud." KanQ (12:2) Spr 80, p. 107.
"Zallie Rulo." KanQ (12:2) Spr 80, p. 108.

VOLLMER, Judith
"For Ellen, at Lake Wesauking." Cond (6) 80, p. 70.

Von GIERKE, Karin
"Cassandra" (tr. of Thomas Brasch). Field (22) Spr 80, pp.

17-21.

Von HUTTEN, Katrine
"Memory Of" (tr. by Norbert Krapf). Stand (21:3) 80, p. 14.
"Statement of Place" (tr. by Norbert Krapf). Stand (21:3) 80, p. 15.
"When I Was Little" (tr. by Norbert Krapf). Stand (21:3) 80, p. 14.

Von SLAGLE, Geoffrey
"Easter 1980." Poem (40) N 80, p. 14.
"To a Graveyard Angel." Poem (40) N 80, p. 15.

VOZNESENSKY, Andrei
"The Great Confrontation" (tr. by William Jay Smith and Vera Dunham). Atl (245:4) Ap 80, p. 117.

WAAGE, Fred
"Annunciation, 1524." SouthernPR (20:2) Aut 80, p. 50.

WADE, Cory
"The Society of Jesus." WestHR (34:1) Wint 80, p. 59.
"Wheel in the Sky." GeoR (34:1) Spr 80, p. 112.

WADE, John Stevens
"Mouse." Poem (40) N 80, p. 51.

WAGNER, Kathy
"Returning to the City by Boat." SouthernPR (20:2) Aut 80, p. 11.

WAGONER, David
"Applying for a Loan with the Help of the Dictionary of Occupational Titles." ConcPo (13:2) Aut 80, p. 5.
"The Arsonist." Salm (50/51) Aut 80-Wint 81, p. 37.
"Bears." Atl (246:3) S 80, p. 64.
"Bittern." NewYorker (56:38) 10 N 80, p. 187.
"By a Lost Riverside." MissouriR (4:1) Aut 80, p. 7.
"Caterpillar Song." Poetry (135:4) Ja 80, p. 220.
"Chorus." GeoR (34:4) Wint 80, p. 886.
"Craneflies." PoNow (27) 80, p. 4.
"The Death of a Crane Fly." NewYorker (56:34) 13 O 80, p. 160.
"Downstream." NewRep (183:10/11) 6-13 S 80, p. 28.
"Driftwood." Atl (246:6) D 80, p. 79.
"For a Jumping Spider." PoNow (27) 80, p. 4.
"For a Woman Who Dreamed She Was a Mermaid." PoNow (28) 80, p. 5.
"For a Woman Who Said I Wasn't Romantic." Antaeus (38) Sum 80, p. 130.
"The Garden of Earthly Delights." NewYorker (56:44) 22 D 80, p. 34.
"In Distress." Kayak (54) S 80, p. 52. (Found poem.)

WAHLE   384

"In Sand and Wind. " Antaeus (38) Sum 80, p. 129.
"In the Country of Old Men. " Ploughs (6:2) 80, p. 81.
"The Last Laugh. " Poetry (137:2) N 80, p. 87.
"The Lookout. " Salm (50/51) Aut 80-Wint 81, p. 38.
"Marsh Hawk. " Harp (261:1566) N 80, p. 88.
"Moth Song. " Poetry (135:4) Ja 80, p. 222.
"My Father's Garden. " MissouriR (4:1) Aut 80, p. 9.
"My Father's Ghost. " Poetry (137:2) N 80, p. 90.
"My Fire. " WestHR (34:4) Aut 80, p. 361.
"My Mother's Garden. " MissouriR (4:1) Aut 80, p. 8.
"My Physics Teacher. " Poetry (137:2) N 80, p. 91.
"Note with the Gift of a Bird's Nest. " Poetry (137:2) N 80, p.
    92.
"Nuthatch. " NewYorker (56:38) 10 N 80, p. 187.
"The Orchard of the Dreaming Pigs. " PoNow (27) 80, p. 28.
"Palindrome--Inside Out. " Poetry (137:2) N 80, p. 93.
"The Resting Place. " Harp (261:1566) N 80, p. 88.
"Return to the Swamp. " NewYorker (56:11) 5 My 80, p. 48.
A Sea-Change: A Sequence of Poems. PraS (54:2) Sum 80, pp.
    41-48.
"The Shooting Lesson. " ChiR (31:4) Spr 80, p. 134.
"Spider Song. " Poetry (135:4) Ja 80, p. 221.
"Staying Alive in a Clear-Cut Forest. " ChiR (31:4) Spr 80, p.
    135.
"Staying Found. " WestHR (34:4) Aut 80, p. 363.
"Total Eclipse. " ConcPo (13:2) Aut 80, p. 5.
"Under the Sign of Moth. " Tendril (9) 80, p. 162.
"Under the Sign of the Moth. " Poetry (135:4) Ja 80, p. 218.
"Walking in Broken Country. " PoNow (27) 80, p. 28.
"Weeds. " MissouriR (4:1) Aut 80, p. 10.

WAHLE, F. Keith
"Modern Lives. " PartR (47:2) 80, p. 228.

WAIN, John
"Visiting an Old Poet. " CarlMis (18:2) Sum 80, pp. 123-132.

WAINWRIGHT, Letitia L.
"Drought. " Prima (5) 79, p. 47.

WAKEMAN, John
"Love in Brooklyn. " Poetry (135:5) F 80, p. 266.

WAKOSKI, Diane
"Breakfast. " SouthernPR (20:2) Aut 80, p. 5.
"Frog Mozart. " StoneC (7:3) D 80, p. 43.
"My Mother's Milkman. " Tendril (9) 80, p. 163.

WALCOTT, Derek
Eight poems. Antaeus (37) Spr 80, pp. 7-17.
"Hurucan. " NewYRB (27:19) 4 D 80, p. 42.
"Jean Rhys. " NewYorker (56:10) 28 Ap 80, p. 48.
"Letters from the Ming Dynasty" (tr. of Joseph Brodsky).

NewYorker (55:50) 28 Ja 80, p. 32.
"The Liberator. " Columbia (5) Aut-Wint 80, p. 7.
"The Man Who Loved Islands. " AmerPoR (9:3) My-Je 80, p. 48.
"North and South. " NewYorker (56:43) 15 D 80, p. 36.
"Old New England. " NewYorker (56:17) 16 Je 80, p. 34.
"The Season of Phantasmal Peace. " NewYorker (56:36) 27 O 80,
    p. 54.
"Upstate. " NewYorker (56:3) 10 Mr 80, p. 46.

WALD, Diane
"Customs. " PoNow (29) 80, p. 45.
"The Jetty. " MissouriR (3:2) Wint 80, p. 23.
"A Landscape, Grateful. " MissouriR (3:2) Wint 80, p. 24.
"On an Untitled Photo: Three Pages Held Up to the Sky" (for
    Bob). MassR (21:4) Wint 80, p. 723.

WALDEN, Edith
"The Wolf Prince. " Pig (7) My 80, p. 15.

WALDMAN, Anne
"A Dialogue Between the Self and the Soul. " SunM (9/10) Sum
    80, p. 176.
"Glacier. " Ark (14) 80, p. 393.
"Prehensile. " Ark (14) 80, p. 391.
"Shadow. " SunM (9/10) Sum 80, p. 175.
"Two Hearts. " SunM (9/10) Sum 80, p. 174.
"Valentines. " SunM (9/10) Sum 80, p. 173.
"Winter" (tr. of Pierre Reverdy w. Douglas Haynes). Ark (14)
    80, p. 394.

WALDRON, Sharon
"Death After the Run. " UTR (6:3/4) 80, p. 63.

WALDROP, Keith
"Chromatic Study" (for Heide Ziegler). OP (30) Aut 80, p. 4.
"Drift. " OP (30) Aut 80, p. 3.
"The Ruins of Providence. " OP (30) Aut 80, p. 7.

WALDROP, Rosmarie
from Providence in Winter: "Come Dawn. " OP (30) Aut 80, p.
    10.
from Providence in Winter: "Come Dreams. " OP (30) Aut 80,
    p. 13.
from Providence in Winter: "Escape. " OP (30) Aut 80, p. 11.
from Providence in Winter: "Sun. " OP (30) Aut 80, p. 8.

WALKER, Brad
"Rattlers. " PoetryNW (21:3) Aut 80, p. 44.

WALKER, David
"Late Harvest, War Autumn. " NewEngR (3:2) Wint 80, p. 265.
"Woman at the Window. " GeoR (34:3) Aut 80, p. 509.

WALKER, Janet A.
from the Izumi Shikibu nikki: (a, b, c, d, e) (tr. from the
Japanese). LitR (23:4) Sum 80, p. 476.

WALKER, Jauvanta
"When Death Comes." CapeR (16:1) Wint 80, p. 39.

WALKER, Jeanne Murray
"Angels." CarolQ (32:3) Aut 80, p. 94.
"Elegy for a Student." SouthernHR (14:4) Aut 80, p. 337.
"How Things Happen." AmerPoR (9:1) Ja-F 80, p. 47.
"Knowledge of Trees: University of Pennsylvania, 1979."
MassR (21:1) Spr 80, p. 136.
"Pantoun." SouthernHR (14:2) Spr 80, p. 167.
"Summer Song: To My Daughter." SouthernHR (14:4) Aut 80, p.
318.
"Tuesday Evening of Easter Week." ChrC (97:12) 2 Ap 80, p.
370.
"Useful Work." PoNow (29) 80, p. 41.

WALKER, Ken
"Orion Rising." NewL (46:4) Sum 80, p. 62.

WALKER, Kirk
"Separation." SlowLR (4) 80, p. 54.

WALKER, Ted
from A Zodiac Suite: "The bull." BosUJ (26:3) 80, p. 200.
from A Zodiac Suite: "The ram." BosUJ (26:3) 80, p. 200.

WALLACE, Jon
"The Linebacker at Forty." KanQ (12:1) Wint 80, p. 140.

WALLACE, Robert
"August: Decline and Fall." PoNow (26) 80, p. 28.
"Driving By." PoNow (26) 80, p. 28.
"Postcards." ThRiPo (15/16) 80, p. 61.
"Sea Turtles." PoNow (26) 80, p. 28.
"Time and Order." PoNow (28) 80, p. 4.

WALLACE, Ronald
"Apples." KanQ (12:3) Sum 80, p. 116.
"The Assistant Professor's Nightmare." SouthwR (65:1) Wint 80,
p. 57.
"Father and Son." MidwQ (21:2) Wint 80, p. 250.
"Moving into the Basement." PoetC (12:1) 80, p. 11.
"My Father's Son." KanQ (12:3) Sum 80, p. 115.
"On the River." SoDakR (18:2) Sum 80, p. 4.
"1001 Nights." PoetryNW (21:2) Sum 80, p. 36.
"Prayer for Fall." Poem (40) N 80, p. 23.
"The Real Thing." MidwQ (21:2) Wint 80, p. 252.
"September Rain." PoetryNW (21:2) Sum 80, p. 36.
"Starry Night." MidwQ (21:2) Wint 80, p. 251.

"Thanksgiving: St. Louis. " Poem (40) N 80, p. 22.
"Wild Strawberries. " QW (11) Aut-Wint 80-81, p. 57.

WALLACE-CRABBE, Chris
"Hospital Hour. " CarlMis (18:2) Sum 80, p. 155.
"Landscape with Classic Figures. " CarlMis (18:2) Sum 80, p.
    156.
"Provincial Distinctions. " NewL (46:3) Spr 80, p. 31.

WALSER, Robert
"The Handharp" (tr. by Tom Whalen). PoNow (28) 80, p. 45.

WALSH, Marty
"Passage. " Poem (40) N 80, p. 4.

WALSH, Phyllis
"Cliff Dwellers. " CreamCR (5:1) Wint 79, p. 108.

WALTER, R. R.
"To Anne Sexton: Bloomington. " BallSUF (21:1) Wint 80, p. 52.

WANDYCZ, Krystyna
"The Assumption of Miriam from the Street in the Winter of
    1942" (tr. of Jerzy Ficowski w. Keith Bosley). PortR (26)
    80, p. 302.
"The Way to Yerushalayim" (tr. of Jerzy Ficowski w. Keith Bos-
    ley). PortR (26) 80, p. 301.

WANG, David Rafael
"Have Tool, Will Travel. " PoNow (27) 80, p. 38.
"Phaeton Alive. " PoNow (27) 80, p. 38.
"The Untouched. " PoNow (27) 80, p. 38.

WANG Hui-ming
"on top of the Mountain" (tr. fr. the Chinese). NewL (46:4) Sum
    80, p. 43.
"Possess nothing. Own none. " NewL (46:4) Sum 80, p. 63.

WANG, Marit Monsen
"Navigare necesse est" (tr. by author). PortR (26) 80, p. 284.

WANIEK, Marilyn Nelson
"The Goose Invited All the Pigs" (tr. of Halfdan Rasmussen w.
    Pamela Lee Espeland). CarlMis (18:2) Sum 80, p. 5.
"Little Cloud" (tr. of Halfdan Rasmussen w. Pamela Lee Espe-
    land). CarlMis (18:2) Sum 80, p. 5.
"Poor Old Blue Monday" (tr. of Halfdan Rasmussen w. Pamela
    Lee Espeland). CarlMis (18:2) Sum 80, p. 6.
"The Winter's Cold in Norway" (tr. of Halfdan Rasmussen w.
    Pamela Lee Espeland). CarlMis (18:2) Sum 80, p. 5.

WANNBERG, Scott
"Closing Country. " Bachy (17) Spr 80, p. 146.

"Flanagan's Movement" (for Bob Flanagan). Bachy (17) Spr 80,
    p. 142.
"Haiku for Nervous Father. " Bachy (17) Spr 80, p. 143.
"Jack Saxaphone" (for Jack Grapes). Bachy (17) Spr 80, p. 144.
"Lesser Saints. " Bachy (17) Spr 80, p. 143.
"Smiling Samurai. " Bachy (17) Spr 80, p. 143.

WANTLING, William
"From a Veteran of the Third World War. " Sam (98) 80, p. 32.
    found poem
from San Quentin's Stranger: "The Cold War. " Sam (98) 80, p.
    32.

WARD, Jerry W.
"And Just Because My Friends. " BlackALF (14:3) Aut 80, p.
    123.

WARD, Robert
"Tenant Farmer. " KanQ (12:2) Spr 80, p. 6.

WARN, Emily
"Living with a Soft Sculptress. " Pig (7) My 80, p. 88.
"Stingy Weather. " Pig (7) My 80, p. 62.

WARNER, Val
"The Landlord. " GRR (11:2/3) 80, p. 15.

WARREN, Eugene
"Bitter Fire. " Focus (14:86) Ap 80, p. 14.
"Breathing Dreams. " Focus (14:86) Ap 80, p. 14.
"Distance. " Focus (14:86) Ap 80, p. 14.
"Soma. " Focus (14:86) Ap 80, p. 14.

WARREN, Larkin
"Wingwalkers. " QW (11) Aut-Wint 80-81, p. 56.

WARREN, Robert Penn
"After Restless Night. " Salm (50/51) Aut 80-Wint 81, p. 15.
"Ballad of Your Puzzlement. " GeoR (34:1) Spr 80, p. 11.
"Chthonian Revelation: A Myth. " YaleR (70:1) Aut 80, p. 95.
"Cocktail Party. " SouthernR (16:2) Spr 80, p. 381.
"Commuter's Entry in a Connecticut Diary. " SouthernR (16:2)
    Spr 80, p. 383.
"Deeper. " SouthernR (16:2) Spr 80, p. 377.
"Dream, Dump-Heap, and Civilization. " SouthernR (16:2) Spr 80,
    p. 382.
"Empty White Blotch on Map of Universe: A Possible View. "
    Atl (245:6) Je 80, p. 58.
"Immanence. " GeoR (34:4) Wint 80, p. 732.
"Last Night Train. " NewYorker (56:15) 2 Je 80, p. 36.
"Looking Northward, Aegeanward: Nestling on Sea Cliff. "
    NewYorker (56:37) 3 N 80, p. 50.
"Passersby on Snowy Night. " SouthernR (16:2) Spr 80, p. 378.

"Question You Must Learn to Live Past. " <u>Salm</u> (50/51) Aut 80-
   Wint 81, p. 11.
"Safe in Shade. " <u>GeoR</u> (34:2) Sum 80, p. 313.
"Sila. " <u>Atl</u> (245:3) <u>Mr</u> 80, p. 70.
"Sky. " <u>NewYorker</u> (56:7) 7 Ap 80, p. 38.
"Summer Afternoons and Hypnosis. " <u>NewYorker</u> (56:26) 18 Ag
   80, p. 34.
"Vermont Ballad: Season Change. " <u>Salm</u> (50/51) Aut 80-Wint
   81, p. 13.
"What Was the Thought?" <u>Salm</u> (50/51) Aut 80-Wint 81, p. 12.
"Why?" <u>SouthernR</u> (16:2) Spr 80, p. 379.

WARREN, Rosanna
"Daylights" (for Tristan Corbière). <u>Shen</u> (31:2) 80, p. 15.
"Music for Railroad, Telephone Wire, and Easter. " <u>Nat</u> (230:19)
   17 My 80, p. 601.
"Virgin Pictured in Profile" (for Ariel and Huxley Miller). <u>Atl</u>
   (245:4) Ap 80, p. 91.

WARSHAWSKI, Morrie
"Caprice. " <u>Tele</u> (16) 80, p. 88.
"The Idea of Floating" (for Charlotte Blob). <u>Tele</u> (16) 80, p. 88.

WASHINGTON, Marcherie
"We bounce over potholes and. " <u>HangL</u> (38) Aut 80, p. 69.

WATERMAN, Cary
"Love Poem" (for M.). <u>Tendril</u> (9) 80, p. 166.
"Me, Learning to Dance. " <u>DacTerr</u> (17) 80, p. 84.

WATERMAN, Charles
"At the R & D Cafe in Cleveland, Minnesota. " <u>Northeast</u> (3:8)
   Wint 80, p. 51.
"Teaching Physics to Bridget at the Cellar Stove. " <u>CarlMis</u> (18:2)
   Sum 80, p. 169.

WATERS, Mary Ann
"Love Scene. " <u>PoetryNW</u> (21:2) Sum 80, p. 11.
"The Shaping. " <u>PoetryNW</u> (21:2) Sum 80, p. 9.

WATERS, Michael
"Singles. " <u>OhioR</u> (25) 80, p. 101.
"Why God Invented the Clock-Radio. " <u>Bits</u> (11) 80.

WATSON, Charlotte D.
"In Memory of African Youth. " <u>Obs</u> (5:1/2) Spr-Sum 79, p. 112.

WATSON, Craig
"Poem Ending He Should Die. " <u>SunM</u> (9/10) Sum 80, pp. 161-
   165.

WATSON, Elaine
"Museum Piece No. 16228. " <u>BallSUF</u> (21:2) Spr 80, p. 11.

WATSON, Lawrence
"Evening. " KanQ (12:3) Sum 80, p. 116.
"Fishing Lesson." BelPoJ (30:3) Spr 80, p. 29.

WATSON, Robert
"Abandoned Husband. " Poetry (135:5) F 80, p. 290.
"God as a Magician. " Poetry (135:5) F 80, p. 287.
"A Good Life. " GeoR (34:2) Sum 80, p. 322.
"Henry Flagler's Song. " SoCaR (13:1) Aut 80, p. 50.
"Lost. " Poetry (135:5) F 80, p. 288.
"Panthers at the Sherry Netherland Hotel. " NewYorker (56:9)
    21 Ap 80, p. 46.
"Repossessed. " Poetry (135:5) F 80, p. 289.
"A Simple Meal. " SoCaR (13:1) Aut 80, p. 51.

WATTERS, D.
"The Foreman. " PottPort (2) 80-81, p. 19.

WATTS, Enos
"Crucible. " PottPort (2) 80-81, p. 12.
"Snowstorm: The Survivors. " PottPort (2) 80-81, p. 28.
"To a Little One. " PottPort (2) 80-81, p. 51.

WATTS, Harriet
"Craft and Industry" (tr. of H. C. Artmann). BosUJ (26:3) 80,
    p. 98.

WAUGAMAN, Charles A.
"Roller Rink. " CapeR (16:1) Wint 80, p. 21.

WAYMAN, Tom
"Figuring. " ConcPo (12:2) Aut 80, p. 45.
"for the younger writers. " Kayak (55) Ja 81, p. 54.
"taking the dead out of my address book. " Kayak (55) Ja 81, p.
    55.
"What the Writing Students of Detroit State Think of Philip Le-
    vine. " MassR (21:3) Aut 80, p. 596.

WEAVER, Dave
"Between Steps. " EngJ (69:5) My 80, p. 59.

WEAVER, Roger
"Who Bridles Us for This Ride?" ConcPo (13:2) Aut 80, p. 39.

WEBB, Bernice Larson
"Cherry Worm. " StoneC (7:2) My 80, p. 18.

WEBER, Elizabeth
"The Dshwari Cloister Ruins" (tr. of Sarah Kirsch). CutB (14)
    Spr/Sum 80, p. 41.
"The Night Spreads Out Its Fingers" (tr. of Sarah Kirsch).
    CutB (14) Spr/Sum 80, p. 40.
"Sachertorte. " Columbia (4) Spr-Sum 80, p. 83.

"Summons Chant" (tr. of Sarah Kirsch). CutB (14) Spr/Sum 80, p. 39.

WEBER, Ron
"Landscape with Hearts and Flowers. " Tele (16) 80, p. 47.

WEDGLEY, Stephen
"do you like my ears?" PoNow (29) 80, p. 42.
"her fingers. " PoNow (29) 80, p. 42.
"There it goes. " PoNow (29) 80, p. 42.

WEEDEN, Craig
"Blacklove's Stain. " PoNow (27) 80, p. 34.
"The Boatyard in Winter. " CimR (52) Jl 80, p. 14.
"The Neighborly Thing. " PoNow (26) 80, p. 42.
"Right Where He Left Off. " PoNow (28) 80, p. 32.
"The Salad Chef's Apprentice. " CreamCR (5:2) Spr 80, p. 69.

WEEDON, Syd
"Charlie howled. " Sam (102) 80, p. 52.
"Clone Clone # 7. " Sam (101) 80, p. 46.
"he sat alone. " Sam (101) 80, p. 2.
"it would be a pitiful way to spend. " Sam (98) 80, p. 20.

WEEKS, Ramona
"Night Song. " Pig (7) My 80, p. 52.

WEIDMAN, Phil
Blind Man's Bluff. WormR (79) 80.   Entire issue.
Ten poems. WormR (80) 80, p. 148.

WEIGEL, Tom
"Beach Front. " Tele (16) 80, p. 38.
"Let's Turn Here" (w. Michael Scholnick). Tele (16) 80, p. 37.
"New York Poem. " Tele (16) 80, p. 38.

WEIGL, Bruce
"Flight. " QW (10) Wint-Spr 80, p. 71.
"Misdirection. " QW (10) Wint-Spr 80, p. 72.
"Mona Lisa. " PoNow (27) 80, p. 14.
"The Streets. " NewEngR (3:2) Wint 80, p. 271.

WEIL, Eric
"Before Cooking an Eggplant. " Poetry (136:2) My 80, p. 65.
"The Path of the Headlights. " Poetry (136:2) My 80, p. 63.

WEIMAN, Andrew
"Andy-Diana DNA Letter. " Poetry (137:2) N 80, p. 94.

WEINBERGER, Eliot
from Chinese Music: "Striving to avoid ambition. " Ark (14) 80, p. 395.
"The Dead of the Revolution" (tr. of Homero Aridjis). Montra

(7) 80, p. 85.
from A Draft of Shadows: "Homage to Claudius Ptolemy" (tr. of
    Octavio Paz). Ark (14) 80, p. 307.
from A Draft of Shadows: "In Defense of Pyrrho" (for Juliun)
    (tr. of Octavio Paz). Ark (14) 80, p. 308.
"How dry I am. " Montra (7) 80, p. 198.
"Journey Book: Mexico" (tr. of Beatrice Caracciolo w. Gustaf
    Sobin). Montra (7) 80, p. 83.
"Landscape" (tr. of Homero Aridjis). Montra (7) 80, p. 89.
"Mexico City" (tr. of Homero Aridjis). Montra (7) 80, p. 88.
"San Miguel in the Backyard" (tr. of Homero Aridjis). Montra
    (7) 80, p. 87.
"Tezcatlipoca" (tr. of Homero Aridjis). Montra (7) 80, p. 84.
"Zapata" (tr. of Homero Aridjis). Montra (7) 80, p. 86.

WEINER, Hannah
"Little Book Indians. " Tele (16) 80, p. 10.

WEINERS, John
"Hunger. " PoNow (27) 80, p. 40.

WEINGARTEN, Roger
"Clay Tenements. " Poetry (135:5) F 80, p. 259.
"Dear Roger. " Shen (31:1) 79, p. 91.
"Night Signals. " QW (10) Wint-Spr 80, p. 33.
"Tunnel Effect. " Poetry (135:5) F 80, p. 257.

WEINMAN, Billy Razz
"Returning forever from Winfield. " ThRiPo (15/16) 80, p. 65.

WEINMAN, Paul
"See If It Fits. " SmPd (49) Spr 80, p. 23.
"Snow Covers Nothing. " StoneC (7:1) F 80, p. 21.
"Though Its Teeth. " Pan (21) 80, p. 6.
"Three Fingers. " PikeF (3) Wint 80, p. 27.

WEISMAN, Ann
"Spiritus" (w. Alice Price). Nimrod (24:1) Aut-Wint 80, p. 110.
"When the Veil Lifted" (w. Jim Roper). Nimrod (24:1) Aut-Wint
    80, p. 106.

WEISS, David
"Kenchana Wunggu" (for P. R.). Agni (13) 80, p. 34.
"The Landlord. " Poetry (135:5) F 80, p. 274.
"On the Marshes at Dawn. " GeoR (34:4) Wint 80, p. 754.

WEISS, Sanford
"The Art of Dreaming. " PoNow (27) 80, p. 10.
"My Mother's Piano. " PoNow (27) 80, p. 10.

WEISS, Theodore
"By the Sea. " Ark (14) 80, p. 396.
"En Route" (for Kathleen & Harry). Tendril (9) 80, p. 168.

WEITZEL, Allen Field
"through the ages. " BallSUF (21:3) Sum 80, p. 36.

WEITZMAN, Sarah Brown
"the reading test. " WindO (37) Aut-Wint 80, p. 10.

WELCH, Don
"The Best Ones. " Northeast (3:8) Wint 80, p. 21.
"The Blind Girl. " Northeast (3:8) Wint 80, p. 19.
"Early Spring. " SmF (11/12) Spr-Aut 80, p. 55.
"The Geese. " SmF (11/12) Spr-Aut 80, p. 51.
"In the Indian Bar at Whitby. " Northeast (3:8) Wint 80, p. 21.
"Love Song. " SmF (11/12) Spr-Aut 80, p. 52.
"Nebraska. " Northeast (3:8) Wint 80, p. 18.
"Poet in Residence at a Country School. " Northeast (3:8) Wint
   80, p. 20.
"The Rabbit. " Poem (39) Jl 80, p. 14.
"The Rarer Game: A Sequence of Poems About Birds and an
   Animal. " Nimrod (24:1) Aut-Wint 80, pp. 6-9.
"Singing a Bird's Song. " Poem (39) Jl 80, p. 13.
"The Treehouse" (for my children). SmF (11/12) Spr-Aut 80, p.
   53.
"Upon Finally Winning Something Big at the Fair. " DacTerr (17)
   80, p. 85.

WELCH, Liliane
"Teaching School in the Gaspe. " StoneC (7:2) My 80, p. 27.

WELISH, Marjorie
"Inquire Here. " SunM (9/10) Sum 80, p. 127.
"Songwriting. " SunM (9/10) Sum 80, p. 126.

WELLER, Chris
"Borderline. " EngJ (69:5) My 80, p. 58.

WELLMAN, Wade
"Dante and the Virgin. " LittleM (12:3/4) 80, p. 71.

WELLS, Thomas
"Nice Images. " Vis (1) 79.

WELLS, Will
"Gathering Darkness. " SouthwR (65:3) Sum 80, p. 266.

WELSH, Carole Kariamu
"Sudeka 1. " Obs (5:3) Wint 79, p. 101.
"Sudeka 2. " Obs (5:3) Wint 79, p. 102.
"Sudeka 3. " Obs (5:3) Wint 79, p. 102.
"Sudeka 4. " Obs (5:3) Wint 79, p. 103.
"Textured Women. " Obs (5:3) Wint 79, p. 104.

WEST, Jean
"Precious Metal. " Confr (20) Spr-Sum 80, p. 41.

WESTERFIELD, Nancy G.
"Arkansas: The Sanctuary." SouthernHR (14:3) Sum 80, p. 233.
"The Avon Lady." Confr (20) Spr-Sum 80, p. 26.
"Climbing to a Pictish Hill Fort." SouthernHR (14:3) Sum 80, p. 232.
"Fitting the Artificial Breasts." Pan (21) 80, p. 20.
"Laying a Cornerstone." Comm (107:11) 6 Je 80, p. 340.
"Sampler." FourQt (29:2) Wint 80, p. 32.

WESTFALL, Kathleen
"Farm Rd 60." Wind (38) 80, p. 71.

WESTLAKE, Wayne
Three Haiku. Northeast (3:8) Wint 80, p. 33.

WESTWOOD, Norma J.
"Father." ChrC (97:37) 19 N 80, p. 1126.
"Game." StoneC (7:1) F 80, p. 23.

WEXELBLATT, Robert
"The Cartographers." FourQt (29:4) Sum 80, p. 19.

WEXLER, Philip
"Concert." Vis (2) 80.

WEYLER, Paula
"Menagerie Room." Wind (37) 80, p. 14.

WHALEN, Philip
"Obsolete Models." Ark (14) 80, p. 398.

WHALEN, Tom
"The Check-up." PoNow (29) 80, p. 41.
"The Handharp" (tr. of Robert Walser). PoNow (28) 80, p. 45.
"The Wreck." PoNow (29) 80, p. 41.

WHEALDON, Everett
"No Mystery." Sam (98) 80, p. 47.

WHEATCROFT, John
"Lower G.I. Series." HiramPoR (28) Spr-Sum 80, p. 38.

WHEDON, Tony
"Hospital." PoetC (12:1) 80, p. 31.

WHEELER, Susan
"The Target Man." Shen (31:2) 80, p. 30.

WHEELER, Sylvia
"Father Poem III." DacTerr (17) 80, p. 86.

WHISLER, Robert F.
"Debts." ArizQ (36:3) Aut 80, p. 210.

"Lorelle. " CropD (2/3) Aut-Wint 80, p. 40.
"Reflections in a Mirror, a Trilogy for W. S. " SouthernPR
    (20:1) Spr 80, p. 55.
"Snowmen. " BallSUF (21:1) Wint 80, p. 54.

WHISNANT, Luke
"A Flight. " SouthernPR (20:2) Aut 80, p. 58.

WHITCOMB, Kathy
"Amazon. " PikeF (3) Wint 80, p. 16.

WHITE, Fred D.
"Far from Home. " Pan (21) 80, p. 5.

WHITE, Gail
"A Vision of Hell. " ChrC (97:34) 29 O 80, p. 1038.

WHITE, James
"The Arc-Welder's Blue" (for Paul Morris). CarlMis (18:2) Sum
    80, p. 173.

WHITE, James L.
"Naming" (for Marie White). OhioR (25) 80, p. 24.
"Vinegar. " PraS (54:1) Spr 80, p. 16.

WHITE, Mary Jane
"Of Encyclical Technique. " WatT (1) Aut 80, p. 3.
"Sick Child. " WatT (1) Aut 80, p. 5.
"Wanting a Bright Baby. " WatT (1) Aut 80, p. 4.

WHITE, Nancy
"The Dance Party. " PoNow (29) 80, p. 42.

WHITE, Roger
"Louis G. Gregory. " WorldO (14:1) Aut 79, p. 8.

WHITE, Steven
"The Angels in Quito. " Aspen (10) Wint 80, p. 51.
"Lazarus" (tr. of Alvaro Urtecho). NowestR (18:3) 80, p. 70.
"Slaughterhouse. " Aspen (10) Wint 80, p. 52.
"Summer Street" (tr. of Ana Ilce). NowestR (18:3) 80, p. 69.

WHITE, William M.
"Dark at the Top of My Stairs. " SouthwR (65:4) Aut 80, p. 398.
"Summer of Pure Ice. " SouthernR (16:3) Sum 80, pp. 608-614.

WHITEHEAD, James
"A Local Man Ponders a Letter He Has Received from a Liberal
    Woman He Continues to Admire" (for John Little). QW (10)
    Wint-Spr 80, p. 34.

WHITEN, Clifton
"Jocasta, Aged 45-50. " ConcPo (12:2) Aut 79, p. 58.

WHITING, Nathan
"An Early Morning Cat." HangL (38) Aut 80, p. 49.
"Girl's Game." HangL (38) Aut 80, p. 50.
"Names." HangL (38) Aut 80, p. 51.
"The Slum Lords of Richmond." HangL (38) Aut 80, pp. 52-56.

WHITING, Shirley
"The Mender." DacTerr (17) 80, p. 87.

WHITMAN, Ruth
"Arrow." BelPoJ (31:1) Aut 80, p. 36.
"Holding Up the Bridge." BelPoJ (31:1) Aut 80, p. 35.

WHITTINGTON, Gary
"The Flower Burial." AntR (38:4) Aut 80, p. 470.
"God." AntR (38:4) Aut 80, p. 469.

WHITTLE, Elizabeth
"utah dalton" (for helen schneedberger). Wind (37) 80, p. 57.

WICKERT, Max
"Dawn Song" (in honor of Hugh MacDiarmid). Pequod (11) 80, p.
    8.
from The Pat Sonnets: (1, 2, 4, 5, 6, 7, 8, 9). Poetry (137:1)
    O 80, p. 19.

WIEBE, Dallas
"Calcutta Jump." SouthernPR (20:1) Spr 80, p. 67.
"The Rise of the Dutch Rest Room." SouthernPR (20:1) Spr 80,
    p. 66.

WIENS, Paul
"Sie nahmen mich mit." PortR (26) 80, p. 142.

WIER, Dara
"All You Have in Common." Columbia (5) Aut-Wint 80, p. 59.
"Breath and Depth of Field." VirQR (56:1) Wint 80, p. 65.
"The Intercession of Light." VirQR (56:1) Wint 80, p. 64.
"Where There Was Stillness." NoAmR (265:1) Mr 80, p. 57.

WIESER, Nora
"From you from me painted dwellers" (tr. of Nancy Bacelo).
    PortR (26) 80, p. 447.
"I need you" (tr. of Cristina Meneghetti). PortR (26) 80, p. 445.
"The Shrew Who Married God" (tr. of Belkis Cuza Malé).
    PortR (26) 80, p. 60.
"Waltz of the Angelus II" (tr. of Blanca Varela). PortR (26) 80,
    p. 287.

WIGGINS, Diane Leslie
"an old woman dying." BelPoJ (31:1) Aut 80, p. 8.
"running." BelPoJ (31:1) Aut 80, p. 7.

WIGGINS, Jean
   "The Holly Tree." FourQt (30:1) Aut 80, p. 2.

WILBUR, Richard
   "Andromache" (tr. of Jean Racine). Poetry (136:1) Ap 80, p. 31.
   "Transit." Tendril (9) 80, p. 170.

WILD, Peter
   "Andrew." CharR (6:2) Aut 80, p. 23.
   "Climbers." PraS (54:4) Wint 80-81, p. 95.
   "Cockerpoos." Im (7:1) 80, p. 8.
   "Daffodils." ThRiPo (15/16) 80, p. 67.
   "Dolphins." PoNow (27) 80, p. 13.
   "Goiter." PoNow (28) 80, p. 15.
   "Ouija." Im (6:2) 80, p. 3.
   "Recidivists." MassR (21:3) Aut 80, p. 568.
   "Sweetbread." ThRiPo (15/16) 80, p. 68.
   "Widow." LitR (23:3) Spr 80, p. 402.

WILDER, Rex
   "Desertion: Day and Night at the Piggery." CreamCR (5:1) Wint
     79, p. 30.

WILER, John
   "The Waterboy." US1 (12/13) Aut-Wint 80, p. 12.

WILJER, Robert
   "Moose." Poetry (136:2) My 80, p. 72.

WILKINS, Paul
   "Hall of Mirrors." GRR (11:2/3) 80, p. 89.
   "Home." GRR (11:2/3) 80, p. 91.
   "The Lives." GRR (11:2/3) 80, p. 92.

WILKINSON, Robert
   "Elegy: Spoiled Meat." PoetryNW (21:1) Spr 80, p. 49.
   "Fishing." OP (29) Spr 80, p. 35.
   "Ilixit." OP (29) Spr 80, p. 34.
   "Landlords." Bits (11) 80.
   "The Other One." OP (29) Spr 80, p. 35.
   "Poem-Shoe." OP (29) Spr 80, p. 33.

WILKINSON, Tom
   "Snake Man." CreamCR (5:1) Wint 79, p. 15.

WILL, Frederic
   "The dark forces, yes that's it." Aspect (76) S-D 79-80, p. 33.
   "He Listened." AmerPoR (9:2) Mr-Ap 80, p. 28.
   "He wondered and wondered ... etc." Aspect (76) S-D 79-80, p.
     31.
   "His big inhibited afterdinner smile." Aspect (76) S-D 79-80, p.
     32.
   "In the Little European Square." PoNow (27) 80, p. 33.

"Neruda's urine. " Aspect (76) S-D 79-80, p. 34.
"The new sounds in the garden. " Aspect (76) S-D 79-80, p. 33.
"Patio Metaphysics. " AmerPoR (9:6) N-D 80, p. 48.
"Phase New IV: Breaking Up Breaking Up Breaking Up. "
    PoetryNW (21:3) Aut 80, p. 17.
"Tom's own little metaphysical inquiry. " Aspect (76) S-D 79-80,
    p. 32.

WILLARD, Nancy
"Blake's Wonderful Car Delivers Us Wonderfully Well. " MassR
    (21:4) Wint 80, p. 780.
"First Goddess: Deverra. " Field (23) Aut 80, p. 36.
"Lightness Remembered. " Field (22) Spr 80, p. 51.
"Night Light. " Field (22) Spr 80, p. 49.
"No-Kings and the Calling of Spirits. " Field (23) 80, p. 39.
"Saint Pumpkin. " Field (22) Spr 80, p. 53.
"Second Goddess: Juno Lucina. " Field (23) Aut 80, p. 38.
"The Sun and Moon Circus Soothes the Wakeful Guests. " MassR
    (21:4) Wint 80, p. 781.

WILLIAMS, C. K.
"Flight. " AmerPoR (9:3) My 80, p. 3.
"Floor. " AmerPoR (9:3) My-Je 80, p. 3.
"The Gas Station. " AmerPoR (9:3) My-Je 80, p. 4.
"On Learning of a Friend's Illness" (for James Wright).
    AmerPoR (9:3) My-Je 80, p. 5.

WILLIAMS, Elizabeth
"After Missing the Last Train Back to Paris. " CreamCR (5:1)
    Wint 79, p. 33.
"Wolf Lake Autumn. " CreamCR (5:1) Wint 79, p. 34.

WILLIAMS, Jonathan
"A Postcard Poem for KR, Survivor, Off There in the Land of
    Gallo's Heartless Burgundy. " Ark (14) 80, p. 401.
"Ten Gists for Kenneth. " Ark (14) 80, p. 399.

WILLIAMS, Kelley
"I seek my harvests. " Prima (5) 79, p. 44.
"Under Eyelids. " Prima (5) 79, p. 44.

WILLIAMS, Linda
"From a Train Station. " PraS (54:4) Wint 80-81, p. 67.

WILLIAMS, Miller
"About the Airplane, Then. " CharR (6:2) Aut 80, p. 9.
"A Bad Moment" (tr. of Giuseppe Gioachino Belli). Poetry (136:
    1) Ap 80, p. 8.
"The Beasts of the Earthly Paradise" (tr. of Giuseppe Gioachino
    Belli). Poetry (136:1) Ap 80, p. 5.
"Believing. " SouthernR (16:3) Sum 80, p. 599.
"Believing in Symbols. " CharR (6:2) Aut 80, p. 8.
"Cain" (tr. of Giuseppe Gioachino Belli). Poetry (136:1) Ap 80,

p. 6.
"Death with a Coda" (tr. of Giuseppe Gioachino Belli).   CutB (14)
   Spr /Sum 80, p. 49.
"Ghosts. "   SouthernR (16:3) Sum 80, p. 597.
"Good Weather" (tr. of Giuseppe Gioachino Belli).   CutB (14)
   Spr /Sum 80, p. 47.
"The Grownup Sons" (tr. of Giuseppe Gioachino Belli).   CutB (14)
   Spr /Sum 80, p. 48.
"Memory" (tr. of Giuseppe Gioachino Belli).   Poetry (136:1) Ap
   80, p. 7.
"The News. "   SouthernR (16:3) Sum 80, p. 602.
"Pity and Fear. "   NewEngR (3:2) Wint 80, p. 174.
"Professor. "   CharR (6:2) Aut 80, p. 9.
"Religion Explained and Defended" (tr. of Giuseppe Gioachino
   Belli).   CutB (14) Spr /Sum 80, p. 46.
"The Resurrection of the Flesh" (tr. of Giuseppe Gioachino Belli).
   Poetry (136:1) Ap 80, p. 9.
"The Survivor. "   NewEngR (3:2) Wint 80, p. 175.
Thirteen poems (tr. of Giuseppe Gioachino Belli).   QW (10) Wint-
   Spr 80, pp. 56-62.
"Trying to Remember. "   Bits (11) 80.
"The Well-Ordered Life. "   SouthernR (16:3) Sum 80, p. 601.
"Words. "   SouthernR (16:3) Sum 80, p. 600.

WILLIAMS, Regina
   "Uncle Henry's Conjugal Visits. "   BlackALF (14:4) Wint 80, p.
   171.

WILLIAMSON, Alan
   "For Robinson Jeffers. "   Ploughs (6:2) 80, p. 78.
   "House-Moving from Tournon to Besancon" (for Bradford Cook).
      ParisR (77) Wint-Spr 80, p. 155.
   "Leaving for Islands. "   Ploughs (6:2) 80, p. 80.
   "Obsession. "   NewRep (183:8) 23 Ag 80, p. 28.

WILLIAMSON, Kim
   "Basically This Morning Is Cold. "   Wind (36) 80, p. 16.

WILLSON, A. Leslie
   "the hopes" (tr. of Dieter Fringeli).   PortR (26) 80, p. 385.

WILMOT, John, Earl of Rochester--see ROCHESTER, Earl of

WILNER, Eleanor
   "Mt. Fuji and the Martial Arts. "   AmerPoR (9:2) Mr-Ap 80, p.
   28.

WILSON, Dolores
   "On Bolts A Man for All Seasons. "   EngJ (69:5) My 80, p. 52.

WILSON, Donald
   "Flashlight Vision. "   KanQ (12:1) Wint 80, p. 120.

WILSON, Edward
"Dogwoods. " Poetry (137:1) O 80, p. 8.
"For the Woman in Her Station Wagon Weeping at a Red Light. "
SouthernPR (20:2) Aut 80, p. 7.

WILSON, Emily Herring
"Ann Eliza Young. " PoNow (26) 80, p. 28.
"Driving Home. " PoNow (26) 80, p. 28.
"Sisters. " PoNow (26) 80, p. 28.

WILSON, Graeme
"Anguish" (tr. of Ono no Komachi). DenQ (15:3) Aut 80, p. 84.
"Bedlam Heart" (tr. of Kiowara no Fukayabu). DenQ (15:3) Aut
80, p. 81.
"Blue Fox" (tr. of Ote Takuji). WestHR (34:4) Aut 80, p. 335.
"Contentment" (tr. of Kino Tomonori). DenQ (15:3) Aut 80, p.
82.
"Curves" (tr. of Yamamura Bocho). WestHR (34:4) Aut 80, p.
335.
"Flower Basket" (tr. of anonymous). DenQ (15:3) Aut 80, p. 84.
"Foolish Women" (tr. of The Monk Kengei). DenQ (15:3) Aut 80,
p. 83.
"Graveyard" (tr. of Saito Mokichi). WestHR (34:4) Aut 80, p.
334.
"Ivies" (tr. of anonymous). DenQ (15:3) Aut 80, p. 81.
"Last Poem" (tr. of Ariwarino Narihira). DenQ (15:3) Aut 80,
p. 85.
"Learning by Touch" (tr. of Takamura Kotaro). WestHR (34:4)
Aut 80, p. 334.
"Love Letters" (tr. of Lady Fujiwara no Yoruka). DenQ (15:3)
Aut 80, p. 80.
"Making Love in Darkness" (tr. of anonymous). DenQ (15:3) Aut
80, p. 82.
"Mirror Weather" (tr. of Kino Tsurayuki). DenQ (15:3) Aut 80,
p. 85.
"My Cat" (tr. of Miyoshi Tatsuji). WestHR (34:4) Aut 80, p.
336.
"Pathway" (tr. of Yoshimine no Munesada). DenQ (15:3) Aut 80,
p. 80.
"White Chrysanthemum" (tr. of Oshikoshi no Mitsune). DenQ
(15:3) Aut 80, p. 83.

WILSON, Jonathan
"Beneath the Temple Mount. " Stand (21:4) 80, p. 37.

WILSON, Keith
"Child's Tale. " PoNow (26) 80, p. 29.
"Northern New Mexican Funeral. " HangL (38) Aut 80, p. 57.
"Sheepherder's Song. " HangL (38) Aut 80, p. 58.

WILSON, Miles
"Riders. " SoDakR (18:3) Aut 80, p. 5.
"Slash Burning. " PoetryNW (21:3) Aut 80, p. 13.

WILSON, Rob
  "The Flatlands. " PartR (47:1) 80, p. 125.

WILSON, Robley Jr.
  "Against Violence. " MalR (54) Ap 80, p. 151.
  "Elegy" (tr. of Aleksandr Pushkin). CutB (14) Spr /Sum 80, p.
    100.
  "The Labor Camp. " GeoR (34:1) Spr 80, p. 38.
  "The Opera. " Poetry (136:4) Jl 80, p. 207.
  "Porcupines. " Poetry (136:4) Jl 80, p. 208.
  "Snail. " MalR (54) Ap 80, p. 152.
  "Something of Love. " MichQR (19:4 /20:1) Aut-Wint 80-81, p.
    529.
  "The Warrior. " MalR (54) Ap 80, p. 150.
  "The Word 'Love.' " MissouriR (4:1) Aut 80, p. 17.

WINDER, Barbara
  "Fires in the Mind. " PoetC (12:1) 80, p. 6.
  "The Limits of Equitation. " KanQ (12:2) Spr 80, p. 54.

WINDLE, Susan
  "Identifying the Brown Thrasher. " Prima (5) 79, p. 45.

WINN, Howard
  "My Father Stands on His Head for My Young Daughter. "
    SouthernHR (14:3) Sum 80, p. 209.
  "Pop Love. " WindO (36) 80, p. 34.

WINNER, Robert
  "The Chain Gain. " PoNow (29) 80, p. 30.
  "Driving in a Storm. " SlowLR (4) 80, p. 18.
  "Evening. " SlowLR (4) 80, p. 17.
  "Penguins. " PoNow (29) 80, p. 30.
  "The Ruler. " AmerPoR (9:5) S-O 80, p. 36.
  "The Shark. " OhioR (24) 80, p. 94.

WINTERS, Anne
  "The Key to the City. " Ploughs (6:2) 80, p. 132.
  "Two Derelicts. " NewRep (183:24) 13 D 80, p. 38.

WINTERS, Bayla
  "Like a Worn Welsh Logo.... " PikeF (3) Wint 80, p. 11.

WISCHNER, Claudia March
  "Hydromancy" (for S.). PoetryNW (21:4) Wint 80-81, p. 26.

WISOFF, Ellen
  "Child's Play (Canzone). " SunM (9 /10) Sum 80, p. 115.

WISTI, Mark
  "God is drunk today. " MinnR (NS 15) Aut 80, p. 22.

WITHERSPOON, G. Ashanti
  "Cue Ball Loneliness. " PikeF (3) Wint 80, p. 28.

"The Ghetto Ghost." PikeF (3) Wint 80, p. 28.

WITSCHEL, John
"on red dog mesa." Kayak (53) My 80, p. 21.
"taking measure." Kayak (53) My 80, p. 20.

WITT, Harold
"Bicep." Poem (40) N 80, p. 60.
"Donald Dimvue, Professor of History." WormR (78) 80, p. 79.
Eight poems. PoNow (27) 80, pp. 5, 36.
"Fad." Harp (261:1567) D 80, p. 89.
"Granite." ConcPo (13:2) Aut 80, p. 96.
"Gunning." Poem (40) N 80, p. 61.
"The Harpist." PoetryNW (21:3) Aut 80, p. 34.
"January First." Wind (38) 80, p. 72.
"Lana Olson." Im (7:1) 80, p. 12.
"Lanky Hank Farrow." PoNow (28) 80, p. 33.
"Mrs. Asquith Tries to Save the Jacarandas." WormR (78) 80,
   p. 79.
"'One Eye' Guy Burns." PoetryNW (21:3) Aut 80, p. 35.
"Snow Queen." NewL (46:4) Sum 80, p. 105.
"Surprise." Wind (38) 80, p. 72.

WITT, Sandra
"Letter to Major George Thomson from Jenny." CutB (15) Aut /
   Wint 80, p. 81.

WITTE, John
"The Alphabet Snake." VirQR (56:2) Spr 80, p. 268.
"The Child Who Rolled Back His Eyes." VirQR (56:2) Spr 80, p.
   269.
"Gravity." GeoR (34:1) Spr 80, p. 130.
"If a Man." ParisR (78) Sum 80, p. 188.
"Leaving the Island." NewYorker (55:48) 14 Ja 80, p. 36.
"Love Poem." AntR (38:3) Sum 80, p. 339.
"Night Flight." AmerPoR (9:5) S-O 80, p. 10.
"Oak Apples." AntR (38:4) Aut 80, p. 462.
"Variations on an Old Woman." OhioR (24) 80, p. 40.
"What the Birds Said." OhioR (24) 80, p. 41.

WITTENBERG, Rudolf
"Break." Confr (20) Spr-Sum 80, p. 25.
"Fragmented Night." Poem (38) Mr 80, p. 62.
"October Bikeride." Poem (38) Mr 80, p. 61.

WOESSNER, Warren
"Center Junction." PoNow (26) 80, p. 12.
"The Disappearance of Father." DacTerr (17) 80, p. 88.
"Heard in Galena, Illinois." PoNow (27) 80, p. 28.
"Honey Creek." PoNow (27) 80, p. 28.
"The Midnight Bus." PoNow (27) 80, p. 28.
"Over." PoNow (27) 80, p. 28.
"Parfrey's Glen." PoNow (26) 80, p. 12.

WOJAHN, David
"Allegory: Attic and Fever." Salm (47/48) Wint-Spr 80, p. 51.
"The Astral Body." Ploughs (6:2) 80, p. 117.
"Border Town Evening." QW (10) Wint-Spr 80, p. 121.
"Climbing Down" (for Mick Fedullo). MissouriR (3:2) Wint 80, p. 36.
"Cold Glow: Icehouses." NoAmR (265:3) S 80, p. 13.
"In Summer." Northeast (3:8) Wint 80, p. 55.
"Noon: On the Death of the Poet Cesare Pavese, Turin, 1950." PoetryE (1) 80, p. 59.
"The Sad Composure." Northeast (3:8) Wint 80, p. 55.
"The Stories Behind Them." PoNow (29) 80, p. 42.
"Weldon Kees in Mexico, 1965." Columbia (4) Spr-Sum 80, p. 7.

WOLF, Leslie
"A Moment with Robin Hood." PartR (47:1) 80, p. 123.

WOLF, Manfred
"The leafless light" (tr. of Hanny Michaelis). PortR (26) 80, p. 273.
"Whoever closes the curtains" (tr. of Hanny Michaelis). PortR (26) 80, p. 274.

WOLF, Marcia
"And the Lord Spoke to Moses." Im (6:8) 80, p. 9.

WOLFE, Edgar
"Sparrows in College Ivy." KanQ (12:1) Wint 80, p. 93.

WOLFER, Cynthia
"The Party." Sam (98) 80, p. 56.

WOLFERT, Adrienne
"The Heart Beats." Poem (38) Mr 80, p. 26.
"Like Four O'Clocks." Poem (38) Mr 80, p. 28.
"On the Discovery of a Human Fossil." Poem (38) Mr 80, p. 27.

WOLFF, Daniel
"Autumns Used to Darken with Meaning." Spirit (5:1/2) Aut-Wint 79-80, p. 34.
"Heaven in Ordinaire." Ploughs (6:2) 80, p. 119.
"The Universal Joint." Ploughs (6:2) 80, p. 120.

WOLFF, Henry
"Gutveig." NewL (46:3) Spr 80, p. 90.

WOLITZER, Hilma
"The Monster." PraS (54:4) Wint 80-81, p. 26.

WOOD, John A.
"A Dance for My Father." SouthernR (16:1) Wint 80, p. 149.
"In My Green Memory I Recall You Most Vividly, My Dear." SouthernR (16:1) Wint 80, p. 147.

"Morning from My Office Window. " SouthernR (16:1) Wint 80, p. 150.

WOOD, Peter
    "Gull. " US1 (12/13) Aut-Wint 80, p. 5.
    "She Says Seychelles. " US1 (12/13) Aut-Wint 80, p. 5.

WOOD, Renate
    "The Experiment. " Aspen (9) Spr 80, p. 45.
    "Points of Entry. " Aspen (9) Spr 80, p. 43.
    "Trying to Pin You Back into the Sky" (for Nancy Koerner).
        Aspen (9) Spr 80, p. 44.
    "Tunnelvision: Berlin 1945. " Aspen (9) Spr 80, p. 46.

WOOD, Susan
    "After You. " MissouriR (4:1) Aut 80, p. 14.
    "As It Happens. " MissouriR (4:1) Aut 80, p. 16.
    "Elegy for My Sister. " MissouriR (4:1) Aut 80, p. 13.
    "I Want to Believe It. " MissouriR (4:1) Aut 80, p. 12.

WOODARD, Deborah
    "Marradi" (tr. of Dino Campana). Durak (5) 80, p. 50.
    "O Poetry You Won't Return Again" (tr. of Dino Campana).
        Durak (5) 80, p. 51.

WOODBURY, James E. A.
    "American Apocalypse. " NewRena (12) Spr 80, p. 40.
    "1939-1940. " NewRena (12) Spr 80, p. 39.
    "When the Heart's Blood Pulsed in Three-Quarter Time. "
        NewRena (12) Spr 80, p. 41.

WOODCOCK, George
    "Kreutzer Sonata. " Ark (14) 80, p. 402.
    "The Mountain Road. " Ark (14) 80, p. 403.

WOOLFOLK, Ann
    "The Second Hunter. " US1 (12/13) Aut-Wint 80, p. 8.
    "Twister. " US1 (12/13) Aut-Wint 80, p. 8.

WOOLLS, Reine Cross
    "Images. " CropD (1) Spr 80, p. 18.

WORLEY, James
    "Back from the War. " ChrC (97:30) 1 O 80, p. 914.
    "Paid Attention. " ChrC (97:17) 7 My 80, p. 520.
    "Statement. " ChrC (97:23) 2-9 Jl 80, p. 701.

WORLEY, Jeff
    "Ash Street Poem. " PoetC (12:3) 80, p. 9.
    "The Last Poem About the Moon. " PoetC (12:3) 80, p. 8.
    "The Something. " PoetC (12:3) 80, p. 10.

WORMUTH, Diana
    "The Baker" (tr. of Artur Lundkvist). OntR (12) Spr-Sum 80,

p. 23.
"Furioso" (tr. of Artur Lundkvist). <u>OntR</u> (12) Spr-Sum 80, p. 25.
"Mill Memory" (tr. of Artur Lundkvist). <u>OntR</u> (12) Spr-Sum 80, p. 24.
"Temples" (tr. of Artur Lundkvist). <u>OntR</u> (12) Spr-Sum 80, p. 21.

WORSLEY, Alice F.
"Our Love Was Sudden as Radishes. " <u>KanQ</u> (12:1) Wint 80, p. 62.

WOSTER, Kevin
"Coming Home. " <u>CapeR</u> (16:1) Wint 80, p. 26.
"Freezing. " <u>CapeR</u> (16:1) Wint 80, p. 27.
"A Gift of Science. " <u>CapeR</u> (15:2) Sum 80, p. 6.
"Leaving with 35 W. " <u>CapeR</u> (15:2) Sum 80, p. 5.
"November Night. " <u>CapeR</u> (16:1) Wint 80, p. 25.

WRAY, Elizabeth
"The Limits of the Town. " <u>NewL</u> (46:4) Sum 80, p. 19.

WRIGHT, A. J.
"An American Still Life. " <u>CropD</u> (2/3) Aut-Wint 80, p. 32.
"Apotheosis. " <u>WindO</u> (36) Spr-Sum 80, p. 41.
"Parahumans Walk Among Us. " <u>CropD</u> (2/3) Aut-Wint 80, p. 12.

WRIGHT, C. D.
"Blazes. " <u>QW</u> (10) Wint-Spr 80, p. 73.
"Headquarters of the Blues. " <u>QW</u> (10) Wint-Spr 80, p. 75.
"The Secret Life of Musical Instruments. " <u>QW</u> (10) Wint-Spr 80, p. 74.

WRIGHT, Carolyne
"Snow Before Sleep: A Letter to Nicholas in Winter. " <u>QW</u> (11) Aut-Wint 80-81, p. 35.

WRIGHT, Charles
"California Spring. " <u>NewYorker</u> (56:18) 23 Je 80, p. 30.
"Called Back. " <u>Tendril</u> (9) 80, p. 171.
"Dead Color. " <u>WatT</u> (1) Aut 80, p. 41.
"Dog Day Vespers. " <u>NewYorker</u> (56:18) 23 Je 80, p. 30.
"Dog Yoga. " <u>Field</u> (22) Spr 80, p. 83.
"Gate City Breakdown. " <u>PoetryNW</u> (21:2) Sum 80, p. 26.
"Laguna Dantesca. " <u>NewYorker</u> (56:18) 23 Je 80, p. 30.
"The Monastery at Vrsac. " <u>Field</u> (22) Spr 80, p. 82.

WRIGHT, Charles David
"Everybody Will Write Poetry" (tr. of Branko Miljković w. Vasa D. Mihailovich). <u>PortR</u> (26) 80, p. 479.

WRIGHT, Franz
"After. " <u>Durak</u> (4) 80, p. 51.

"Brussels, 1971" (for Carolyn). AntR (38:2) Spr 80, p. 171.
"The Journey. " AntR (38:2) Spr 80, p. 172.
"The Neighbor" (tr. of Rainer Maria Rilke). CutB (14) Spr /Sum 80, p. 38.
"Trespassing on 58: Poem for Two Voices. " Durak (4) 80, p. 52.
"View from an Institution" (for B). VirQR (56:1) Wint 80, p. 68.
"The Visit. " VirQR (56:1) Wint 80, p. 67.

WRIGHT, James
"And me there alone at last with my only love. " Poetry (136:3) Je 80. Back cover.
"Between Wars. " Poetry (136:3) Je 80, p. 125.
"Chilblain. " Harp (260:1561) Je 80, p. 70.
"A Dark Moor Bird. " Hudson (33:2) Sum 80, p. 178.
Eight poems. Antaeus (36) Wint 80, pp. 37-43.
"Entering the Temple in Nimes. " NewYorker (55:48) 14 Ja 80, p. 30.
"A Farewell: To the Mayor of Toulouse. " Hudson (33:2) Sum 80, p. 180.
"The Journey. " NewYorker (56:1) 25 F 80, p. 46.
"Rain on the Spanish Steps. " Hudson (33:2) Sum 80, p. 178.
"Reading a 1979 Inscription on Belli's Monument. " Hudson (33:2) Sum 80, p. 177.
"Venice. " Poetry (136:3) Je 80, p. 126.
"The Vestal in the Forum. " Hudson (33:2) Sum 80, p. 180.
"Wherever Home Is. " Hudson (33:2) Sum 80, p. 179.
"A Winter Daybreak Above Vence. " Harp (260:1561) Je 80, p. 70.

WRIGHT, Jeff
"As Pink Is My Witness. " Tele (16) 80, p. 25.
"Halloween, 1978. " Tele (16) 80, p. 25.
"Postcard to Anselm. " Tele (16) 80, p. 25.

WRIGHT, Judith
"Eli, Eli. " NewL (46:3) Spr 80, p. 35.

WRIGHT, Wayne
"Growl. " PottPort (2) 80-81, p. 13.
"Lexicon. " PottPort (2) 80-81, p. 38.

WRIGLEY, Robert
"Prediction. " QW (11) Aut-Wint 80-81, p. 88.

WUBISHET, Girma
"It Comes to This. " Obs (5:1/2) Spr-Sum 79, p. 108.

WUEST, Barbara
"Going. " CapeR (16:1) Wint 80, p. 5.
"Links. " CapeR (16:1) Wint 80, p. 4.

WURM, Franz
"Konjunktur. " PortR (26) 80, p. 381.

WYATT, David
  "Keepers of the River" (for Chuck Barlow). Annex (2) 79, pp.
    39-67.

WYATT, Jiri
  "Tenants of the House. " NewYorker (56:4) 17 Mr 80, p. 88.

WYNAND, Derk
  "The Magician's Wife. " OntR (12) Spr-Sum 80, p. 31.

WYNDHAM, Harald
  "Dreams of Immortality, Etc." Im (7:1) 80, p. 4.
  "Landscapes. " Im (7:1) 80, p. 4.

YAEGER, Patricia
  "Her Attic. " SouthernPR (20:2) Aut 80, p. 31.

YA Hsien
  "Red Corn" (tr. by author). PortR (26) 80, p. 394.
  "Wartime" (tr. by author). PortR (26) 80, p. 392.

YALIM, Oscan
  "Duel" (tr. of Cemal Sureya w. William Fielder and Dionis Cof-
    fin Riggs). DenQ (15:2) Sum 80, p. 87.
  "San" (tr. of Cemal Sureya w. William Fielder and Dionis Coffin
    Riggs). DenQ (15:2) Sum 80, p. 86.

YAMRUS, John
  "I Was 13, Maybe 14, and. " Sam (101) 80, p. 58.

YATES, David C.
  "Wakefield Returns. " ColEng (41:7) Mr 80, p. 802.

YATES, J. Michael
  "I am speaking to you with my death between us. " NewOR (7:2)
    80, p. 182.

YATES, James
  "Chaplin. " PoNow (29) 80, p. 43.
  "Hitchhiking to a Funeral. " PoNow (29) 80, p. 43.
  "It's a Boy. " PoNow (29) 80, p. 43.
  "Watching One Become Two. " PoNow (29) 80, p. 43.

YATES, Lynda
  "The Disordering. " SouthernR (16:1) Wint 80, p. 160.
  "In the Middle of a Plowed Field, a Rock. " GeoR (34:2) Sum 80,
    p. 360.
  "Naked Like This. " Confr (20) Spr-Sum 80, p. 59.

YAU, John
  "Chinese Villanelle. " SunM (9/10) Sum 80, p. 125.
  "Ten Songs. " PartR (47:1) 80, p. 127.

YEATS, Cameron W.
"A Box. " CropD (2/3) Aut-Wint 80, p. 33.

YEATS, William Butler
"The Watch Fire. " Poetry (135:4) Ja 80, p. 223.

YENSER, Stephen
"Ember Week, Reseda. " YaleR (70:2) Wint 81, p. 262.
"Fundamental. " Nat (230:19) 17 My 80, p. 600.

YORUKA, Lady Fujiwara no
"Love Letters" (tr. by Graeme Wilson). DenQ (15:3) Aut 80, p.
   80.

YOSHIMASU, Gozo
"Adrenalin. " PortR (26) 80, pp. 233-238.

YOTS, Michael
"At Edgar Bergen's Funeral. " PoNow (29) 80, p. 44.
"It Goes with the Territory. " Wind (36) 80, p. 67.
"Juarez, Nogales, Tijuana, Et Al. " Wind (36) 80, p. 67.
"Reviewing the Game Films. " PoNow (29) 80, p. 44.

YOUNG, Al
"Mid-Life Crisis: A Critical Review. " Thrpny (2) Sum 80, p.
   22.

YOUNG, David
"How Music Began. " PoNow (28) 80, p. 28.
"Jaywalker. " PoNow (28) 80, p. 28.
"Three Private Madrigals" (tr. of Eugenio Montale w. Vinio
   Rossi). Field (23) Aut 80, p. 43.

YOUNG, Gary
"Equinox. " PoNow (26) 80, p. 33.
"Prayer. " Poetry (135:6) Mr 80, p. 323.
"Sleeplessness. " PoNow (26) 80, p. 33.
"To an Estranged Wife. " Poetry (135:6) Mr 80, p. 324.
"Walking Home from Work. " NewOR (7:1) 80, p. 57.

YOUNG, Geoffrey
"Side by Side. " CarolQ (32:1) Wint 80, p. 92.

YOUNG, Karl
"Second Hymn to Janus. " SunM (9/10) Sum 80, p. 26.

YOUNG, Virginia Brady
Three Haiku. Northeast (3:8) Wint 80, p. 33.

YOUNGBLOOD, Sarah
"John Keats on a Barn-Roof in Maine. " MassR (21:2) Sum 80, p.
   314.
"Mr. Jefferson's Horses. " MassR (21:2) Sum 80, p. 315.

YU Kwang-chung
"All That Have Wings" (tr. by author).   PortR (26) 80, p. 391.

YUZURU, Katagiri
"At Kitkitdizze. " Ark (14) 80, p. 253.
"Love Song. " Ark (14) 80, p. 254.
"Spring in Iowa, 1971. " Ark (14) 80, p. 252.

ZACH, Natan
"To be lord and master in your own house. " PortR (26) 80, p.
    210.
Twelve poems (tr. of Amir Gilboa w. Jon Silkin and Bat-Sheva
    Sheriff). Stand (21:4) 80, p. 4.

ZACK, David
"Extraterrestrial Object. " SouthwR (65:4) Aut 80, p. 384.

ZADE, Wayne
"The Telling. " PoNow (29) 80, p. 44.

ZADRAVEC, Katharine
"Penance. " Comm (107:11) 6 Je 80, p. 340.

ZAJC, Dane
"The Silent Grindbeetle. " PortR (26) 80, p. 488.

ZALUDA, Scott
"Outline for a Longer Prayre. " CutB (15) Aut/Wint 80, p. 77.

ZAMVIL, Stella Savage
"Lucky Strike Green. " Sam (98) 80, p. 42.

ZANCANELLA, Don
"To My Brother in LaBarge. " Aspen (10) Wint 80, p. 82.

ZANN, Paul
"Envy. " PottPort (2) 80-81, p. 47.
"Farewell. " PottPort (2) 80-81, p. 42.
"Fear and I. " PottPort (2) 80-81, p. 46.

ZARANKA, William
"At the National Park. " Wind (37) 80, p. 58.
"Ice Age. " Wind (37) 80, p. 58.

ZAVATSKY, Bill
"Vowels" (tr. of Arthur Rimbaud). Durak (4) 80, p. 46.

ZAVRIAN, Suzanne Ostro
"Alan. " Tele (16) 80, p. 50.
"Don. " Tele (16) 80, p. 51.
"Requiem. " Tele (16) 80, p. 51.
"The Waters of Manhattan" (for Danny). Tele (16) 80, p. 50.

ZAWADIWSKY, Christine
"Howling. " Pan (21) 80, p. 24.

ZDANYS, Jonas
"A Poem About Memory" (tr. of Tomas Venclova). PortR (26)
80, p. 264.

ZEBRUN, Gary
"After Christian Orgies in the Catacombs. " SewanR (88:2) Spr
80, p. 183.
"Along the Hudson. " PoNow (29) 80, p. 44.
"Discovery" (for John and Barbara). Comm (107:8) 25 Ap 80, p.
238.
"Field Daughter. " SewanR (88:2) Spr 80, p. 182.
"Gallery, Lackawanna, N. Y. " AmerS (49:2) Spr 80, p. 208.
"No Memory of Dying. " NewRep (182:15) 12 Ap 80, p. 39.

ZEFF, Michele
"Dialogue Before a Wall of Masks at the Museum" (w. James
Polan). Nimrod (24:1) Aut-Wint 80, p. 107.

ZEKOWSKI, Arlene
"salt from sacraments. " Kayak (54) S 80, p. 54.

ZEPPA, Mary
"Anna Reuss. " Im (6:2) 80, p. 11.
"Better to Marry than to Burn. " Im (6:2) 80, p. 11.

ZIEGLER, Alan
"Making It. " PoNow (27) 80, p. 14.
"While She Is with Him. " PoNow (27) 80, p. 14.

ZIMAN, Larry
"Day. " WormR (78) 80, p. 76.
"I. " WormR (78) 80, p. 76.

ZIMMER, Paul
"A Final Affection. " CharR (6:1) Spr 80, p. 23.
"When Angels Came to Zimmer. " CharR (6:1) Spr 80, p. 24.
"Work. " PoNow (26) 80, p. 17.
"Zimmer in the Old Scholar's Study. " PoNow (26) 80, p. 17.

ZIMMERMAN, Laura
"Still Life. " Tendril (7/8) Spr-Sum 80, p. 82.

ZIMROTH, Evan
"Another Trashy Aubade. " Poetry (135:5) F 80, p. 276.
"Lilly's Song. " Poetry (135:5) F 80, p. 280.
"The Menhirs of Carnac. " SewanR (88:1) Wint 80, p. 31.
"On Hearing that Childbirth Is Like Orgasm. " Poetry (135:5) F
80, p. 279.
"Tall Woman in Song. " SewanR (88:1) Wint 80, p. 32.
"Unfinished Portraits. " Poetry (135:5) F 80, p. 277.

ZIMUYA, Bonus
"Cattle in the Rain" (tr. by Robin Graham). Stand (21:1) 79-80,
    p. 51.
"My Home" (tr. by Robin Graham). Stand (21:1) 79-80, p. 50.
"No Songs" (tr. by Robin Graham). Stand (21:1) 79-80, p. 52.

ZINNES, Harriet
"Hi!" PoNow (27) 80, p. 15.
"Mirror." Im (6:2) 80, p. 4.

ZIRLIN, Larry
"Body And." Im (7:1) 80, p. 5.

ZISQUIT, Linda
"Dead Center." Stand (21:4) 80, p. 38.

ZLOBEC, Ciril
"Evening." PortR (26) 80, p. 486.

ZMUDA, Bob
"Love Song." PartR (47:1) 80, p. 131.

ZOLYNAS, Al
"Cat Puke and Flies Poem." PoNow (28) 80, p. 18.
"How It Is." PoNow (28) 80, p. 18.
"A Nightmare Concerning Priests." PoNow (28) 80, p. 28.
"One Man's Poison." PoNow (28) 80, p. 28.
"Two Childhood Memories." PoNow (28) 80, p. 28.

ZUBER, Isabel
"For the Children." Wind (37) 80, p. 60.
"The Maker of Sleds." SmF (11/12) Spr-Aut 80, p. 46.

ZU-BOLTON, Ahmos II
"Ain't No Spring Chicken." OP (29) Spr 80, p. 4.
"Beachhead Preachment." OP (29) Spr 80, p. 9.
"A Crucifix for DeRidder or The Governor of Ollie Street Re-
    turns." OP (29) Spr 80, p. 8.
"A Galveston Rock of Ages." OP (29) Spr 80, p. 6.
"A Neo-Folklore." OP (29) Spr 80, p. 3.

ZUKOR-COHEN, Maree
"The Birth." CropD (2/3) Aut-Wint 80, p. 28.
"Bone Dance." Vis (4) 80.
"Transparencies." Vis (3) 80.

ZWEIG, Paul
"The End Circulates in the Wide Space of Summer." NewYorker
    (56:28) 1 S 80, p. 32.
"A Fly on the Water." Tendril (9) 80, p. 172.

ZYDEK, Fredrick
"Ichthyosaurus." SouthwR (65:1) Wint 80, p. 28.

"Lights Along the Missouri" (for Pat Borgstrom). <u>Annex</u> (2) 79, pp. 73-107.

"Roots" (for Charles Fortson). <u>CapeR</u> (15:2) Sum 80, p. 33.

"Singing in the Spirit at Duchesne." <u>WorldO</u> (14:2) Wint 80, p. 6.

"Thirteenth Meditation: The Finest Fire." <u>CalQ</u> (16/17) 80, p. 130.